A DICTIONARY OF CANADIAN ARTISTS

COMPILED BY

COLIN S. MACDONALD

VOLUME THREE

(PART ONE)

Canadian Paperbacks,
Ottawa

First Edition 1971
Printed in Canada

Library of Congress
Catalogue No. L.C. 67-8044
SBN 0-919554-05-9

A DICTIONARY OF
CANADIAN ARTISTS

To

my mother

CATHERINE HELEN MACDONALD

————————

and my sister and brother-in-law

ILEACH and JOHN HART

ACKNOWLEDGEMENTS

I wish to express my indebtedness to all who have made possible this compilation:

To Dr. R.H. Hubbard, Chief Curator of The National Gallery of Canada for permission to use material from the National Gallery of Canada publications; Mr. Alan Jarvis and Mr. Paul Arthur of *Canadian Art* magazine for permission to use material from their publications; to Mr. M.W. Thistle, Manager, Public Relations Office, National Research Council of Canada, for his vital constructive criticism; Mr. J. Russell Harper, author of *Painting in Canada/A History*, for his key suggestions in the early stages of the manuscript; to the following for permission to quote passages from their writings on Canadian artists: Mr. William Colgate, author of *Canadian art, its Origin and Development;* Mr. Graham McInnes, author of *Canadian Art;* Mr. Robert Ayre of the *Montreal Star;* Mr. Robert Fulford, Editor, *Saturday Night; The Toronto Star;* Mr. Harry Malcolmson of the *Toronto Telegram; The London Free Press; Saturday Night; The Gazette, Globe And Mail;* for permission to quote passages from their art reviews and columns; Mr. W.J. Withrow, Director of the Art Gallery of Ontario; Mr. Lawrence Sabbath of Montreal; to the following publishers; Burns and MacEachern Limited for excepts from Paul Duval's *Canadian Drawings and Prints, Canadian Water Colour Painting, Group of Seven Drawings;* The MacMillan Company of Canada Limited for excerpts from *Canadian Art* by Graham McInnes; Clarke, Irwin & Company Limited for excerpts from *A Painter's Country* by A.Y. Jackson and *Growing Pains* by Emily Carr; to Ryerson Press for excerpts from their publications on Canadian artists too numerous to mention here (acknowledgements to their authors appear in the text); to *MacLean's* magazine for excerpts from articles dealing with Canadian artists (acknowledgements to their authors appear in the text); *Weekend Magazine* for excerpts from their publications (acknowledgements to their authors appear in the text); to Mrs. Mary N. Balke, Librarian, National Gallery of Canada, and its former librarian, Miss Christa Dedering; to the following who have supplied information at various times; Mr. Paul Duval, author of many articles and books on art; Mr. Richard B. Simmins, author, lecturer, critic on art, and Miss Norah McCullough, Western Representative, National Gallery of Canada, and Mr. J. Stanford Perrot of the Southern Alberta Institute of Technology, to the following art societies; Royal Canadian Academy, Canadian Group of Painters, Canadian Society of Painters in Water Colour, Nova Scotia Society of Artists, Ontario Society of Artists, Manitoba Society of Artists, Saskatchewan Society of Artists, Alberta Society of Artists, British Columbia Society of Artists, Federation of Wood Carvers, Young Commonwealth of Artists for information on Canadian artists abroad; to Mr. Raymond Poulin and Mrs. Moy Smith of Montreal also Michel Champagne, Cultural Agent for the Department of Cultural Affairs of the Province of Quebec, who have provided information on Quebec artists; to over 400 Canadian artists from every province in Canada and scores of art dealers who have contributed information on art and artists in Canada.

Colin S. MacDonald
Editor

JACOBI, Otto Reinhold
1812-1901

Born at Konigsberg, Prussia, the son of Ehlert Reinhold Jacobi, a malt brewer and Johanne Louise Linck.[1] He received his education at Konigsberg where he became a teacher (probably of art). He then studied art at the Academy of Berlin and in 1832 (at the age of 20) he won a 1,000 dollar prize to study three years at Dusseldorf.[2] While he was at the Dusseldorf school he was appointed (c. 1837) court painter at Wiesbaden, a position he held for twenty years. His work became well known in his own country and he received numerous commissions from royalty. He became known in England and later Canada. It was someone in Canada familiar with his work who suggested he be invited to come to Canada and paint a scene of the Shawinigan Falls. This scene would then be presented to the Prince of Wales during his official Canadian reception.[3] Jacobi arrived in Canada in 1860 and completed this commission but instead of returning to Germany where he had established himself he stayed on in Canada.[4] Newton MacTavish[5] described this period as follows, "His paintings of this period and even of the period embracing the next ten years, display a good sense of colour values, though they may be found lacking in originality and variety of design. Some of his paintings are notable for their delightful tones of gray, but most of them are emphatic exponents of the merits of red and orange. In Jacobi Shawinigan Falls must have aroused genuine enthusiasm, for the painting of waterfalls became with him a veritable passion. . . . One of his favourite compositions was an orange sunset, with some indication of trees on either side and a waterfall down the middle. This somewhat sentimental bit of landscape he repeated many times, with, of course, enough variation. . . ." Jacobi lived in Montreal where he worked for Notman and Fraser.[6] Then he moved to Toronto where he became a charter member of the Royal Canadian Academy in 1880 and was president of this society from 1890-1893. He was among the first exhibitors at the Ontario Society of Artists and was one of the first teachers (of water colour drawing) at the Ontario School of Art which was founded by the Ontario Society of Artists. He was a better painter than a teacher and it seems he was not able to impart his fine water colour technique to his pupils. For this reason he left the Ontario School of Art but later taught pupils privately including Henry Sandham.[7] Discussing his work Edgar Andrew Collard[8] noted "He would paint in oils, sometimes on canvases of tremendous size. Or he would paint in watercolors, often minute little pictures, measuring only a few inches. But whether the scale was large or small, he achieved a sense of sublimity, perhaps with a certain touch of romantic wistfulness." Jacobi's paintings were in some demand in the auction rooms[9] of Montreal and Toronto and are still sought after today. He was married in Germany in 1837 and had one son who came to America and took up ranching in the Dakota country. It was at his son's ranch in 1901 that Jacobi died at the age of 89. Robert Harris painted an excellent portrait of Otto Jacobi in 1892. This portrait was acquired by the Royal Canadian Academy who made a gift of it to the National Gallery of Canada around 1900.[10] Jacobi is represented in the National Gallery of Canada, the Art Gallery of Ontario, The Agnes Etherington Art Centre (Queen's University, Kingston); The Montreal Museum of Fine Arts; The Museum of the Province of Quebec; in many private collections in Montreal, Toronto, and Ottawa. Reproductions of Jacobi's paintings can be found in the following books.[11] (see below).

References

[1] *A Standard Dictionary of Canadian Biography* (Canadian Who Was Who) Vol. 2, biography by William R. Watson, O.B.E., Toronto, 1934, P.207

JACOBI, Otto Reinhold (Cont'd)

[2] *Universal Cyclopaedia*, Charles Kendall Adams, LL.D., Ed., and R. Johnson Ed. of Revision, D. Appleton & Co., New York, 1902, P.628

[3] see[1]

[4] see[1], P.208

[5] *The Fine Arts In Canada* by Newton MacTavish (NGC Trustee), MacMillan, Toronto, 1925, P.11

[6] *Canadian Water Colour Painting* by Paul Duval, Burns & MacEachern, 1954, 7th page of text

[7] see[5], Page 13

[8] *The Gazette*, Montreal, Nov. 20, 1954, "All Our Yesterdays" by Edgar Andrew Collard

[9] *Canadian Art, Its Origin and Development* by William Colgate, Ryerson (1943) Ryerson Paperbacks, 1967, P.34

[10] *National Gallery of Canada Catalogue of Paintings & Sculpture, Volume 3*, by R. H. Hubbard, 1960, P. 115

[11] *Canadian Water Colour Painting* by Paul Duval, Plate 16
Painting In Canada/A History by J. Russell Harper, Plate 171, plate 176
The Art Gallery of Toronto (Catalogue) 1959, Page 49
Three Hundred Years of Canadian Art (Catalogue, NGC) 1967, Page 81
Agnes Etherington Art Centre (Catalogue, Queen's Univ., Kingston, Ont.) 1968, No. 62
NGC Catalogue of Paintings & Sculpture, P. 146, P. 394
The Fine Arts In Canada by Newton MacTavish, P. 9
A Century of Colonial Painting (NGC Catalogue) by J. Russell Harper, see back cover
Canada And Its Provinces, Vol. 12, Painting & Sculpture by E.F.B. Johnston, P. 604

JAENICKE, Beulah Irene (Mrs. Edward J. Rosen)
b.1918

Born at Leader, Saskatchewan, she studied in Vancouver, B.C., at the Canadian Institute of Associated Arts under Clark Stevenson in Life Drawing; J.W.G. MacDonald in Design and Colour, and G.H. Tyler in Painting. She exhibited at the Vancouver Art Gallery and with the Montreal Art Association. In 1942 she enlisted in the Canadian Women's Army Corps and became 2nd Lieutenant the following year. She worked with the promotion section of the directorate of army recruiting at Ottawa and, in 1945 was married to Capt. Edward J. Rosen, a psychiatrist with the R.C.A.M.C. at the Rideau Military Hospital, Ottawa.[1] She contributed cartoons to the Canadian Army training paper "Khaki". She may be painting under her married name but no recent information is available on this artist.

References

National Gallery of Canada Information Form rec'd May 30, 1938

Vancouver Sun, Van., B.C., Aug. 19, 1944 "CWAC Artist Depicts Headquarters" (photo of artist with her work)

The Ottawa Citizen, Ottawa, Ont., Jan. 19, 1944 "Beulah Jaenicke Artist, Assisting Army Promotion"

Standard Freeholder, Cornwall, Ont., Jan. 20, 1944 "C.W.A.C. Officer Is Able Artist Canadian Army"

[1] *Gazette*, Rivers Manitoba, Feb. 9, 1944 "Western Artist"
The Ottawa Journal, Ottawa, Ont., Aug. 4, 1945 "Rosen-Jaenicke

JALAVA, Erkki

Born in Finland, he studied five years at the Art Academy in Stockholm, Sweden. He then painted in France, Spain, Norway, Turkey, Sweden and came to Canada in 1954. He settled in a suburb of Toronto with his wife and children. Each summer he has gone to Parry Sound to paint landscapes and many sketches which he completes during the winter months. He also does abstract painting but more to please himself. He has exhibited his work at the floral shop in the Royal York Plaza and probably elsewhere.

Reference

Weston Times-Advertiser, Toronto, Ontario, May 22, 1964 "Night Beat (Suburban Art-Music-Drama)" by Leo Donoghue

JAMES, Ann
b.1925

Born in Hove, Sussex, England, she studied at the Brighton School of Art and came to Canada in 1945. She lived in Vancouver for a while but later moved to Regina, Saskatchewan. She studied at the University of Saskatchewan (Regina Campus Art School) under Arthur McKay, Kenneth Lochhead, Ric Gomez and Jack Sures. A painter and potter she has participated in a number of exhibitions including the Saskatchewan Arts Board Show (1965), Diamond Jubilee Show (1966) where her painting won the critic's selection (Clement Greenberg). She held a one man show at the Regina Public Library in 1968 where her work was reviewed with strong reactions (see review by Katie Fitzrandoph).[1] Ann James shares a studio with Beth Hone in Regina. This studio was formerly a church. Explaining the artist's work Ruth Willson[2] of the Regina Leader Post noted, "Ann's is avant-garde. . .so avant-garde that her show at the library scared some people, she said. It assaults the emotions. If you can see the sarcasm and the satire in some of these creations, they'll evoke instantaneous laughter. If you can't, they're liable to make you angry. In 'Jack and Jill', for example, Ann strips the pretty myth away and shows the nursery rhyme for what it is, a horror story. She does similar things in other pieces, twisting what we thought was truth around to reveal it as a lie." Ann James has travelled extensively in Europe and the Orient to visit galleries and museums. Although she has been painting for many years she just began working in pottery in 1967. Her main interests lie in sculpture and sculptural paintings using the materials of clay, foam-fibreglass and polyester resins.[3] She has been teaching children's classes in creative ceramics. She is a member of the Toronto Potters' Guild and the American Craftsmen's Council (N.Y.).

References

[1] Regina Leader Post, Sask., Oct. 1, 1968 "Nothing tame about James art at Central Library" by Katie Fitzrandoph

[2] Ibid, Oct. 12, 1968 "Artists transform old church into studio" by Ruth Willson

[3] National Gallery of Canada Information Form rec'd May 13, 1968

JAMES, Mary Stewart
b.1903

Born at London, Ontario, she studied silver-smithing under Miss Ruth Eisenhauer, Miss Vera Cummings, Mrs. Eberhard Peill and Mr. E.N. Roulston at the Province

JAMES, Mary Stewart (Cont'd)

of Nova Scotia's Department of Adult Education. In 1957 she won Second Prize for her silverwork in the Canadian Handicraft Guild Exhibition (New Brunswick Branch) and in 1958 received an Award of Merit from the World's Fair, Brussels, Belgium. Two of her silver works were exhibited at Expo '67, Montreal, and one of these pieces was purchased by the National Gallery of Canada and is on permanent display at the National Museum, Ottawa. She has given lectures and demonstrations of silver-smithing to the South Shore Art Group of Lunenburg, N.S. Her work has also been exhibited at the Stratford Festival, National Gallery of Canada, Festival of the Arts (Tatamagouche, N.S.) and the Centennial exhibition at the Halifax Public Library. She is the wife of Lt. Col. Arthur A. James, M.D. (R.C.A.M.C. retired). A Charter Member of the Metal Arts Guild of Nova Scotia; member, Nova Scotia Handcraft Guild, and the Arts and Crafts Committee of the Fisheries Ex. of Lunenburg. She lives at Lunenburg, N.S.

References

National Gallery of Canada Information Form rec'd July 13, 1967

Handcrafts, Vol. 17, No. 2, April, 1959 published by Nova Scotia Department of Adult Education (see cover and article inside)

JAMESON, Lionel B.

b. (c) 1908

Born in Regina, Saskatchewan, he was educated at Regina Collegiate Institute, Regina Technical School, and studied commercial art at Edmonton under Frank Turner; the Livingston Academy of Arts and Sciences at Washington, D.C., and worked as an artist with the Washington *Times-Herald*. In 1929 he was employed with the Major-Chandlee Studios at Washington; 1930 was assistant instructor in commercial art at the Livingston Academy and at the same time attended classes at the Corcoran Art Gallery, Washington. He did considerable freelance work and contributed nature drawings and paintings to *Nature Magazine*. By 1930 he was in Ottawa, Canada, where he also did free lance work and was then employed by the Canadian Society of Technical Agriculturists on the World's Grain Exhibition and Conference at Regina. He has done commercial art work in various artists' media illustrating scientific bulletins and text books for the provincial and federal governments. In 1942 he was appointed artist with the entomological branch of the Department of Agriculture (Ottawa), succeeding the late Frank Hennessey. No recent information is available on this artist.

Reference

The Ottawa Citizen, May 27, 1942 "Lionel B. Jameson Named Artist with Agriculture Department"

JAMIESON, Martha Greening

b.1918

Born in Calgary, Alberta, she studied at the Ontario College of Art under F.S. Haines, George Pepper, Cameron Paulin, John Alfsen, Rowley Murphy, Eric Aldwinckle, Franklin Carmichael, Charles Comfort; in Kingston, Ontario, under André Biéler and Goodridge Roberts.[1] She also studied at the Art Students'

JAMIESON, Martha Greening (Cont'd)

League, N.Y.C.[2] She became music librarian at Queen's University and interested in the theatre. She received a British Council Scholarship to study scene designing in England in 1949 at the Old Vic Theatre School in London.[3] She returned to Kingston where she has been active as set designer also designer of costumes and properties for theatre productions at Queen's University; at the Stratford Festival Theatre (Ontario) and the Canadian Repertory Theatre.[4] In 1968 seventy-six of her theatre drawings and water colours were exhibited at the Agnes Etherington Art Centre where Barry Thorne[5] of the *Kingston Whig Standard* noted, "The remarkable thing about Miss Jamieson's fluid drawings is that they are also interpretations of the roles of the characters who will wear the costumes. It would be theoretically possible to cast the characters on the basis of the drawings, because they attempt to express symbolic meaning or a feeling about the play from which the characters involved are taken." She completed a mural for the Students' Memorial Union (C.O.T.C. room) at Queen's University entitled "Canadian Armed Forces, Europe 1939-45".

References
[1] National Gallery of Canada Information Form rec'd Dec.12, 1941
[2] *Whig-Standard*, Kingston, Ont., Sept. 27, 1949 "Kingston Artist Will Study On Scholarship In England"
[3] Ibid
[4] Ibid, Dec. 14, 1968 "Martha Jamieson drawings" by Barry Thorne
[5] Ibid

JANES, Phyllis Hipwell (Mrs. James)

Born at Alliston, Ontario, she attended the University of Toronto where she received her B.A., then studied two years at the Ontario College of Art under Arthur Lismer and A.Y. Jackson.[1] She received much encouragement from the late Douglas Duncan of the Picture Loan Society[2] and held an exhibition of her chalk drawings there in 1950.[3] Rose MacDonald[4] on viewing this exhibition noted, "The artist uses the pastel medium altogether, at least in so far as the present show is concerned. She approaches her subjects, children usually, with humor and, as befits the mother of three young sons, with understanding of the outlook of the young upon their world." Other of Phyllis Janes' subjects included street scenes and barnyard life as seen at the CNE Winter Fair. She became a member of the Canadian Society of Graphic Art in 1952 and of the Ontario Society of Artists in 1958. She has exhibited with the Royal Canadian Academy, the Canadian Group of Painters, the Montreal Spring shows, at Victoria College and the Art Gallery of Ontario (4 Canadians) and elsewhere. She is represented in public and private collections across Canada.

References
[1] National Gallery of Canada Information Form rec'd Apr. 13, 1951
[2] Ibid
[3] Picture Loan Society exhibition notice "Chalk Drawings" by Phyllis Janes Oct. 28, to Nov. 10, 1950 with reprod. of her drawing "Hallowe'en"(1948)

JANES, Phyllis Hipwell (Cont'd)

[4]*Evening Telegram*, Toronto, Ont., Oct. 28, 1950

see also

The London Free Press, Lond., Ont., Mar. 14, 1959 (reproduction of her lithograph "Wet and Cold" a study of a child re: C.S.G.A. exhibit)

Sault Ste. Marie Star, Ont., Apr. 22, 1959 (reprod. of her lithograph "Dividing The Spoils" a study of two boys re: C.S.G.A. exhibit)

Fredericton Daily Gleaner, N.B., Feb. 9, 1960 (reprod. of her "Nervous Entertainer" re: C.G.P. exhibit)

JANITSCH, Marguerite D.

Born in Quebec, P.Q., she studied at the Ecole des Beaux Arts, Quebec, under Prof. Jean Paul Lemieux, Jean Soucy and at Western University, London, Ontario, under Prof. Louis Belzile. She received the following prizes for her paintings: First Prize, University of Western Ontario, 1956; Second Prize, Ecole B.A. Cours Libre, 1957; First Prize, Ecole B.A. — Cours Libre, 1958; First Prize, Ecole B.A. — Cours du soir, 1958; First Prize, Concours Jardin Zoologique, 1958. She has exhibited at the Spring Exhibition of the Montreal Museum of Fine Arts, 1958. Member of the Société des Arts Plastiques. Lives in Quebec City.

Reference

National Gallery of Canada Information Form rec'd during 1958.

JANVIER, Alex Simeon

b.1935

Born on Le Goff Reserve, Alberta, his talent was discovered by Rev. Father Bernet-Rolande at the Blue Quill Indian Residential School.[1] He later studied at the Southern Alberta College of Art, Calgary, under Illingworth Kerr, Stanford Perrot, Kenneth Sturdy, Ronald Spickett, Marion Nicoll, Robert Oldrich, W. Drohan and Stanford Blogett.[2] Janvier won many awards during his study at the College and received a four year diploma in Fine Art and Craft. Afterwards he taught art with the Extension Department of the University of Alberta at Edmonton; also at the Edmonton Art Gallery; Edmonton City Recreation Department (two years).[3] His work entitled "Our Lady of Teepee" was chosen to represent Canadian Native Painting in the Vatican in 1950. Averaging 80 percent at college he still could not find anyone who would hire him in his chosen field and even had trouble finding a hotel room in which to stay during his job hunting in the city. Finally he decided to return to the Reserve and raise cattle with his brother. But in 1964 through the assistance of a friend he held his first one man show at the Jacox Gallery in Edmonton. Dorothy Barnhouse[5], *Edmonton Journal* art critic, noted of this show, "The cleanly patterned water colors do not lean on the cliché symbolism of most native art. Rather, they achieve a kind of 'nature mysticism' through simplification and near-abstraction of organic forms. . . .Color plays a minor role. Sometimes it is limited to monochrome or earth colors or primaries subdued and steadied with black and brown. Occasionally, brilliant reds, yellows, blues, attain fluorescent proportions, as in 'City Lights' ". By 1966 Janvier was working for the Department of Indian Affairs, as an arts and craft consultant, travelling throughout Alberta looking for promising talent and generally encouraging Indians with artistic potential and arranging exhibitions of their works.[6] In his own painting however Alex

JANVIER, Alex Simeon (Cont'd)

Janvier has found peace and contentment on the land where he feels he has done his best works of art. He still considers his home to be Le Goff Reserve at Le Goff, Alberta. He is represented in a number of collections including the collection of the Rt. Hon. and Mrs. L.B. Pearson, Ottawa.[7]

References

[1] *Edmonton Journal*, Edmonton, Alta., Feb. 20, 1964 "Edmonton Showing Planned by Artist" by Frank Hutton

[2] National Gallery of Canada Information Form rec'd Mar. 9, 1964

[3] Ibid

[4] *Edmonton Journal*, July 1, 1964 "Alberta Artist Finds Frustration In Search For Work In his Field" by Dorothy Barnhouse and Peggy Paulson

[5] Ibid

[6] St. Paul *Journal*, Alta., July 21, 1966 "Alex Janvier To Exhibit Art Toronto"

[7] Ibid, May 21, 1964

JAQUE, Louis (Louis-Jacques Beaulieu)
b.1919

Born in Montreal, P.Q., he studied at the Institut des Arts Appliqués (formerly Ecole du Meuble) where he was influenced by a course on the history of art given by Maurice Gagnon.[1] He started painting seriously in 1944 following his army service.[2] About 1960 he attracted attention with his oriental looking gouaches which he sometimes created with a granular consistency. They were described as a symphony of blue, indigo and mauve contrasts. He exhibited this work at the Galerie Libre in December. He designed furnishings for Canadian embassies in China and Norway.[3] By 1965 he had done considerable work in inks and oils in which he found the shapes of spheres (suns and moons) of particular interest. Viewing his work at the Galerie Camille Hebert Réa Montbizon[4] noted, ". . .this show at Hebert's is something of an exercise in dualism. While the one half containing the large oils is clean, cool and sober, the other half, composed of colored inks in correspondingly smaller format, presents itself as ambiguous, mystifying and dreamlike. These paintings are like vedute of some intimate memories. Only the presence of the disc reminds one of the larger works. In the inks it appears as opening into space or as mass afloat, shaped into solid bodies. Here, line and mass are skilfully interchanged, with line, forkelled or fringed, broken, feathery or spiraling, playing a role of equal importance. . . .Color is used most sparingly and elegantly, on occasion for no more than accent, while the heavy blacks provide the drama as well as carry the plot. Under Louis Jaque's sensitive touch some of these ink paintings become perfect gems." Jaque has received the following honours: Concours Artistique de la Province de Quebec (1949), Jessie Dow Prize at the Montreal Spring Show (1960) and a Canada Council grant (1964). He lives in Montreal and teaches at l'Institut des Arts Appliqués. He is the brother of artist Paul V. Beaulieu.

References

[1] National Gallery of Canada Information Form rec'd Aug. 19, 1965; June 23, 1958

[2] Ibid, June 23, 1958

[3] *Le Devoir*, Mtl. P.Q., Dec. 15, 1960 "A La Galerie Libre – Exposition Jacque"

JAQUE, Louis (Cont'd)

[4]*The Gazette*, Mtl., 8 May, 1965 "The Cool And The Intimate" by Réa Montbizon
see also
La Presse, Dec. 7, 1960 "Les Gouaches De Louis Jaque"
Ibid, Dec. 8, 1962
The Gazette, Mtl., Apr. 6, 1963 "Louis Jaque"
Actualité, Mtl., May 1963
Montreal Star, Mtl. May 5, 1965 "Art Scene – Three Exhibitions" by Robert Ayre
Le Petit Journal, Que., P.Q., May 16, 1965 "Louis Jaque, un peintre qui joue avec les soleils" par Paul Gladu
St. Jerome L'Echo du Nord, Que., P.Q., Aug. 14, 1968 "A la Galerie l'Apogée de Saint-Sauveur-des-Monts – Pendant le mois de août, Louis Jaque y expose de ses oeuvres"
Ibid, Aug. 21, 1968 "Saint-Sauveur"

JARAIN (Jacques Rainville)
b. (c) 1934

Born at St. Jean, Quebec, he completed his early studies there and then entered the Ecole des Beaux-Arts where he attended classes for two years and was a fiery student. He consequently did not continue with his courses but went on with his painting. His work was equally as fiery or forceful and he experimented with different techniques including the working on unexposed negatives. Later he found plate glass a satisfactory medium for his painting (a technique called "le clairisme") using opaque materials and applying them so that parts of the painting would be transparent. Astrology and mysticism (occultism) are evident in his work. He has receive much assistance from his colleague Gilles Lord. Jarain has been teaching decoration for the folklore Federation of Quebec and was teacher of plastic arts for the diocesan federation of playground supervisors. He won honourable mention in the festival of dramatic art for his set decoration for Arthur Adamov's play *Ping Pong*.

References
Le Canada Français, St. Jean, Que., Feb. 27, 1964 Ibid, Mar. 12, 1964

JARNUSZKIEWICZ, Wocjiec

Born in Poland, he received his training while working with his father, an iron worker. Following World War II they worked on the decorative metal designs of buildings in old Warsaw and he came to Canada in 1963. He then worked in wrought iron shops in Quebec City before opening a studio at Granby, Quebec, with Jean Michel. They were last reported to be moving to Montreal. His wrought iron "Icarus II" was exhibited at Expo '67.

References
Public relations release by Shirley Sklov for Galerie des Artisans, 2025 Peel St., Montreal, P.Q.

Canadian Fine Crafts (book for Canadian Government Pavilion of Expo '67) by Moncrieff Williamson (obtainable from Queen's Printer of Canada)

542

JARVIS, Alan Hepburn

b.1915

Born in Brantford, Ontario, the son of Charles Arthur Jarvis, optometrist, and Janet Stewart Mackay; his father died in 1918 and the Jarvis family moved to Toronto.[1] He attended Parkdale Collegiate and then entered the University of Toronto. During his freshman year he met Douglas Duncan, founder of the Picture Loan Society and art patron.[2] It was through Duncan that he met gallery owners and painters and during the evenings he studied sculpture techniques at the Central Technical School under Elizabeth Wyn Wood Hahn. It was through Douglas Duncan that he also met David Milne.[3] Milne became an important influence in Jarvis' life. In 1936 Jarvis travelled through Europe by auto where he photographed Romanesque church sculpture. He graduated from the University of Toronto in 1938 with his B.A. majoring in philosophy and psychology. He won a Rhodes Scholarship and attended Oxford University but the war in 1939 brought the end of his studies. He returned to Canada where he continued his postgraduate studies at the University of Toronto and later won a fine arts fellowship to New York University. There he specialized in museology, early Christian art and English 18th Century art and graduated in 1941.[4] He returned to England where he joined the personnel department of Parnall Aircraft Limited (producers of the Lancaster Bomber). This led to his appointment as special assistant and later private secretary to Sir Stafford Cripps, Minister of Aircraft Production. He worked for Cripps from 1941 to 1945 and edited a collection of Minister's speeches under the title "Democracy Alive" (1946). He became Director (1945-47) of Public Relations of the Council of Industrial Design, England, who were particularly concerned with the improvement of designs of goods being exported from Britain. He wrote *The Things We See* (1946) the first in a series of seven books on design published by Penguin Books Limited, England. He was made Director of Pilgrim Pictures (1947-50); followed many other activities including; Quizmaster for the BBC program "Under Twenty Questions"; Chairman of London's Group Theatre; Trustee The Mermaid Theatre; Director of British Handcraft Export Corporation; Head of Oxford House (where derelicts were cared for in the London slum area) but during all this time he kept at his sculpture and was afforded excellent opportunities to do portraits of outstanding people including: a posthumous head of Sir Stafford Cripps (exhibited at the Royal Society of British Artists); Peter Ustinov (actor, producer, playwright); Kirsten Flagstad (opera singer); William Rootes (auto maker); Sir Eric Bowater (paper magnate) and others. In 1955 he was appointed director of the National Gallery of Canada where he succeeded in bringing art to the people through a greater number of extension programs, lectures, and T.V. appearances and presented "The Things We See" produced in Ottawa and seen throughout Canada. Carl Weiselberger[5] who was then art critic for *The Ottawa Citizen* quoted Jarvis as follows, "My idea is still, rather than 'elevating' public taste, to increase people's enjoyment in looking at everything around them: landscapes, houses, everyday things embodying industrial design, and finally the fine arts – painting, drawing, sculpture." In Ottawa behind the scenes Jarvis continued with his sculpture. He married Elizabeth Devlin in 1955 and resided in Rockcliffe until a year or so after his resignation from the National Gallery in 1959. During the years he was Director of the Gallery he had made it more alive and even secured a restaurant for the new Gallery quarters in the Lorne Building. Peter C. Newman[6] explained how he succeeded as follows, "When the new National Gallery building was being planned, Department of Public Works architects firmly decided against including the restaurant requested by Jarvis. He was told government regulations specifically

JARVIS, Alan Hepburn (Cont'd)

state that the only federal buildings which can have public eating facilities are transportation terminals. Jarvis insisted. 'A restaurant,' he said, 'is an absolutely essential antidote to museum feet.' Government officials again ruled no restaurant. Eyebrows quirked, Jarvis calmly replied: 'No restaurant, no Jarvis.' Alan Jarvis was elected Chairman of the Society for Art Publications in 1959, producers of *Canadian Art* of which he also became Editor. In March of 1962 after exhibiting in Montreal and Toronto, he opened his one man show of sculpture at the Robertson Galleries, Ottawa, when Carl Weiselberger[7] noted, ". . .as a portrait-sculptor Alan Jarvis believes in a realistic rendition of the human head. It is still interesting enough to be studied and explored without radical distortion, a world of eternal wonder if you portray it as it looks to the artist and — to the sitter, who after all wants to recognize his own face. . . ." The exhibition included portraits of Peter Gordon (Ottawa); young A.J. Freiman (Ottawa); Barbara Chilcott (actress); Mrs. Harry Davidson (Ottawa); Miss Lola Rasminsky (daughter of the Governor of the Bank of Canada) and photographs of his earlier works: Sir Stafford Cripps, Sir Eric Bowater, Peter Ustinov, Dr. Cyril James (Principal of McGill University), Samuel Bronfman and others. Later that year Jarvis was awarded an honorary doctor of laws degree from Waterloo Lutheran University. In 1964 he completed a heroic-size head and shoulders of Major General F.F. Worthington and the work was placed in the Worthington Park at Camp Borden. This work had been commissioned by The Royal Armoured Car Association. In addition to his many speaking engagements, lectures, writing commitments with newspapers, he became general editor for a series of books (The Gallery of Canadian Art) published in 1962 by the Society for Art Publications and McClelland and Stewart. He was also the author of one of these books dealing with the life and work of David Milne.[8] This is an excellent book, as are the others of this series. In 1968 he received a Canada Council Grant to re-open his sculpture studio while he continues to work on another book. Many of his articles can be found in issues of *Canadian Art* magazine or *Arts-Canada* as it is now called (edited by Anne Brodsky). His sculpture and silversmith works are in Canadian, American, and British collections.[9]

References

[1] *MacLean's Magazine*, Nov. 22, 1958 "Is Jarvis Mis-spending Our Art Millions? " by Peter C. Newman (photography by Jack Olson) P.42

[2] Ibid, P.42

[3] Ibid

[4] *Canadian Art*, Vol. 12, No. 3, P.130 "Coast To Coast In Art" "Alan Jarvis Appointed Director of the National Gallery of Canada"

[5] *The Ottawa Citizen*, March 14, 1962 "Critic Surprises As Sculptor" by Carl Weiselberger

[6] see[1]

[7] see[5]

[8] *David Milne* by Alan Jarvis, Society For Art Publications/McClelland and Stewart Limited, 1962

[9] see[4]

JARVIS, Donald Alvin

b.1923

Born in Vancouver, B.C., he was particularly interested in drawing at an early age and when he was 19 entered the Vancouver School of Art (1941) where he studied for a year under B.C. Binning, J.L. Shadbolt, C.H. Scott, Amess and others.[1] His

JARVIS, Donald Alvin (Cont'd)

art education was interrupted probably because of the war. He returned to the Vancouver School of Art in 1946 and completed his course in 1948 when he won an Emily Carr Scholarship.[2] With this scholarship he studied in New York City under Hans Hofmann. *Canadian Art*[3] magazine had noted his work under the section "Directions In British Columbia Painting" where his "Victory Square" appeared and was captioned, "the post-impressionist tradition thoroughly absorbed and given a new adaptation to our environment." By 1948 he had left his post-impressionistic tradition for a style partly or wholly derived from his study and environment in New York. A one man show of his oils, water colours, and drawings took place at the Vancouver Art Gallery and the University of British Columbia in the winter of 1949-50. *Canadian Art*[4] magazine viewing this show found, "In all of three mediums employed, but most richly in his oils, his forms, which were once muted and tonal, now glow in rich intensities, while his meaning, now less obvious, remains deeply charged with an emotion which arises from the play of his imagination on his environment." Two of his abstract renditions of the city were purchased by the National Gallery of Canada (one oil on canvas and one drawing). Both works seemed to be a commentary on the imprisonment of the individual by modern society with its dominant towers not unlike perhaps the Tower of Babel; the height and impressiveness of which was intended to keep certain ancient tribes together as a power to dominate the rest of the world. In the process of attempting to build the tower they were punished by God by not being able to communicate with one another. Modern man imprisoned in our Babel like society of materialistic preoccupation of mass production and the quest for the almighty dollar, stalks through our cities like a robot unable or unwilling to communicate with his neighbor. But while Jarvis painted man in the city he also painted landscapes of British Columbia some being described by Robert Fulford[5] in 1961 as follows, "He has turned to the coast forests and beaches, the forms of trees, stumps and driftwood, as well as aspects of the city and its people. He concentrates as he says, on 'the passage of the seasons; the relation between the sea and the land; between nature and man-made forces; the processes of life.' ". By 1963 he had moved deeper into the realm of abstraction and his paintings were described by Joan Lowndes[6] as follows, "Two new motifs are emerging: a tangle of underbrush, its vitality expressed by a sinuous black mesh that covers the entire canvas; and the relation of two forms. In *Encounter 1* we see the latter close to nature; one felled tree, one erect, meeting in a tender rosy-mauve haze. *Encounter II* has become something quite different: belligerent personalities, both upright, whose clash generates flakes of orange light. This is an area full of dramatic possibilities which Jarvis is just beginning to explore." Jarvis was appointed Instructor in Drawing and Painting at the Vancouver School of Art in 1951 and is now Head of that department; received a Canada Council Senior Arts Fellowship in 1961; exhibited in the National Gallery of Canada Biennials 1955, 57, 59, 61, 63; Lugano, Switzerland 1956; Inter-American Exhibition of Painting and Graphic Art, Mexico, 1958 and others; one-man shows: Vancouver Art Gallery 1949, 1955; U.B.C. Fine Arts Gallery 1949; Victoria Art Gallery 1955; New Design Gallery, Vancouver, 1958, 1962. He is represented in the following public collections: Vancouver Art Gallery; Victoria Art Gallery; Winnipeg Art Gallery; Victoria College; C.I.L. Collection; The National Gallery of Canada (by three or more works); The Agnes Etherington Art Centre, and in many private collections. One of his most recent exhibitions took place at the Bau-XI Art Gallery, Vancouver, in the autumn of 1968. He is a member

JARVIS, Donald Alvin (Cont'd)

of the Canadian Group of Painters, the British Columbia Society of Artists, and the Royal Canadian Academy (A.R.C.A. 1962). He lives in Vancouver.

References

[1] Information on Donald Jarvis submitted to the National Gallery of Canada by Dr. Naomi Jackson Groves, Jan. 3, 1964; also document from artist

[2] Ibid

[3] *Canadian Art*, Volume 5, No. 1, Autumn, 1947 "Directions in British Columbia Painting" P.4

[4] Ibid, Vol. 7, No. 3, "Coast to Coast In Art" P.115

[5] Ibid, Vol. 18, No. 1 "A Survey Of The Work Of 24 Young Canadian Artists" by Robert Fulford, P.28 (D.A. Jarvis)

[6] Ibid, Vol. 20, No. 1 "Art Reviews" "Don Jarvis at the New Design Gallery, Vancouver" by Joan Lowndes

see also
Catalogue – *Agnes Etherington Art Centre*, Queen's University at Kingston, Ontario, 1968, P.63

The Arts In Canada, Ed. by Malcolm Ross, "Painting" by Robert Ayre, 1958, P.32 (ill)

Canadian Art, Vol. 15, No. 1 "Recent Acquisitions by The National Gallery of Canada" P.55 (ill)

National Gallery of Canada Catalogue of Paintings and Sculpture, Vol. 3, Canadian School, by R.H. Hubbard, P.146-7

The Arts In Canada (obtainable from the Queen's Printer/Federal) "Contemporary Art Since 1930" P.102

JARVIS, Lucy Mary Hope

b.1896

Born in Toronto, Ontario, she studied at the Havergal Ladies College in Toronto and then attended the Art School of the Boston Museum of Fine Arts (1925-29).[1] She specialized in the painting of children's portraits in Toronto following her study in Boston.[2] In 1931 she exhibited with the Royal Canadian Academy and subsequently spent a year painting in a Nova Scotia fishing village; instructed in art at King's Hall, Compton, Quebec; was cataloguer and draftsman for the Royal Ontario Museum, Toronto; full time painter at Brantford, Ontario, where she held a solo exhibit of her work. In 1940 she was in Fredericton, N.B., where she painted, exhibited, and started, with Pegi Nicol MacLeod, the Observatory Art Centre at the University of New Brunswick. She also kept the University Art Department in operation. By 1942 she was operating a rural circuit for the National Film Board and the War Information Services. In 1944 she became Art Instructor for the Provincial Normal School in Fredericton.[3] She was appointed Director of the Art Centre of the University of New Brunswick in 1946, a position she held until 1960 when she returned to full time painting.[4] In 1954 Avery Shaw[5] writing on New Brunswick painters referred to 'The poetry of Lucy Jarvis's landscapes.' With the aid of a Canada Council grant and the assistance of friends at the University of New Brunswick Art Centre, she travelled in Europe during 1961.[6] There she painted and studied at the studio of André Lhote and the Grand Chaumière; travelled in England, Spain, Switzerland, Germany and Austria where she studied under Oskar Kokoschka at the Salzbourg Art Seminar.[7] She returned to Canada in August of 1961 and established a studio at Pembroke Dyke near Yarmouth, N.S.[8] A showing of her paintings took place at the University of New Brunswick in 1962 which included 40 works (16 oils, 14 water colours, 10 drawings) of portraits, figure

JARVIS, Lucy Mary Hope (Cont'd)

studies, and landscapes. The late Jack Humphrey viewing that show noted, "Lucy loves what she paints and does not work with competitive ambition or rivalry which compels some of today's contemporary painters." Humphrey also noted that there was in her work 'good colour and good paint.' Her works are in the collections of the New Brunswick Provincial Museum; Hart House, University of Toronto; University of New Brunswick Teachers' College and many private collections. Her latest exhibition was shown at the Unitarian House, Fredericton, N.B., in 1968.

References

[1] National Gallery of Canada Information Form received May, 1931, also see *Fredericton Gleaner* May 7, 1960

[2] *Fredericton Gleaner*, March 8, 1951 "U.N.B. Art Director Has Exhibition"

[3] Ibid, May 7, 1960 "Miss Lucy Jarvis Leaves UNB Art Centre Shortly; Plans Return to Painting" by Ted Guidry

[4] Ibid

[5] *Canadian Art*, Vol. XI, No. 4, Summer 1954, "Painters of New Brunswick" by Avery Shaw, P.151, 153

[6] *Fredericton Gleaner*, March 21, 1962 "Painting Exhibit Opened"

[7] Ibid

[8] Ibid

[9] Ibid, Nov. 29, 1968 "Exhibition Opens On Sunday"

JASMIN, André
b.1922

Born in Montreal, Quebec, he received his B.A. from the University of Montreal and then studied two years at l'Ecole du Meuble under Borduas, Pellan, Maurice Gagnon (art history) and Parizeau (architecture). He became active in the field of costume and set designing and did costumes and set designs for "Les Compagnons" of Montreal who presented *Les Fourberies de Scapin* in New York City in 1945. He also designed costumes and sets for two Canadian ballets: *La Gaspésienne* and *Papotages* for the Ruth Sorel Company. In his painting, he held his first one man show of ink drawings, charcoals, and water colours in Montreal in 1947. Other one man shows followed in 1948, 1951, 1952, 1955, 1956 while he also participated in group shows in Montreal, Quebec City, Toronto, Winnipeg, Calgary and Ottawa at the National Gallery. His 1956 solo show was given at The Collector's Gallery, New York City, and the foreword for the exhibition catalogue was written by Jean René Ostiguy, of the National Gallery of Canada. His work has been influenced by Braque, also Rouault but much of his work is non-figurative. He exhibited at Centre d'Art du Mont-Royal his non-figurative paintings in 1965. He is respected not only as a serious painter but as a teacher. He is Professor of Art History at the Ecole des Beaux-Arts, Montreal, and gave a series of gallery talks at the National Gallery of Canada on Cézanne, Tintoretto, Rembrandt, Chagall, Bonnard, Pellan, Borduas, and Riopelle during the fall of 1966.

References

Catalogue booklet *Exhibition of Paintings by André Jasmin*, The Collector's Gallery, 49 West 53rd St., New York City Oct. 1-15, 1956 "The Private Language of André Jasmin" by Jean René Ostiguy, National Gallery of Canada.

Press Release (NGC) Oct. 12, 1966 by L.G. James, Public Relations Officer

Le Petit Journal, Montreal, Sunday, April 25, 1965 "Musique peinte de Jasmin: couleur, trait prestigieux" par Paul Gladu

JASMIN, Edouard
b. (c) 1905

Born at Bois-Franc, Quebec, he was educated at the classical college of St. Thérèse. Following his studies he became a missionary in China where he lived for fifteen years. He returned to Quebec, married, and operated an oriental curios shop and learned how to make decorative objects which he sold. He then took evening courses at the Ecole des Beaux-Arts, Quebec. For a time he sold imported teas, coffees, and spices in his shop but when the war disrupted the import business he converted his shop into a restaurant. His restaurant was frequented by artists like Dumouchel, Bellefleur, Giguere, Filion and others and one day Alfred Pellan looked with great interest at the restaurant walls which Jasmin had decorated with graffiti. His association with the artists led to him becoming a professional artist at the age of 57. He has exhibited his work at Galerie Rita Huot and has taught privately. He has been working with a technique using the mixture of fish glue, sand and varnish. Several months of the year he works as artist for the Municipal Park Service of Quebec City.

Reference

La Presse, Sept. 8, 1962 "les beau-arts — Edouard Jasmin: inventeur de formes et de couleurs . . . " par Claude Jasmin

JAWORSKA, Ewa (Mrs.)

Born in Poland she came to Canada around 1949. She won first prize for her display of pottery at the "New Canadians" exhibit sponsored by the Canadian Handicraft Guild in Montreal, January, 1954, and subsequently held an exhibition of her ceramics at the Robertson Galleries, Ottawa. She was last reported as living in Ottawa.

Reference

Ottawa Evening Citizen, May 28, 1954 "Polish-Born Artist Shows Her Ceramics"

JEAN, Marcel
b.1937

Born in Quebec City, he studied at the Ecole des Beaux Arts and graduated with his diploma in 1959. He also received the Bronze Medal awarded by the Lieutenant-Governor the same year. In 1960 he received his teacher's diploma and in 1964 was appointed a professor at the Ecole des Beaux-Arts of Quebec. He exhibited his paintings, reliefs and drawings (1959 to 1967 period) at the Museum of the Province of Quebec during 1967. He has won many awards for his work including: Third Prize, Quebec Provincial Competition for painting (1961); Second Prize, same competition, for painting (1962); Second Prize in the Laval University competition (1964); Second Prize in the Graphics sections of the Quebec Provincial competition (1965) (1966); and had his work chosen in the Reeves & Sons competition for presentation to the permanent collection of the Museum of the Province of Quebec (1967). Generally Jean's works have been described as particularly intellectual, pure abstraction concerned with geometric constructions. He is also represented in the Museum of Contemporary Art, Montreal.

JEAN, Marcel (Cont'd)

References
   Quebec Chronicle-Telegraph, Sept. 28, 1961 "City Artist Places Third In Provincial Competition"
   Le Soleil-l'Evenement, 4 March, 1967 article by Claude Daigneault
   Ibid, Oct. 31, 1967 "Remise D'Un Dessin" photo of artist with M. Jean Soucy (director of the Quebec Provincial Museum) and M. David Hackett (Pres. Reeves & Sons) and caption.
   L'Action, Quebec, P.Q., Oct. 31, 1967 (a photo as above) with caption

---

JEAN-LOUIS, Don
b.1937

Born in Ottawa, Ontario, he received his education there and then followed his own self teaching plan as he explained for *The Canadian Architect*[1] (1962), "Although I started drawing at an early age, I feel it is only in the last three years that I have developed a firm basis for direct progression. It seems to me that the period between when I started to draw until three years ago was a time of preparation. It was not until I had gone through a very strong emotional experience that I decided my direction. The result of this experience ended in an elegy – a poetic lament – not for the dead but for the living." His first one man show of drawings was held at The Isaacs Gallery, Toronto, in 1961.[2] He held another one man show at the Isaacs in 1963 as well as at the Town Cinema, Toronto. In 1964 he held his third solo exhibit at the Isaacs Gallery when Kay Kritzwiser[3] of the Toronto *Globe & Mail* noted, "When he paints, he becomes an X-ray machine, a magnifying glass, a microscope. For him a tree seethes with movement. An apple is full of organic movement . . . . Man is so assailed by the acceleration of time and space, he is moving away from his human ability to choose, substituting the machine's ability to select." She quoted Jean-Louis as follows, "We have no time to reflect. No time to be silent. In my painting I try to listen to the music of silence – the organic silence of the landscape." During this same year Jean-Louis was chosen by The National Gallery of Canada to represent Canada in the Lugano International Exhibition of Prints and Drawings at Switzerland. By 1967 he was working with plastic sculpture in which he borrowed the technical processes of commercial sign-makers. This work prompted the following comments from the *Toronto Daily Star*,[4] "What we have here, then, is, like Pop Art, a challenge to the standard artistic sensibility. But where Pop asks us only to receive mass culture into the art gallery, Jean-Louis takes the further step of inviting nature to join in the process." His most recent exhibition was held at the 20-20 Gallery, London, Ontario, in the late winter of 1969. Jean-Louis is represented in The National Gallery of Canada, The Montreal Museum of Fine Arts, and elsewhere as well as in many private collections. He lives in Toronto, Ontario.

References
   [1] *The Canadian Architect*, January, 1962 (six reproductions of his work)
   [2] Exhibition sheet – Isaacs Gallery, 1964
   [3] *Globe & Mail*, Sat., Dec. 5, 1964 "At The Galleries" by Kay Kritzwiser

JEAN-LOUIS, Don (Cont'd)

[4]*Toronto Daily Star*, Apr. 15, 1967

see also

Toronto Daily Star, July 29, 1967 "Will technology replace plain old artistry? " by Gail Dexter

London Evening Free Press, Feb. 24, 1969 "Plastic art brings praise from critic" by Lenore Crawford

The Gazette, Montreal, Mar. 7, 1969 "This was Don Jean-Louis at the 20-20" by Rod Wachsmuth

Canadian Water Colours Drawings & Prints 1966 (catalogue NGC) No. 30

Canadian Art, Vol. 21, No. 2, Mar. Apr. 1964 "How 20 Canadians Draw The Line" by Arnold Rockman, P.86

JEFFERIES, Gloria

b.1923

Born in Toronto, Ontario, she studied at the Western Technical School, Toronto, and at the Ontario College of Art evenings under John Alfsen and Emanuel Hahn. In 1940 she won the Rolph, Clarke, Stone Scholarship. At first she worked in the field of commercial art but later began making small sculpture out of stone, etc., and carvings in wood. By 1948 she had her studio in the basement of the Royal Ontario Museum where she was engaged at making reproductions of museum pieces including a horse's head (Han dynasty 220BC – 200AD), a wooden idol (Goddess of Mercy, Quan Yin), miniature copies of Canadian animals with authentic colouring (family of black bears, sleeping white – spotted fawns, a mother husky dog with pups, a beaver, and others).[1] She went to Mexico where she studied under Jose Gutieriz who was particularly interested in painted sculpture.[2] From this experience she produced tropical fish using turquoise, coral, and other colours for the markings of the fish. The Toronto *Saturday Night*[3] in 1948 noted of her "Eskimo Madonna", " . . . she can endow a human subject with rare depth and simplicity."

References

National Gallery of Canada Information Form rec'd June 12, 1944

[1]*Toronto Evening Telegram*, March 22, 1950 "Sculptress Carves Model Animals" by Marilyn Bell

[2]Ibid

[3]*Saturday Night*, Toronto, Ont., Dec. 25, 1948 (a large reproduction of 'Eskimo Madonna' – photo by Lockwood Haight Panda Studios)

see also

The London Free Press, London, Ont., Oct. 7, 1948 "Sculptor to Give Lecture Friday"

Ibid, Sept. 25, 1948 "In Museum Display" (a reproduction of her 'Eternal Woman')

JEFFERIES, G.F.

b.1914

Born in Halifax, N.S., he studied at the Nova Scotia College of Art and entered the field of commercial art. He worked for the Robert Simpson Eastern Limited as display manager. In his painting he has done free lance work and has his own studio. He does water colours, oils, and silk screens. He has taught silk screen

JEFFERIES, G.F. (Cont'd)

technique and display work at the Nova Scotia College of Art and is also an instructor in signs and show card writing during the evenings at vocational schools. He is a member of the Nova Scotia Society of Artists and lives in Halifax, N.S.

Source
Document from artist.

JEFFERYS, Charles William
1869-1951

Born in Rochester, Kent, England, the son of Charles T. Jefferys, a builder, and Ellen Kennard. Jefferys grew up in an area surrounded by historical ruins[1] and was a neighbour of the great author Charles Dickens.[2] He left England with his family and they settled in Philadelphia, U.S.A., where they were near relatives;[3] later they moved to Hamilton, Ontario, and finally Toronto around 1880.[4] Charles attended the Winchester and Dufferin Street School in Toronto and was often called upon to decorate the blackboards for special occasions.[5] His chalk drawings covered such events as "The Landing of Caesar", "Wolfe at Quebec", "The Battle of Queenston Heights" and his school books were filled with his own conceptions of events and how places must have looked.[6] His schoolmates would willingly pay him a few pennies to decorate their books. Also destined to become an outstanding Canadian artist was Frederick Brigden, a fellow schoolmate, and their paths were to cross many times throughout their careers. When Jefferys had finished school his father got him a job with the Toronto Lithographing Company as an apprentice. There he learned to draw on stone and to design show cards, calendars and even labels on tomato cans.[7] His employer later rented his services to *The Globe* to make sketches of the daily events.[8] About this time (1887) he was taking instruction in drawing with other students (including F.S. Challener) from G.A. Reid who had studied under Thomas Eakins in Philadelphia and Benjamin Constant in Paris.[9] Reid and his wife however, departed for Europe in 1888 so Jefferys, Challener, and other students went over to the Toronto Art Students' League which had been newly established. There Jefferys met Charles MacDonald Manly who taught him the essentials of water colour painting.[10] Other students at the League included David Thomson, J.D. Kelly, William Cruikshank, Robert Holmes and A.H. Howard.[11] In 1889 he painted and sketched in the Richelieu River country and among other things there did some very fine sketches of old churches which appeared in the League Calendar issues.[12] In the fall of 1892 Jefferys went to the United States where he found a job with *The New York Herald*.[13] While there he contributed an illustration to the first Toronto Art League Calendar in 1893. His wife Jean F.M. Adams died in 1900 at their home in New Jersey and not long afterwards Jefferys returned to Toronto.[14] His wife had been an artist in her own right and had contributed to issues of the Art League Calendar. In 1889 Jefferys visited the old city of Quebec with Charles MacDonald Manly. There, he made many sketches in black and white of historical dwellings and locations, even the sailing ships in the harbour.[15] In 1890 he toured the Maritime Provinces making sketches of that area of Canada for *The Globe*. In 1900 he returned to the Richelieu River country and in 1901 was commissioned to illustrate the tour of the Duke and Duchess of Cornwall and York and travelled across Canada with the news party. It was then that he saw the prairies for the first time, a subject to which he would return again and again for his paintings and drawings. It was his paintings of the prairies that were considered to be his best. From 1902 to 1903 Jefferys contributed art features to *The Moon* edited by Knox Magee. The magazine was short lived, perhaps because it was ahead of its time.[16] Magee was an exponent of an independent Canada, and in politics he was a free thinker.[17] But Magee continued to make his contribution to Canadian literature as a forceful writer. Jefferys was active in book illustration and did illustrations for many books including Marjorie Pickthall's *Dick's Desertion*, a boy's adventures in the Canadian forests (1905); *The Straight Road* (c1906); *Billy's Hero, or The Valley of Gold* (1908); and David Boyle's *Uncle Jim's Canadian Nursery Rhymes* (1908) which Sybille Pantizzi[18] felt were his best coloured illustrations. Jefferys married Clara A.B. West of Winnipeg in 1908. The same year he helped found the Arts & Letters Club. He made further trips to the prairies and foothills country in 1907 and 1910. For the publisher Robert Glasgow he did illustrations for *Makers of Canada* published between 1903 and 1911 in 21 volumes; *Chronicles of Canada* published between 1914 and 1916 in 32 volumes; *Chronicles of America* and *Pageant of America*. Around 1915 Jefferys did 102 drawings for *Sam Slick* by Judge Thomas Haliburton which was to be published by Glasgow, Brook and Company but before the work went to press the firm ceased to operate in Canada and Jefferys' illustrations were taken to New York City. Robert Glasgow of the firm, died in 1922 and the work for which Jefferys had spent many months of diligent study was forgotten. Dr. Lorne Pierce of Ryerson Press, after the death of Jefferys, provided information on the missings drawings to the Imperial Oil Company of Canada. This company then purchased the drawings which were still in New York. In 1956 Ryerson Press finally published *Sam Slick in Pictures* by Thomas C. Haliburton, edited by Malcolm Parks, illustrated by C.W. Jefferys. Near the end of the First World War Jefferys, unable to go overseas, was employed by the Canadian War Records to make pictures of military training in Canada at Petawawa Camp and at Niagara. These studies include lithographs, drawings, water colours, and a large oil (60" x 76") entitled "Polish Army Bathing At Niagara Camp" now in The Canadian War Memorials Collection (1914-18) at the National Gallery of Canada. In 1921 recognition of him as a historical artist led to his commission by the Ontario Department of Education to illustrate George M. Wrong's *Ontario Public School History of Canada* published by Ryerson Press. He produced many other illustrations for Ryerson and Musson publishers. In 1927 he did pictures illustrating the history of Canada for the Diamond Jubilee of Confederation published by *The Toronto Star*. In 1929 he completed two large murals (10 x 14 ft) and was assisted greatly by F.S. Challener, for Manoir Richelieu at Murray Bay, Quebec; one depicting the arrival of Gaultier de La Comporte in 1672; the other of the arrival of Captain John Nairne in 1761 who purchased the seigniory at Murray Bay.[21] In 1930 Jefferys wrote and illustrated *Dramatic Episodes in Canada's Story*, a 75 page book published by *The Toronto Star*. In 1930 and 1931 Jefferys created four panels (7 x 10ft.) for the Writing Room of the Chateau Laurier Hotel in Ottawa, depicting moments in the history of the Ottawa River. While working on the murals he took ill and had to get away to a warmer climate. He stayed in Jamaica while his friends Frederick Haines and Herbert Palmer both R.C.A.'s carried on with the work. Jefferys returned and completed the job and brought back a number of water colour sketches which were exhibited at the Mellors Gallery in Toronto.[22] The four panels were removed from the Chateau Laurier in 1962 when alterations to the hotel were made. Three of the murals were saved by the National Capital

Commission and National Gallery Conservationist Nathan Stolow. They were unable to do anything with a fourth panel which was irretrievably damaged. In 1934 Ryerson Press published *Canada's Past In Pictures*, a 131 page book written and illustrated by Jefferys. He designed in 1937 four large relief panels depicting historical events for the Memorial Arch at Niagara Falls. The work was then executed by Emanuel Hahn. Jefferys in 1938 was appointed historical consultant for the Dominion Government when they undertook the reconstruction of Champlain's Habitation of Port Royal on the north shore of Annapolis Basin, Nova Scotia. The architect of this work was Kenneth D. Harris of the surveys and engineering branch of the Department of Mines and Resources, Ottawa. Jefferys retired in 1939 from the Department of Architecture of the University of Toronto where he had been instructor of drawing and painting since 1912.[23] In 1941 he was a contributing artist to an excellent book entitled *Canada: The Foundations Of Its Future* by Stephen Leacock published by The House of Seagram in a limited edition. Other contributing artists were Stanley Royle, A. Sheriff Scott, F.H. Varley, H.R. Perrigard, W.J. Phillips, James Crockart and Ernst Neumann. In 1942 Jeffery's first volume of *The Picture Gallery of Canadian History* (268 pages) was published by Ryerson Press, containing drawings taken from old prints and paintings or from surviving objects of the past in Canada, including buildings, furniture, tools, weapons, costumes, vehicles and imaginative pictures of episodes and phases of Canada's history which he made during his career. An appendix in the volume lists the sources of information including bibliography, list of museums and collections of historical objects and pictures with comments on the material contained in the museums. This first volume covers the period of discovery of Canada to 1763. The second volume, published in 1945, covers the period 1763 to 1830 and shows the events of the period, and scores of long-discarded and forgotten things of pioneer life (271 pages including source listings). The third volume appeared in 1950 and covered the period 1830 to 1900 in 252 pages. In all three volumes Jefferys was assisted with the illustrations by T.W. McLean. The total work consists of 2000 separate drawings giving us one of the finest sources of information of our frontiersmen, settlers, explorers, pioneers, farmers, trappers, woodsmen, roadbuilders, surveyors and homemakers. In 1948 a retrospective show of his work was held at The Little Gallery in Toronto just next door to G.A. Reid's old residence. Viewing this show *The Toronto Telegram* noted, "The delicately detailed black and whites, ink and pencil, seem mostly to be earlier work; some of the larger oils belong to the early 40's. The occasional historical drawings recalls Mr. Jefferys' authority as an historical artist, a field in which he has been a muralist as well. There is an almost lyrical quality in such landscapes as 'Maples and Beeches' with its soft suffusion of light on the tender palette of nature." In 1949 a stamp based on his painting "The Founding of Halifax, 1749" in the Art Gallery of Ontario, was released by the Canadian post office department to commemorate the biennial of Halifax, 1749 to 1949.[24] Following Jefferys' death in 1951 the Saint John, N.B., *Telegraph-Journal* in an editorial wrote these words, "What probably has struck hundreds of thousands of Canadians most forcibly about Mr. Jefferys' work is its realism. He made the history of this land come alive again in the minds of school children and of grown-ups alike. He eschewed any excess of formality and splendor, in vivid contrast with the heavy drama of most great historical paintings, to leave us and our posterity with the feeling that Canadian pioneers were not so much demi-gods and king-makers as plain people full of courage and hope

JEFFERYS, Charles William (Cont'd)

Canadian history would be much less interesting to contemporary students if the pedestrian prose of our historians had not been relieved by the living art of Mr. Jefferys. Himself an immigrant from England, he enriched this country's heritage by dramatizing it for the nation's people."[25] In 1958 *Fences* by Harry Symons, illustrated by Jefferys, was published by Ryerson Press (a magnificent study of the history of fences in Canada). Just before his death Jefferys had been working with the Imperial Oil Company in the gathering together of his life's work. Today Imperial Oil has 1,200 of his drawings and paintings including the portfolio of 102 drawings he did for the Sam Slick stories. Reproductions have been made available to cultural and educational organizations by this firm. A plaque to honour C.W. Jefferys was unveiled on August 30, 1960, on the grounds of his former residence at 4111 Yonge Street, North York township. The ceremony was sponsored by the North York Historical Society. Mr. Robert Stacey, grandson of the artist, unveiled the plaque.[26] Jefferys was survived by five daughters: Mrs. Charles Thompson (Toronto); Mrs. Edward Helm (California); Mrs. Alexander Fee (York Mills, Ont.); Mrs. Harold Stacey (Long Island) and Mrs. O.W. Allen (Edmonton).[27] A listing in 1951 by the *Ontario Library Review* showed the following private collectors of his works: F.B. Bowden, Esq. (Toronto); William Colgate (Toronto); W.H. Cranston, Esq. (Ottawa); Mrs. E.F. Ely (Toronto); Dr. & Mrs. G.A. Fee (Toronto); Dr. T. H. Hogg (Toronto); Dr. K.G. Makenzie; the late Lorne Pierce; Mrs. H. Stacey (Long Island, N.Y.); Mrs. C.A. Thompson (Toronto); F.G. Venables (Toronto); Mrs. Robert Glasgow (Montreal); Mrs. R.J. Dilworth (Toronto); A.B. Fisher, Esq. (Toronto); Ivor Lewis (Toronto). Jefferys is also represented in a number of other private collections including that of Mr. & Mrs. Jules Loeb. The public collections in which he is represented include: Art Gallery of Ontario; City Hall, Toronto; Faculty Union, University of Toronto; Hudson's Bay Company, Winnipeg; National Gallery of Canada, General Collection; Normal School, Ottawa; Peel County Art Collection (W. Perkins Bull), Brampton, Ont.; Provincial Government of Ontario; Public Archives of Canada; Agnes Etherington Art Centre (Queen's University at Kingston, Ont.); R.C.A. Diploma Collection at the National Gallery of Canada; Saskatoon Memorial Art Gallery at Nutana Collegiate Institute, and elsewhere. Jefferys was a member of the following societies: Ontario Society of Artists (1902 – Pres. 1913-1919); Royal Canadian Academy (A.R.C.A. 1912 – R.C.A. 1925); Graphic Arts Club which became the Canadian Society of Graphic Art (Pres. 1903-4); Canadian Society of Painters in Water Colour (founder member 1925 – Pres. 1928-31); Toronto Art Students' League (1886-1904); Arts and Letters Club, Toronto (founder member 1908 – Pres. 1924-26); Canadian Society of Applied Art; Ontario Historical Society (honorary life member – Pres. 1942-43); Canadian Authors' Association (founder member); Champlain Society (council member); Faculty Union, University of Toronto (honorary life member); Our Club, Toronto (a discussion group composed of outstanding men in the fields of the various arts and sciences). Jefferys exhibited many times with the various art societies of which he was a member. During his career he was awarded the following honours; LL. D., Queen's University, Kingston, 1931; honorary chieftain of the Mohawks of the Grand River Valley and was given the name Ga-Re-Wa-Ga-Yon.[28]

References

[1] *School Progress*, November, 1937, "C.W. Jefferys, R.C.A., LL.D. A Great Canadian Artist and Educationist" by Albert H. Robson, P.15
[2] *The Telegram*, Toronto, Ont., Aug. 25, 1945 "Charles W. Jefferys"

JEFFERYS, Charles William (Cont'd)

[3] *Ontario History*, Vol. XL 1 (1949), No. 4, C.W. Jefferys, O.S.A., R.C.A., LL.D. by Lorne Pierce

[4] Ibid

[5] see[1]

[6] *Chronicle-Telegraph*, Quebec, P.Q., Sept. 25, 1942 "Canadian Artist Author Versatile"

[7] *C.W. Jefferys* by William Colgate, Ryerson, Tor., 1945, P.3

[8] Ibid, P.4

[9] *G.A. Reid* by Muriel Miller Miner, Ryerson, Tor., 1946, P.46, 49

[10] see[7], P.5

[11] see[7], P.5

[12] *C.W. Jefferys* by William Colgate as in [7], P.13

[13] Ibid, P.11

[14] Ibid, P.11

[15] Ibid, P.13

[16] Ibid, P.16

[17] *Canadian Men and Women Of The Time*, Morgan, 1912 (see Magee, P.724)

[18] *The National Gallery of Canada Bulletin 7/1966* "Book Illustration and Design by Canadian Artists 1890-1940" by Sybille Pantazzi (Librarian, The Art Gallery of Ontario)P.7

[19] *Check List Of The War Collections* by R.F. Wodehouse, NGC, Queen's Printer, 1968

[20] as in[7], P.26 also article in Winnipeg *Tribune*, Aug. 9, 1930 by Walter J. Phillips

[21] Winnipeg *Tribune*, Aug. 9, 1930, article on Jefferys by Walter J. Phillips

[22] as in[7], P.26

[23] *Encyclopedia Canadiana*, 1962, Grolier (Can.) C.W. Jefferys by Emily Herbert, P.346

[24] *The Ottawa Citizen*, May 2, 1949 (photo of stamp by CP) small caption.

[25] *Telegraph-Journal*, Saint John, N.B., Oct. 13, 1951 "He Made Our History Live"

[26] *Toronto Daily Star*, Aug. 31, 1960 "Plaque Honors Star Artist"

[27] *Globe & Mail*, Toronto, Ont., Oct. 9, 1951 "Noted Canadian Artist Made History Popular"

[28] *Mayfair*, Toronto, Ont., December, 1951 "The Mohawks' Great Battle Chief"

see also
Imperial Oil Company (Toronto) for portfolios of C.W. Jefferys' drawings
A Century of Canadian Art (catalogue) 1938, P.20, from Queen's Printer
Canadian Art by Graham McInnes, MacMillan (1950), P.62
Canadian Drawings & Prints by Paul Duval, Burns & MacEachern (Tor.) 1952
Canadian Water Colour Painting by Paul Duval, Burns & MacEachern, 1954, see text and plate 21
A Painter's Country by A.Y. Jackson, Clarke, Irwin & Co., Ltd., 1958, P.123
The Art Gallery of Toronto catalogue of Painting & Sculpture (1959)
The National Gallery of Canada Catalogue of Paintings & Sculpture, (1960) *Volume 3, Can. School* by R.H. Hubbard, P.147-8, 394, 428
Painting In Canada/A History by J. Russell Harper, U. of T. Press, 1966, see index also plate 239 on Page 266
The Formative Years/Canada 1812-1871, Ryerson, Tor., 1968, Illustrations by C.W. Jefferys from the collections of Imperial Oil Limited.
Agnes Etherington Art Centre, Queen's University At Kingston (cat.) 1968
Canadian Art Its Origin And Development by William Colgate, Ryerson Paperbacks, 1967 see index.
Ontario Library Review, May, 1951 Jefferys, Charles William (much information in this biography)

JEFFREY, Alice

A west coast Indian artist and totem pole designer who demonstrated her skills at the "B.C. Unlimited" exhibition during the first week of June, 1967, at the Hudson Bay Company store in Vancouver.[1] Her work was very well received at this show.

JEFFREY, Alice (Cont'd)

Her designs have been collected by two Vancouver people Inga Nielsen and Les Lavers, who are interested in translating her designs and the designs of other Indian artists into high fashion colours for prints. It was mentioned that Alice Jeffrey was contemplating a tour of Canada and the United States because of the demand for her work.[2]

References
[1]*News* Prince Rupert, B.C., June 9, 1967 "Master Artist At Work" (photo of artist at work with several of her designs around her desk)
[2]*Victoria Colonist*, July 19, 1967 "Natives To Set Style? "

JEFFRIES, Donald Clark
b.1914

Born in Sussex, New Brunswick, he attended the Sussex Grammar School and Teachers' College, Fredericton, then taught in rural schools also schools at Sussex and Moncton, N.B. He then served with the Royal Canadian Air Force from 1942 to 1945 where he was a bombing instructor.[2] Following his discharge he taught at Macdonald College (McGill University) and then went to New York to continue his studies at Columbia University. He studied under Ziegfeld, Martin, Malderelli and received his B.S. and M.A. in Fine Arts and Fine Arts Education.[3] He exhibited his painting and sculpture in New York before returning to Canada.[4] He was appointed teacher of art, handwriting, and English at Teachers' College at Fredericton, N.B. in 1947.[5] In 1950 a solo show of his non-objective paintings and sculpture, also a few abstractions and representational forms, took place at the Fredericton Observatory Art Centre when the *Gleaner*[6] noted ". . . these paintings contain mood, feeling and expression. They stimulate consideration of architecture and reveal the pleasure to be derived from the contemplation of space relations — shapes, textures and combinations of colour." In 1951 he held what is considered the first exhibition of non-objective painting in Halifax at the Granville Galleries. The *Halifax Mail Star*[7] commented, "Several of the paintings show a great concern for three-dimensional effects and modelled form — possibly influenced by his concern for problems of sculpture. Some examples of his earlier work in realistic and abstract sculpture are also on view . . . . The exhibition is stimulating and varied." He was reported last, as Professor of Art Education at the Nova Scotia College of Art, Halifax.

References
[1]*The Forum*, Fredericton, N.B., November, 1947 "Donald Jeffries Is Art Teacher"
[2]Ibid
[3]National Gallery of Canada Information Form rec'd June 13, 1951
[4]see[1]
[5]see[1]
[6]*Gleaner*, Fredericton, N.B., Jan. 14, 1950 "Exhibition Opened Today At Art Centre"
[7]*Mail Star*, Halifax, N.S. Feb. 7, 1951 "D.C. Jeffries Presents Art Exhibition

JENKINS, George
b.1920
Born at Wilkie, Sask., he spent his childhood at Lloydminister, served overseas with the Canadian Army during World War Two, returned home and eventually settled in Victoria, B.C., where he has held several one-man shows. Has been painting since 1948 and full time since 1963. Has won several important prizes from juried shows. Considers himself an "Abstract-realist" in the tradition of Andrew Wyeth. Exhibited at Charles and Emma Frye Art Museum, Seattle; Mendel Art Gallery, Saskatoon (1970). In perm. coll. of Mendel Art Gallery, and Great West Life (Winn., Man.).

References
> *Herald*, Penticton, B.C., Aug. 16, 1967 "Coast Artist Displays Work"
> Catalogue – *An Exhibition of Paintings by J. George Jenkins*, by J. Climer, Director, Mendel Art Gallery, Sept., 1970

JENSEN, Bent

A Winnipeg artist who painted the crest of the City of St. Boniface. The crest was originally designed by the Roman Catholic Archbishop Tache, and Jensen's crest painting was presented to The City of Mount Royal, a sister city of St. Boniface as part of the twinning ceremonies originated by the Union of Quebec Municipalities.

Reference
> *Free Press*. Winnipeg, Manitoba, September 6, 1967 (photo of artist, crest, and Mayor of St. Boniface)

JENSEN, LeRoy
b.1927
Born in Vancouver, B.C., he first studied painting in Japan where he lived, later in Europe at the Royal Academy at Copenhagen, under Axel Joersensen and Willhelm Lundstrom, then two years under André Lhote in Paris.[1] He returned to Canada and in 1953[2] settled in Vancouver, B.C., where he taught three years at the University of British Columbia, Department of Extension. He subsequently taught at The Banff School of Fine Arts. He has exhibited his work across Canada. *The Vancouver West Ender*,[3] B.C., described his work as follows, "Paintings and drawings by LeRoy Jensen are generally representational, vitally interesting in human values so that the human figure plays an important role in so much of his works. He seeks always a balance between the elements of abstraction, reality, form and spirit, working often in the field of etching, engraving, lithography, mural and fresco." He exhibited his work at the Gallery of B.C. Arts in West Vancouver in 1968. He is a member of the B.C. Society of Artists, Federation of Canadian Artists and the Okanagan Contemporary Artists. He lives in Kelowna, B.C.

References
> [1]National Gallery of Canada Information Form completed May 10, 1967
> [2]Penticton *Herald*, May 3, 1963 "Many Enjoying Two-Man Display"
> [3]*Vancouver West Ender*, B.C., Dec. 4. 1968 "L. Jensen Work at Local Gallery"
> see also
> *News*, Powell River, B.C., Aug. 7, 1960 "Exhibition of paintings and drawings by LeRoy Jensen"
> *Daily Courier*, Kelowna, B.C., Nov. 4, 1961 "Coast Artist LeRoy Jensen Has The Touch" by Anne Smellie

JENSEN, LeRoy (Cont'd)

Ibid, May 29, 1962 "Modern Paintings Of LeRoy Jensen Now In Library"
Penticton Herald, Penticton, B.C., May 2, 1962 "Kelowna Artist's Large Exhibition"
The Vernon News, B.C., March 23, 1964 "Eastern Western Art Made Fine Exhibition"
Vancouver Province, Van. B.C., May 8, 1965 "The views are similar but the results differ"
by Belinda MacLeod

JÉRÔME, Frère   (see PARADIS, Frère Jérôme)

JÉRÔME, Jean-Paul

b.1928

Born in Montreal, P.Q., he became fascinated with the work of Van Gogh before he entered art school.[1] He studied at the Ecole des Beaux-Arts (1944-49) where he received his diploma. After his graduation he did little or no painting. Returning to his easel he had his paintings accepted for the annual Montreal Spring Shows of 1951, 52, and 53. He exhibited as well in the Quebec Provincial Exhibition of 1952 and in 1954 held his first one man show at Gallery XII of the Montreal Museum of Fine Arts. His paintings of this period were derived from the influences of artists like Mondrian, Doesburg, Kandinsky, Malevitch as well as the Cubists.[2] In his methodical study of space he was moved in 1955 to compose in collaboration with Belzile, Jauran (Rodolphe de Repentigny) and Toupin the *Manifeste des Plasticiens* a reaction against the paintings of the Borduas camp which the Plasticiens considered overly facile.[3] In 1956 Jérôme became a member of the Non-Figurative Artists Association of Montreal. This same year he sailed for France to pursue further study in art and also travelled in Italy, Switzerland and Austria. It was in 1957 during his one man show at Galerie Arnaud that Jean Simard, noted Montreal art critic, first saw Jérôme's paintings and was struck by the intensely Canadian and northern colours of his work.[4] Jérôme returned to Montreal in 1958 and in 1959 held a solo show at the Denyse Delrue Gallery for which a catalogue was produced with text by Simard. It was here that Simard[5] explained how he found Jerome's work bewitching, filled with dreams, nostalgia, solitude and love. And how the artist divided his composition into two unequal rectangles which he then carefully filled with raw colours.[5] Dorothy Pfeiffer[6] of *The Gazette* found that his work reminded her of Bible scenes especially his paintings of reeds. Other works which had the qualities of the Northern Lights made her think what good designs for stained-glass windows in modern cathedrals they would make. Jérôme had on his return to Montreal joined the staff of the Ecole des Beaux-Arts, Montreal, while he also continued with his development as painter. In 1960 he held a solo show of abstract pastels at Galerie Libre. It was in these pastels that the reviewer for *La Presse* found the qualities which indicated to him that Jérôme would make a good theatre decorator because of his sense of space, sense of depth, and a sense of a certain living breathing relief enveloped by mystery and drama, with his colours admirably chosen for the play of lighting.

References

[1] *La Presse*, Mtl., P.Q., Dec. 11, 1954 article by R. de Repentigny
[2] *Ecole De Montreal* by Guy Robert, Editions Du Centre De Psychologie Et De Pedagogie, Montreal, P.21, 22

JÉRÔME, Jean-Paul (Cont'd)

[3]*Le Petit Journal*, Mtl., P.Q., Nov. 6, 1960 "Un   poète de la lumière et un magicien du mouvement" par Paul Gladu

[4]*Jean-Paul Jérôme*, par Jean Simard, La Galerie Denyse Delrue, Mtl., P.Q., April, 1959

[5]Ibid

[6]*The Gazette*, Mtl., P.Q., May 23, 1959 — Art — "Jean-Paul Jérôme" by Dorothy Pfeiffer

[7]*La Presse*, Mtl, P.Q., Nov. 12, 1960 "Jean-Paul Jérôme"

see also

La Presse, Mtl., P. Q., Dec. 1, 1954 "La peinture, 'un jeu de l'esprit', affirme le plasticien Jérôme"

Ibid, Dec. 4, 1954 "Première exposition au Musée"

Le Devoir, Mtl., P.Q., Nov. 15, 1955 "Une expérience décevante" par Noël Lajoie

La Presse, Nov. 16, 1955 "Vigoureuse élimination de la sensiblerie dans la peinture de Jérôme" par R. de Repentigny

Ibid, Oct. 17, 1957 "Exposition du peintre J.-P. Jérôme à Paris"

Ibid, May 19, 1959 "Jérôme fait sa rentrée à la galerie Delrue"

Le Petit Journal, Mtl., P.Q., May 24, 1959 "Dans un studio de Paris, Jérôme découvre la . . . nature canadienne" par Paul Gladu

Le Devoir, Mtl., P.Q., May 27, 1959 "Formes et Couleurs" par René Chicoine

La Presse, Mtl., P.Q., May 30, 1959 "Tableaux de Jérôme et fleurs; virage à l'École des Beaux-Arts" par R. de Repentigny

---

JETTEN, Doreen (Mrs.)

Born in Kampali, Uganda, she was educated in Cambridge, England, and took nursing education in London, England. She came to Canada and settled at Port Arthur in 1953, and started painting the same year. Working in oils and acrylics she paints abstracts and landscapes and has taught art at Selkirk Collegiate and Vocational Institute, Fort William. She has exhibited her work in group shows at the Great Hall, Lakehead University. She lives at Port Arthur, Ontario.

Reference

News-Chronicle, Port Arthur, Ont., July 17, 1968 "Known Artist Will Show Work"

JOBIN, Ivan

b.1885

Born in Montreal, P.Q., he studied drawing at the Monument National and later took private study and also visited workshops of many artists.[1] A painter and sculptor he taught wood carving for fifteen years for the Catholic School Commission. He went to France (c. 1946) where in 1956 he held a one man show of his work at "Les Amitiés Françaises" gallery.[2] The exhibition of fifty-four pastels, water colours, washes and ink drawings was opened by the Canadian Ambassador to France.[3] Jobin produced a series of paintings of churches of France as well as lunar landscapes as seen through various telescopes.[4] He is mainly a landscapist in the traditional school and put forward the theory that only man not nature produces the straight line. His book *The Straight or Curved Line* was published sometime before 1936.[5] In an article by S. Handman in *The Montreal Star* in 1936, it was noted that Jobin was married with two children and spent most of his time at his country house at Chambly Canton, Quebec.[6]

JOBIN, Ivan (Cont'd)

References

[1] National Gal. of Can. Info. Form (undated)

[2] A Montreal newspaper (clipping) 19 Oct., 1956 "Un peintre canadien expose des paysages lunaires à Paris"

[3] Ibid

[4] Ibid

[5] *The Montreal Star*, April 15, 1936 "Cameos – Ivan Jobin, Mystic" by S. Handman

[6] Ibid

JOBIN, Louis
1845-1928

Born at Saint Raymond, Quebec, County of Portneuf, his family moved to Pointe-aux-Trembles in the same county, when Jobin was about four.[1] Later Jobin served a three year apprenticeship under the master wood-carver François-Xavier Berlinguet (Berlinguet's mentor, his own father, had studied under Thomas Baillargé, a leading architect-carver of the early 19th Century).[2] Jobin's schooling therefore had been in the finest of traditions – going back to the Cap-Tourmente school founded by Msgr. de Laval in 1673 (this derivation had been traced by the late Dr. Barbeau).[3] For over forty years Jobin made his living principally by the carving of figureheads, nameboards, and stern-work for the decoration of wooden sailing ships at Quebec City and then in New York where he spent a year. He returned to Montreal and opened a shop, still engaged in marine decoration. With the coming of the steam ships, business for the wooden ships became slower and slower and Jobin turned to other types of commissions. He carved everything from cigar store Indians (which are now a very very rare collector's item) to a figure of a notary for a notary's door. Finally with the scarcity of work in ship decoration he returned to Quebec City and took on more and more commissions for churches. In great demand were his carved figures of Christ, the Virgin Mary, the apostles and many saints. An interesting commission was handed him in 1879 by Charles Napoleon Robitaille (who had prayed to the Virgin Mary, twice, when in danger, and twice was snatched from the clutches of death). Robitaille had Jobin carve a 25 foot statue of the Virgin Mary which was placed on top of the 1500 foot cliff of Cape Trinity overlooking the Saguenay River. The work was completed in 1881 and was unveiled by Bishop Racine. To this day the statue has been carefully preserved. Blodwen Davies[4] in her book *Saguenay* relates how the huge statue was erected, "The figure was made in three sections, in order to make the task of getting it up on the rocks possible. It was carried by schooner up the river to the foot of Trinity, and then a party of workmen were set to work on the job of cutting a trail through the woods and over the rocks to the selected spot. The men had to build a sort of wooden railway, over which the huge carved blocks could be dragged by block and tackle from ledge to ledge . . . . The wooden figure is sheathed in lead and frequently painted." She also noted that it was then thought to be one of the largest Madonnas in the world, and up to that time had been cared for by the Robitaille family.[5] Jobin had carved this large statue in his workshop at St. Joachim just outside Ste. Anne-de-Beaupré.[6] Jobin finally settled at Sainte-Anne-de-Beaupré where he had a small shop. Here he was discovered, as

JOBIN, Louis (Cont'd)

Blodwen Davis recalled, " . . . when he was old and bent, historians and art collectors suddenly began to search for samples of his work. Few seem to realize that this celebrated Virgin is his." The historian who made him known nationally, was Marius Barbeau who in 1925 in the company of A.Y. Jackson and Arthur Lismer found him in his small shop. Jackson selected a cherub from the rear of Jobin's shop and secured it for the Art Gallery of Toronto at his (Jackson's) suggested price of seventy-five dollars.[7] Barbeau returned to Jobin's shop in the succeeding months, before Jobin's death in 1928, and traced the whereabouts of Jobin's numerous works (Victoria Heyward also searched for this work). Jobin's records were meagre after a fire in his shop which destroyed most of the record books. But one book remained which had 18 pages of neat writing that recorded twelve years of his work, 1913 to 1925, and revealed his output of 21 statues in 1914, 30 statues in 1916, 17 statues in 1919 and 23 statues in 1920 (when he was over 75 years old). Often Jobin left his initials off his work making the task of identifying the various pieces of sculpture he had done very difficult for the historians. The National Gallery of Canada acquired two of his works in 1929 "The Good Shepherd" and "The Virgin".[8] Subsequently the Gallery acquired another four statues, three from A. Sidney Dawes of Montreal, and a fourth from Mr. Herbert Schwartz.[9] Two of the Dawes donations include St. Peter and St. Paul, carved from pine, each 6 ft. high. In the parishes of Rivière-du-Loup and St. Henri de Levis, Dr. Barbeau found 75 statues. A number of them were eight to ten feet high (for niches near the ceiling or in the choir) others were two or three feet high (for the decoration of altars).[10] Other of Jobin's works include: a statue of Our Lady of the Sacred Heart with child (covered with lead) for the home at Levis; statue of Frontenac and Elgin for the seminary of Sherbrooke (covered in copper); statue of Saint Anne (covered with copper) for Montebello; statue of Saint Michael, 6 ft. (covered in copper) for les Chutes-à-Blondeau, Ontario; statue of Lady of the Sacred Heart of Montmartre, 13 ft. (covered in copper and gilded) for the church of St. Alphonse, Minnedosa, Manitoba; a statue for Hamilton, Ohio; several statues for Nicolet and Bécancour; four angels for the sanctuary of the church of Faubourg, Saint-Jean; statue of Notre Dame de Lourdes (painted white) 6 ft. bought by Mme. Bossé of Quebec for Labrador; two angels 7 ft. for Mr. Martel curé of Saint-Isidore, Chicoutimi; statue of Saint Anne, 5½ ft.(painted white) for Mr. Maytor, Ashland, Wisconsin; two angels with trumpets, 7 ft., and 10 ft. covered in copper and gilded for a steeple at Holyoke, Mass.; head of a child for the Duke of Devonshire; two heads were acquired by the late Dr. Marius Barbeau; two judgement angels with trumphets in the Deschambault cemetery at Portneuf; an altar piece for the church of l'Isle-aux-Coudres.[11] Jobin died at Ste. Anne de Beaupré just three years after Dr. Barbeau's visit, a visit that if it had occurred a few years later might have left us with considerably less information on one of the last of the great race of woodcarvers in Canada. Jobin is also represented in the National Museum of Canada and the Museum of the Province of Quebec.

References

[1] *La Presse*, Montreal, P.Q., Aug. 26, 1933 "Un grand artisan; Louis Jobin" par Marius Barbeau

[2] Ibid

[3] *Family Herald*, Montreal, P.Q., May 2, 1934 "Medieval Wood-Carver In Laurentians" by Marius Barbeau

JOBIN, Louis (Cont'd)

[4] *Saguenay; River of Deep Water Waters* by Blodwen Davies, copyw. by Canada Steamship Lines, published by McClelland & Stewart Limited, 1930, P.192-3

[5] Ibid, P.193

[6] Ibid, P.193

[7] *A Painter's Country* by A.Y. Jackson, Clarke, Irwin, Tor., 1963, P.68

[8] *The National Gallery of Canada Catalogue, Vol.3* by R.H. Hubbard, P.349

[9] *Le Droit*, Ottawa, Ont., Sept. 12, 1963 "Dons au Musée National"

[10] *Vancouver Province*, Van., B.C., Jan. 9, 1942 "French Canadian A Master Carver" by Marius Barbeau

see also

The Macmillan Dictionary of Canadian Biography Edited by W. Stewart Wallace, 1963, P.348-9

Canadian Art Its Origin and Development by William Colgate, P.115

The Arts In Canada prepared by the Canadian Citizenship Branch, Dept. Citizenship and Immigration, Ottawa, 1958, obtainable from Queen's Printer, P.24-5

Three Hundred Years of Canadian Art a catalogue by R.H. Hubbard and J.R. Ostiguy, Queen's Printer, 1967 Page 88, cat. nos. 138, 139, 140.

The Development of Canadian Art by R.H. Hubbard, Queen's Printer, 1963, P.43, 44

JOE, Philip

b. (c) 1945

A Yukon Indian who paints oil pastels on moosehide which is then stretched on a wooden frame by means of moosehide thongs. This work is being promoted by the Vocational Guidance Counselor Harold G. Kendall of the Yukon Indian Agency. An assembly-line of local families has been organized to produce various parts of the pictures. Some of the moosehide paintings are stretched on snowshoe shaped frames.

Reference

Star, Whitehorse, Yukon, Jan. 17, 1966 (photo of artist, his work, and Harold Kendall of the Yukon Indian Agency)

JOHNS, A. Wilfrid

One of his paintings is in the collection of the University of Victoria, B.C., and depicts the scope of a modern university. Measuring nine by six feet the mural hangs on the second floor of the Ewing Building with other paintings of the University's collection. Johns was in 1960 a professor of art education at the University.

References

Victoria Daily Times, Mar. 22, 1960 " 'Bustling' Mural Unveiled Wednesday"

Ibid, Mar., 25, 1960 "My Jigg's Eye View of Culture" by Stott

---

JOHNSON, Bruce Henderson

b.1926

Born in Toronto, Ontario, he went to sea at the age of fifteen then joined the R.C.A.F. and served as an aerial gunner during the Second World War. He received

JOHNSON, Bruce Henderson (Cont'd)

his discharge in 1945 and went to work as an apprentice artist in a Toronto engraving house.[1] He learned by practical experience instead of attending formal art classes. He has worked in various commercial illustration studios and advertising agencies. Following his marriage he moved to Montreal where he established himself as a freelance artist. Since 1950 he has done commissions for all the major Canadian magazines which included editorial and general commercial illustration.[2] His work began appearing in *Weekend Magazine* about 1957.[3] In 1963 Johnson moved to Franklin Centre, 40 miles southwest of Montreal, where his children enjoy growing up in the country atmosphere which he described as "A small brook, eight rolling acres of trees and a neighbor with a friendly horse."[4] This atmosphere prompted him to create a picture story for *Weekend Magazine's* issue No. 32 of 1964 entitled "When Children Discover The Country". Johnson's illustrations are full of colour and life; a few of them are listed below.[5] His Montreal sketches have appeared on the editorial pages of *The Montreal Star*.

References

[1] National Gallery of Canada Information Form (undated) also *Weekend Magazine*, Dec., 23, 1967 "The Art Of The Matter" a biographical sketch of Bruce Johnson by Craig Ballantyne, Editorial Director of *Weekend Magazine*.

[2] Nat. Gal. Can. Info. Form as above

[3] *Weekend Magazine* as above

[4] Ibid

[5] Issues of Weekend Magazine in which Johnson's work appears:

Harry J. Boyle's "Merry Christmas At Lee's Cafe" (No. 51, 1964);

Robert McKeown's "Ottawa's Red Spies: Wicked, Wacky and Ever Present" (No. 15, 1965);

Margo Oliver's "Fall For Vegetables" (No. 36, 1965);

Max Braithwaite's "Prairie School teacher" (three parts, No. 37, 38, 39, 1965);

A picture story of how Johnson's three children search for the perfect Christmas tree at their country home (No. 52, 1965);

Cyril Robinson's "Two Who Survived" (No. 10, 1966);

Patrick Nagle's "The Man Who Lived With War" the story of Raymond Collishaw, flying ace (No. 36, 1966);

"The Farm Fair" Johnson's impressions of a country fair (No. 38, 1966);

"Christmas In The Country" picture story by Johnson (No. 52, 1966);

Jack Carroll's "Portrait Of A Poolroom Hustler" (No. 9, 1967) and many others.

JOHNSON, Douglas

b. (c) 1924

Born at Smithville, Ontario, he lived on a farm and attended a rural school. About 1941 he went to work for a local weekly newspaper where he did everything from operating the linotype machine to sweeping the floor. In 1942 he enlisted in the army in which he served until 1946. He returned to the newspaper, and in 1947 enrolled at the Ontario College of Art where he studied lettering, sculpture, interior and three-dimensional design, industrial design and the history of art. He graduated from the College with honours in 1951. He worked for the Department of Trade and Commerce, Ottawa, 1952-6, then moved to Montreal where he is presently employed with the Canadian National Railways making complicated charts. In the evenings he follows his career of painter mainly in the abstract. He has had a solo exhibition in a Montreal theatre. A photographer as well he held a one man show of his prints in Ottawa.

JOHNSON, Douglas (Cont'd)

Reference
   Review, Smithville, Ontario, Jan. 27, 1960 "Former Smithville Boy Talented Artist"

JOHNSON, Edwin J.
b.1889

Born in Brigden, Ontario, he has been a farmer and artist all his life. When he first started to paint scenes he used pastels and did pen and ink drawings, but most of his work has been done in oils. His scenes are about threshing, logging, barn-raising, plowing with horses, and oil field operations at Lambton, modern rural landscapes and other subjects. At first he began selling and giving his works to friends but finally knowledge of his paintings extended beyond his region. Today collectors of his works can be found in United States, Britain, and across Canada. His wife looks after the sales of his paintings and usually selects titles for most of them. Edwin Johnson is represented in the Oil Museum of Canada, Oil Springs, Ontario. It is estimated that he has done 461 paintings, most of them depicting pioneer life in Lambton County, Ontario. His home is at R.R.1, Brigden, Ontario. Now that he is 80 years old he only paints a few hours a day.

References
   Sarnia Canadian Observer, Sarnia, Ont., Sept. 15, 1960 "He's A Farmer-Artist"
   London Evening Free Press, London, Ont., Feb. 6, 1969 "Brigden man's 461 paintings compendium of Lambton history" by Bill Morley

JOHNSON, Esther

She designed windows for St. Bartholomew's (Anglican) Church in Toronto and has also worked with Yvonne Williams in the decoration of this church.

Reference
   Globe & Mail, Toronto, Ont., April 26, 1958 "Inexpensive Windows Are Chosen by Church"

JOHNSON, Kathleen Beatrice
b.1917

Born in York Township, Ontario, she studied at the Ontario College of Art (1932-6), under Yvonne McKague Housser and Grace Coombs, where she received a Junior Scholarship. She became active in Willowdale art circles and was a founding member of the Willowdale Group of Artists (Pres. 1954-55). Subsequently she became a member of the Society of Canadian Artists (1958) and was its membership convenor, 1959-60. Kathleen Johnson has been working in mixed media and acrylic and received the Carling's Mixed Media Award in 1965. She exhibited with the Colour and Form Society at Hart House (1968) and Waterloo University (1968). She was a member of the Ontario Institute of Painters (1961) but resigned in 1965. Her first one man show of paintings was held at the Don Mills Library in 1966 which was followed by a one man show at the Sobot

JOHNSON, Kathleen Beatrice (Cont'd)

Gallery in 1968. She is represented by the Sobot Gallery. Her work hangs in the permanent collection of Ontario House, London, England. She teaches art for Adult Education programs and lives at Willowdale, Ontario.

Reference
    National Gallery of Canada Information Form rec'd c.1968

JOHNSON, William James
b.1927

Born at Windsor, Ontario, he was active with the Maritime Art Association while a member of the R.C.A.F. stationed at Summerside, P.E.I. An electronics officer in the Air Force he retired in 1964 when he returned to Windsor. He completed study at a teachers' college and attended a summer course in painting at the Ontario College of Art. He has done some outstanding work in portraiture and is represented in the permanent collection of the Fathers of Confederation Memorial Gallery in Charlottetown. He lives at London, Ontario.

References
    National Gallery of Canada Information Form rec'd in 1964
    Journal-Pioneer, Summerside, P.E.I., March 25, 1963 "Painting Is Accepted For Exhibition"
    Ibid, Feb. 7, 1964 "Course In Drawing, Painting Slated For Summer Street School"
    Ibid, May 8, 1964 "Painting Is Accepted by Fred. Gallery"
    Guardian & Patriot, Charlottetown, P.E.I., July 22nd, 1964 "Airman Artist Began Career When Treated For Arthritis"
    Windsor Daily Star, Windsor, Ont., Aug. 7, 1964 "Painting Donated to Centre" (Senator Orville Phillips of Summerside, P.E.I., purchased Johnson's 'Fisherman's Son' then donated it to Fathers of Confederation Centennial Centre at Charlottetown)
    The London Free Press, London, Ont., July 8, 1965 "Schooling Precedes Teaching"

JOHNSTON, Dorothy Paine (nee Dorothy Dunn)
b.1925

Born in Harcourt, New Brunswick, she graduated from the University of Manitoba, Winnipeg, in Interior Design from the School of Architecture in 1956 and in Fine Arts, 1965, when she studied under Ivan Eyre, Ron Burke, Cecil Richards, Charles Scott and Kenneth Butler. A ceramic sculptress her work has been sold and widely distributed in Canada and the United States (Los Angeles, Chicago and New York). One man shows of her work have been held at the Yellow Door Gallery (1965), the Leisureland Show (1967) and the Fleet Gallery (1968) in Winnipeg. She has been working mainly with stoneware clay as a medium in which she fashions a variety of shapes or objects ranging in size from one inch to over three feet. Recently she has been experimenting with melting Italian lime-based glass in stoneware clay. One of her other experiments will be to combine stoneware forms with old wood and metal (cedar fence posts with ceramic heads). She is represented in the permanent collection of the Department of External Affairs (overseas). She has written a thesis on ceramic sculptural murals on which she has done considerable work. Most of her work is untraditional in concept and is highly creative. She has given lectures in Manitoba on glass as an art form, also the history of art and its relation to political history. She lives in Winnipeg.

JOHNSTON, Dorothy Paine (Cont'd)

References
> National Gallery of Canada Information Form rec'd July 17, 1967
> *Winnipeg Free Press*, Man., June 5, 1965 "Coherence In The Joy" a review by Ken Winters
> Ibid, June 29, 1968 "Transition In Sculpture" by Peter Crossley

JOHNSTON, Frances-Anne (Mrs. Franklin Arbuckle)
b.1910

Born in Toronto, Ontario, the daughter of the late Franz Johnston (noted Canadian artist) and Florence Jamieson, she received her education at the North Toronto Collegiate and at the Ontario College of Art where she won two scholarships. She met her husband Franklin Arbuckle at the Ontario College of Art. They married five years later in 1934 after the worst part of depression had passed and settled down in Toronto. She was particularly interested in landscapes which she did very well but in 1937 her first daughter was born and she was no longer free to paint out-of-doors. She turned to painting interior studies and today is one of Canada's most accomplished artists in this subject. For many years she was known for her Christmas cards and much later did a series of Canadian Wild Flower studies for Murray's Restaurants which were reproduced as part of the decoration for the menus. Her husband was moved to Montreal in 1941 while an employee of Bomac Engravers' and they lived there until 1958 when they returned to Toronto. Much of her time has been taken up with the raising of her two daughters and it was not until the last few years that she has been able to devote more of her time to painting. She has exhibited, over the years, with the Royal Canadian Academy and with other societies. She was elected an A.R.C.A. in 1949 and R.C.A. about 1963. She is represented in a number of galleries including the Roberts Gallery (Toronto), the Eaton's Fine Art Gallery (Toronto), Wallack Galleries, Ottawa.

References
> *MacLean's Magazine*, Feb. 28, 1959 "The Franklin Arbuckles" by Barbara Moon
> Royal Canadian Academy exhibition catalogues
> Ontario Library Association biographies (1951)
> Viewing the artist's work in the Roberts and the Eaton's galleries.

JOHNSTON, Francis Hans (Frank H. Johnston) (Franz Johnston)
1888-1949

Born in Toronto, Ontario, the son of Hans Hamilton Johnston and Mary Elizabeth Roderick (both parents from Ireland) he was educated at the Givins Street School, Toronto, the Central Technical School under Gustav Hahn, the Central Ontario School of Art under William Cruikshank and G.A. Reid.[1] He served his apprenticeship with Brigden's Limited in Toronto.[2] He became employed by the Grip Engraving Company sometime in 1908.[4] He then went to the United States where he continued his studies, and later attended the Pennsylvania Academy of Fine Art under the late Phillip Hale and Daniel Garber.[3] He moved to New York where he worked in the Carleton Illustrators Studios, a firm which was associated with the Carleton Studios in London, England. He then returned to Toronto.

In 1918 Johnston was commissioned by the Canadian War Memorials to record the activities of Canadian flying personnel training for overseas duty.[5] During this period he produced seventy-three (or more) works including water colours, temperas, and oils. Many of these paintings although of a documentary nature were brilliantly created through masterful composition and colouring (see *Check List Of The War Collections* by Major R.F. Wodehouse-NGC-). Johnston's paintings are among the finest in the war collections. Following his service with the Canadian War Memorials he returned to Toronto where he probably spent some time at the Studio Building. In 1918 he accompanied Lawren Harris, J.E.H. MacDonald, Dr. James MacCallum in their first box-car trip to Algoma. This region of northern Ontario was an area of beauty in autumn. The trees of gold, yellow, and crimson covering the majestic mountains and edges of the lakes and rivers moved the artists to create some of their finest canvases. Johnston returned to Algoma in 1919 with Jackson, MacDonald, Harris and Dr. MacCallum who probably joined them later. This group went again in 1920. Johnston made scores of drawings and paintings of Algoma but few of them were reproduced in Canadian art history books with the exception of his "Fire Swept, Algoma"[6] (NGC Coll.); "God's Country"[7] (Mr. & Mrs. J. Loeb); "In Algoma"[8] and "Northern Cabin"[9]. In 1920 Johnston became a founding member of the Group of Seven (others were: J.E.H. MacDonald, A.Y. Jackson, Frank Carmichael, F.H. Varley, Arthur Lismer, Lawren S. Harris) and he exhibited in their first exhibitions but in 1922 his association with the Group of Seven ended. They had become a target of attacks by critics and somehow their group spirit seemed to limit Johnston from doing what he wanted to do. He was every bit as eager to express his love of the Canadian wilds as they were but he wanted to paint in a less controversial style. Johnston held a solo exhibit of his work at the T. Eaton Company in December, 1920, when *The Mail & Empire*[10] noted, "The position of Frank H. Johnston, A.R.C.A. among local artists is unique. Mr. Johnston is always classed as one of the much discussed 'group of seven,' but he has never got out of touch with the picture lovers who cannot quite get the viewpoint of his ultra-radical companions . . . . He has the secret of the living, vivid coloring of the Northland, and catches the feeling of the wild spaces." Johnston left Toronto when he was appointed Principal, the Winnipeg School of Art. He kept up his activities as a painter and held an exhibit of 326 of his paintings at the Winnipeg Art Gallery of which Arthur Stoughton[11] of the *Free Press* noted, "The greater number of the pictures are done in tempera, although this show presents evidence of the versatility of this man. He seems to have tried every color medium with good results. Here, in No. 304, is a massive oil painting with all the solidity which that material may present. Here, in No. 60 and in 280, are the wettest of transparent water colors, composed of washes of most elusive tints, devoid of outline. Then there are watercolors, as in No. 281 done in that method of broken color, dear to the heart of the impressionist or pointillist, in which spots of pure color put side by side blend in the eye of the observer. Again there are some dozen pastels which have a three-fold interest — first, from their good quality, second, because they present the artist's first impressions of Winnipeg, and, third, as being his first essays in this medium." In December of that year Johnston held another exhibition of his paintings particularly of Western Canada which were described as having "the stimulus of the great spacious plains", "magnificent cloud effects",

JOHNSTON, Francis Hans (Cont'd)

"glowing sunsets and enveloping sunshine".[12] He was principal of the Winnipeg School of Art from 1920 to 1924 and by 1927 was back in Toronto where he became principal of the Ontario College of Art. About 1926 he changed his name from Frank to Franz because he was told by a numerologist friend in New York that the name Frank would never bring him success. Johnston wrote down the name Franz (name of a community east of White River, Ont.) and his friend told him it was an excellent choice. His canvases from then on were signed Franz Johnston. He was principal of the Ontario College of Art from 1927 to 1929. He exhibited his work throughout his career with the Ontario Society of Artists and the Royal Canadian Academy as he was a member of both societies (O.S.A.) (A.R.C.A.). In 1931 the Simpson's Fine Arts Gallery created a new Franz Johnston Room for the express purpose of selling his paintings.[13] Johnston established a summer school of art at Georgian Bay (1930-40) where he was closer to that part of Ontario he loved to paint. In 1940 he closed his summer school and settled at Wyebridge in the same region. He began his trips into the Far North in the thirties and his work of this period was exhibited at several galleries including the Malloney gallery in Toronto. In 1938 Augustus Bridle[14] in *The Toronto Star* noted Johnston's exhibit at Malloney's as follows, "Canada's farthest-north regular painter has for three years brought the land of crackling sub-zero, shivering spruces and truculent huskie dogs into picture shows here . . . . What he has already painted of actual life in the Nipigon Country, as shown in this super-brilliant, intimate picture-saga at Malloney's, is to him a mere prelude to what he intends to paint of Canada's so-called 'lost frontier.' " In 1939 he was commissioned by Gilbert Labine (Vice-Pres. of Eldorado Gold Mines) to go to the Canadian Arctic to paint nature, trappers, miners and native types in all seasons and after five months completed 100 sketches. Working in 35 to 40 below zero weather, he mixed his pigments, which had become like jelly, with pure turpentine. When he painted he covered his hand in a lumberman's sock through which he manipulated his brush.[15] Many of these works were exhibited at Malloney's in December of that year. In 1940 he completed a large canvas entitled "Shack In The Woods" which he considered his masterpiece. He took it to a Toronto art dealer to sell and was in the process of dickering for the best price when a man (from New York) entered the gallery and asked Johnston how much he wanted for the painting. Johnston stated 850 dollars and the man purchased the work on the spot. Later reproductions of this painting were sold by the thousands with Johnston receiving no royalties from their sales.[16] In 1942 he exhibited his work at Eaton's, particularly scenes of the Wyebridge area, also some arctic paintings. He again exhibited at Eaton's in 1943 when Augustus Bridle[17] found in his paintings "Green-blue skies and lavender snows; blue snow-wraiths in the shadow against a blaze of early morn golden light; ravishing snakes of water as opalescent as rainbow-backed beetles; tousles of brushwood that look like jackpine or tamarac because painted so vividly . . . . These are a few of the Wye-fantasias." Of the eighty paintings he exhibited, fifty percent were sold within three weeks. They ranged in price from fifty to one thousand dollars each.[18] In 1948 Johnston moved from Wyebridge to Midland, Ontario, but not long afterwards suffered a stroke. His paintings were in popular demand until his death. In July the Owen Sound *Sun-Times* noted his passing as follows, "It may be said that, in a sense, Franz Johnston dedicated his professional life to Canada, for he had a deep appreciation for what this country had to offer. This sense of

JOHNSTON, Francis Hans (Cont'd)

dedication was exemplified in his works. He painted Canadian things because he knew them best and he knew them best because he chose to live and work among the scenes and the people he portrayed . . . . He will be long remembered for his long-established summer art school on Georgian Bay. Here he not only created some of his own most famous paintings, but also guided the steps of many other painters along the pathway to success." The bulk of Johnston's paintings still in his possession at the time of his death were purchased by Laing Galleries, Toronto.[20] A plaque was unveiled by Mrs. John Schofield (formerly Mrs. Franz Johnston) on the grounds of his former residence at Wyebridge, Ontario on September 18, 1963. The Roberts Gallery, Toronto, held an exhibition of his work during the same year. Johnston illustrated and did decorations for a number of books.[21] He is represented in the following public collections: Saskatoon Art Centre, Sask.; Winnipeg Art Gallery, Winnipeg, Man.; London Public Art Museum, London, Ont.; Art Gallery of Ontario, Tor., Ont.; McMichael Conservation Collection, Kleinburg, Ont.; National Gallery of Canada (General Collection, and War Collection as mentioned above); and probably other public collections, also the following private collections: J. G. McKurdy, Regina Sask.; Arthur Cutten Jr.; Mr. & Mrs. Jules Loeb, Hull, Quebec; formerly in the collection of the late Dr. Tait Mackenzie; Franz Lawren Johnston (his son) Grimsby, Ontario; others of his surviving relatives; William G. Street, Richmond Hill, Ontario. At the time of his death Johnston was survived by: his wife (now remarried); four children — Frances-Anne Johnston, A.R.C.A. (wife of Franklin Arbuckle, R.C.A.) Toronto; Mrs. James Stevenson (Toronto); Paul Roderick (an artist who paints under this pseudonym); Franz Lawren Johnston (see above); a brother Harry Johnston (Toronto). A retrospective exhibition of his work was organized by his son Paul at the Rothman Art Gallery, Stratford, Ontario, and opened in September, 1970. Paul Roderick is also preparing a book on his father.

References

[1] National Gallery of Canada Information Form rec'd May 14, 1915
Evening Telegram, Toronto, Ont., July 11, 1949 "Artist Franz Johnston, 61, Dies" by Rose MacDonald
[2] *Globe & Mail*, Toronto, Ont., July 11, 1949 "Noted Canadian Artist, Franz Johnston Dead" by Ken W. MacTaggart
[3] NGC Inf. Form as in[1]
[4] *September Gale* by John A.B. McLeish, J.M. Dent & Sons Ltd., 1955, P.24, 25
Group Of Seven Drawings by Paul Duval, Burns & MacEachern, 1965, 3rd page of text
J.E.H. MacDonald, R.C.A., 1873-1932 (Catalogue) P.13
Canadian Landscape Painters by A.H. Robson, Ryerson, 1932, P. 136
The Group of Seven by Peter Mellen, McClelland & Stewart Ltd., Tor. 1970, P. 21
[5] *The Group of Seven* by Dennis Reid, NGC, 1970, P. 119, 120
[6] *Canadian Painters* by Donald W. Buchanan, Phaidon, NYC, London, 1945, Plate 54
The Development of Canadian Art by R.H. Hubbard, Queen's Printer, 1963, P.96
Nat. Gal. Can. Catalogue, Vol. 3 by R.H. Hubbard, P.149
Three Centuries of Canadian Art by R.H. Hubbard & J.R. Ostiguy, P.129
[7] *Painting In Canada/A History* by J. Russell Harper, U. of T., 1966, P.289
[8] *Group of Seven Drawings* by Paul Duval, Burns & MacEachern, 1965, P.11 & 12
[9] Ibid
[10] *The Mail & Empire*, Tor., Ont., Dec. 18, 1920 "Wealth Of Color Seen In Paintings"
[11] *Free Press*, Winnipeg, Man., Jan. 28, 1922 "Winnipeg Art Topics" by Arthur Alexander Stoughton

JOHNSTON, Francis Hans (Cont'd)

[12] Ibid, Dec. 8, 1922 "Frank H. Johnston Exhibition One Of Year's Local Art Events" by Arthur Alexander Stoughton

[13] *Canadian Homes and Gardens*, March, 1931 "Announcing the New Franz Johnston Room in the Fine Arts Gallery"

[14] *The Toronto Star*, Dec. 7, 1938 "Johnston Exhibits Trail Extravaganza"

[15] *Globe & Mail*, Tor., Ont., Oct. 24, 1939 "Johnston Paints With Turpentine"

[16] Unidentified clipping from Fort William area — article entitled, "Shack In Woods Made Mint for Another" by John Friesen

[17] *The Toronto Star*, Mar. 23, 1943 "Many-Trails Franz Shows Canada Revue" by Augustus Bridle

[18] *Free Press*, Midland, Ont., Mar. 31, 1943 "Franz Johnston's Art Show Proves Toronto Sensation Fifty Per Cent Pictures Sold"

[19] *Sun-Times*, Owen Sound, Ont., July 16, 1949 "Franz Johnston — Painter of the Canadian Scene"

[20] *Globe & Mail*, Tor., Ont., July 12, 1949 "Rich Legacy Left Canada by Artist of the North" (two photos with captions)

[21] *Canadian Folk Songs* (Old & New) selected and translated by J. Murray Gibbon, Decorations by Frank H. Johnston, J.M. Dent & Sons Ltd. (Lond. & Tor.) 1927

Friendly Acres by Peter McArthur with decorations by Franz Johnston, The Musson Book Co. Ltd., Publishers, 1927

The Beauport Road by J.E. LeRossignol, decorations by Franz Johnston, McClelland & Stewart Ltd., Tor., 1928

The Flying Canoe by J.E. LeRossignol, decorations by Franz Johnston, McClelland & Stewart Ltd., Tor, Ont., 1929

The Wayside Cross by Mary E. Waagen, illustrations by Franz Johnston, The Musson Book Co. Ltd., Tor., 1929 (see NGC Bulletin 7/1966 P.16)

see also

The Fine Arts In Canada by Newton MacTavish, MacMillan, Tor., 1925, P.154

A Century Of Canadian Art (catalogue, 1938, Tate Gal. exhibit) Queen's Printer, P.21

Canadian Art: Its Origin And Development by William Colgate, Ryerson, Tor., 1943 (Paperback 1967), P.36, 69, 71, 78, 81, 82, 88-90, 177, 178, 221

Canadian Art by Graham McInnes, MacMillan, Tor., 1950, P.54, 57, 60

A Painter's Country by A.Y. Jackson, Clarke, Irwin, Tor. 1963, P.47-8, 54-5, 78, 114

The McMichael Conservation Collection, notes by Paul Duval, Clarke, Irwin, Tor., 1967

Encyclopedia Canadiana, Grolier, Vol. 5, 1962, P. 357

The Group of Seven by Thoreau MacDonald, Ryerson, Tor., (Third Ed.1952), P.6

JOHNSTON, James Dalzell

b.1918

Born at Birnie, Manitoba, he began painting in 1945 and studied at the Vancouver School of Fine Arts under B.C. Binning, J.L. Shadbolt, Fred Amess, Charles Scott, others, and graduated in 1948. He has been chiefly interested in painting the human figure in natural or man made environments. He found his subjects along the west coast, then the interior of British Columbia; later Toronto, Ontario and was last reported living in Moose Jaw, Saskatchewan where he was organizer of the Moose Jaw City Arts and Crafts (1952), Advisor of the Moose Jaw Arts and Crafts Co-ordinating Council (1953) and a member of the Moose Jaw Fine Arts Guild, Recreation Supervisor in the City of Moose Jaw. He won a prize for his painting "Duel at Brockton Point" at the Canadian Society of Graphic Art's exhibit in September of 1957 (first prize went to Jack Bush of Toronto).

References

National Gallery of Canada Information Form rec'd May 16, 1953

The Province, Vancouver, B.C., Sept. 4, 1957 "Artist awarded prize of $50"

JOHNSTON, Paul Roderick (see Paul Roderick)

JOHNSTON, Robert Edwin

1885-1933

Born in Toronto, Canada, the brother of Franz Johnston, A.R.C.A., he studied in Toronto under William Cruikshank and C.M. Manly and in London, England, at the Bolt Court School under Cecil Rae; the Regent Street Polytechnic under Watson; Westminister College of Art under Walter Sickert and in New York, U.S.A., under Harry Wickey.[1] He returned to Canada where he made his living as a commercial artist, illustrator (working in oils) and also cartoonist for the Toronto *Saturday Night*.[2] Later he went to the United States (c.1911) and resided at Leonia, New Jersey (not far from New York City).[3] In 1925 he was awarded $1000 Purchase Prize for the decoration of the Walt Whitman Hotel at Camden, N.Y. (a mural depicting the poet in an allegorical setting).[4] Johnston died at his home in Leonia.

References
[1] National Gallery of Canada Information Form rec'd Feb.9, 1927
[2] *The Globe*, Tor., Ont., Nov. 30, 1933 "Robert E. Johnston" (obituary)
[3] as in[1]
[4] *Star Weekly*, Tor., Ont., Oct. 24, 1925 "Pick Canadian Artist To Honor Famous Poet"
see also
Canadian Landscape Painters by A.H. Robson, Ryerson, 1932, P.136
Canadian Art; Its Origin and Development by William Colgate, Ryerson, 1943, P.69, 221

JOHNSTONE, John Young

1887-1930

Born in Montreal, Quebec, he studied at the Art Association of Montreal under William Brymner, R.C.A., and in Paris at the Académie de la Grande Chaumière under Pau, Casteluche, Simon, and Ménard.[1] His style was rather beautiful being a simplified realism also with the influence of the Impressionists. He was most successful in his early thirties. He exhibited his paintings at the Montreal Spring Shows and with the Royal Canadian Academy. He was elected A.R.C.A. in 1920. Newton MacTavish[2] included him amongst the very fine painters in Canada in 1925 and his painting "A Quebec Village" (an oil on panel) was reproduced in Mac-Tavish's *The Fine Arts In Canada*.[3] The National Gallery of Canada acquired four of his canvases – two street scenes entitled "Quai Des Augustins Bruges" (acq. 1915) and "Bonsecours Market" (acq.1916) – a harbour scene "Le Bassin Louise, À Québec" (acq.1922) and a rural scene "The Road, Saint-Joachim, Quebec" (acq.1924).[4] In 1930 he went to Havana, Cuba, and somehow became destitute and died there at the age of 43.[5] Those who still enjoy his paintings wonder if his tragic end could not have been prevented.

References
[1] *The Fine Arts In Canada* by Newton MacTavish, MacMillan, Tor., 1925, P.171
[2] Ibid, Chapter 23 "Others Of Importance", P.147
[3] Ibid, P.69
[4] *National Gallery of Canada Catalogue, Volume 3*, by R.H. Hubbard, P.150
[5] *The Globe*, Tor., Ont., Feb. 14, 1930 "Canadian Artist Dies In Poverty"

JONE, Wing

b.1922

Born in Toronto, Ontario, he served with the Canadian Army in India (1944-6) where he had the opportunity to design, construct and decorate sets for camp shows. When he returned to Canada he studied evenings and also part time at the Vancouver School of Art (1947-53); the Polytechnic School of Art, London, England (1955-56) and on a scholarship at the Instituto Allende, Mexico (1958) under James Pinto. He was last reported living in Vancouver, B.C. No recent information is available on this artist.

Reference

National Gallery of Canada Information Form rec'd June 30, 1959

JONES, Dennis Gordon

b.1932

Born in London, England, he was brought up in India and later studied at the Farnham School of Art, Surrey, England, and also under Paul Sharp and Harold Cheeseman. He travelled and painted in Europe from 1953 to 1955. He came to Canada in 1958 and settled in Montreal. Recently, in his painting, he has been interested in geometric abstraction and has held one man shows at the Galerie Libre, Montreal (1964) (1965), at the Sobot Gallery, Toronto (c.1965) and in many group shows including Paintings by Young Quebec Artists organized by the National Gallery of Canada. He is represented in the collections of the National Gallery of Canada (drawing), the Dominion Gallery, Montreal, and in many private collections in Montreal; Toronto; New York City; London, England; San Francisco; Chile, and elsewhere.

References

National Gallery of Canada Information Form c.1966

Catalogue sheet – *Paintings by Young Quebec Artists* (an exhibition organized for the Western Canada Art Circuit through the cooperation of Galerie Libre, Galerie Agnes Lefort, and Norah McCullough of The National Gallery of Canada.

JONES, Edith (Mrs.)

She resides in Sidney, B.C., and started painting about 1953. She studied under Herbert Siebner and Arnold Burrell and has been particularly interested in land-scape and plant themes. Using these subjects she has done extensive work with sink-screen prints and received honourable mention in the Jury Shows of the Art Gallery of Greater Victoria in 1967. She was awarded First Prize in the 1964 Alberni Valley exhibition. Her serigraphs are in the collection of the Art Gallery of Greater Victoria.

References

Bulletin: Art Gallery of Greater Victoria, Sept.-Oct. 1967

Saanich Review, Sidney, B.C., May 15, 1963 "Sidney Artist Gains Acclaim At Jury Show For 'Forms In Moss' "

The Daily Colonist, Victoria, B.C., Oct. 29, 1967 "Sidney Artist Exhibits Silk Screens" by Ina D. D. Uhthoff

JONES, Fran (Frances Martha Rosewarne)
b.1916

Born at Smiths Falls, Ontario, she studied at the Ontario College of Art (1936-39) under John Alfsen, Frank Carmichael, Rowley Murphy, Eric Aldwinckle, Fred Haines; Gustav and Emanuel Hahn, Charles Comfort, George Pepper, Yvonne McKague and took the history of art under Prof. Alford; she graduated from the College in 1940 with her A.O.C.A. (receiving honours in water colours, and figure drawing). Subsequently she attended summer school at Queen's University in 1952 where she studied under Stanley Cosgrove and Grant MacDonald; the summer of 1954 at the Art Students' League under Will Barnett and Bernard Klonis; at Queen's again in 1957 under Gustav Weisman and André Biéler; and she took a number of other courses on art and art history. A commercial artist she has worked with the National Film Board (1945-46); Murphy Gamble (1946-47); Advertising Manager for R.J. Devlin & Co., Ottawa (1947-49); Exhibition Commission (1949); A.J. Freiman Ltd. (1950); Queen's Printer (1953-58). As a painter and graphic artist she is best known for her colour prints. Her work was once described by Harry Bruce of *The Ottawa Journal* as follows, " . . . Taking up one of an assorted collection of fine German steel gouges and knives, she begins her careful hacking away of everything she wants left white. When she had dug out out separate cuts for each color, she 'beds one down' and rolls ink across the carved face. The paper is tacked into place over the wet engraving. Next Tool? A teaspoon. The bowl of a teaspoon is not a very substantial printing press, but Miss Jones rubs and taps every inch of the paper against the linoleum. This done she deftly slips the cut from under the paper, rolls another wet color on her second cut, slides it under the paper, and again applies the teaspoon treatment. The more colors used, the more difficult it becomes to accomplish a neat 'registration'. Miss Jones has made five-color prints but she prefers to use only two." She exhibited her colour prints at the Lofthouse Galleries, Ottawa, in the spring of 1969. A member of the Canadian Society of Graphic Artists (Toronto, 1956) she has exhibited often with this society and with: First and Second Burnaby Print Shows; Montreal Spring Shows (1956, 57, 60); Canadian Water Colours, Drawings and Prints (1966); Art Gallery of Hamilton (1952-57); was one of three Canadians chosen to send work to the Second Biennial of Graphic Art at the Museum of Modern Art, Tokyo, Japan, in 1960. She had held office with the Canadian Federation of Artists (Treas. 1945-56); Ottawa Art Association (Publicity 1954-56). She is married to artist Bob Rosewarne and they live in Ottawa.

References
National Gallery of Canada Information Forms rec'd 21 June, 1966 & July/58
The Ottawa Journal, Ottawa, Ont., Oct. 26, 1957 "Linoleum Cutting A Fine Art Producing Multi-Color Prints" by Harry Bruce.
Ibid, Oct. 24, 1970 "Ottawa Artists (3) – Prints Convey Reactions To World Around Her" by Valerie Knowles

JONES, Harry Ernest

b.1892

Born in Berkshire, England, he served in the First World War with the infantry and later the flying corps. He studied at Wantage, Oxford before coming to Canada in 1910 and settled in Edmonton.[1] He studied under A.C. Leighton of Calgary and became a member of the Edmonton Art Club (1933) and the Alberta Society of

JONES, Harry Ernest (Cont'd)

Artists (1934).[2] During the Second World War he enlisted in the R.C.A.F. and was attached to the recruiting section with the rank of Flight Lieutenant.[3] In 1941 he exhibited his oils and water colours at the Vancouver Art Gallery when Palette[4] of the Vancouver *Province* noted of his work, "Direct and vigorous in expression, a fine lyrical element runs through most of his work which extends in subject matter from the prairies and Rocky Mountains of the Coast and up to the Northwest Territory." No recent information is available on this artist.

References

[1] National Gallery of Canada Information Form
[2] Ibid
[3] *The Province*, Van., B.C., June 27, 1941 "R.C.A.F. Officer Wins Praise For Exhibit of Fine Paintings" by Palette
[4] Ibid
see also
The Vancouver Sun, Van. B.C., June 25, 1941 "Five Paintings by RCAF Man Now on Show at Art Gallery" by Mildred Valley Thornton

JONES, Helen (Mrs. H.M. Jones)
b.1909

Born at Arkona, Ontario, she studied at the Ontario College of Art also under Paul-Emile Borduas, David Partridge and Tony Urquhart. She has won awards at the Alan Gallery and the Doon School of Fine Arts also the Yale and Town Award (1958) of the Niagara District. Her work has been chosen for travelling exhibitions of the Canadian Society of Painters in Water Colour. One man shows of her work have taken place in Washington, D.C., Hamilton, and St. Catharines, Ontario. She lives at Grimsby, Ontario.

References

National Gallery of Canada Information Form rec'd in 1960
Independent, Grimsby, Ont., April 5, 1967, "Helen Jones Exhibition in E. York"

JONES, Henry Wanton
b.1925

Born at Waterloo, Quebec, he was brought up on a farm and attended the district school where he would earn his spending money drawing pictures of dogs and other animals for the boys during his free moments. He went to Montreal where he was hired as a clerk at Morgan's and began studying painting at night schools. He studied at the Montreal Museum School of Fine Arts under the late Dr. Arthur Lismer, Gordon Weber, Jacques de Tonnancour and Eldon Grier.[1] A painter and sculptor, he became a member of the Canadian Group of Painters in 1955 and the Quebec Sculptors' Association in 1962.[2] In 1957 he had held a one man show of paintings and sculpture at Galerie Agnes Lefort and Robert Ayre[3] noted this show as follows, "His constructions are a sort of metal calligraphy, delightfully airy and witty, and his pictures — there are 28 in this, his first important one-man show — are the work of a painter of discrimination. It may be a matter of personal preference, but I like his pale compositions — 'Interior', 'Still Life Near a Summer

JONES, Henry Wanton (Cont'd)

Landscape', 'Island of White Shapes', 'Self Portrait with Still Life' — better than such colorful works as 'Musician', 'Interior with Cats', 'Personnage près de la Fenêtre' and 'Nude' . . . . He uses the human figure and the still life in the others, but the forms are better digested; the outlines are faint, the colors muted, with a good deal of white with grey and warmed with yellow. Here is refinement that makes me think of the English painter Ben Nicholson . . . ." In 1958 Jones participated in the first annual exhibition and sale of works by Quebec artists at the Montreal Museum of Fine Arts. This exhibition was opened by Montreal's Mayor Fournier. Also in 1957 Jones joined the teaching staff of the Montreal Museum School of Fine Arts where he has taught painting, design, and more recently, sculpture. He has been teaching sculpture at Sir George Williams University for nearly two years. Jones has exhibited with the Royal Canadian Academy (from 1964 on); the Concours de Quebec (1965 and on); the City of Montreal (1959-60-61); Canada House at New York (1963); Sculpture 67 held at the Toronto City Hall and he is represented in the following collections: Sir George Williams University; The Bundy Art Gallery, Vermont, U.S.A.; and in many private collections including: Freygood (Mtl.); Grier (Mtl.); Dobush (Mtl.); Mrs. Eaton (Tor.); and others.[4] He married Paula L'Abbe (an artist) in 1953. He has been making jewellery and his wife Paula helps in the mounting of the jewellery as well as in the making of ceramics which they create together. Jones exhibited at the Waddington Gallery, Montreal, in February, 1969. He and his wife live in their studio on Stanley Street, Montreal.[5]

References

[1] National Gallery of Canada Information Form rec'd July 11, 1967
[2] Ibid
[3] *The Montreal Star*, Mtl., P.Q., Oct. 19, 1957 "Riopelle, Jones, Tondino and Others on Display" by Robert Ayre
[4] see [1]
[5] *London Mail*, Granby, P.Q., Mar. 18, 1964 "Henry Jones renowned Canadian Artist
see also
The Montreal Star, Nov. 9, 1963 "Montrealer Wins $1,000 Art Award"
Le Nouveau Journal, Oct. 14, 1961 "Peinture Fraiche "par Jean Sarrazin
Leader-Mail, Granby, Oct. 18, 1961 "Waterloo artist gains distinction in Art World"
Le Droit, Ottawa, Ont., Oct. 13, 1961 "Menses et Jones exposent à la Galerie XII"
The Telegram, Toronto, Ont., Apr. 12, 1958 "Accent On Art" by Paul Duval
The Gazette, Montreal, P.Q., Jan. 25, 1958 "Quebec Artists' Show, Sale Lauded By Mayor Fournier"
La Presse, Montreal, P.Q., Oct. 19, 1957 "Jimmy Jones, peintre et sculpteur, à la galerie Lefort"

JONES, Hugh Griffith

1872-1947

Born at Randolph, Wisconsin, U.S.A., he received his education at the University of Minnesota then trained for an architect with George E. Bertrand of Minneapolis, Minn., before moving to Chicago where he practised for five years.[1] After operating a building specialty business for several years he moved to New York where he worked with architects Lowe, Flagg and Brite.[2] It was in 1899 that he attended the life class of the "Sketch Club" of New York (an architects' club) and that same year, and in the following years, he exhibited his work with the annual exhibitions

JONES, Hugh Griffith (Cont'd)

of the New York Water Color Club and American Water Color Society.[3] He came to Canada in 1908 as chief designer for the architectural department of the Canadian Pacific Railway and after a year was appointed assistant chief architect.[4] He distinguished himself in this field and in 1932 at the age of 60 retired. In 1934 he collaborated with Edmond Dyonnet in the writing of the history of the Royal Canadian Academy. He held one man shows of his paintings at the Arts Club, Montreal, the Art Association of Montreal Spring Exhibitions and once or twice at the Toronto Exhibition and National Gallery of Canada travelling R.C.A. exhibitions. Showings of his paintings were held at the Arts Club, Montreal, the Art Association of Montreal (1925, 27, 33, 35, 39) mostly of Laurentian or foreign subjects in water colour. His 1939 exhibit at the Art Association of Montreal was noted by the Montreal *Gazette*[5] as follows, "Vivid jottings done during Italian travel and Laurentian scenes are the subjects of this collection, which is one of evenly high standard and rich in interest . . . These notes of travel are of compact size. Just as Morrice found the thumb-box sketch the ideal size for the swift recording of tonal impressions, so Hugh Jones has been able to wash in with spontaneity and transparency a multitude of 'bits' that have seized his fancy and very definitely give enjoyment to those who view these. Not that their scale has cramped him. There are Italian vistas that carry the eye for miles across plain and hill, and the illusion of distance is convincingly conveyed. In 1945 he exhibited about twenty oils which he did while visiting the Dalmation Coast (each painting measuring 22" x 28"). The Montreal *Gazette*[6] again noted, "Certainly the region is varied and interesting sketching ground since the shores and valleys sheltered from the bitter Bora winds from the north seem almost tropical in respect with palm trees, umbrella pines and rich vegetation flourishings. Gardens are masses of flowers in February, while less than a mile away around a headland or up the mountainside, there is dreary, rocky bleakness . . . . The harbor, the medieval walls, the forts and some of the bays have occupied his brush, all good compositions set down in refreshingly clean color. There is a glow to the paint in 'Three Bell Chapel, Ombla Road, Ragusa' with a woman and a child about to enter the white walled building with its golden-tiled roof, while in the distance is a hint of water and a white sail . . . (the article went on to discuss other paintings in the exhibition)." Jones painted hundreds of water colours during his lifetime and many of them were exhibited at the Art Association of Montreal. He was elected a Fellow of the Royal Institute of British Architects (1921); member of the Royal Canadian Academy (1926); the Royal Architectural Institute of Canada and the Quebec Association of Architects. He died in Montreal at the age of 75.[7] He was survived by his widow, the former Harriette Elizabeth MacConnell. He is represented in the collection of the Art Association of Montreal by two water colours and an oil; the Nat. Gal. Can. by an architectural drawing and in many private collections. A memorial exhibition of his work (architectural drawings and paintings) was held at Montreal Museum of Fine Arts in December of 1947.[8] Also another exhibition at the Arts Club, Montreal, in 1957.[9]

References

[1] National Gallery of Canada Information Form rec'd June 10, 1925
[2] *The Gazette*, Mtl., P.Q., Feb. 25, 1939 "Canadian Art and Artists — Hugh G. Jones, R.C.A., F.R.I.B.A. Architect and Painter" by Richard H. Haviland
[3] Ibid
[4] Ibid

JONES, Hugh Griffith (Cont'd)

[5] Ibid, Jan. 21, 1939 "Hugh G. Jones, R.C.A. Shows Watercolors"
[6] Ibid, Jan. 13, 1945 "Fine Arts – Scenes of Dalmatia By Hugh G. Jones"
[7] The Montreal Star, Feb. 17, 1947 "Hugh G. Jones Dies At Home" also The Gazette, Feb. 18, 1947 "Architect, Artist Hugh G. Jones, Dies"
[8] The Montreal Star, Dec. 15, 1947 "Water Colors by Hugh G. Jones" by H.P.B.
[9] The Gazette, Oct. 5, 1957 "Arts Club Showing Hugh G. Jones' Work"
Ibid Oct. 12, 1957 "Good Watercolors by Hugh G. Jones"

JONES, Phyllis Jacobine (Jacobine Jones)
b.1898

Born in London, England, of Danish and English origin, she studied at the Regent Street Polytechnic, London, under Harold Brownsword and there she won a gold medal for her animal modelling. She then studied in Italy, Denmark, and France where she exhibited at the Salon.[1] Her figure of St. Joan (which she carved in Rouen stone) was exhibited at the Royal Academy, London, and was later exhibited at the Royal Scottish Academy, Glasgow, and purchased by that city for the Kelvin Museum.[2] She came to Canada in 1932 and settled in York Mills, Toronto. She continued to do animal sculpture at the Ontario Agricultural College at Guelph where she was allowed space and facilities in 1933 to make studies of the various animals. The animal sculpture which she did there during that period is now part of the College's permanent collection.[3] In the years that followed she worked in bronze, marble, wood, and plaster, creating a variety of sculptural works in every size from small pieces to large bas-relief panels.[4] In 1938 two of her bronze animal sculptures were chosen for exhibit at "A Century of Canadian Art" held at the Tate Gallery, London, England.[5] The following year she joined other artists in the production of work for the Canadian Pavilion at the New York World's Fair.[6] Photographs in the Canadian Geographical Journal and the Saturday Night showed her at work on two of her huge statues of allegorical figures "Jack Canuck" and "Electric Power".[7] In 1950 she completed figures of Champlain, Wolfe, Simcoe and Brock (each 9 ft. high) for the outside of the Archives Building of the University of Toronto. The idea for the historical figures had been put forward by architects Mathers and Haldenby. In the production of the figures Miss Jones did them first in clay, then cast the figures in plaster of Paris and finally moved the plaster of Paris figures to the scaffolding at the building where stone carvers with dividers and other precision instruments transferred details of the figures into exact copies of Queenston limestone. The finer details of hands and faces were finished by Miss Jones. Each figure measures nine feet by one foot.[8] In 1951 she completed a great marble relief for the Bank of Nova Scotia's banking room in Toronto (King and Bay Sts.) depicting human figures in action at various industries with which the Bank of Nova Scotia has been associated over the years. She completed this job in the remarkable time of only 15 months. A working model, one quarter size was made in plastilina (synthetic clay). A plaster relief was made from this model. The plaster relief was completed in flawless detail and was then measured carefully by a method known as "pointing" (actual points of ink are marked where measurements are made). These measurements are multiplied by four to the full size of the work and a drawing of the full size work completed. From this drawing the plaster foundation for the actual plaster cast was built. Miss Jones then completed the clay model (in eight sections to facilitate handling) and

577

JONES, Phyllis Jacobine (Cont'd)

casts of these sections were then made. Marble cutters did the finished work by copying the eight full size sections. A good coverage of the various stages of production of this marble relief appeared in *Mayfair*[9] magazine of May, 1951. In 1954 she completed a panel 15 ft. long and 9 ft. high for the Confederation Life Building, Toronto. Pearl McCarthy[10] described this work as follows, "The subject is the father of the family as protector and provider. The father stands in the centre of the panel with one arm on the shoulder of his young son and the other on his bow, with the deer he has brought home slung over his shoulder. The mother with a baby dominates the left side of the panel, while on the right, a daughter attends a primitive cooking pot. It is in four-inch relief, and in a style which may be described as classical with a sense of easy freedom." This "easy freedom" has been a characteristic of all of Miss Jones' work. Other commissions completed by her include: Bank of Canada, Wellington Street, Ottawa (medallions on bronze doors) done in 1938; Our Lady of Mercy Hospital, Sunnyside Ave., Toronto; Gore Vale Fire Insurance Building, Galt, Ontario; St. Thomas Hospital, St. Thomas, Ontario (nine panels in Queenston limestone); Bank of Montreal, Toronto, Cor. of King and Bay Sts. (two panels of a total work of 12 panels executed by six sculptors) where she worked along side Emanuel Hahn (in charge), Donald Stewart, Elizabeth Wyn Wood, Florence Wyle, Frances Loring. Other commissions included a sculpture for the Metropolitan Toronto Home For The Aged at Newmarket (a beaten copper sculpture with masses and curves suggesting generosity and shelter); Trinity College chapel (a tympanum in the east porch of the chapel) U. of T., 1957. She also did sculpture for the Crysler Memorial Park, Morrisburg and models for several war memorials. During her career she has held only two one man shows — one in 1936 at the Mellors Gallery, Toronto, and the second at Rodman Hall, St. Catharines, Ontario, in May of 1969. Reviewing this one man show Joan Phillips[11] of *The St. Catharines Standard* noted, "Many of the pieces in the show opening tonight are on loan from collections throughout Ontario. Others are ones the petite sculptress, still spry and active in her late 60's has been working on during the last year." Joan Phillips went on to quote Jacobine Jones explaining her scarcity of smaller works as follows, "I've been so busy with the big architectural work, panels, that I haven't had much time to do the small stuff, which I enjoy doing, ..." Writing on Miss Jones in 1948 Josephine Hambleton[12] noted, "She . . . has established not only for herself, but for Canadian architectural sculpture, a very high reputation." There have been few publications dealing solely with sculpture in Canada, and for this reason there has been little published material of a definitive nature on her work. In 1943 William Colgate[13] in his *Canadian Art, Its Origin and Development* touched upon most of her major achievements up to that time. She was elected A.R.C.A. 1943, R.C.A. 1954; also a member of the Sculptors' Society of Canada. Her "Black Cavalry" (an equestrian portrait of a Nubian warrior) was reproduced in the above book by Colgate.[14] She has produced many works since then and a number of commissions in the St. Catharines area. Jacobine Jones is also known for her teaching of many students at the Northern Vocational School, Toronto, and at the Ontario College of Art where she was Director of Sculpture from 1951 to 1953. Her recent one man show was arranged through the efforts of Peter Harris, Director of Rodman Hall, St. Catharines, Ontario. She lives at Niagara-on-the-Lake, Ontario. Her works are in the collections of: The National Gallery of Canada (R.C.A. Diploma Collection — bronze equestrian figure), the Art Gallery of Hamilton, other public galleries and in many private collections.

JONES, Phyllis Jacobine (Cont'd)

References
[1] National Gallery of Canada Information Form rec'd Feb. 2, 1939
[2] Ibid
[3] *Globe & Mail*, Tor., Ont., Nov. 28, 1936
[4] *Canadian Art, Its Origin and Development* by William Colgate, Ryerson, Tor., 1943, Ryerson Paperback, 1967, P.207
[5] *A Century of Canadian Art*, 1938, The Tate Gallery, London, England (this catalogue obtainable from Queen's Printer, Ott.)
[6] *Canadian Geographical Journal*, July, 1939 "Canada's Participation In The World's Fair" by J. G. Parmelee, P.96
[7] as above and *Saturday Night*, Mar. 2, 1940 "Jacobine Jones Sculpture" by Jacobine Jones
[8] *Evening Telegram*, Tor., Ont., Oct. 18, 1950 "Carved In Stone" also *Globe & Mail*, Tor., Ont., Oct. 18, 1950 "Sculptors Labored For 11 Months To Insure Subjects Matched Periods" by Pearl McCarthy
[9] *Mayfair*, May, 1951 "Tiny Woman Produced Heroic New Sculpture" (photos by Nott & Merrill) see also *Globe & Mail* Tor. Ont., Sept 20, 1951 (large photo of finished work)
[10] *Globe & Mail*, Tor., Ont., Mar. 6 1954 "Art & Artists — Fifteen-Foot Panel In Stone A New Sculpture for Toronto"
[11] *The St. Catharines Standard*, May 2, 1969 "Jacobine Jones' Exhibition — It's Her First In 33 Years" by Joan Phillips
[12] *The Ottawa Citizen*, Nov. 6, 1948 "Ottawa, A City of Fountains? by Josephine Hambleton
[13] *Canadian Art, Its Origin and Development* by William Colgate, P.205
[14] see[1], P.206
see also
National Gallery of Canada Catalogue, Vol. 3 by R.H. Hubbard, 1960, P.395
The Arts In Canada, Edited by Malcolm Ross, MacMillan Co. of Can., 1958 'Sculpture" by William S.A. Dale, P. 38
Canadian Art by Graham McInnes, MacMillan, Tor., 1950, P.96
Royal Canadian Academy of Arts Annual Exhibition Catalogues
catalogue — *Jacobine Jones*, An exhibition of sculpture, Nov. 17 to 30th 1936, Mellors Galleries, Tor., Ont.

JONES, Maria (Mrs. John Jones)

A potter whose work was chosen for exhibit across Canada by judges of the Canadian Biennial Pottery Show. She studied under Osie Osborne of Victoria, B.C., and on an 18 month visit to England she attended the Brighton School of Arts and Crafts where she continued studies in pottery. She lives at Port Alberni, B.C., where she is teaching pottery at night classes under the sponsorship of the Adult Education Department of the local School District.

Reference
Alberni Valley Times, Port Alberni, B.C., March 5, 1969 "Canada-Wide Show — Local Potter's Work Chosen"

JONES, Rupert

b.1924

Born at Sandys Parish, Bermuda, he received his early education at the West End School, Bermuda, and at the Central School of Pembroke Parish, then at the Sandys Secondary School. He worked in an architect's office where he assisted with land surveying and later worked for a paint and decorating company doing show-

JONES, Rupert (Cont'd)

cards and lettering. He was associated for a time with a theatrical group designing stage sets in Bermuda. He came to Canada in 1952 and settled in Montreal where he studied for four years at the Montreal Museum of Fine Arts' School of Art and Design. He won a prize in the 77th Annual Spring Exhibition of the Montreal Museum of Fine Arts for his sculptured head entitled "Diana". Jones has taught sculpture in the Children's Classes in the Art Centre of the Montreal Museum of Fine Arts formerly under the direction of the late Dr. Arthur Lismer. He is a member of the Quebec Society of Sculptors and lives in Montreal.

References

Biographical sheet (in the artist's file of the NGC Library)
Montreal *Gazette*, Mtl., P.Q., Apr. 4, 1960 "Native Wins Top Sculpture Prize"
La Presse, Mtl., P.Q., Apr. 4, 1960 (photo of artist at work and one of his sculptures "Diana")

JONGERS, Alphonse

1872-1945

Born at Mézières, France, the seventh son of Jean Jacques Jongers and Marie de Schomberg, he studied at the University of Paris where he received his Bachelor of Literature. He then studied art at the Ecole des Beaux Arts, Paris (1889-1892) under Cabanel, Delaunay, Moreau and received a scholarship for further study. He spent two years in Madrid, Spain, where he made copies of the work of Velazquez. He met John Singer Sargent there (an American society portraitist) and they later went to England to paint. Jongers came to Canada in 1896 and settled in Montreal where he opened a studio.[3] In 1900 he moved to New York where he established himself as a portrait painter of note. He was commissioned by various members of the Vanderbilt family for portraits and also painted the portrait of William H. Taft, President of the United States. While in the States he married and lived at Newport where he did portraits of a number of society figures. He returned to Montreal in 1924 and set up a studio and home in the Ritz Carlton Hotel.[4] In 1937 he was awarded the Legion of Honor by France for his achievement as a painter. He painted many portraits in Montreal. His fee ranged from $3,000 to $5,000 but he painted many of his friends for nothing.[6] At one time he had a waiting list of 17 people for portraits.[7] He had invested a considerable sum in stocks and when the market crash of 1929 happened, Jongers had to give up his expensive living. He left the Ritz Carlton but when times improved he returned to this hotel where he lived until his death at the age of 73. Amongst those who sat for him were: Lord Bessborough (former Governor General of Canada); Lady Bessborough; Lord Tweedsmuir (former Governor General of Canada); Chief Justice R.A.E. Greenshields; Sir Andrew Macphail; Sir Charles Gordon; Dr. W.W. Chipman; Dr. E.W. Archibald; Norman Dawes; Col. George Cantlie; J.E. Aldred; Dr. Lionel Lindsay; Miss Jennie Webster; Mme. Paul Rodier; John Gilmour; René Turck (Consul-General of France); Air Marshal Billy Bishop; F.N. Southam (newspaper, publishing and financial personality); D. Forbes Angus; Adelard Godbout (a former Premier of Quebec) and many others. At the time of his death the Montreal *Gazette*[8] in an editorial noted, "His portraits were marked by strength and realism, with a superb sense of color. An older generation regards his portraits of the late Sir Andrew Macphail, Mr. Willie Hope and Chief Justice Greenshields as outstanding examples

JONGERS, Alphonse (Cont'd)

of the portrait painter's art. Alphonse Jongers lived to the age of seventy-two, but almost to the end of a full and a busy life, his devotion to his work never ceased nor slackened. He passes on assured of an outstanding place among the Canadian artists of his time." Jongers was elected an Associate of the Royal Canadian Academy in 1937 and full member in 1938, also an Associate of the National Academy of Design, New York City. He is represented in the following public collections: in the U.S.A., Metropolitan Museum, New York; the National Gallery, Washington, D.C.; Brooklyn Museum, N.Y.; in Canada at the National Gallery of Canada (R.C.A. Diploma Collection) and elsewhere. He died in Montreal and was buried in the Mount Royal Cemetery. A memorial exhibition of his work was held at the Art Association of Montreal in December of 1947.

References

[1] National Gallery of Canada Information Form rec'd Feb. 3, 1927

[2] Baie-Comeau *L'Aquilon*, P.Q., Sept 3, 1958 "Parmi les peintures de l'Exposition"

[3] see [1] and [2]

[4] see [1] and [2]

[5] *The Gazette*, Mtl., P.Q., Mar.19, 1937 "France Decorates Montreal Painter"

[6] *Memoirs of a Canadian Artist* by Edmond Dyonnet (original manuscript P. 70)

[7] Ibid

[8] *The Gazette*, Mtl., P.Q., Oct. 3, 1945 "Alphonse Jongers, R.C.A."

[9] *The Montreal Star*, Mtl. P.Q. Dec. 17, 1947 "Works of Jongers Are Exhibited" also *The Gazette*, Mtl., P.Q., Dec. 13, 1947 "Portraits by Jongers Interesting Exhibition" *The Montreal Standard*, Dec. 20, 1947 "Jongers' Works Now on Exhibit"

see also

Canadian Art, Its Origin and Development by William Colgate, Ryerson, 1943, Ryerson Paperbacks, 1967

National Gallery of Canada Catalogue, Volume 3 by R.H. Hubbard, P.395

The Montreal Standard, Jan. 10, 1948 "Alphonse Jongers" story by Zoe Bieler (Standard staff writer)

JOPLING, Frederic Waistell
1860-1945

Born at Kensington, England, he came to Canada in 1874 and settled in Toronto, Ontario. In 1877 he entered the Ontario Society of Artists art school and studied under Lucius O'Brien and John Fraser until 1878.[1] In 1880 he arrived in New York City where he studied at the Art Students' League under Walter Shirlaw, William Sartain and William Chase, until 1883. He remained in New York City for thirty-two years where he worked as an advertising artist for railway and steamship companies also on the staff of the New York Herald.[2] He sold his work as well, to *Harper's Weekly* and *Colliers*. He later worked for several large photo engraving and printing houses in the United States including the American Bank Note Company. Returning to Canada in 1912 he settled in Toronto. Many years later Pearl McCarthy[3] noted, "F.W. Jopling has spent a lifetime etching the romance of history and of scenes. Hundreds and hundreds of copper plates keep, in lasting form, this record of a world which the artist has found fascinating . . . . But Mr. Jopling, 82, is living a strong, artistic life now, as may be seen by visiting the Roberts Art Gallery on Grenville Street, where a large collection of his etchings is on view. He did an extensive series of pictures of the Royal tour last year, having been accorded special facilities for his work, and these etchings include Washington and the President's Hyde Park home as well as Canadian scenes. The outstanding

JOPLING, Frederic Waistell (Cont'd)

point in his historical pieces is his ability to suggest the glamour in the fact. Because his catholic interest has taken in everything from the building of the Welland Canal to interior views of Osgoode Hall and views of life classes in a studio, there is a wealth of subject interest." Frederic Jopling died in Toronto at the age of eighty-five.[4]

References
[1] National Gallery of Canada Information Form rec'd Feb. 8, 1927
[2] Ibid
[3] *Globe & Mail*, Tor., Ont., May 11, 1940 "Art and Artists" by Pearl McCarthy
[4] *The Toronto Star*, April 11, 1945 "F.W. Jopling Buried Was Noted Artist"
A group of his etchings won recognition from King George V at the Wembley exhibition of 1924.

JORGENSEN, Flemming

b.1934

Born at Aalborg, Denmark, he served four years apprenticeship in Denmark at display and design work. He came to Canada in 1956 and settled in Victoria, B.C.[1] He studied under Herbert Siebner for three years (1958-61). Jorgensen's paintings vary from landscape and figure studies to abstract compositions. He exhibited jointly with Michael Morris in 1959 at the Apollo Art Galleries. Viewing this show Moncrieff Williamson[2] noted, "His handling of oil paint-casein and wax, a tricky medium mixture which Mr. Siebner's students go for in a big way, is quite excellent. He has an air of promise as colorist (are these ice-blue blues Danish in subconscious inspiration?) and I feel that once he has learned to give a bit more body to his pigment, then the textural surfaces will be far more happy to observe." By 1966 Jim Rae[3] of the Saanich *Dogwood-Star* in an article on the artist described his work as follows, "Jorgensen appears . . . to revel in the loud and often clashing colors that Siebner shuns. His paintings, especially his most recent ones, are gay as any Christmas card — but the ideas or feelings they express are subtle and elusive. This, according to the artist, is just as it should be. 'There should always be a note of mysteriousness about a painting,' Jorgensen says." He exhibited an ink wash at the Canadian Water Colours Drawings and Prints 1966 at the National Gallery of Canada and in 1968 showed his recent work at Pandora's Box, Victoria, B.C. and The Print Gallery, Victoria.[4] Jorgensen lives at Saanichton, B.C. where he was recently married.

References
[1] National Gallery of Canada Information Form rec'd Mar. 18, 1964
[2] *Victoria Daily Times*, Oct. 24, 1959 "Two Man Show Reveals Exceptional Promise" by Moncrieff Williamson
[3] *Dogwood-Star*, Saanichton, B.C., Thurs. Feb. 10, 1966 "Flamboyant Dane Enlivens Saanich Art" by Jim Rae
[4] *Victoria Daily Times*, Vic., B.C., Mar. 30, 1968 (photo of drawing-collage)
see also
Catalogue *Canadian Water Colours Drawings and Prints, 1966* NGC or Queen's Printer.

JOSO

A guitar player, he has performed at the Act One coffee house in Yorkville, Toronto. He is also a sculptor. He exhibited his sculpture of 'Byzantium Women' (done in clay with oil and wax polish — and some with ceramic glaze) at the Pollock Gallery, Toronto, in April of 1968. His style is modern and intriguing.

References
The Toronto Telegram, Tor, Ont., Apr. 5, 1968
Pollock Gallery exhibition notice announcing exhibition for Apr. 1 to Apr. 13th.

JOURDAIN, Jacques

A Quebec City artist who studied there at the Ecole des Beaux-Arts under Jean-Paul Lemieux, Jean Soucy and Benoit East and graduated in 1956.[1] He won first prize at the Quebec Provincial Exhibition in 1957 and in 1958 showed his paintings with the work of Montreal photographer Larose, at the Canadian Club under the auspices of Les Amis de l'Art.[2] In 1958 he took part in the Exposition des Moins-de-trente-ans (under-thirty exhibit) at Ile Ste-Hélène and also took first prize at the regional exhibition of Three Rivers.[3] In 1960 several of his works were chosen by the Montreal Museum of Fine Arts 77th Spring Show. He held a solo exhibit of about 70 pictures at the St. Joseph's Seminary, Three Rivers, of oils, gouaches, charcoal sketches and workshop studies.[4] He was awarded Second Prize in 1962 at the Quebec Provincial Contest and held his first Montreal one man show at Galerie Martin, when his work was noted by Dorothy Pfeiffer[5] as follows, "Jourdain works for the most part in printer's colorful inks. Beginning as a painter of naturalistic style — he held an exhibition of his works in this category at the Quebec Palais Montcalm — he appears today to be evolving gradually through semi-abstraction to attempted non-representation. Jourdain's work shows considerable promise . . . . His compositions — while pleasantly inventive — occasionally seem uncertain. He has an excellent grasp of the possibilities of abstract perspective and of planes; also a pleasantly instinctive feeling for line and mass which today is marred only by uncertainty." By 1968 after a number of other one man shows he exhibited at Galerie Zanettin[6] and the same year won a Price Fine Arts award.[7] In 1969 he exhibited at the Salon Pic du Centre Culturel, Three Rivers, a number of works produced by his use of printer's inks on zinc sheets which give his work interesting qualities, simple composition, and a richness of colour schemes.[8] Lives in Quebec City.

References
[1] *Le Nouvelliste*, Que., P.Q., April 8, 1961 "Jourdain, peintre de la nature québecoise — Vernissage ce soir" par Pierre L.-Desaulniers
[2] Ibid
[3] Ibid
[4] Ibid
[5] *The Gazette*, Mtl., P.Q., "Quebec Painter's Show" by D.Y.P.
[6] *Le Soleil*, Que., P.Q. "Les toiles de Jacques Jourdain à la galerie Zanettin"
[7] *Le Nouvelliste*, Jan. 11, 1969 "Les peintures de Jacques Jourdain offrent un éventail de formes pittoresques et de couleurs éclatantes" par René Lord

JOURDAIN, Jacques (Cont'd)

[8]Ibid

see also

Le Nouvelliste, April 1, 1961 "Le peintre Jacques Jourdain exposera pour la première fois dans sa ville natale"

Ibid, April 10, 1961 "Jacques Jourdain: une découverte parmi les peintres trifluviens" par Pierre L.-Desaulniers

Ibid, April 11, 1961 "Jacques Jourdain est resolument impressionniste"

Ibid, March 21, 1962 "Jacques Jourdain exposera 40 oeuvres à Québec"

Ibid, March 30, 1962 "Jacques Jourdain expose au Séminaire pour quatre jours" par Pierre L-Desaulniers

Chronicle-Telegraph, Mar. 22, 1962 "Sensitive Work In Monochrome"

Le Nouvelliste, Feb. 24, 1968 "Vernissage des oeuvres de M. Jacques Jourdain"

JOURDAIN, Roger (Rev. Father Roger Jourdain)
b.1914

Born in Montreal, P.Q., he received his education in Quebec while taking his Bachelor of Arts degree. He also studied art under Rudolphe Dugway at St. Antoine College. He has studied in Paris under modern and classic artists. In Canada he has decorated eight churches in Saskatchewan but also continues to fulfil his parish duties at St. Vital at North Battleford. His work has been shown at the James Art Studio in Saskatoon where it was favourably received. He is represented in private collections in New York, Toronto, Montreal, Saskatoon and North Battleford mainly by landscapes and abstract paintings. He is however regarded as a specialist in interior decoration for churches.

Reference

Battleford News-Optimist, North Battleford, Sask., April 19, 1963 "Battleford Priest Called New Art Star"

JOY, John
b.1925

Born in Toronto, Ontario, he studied at the Central Technical School under Peter Haworth, Doris McCarthy, and Carl Schaeffer, also at the Ontario College of Art. A portrait and landscape painter in oils, water colours, charcoal and pen and ink his work has been well received. Special note has been paid to his winter scenes, weather beaten houses, barns and ancient farm machinery. He has held a number of one man shows including the following; at North York Public Central Library at Willowdale (Nov. 1964), the Markham Centennial Library, Ontario (Sept. 1968) and a two man show at the Sobot Gallery, Toronto (Tor. Apr. 1965). Joy has given a number of demonstrations throughout Ontario and is represented by the following galleries: Malloney's Gallery at Ontario House, London, England; the Sobot Gallery (Tor. Ont.); the Lillian Morrison Gallery (Tor. Ont.) and the Tamarack Studio in Banff, Alta. He is represented in the permanent collection of the Educational Corporation, Chicago, Illinois (a painting of Algoma was chosen for the Corporation's World Book Encyclopedia) and in many private collections particularly at Markham, Ontario.

JOY, John (Cont'd)

References

National Gallery of Canada Information Form rec'd Oct., 1965
Willowdale Enterprise, Willowdale, Ont., Nov. 4, 1964 "All Mediums In Art Show"
Chatham News, Ont., Jan. 5, 1968 "Library Event Features Art"
Markham Economist and Sun Markham, Ont., Sept. 12, 1968 "Local Scenes On Exhibit"

JUDAH, Doris Minette (née Trotter)

b.1887

Born in Montreal, P.Q., she studied drawing under Edmond Dyonnet and modelling under Albert Laliberté at the Monument National and the Ecole des Beaux-Arts. During her study she won a gold medal from the Conseil des Arts et Métiers for achievement in life class (1918-19). She became honorary Director of the Rochester Art Association and Modeling School, Rochester, Minn., U.S.A. (1924-25) while continuing to exhibit her work at various centres. In 1936 she held a solo show of sculpture and plaques at The Coffee House, Union Street, Montreal. Included in the showing were busts of: Miss Winnifred Kydd, C.B.E., M.A. (Pres. Nat. Council of Women; Dean of Women at Queen's University); Brig. Gen. H.S. Birkett, C.B.,V.D., M.D., LL.D., F.R.C.S. (C), F.A.C.S.; Lt. Col. W.W. Burland; Dean H.M. MacKay, B.A., B.Sc., LL.D., M.Am. Soc., C.E.; Miss Catherine I. Mackenzie (Principal – High School for Girls); Harold Hibbert, D.Sc., Ph.D., F.R.S.C. (Prof. of Industrial & Cellulose Chemistry – McGill Univ.). Doris Judah is the wife of E. Lionel Judah.

References

National Gallery of Canada Information Form rec'd 1932
La Presse, Jan. 11, 1936 "Doris-M. Judah, sculpteur"
Exhibition of Sculpture by Doris M. Judah (catalogue sheet) Jan. 1st-31st, 1936, The Coffee House, 1191 Union St., Mtl., P.Q.
Royal Canadian Academy of Arts (catalogue) 1931
She also exhibited with the Art Association of Montreal

JUHASZ, Paul

b.1911

Born in Györ, Hungary, he studied at the Textile Technical and Designing School in Hungary and came to Canada in 1951. He has shown his work at the Canadian National Exhibition (1966), the National Gallery of Canada, Ottawa (1966-67) and is on the faculty of Architecture at the University of Toronto. He was awarded first prize in textile designing at the Canadian National Exhibition in 1966. He is a member of the Canadian Handicrafts Guild and lives in Toronto.

Reference

National Gallery of Canada Information Form rec'd July 13, 1967

JUHASZ, Peter

B.1921

Born at Olahszentgyorgy, Transylvania, he studied at the Belle-Arte Academy in Bucharest, Roumania, and at the University of Budapest. A painter, sculptor and

JUHASZ, Peter (Cont'd)

graphic artist, he has exhibited his work widely in Europe, United States and is represented in private and public collections in Roumania, Hungary, Austria, France, U.S.A. and Canada. He came to Canada in 1957 and became a Canadian citizen in 1962. He exhibited his graphics and paintings at the Fine Art Gallery of the Central Library of Metropolitan Toronto where a variety of subjects were shown including landscapes, still life studies, children, figures, nudes, flower studies and a number of portraits, in all about 152 paintings and graphics. He is a member of the Alberta Society of Artists.

Reference

Catalogue – The Fine Art Gallery of The Central Library of Metropolitan Toronto dated Sunday December 16 (the year was unspecified)

JULIEN, Octave-Henri

1852-1908

Born in Quebec City, P.Q., the son of Henri Julien (who was a manager of Desbarats Co., King's Printer) and Zoé Julien (his mother had the same surname as his father although not related).[1] Henri Julien attended schools in Quebec City and in Ottawa at the University of Ottawa. At the age of 16 he entered the engraving firm of George E. Desbarats Co. of Montreal after his family finally settled in that city. This firm published *The Canadian Illustrated News*, *L'Opinion publique* and *The Hearthstone* (or later *The Favourite*).[2] He worked in a number of engraving departments of Desbarats and then began to draw and sketch and it was not long before his sketches appeared in the papers produced by Desbarats.[3] In 1874 Julien took time out from Desbarats to accompany the first expedition of the Royal Northwest Mounted Police to supress liquor traffic on the Prairies and while in the West enjoyed an experience of a lifetime. Frederick Yorston[4] of *The Montreal Standard* commenting on Julien's career many years later noted, "His sketches of the Indians and the life of the plains were famous throughout the continent. Mr. Julien related many an amazing tale of the then great unknown land, and his story of a buffalo hunt at Fort Garry was a classic." On his return to the East Julien went back to work for the firm Desbarats who were later bought out by George Burland. Later he was offered a job on the permanent staff of *The Montreal Star* by its proprietor, Mr. Hugh Graham, and he accepted. Yorston,[5] Editor-in-Chief of *The Montreal Standard* described an incident during Julien's long service with the *Star* as follows, "His portraits were unequalled and he could delineate a man's features with amazing rapidity. A little incident will show his skill. During the visit to Montreal of the celebrated Dr. Lorenz, Mr. Julien went to the operating theatre of one of the local hospitals. He made a couple of sketches of the famous surgeon at work. Then he left the operating theatre and was proceeding out when he was stopped by one of the doctors of the staff. This gentleman seemed displeased that a newspaper artist should have invaded the operating theatre. He asked Mr. Julien to allow him to see the sketches. Mr. Julien, who had a soul above suspicion, handed the rough drawings to the doctor, who looked at them, then tore the paper in pieces and threw the scraps on the floor. Mr. Julien made no comment, turned on his heel and left the building. He returned to his office and from memory made a drawing which was a perfect portrait of the great surgeon, and one which attracted the most favourable comment from those who had had an opportunity of seeing Dr. Lorenz.'' Julien knew every phase of newspaper production: the first sketch, making the plate, working in every form of known engraving processes also for stone work and general lithography. His rare skill with pen and pencil and the above knowledge of the various processes made him a unique asset in the publishing industry. But Julien was also loved by his friends and newspaper associates. His cartoons were not dependent on the harsh distortion of features of his subjects but of a greater skill of catching very human glimpses of his political subjects in normal or comical poses. In 1938 Dr. Marius Barbeau[6] described Julien's newspaper career as follows, "From the moment Julien became a newspaper illustrator, he was always harried by the inexorable clock (talonné par l'heure inexorable), and by the needs of his large family. He invariably had to despatch his drawings before he had time to finish them to his liking. During the sessions of Parliament at Ottawa, he worked in a small room, at the old Russell House, the clock ticking close to him and reminding him that he must run to the station with his last cartoon, if it were to appear in *The Montreal Star* the next day. Under pressure he developed a skill that was amazing: a high speed in taking 'shorthand' notes from his living models, a memory of facial expression and of gestures, and a sense of instantaneous characterization. Kindly humour, fun, and good fellowship enabled him throughout that steady outpouring to interest and amuse often at the expense of other people but without ever hurting them. Indeed everyone was proud to be the object of his passing attention." It was in 1886 that Julien became chief of the *Star's* art department, a capacity which he filled until his death in 1908.[7] He also did book illustrations for Adolphe Poisson's *Sous Les Pins* in 1902 and Louis Frechette's *La Legende D'Un Peuple*, 1908 and probably for other publications. As a painter he also showed marked ability and if he had had more time to carry through his ideas for paintings he would have been equally esteemed in both fields. He did mostly water colours and a few oils, and many pencil drawings of the Habitant's life and character. A good number of his water colours were of men fishing on the river near Ste. Rose where he had a summer home and spent most of his leisure time fishing. An exhibition of his drawings, water colours and oils of French Canadian life was held at The Arts Club, Montreal, in October of 1936.[8] They were mainly from the collection of his daughter Miss Jeanne Julien who then owned 76 of the 98 works on exhibit. Henri Julien married Marie-Louise Legault dit Deslauriers and they had 18 children of whom eight survived infancy (one son and seven daughters). His wife died in 1924. Whether his other works were in the possession of his surviving family or their offspring besides his daughter Jeanne is not known but Alan Jarvis in an article on Julien for *Weekend Magazine*[9] in 1961 noted that a collection of 130 of Julien's works owned by the Julien family was sold in 1936 to Raoul Barbin (Quebec artist) and that this collection was later purchased by Paul Cardinaux who was the owner at the time of Jarvis' article. The late Dr. Marius Barbeau wrote in 1938 that he had traced 700 of Julien's drawings to a storage room.[10] Also in 1936 the Quebec Provincial Museum exhibited 80 of his sketches of members of Parliament during the Laurier era also sketches of legends and customs of Old Quebec.[11] In 1938 an important tribute was paid to Julien by The National Gallery of Canada who organized an exhibition of 135 pen and ink, chalk, water colour, pencil, coloured chalk, oils and wash drawings. This exhibition was opened by the then Minister of Public Works, Hon. P.J.A. Cardin. Here a series of 15 reproductions of his work and one original drawing of Sir Wilfrid Laurier were shown. The reproductions included drawings of Sifton,

Borden, Blair, Tarte, Mulock and others. There were also drawings of events of the time: "The Mintos Arrive At Quebec", "Countess and Earl Grey At The Théatre Des Nouveautés", "Hon. Mr. Borden Presented In The House Of Commons By Hon. Mr. Foster and Hon. Mr. Monk", "Return Of The Canadian Troops From South Africa", and so on. The exhibition was made up from private and public collections of the following: The Musée de la Province de Québec, Art Association of Montreal, The McCord National Museum of McGill University, The Arts Club, Montreal, Raoul Barbin, Esq., Montreal; J. Arthur Dupont, Esq., Montreal; Joseph Lebrun, Esq., Montreal; W.S. Maxwell, Esq., Montreal; The Misses Mignault, Montreal; Louvigny de Montigny, Esq., Ottawa; Ward C. Pitfield, Esq., Montreal; C.W. Simpson, Esq., R.C.A., Montreal; Antoine Valiquette, Esq., Montreal. This memorial exhibition was also shown in Toronto and Montreal. In 1941 Marius Barbeau's very human and definitive book *Henri Julien* was published as part of the Ryerson's Canadian Art Series and was very well received. R.C.[12] of *The Montreal Standard* noted, " . . . Mr. Barbeau is to be congratulated on the very fine summary and the choice of the many contrasting illustrations of Julien's work given us here . . . . Julien's lovableness is noted by the late Lord Atholstan in a letter to Madame Julien on his death, in which he said in part — 'The poor Henri loved you so tenderly . . . . He was an extraordinary man, joining to his great talent the most charming disposition. He had won universal admiration, and the true affection of all those who knew the kindness of his heart . . . . ' " It has been said that Henri Julien was the first black and white artist on the North American continent and the most prolific. He died at the age of 56 after leaving the office of *The Montreal Star* to arrange for a little holiday he had earned. He dropped on the sidewalk just before reaching the Canadian Pacific Railway Office.[13] Dr. Barbeau[14] in his book wrote, "His premature death was brought about by over-work. 'He was well built, like an athlete, all muscles, little flesh,' according to a member of his family. 'But in the winter of 1908, while in Ottawa, he had suffered a severe attack of influenza, and, before he had time fully to recover, he had to work strenuously on the Tercentenary of Quebec. Much weakened after returning to his job in Montreal, he was trying to fight it off when he collapsed on the street, his heart having failed him.' " Over the years many tributes have been paid to this gifted and much loved Canadian.

References

[1] *A Standard Dictionary of Canadian Biography*, Vol. 2, 1938, Tor., Julien, Henri by William R. Watson, P.212 also *The Montreal Standard*, Sept. 7, 1935 (as below)

[2] *The Montreal Standard*, Sept. 7, 1935 "Anniversary Of Henri Julien's Death" by Frederic Yorston (Editor-In-Chief of the *Standard*)

[3] Ibid

[4] Ibid

[5] Ibid

[6] *Henri Julien, 1851-1908* (Catalogue Memorial Exhibition, Ottawa, 1938) text by Marius Barbeau (Foreword by Eric Brown), P.6

[7] *The Montreal Standard* as in[2]

[8] *Exhibition on Drawings, Watercolours and Oils of French Canadian Life by Henri Julien* held In The Arts Club, Sunday Oct. 4th until Oct. 30th, 1936 with foreword by Robert W. Pilot, R.C.A. (catalogue)

[9] *Weekend Magazine*, Vol. 11, No. 26, 1961 "Lively Portraits Of Canada's Political Past" by Alan Jarvis

[10] *Henri Julien* (catalogue) as in[6] P.7

JULIEN, Octave-Henri (Cont'd)

[11] *Quebec Chronicle-Telegraph*, Quebec, P.Q., Nov. 14, 1936 "Fine Collection Of Drawings Is Shown at Museum"

[12] *The Montreal Standard*, Feb. 28, 1942 "Booklet On Art of Henri Julien" (Book Review by R.C.)

[13] *The Montreal Standard* as in[2]

[14] *Henri Julien* by Marius Barbeau, Ryerson, Tor., 1941, P.40-1

see also

bibliography of *Henri Julien* (above) P.43

Canada And Its Provinces, Vol. 12, 1914, Painting And Sculpture In Canada by E.F.B. Johnston P.608, 631

The Fine Arts In Canada by Newton MacTavish, 1925, P.64

Canadian Art, Its Origin And Development by William Colgate, 1943, Ryerson Paperback 1967, P.118-119, 220.

The Arts In Canada, Dept. Citizenship & Immigration, Ottawa, 1958, P.64

The Macmillan Dictionary of Canadian Biography Edited by W. Stewart Wallace, 1963, P.357

Canadian Landscape Painters by A.H. Robson, Ryerson, Tor., 1932

Contes D'Autrefois by Louis Fréchette, Honoré Beaugrand, Paul Stevens, Éditions Beauchemin, Montreal, P.Q., 1946

Canadian Drawings And Prints by Paul Duval, Burns & MacEachern, Tor., 1952, Second and Third pages of text, pen drawing – plate 2

A Painter's Country by A.Y. Jackson, Clarke, Irwin, Tor., 1963, Page 123

The Development Of Canadian Art by R.H. Hubbard, Queen's Printer, 1963, P.75, plate 122

Painting In Canada/A History by J. Russell Harper, U. of T. Press, Tor., 1966, P.242 (Harper gives a good account of Julien and two fine examples of Julien's work also appear in this book, plates 218 and 219)

JUNEAU, Denis

b.1925

Born in Verdun, Quebec, he entered the Ecole des Beaux-Arts in 1943 where he studied seven years in the techniques of drawing, decolourization (from fading, bleaching), painting, and advertising under Alfred Pellan, Julien Hébert, Maurice Raymond, Jean Simard, Jean Faucher, Renée Chicoine and others also sculpture under Sylvia Daoust and Armand Filion. He then served his apprenticeship in silver work under George Delrue and studied draughting with Gilles Beaugrand. He went to Italy in 1954 where he continued his studies until 1956. He was particularly interested in the confrontation of art and industrial techniques and carried out studies in this field at the Centro Studi Arte Industria de Novara where he worked under the direction of the founder of the school Nino di Salvatore (abstract painter and designer). One of Juneau's metal sculptures was exhibited at Cantu, Italy, in 1957. Returning to Canada he held a one man show in Montreal in 1958 where in the following year he became a member of the Non-Figurative Artists Association of Montreal and exhibited with them at the Montreal Museum of Fine Arts. Juneau is known in the field of industrial aesthetics by architects and decorators, also for his sculpture, paintings and murals by the general public. He has participated in a number of group shows including The Third and Seventh Biennial Exhibitions of Canadian Art/Painting; Panorama 11 (1955-65) at Musée d'Art Contemporain de Montreal (1967); 88th Royal Canadian Academy of Arts Exhibition (1967); group showing at the Carmen Lamanna Gallery, Toronto (1968); The Three Schools, Toronto (1968); Deck-the-Grange Committee (Women's Committee Art Gallery of Ontario) (1968); Seven Painters from Montreal, Massachusetts Institute of Technology, Hayden Gallery (1968). His one man shows of paintings, sculpture and drawings have taken place at the following places: Galerie Denyse Delrue, Montreal

JUNEAU, Denis (Cont'd)

(1958); Galerie Norton du Musée des Beaux-Arts, Montreal (1962); Galerie Nova et Vetera, Montreal (1962); Galerie Denyse Delrue, Montreal (1963); Galerie du Siècle, Montreal (1967); Galerie Carmen Lamanna, Toronto (1968); Galerie le Gobelet, Montreal (1969). His honours include: Canada Council Grants (1961-2) (1963-64) (1968-69); Honourable Mention Alcan architectural competition, 1957; Grand Prize for the trophy to be given to the winner of the Province of Quebec Town Planning Competition, 1965; Mention, Artistic Competition of Quebec, 1967; Mention, Shaw, Winnipeg, 1968. He is represented in the Musée d'Art Contemporain, Montreal; Montreal Museum of Fine Arts; Ontario Council of Arts; National Gallery of Canada; Minister of Cultural Affairs collection, Quebec; St. Lawrence Columbium and Metals Corp.; Rothmans of Pall Mall Canada Limited. Lives in Montreal.

References

The Third Biennial Exhibition of Canadian Art, 1959 (Catalogue No. 30)

The Non-Figurative Artists' Association of Montreal by Claude Picher, Queen's Printer, Ottawa, 1960

Panorama Peinture au Québec, 1940-66

Art d'Aujourd'hui, revue d'art française, Novembre 1958

Journal Royal Architectural Institute of Canada, February, 1962

La peinture Canadienne Moderne, De Luca editor, juin-août, 1962

Ecole de Montréal by Guy Robert, Editions du Centre De Psychologie Et De Pedagogie, Montreal, Canada, 1964, P.22, 54.

Seventh Biennial of Canadian Painting, 1968 (catalogue) P.46, Cat. 98

Painting in Canada/A History by J. Russell Harper, U. of T. Press and Les Presses de l'université Laval, 1966, P.412

Document from artist, 1969

Maclean's, July, 1969 article by Robert Millet

JUTRAS, Joseph

b.1894

Born in Montreal, P.Q., he was first a real estate salesman then a window dresser, ketchup company salesman, perfume manufacturer and when business generally dropped to a standstill during the depression years Joseph Jutras turned to the sale of his paintings. He had studied art three years at the Monument Nationale, and in 1924 had exhibited his work at the Montreal Museum of Fine Arts. He sold two of his paintings, winter scenes, to the Quebec Provincial Government and they are now believed to be in the collection of the Quebec Provincial Museum. He had been guided during his art studies by Joseph St. Charles, Alfred Laliberté and at various times he received help from A.Y. Jackson, Maurice Cullen and John Johnstone. In 1932 he exhibited his paintings first in the streets of Montreal and continued to do this over the years especially around Dominion Square. It is not known whether he is still alive (would be 75) and if so whether he still sells his paintings in the same manner. He specialized in landscapes and always tried to work from nature. He was particularly interested in subjects of historical value. No news has been received about him in recent years.

References

The National Gallery of Canada Information Form rec'd Jan. 29, 1927

The Montreal Standard, Oct. 9, 1948 "Artist Exhibits Wares on Streets" by Clayton Gray (photo of artist with his work and article)

KADLEC, Dusan
b.(c)1942

He arrived in Canada from Czechoslovakia in 1968 and has already established himself as an artist of importance in Canada. In 1968 he was working in Nova Scotia and had just completed a portrait of Annapolis Valley industrialist John E. Schaffner of Port Williams, Kings County, N.S. He studied at the College of Arts, Prague, and continued his studies at the Academy of Creative Arts, Prague, where he received his Master of Fine Arts degree in painting. He did paintings and drawings for Czechoslovakian television and was art advisor for progressive beat music orchestra in Prague. He was one of the artists working on the outstanding Czechoslovakian Pavilion at Expo '67. He was awarded a bronze medal for his participation in International Exposition of Jewelry in Jablonce and Nisou. He came to Canada with his wife Marika and their two children and he is looking forward to working in commercial art to supplement his professional career.

Reference

    Halifax Chronicle Herald, Halifax, N.S., Dec. 19, 1968 "Young Czech Artist completes His First Portrait In Canada" (report from Kentville, N.S.)

KAGVIK, Davidee

An Eskimo sculptor from Great Whale River on the lower Hudson Bay coast of Quebec. He makes his living as a carver but is also a builder of kayaks. In January of 1968, 37 of his stone carvings were presented at the Lofthouse Galleries Limited, Ottawa, when Jenny Bergin[1] in *The Ottawa Citizen* noted "Hunters, fishermen, women and walruses, all the traditional subjects of the Eskimo artist, are seen and portrayed in the deceptively simple manner associated with these Northern people. It is deceptive because the uncluttered lines, natural balance and intrinsic regard for material combine to give the end result an easy, flowing quality which is apparently effortless. All of Kagvik's carvings are small: they have a temptingly portable character in the age-old tradition of Eskimo sculpture, demanding to be picked up and handled . . . . Sharply incised lines contrast with fine, highly-polished planes to produce a decorative quality which in no way detracts from the massiveness and weight of the carving, but rather serves to enhance it." Kagvik is represented in the permanent collection of the Museum of Modern Art in New York City. His Ottawa exhibit was made possible by Alma Houston, the staff of the Canadian Arctic Producers, and Duncan deKergommeaux, Canadian artist and proprietor of the Lofthouse Galleries who prepared an informative catalogue.

References

    The Ottawa Citizen, Ottawa, Ont., Feb. 13, 1968 "Eskimo carving exhibit at Lofthouse Galleries" by Jenny Bergin

    Davidee Kagvik, Sculpture (catalogue) exhibit Feb. 12 to March 9, 1968, at the Lofthouse Galleries Ltd., Ottawa (text by Duncan deKergommeaux)

    see also

    The Ottawa Journal, Feb. 13, 1968, Ottawa, Ont. "Top Eskimo Sculptor Exhibits in Ottawa" by W.K. Ketchum

KAHANE, Anne (Mrs. R. Langstadt)
b.1924

Born in Vienna, Austria, she came to Canada as a small child (1925) and moved to Montreal with her mother when she was five. Later she attended the Strathcona Academy and took night courses in traditional sculpture for a year at the Ecole des Beaux Arts, Montreal. Not satisfied with traditional sculpture she tried commercial art school where she studied for two years.[1] She was then persuaded by her mother to broaden her horizons at the Cooper Union Art School, New York City where she studied from 1945 to 1947.[2] There she took a general course in architecture, industrial design, commercial art and wood carving. She returned to Montreal and worked as a free-lance commercial artist but her friends discovering her sculpture which she had brought home, urged her to concentrate in this field. She was at the time painting and remained occupied with this medium until her final realization that sculpture was the medium in which she would find herself.[3] By 1950 she was deeply involved with modern sculpture and in 1953 achieved remarkable success with her winning of a prize at the first International Sculpture Competition held in London, England. The competition was organized by the Institute of Contemporary Arts of London, and the theme of the competition was "The Unknown Political Prisoner". More than three thousand five hundred works were submitted from 57 countries. In the preliminaries, Canada had 41 entries, Germany 607, Great Britain 513, United States 400, France 307, Italy 296. In the finals Canada had only three entries to go overseas — the work of Julien Hebert, Robert Norgate and Anne Kahane. Robert Ayre[4] noted the following of Anne Kahane's marquette 'Prisoner', "In Miss Kahane's sculpture you see the outline of a man; you recognize the weary head, you feel the tension of the hands downthrust toward the earth, as if to compensate for the sagging knees, and force the suffering body to remain upright; the prison bars, which are also the binding chains, are one with the ribs and they extend into the sharp spikes which are the symbols of torture; the work is a powerful synthesis, and impressive and moving realization of the theme. The marquette is, of course, a small thing, made of copper tubing and plastic wood, but although the sculptor has had no experience of monuments or heroic works of any kind, 'Prisoner' is essentially big and could only gain in impressiveness by being enlarged." In 1956 Anne Kahane completed a sculpture made up of a group of figures (3-1/4 ft high) with a total length of 10 feet for an office building at 310 Victoria Avenue in Montreal. Her theme was to portray nine or so people brought together in conversation. *The Montreal Star*[5] described the work as follows, ". . . the semi-abstract treatment is in keeping with the architecture, its clean lines, the contrast of textures of metal, stone and wood. While keeping firmly within the rectangle, Miss Kahane has worked out a satisfying variety and rhythm of shapes and spatial relationships and has added to the interest by contrasting two woods, mahogany and redwood." The sculpture had been commissioned by David K. Linden, architect and town planning consultant, who designed the building. This same year she won first prize for her group of figures entitled "The Ball Game" (figures two feet high in a line six feet long, carved in redwood). An exhibition of her work was held at Greenwich Gallery, Toronto, in 1958. This same year five of her works were chosen for exhibit at the Canadian Pavilion of the World's Fair held at Brussels. From there her work was sent to the Canadian Pavilion at the Venice Biennale, Italy, where she was the only exhibitor of sculpture and one of the four Canadian artists exhibiting. Joan Capreol[6] in the *Globe and Mail* described her five works as follows, ". . . her five works in the

Venice Biennale have one characteristic in common with her Prisoner — a close-ness to humanity. Perhaps the most striking is the 'Woman in Italy' — a 38-inch tall figure in mahogany, holding a shopping bag in sheet brass. Here is a serenity and resignation which you do not see in North American women. 'I sketched Italian women when I was there two years ago and did this figure from a Florence sketch,' said Miss Kahane. The other four Venice pieces are groups of people — complex compositions in redwood which appear simple and pure in line and form, and which Anne Kahane herself finds more interesting because she sees people in the city around her, not as individuals but as anonymous members of groups, talking, riding, sitting, walking together." Her work also caught the critical interest of Dr. William S.A. Dale in his section on Sculpture for Malcolm Ross' *The Arts In Canada*.[7] In 1959 her sculpture "Follow The Leader" won her an award at the 76th annual spring exhibition at The Montreal Museum of Fine Arts[8]. Her work was presented at the Isaacs Gallery when Paul Duval[9] explained "Miss Kahane buys the planks for her sculpture from a local lumberyard. Poplar is her favorite material at this time, although she also works in pine, walnut and maho-gany. Her carving is executed with standard chisels, gouges and mallets." In 1960 Charles Spencer[10] in *The Studio* was impressed with her work and explained "She creates her statues and groups by a building-up process bringing together shaped pieces which are glued together into one form. In this way she is not confined to the size of any particular block of wood and she finds that her method allows greater freedom of expression. Even the sketches for a final work are usually done in wood and not with pencil and paper." He concluded his article by saying, "There is nothing coy or mannered in her approach to the human figure or the human scene. The choice of subjects denotes a fresh, warm personality, whilst the intricate interlocking of the figures, and the bold patterning of the related masses, reveals a gifted and mature experimental artist." At the first Wood Sculpture Exhibit at the Beaverbrook Art Gallery the same year she won first prize for her "Slumber". Eleven of her works were exhibited at the McIntosh Memorial Art Gallery at the University of Western Ontario with the work of five other sculptors in 1961. Robert Fulford[12] did a very fine write up in *Canadian Art* also good photos of her work accompanied the article. She received a Canada Council Senior Arts Fellowship (1960-61). By 1962 she decorated her sculpture with less paint. In 1963 she exhibited her work at the Denyse Delrue Gallery, Montreal, when Dorothy Pfeiffer[12] of *The Gazette* found in her work, "An incredible amount of sensitive cutting, chiselling, smoothing, modelling and rubbing with beeswax has gone into the realization of her present works, nearly all of which present the gradual emergence of humanity . . . . " In the next few years she completed commissions for: La Grande Salle at the Place des Arts, Montreal; the Winnipeg International Air Terminal (a large carving, a memorial to Captain F.J. Stevenson, founder of the original airport);[13] the Winnipeg General Hospital; Expo '67 "Man on his head" very well reproduced in *Canadian Sculpture Expo 67*[14] (plate No. 17). She is represented in the National Gallery of Canada by her wood sculptures "Queue" a group of figures 25" x 48" and "Summer White" two figures 38" high;[15] Art Gallery of Ontario, Tor.; Winnipeg Art Gallery; Vancouver Art Gallery; Mount Allison University; McMaster University; University of Western Ontario; Sir George Williams University; Art Museum in London, Ont.; Agnes Etherington Art Centre (Queen's University), Kingston, Ont.;[16] and in many private collections. She also won First Prize for sculpture at The Winnipeg Show

KAHANE, Anne (Mrs. R. Langstadt) (Cont'd)

1955, 1956, 1957. She is an Assoc. of the Royal Canadian Academy and member of the Sculptors' Society of Canada. She lives in Montreal and is married to free lance writer and art director Robert Langstadt.

References

[1] *Canadian Art*, Vol. 10, No. 4 "Anne Kahane – An Art of These Times" by Robert Ayre, P.144-147

[2] Ibid also NGC Information Form rec'd June 12, 1964

[3] Ibid, P.145-146

[4] Ibid, P.145

[5] *The Montreal Star*, Sept. 1, 1956 (photo of work in office building lobby)

[6] *Globe & Mail*, Tor. Ont., Sept. 20, 1958 "Kahane Works in Venice Exhibit" by Joan Capreol

[7] *The Arts In Canada* Ed. by Malcolm Ross "Sculpture" by William S.A. Dale, P.41

[8] *The Gazette*, Mtl. P.Q., Apr. 3, 1959 "City Sculptress Wins Art Prize"

[9] *The Telegram*, Tor., Ont., Oct. 17, 1959 "Life Cues Her Carving" by Paul Duval

[10] *The Studio*, Vol. 160, July, 1960 "Anne Kahane – Canadian Sculptor" by Charles S. Spencer

[11] *Canadian Art*, Vol. 18, No. 1 "A Survey Of The Work Of 24 Young Canadian Artists" notes by Robert Fulford, P.30, 31

[12] *The Gazette*, Mtl., P.Q., Mar. 30, 1963 "Art" by Dorothy Pfeiffer

[13] *Canadian Art*, Vol. 21, No. 3 "Art At The Airports" by Evan H. Turner, P.137

[14] *Canadian Sculpture Expo 67* Ed. by Natan Karczmar, Introd. by William Withrow, Graph, Montreal, 1967

[15] *National Gallery of Canada Catalogue, Vol. 3* by R. H. Hubbard, P.350

[16] *Agnes Etherington Art Centre* (catalogue) 1968 by Frances K. Smith foreword by J.A. Corry; Introduction by Ralph Allen, see Kahane, No.67

see also

National Gallery of Canada Catalogue sheet "A Trio of Canadian Sculptors" (Jack Hardman, Anne Kahane, Cecil Richards) by Norah McCullough

Canadian Art, Vol. 15, No. 3 "Comments by a Belgian Art Critic" P.189

Ibid No. 4 "Can Toronto Overtake Montreal As An Art Centre? " by Hugo McPherson, P.269

KAJANUS, Johanne

Born in Oslo, Norway, of Norwegian father and French mother, as a little girl she was taken to France with her parents. Her father was an eminent conductor and founder of the Helsinki symphony orchestra. Her mother gave her her first drawing lessons and at fifteen she finished her secondary studies and held her first sculpture show at Antibes, a show which led to her being accepted at the Ecole des Arts Decoratifs of Nice where she studied before entering the Ecole des Beaux-Arts of Paris. She received honourable mention at the Salon des artistes français de Paris, and it was after this show that she received many commissions to sculpt the heads of French political and professional personalities. She won a medal at the Exposition Universelle de Paris in 1937 where she later met and married a Norwegian engineer, Kaare Hultgreen. Later she returned to Norway with her husband and four children. Although she still did sculpture, she no longer took part in exhibitions. After the loss of two of her children and the growing up of the other two she established in Moss (a suburb of Oslo) a fine arts school where she taught drawing, painting and sculpture. Her husband died (at 46) and she returned to Paris in 1959. Making a living was difficult but her two children helped. In 1962

KAJANUS, Johanne (Cont'd)

they arrived in Canada and settled in Montreal where after working as a decorator of lamp bases at $1.25 an hour, a nurses' aide at the Royal Victoria Hospital, she finally received commissions for sculptured portraits. She became an associate of a new French Canadian company "Le Domaine d'Art et de Sculpture" a group dedicated to maintaining professional standards in the making of fountains, monuments, decorative frescoes, and other types of commissions.

Reference
   La Patrie, Mtl., P.Q.., Thurs. Sept. 5, 1963 "Johanne Kajanus"

KAKINUMA, Thomas
b.1908

Born at Tochigi-Ken, Japan, he came to Canada in 1937 and was made a naturalized Canadian in 1951.[1] He studied at the Ontario College of Art and graduated in 1947 with honours in Fine Art.[2] He took further studies at the Art Students' League under Yasuo Kuniyoshi, 1948-50, then returned to Canada and studied pottery part time at the Ontario College of Art and U.B.C.[3] He has taught pottery at the Banff School of Fine Arts and ceramics at the University of British Columbia (1965-69). His ceramic sculpture and pottery have been well received. His solo exhibits include: U.B.C. Art Gallery, 1956; Laing Gallery, Toronto, 1960; Kagoshima City, Japan, 1961; Vancouver Art Gallery, 1962; Victoria Art Gallery, 1963; Burnaby Civic Art Gallery, 1964; New Design Gallery, Vancouver, 1965; Hamilton Art Gallery, 1966; Canadian Handicraft Guild, Montreal, 1966; Canadian Handicraft Guild, Toronto, 1966; Robertson Galleries, 1967. *The Toronto Daily Star*[4] noted, "He brings unusual charm and vivacity to his owls and penguins, hens and fish, and if he lacks originality in his forms he makes up for it in sheer virtuosity. His vases of which there are a half-dozen or so in the exhibition, can't be criticized on any grounds I know. They have a classical shape and homespun vigor, and their leaf-and-twig patterns seem to me to be rendered perfectly." His awards include: Grand Award at Canadian Ceramics, 1957 (Toronto); Silver Medal at International Ceramics, 1962 (Prague); Best Ceramic Sculpture, Canadian Ceramics, 1963 (Montreal); Purchase Awards of the Vancouver Art Gallery, University of British Columbia, Winnipeg Art Gallery.[5] He is represented in the permanent collection of the International Ceramic Museum of Faenza, Italy (1959). He received a Canada Council Senior Fellowship to study ceramics in Mexico and Japan (1960-61). He lives in Burnaby, B.C.

References
   [1] National Gallery of Canada Information Form rec'd Oct. 1965
   [2] Ibid
   [3] Ibid
   [4] *Toronto Daily Star*, Tor., Ont., May 21, 1960 (small article and small photo)
   [5] Biographical card and exhibition notice by The Robertson Galleries "Thomas Kakinuma" April 2nd – 15th

KALLMEYER, Minnie

1882-1947

Born in Detroit, Michigan, U.S.A. she came to Canada as a young girl and studied at the Central Ontario School of Art, Toronto, under F. McGillivray Knowles and privately with J.W. Beatty; also in Munich with Prof. Walter Thor and in Paris under Richard Miller.[1] She exhibited her work with the Ontario Society of Artists and became a member of that society in 1922.[2] During an exhibition of her work at Eaton's Fine Art Galleries in 1933 the *Globe & Mail*[3] noted, "Miss Kalmeyer knows her Canada in many localities and moods, and her work is rich in color and broad in treatment. For general home decoration, she is most happy in her medium-sized pictures, which seems to 'compose' better than the larger works, though the latter are rich in carrying power. Many of the studies in the present exhibition represent the Nova Scotian coast and fishing scenes . . . . There are sketches from Georgian Bay and England, and a flower-hung Devonshire cottage is beautiful in its simple, decorative quality." Newton MacTavish[4] in 1925 placed her among the ranks of Canadian women painters of acknowledged ability. She is represented in the National Gallery of Canada by a medium sized canvas entitled "Hartung's Wharf, Boothbay Harbor, Maine".[5] She died in Toronto and was survived at that time by a sister Miss Clara Kallmeyer who was living with her in Toronto.[6]

References
  [1] National Gallery of Canada Information Form rec'd May 24, 1944
  [2] *The Toronto Star,* Tor., Ont., Apr. 22, 1922 "Was Born at Riga Paints Horses Here" (a joint announcement of new memberships to the Ontario Society of Artists — André Lapine and Miss Kallmeyer)
  [3] *Globe,* Tor., Ont. Nov. 11, 1933 "Art and Artists"
  [4] *The Fine Arts In Canada* by Newton MacTavish, MacMillan, Tor., 1925, P. 146
  [5] National Gallery of Canada Catalogue, Vol. 3, Can. School by R.H. Hubbard, P. 151
  [6] *Glove & Mail*, Tor., Ont., Mar. 24, 1947 "Toronto Artists Won Distinction"

KALOUT, Pacome

An Eskimo sculptor who died early June, 1968.

Source
  Reference Department, Main Branch, Ottawa Public Library.

KALVAK, Helen

b.(c)1903

A Holman Island Eskimo and sole child of her parents whom she accompanied on 'the hunt' where she observed Eskimo and animal life. She shot her first caribou with bow and arrow at the age of 11. With her knowledge of hunting, Eskimo folklore, and witchcraft she was encouraged to draw by Rev. Father Henry Tardy an Oblate missionary and founder — manager of the Holman Eskimo Co-operative. Her talent was discovered by Fr. Tardy about 1962. She received some instruction from a teacher at the Co-operative and two years later was producing eight to ten pieces of graphic art per week with considerable originality aided by her experiences. She opened a display of the Holman Island Graphics at the Edmonton Art Gallery in March of 1968 where some of her works were on display.

KALVAK, Helen (Cont'd)

References
   Edmonton Journal, Edmonton, Alta., Mar. 2, 1968 "Eskimo Artist Visits City With 'ulu" Show"
   Ibid, Mar. 14, 1969 "At almost 70 Kalvak became an artist" by Art Sorensen

KAMIENSKI, Jan

One of Canada's noted political cartoonists and illustrators who has been on the staff of *The Winnipeg Tribune* since about 1958. His fine illustrations have appeared in *Weekend Magazine* and they reveal the artist's extensive research into the story background in making his illustrations. A specific example was his illustrations for Barry Craig's "Unsophisticated Lady Of The Lake" which appeared in the above magazine telling the story of the *MS. Keenora* a passenger and freight ship on Lake Winnipeg. Kamienski has a masterful technique, simplified style, and a good likeness of his subjects whether it be people or their surroundings. He exhibited his cartoons under "Politics '65" at *The Yellow Door Gallery* in October, 1965. He was chosen top Canadian newspaper cartoonist for his cartoon "The Three Musketeers" at the Toronto Men's Press Club's 15th annual National Newspaper Awards competition. Earlier he won one thousand dollars in a competition sponsored by the City of Montreal.

References
   The Winnipeg Tribune, Winnipeg, Man., Sat., Oct. 16, 1965 "West's first cartoon exhibit" (photo of artist and article)
   Weekend Magazine, No. 25, 1966 "Unsophisticated Lady Of The Lake" by Barry Craig – illustrated by Jan Kamienski

KAMPMANN, Dürten
b.194-

Born in West Berlin, Germany, she came to Canada in 1956 and attended the Winnipeg School of Art (University of Manitoba) under Cecil Richards and the University of British Columbia under Olivier Stiebelle also in San Francisco and in France. She became a naturalized Canadian in 1962. A sculptress in a variety of media including stone and wood she won two scholarships for summer school of arts at Vancouver and First Prize for the best sculpture done at the Winnipeg Art School. Her work has been exhibited at the Seventh Annual Winnipeg Show and, in San Francisco at the San Franc. Art Festival, 1966. She is represented in the collection of Arthur Vincent of Winnipeg; the Sutter's Art Gallery, San Francisco and elsewhere. Has been living in San Francisco, California.

Source
   National Gallery of Canada Information sheet.
   see also
   Artforum, 1963

KANANGINAK

b.(c)1937

An Eskimo artist from Cape Dorset, Quebec, who is a member of the West Baffin Co-operative. He is a designer, graphic carver, and soapstone carver. His work can be seen at the Canadian Handicraft Guild Shops, Ottawa, Stratford Festival Theatre, and elsewhere. He attended the opening of an exhibition at the Canadian Handicrafts Shop, Wellington Street, Ottawa, in 1965 when former Federal Northern Affairs Minister Arthur Laing opened the shop.

References

The Ottawa Journal, July 20, 1965 "Eskimo Is Hunter, Artist And Ambassador as Well" by Bryan Hay (of the *Journal*)

Stratford Beacon-Herald, Stratford, Ont., July 19, 1965 "Eskimo Artist Feature Of Handicraft Exhibit"

KANE, Paul

1810-1871

Born at Mallow, Cork County, Ireland, the son of Michael Kane who had come to Ireland with the Royal Horse Artillery in 1798 and had later retired and settled at Mallow where he engaged in business.[1] Michael Kane originally spelled his family name Keane. Perhaps through repeated errors in registers he decided to give in to the simpler phonetical spelling. This retired soldier had four sons and one daughter: Paul, James (who died in Bellevue Hospital, N.Y., 1829); Fred (died from a fire at Warren, N.Y., 1847); Oliver (who died in Ireland before the family left for Canada) and Mary (whose death date we do not have).[2] It is through Mary that certain facts about the Kane family are known. She married Daniel Bancroft in 1831 and their son Marshall S. Bancroft passed these facts to J. Addison Reid who in turn passed them on to Lawrence J. Burpee, noted scholar on the history of exploration in Canada.[3] It was Burpee who wrote the introduction of *Wanderings of An Artist* published by the Radisson Society of Canada in 1925. Burpee's introduction also appears in the 1968 Hurtig Edition which includes the following facts: Paul Kane's father when he came to Canada settled in York (Toronto) in 1818 or 1819 and established himself as a wine and spirit merchant. He had a store on the west side of Yonge Street between King and Adelaide.[4] He died in 1851 at the age of 78.[5] Paul attended the District Grammar School where he showed an interest in drawing and was encouraged by the drawing master Mr. Drury. Paul left school in 1826[6] and went to work at Conger's furniture factory where he remained until 1830.[7] During his school years he spent much time with the Mississauga Indians. Many years later in his preface for his *Wanderings of An Artist* he stated, "I had been accustomed to see hundreds of Indians about my native village, then Little York, muddy and dirty, just struggling into existence, now the City of Toronto, bursting forth in all its energy and commercial strength. But the face of the red man is now no longer seen. All traces of his footsteps are fast being obliterated from his once favourite haunts, and those who would see the aborigines of this country in their original state, or seek to study their native manners and customs, must travel far through the pathless forest to find them."[8] He worked at Conger's for four years and soon realized that he had to find some way of making more money in order to study painting abroad. He spent the next few years at Cobourg, Ontario, where he painted a number of portraits including those of Sheriff and Mrs. Conger (his old boss), Mrs. Percy and Sheriff Ruttan, Mrs. F.S. Clench, Mrs. William Weller and

KANE, Paul (Cont'd)

others.[9] He returned briefly to Toronto and then he left for Detroit (1836) and from there to other parts of the United States. He sailed for Marseilles, France, from New Orleans in 1841, in search of knowledge about the great works of art throughout Europe. He kept a diary of his experiences but unfortunately it was lost.[10] Through a personal friend of Kane, Dr. Wilson who was a Professor of History and English at the University of Toronto, we learn that Kane visited Paris, Genoa, Milan, Verona, Venice, Bologna, Florence, Rome and Naples where he made copies of famous paintings including Raphael's Madonna (in the Pitti Palace), portraits of Popes Paul II and Julius II, self portraits of Leonardo da Vinci and Rembrandt (in the Florentine gallery); the Madonna by Murillo (in Corsini Palace of Rome); portrait of Pope Gregory XVI by Bustato.[11] In Italy he met the Scottish artist Stewart Watson and they returned to London, England where they shared a studio and lodgings at the home of a Mr. Martin on Russell Street near the British Museum. He also met another Scottish artist Hope James Stewart who returned to Edinburgh and kept in touch with him by letter.[12] Kane returned to Canada in 1844 and by then had decided to undertake to paint the Indian, which task he described as follows, "The principal object in my undertaking was to sketch pictures of the principal chiefs, and their original costumes, to illustrate their manners and customs, and to represent the scenery of an almost unknown country."[13] In 1845 Kane set out for Lake Simcoe with a portfolio, a box of paints, a gun and ammunition. He travelled to Orillia by boat; crossed over to Sturgeon Bay on Lake Huron where he hired a guide and a canoe and reached Penetanguishene. There he caught a packet boat for Owen Sound. At Owen Sound he met three men bound for a council of chiefs at Saugeen who were negotiating a sale of land to the Provincial Government. Kane proceeded with the trio and his Indian guide all night through the woods and swamps in the rain which came down in 'torrents'.[14] They arrived the following morning after a hectic night. There Kane sketched Indian chiefs: Maticwaug (Ojibway); Maskuhnoonjee; a chief's daughter; another chief Wah-pus and his immense task had begun. He returned the way he went with a companion named Dillon[15] and when they reached Penetanguishene they stocked up on provisions and headed for Manitoulin Island. Kane made sketches of Indian encampments along the way like "Encampment amongst the Islands of Lake Huron" (sketch No. 1 in his book).[16] After 200 miles of canoeing they reached Manetouawning on Manitoulin Island. This was a settlement of 2000 Indians lodged in forty or fifty log-houses built for them by the Provincial Government. One of the chiefs he sketched Awbonwaishkum (sketch No. 2) he considered possessed the "characteristics of the Indian to a striking degree."[17] He also sketched a pipe the chief had carved. The bowl of the pipe had a striking resemblance to the head of an Egyptian sphinx. The chief explained however that the design (sketch No. 3) had been passed down by previous generations.[18] Kane remained in Manitoulin Island for two weeks. His companion Dillon left the island by schooner. Kane himself went to Sault Ste. Marie on board the steamer "Experiment". His canoe was also taken on board. At Sault Ste. Marie he got the friendly advice of a gentleman to apply to Sir George Simpson, Governor of the Company located at Lachine, Quebec, before travelling west into the interior. From Sault Ste. Marie he took the steamer to Mackinaw (Mackinac) where Lake Huron and Lake Michigan meet. There the Ojibways and Ottawas had gathered to receive their pay "for lands ceded to the United States." In his diary he wrote "I at once pitched my tent in their midst, and commenced to sketch their most remarkable

KANE, Paul (Cont'd)

personages."[19] As he sketched, the wild Indian dogs began to feed on his provisions so he had to move his tent away from the others. The dogs were kept "for the purpose of hunting and drawing their sleds in winter" and were therefore important for the Indians' existence. After moving Kane was sketching by the light of a candle (stuck in the ground in his tent) when one of these dogs dashed into his tent and snatched his candle, leaving him in the dark. The next day the dog returned and he shot at it not to kill but as he explained, "I thought to inflict summary justice upon the marauder, and fired the contents of my pistol into his carcase. Beyond my expectations, which had only been to wound, I saw that I had killed him, and was immediately assailed with a demand, from the owner of the dog and his wife, for payment for the loss of his services, which I agreed to liquidate on their paying me for the losses I had sustained in hams and other provisions which their dog had stolen from me. Hereupon they balanced accounts, and considered that we were about even, giving me an invitation to join them at supper, and partake with them of the slaughtered animal, in which operation I afterwards saw them happily engaged."[20] There he sketched the chief "Mani-tow-wah-bay". After three weeks at Mackinaw, Kane went on to Green Bay, through the Fox River to Lake Winebago to see the Monomanee Indians gathered to receive pay for lands they had sold to the United States government. He passed a trading post where many Indians were 'lying about in a state of beastly intoxication' having been given liquor by the white man. He continued on up a stream until he reached the Monomanee camp. On the way he had seen Indians spearing salmon by night and he described the scene as follows, ". . . this has always a very picturesque appearance, the strong red glare of the blazing pine knots and roots in the iron frame, or light-jack, at the bow of the canoe throwing the naked figures of the Indians into wild relief upon the dark water and sombre woods."[21] At the Monomanee camp of 3,000 Indians he sketched chiefs and others. During the council held before the payment the Indians aired their various complaints, one being that money paid to them passed through too many hands and through this process much of it was lost to them.[22] Kane sketched an Indian gambler named "Coe-coosh" from the Pottowattomie tribe notorious for their gambling and fleecing of the Monomanees. He also sketched "Kitchie-ogi-maw" (the Great Chief), "Mauza-pau-Kan" (Brave Soldier). When the Indians received their pay great quantities of liquor appeared in the camp and drunkenness soon prevailed. Kane recognizing a dangerous environment left the scene and made his way back to Toronto. In March of 1846 he went to Lachine to see Sir George Simpson and showed him his sketches. He explained to Sir George that he wanted to record the life of the Indian in the interior. Sir George was very interested in Kane's paintings and commissioned him to paint twelve either for himself or the company. He also gave Kane a letter of introduction to travel by Hudson's Bay boats and canoes and to stay at the various posts along the way. He returned to Toronto and in May of the same year he joined Simpson and his party at the dock and they proceeded with the long range goal of intercepting a brigade of Hudson's Bay canoes at Sault Ste. Marie. This was to be done by taking a steamer to Mackinaw and from there to Sault Ste. Marie. At Mackinaw Kane was given the time of departure of the steamer which was the next morning. Kane then went ashore. Arriving at the wharf at the appointed time in the morning he found that the steamer had departed twenty minutes ahead of time. He hired a skiff which had only a blanket for a sail and he found three lads in their late teens whom he paid well for the risk involved and they set out on the 45 mile trip with only a

600

single loaf of bread, a little tea and sugar for stores. With only a 20 minute stop for tea and bread they proceeded all night in record time and reached their objective the next morning. Much to the astonishment of Simpson, Kane again appeared. The brigade of canoes which Simpson had hoped to intercept had passed through two days previously. Not having any room for Kane he proceeded with his own canoes to catch up to the brigade. Kane had to follow in the schooner "White Fish" bound for Fort William. When the schooner reached Fort William and Kane presented his letter of introduction he obtained a canoe and caught up to Simpson and the brigade. Lawrence Burpee,[23] historian, described the next leg of his trip as follows, "They followed what is known as the Kaministikwia route, first discovered by the French, subsequently abandoned in favour of the Grand Portage route, and re-discovered and re-established by the North-West Company when Grand Portage became territory of the United States. Their way lay up the Kaministikwia river, thence by a series of small lakes and streams over the height of land and down to Rainy Lake. After a brief rest at Fort Frances, they descended Rainy River to the Lake of the Woods, and Winnipeg River to Fort Alexander near its mouth. All along the route Kane took advantage of every opportunity to make sketches of the Indians and their camps, the portages, and bits of characteristics scenery." At Fort Alexander Kane left the brigade and engaged a party of Indians to take him as far as Fort Garry (Winnipeg). There he joined a band of half-breeds in a buffalo hunt and described the event as follows,[24] "Their buffalo hunts are conducted by the whole tribe, and take place twice a year, about the middle of June and October, at which periods notice is sent round to all the families to meet at a certain day on the White Horse Plain. Here the tribe is divided into three bands, each taking a separate route for the purpose of falling in with the herds of buffaloes. These bands are each accompanied by about 500 carts, drawn by either an ox or a horse . . . . I[25] arrived at the Pambinaw River, and found the band cutting poles, which they are obliged to carry with them to dry the meat on, as, after leaving this, no more timbered land is met with until the three bands meet together again at the Turtle Mountain, where the meat they have taken and dried on the route is made into pemmican." On page fifty of Kane's book he describes how pemmican is made and carried around. He joined a band of about two hundred hunters besides women and children who were also accompanied by an immense number of dogs from the settlement. The dogs fed on the waste parts of the butchered animals. They passed Dry Dance Mountain and proceeded into Sioux country. They were visited by twelve Sioux chiefs with whom the half-breeds had been at war. The Sioux wanted to make peace but while seated around for discussion a body of a half-breed was found nearby and brought to the camp. This ended the talks and the Sioux were lucky to escape with their lives. A warning that no peace could be made until satisfaction for the dead man was had were the last words given by the half-breeds. Three days afterwards scouts of the half-breed hunting party signalled that enemies were approaching. This was done by throwing handfuls of dust in the air (buffalo sightings were signalled by scouts running their horses to and fro). A band of one hundred of the half-breeds' best riders rode out to the area and took cover below a bank of a small stream then sent out two decoys. The decoys brought the Sioux charging upon them and the Sioux were met by a volley of a hundred rifles. The Sioux fled leaving eight dead. Burpee[26] continued the description of Kane's journey as follows, "Learning that a small sloop was about to sail from Lower Fort Garry to the north end of Lake Winnipeg, he rode down and embarked on her for

Norway House, where he remained until the middle of August waiting for the brigade on its way inland from York Factory. Leaving Norway House, they crossed the foot of Lake Winnipeg, portaged round Grand Rapids, and ascended the Saskatchewan to Carlton House, where they left the boats and proceeded on horseback to Fort Edmonton, witnessing by the way the ancient Indian method of trapping buffalo by means of a pound, and sketching some of the chiefs of the Cree Indians. From Fort Edmonton, they started on horseback for the Athabaska and entered what is today known as Jasper Park. It was now the beginning of November, they had to travel up to Athabaska Pass through heavy snow, and the horses were abandoned in favour of snowshoes. A difficult journey carried them over the summit and down the Pacific slope to Boat Encampment on the Columbia. Here they again took boats and descended the river to Fort Vancouver, where they arrived December 8th." The Fort was situated on the North bank of the Columbia River about six miles above its junction with the Willamette River where the city of Vancouver, Washington, stands today. There he made a sketch of the Flathead chief Casanov who was head of Chinooks and Klickataats (both tribes Flatheads) in the immediate vicinity of the Fort (for Casanov see sketch No. 8). Here Kane noted that Casanov had at one time 1000 warriors and himself had ten wives, four children, and eighteen slaves.[27] The whites then settled in the area and brought fever that left the Chief with one wife, one child and two slaves. Kane also tells us that the Chief had at one time a hired assassin who killed persons thought to be obnoxious by the Chief. The story goes that this hired assassin finally fell in love with one of the Chief's wives and took her away with him. The Chief who was furious later caught up with them at separate times and killed them both.[28] From Fort Vancouver Kane proceeded to Oregon City, located today in the State of Oregon, with Mr. Mackenlie, Chief Trader of Fort Vancouver, and on their trip they experienced temperatures of seven below zero.[29] At Oregon City he stayed in the house of Mr. Mackenlie for three weeks then he ascended the Walhamette River with a Jesuit missionary named Father Acolti and they proceeded to the Roman Catholic mission operated by six Sisters of Charity. At the mission the nuns taught forty-two pupils both red and white. On his return Kane sketched the Klackammuss Indians and watched them gamble four small stocks in their hands. The stocks are placed under a mat in positions which the other party must guess (see page 134 for details). After returning to Fort Vancouver Kane set out for Vancouver Island in a small wooden canoe with two Indians. They departed on March 25th and on the way the artist sketched a volcano (Mount St. Helen's) at the mouth of the Kattlepoutal River. By March 27th they were on the Cowlitz River where Kane inspected an Indian burial ground which he sketched (No. 9 in his book).[30] They then crossed by horseback over country to the Nasqually River and on to Puget Sound which is today bordered by Tacoma and Seattle. From there Kane travelled to Fort Victoria on Vancouver Island. He made the trip by canoe with six Indians paddling.[31] From Fort Victoria he made trips up the eastern side of Vancouver Island and over to the main land where he visited Indian villages and made sketches of their inhabitants. At Victoria he met an old Nasqually chief who had come down to the coast in search of his favourite wife who had been carried off and sold on Vancouver Island. Kane[32] relates, "I asked him how he had managed to escape on coming down, and he showed me an old piece of newspaper, which he said he held up whenever he met with strange Indians, and that they, supposing it to be a letter for Fort Victoria, had allowed him to pass without

KANE, Paul (Cont'd)

molestation." Albert H. Robson[33] noted author on Canadian art tells of Paul Kane's return east as follows, "On July 1, 1848, Kane began his return journey up the Columbia River and through the mountains to Fort Edmonton, arriving on December 5. After spending Christmas and New Year's at this Post, he travelled to Fort Pitt where he lingered a month sketching the Cree Indians before returning to Edmonton. On April 12 he left for Rocky Mountain House, 180 miles up the Saskatchewan, to study the Blackfeet Indians and from there joined the York Factory Brigade, going to Norway House, which was reached on June 18. From Norway House he returned to Toronto passing over the same route he had traversed on his outward journey, arriving home in October." Kane brought back more than five hundred sketches enough to keep him supplied with material for painting for the rest of his life. His commissions included: 12 paintings for Sir George Simpson; 12 paintings for the Library of the Legislature of Upper Canada (11 of these are now in the National Gallery of Canada, 1 being destroyed by fire at Quebec City or Ottawa); 100 oil paintings of Indian life and character and western scenes for George William Allan (this collection was later purchased by Sir Edmund Osler of Toronto and presented to the U of T's Royal Ontario Museum); 300 of Kane's field sketches were also turned over to the Royal Ontario Museum by Major Raymond Willis, a descendant of the Hon. George W. Allan. Kenneth E. Kidd[34] of the Museum described the sketches as follows, "All . . . are characterized by a freshness and vitality which immediately attract one; if we can imagine the arduous circumstances under which the artist must have worked at them – in a moving canoe, in the excitement of a buffalo hunt, or in the intense cold, or again, under the suspicious eyes of hostile Indians – we must concede his ability to capture not only delightful bits of scenery but the significance of the action or the view before him as well." Kidd,[35] in an article for *Canadian Art* magazine, described Kane's 1845 sketches as follows, "Kane used his pencil with almost photographic effect in depicting river and boating scenes, rocks and Indian camps. Usually no unnecessary or extraneous matter was put in; the scenes contain the essentials required to give a clear concise report. There is a fine gradation of shading in these, which Kane was never able to achieve in any of his oils, and which contributes to making many of these field sketches more satisfying to us than much of his studio work. The water-colour-and-pencil combination was used chiefly at this stage for producing portraits and representations of handicrafts, although a few landscapes, such as that of Sault Ste. Marie, are also done in this medium . . . . When he set off for the North-west coast in 1846 on his longer trip, most of his meagre equipment quickly became exhausted, for he was forced to use scraps of notepaper, some of it even lined in blue before the end of his journey. His water colours, fortunately, did not run out, and thus the intrepid artist-explorer was able to record a truly great number of scenes along the way." The remaining bulk of Kane's sketches were owned by his grandson, Paul Kane, a Winnipeg lawyer who also owned Kane's diary. The grandson offered this collection of sketches to the Canadian Government in 1935 for $250,000. Prime Minister Bennett told him he would be prepared to pay $125,000 for them but before any transaction had taken place the government changed hands. Other offers were made to Canadian Galleries including the National Gallery of Canada who were interested only if they could choose the ones they wanted rather than to purchase the lot. Eventually the collection (230 water colour, oil and pencil sketches, four large oil paintings and manuscript of *Wanderings Of An Artist* were sold to H.J. Lutcher Stark, oil millionaire of Orange,

KANE, Paul (Cont'd)

Texas for $100,000. The transaction was handled through Edward Eberstadt & Sons of New York.[36] Since the death of Mr. Stark the collection has been the property of the H.J. Lutcher Stark Foundation of Orange, Texas.

References

[1] *Wanderings Of An Artist Among The Indians Of North America* by Paul Kane, M.G. Hurtig Ltd., Edmonton, Alberta, 1968, Introduction by Lawrence J. Burpee Page xxi

[2] Ibid

[3] *The Oxford Companion to Canadian History and Literature* by Norah Story, Oxford University Press, (Canadian Branch) 1967, P.116, 117

[4] Ibid, xxi

[5] Ibid, xxii

[6] *Paul Kane* by Albert H. Robson, Ryerson, 1938, P.4

[7] Ibid, P.4

[8] *Wanderings Of An Artist* as in [1], Author's Preface, P.1 xii

[9] Ibid, xxvi also *Toronto Daily Star*, Tor., Ont., Sept. 3, 1960 "Old Times In Ontario" by Edwin Guillet (Res. Historian Archives of Ontario)

[10] Ibid, xxvii

[11] Ibid, xxviii

[12] Ibid, xxix also *Paul Kane* by Albert H. Robson, P.6

[13] Ibid, Author's Preface, 1 xii

[14] Ibid, P.1

[15] Ibid, P.4

[16] Ibid, P.5

[17] Ibid, P.9

[18] Ibid, P.9

[19] Ibid, P.18

[20] Ibid, P.19

[21] Ibid, P.21-22

[22] Ibid, P.23

[23] Ibid, xxxi, xxxii

[24] Ibid, P.51

[25] Ibid, P.52

[26] Ibid, xxxii, xxxiii

[27] Ibid, P.118

[28] Ibid, P.120

[29] Ibid, P.131

[30] Ibid, P.139

[31] Ibid, P.144

[32] Ibid, P.171

[33] *National Gallery of Canada Catalogue, Vol. 3* by R.H. Hubbard, P.152-156

[34] *Bulletin of the Royal Ontario Museum of Archaeology,* Tor., No. 23, May 1955, "Paul Kane, Painter Of Indians" by Kenneth E. Kidd, P.11

[35] *Canadian Art*, Vol. 8, No. 4, Summer 1951 "Paul Kane — A Sheaf of Sketches" by Kenneth E. Kidd, P.166-167

[36] *Edmonton Journal*, Edmonton, Alta., Nov. 8, 1957 "Texas Oilman Buys Frontier Artist's Works" (a CP release Winnipeg)

New York Times, NYC, Oct. 27 1957 "Texan Acquires Sketches of West"

Winnipeg Tribune, Winnipeg, Man., Nov. 7, 1957 "Texan Buys $100,000 Art Trove"

see also

Canada And Its Provinces, Volume XII "Painting And Sculpture In Canada" by E.F.B. Johnston, Glasgow, Brook, Tor., 1914 P.596, 602

The Fine Arts In Canada by Newton MacTavish, MacMillan, 1925, 3-7

Encyclopedia Of Canada, Volume 3, Ed. W. Stewart Wallace, Univ. Assoc. of Can., 1948, P.321

KANE, Paul (Cont'd)

Canadian Landscape Painters by A.H. Robson, Ryerson, Tor., 1932

The Growth Of Canadian Painting by Donald W. Buchanan, Collins, Tor., 1950, P.18, 19, Plate 1 of Monochrome Illustrations

The Arts In Canada, Canadian Citizenship Series Pamphlet No. 6, Ott. 1958 P.39, 40, 41

Encyclopedia Canadiana, Volume 5, Grolier, Ottawa, 1962, P.386

The MacMillan Dictionary of Canadian Biography, Ed. W. Stewart Wallace, MacMillan, Tor., 1963, P.358

The Development Of Canadian Art by R.H. Hubbard, Queen's Printer, 1963, P.60-1

Canadian Art Its Origin And Development by William Colgate, Ryerson Paperbacks, 1967, (see index)

Three Hundred Years of Canadian Art (catalogue) by R.H. Hubbard and J.R. Ostiguy, Queen's Printer, 1967, P.64-5

Agnes Etherington Art Centre, Queen's University At Kingston Permanent Collection, 1968 by Frances K. Smith, Item 74

Painting In Canada/A History by J. Russell Harper, U. of T. Press, 1966, P.147, 148, 149, 150, 151.

―――――――――

KANTAROFF, Maryon

b.1933

Born in Toronto, Ontario, she graduated from the University of Toronto in Art and Archaeology in 1957.[1] She then worked as Assistant Curator of the Art Gallery of Ontario but decided to take a post graduate course at the Chelsea College of Art, and at the British Museum.[2] During this period she became interested in sculpture which she studied and worked at for six years. She has exhibited her work in several galleries in the United Kingdom; done some work for television also architectural commissions. An exhibit of her work took place in the Main Lobby of the Toronto City Hall in August, 1968, when Kay Kritzwiser[3] of the *Globe & Mail* noted, "Her current exploration in aluminum and cast fibreglass, in resin and cement, made a strong frieze in the City Hall's main lobby this week. But guests invited to a wine and cheese party by Aldermen Hugh J. Bruce and Michael Grayson, to see Miss Kantaroff's sculptures, were also shown the obverse of her creative coin; a representational head of Tony Amodeo, Toronto, which will be cast in bronze . . . . 'Of course it's strictly academic,' Miss Kantaroff said of the head. 'I don't feel I have the right to do anything but academic representation in portraiture.' Her beautiful eyes flickered mischievously. 'Not when it's for a client." She has gained an international reputation as an artist who works in steel, resin and cement. She has been awarded several architectural commissions in Canada. Her sculpture has been shown also in Milan and Munich. She lives in the Chelsea area of London, England.

References

[1] *The Toronto Telegram*, Tor., Ont., Sat., Apr. 20, 1968 "Sculptors . . . and one who came back" by Margaret Penman

[2] Ibid, also *Quebec Le Soleil*, Quebec, P.Q., Oct. 28, 1965 "Une Canadienne à la Biennale d'Art abstrait"

[3] *The Globe & Mail*, Tor., Ont., Aug. 17, 1968 "Panorama for Toronto's City Hall-At The Galleries" by Kay Kritzwiser

[4] *The Toronto Telegram*, Mar. 14, 1969 "Munich display for sculptor Kantaroff"

KARDOS, Ladislas
b.1909

Born in Budapest, Hungary, he lived in Vienna and Paris in his youth.[1] During the Second World War he served in the French army in North Africa.[2] In 1951 he settled in Vancouver, B.C., where he was in the lumber business until an aeroplane accident required him to leave his business in the hands of colleagues for eight months.[3] It was during this period in 1957 that he began to paint full time although he had always been interested in painting. His work has been executed mainly in oils from the semi abstract and impressionistic approach. His subjects include streets, docks, harbours or villages of many countries he has visited. Ian McNairn[4] of the University of British Columbia noted, "The poetic experience is a major part of the nature of art. It is quite appropriate therefore that Ladislas Kardos should think of his art as basically poetic. Perhaps we have been too slow to relate the aesthetic experience of painting to that of poetry but it is never too late to learn . . . . Two elements are shared in essence by the arts, and as far as the work of Kardos is concerned, shared by painting and poetry. First of all is the element of form. His paintings are organized into a sensitive rhythmic pattern. Usually the basic pattern is simple but the appeal is not in this first pattern but the rhythms within it. Symmetry and simple horizon, whether described or suggested, are generally ignored in contemporary abstractions. It is refreshing then to discuss an artist who recognized the aesthetic values in these classical forms . . . . The second element which his paintings share with poetry is imagery. His subjects are a translation of nature into a truly poetic vision. Three themes dominate his work — flower studies, broad visionary landscapes and hill towns, often by the sea. There is no specific description of the subject — there are no particulars, only suggestions. Through suggestion we approach a universal experience which is nonetheless personal — the kind of experience mankind is constantly searching for." Kardos has exhibited his paintings in many group shows including: Western Art Circuit (1962); Faculty Club, Vancouver (1963) and other exhibits abroad. His one man shows include those at Galerie Bernheim-Jeune, Paris (1964); International Gallery, New York (1964); Museum of Fine Arts, Eugene, Oregon (1964); Galerie Gerard Mourgue, Paris (1965); Argus Gallery, Melbourne (1965); Jack Hambleton Galleries, Kelowna, B.C. (1965); Institute for Cultural Relations, Budapest (1966); Commonwealth Inst., London, England (1966); Galerie Martal, Montreal, P.Q. (1967); Gallery of the Golden Key (1968); Galerie Cultura Libertad, Lima, Peru. He is represented in the following collections: Museum of Modern Art, Paris France; Museum of Contemporary Art, Montreal; Museum of Fine Art, Eugene, Oregon; Faculty Club, Vancouver, B.C.; University of British Columbia, Vancouver; Confederation Art Gallery, Charlottetown, P.E.I. and in many private collections.

References

[1] National Gallery of Canada Information Form rec'd October, 1965 also *Ladislas Kardos* (catalogue) Commonwealth Inst. Art Gallery, Kensington High Street, London, W. 8, England

[2] *Ladislas Kardos* (as above)

[3] *Kelowna Courier*, Kelowna, B.C., Fri., July 23, 1965 "Plane Crash Opens Door For New Artistic Career"

[4] *L. Kardos: Paintings*, with introduction by Ian McNairn, paintings by Kardos, poetry by Marya Fiamengo, Cesar Vallejo, Ralph Gustafson, Klanak Press, Vancouver, 1963

see also

Vancouver Life, Nov., 1967, "Kardos: the cosmopolitan who creates cities" by E. Johnson

Le Soleil, Que., P.Q., May 2, 1964 "Un peintre canadien à Paris"

Ibid, Sept. 23, 1964 "Kardos peintre de la cité" par Gaston L'Heureux

Lethbridge Herald, Leth., Alta., Oct. 4, 1963 "Special Display On Art At Library"

KARLIK, Pierre

b. (c) 1931

An Eskimo sculptor from Rankin Inlet, North West Territories, Canada, who has done large and small carving of Arctic animals. He completed a 600 lb. walrus for the Municipal Offices of Etobicoke, Ontario, and was recently commissioned to carve an 8000 lb. walrus sculpture for the 20 story building of Aquitaine Company of Canada Limited at Calgary, Alberta (a French owned oil corporation). A large piece of medium-soft rock will be taken from a quarry at Broughton Station, Quebec, and either shipped to Calgary or Churchill, Manitoba, for the actual work. Karlik wanted to do the work in Churchill because he found Calgary too warm.

References

Barrie Examiner, Barrie, Ont., Dec. 12, 1968 "Eskimo Sculptor"
Le Droit, Ottawa, Ont., Dec. 19, 1968 (large photo of artist with model in hand – also caption)
Time, December 27, 1968 "The Biggest Walrus" P.10

KARMAN, Robert

b.1933

Born in Montreal, Quebec, he is a self taught artist who has made his living as a commercial artist. He has become known for his landscape painting. He settled in Scarborough, Ontario, until 1961 when he took his wife and family to Europe to broaden his horizons as a painter. His semi abstract landscapes are well done and show good taste. His paintings have been exhibited at the 78th Spring Show (Montreal); 9th Annual Winter Exhibition (Hamilton); 86th Annual Ontario Society of Artists exhibition (Toronto) and elsewhere.

References

National Gallery of Canada Information Form rec'd June 23, 1958 a reproduction from a Brigden Calendar of Advertising Production Service (date unknown)
Scarborough News, Ont., Mar. 23, 1961 "Artist In A Rut Seeks Inspiration In Europe"

KARVONEN, Mirja Lydia

b.1918

Born at Kisko, Finland, she studied at the Fredrika Wetterhoffin Kotiteollisuuso-pisto, Finland, and the Walstedts Textilverkstad, Holsaker, Sweden. She came to Canada, with her husband Urho in 1958. A weaver, she exhibited her work at the 9th and 10th Annual Weaving Exhibitions (1961, 1962) at London, Ontario; Fine Arts Gallery, University of British Columbia, Van. (1962); B.C. Craftmen (1964) at The Vancouver Art Gallery; 12th Annual Weaving Exhibition (1964), Van.B.C.; German Industries Fair – Canadian Exhibit section (1964); International Arts and Crafts Fair, Florence (1965); Canadian Fine Crafts (1966-7) at The National Gallery of Canada; Studio Fair (1967), Van., B.C. and she has received many honours at these exhibitions. She lives in North Vancouver, B.C.

Reference

National Gallery of Canada Information Form rec'd July 7, 1967

KASHETSKY, Joseph

b.1941

Born at Saint John, N.B., he studied art for four years at the Saint John Vocational School under Ted Campbell and Fred Ross. A painter he has held one man shows in Montreal; the New Brunswick Museum, and the Mount Allison University in 1961.[1] He has worked as a commercial artist in Saint John, N.B. and was awarded a Canada Council grant in 1967 for a year's work in art. He held a one man show at the Morrison Art Gallery, Saint John in October of 1968 when the *Evening Times Globe*[2] noted, "The abstract form has always been his medium and he is quick to say there is no hidden symbolism in his work. His drawings are meant to please the eye through balance and clarity of design . . . . There is definitely a richness in the work of this 27-year-old artist." Another one man show of his work was held in May of 1969 at New Brunswick Museum organized by the Department of Art of the Museum. Ian G. Lumsden[3], Curator of Art at the Museum wrote the foreword for the catalogue in which he noted, "The vacuity of his figures project, at once, both a tragic and exquisite mien. The torment and anguish reflected in his figurative works exhibit a concern for the persecuted factions of humanity throughout history, and the alienation of the artist from the mundane details of day to day existence. Though his Jewish heritage is an integral part of his work, his interest extends beyond religion and race to mankind in general. In a milieu which relies so heavily on the regional, it is refreshing to see an artist whose work attains a level of universal import." Included in his exhibit were still lifes, nudes, figure studies, 'house portraits', structure studies, interiors and other subjects. He was awarded a Canada Council Grant for the period 1969-70. One of his relief compositions decorates the head of the main stairs in the Student Union Building of the University of New Brunswick at Fredericton. It was given as a gift by the Class of '69. He is represented in the permanent collection of the New Brunswick Museum.

References

[1] Catalogue of 74 *Paintings and Drawings by Joseph Kashetsky* for the exhibition organized by the Department of Art of The New Brunswick Museum (foreword by Ian G. Lumsden, Curator of Art) also catalogue for the exhibition *Joseph Kashetsky* at The New Brunswick Museum and Mount Allison University (1961)

[2] *Evening Times Globe*, Saint John, N.B., October 26, 1968 "One-man Show For Young Artist"

[3] see[1]

KAUFMAN, Helen

Originally from Poland she exhibited 42 of her paintings at the Borocov Centre, Toronto, in October of 1963 when J.S. of the *Canadian Jewish Outlook* noted, " . . . her works show that she has much to say by way of pencil and paint. Although largely abstract in nature, her canvases communicate what she is aiming at . . . one can't help feeling caught up by the richness of her themes and her colorfullness. . . . We are personally not for abstract art, and we feel that Helen Kaufman finds her best work when she pursues a middle course between abstract and realistic portrayal, tending toward the more representational. However that may be, there is no denying that in her we have an artist who will surely make a fine contribution to the Canadian art scene."

Reference

Canadian Jewish Outlook, Toronto, Ont., November, 1963 "A Painter Of Promise" by J.S.

KAUFMANIS, Rusins (Rusins)

A well-known Canadian caricaturist who has exhibited his work in several cities including Toronto in the foyer of Eaton's-College street store. Many notable political figures have been the subject of his pen over the years. His cutting satirical cartoons appear on the Editorial Page of *The Ottawa Citizen* almost daily. He lives in Ottawa.

References
> *Globe & Mail*, Tor., Ont., Oct. 19, 1957
> *The Ottawa Citizen* (see daily issues)

KAY, Louis

An artist from Toronto who did life sized portraits of the Fathers of Confederation for a collection of Canadian historical material centered on the Canadian graphic arts gathered by Rolph, Clark, Stone Limited as a centennial project. Kay was originally from Hungary.

Reference
> *The Mail-Star*, Halifax, N.S., Oct. 21, 1964 "History Recalled By Art Collection"

KEARNS, Murray William
b.1929
Born in Toronto, Ontario, he studied at the Ontario College of Art under J.W.G. MacDonald, Rowley Murphy, Carl Schaeffer, Jack Martin, Harley Parker and George Pepper. He is known for his etchings and in 1951 wrote an article on "Methods of Etching" for *The Canadian Forum*. His article was accompanied by a reproduction of one of his etchings entitled "Baldwin Market" which indicates that he is an excellent artist and etcher. He is a member of the Federation of Canadian Artists and lives in Toronto. No recent information is available on him.

References
> National Gallery of Canada Information Form rec'd May 1, 1950
> *The Canadian Forum*, Tor., Ont., May, 1951 "Methods of Etching" by Murray W. Kearns, P.38

KEATING, Frank
b.1892
Born in St. John's, Newfoundland, he received artistic encouragement from his mother who sent him to the Newfoundland Art School at St. John's. His father, John Keating, was Deputy Minister of Finance for Newfoundland and was so involved with politics that he did not notice his son's interest in art. After Frank

KEATING, Frank (Cont'd)

ran away to sea at the age of 15, his father brought him back, but after this happened a few times his father decided to let him have his way. Since that time Frank Keating has spent over twenty-five years at sea mainly serving with the Belgian Mercantile Marine. Between trips to sea he worked as a newspaperman, an interpreter with the U.S. army (1917-18), an art director in a couple of large department stores and a few other occupations. He was awarded a bronze medal in 1909 by the Cloth Workers' Company, London, England, for a series of murals. During his exhibit of 37 oils at the James MacConnell Memorial Library in Sydney, Cape Breton Island, in August of 1968, F.H. Stevens[1] of the *Sydney Breton Post* noted, "It happens that the writer crossed the Atlantic 38 times in the course of serving aboard a U.S. Navy transport in the First World War and after the 1918 Armistice, and four times in civilian life thereafter. In looking at the Keating paintings Tuesday one joyfully recognized his seascapes as the real thing. This was it veritably in such paintings as 'After the Squall's Over', 'Olive Sea', 'Weather', etcetera. Memories were stirred vividly . . . to feel in recollection the heave of the deck beneath your feet, to breathe again that wild, free pure ocean air and see again the true colours of the ocean. The Keating paintings range from the large, bold and spectacular to the small, delicate and intimate . . . . Not that one expected it to be less than good, but the consoling fact of the current exhibition at Sydney's public library is that it exceeds one's expectations." In November of 1968 he exhibited his paintings at the Arts and Culture Centre, St. John's, Newfoundland, when Marlayne Clarke[2] of the *Evening Telegram* noted, "The sea theme runs through all Frank's paintings, many of them are seascapes, boats and one is a shipboard scene. He said the interesting effects he has achieved with his canvases are the result of experimentation. Some of his paintings are combinations of water colors, oil, and fabrics. He also uses different techniques of applying the media such as spray painting and several of his paintings have fold-off panels. Many of the paintings have strong contrasts giving a 'realer than life' impression. Throughout the paintings there is a current of humor. I had to chuckle when I saw the one of old Mother Hubbard going to her cupboard to get her dog a bone. A fold-off cupboard door reveals a bottle of French red wine — Beaune (pronounced 'Bone')." Frank Keating does not stay too long in any one place but he may be found at St. John's, Newfoundland or perhaps Antwerp, Belgium.

References
[1] *Cape Breton Post*, Sydney, N.S., Aug. 7, 1968 "Graphic Touch . . Artistic Conquest" by F.H. Stevens
[2] *Evening Telegram*, St. John's Nfld., Tues., Nov. 12, 1968 "Frank Keating paints life the way he sees and feels it" by Marlayne Clarke

---

KEATLEY, Gwen

A graduate of the Ontario College of Art she is on the staff of the Sault Ste. Marie *Daily Star*. During an exhibit of her work in December of 1959 at the local YMCA she was asked by Nan Rajnovich another *Star* reporter, how she expected to communicate in non-objective painting which denies the use of symbols of recognizable reality. Gwen Keatley's answer was, "I really don't see what that's got to do with

KEATLEY, Gwen (Cont'd)

me, that is this worry about communication. I am not a world facelifter type at all. There is no existentionalistic philosophy between the brush strokes. Painting to me is not a ways or means to the salvation of man. It is simply decorative . . . . The first painting that ever impressed me was a Kandinsky . . . . Shortly afterward, I saw a painting titled Metaphysical Atmosphere. It was huge with a big black rectangle hanging from over a grey sky waterscape. The black effort was, I suppose the gates of heaven. This painting decided for me that I would never be a story-teller and yet I have gone slightly story-tellerish on Christ. But it depicts the fear that is in all of us — honest fear — conscious fear. I am not preaching. This fear is there. I like it. I paint it . . . . When I think about those artists who communicate to me either directly or through painting I can't get very far away from Canada. Graham Coughtry, Jock Macdonald and David Milne."

Reference
> *Daily Star*, Sault Sainte Marie, Ont., Dec. 11, 1959 "I Exist as of The Moment" "G. Keatley Painting in One-man Show" by Nan Rajnovich (an interview set down by questions and answers of which the above is only small excerpt)

KEDDIE, Kate M.

b.1887

Born at Seven Islands, Quebec, the daughter of James A. Wilson, a chief factor of Hudson's Bay posts in northern Quebec and later Labrador. At Cumberland House, Saskatchewan, she met and married Philip Keddie who later died in the late 1920's. In 1930 she joined the staff of the International Grenfell Association and was sent to North West River, Labrador, as hostess for three years of the local hospital. Later she established a handicraft department for the Grenfell Mission in Cartwright, Labrador, where she became industrial director in charge of handicrafts and in this capacity travelled extensively by dog team or by boat to the various settlements. She retired from this work in 1958 when she began oil painting. She has exhibited at Eaton's art gallery in Winnipeg (29 oil paintings including northern landscape scenes) and probably elsewhere. She is now living in Victoria, B.C.

References
> *The Tribune*, Winnipeg, Man., May 2, 1966 "One-man show at 79 years"

KEENE, Caleb

(c) 1866[1]-19 - -

An Oakville, Ontario, artist who was a painter and lacquer worker. He exhibited his paintings at the Eaton Fine Art Galleries, College Street, Toronto, in the 1930's and 40's. A *Toronto Star Weekly*[2] reporter described his studio as follows, "Mr. C. Keene is a painter of Canada; he loved the woods, the hills and the streams of the Dominion and he has put his love on to canvas. But in addition to the fame he has won for his landscapes he is recognized as the foremost exponent of lacquer work in the Dominion and his reputation in this branch of art is world-wide. A *Star* reporter called upon Mr. Keene and was ushered into his roomy studio. About the room were examples of his work —

KEENE, Caleb (Cont'd)

landscapes of the Laurentians, scenes in France and Belgium and Africa, for Mr. Keene is a great traveller; screens, cabinets and tapestries in lacquer . . . . Perhaps the most intriguing things in the studio were the examples of lacquer work executed by Mr. Keene. He has been a student of this almost forgotten art for a great number of years and his work is considered to be among the finest produced. A large cabinet lacquered in pure vermillion stood at one side of the studio and gave an excellent idea of his capabilities. No Dutch craftsman of the eighteenth century ever turned out a smoother or more beautiful piece of work. The rich varnish felt like polished glass and the embossed design built up by countless brush strokes was superb." During his 1939 exhibit at Eaton Fine Art Galleries, Toronto, his paintings were reviewed by the *Saturday Night*[3] as follows, "Mr. Caleb Keene delights us with a small group of his still-lifes — exquisitely mellow compositions that seem to embody the glow of old silver, the patina of rich bronze, the warmth of faded parchment and the bouquet of rare wine. Mr. Keene's interest lies in the play of texture and surface, and he caresses the objects in his well-seasoned little world with a most loving brush. This is a most appropriate showing for the season of mists and mellow fruitfulness." Caleb Keene was the father of Louis Keene, Canadian artist.

References

[1] Keene's birth date is not certain

[2] *Toronto Star Weekly*, Tor., Ont., April 11, 1925 "Keene's Lacquer Work Is Famed World-Wide"

[3] *Saturday Night*, Toronto, Nov. 18, 1939
see also
Saturday Night, Oct. 31, 1936 (review of an Eaton's show)
Ibid, Nov. 4, 1939 (photo of his work and caption)
Ibid, Mar. 2, 1940 (photo of artist at his easel)

KEENE, Louis

b.1888

Born in London, England, the son of Caleb Keene, Canadian artist, he studied at the Bolt Court School of Photo Lithography; the Chelsea School of Art, London, England; South Africa College of Art.[1] He was cartoonist for the *Cape Argus* in South Africa.[2] He sketched in Europe in 1908, and came to Canada in 1912.[3] He was cartoonist for *Fair Witness*, Montreal, and the *Herald*, Montreal; illustrated his own book *Crumps* and did illustrations for several other books.[4] He served with the First Auto Machine Gun Brigade (Canadian) in Britain also with the Imperial Army (1915); 150th Batallion, Montreal, with the rank of Lieutenant (1916); 20th Machine Gun Company, Siberia, Russia (1916-19). He held a solo exhibit of his landscapes of the Muskoka and Laurentian areas in 1920 at the Eaton Fine Art Galleries, Toronto (was employed with the T. Eaton Company as a specialist in chinaware).[5] During the Second World War he returned to the Canadian army. Became Commanding Officer of the Lorne Scots Regiment, holding the rank of Lieutenant-Colonel. He took this unit overseas in 1940. Subsequently he became Commanding Officer of No. 1 Canadian Repatriation Depot in England. During his service with the army in 1914-18 and 1940-45, he made sketches of activities with which he was connected. Many of his war sketches (First and Second World Wars) are in the National Gallery of Canada war collections.[6] He was last reported living in Toronto.

KEENE, Louis (Cont'd)

References
[1] National Gallery of Canada Information Form (undated) also *Globe & Mail*, Toronto, Ont., Nov. 8, 1938
[2] Ibid
[3] Ibid
[4] Ibid
[5] *Globe & Mail*, Tor., Nov. 8, 1938 "English Artist's Home Amid Trees Breathes Old World Atmosphere"
[6] *Check List Of The War Collections, National Gallery of Canada* by R.F. Wodehouse, Queen's Printer, 1968, P.34-5, 183

KEEVIL, Roland
(c) 1887-1963

Born near London, England, he received a college education and came to Canada in 1905 and homesteaded at O'Malleys, near Pike Lake, Saskatchewan.[1] In 1919 he moved to Saskatoon where he made his living in the farm implement business and later from the Keevil Realty company which he founded.[2] He retired in 1959 and began painting full time. A folk painter, self taught, his work soon charmed many viewers. He painted only in oils as he explained for the booklet *Folk Painters of the Canadian West*[3] "I paint only in oil (with) a camel's (hair) soft brush and roughly, half and half, linseed oil and turps. I have done a few quickies, small ones 8" x 10" at Waskesiu. They took perhaps a couple of hours or less to complete. Could have sold them on the spot for $25.00 each and more. However, I much prefer making a quick, casual pencil sketch, and to paint later from same at my home . . . . People have repeatedly asked, 'How do you get such a vivid effect?' No. 1 I never use anything but new paint each time I paint. No. 2 I always keep the brushes clean. No. 3 My oil and turps are always kept clear. I make no attempt to reproduce exactly what I see ahead of me. These pencil sketches of mine are only a guiding point. Rather do I endeavour to improve on what I see, changing here and there and making more vivid, as the spirit so moves me." A number of his works were purchased in the United States and in various parts of Canada. The National Gallery of Canada purchased his painting "Winter, Kinsmen Park" which was exhibited in the exhibition Folk Painters of the Canadian West held in July of 1959, organized by the Gallery and sent on travelling exhibit. Another of his paintings of the Waskesiu Highway was accepted by Princess Margaret during her tour in Canada. Roland Keevil died at the age of 76 in Saskatoon. He was survived by his wife, Sophia; four daughters, Mrs. E. Wedge, Saskatoon; Mrs F.L.G. Webster, Alberni, B.C.; Mrs. W.F. McWhinney, Calgary; and Mrs. F.H. Munkley, Scarboro, Ontario; two sons, Dr. Norman Keevil, Toronto and Alan Keevil of Calgary; also one sister and two brothers.[4]

References
[1] *Star Phoenix*, Saskatoon, Sask., Apr. 25, 1963 "Roland Keevil, Pioneer Realtor, Painter Dead"
[2] Ibid
[3] *Folk Painters of the Canadian West* Foreword by Alan Jarvis, text by Norah McCullough
[4] see[1]

KEIRSTEAD, James Lorimer
b.1932

Born in Saint John, New Brunswick, he served in the Canadian Army in Korea (1952-53) and the Ontario Provincial Police (1954-65).[1] In Kingston he attended art classes at Queen's University under André Biéler and Ralph Allen.[2] He has been painting seriously since 1956 and earning his living from the sale of his paintings since 1965. Solo exhibits of his paintings have been held at Wallack's Galleries, Ottawa; Gallery of Fine Arts, Jamestown, N.Y.; the Tygeson Gallery, Toronto; the Up and Down Galleries (his gallery) Kingston; The Rideau Gallery, Westport, Ont.; also in Montreal and Niagara Falls. Viewing his 1968 exhibit at the Wallack's Art Galleries, W.Q. Ketchum[3] of *The Ottawa Journal* noted, "James Lorimer Keirstead has many admirers in Ottawa. This is his sixth one-man show under Wallack auspices. Mr. Keirstead is primarily a landscape artist. In depicting the beauty of the countryside in the changing seasons he uses a palette knife with a lavish hand. His still lifes show his obvious love of flowers which he paints with sensitivity. Viewers admired his canvas 'The Maple.' 'Old Frontenac Homestead' captures the elusive charm of weathered buildings of bygone era. 'Garage Westport' and 'Along the Perth Road' have a special appeal as well as 'Hilltop Shack' which stands invitingly in the shroud of winter . . . . He has within recent years attained a technical perfection with an unerring sense of both color and composition." Mr. Keirstead has given lectures, demonstrations, organized exhibitions, and taught art classes in many parts of Ontario. He lives in Kingston where he continues to be very active in the field of visual arts.

References
[1] National Gallery of Canada Information Form rec'd 1965
[2] Ibid
[3] *The Ottawa Journal*, Ott., Ont., Nov. 8, 1968 "Keirstead Paintings On View"
see also
The Ottawa Citizen, Oct. 20, 1964 "OPP officer talented painter of landscapes" by C.W.
Ibid, Oct. 27, 1965 "Young artist best in townscapes" by Carl Weiselberger
Whig-Standard, Kingston, Ont. Sept. 30, 1966 "Exchanged Gun for Palette" by David Cleland
Ibid, Apr. 6, 1966 "Painting Techniques Illustrated By Artist for Nurses' Alumnae" by Ann Levandoski
Pembroke Observer, Mar. 18, 1967 "Paintings By Keirstead, Zeigler, On Exhibit Here" by Penny McCullough

KELLETT, Anne

Born in Bradford, Yorkshire, England, she came to Canada and settled in Brantford, Ontario, where she has been active in drama and in the art of shell work.[1] Viewing her 1967 exhibition at Miss Kellett's home Helen Knight[2] of the Brantford *Expositor* noted, "Miss Anne Kellett displayed about 50 examples of the delicate floral designs in shell work for which she is renowned. Some pieces gleamed in a lapis lazuli effect while others glimmered in a mother-of-pearl luminescence. Trays, candle holders, jewel boxes and exquisite Renaissance wall panels revealed the professional craftsmanship of an artist in shell work. It all began in 1939 when a holidaying friend returned to Brantford with a bag full of shells from Florida and gave them to Miss Kellett, who started on a hobby which developed into an art." Examples of her work are now on permanent display in Ripley Museums in United States and at Niagara Falls, Ontario. She is also represented by outstanding jewellers

KELLETT, Anne (Cont'd)

and other commercial firms in Canada, at Toronto, Hamilton, Brantford and in the United States at New York and Walcula Springs, Florida. She was commissioned by the Brantford Local Council of Women to design and execute a shell work jewel box as the council's gift to H.R.H. Princess Elizabeth on the occasion of her wedding. The box was exhibited at St. James Palace, London, England, among the weddings gifts. A replica of this box is on view each summer in Victoria, B.C., along with replicas of the Crown Jewels. She has exhibited her work at the Canadian National Exhibition (1940) where she won First Prize; London, Ontario (1941, 42, 46); Toronto at the Art Gallery of Toronto (1943); Guild of All Arts, Scarborough, Ontario; Pacific National Exhibition, Vancouver; Brantford Public Library, Brantford, Ont.; and the Glenhyrst Art Gallery, Brantford, Ontario. She lives in Brantford.

References

[1] National Gallery of Canada Information Form rec'd May 9, 1949
[2] *The Expositor*, Brantford, Ont., June 1, 1967 "Artist Displays Collection of Renowned Shell Designs" by Helen Knight

KELLETT, Edith

b.1877

Born in Yorkshire, England, she came to Canada in 1919 and settled at Brantford, Ontario. She studied at the Drexel Institute, Philadelphia, and the Womens School of Design, Philadelphia, under Howard Pyle (painter) and Charles Grafley (sculptor) and others.[1] She received 'Honorable Mention, Miniature on Ivory' at the exhibition of "Americanization Through Art" at Memorial Hall, Philadelphia, 1916.[2] She also exhibited at Carnegie Art Galleries, Pittsburg, Pa.; Royal Academy, London, England (1924); Paris Salon, France (1925, 1928); Canadian National Exhibition, Toronto and elsewhere. The *Saturday Night*[3] in 1924 noted, "A miniature from her gifted brush has recently passed the critical test of this year's judges (of Royal Academy, London, Eng.) and received the approval of that institution of ancient tradition and exalted standard . . . . Along the circumscribed path of this exacting line of art, Miss Kellett has most successfully pursued her way, culling flowers of well deserved merit by the wayside. The most highly prized and the most recently added to her bouquet of honor, was won by a miniature, on ivory, of her sister Vera. This little gem, which won the commendation of this year's judges, well reveals the indisputable genius of its creator." In 1932 she was elected member of the Pennsylvania Society of Miniature Painters and also became a member of the Plastic Club, Philadelphia.[4] She painted about one hundred miniatures. Her sister Vera had in 1938 a small select group of her miniatures.[5] Edith Kellett is represented in the Art Museum, Philadelphia.

References

[1] National Gallery of Canada Information Form rec'd June 2, 1925
[2] Ibid
[3] *Saturday Night*, Sat., Sept. 20, 1924 "Canadian Women in the Public Eye"
[4] Letter to NGC from her sister Anne dated June 14, 1938
[5] Ibid
see also
La Revue Moderne, Paris (c) 1925, P.3

KELLY, Beverley Ann Lambert

b.1943

Born at Biggar, Sask., she studied at the Saskatoon Technical Institute under Robert Murray (1959-60) and the College of Art, University of Saskatchewan under Arthur McKay, Kenneth Lochhead and Ronald Bloore (1961-63) also received her B.A. from the University of Saskatchewan, Saskatoon (1967). She has done both objective and non-objective paintings and drawings and has experimented with coloured transparent tissue papers; collages (non objective) and more recently 'windows' made of canvas painted with layers of acrylic (for the panes) and wood built up with gesso and paste (for the window frames). She has exhibited at the Western Art League Annual, held at the London Public Art Gallery (1966); "Young London" at the 20/20 Gallery, London (1967); also a one man show at the 20/20 Gallery (1968). She received the Reeves Painting Award (1962); Purchase Award (Western Art League) 1966. She is married to Alex Kelly who is completing his Ph.D. in Economics at the University of Western Ontario.

References
    National Gallery of Canada Information Form rec'd in 1968
    see also
    Free Press, London, Ontario, Feb. 23, 1968 "One-man show features one subject: windows" by Lenore Crawford
    Arts/Canada, 1967 "The London Scene"
    Star Weekly, 1968 "Swinging London"

KELLY, John David

1862-1958

Born at Gore's Landing, near Peterborough, Ontario, the son of John Kelly, axe handle maker, lumber worker, and farmer.[1] His father went to Gore's Landing where he was employed in a lumber mill but later returned to Percy Ontario to farm. As a boy John Jr. and his brothers were encouraged by their father to become artists. Two of the boys achieved this goal, John Jr. and Percy (who died in 1948). The third brother Bert (who died in 1941) became an artistic printer.[2] John Jr. received his early education at S.S. No. 6 (The Stone School) near Percy and from there he went on to the Cobourg Collegiate.[3] Afterwards he studied at the Ontario School of Art under Marmaduke Matthews, John Fraser and others, graduating in 1882 with a gold medal.[4] For a year he painted on his own, then he joined the staff of the Grip publishing firm in Toronto where he worked on designs and illustrations.[5] In 1884 he then joined the Toronto Lithographing Company and was assigned to the publication *War News* and was despatched to the west to cover the events of the North West Rebellion of 1885. Subsequently he was assigned to another project which was to deal with the review of the activities of General Middleton's troops at Winnipeg but this assignment never reached the publication stage. His trips west gave him stimulus for his historical paintings which were to occupy his energies for the rest of his life. The Toronto Lithographing Company later became the Stone Lithographing Company and then Rolph, Clark, Stone Limited; the three firms employing Kelly for the remarkable period of 71 years. When he retired from Rolph, Clark, Stone in 1955, he donated his art studio and collection of rare reference books (especially of Canadiana) to the firm's library to aid other company artists.[6] One of his important projects was for the series of 28 historical paintings commissioned by the Confederation Life Association entitled

KELLY, John David (Cont'd)

"Gallery of Canadian History". This collection has been shown throughout Canada, the United States, London, England; has appeared on Confederation's annual calendars, in booklets for service clubs, home and school groups, church groups, art classes, study groups and historical societies.[7] The work of Kelly, for this firm, has been carried on by Rex Woods. When not on loan the paintings are kept on the 10th floor of Confederation Life's head office in Toronto. In 1886 Kelly married Alice Bigelow of New York City and took her to Europe for a honeymoon where he saw the Swiss pictorial railway maps. On his return to Canada he suggested the idea to the Canadian Pacific Railway who commissioned him to do such maps. Collecting material for this project took him across Canada in 1911 and 1929.[8] He produced many wonderful paintings of all the regions of Canada. Of his many historical paintings, it may be of interest to note his "Fathers of Confederation", and the same subject treated by Robert Harris. Most Canadians have come to accept Robert Harris' painting of the Quebec Conference of 1864 as completely authentic in every detail including the background (the building and the view through its windows) but Kelly or an associate researcher, discovered that the three large windows in the Harris work were those of the Charlottetown Legislative Building while looking through these three windows one sees the harbour at Quebec City. Kelly's "Fathers of Confederation" (owned by Confederation Life) depicts the sixteen fathers of the four charter provinces — Ontario, Quebec, New Brunswick and Nova Scotia — at the close of the three weeks of constitutional meetings in Westminister Palace Hotel, London, England in December, 1866. In this painting one can see the great passion Kelly had for detail — figures and the interior of the conference room itself where even the pictures on the walls have singing colours of uniformed dignitaries giving the viewer a feeling that he is sitting in on the meeting. Harris' "Fathers of Confederation" with its minor inconsistancies does not detract from his own meticulous research on the subject and he was without a doubt a superb portraitist. It is not the object here to compare one artist with the other. John David Kelly died in Toronto at the age of 98. At his death the following editorial appeared in the Peterborough *Examiner*[9] " . . . Mr. Kelly's pictures made history more real to hundreds of thousands of Canadians, and provoked in them that kind of nostalgic reverie which art critics especially despise. In consequence the idea grew up that Mr. Kelly was an accomplished artificer, in his particular way, but not an artist in a serious sense. From this opinion we dissent, for a reason which is not easy to explain in words, but which we believe has sufficient merit to make us try. If you look at any of Mr. Kelly's pictures you will see that they are very carefully composed; the composition is academic and old-fashioned, and therefore it does not seem to have attracted much attention. But it is more than merely academic; it is dramatic, and that in no superficial or contrived way. The ordinarily 'dramatic' nineteenth century picture . . . is dramatic in an artificial sense. The figures are posed in tableaux which proclaim their falsity. But in Mr. Kelly's pictures — the famous one of Mackenzie at the Pacific, for example — the drama rises from the subject itself; it is integral, and not peripheral . . . . To put it more simply, Mr. Kelly *felt* the situations which he painted, and all his historical accuracy and old-fashioned technique were at the service of his feeling. To us, and to many others, this feeling is communicated by the pictures themselves." During his life Kelly was active with several art societies. In 1886 he became a charter member of the Art Students' League (other members included: A.H. Howard, Robert Holmes, C.M. Manly, W.W. Alexander, O.R.

KELLY, John David (Cont'd)

Hughes and later David Thomson, F.H. Brigden, W.D. Blatchly, C.W. Jefferys, W.J. Thomson);[10] in 1904 a founding member of the Graphic Art Club (with many of the above A.S.L. members as well as J.W. Beatty, T.W. Mitchell, Ivor Lewis, T.W. McLean, A.H. Robson and others).[11] At the time of his death he was survived by four nephews; Archie McCracken (Roseneath); Ray and Harry Kelly (Warkworth, Ont.); Orville Kelly (Brighton, Ont.); and three nieces: Mrs. William Potter (Warkworth, Ont.); Mrs. W. Whaley (Mimico, Ont.); Miss Beatrice Kelly (NYC, USA).[12] His wife Alice died in 1893 when his only son died at birth. Copies of Kelly's historical paintings have been reproduced in Newfoundland's Confederation Building; City Hall, Halifax, N.S.; City Hall, Van. B.C.; City Hall, Tor., Ont.; two dramatic murals in the Royal York Hotel, Toronto; Crysler Museum in Upper Canada Village near Morrisburg and he is represented in the Art Gallery of Ontario and elsewhere. A memorial plaque to him was unveiled in Percy Centennial School, Warkworth, on August 19, 1968, and the plaque is to be placed in Percy Centennial Park, Warkworth, under the sponsorship of the Centennial Saga Committee of Percy Township, presented by the Archaeological and Historic Sites Board of Ontario under its 'Heritage Foundation'.[13]

References

[1] *Globe & Mail*, Tor., Ont., Dec. 29, 1958 "Painter of Scenes In Canadian History"

[2] *The Calgary Herald*, Nov. 27, 1958 (Tor. CP) "Dean Of Canadian Artists Says Learn To Draw First" see also [3] below

[3] *Sentinel-Star*, Cobourg, Ont., Jan. 8 1959 "Native Of Rice Lake Famous Artist Dies"

[4] *Examiner*, Peterborough, Ont., Apr. 8, 1967 "Percy honors painter" by Aureen Richardson

[5] see [3]

[6] see [3]

[7] *Confederation Life's Gallery of Canadian History* (a booklet with 33 reproductions of historical paintings) Reproductions of the original paintings will be made available to groups or researchers or publishers. They should apply to branch offices of Confederation Life in their districts or to Public Relations Department, Confederation Life, 321 Bloor St. East, Tor. 5, Canada.

[8] *Examiner*, Peterborough, Ont. as in [4] (see subheading "John D. Kelly, A pioneer in historical painting")

[9] Ibid, Dec. 31, 1958 "John David Kelly"

[10] *Canadian Art Its Origin and Development* by William Colgate, Ryerson Paperback, 1967, P.43

[11] Ibid, P.69

[12] *Sentinel-Star*, Cobourg, Ont., Jan. 8, 1959 "Native Of Rice Lake Famous Artist Dies"

[13] *Examiner*, Peterborough, Ont., Aug. 19, 1968 "Painter's Plaque Unveiled in Warkworth"

see also

Encyclopedia Canadiana (historical illustrations)

Confederation, published by Rolland Paper Co. (discussion of "Fathers of Confederation" by Robert Harris, John D. Kelly)

Centennial Saga of Percy Township (includes story about J.D. Kelly with copies of his paintings)

KELLY, Patrick

b (c)1937

Born in England he studied at the Hammersmith School of Art, London, and came to Canada in 1957. His first one man show was held at the Art Emporium, Vancouver, where a dozen of his abstract sculptures and almost fifty paintings were on view.

KELLY, Patrick (Cont'd)

References
> *Vancouver Sun*, Van., B.C., Dec. 1, 1959 "Artist Finishes Sculpture Then Tosses Acid Over it" by Dave Robertson

KELLY-TÉTREAULT, May

She first began working with ceramics as a hobby during a visit to the workshop of Gaétan Beaudin of North Hatley, with a group from "Jeunesses Musicales". For five consecutive years she took summer courses under Beaudin while building up her own workshop and specializing in earthenware. She has made bottles, sets of dishes, ceiling candelabra, table lamps, bird cages, jugs, cookie jars, casseroles, spice pots, beer mugs, liquor decanters, bowls of all sizes, and other items. Her works have toured the Province of Quebec in private exhibitions or through the agency of the Centrale d'Artisanat du Quebec; shown at Toronto, they took a prize from the Canadian Handicraft Guild. She has given courses and demonstrations at the Collège Militaire de Saint-Jean and to Chamber of Commerce groups, home economists, farmers' wives etc. Since her marriage to André Tétreault in 1964 she has become interested in refinishing old Canadian furniture. Loves skiing, and has been a member of ski patrols.

References
> *La Terre de Chez Nous*, Montreal, P.Q. "pages du foyer − May Kelly-Tétreault − céramiste et skieuse" par Jacqueline April

KELMAN, Harry

He studied art and other subjects in the High School of Commerce, Ottawa Technical High School, and then in New York. During the Second World War he toured Canada and went overseas with the Navy Show and on his way home from Germany stayed on in London, England. He returned to Paris where he remained for ten years. He spent the first three years under the sponsorship of the Department of Veterans' Affairs and a French Government grant. He lived at the Maison Canadienne of the Cité Universitaire and worked in various work shops of artists in Paris. He was employed by the American Government with the ECA (Marshall Plan) in the information division. Later he became a free lance artist. He returned to Canada and joined the production department of the Canadian Labour Congress in 1955 where he is also their art director. He won prizes for the following designs: the official ICFTU booklet circulated in Canada and elsewhere; the CIO Labour Fund and International Metal workers poster series; also a number of CIO booklets on industrial unions printed in four languages; the "Freedom Film Strip Series" (42 labour film strips in three languages distributed by the ICFTU); International Solidarity Fund Poster Competition (1959). Kelman exhibited 55 of his paintings at the Social Centre of the University of Montreal in June of 1963. He lives in Ottawa with his wife, Olga Kelman, an artist in her own right, and their two children.

References
> *The Ottawa Citizen*, Oct. 3, 1959 "CLC's Art Director Winning New Acclaim"
> Catalogue sheet − *Kelman* (an exhibition of his work at the University of Montreal 1st to 15th June, 1963)

KELMAN, Olga

b.(c)1925

Born in France she married Harry Kelman in 1947 and came to Canada a few months ahead of him. She has done many paintings and drawings, lino and wood-cuts, mobiles, puppets, carvings and portrait sculptures. She was the subject of an article in *The Ottawa Journal*, January of 1959 when Catherine Langley explained, "Much of her painting since she arrived in Ottawa . . . has dwelt heavily on abstract themes, as she has difficulty in finding suitable models. The Kelman children . . . Paul, and Teena, are restless posers, although portraits of the two are prominently displayed in the studio . . . she has turned to highly individualistic experiments in a number of media, relying on her husband as critic and teacher. In sum, the introspective and lonely work characterizing her Ottawa years may later prove an important period . . . . In Ottawa, she's found a lucrative field in commissioned (television) sets and department store murals. She's in the thick of fashion work, teaches modelling three nights a week, is planning an all French fashion show emphasizing Canadian simplicity and Parisian chic, and designs her clothes" Gertrude Lapointe wrote a second article on her for *Le Droit* in 1963. Olga Kelman lives in Ottawa with her husband and family.

References
The Ottawa Journal, Ottawa, Ont., Jan. 10, 1959 "A Parisienne's World of Art" by Catherine Langley
Le Droit, Ottawa, Ont., Sept. 14, 1963 "Femme aux cent talents" par Gertrude Lapointe

KELSEY, C.W.

An artist from Westmount, Quebec, who has designed a number of stained glass windows including a couplet window for Trinity Church, St. Agathe, in commemoration of the 1951 visit of Queen Elizabeth and the Duke of Edinburgh. The window shows the royal couple entering Trinity Church in the company of church dignitaries. This work was commissioned by Mrs. R. Percy Adams, wife of a former Mayor of Westmount.[1] Kelsey also did a three panel memorial window for St. George's Church, Dominion Square, Montreal, symbolizing the three Canadian armed services, and under the panels are the words, "They fought not for glory nor for wealth nor for honor but for that freedom which no good man will surrender but with his life."[2]

References
[1] *The Herald*, Mtl., P.Q., "Colored Window Marks Royal Visit"
[2] *The Gazette*, Mtl., P.Q., Nov. 11, 1958 (photo of windows and caption)

KELSEY, Leonard Edgar

b.1883

Born in London, England, he studied at the Ruskin College, London, England, and came to Canada in 1909 and settled in Montreal. There he studied under Adam Sheriff Scott, R.C.A. He joined the art staff of the Standard Photo Engraving Company and later the Mortimer Company. In 1917 he opened his own commercial art studio. His father was a sculptor also his grandfather who won a silver medal from the Royal Academy in London.

References
National Gallery of Canada Information Form rec'd Sept. 4, 1945

KEMBALL, Patrick Charles

b.1938

Born at Cranbrook, B.C., he studied at the Alberta College of Art under Ronald Spickett, Marion Nicoll, Kenneth Sturdy and others.[1] His goal has been to paint joy, ecstacy, birth and wonder and the ultimate things in terms of visual symbols. At one time Kemball wanted to become a monk but somehow he became disillusioned and turned to painting.[2] Much of his painting has to do with symbolic, religious expression. In 1968 an exhibition of his paintings was held at the Students' Union Building in Edmonton, Alberta, when Bill Pasnak[3] noted, "He has shed the conventionally acceptable image of Pat Kemball, and taken on the mystical identity of Manwoman. Manwoman is as symbolic as his paintings. The message he has should interest artists, poets, psychologists, theologians and the common man. Manwoman's work, basically, is an expression of symbolic mysticism. It can best be described in relation to the Kundalini, which is taken from the Hindu religion. The Kundalini places seven lotus flowers on the spine, corresponding to seven areas of the body, and each having its own spiritual significance. At the base of the spine is a coiled snake . . . . The seventh (lotus) is on the top of the head. It is the thousand-petalled lotus, symbolising the perfection of God. As the soul moves toward spiritual attainment, the snake uncoils, and moves up through each of the lotuses. Manwoman's paintings express the upward movement of the soul. As it moves upward, all conflicts must be resolved. Perfect harmony must be created for the god-state. Hence the symbolic significance of the name 'Manwoman': the containment of two states in one . . . . As the soul moves up toward the final state of perfection, it reaches a point where it separates from the ego force, and leaves it behind." Many of Kemball's paintings have to do with the various phases of the soul's journey from the first lotus to the seventh. His paintings are done in acrylics, pastels and oils. Kemball lives at Genesee, Alberta.

References

[1] National Gallery of Canada Information Form rec'd May 25, 1964
[2] Ibid
[3] *The Gateway*, Edmonton, Alta., Mar. 8, 1968 "The mystical art of Manwoman" by Bill Pasnak
see also
Edmonton Journal, Edmonton, Alta., Apr. 4, 1968 "Exhibition Has Element Of Mystery" by Dorothy Barnhouse

KEMP, James Alexander

b.1914

Born in Toronto, Ontario, he began drawing with great interest at an early age and at twelve years attended the Ontario College of Art. By the time he was fourteen he was taking private lessons where he studied life drawing.[1] In his academic work he entered the University of Toronto and graduated in 1940 with his Bachelor of Arts.[2] He did commercial art work and edited house publications for the London Life Insurance Company. In 1940 he joined the Royal Canadian Navy Volunteer Reserve and served as a gunnery officer and later as an ordnance inspector. He retired from the Navy with the rank of Lieutenant Commander. During his service he did cartoons for the *Crow's Nest* and other publications. After the war he returned to London, Ontario, where he became manager of publications for the London Life Insurance Company. He began painting in oils under the encouragement of Clare Bice and has been painting seriously since 1950.[3] He was elected

KEMP, James Alexander (Cont'd)

member of the Ontario Society of Artists in 1954. During a solo exhibit of his work at the Thielsen Galleries, London, in 1958, Lenore Crawford[4] of *The London Free Press* noted, " . . . the walls fairly crackled with the excitement of vivid colors, rhythm, delicious humor and, above all, a sense of 'arrival' that prevailed . . . . The collection is notable for the number of landscapes — or, rather, paintings for which landscapes were the springboard for the Kemp semi-abstract style. There also are some fine studies of women in what is now practically a Kemp tradition, including a blue one and a green one just to show the Kemp palette has not forsaken those colors entirely. And there are still lifes; especially interesting is a large study of a table with a bowl of fruit on it." The following month Kemp won an award at the 18th Annual Western Ontario Exhibition for the best oil painting and has since won this award several times. Since 1950 he has exhibited regularly with the O.S.A. and the R.C.A. and other groups. He is represented in the collection of the University of Western Ontario, Waterloo College, Assumption College as well as in private collections in Canada and the United States. He lives in London, Ontario.

References
[1] *The Standard Magazine*, Mtl., P.Q., Saturday, April 14, 1945 "Canadian Navy Artist" by Gerald H. Waring
[2] National Gallery of Canada Information Form rec'd 1961
[3] Ibid
[4] *London Free Press*, London, Ont., Mar. 29, 1958 "London Artists' Show Attracts Large Crowd" by Lenore Crawford
[5] Ibid, May 3, 1958 "Three Londoners Receive Art Exhibition Awards"

KEMP, Robert G.

b.1928

Born in Toronto, Ontario, he studied painting at the Banff School of Fine Arts and completed his course in 1947 also at the Northern Vocational School (four years) where he graduated in 1951. He worked eleven years in advertising art and was art director for two firms in Toronto. He also continued to make trips to various parts of Canada in search of landscapes for his painting. While skiing he discovered in 1956 the rich scenery of Collingwood facing Georgian Bay.[1] In 1961 he settled there at Blue Mountain where he has been painting full time. His studio "The Artist's Studio" is located on the Blue Mountain Winter Park Road. Describing his work in 1969, J.T. MacMurchy[2] of the Collingwood *Enterprise-Bulletin* noted, "He is a dedicated artist, sensitive and shy, but sufficiently practical and commercial that he knows the value of his work and the price he can expect to receive for it — in various forms. Robert Kemp likes to work on location and most of the finished pieces now hanging in his gallery, and in the Tom Thomson Memorial Gallery in Owen Sound, were painted within a 15 mile radius of his home. This man has made a great contribution to the historical background of the area. He has recorded, through his paintings many of the older houses in their natural settings. These examples of older architecture are rapidly disappearing, but fortunately for us, most of them have been perpetuated by Bob Kemp . . . . The products of the Kemp studio are varied in subject, but all are desirable. Some of his originals are now available in print form and hasty notes. This latter work is performed here, at Collingwood Litho or at the offset plant of Jock Bennett at Craigleith." His work

KEMP, Robert G. (Cont'd)

was exhibited at The Tom Thomson Memorial Gallery in a three man show which also included the work of David Holmes (Kingston, Ont.) and Anne March (London, Ont.). In this particular exhibition Kemp's landscapes were executed in pastels tinted with a subtle water colour wash.[3]

References

[1] Markdale *Standard*, Ont., July 11, 1968 "Art Gallery To Remain Open Benefit To Tourists"
[2] Collingwood *Enterprise-Bulletin*, May 8, 1969 "Robert G. Kemp – His Studio Overlooks The Mountain and The Bay" by J.T. MacMurchy
[3] Ibid, April 24, 1969 "Robert Kemp One Of Three Artists At O.S. Gallery"

KENDERDINE, Augustus Frederick
1870-1947

Born near Blackpool, Lancashire, England, one of twelve sons, he received his first art lessons from his godfather, Augustus Lafosse noted Belgium painter who was awarded the Chevalier of the Legion of Honour.[1] It was at the Manchester School of Art that Kenderdine studied under his godfather. Subsequently he went to Paris where he attended classes at the Académie Julian under Jules Lefevre. By the early 1900's he was an established painter of Lancashire scenes (did many hunting scenes) and exhibited at the Royal Academy in 1901.[2] His paintings were acquired by the Grundy Gallery, Blackpool, England, and in the Queen's Park Gallery, Manchester. For a time he had his own art shop. Then he served with a British cavalry regiment and was an instructor in horsemanship in the Duke of Lancaster's Own regiment.[3] He married and in 1907 came to Canada with his wife and children. He settled at Lashburn, Saskatchewan, where he established a homestead-ranch. *The Edmonton Journal*[4] described this experience as follows, "The rolling land, watered by a broad river, bears multitudes of trees. There young Kenderdine placed his ranch, beginning with a few cattle and a still smaller number of horses. He stayed on the land nearly twenty years, learned the cattle business, brought up a family, developed a philosophy and acquired the rugged health which keeps him energetic at sixty." When he had more time for painting Kenderdine began decorating doors of his barns and store-houses. The area in which he had settled was so remote that it took him five days by wagon over trackless prairie land to reach Lloydminster where he purchased his supplies. About 1920 he returned to the Old Country for a visit. On his way he decided to leave some of his paintings with an art dealer in Saskatoon for framing.[5] He had agreed with the dealer that if someone wanted to purchase them it would be agreeable for the dealer to make the transaction. Returning home he checked with the Saskatoon dealer and much to his surprise found that all of his paintings had been sold. With the money from the dealer, Kenderdine had enough to cover the costs of his trip abroad. Some of his paintings had been purchased by the President of the University of Saskatchewan, Dr. Walter C. Murray, for the University buildings. Dr. Murray had also left word with the dealer that he wanted to meet the artist.[6] The meeting took place and Kenderdine was offered a position of instructor in a new art department for the University and he accepted the offer. His son Richard continued to farm the extensive land holding which Kenderdine had acquired.[7] By 1921 he was exhibiting in Saskatoon and was reviewed by the *Phoenix*[8] as follows, "Seven of his pictures are temporarily on exhibit at Tyre's art shop on Twentieth Street. One, a moonlight scene on Fishing

KENDERDINE, Augustus Frederick (Cont'd)

Lake, is remarkable for the richness of its tone, its attractive composition, and its perspective. What is probably the best picture in the collection, as well as the largest, shows an autumn day on the Saskatchewan River at Yankee Bend. Far in the distance can be seen the blue form of Frenchman's Butte, while in the foreground a clump of tall poplars lends grace to the impressive dignity of the landscape. The light is excellent, and the picture is painted in a brilliant style. The outstanding characteristic of Mr. Kenderdine's work is his aerial perspective. A cloud effect and a representation of a brilliant autumn sky make this picture worthy of the highest admiration." In 1926 a number of his paintings were shown in Edmonton, Alberta, at the public library lecture room and then in New York and later Philadelphia.[9] In 1933 he completed two very large canvases (21 feet long) for the reception room of the building which housed the World's Grain Exhibition and Conference at Regina. These works were commissioned by the Dominion Government. He also did a third picture of the World's Grain Show building which was used for the Canadian exhibit at the Chicago World's Fair. Around that time he was commissioned to make twelve illustrations of Saskatchewan scenes for a souvenir book (400 copies printed) for delegates from overseas attending the conference in Regina.[10] Also around this period he did 95 illustrations in line drawing and colour for a school reader published by J.M. Dent.[11] During the late spring, summer and early fall he spent many years at Emma Lake in Northern Saskatchewan and the remainder of the year he taught art at the University of Saskatchewan in Saskatoon. In 1936 he was appointed Director of the Regina School of Fine Art and Gordon Snelgrove was appointed professor of History of Art.[12] They also took over the summer school of art at Emma Lake. This particular school had been founded by Kenderdine in 1935. An exhibit of paintings by Kenderdine, Fred Steiger, James Henderson and Mrs. Hilda Stewart was shown at the Calgary City Council Chamber in 1939 when *The Calgary Herald*[13] noted, " . . . his work seems to combine the basic principles and fine undertone of an older school with the freshness of treatment of the moderns. It is work of which the west may well be proud." By 1946 he had acquired an old R.C.A.F. ambulance which he used as a mobile studio.[14] During his career he painted a number of portraits particularly of Indians. In 1947 while conducting his annual summer school at Emma Lake he took ill and died on August third. He was survived at that time by his wife, his son Richard, who was managing his ranch, two daughters, Mrs. O. Beamish of Lashburn, and Mrs. J. Kenderdine of Tokyo, Japan.[15] An address and memorial service in memory of Gus Kenderdine was held at Murray Point, Emma Lake art camp when James S. Thomson, President of the University of Saskatchewan, addressing the gathering reminisced,"He rode the range and broke the soil. He had felt hope and despair, the joy of achievement and the sorrow of defeat. All the happiness and the heartbreak, the swift gain and the swifter loss he knew and felt so that when he painted a picture of the western prairie and entitled it, 'The Land of Promise,' he was translating a personal experience into a work of art. And thus his painting has a far deeper significance than the solitary work of a gifted craftsman — it is the unique expression of an entire era of social life, as seen and felt by a fine spirit who himself was part of it. The story of Saskatchewan would be incomplete without his work." A memorial exhibition of his work was held at The Art Galleries under The Grandstand Exhibition Grounds, Regina, during July of 1948.[16] A memorial stone was dedicated to his memory at Murray Point in August of 1954. The stone is set in a grove of spruce and poplar beside one of the main buildings of the school. A bronze plaque is set in the stone

KENDERDINE, Augustus Frederick (Cont'd)

inscribed "Gus Kenderdine".[17] He is represented in the National Gallery of Canada (Ottawa); University of Saskatchewan (Regina); the City of Regina; City of Moose Jaw; Grundy Gallery, Blackpool, England; Queen's Park Gallery, Manchester, England; University of British Columbia; Regina College Library; Moose Jaw Library, Edmonton; Memorial Art Gallery, Saskatoon; Glenbow Foundation, Calgary (who have 25 major oils, and 116 minor works and sketches).[18] Other showings of his work have taken place over the years under auspices of the Glenbow Foundation.

References

[1] National Gallery of Canada Information Form (undated) also *Saturday Review*, Winnipeg, Dec. 16, 1933 "Art & Artists"

[2] *Leader Post*, Regina, Sask., Aug. 4, 1947 "Noted Artist Dead"

[3] *Star-Phoenix*, Saskatoon, Sask., Aug. 4, 1947 "Gus Kenderdine Passes"

[4] *The Edmonton Journal*, Alta., Sat., Nov. 25, 1929 "Living on his remote ranch he kept brush and palette busy"

[5] *Herald*, Prince Albert, Sask., April 15, 1936 "Spring's Here; Kenderdine Won't Be Far Behind"

[6] Ibid

[7] Ibid

[8] *Phoenix*, Saskatoon, Feb. 16th, 1921 "Finds Beauty In Landscapes West Of Battleford"

[9] Ibid, July 31, 1926 "Kenderdine Paintings Create Much Interest In Edmonton; Will Show Pictures In East"

[10] *Leader-Post*, Regina, Sask., June 10, 1933 "Paintings 21 Feet Long Show Province Beauties In World Show Building"

[11] Ibid

[12] Ibid, May 19, 1936 "Snelgrove And Kenderdine To Teach In Arts"

[13] *The Calgary Herald*, Dec. 16, 1939 "Prairie Artists Reveal Merit In Exhibit Here"

[14] *Leader-Post*, Aug. 19, 1946 "Art On Wheels"

[15] Ibid, Aug. 4, 1947 "Noted Artist Dead"

[16] Catalogue — Kenderdine Memorial Exhibition at The Art Galleries Under The Grandstand Exhibition Grounds, Regina, July 26th to July 31st, 1948 with foreword by S. Basterfield, Dean of Regina College, University of Saskatchewan (77 paintings shown).

[17] *Herald*, Prince Albert, Sask., Aug. 2, 1954 "Memory Honored Of Art Pioneer"

[18] *Times Herald*, Moose Jaw, Sask., Feb. 1, 1958 " 'Gus' Kenderdine Paintings Range From Paris To Canada"

see also

Canadian Art Its Origin and Development by William Colgate, Ryerson Paperbacks, 1967, P.184-5

The MacMillan Dictionary of Canadian Biography by W. Stewart Wallace, MacMillan, Tor., 1963, P.361-2

The National Gallery of Canada Catalogue, Vol. 3, Can. School, by R.H. Hubbard, P.156

Painting In Canada A History by J. Russell Harper, U. of T. Press, 1966, P.344, 346

KENNEDY, Alex

b.1934

A self taught artist from Fort William who spends much of his time painting in a remote shack on Lake Shebandowan, Ontario. He exhibits his paintings at the Gallery of Fine Arts. Ft. William, Ontario. He has chosen biblical subjects for his paintings which take the form of faces described by Mary MacLean of the Port Arthur *News-Chronicle* as follows, "The beautiful painting of Christ, entitled 'Come' was the favorite, followed by one of an old man, called 'Reminiscence'. 'The Storm on the Sea of Galilee', and 'The Sea of Tiberias'. The 'Faces of Man'

KENNEDY, Alex (Cont'd)

also caused quite a bit of comment, some saying they felt depressed as they studied the painting. A visitor from Toronto said he thought it was the most terrific painting he's ever seen. 'It has such impact.' He looked at it for one hour." In the autumn Kennedy has taken trips to the Franklin Islands in the Arctic to prospect. It is estimated that he has done more than 200 paintings, sketches and sculptures.

References
> *News-Chronicle*, Port Arthur, Ont., May 13, 1966 "Shebandowan Lake Artist Works Best in Wilderness" by Arnie Hakala
> *Times-Journal*, Fort William, Ont., May 28, 1966 "Local Artist's Works On Display Next Week"
> *News-Chronicle*, Port Arthur, Ont., "1,000 Complimentary Viewing Paintings" by Mary MacLean
> *Times Journal*, Fort William, Mar. 8, 1969 (photo of artist with his work; with caption)

KENNEDY, Catherine

Originally from the Isle-of-Lewis, Scotland, she studied at the Glasgow School of Art (1959-61), the Southampton College of Art (1961-62) and the School of Design and Crafts of the Edinburgh College of Art (graduated 1965). She has exhibited her paintings at the Wessex Artists Exhibition at the Art Gallery of Southampton (1962); Robertson Gallery, Ottawa (1966); Colour and Form Society, Toronto (1966); and at the Maison des Arts la Sauvegarde, Montreal (1967). She has exhibited textiles at the Jewish Community Centre, Ottawa (1967); and in Canada Crafts '67 where she won a prize for printed cottons; Galerie des Artisans, Montreal in a two craftswoman show (with Madeleine Moir). She has been teaching at the Municipal Art Centre in Ottawa. She was awarded a Canada Council grant in 1967.

Reference
> Circular – Canadian Guild of Crafts, 2025 Peel St., Montreal 2, P.Q., Feb., 1968

KENNEDY, F. Dawson
b.1906

Born at Peterborough, Ontario, he studied at the Central Technical School, Toronto, under Alfred Howell, L.A.C. Panton, P. Haworth and at the Royal College of Art, London, England under Profs. W. Rothenstein, E.W. Tristram and Randolph Schwabe. He returned to Canada where he was instructor of Design at the Central Technical School for over twenty-three years (first in 1930). He has been active with various art societies, showing his work at their annual exhibitions. He is a member of Canadian Society of Graphic Art (Sec. 1933, 34, 36 – V. Pres. 1936-37); Canadian Society of Painters in Water Colour (Sec. 1950-51; 1951-52; Director, 1952-53); Federation of Canadian Artists (Chairman Ontario Region 1942-43); member of the Canadian Arts Council (1948-52). He is represented in the following galleries by water colour paintings: London Public Library and Art

KENNEDY, F. Dawson (Cont'd)

Museum, London, Ont.; Art Gallery in Gloucester, England, and in various private collections. He lives at Nashville, Ont. No recent information is available on this artist.

Reference
National Gallery of Canada Information Form rec'd July 27, 1953

KENNEDY, Garry Neill
b.1935

Born at St. Catharines, Ontario, he graduated with honours in drawing and painting from the Ontario College of Art in 1960; also from the University of Buffalo, N.Y., where he received his Bachelor's degree in Fine Arts in 1963. He held a solo exhibit of his paintings at Rodman Hall Art Centre at Port Colborne, Ontario and has exhibited his work regularly at the Albright-Knox Members Gallery, Buffalo. He taught painting for the Port Colborne Art Association (1962-63); was assistant art professor at the Northland College, Ashland, Wisconsin, U.S.A., before his appointment as President of the Nova Scotia College of Art in April of 1967.

References
National Gallery of Canada Information Form rec'd Jan. 1963
Halifax *Mail-Star*, April 1, 1967 (photo of artist with notice of his appointment to Presidency of the Nova Scotia College of Art)

KENNEDY, John de Navarre
b.1888

Born in London, England, he settled in British Columbia in 1909 and later moved to Toronto, Ontario, in 1921. He was active in art societies and was a member of the Canadian Society of Painters in Water Colour (1934); Canadian Handicraft Guild (Ontario); Canadian Authors' Association. He was last reported as living in Toronto.

Reference
National Gallery of Canada Information Form rec'd Feb. 12, 1946

KENNEDY, Joseph
b.1945

An artist from Victoria, B.C., who studied at the Vancouver School of Art. He has won two prizes recently: a $1,000 first prize for his painting "Figure" in 1966 at the Victoria Art Gallery and a $100 prize in 1967 for a similar exhibition at the Gallery. He was commissioned by the B.C. Government to do a 50 foot mural for the B.C. Institute of Technology in Vancouver. He is an illustrator with the B.C. department of public works.

References
Times, Victoria, B.C., Oct. 26, 1966 "City Artist Wins $1,000 Prize"
Ibid, May 17, 1967 "No Title But Work A Winner"

KENNEDY, Kathleen Cooley

b.1908

Born in Kingston, Surrey, England, she studied at the Kingston-on-Thames School of Art; Royal College of Art, London, England under Prof. Rothenstein, Prof. E.W. Tristram and Randolph Schwabe. She came to Canada in August of 1932 and settled in Toronto and later Nashville, Ontario. She became a member of the Canadian Society of Painters in Water Colour (1943) and served as its director (1946-47; 1947-48) and secretary (1948-49; 1949-50). Before coming to Canada she had also studied with the Royal Drawing Society. No recent information is available on this artist.

Reference
National Gallery of Canada Information Form rec'd July 27, 1953

KENNEDY, Robert

A Brampton Centennial School art teacher who won the Centennial Plus One professional art contest. Kennedy has painted portraits of Harry Brooks (British property tycoon), Prince Roderick Ghyka of Roumania, and other notables. His work has been exhibited at the Downsview Library and he is head of the art department at the above school.

References
Brampton Daily Times & Conservator, Brampton, Ont., Oct. 11, 1968 "Award To 'Reclining Woman' "
Bramalea-Guardian, Bramalea, Ont., Oct. 16, 1968 " 'Reclining Woman' tops in art show"

KENNEDY, Sybil

b.1899

Born in Quebec City, P.Q., she studied under William Brymner at the Montreal Museum of Fine Arts and later under Alexander Archipenko and John Sloan in New York City.[1] Although living in New York she is a Canadian citizen and exhibits her work in Canada.[2] Her work was shown at the Maynard Walker Galleries, N.Y., in 1937 (solo exhibit); Chicago Institute of Art, 1937 (by invitation); Olympiad Exhibition, London, England, 1948; Gallery XII of the Montreal Museum of Fine Arts in 1951 and at the Dominion Gallery in 1962 when Dorothy Pfeiffer of *The Gazette*[3] noted, "Among the works on view may be remarked the elegant intrigue of her bronze 'The Gossips' with its satiny brown-green patina; the arresting simplicity and powerful distortion of an exhorting 'Moses' with extended raised arm and hand. Also the exaggerated detail of both hands and feet of the despairing figure 'Grief,' which sculpture becomes even more moving when contrasted with the magnificently modelled natural forms in her small bronze 'Hands and Feet'. Miss Kennedy has added new dimensions to her art by presenting her work as cast in unusual materials, such as brass and aluminum. Her bright brass 'Torso,' strangely Victorian in this present day, appears at the same time as both decorative and sensuous." Dr. William S.A. Dale[4] noted how the mannered gestures

KENNEDY, Sybil (Cont'd)

and elongated scale of proportions of her work owed much to the work of Lehmbruck. She has served on the jury of awards (1940 and subsequent years) for the National Association of Women Artists. She is a member of the Royal Canadian Academy (A.R.C.A. 1953); Sculptors' Society of Canada; National Association of Women Artists; Audubon Artists.[5] She is represented in the collection of the Art Association of Montreal and the National Gallery of Canada.[6]

References
[1] National Gallery of Canada Information Form rec'd May 23, 1944; Aug. 30, 1965
[2] Ibid
[3] *The Gazette*, Mtl., P.Q., 29 Sept., 1962 "Sybil Kennedy Exhibition" by Dorothy Pfeiffer
[4] *The Arts In Canada*, Ed. by Malcolm Ross, "Sculpture" by William S.A. Dale, Macmillan, Tor., 1958, P.39
[5] as in[1]
[6] *National Gallery of Canada Catalogue, Volume 3, Can. School* by R.H. Hubbard, Queen's Printer, 1960, P.351
see also
The Ottawa Evening Citizen, Dec. 11, 1948 "Canadian Artist's Work In Bronze" by Josephine Hambleton

KENOJUAK
b (c) 1927

An Eskimo woman who has lived most of her life at Itigakjuak, a hunting camp about thirty miles from Cape Dorset on the west side of Baffin Island.[1] Later she moved into the settlement at Cape Dorset. She has distinguished herself among Canadian Eskimo artists for her sealskin and stone cut prints, copper engravings and fabric designs.[2] One of her stone prints "Enchanted Owl" which she did about 1960 sold in Chicago, U.S.A. for $3,000.[3] Each print is reproduced in 50 impressions. Viewing a showing of Kenojuak's prints at the National Library in Ottawa during 1967, Jenny Bergin[4] noted "The most remarkable feature of Kenojuak's work is that although her environment restricts the range of subjects, her vivid imagination, coupled with a very keen observation of Arctic life, enables her to bring a sense of newness and regeneration into each of her prints. A clear example is 'Bird in My Mind', a stone-cut made in 1961 in which a sophisticated design has been based on the arctic owl, keeping the essence or spirit of the bird while endowing it with a fanciful, decorative quality. These grave, silent birds are featured in many designs, always varied and shown to us in a new light." The above exhibition was opened by The Honourable Arthur Laing, at that time Minister of Indian Affairs and Northern Development. Kenojuak was awarded the Medal of Service of the Order of Canada in 1967. In 1964 the National Film Board of Canada produced the film "Kenojuak" which has made her work known to art lovers throughout the world.[5] She is the wife of Johnniebo and they have four children. In addition to her graphic work Kenojuak has recently turned to creating soapstone sculpture. James Houston has devoted six pages of his book *Eskimo Prints* to her work.[6] It was James Houston who introduced printmaking to the Eskimos.

References
[1] *Lakes District News*, Burns Lake, B.C., Dec. 6, 1967 "Art Show"
[2] Ibid
[3] *The Globe Magazine*, Jan. 18, 1969 article by Dorothy Eber
[4] *The Ottawa Citizen*, Nov. 30, 1967 "Eskimo art 'imaginative' " by Jenny Bergin

KENOJUAK (Cont'd)

[5]Film, "Kenojuak"; 16 mm. and 35 mm., colour, 22 min., National Film Board of Canada, Montreal, 1964

[6]*Eskimo Prints* by James A. Houston, Barre Publishers, Barre Mass., 1967 P. 34-39.

see also

The Montreal Star, Dec. 6, 1967 "Kenojuak just loves that medal" by Robert Ayre

Whig-Standard, Dec. 4, 1967 "Eskimo Art At Centre"

---

de KERGOMMEAUX, Duncan
b.1927

Born at Premier, British Columbia, of Breton descent, he began serious painting about 1953 at Prince Rupert. During the summer of that year he studied at the Banff School of Fine Arts and returned to British Columbia. His early work was very much influenced by the paintings of Emily Carr and Lawren S. Harris and he did hundreds of sketches of trees, figures, and landscapes.[1] He then studied under Jan Zack in Victoria. At the beginning he wanted to become a sculptor but he went on with his studies in painting. Zack opened new vistas for him and following his study in Victoria de Kergommeaux attended a summer session with Hans Hofmann at Provincetown, R.I.[2] In 1953 he won the Victoria Times Mural Competition. In 1954 he travelled to eastern Canada. In 1957 he won an award in the Monsanto Canadian Art Competition. This success was followed by the Purchase Award at the Minneapolis Biennial, 1958. He taught art classes in Ottawa, 1957-8. In 1958 he won a Canada Council award and studied in Mexico. In 1959 he became very interested in Geometrics and has produced two hundred or more of these statements on colour and form.[3] He was back on the West Coast again but returning to Ottawa in 1960 he became active in art circles and participated in the National Gallery of Canada Association's presentation "Artists In Action" held at the Clark Memorial Centre in 1961 where he spoke on abstract art.[4] In 1963 the Blue Barn Gallery in the West End of Ottawa opened with a one man show of his collages which were noted by Dr. Naomi Jackson Groves[5] in *Canadian Art* as follows, "The 20 collages belong to the same creative phase and were produced within the past half year or so. Untitled, they bear their 1962 sequence number, the one here illustrated, for instance, being No. 24/62 — Collage, canvas on masonite, 22" x 72". Most are long horizontals, the background in all cases a rich ebony black, upon which clear-cut verticals, broad or fine, straight or subtly tapered, are placed with fastidious care. The composition is at times quite classical in its balance of strong flanking forms, with slightly more elaborate centered interest, perhaps a circular or ovoid or other almost biological shape which attracts the eye with totemic fascination, so that these completely non-objective combinations produce an effect of mystery . . . . Colour is used most sparingly and singly — restrained sienna, the dying rose beloved of Paul Klee, tiny scarlet strips, once only an emphatic magenta passage. Actually, colour seems no more needed here than on a gleaming piano keyboard of ivory and ebony. Austere simplicity combined with mastery of richly variant form recalls similar qualities in J.S. Bach's series of 'Inventions' — in their own way 'non-objective,' not made for lovers of lushness, but highly satisfying to tastes that favour this form of 'plainness.' The de Kergommeaux 'Inventions,' far from the dangerous borderline of mere decorative facility, bear witness to a sensitive creative mind happily gifted for conveying the harmonies of his own world to the rest of us." His most recent series of statements on geometric themes have to do with the cube.

de KERGOMMEAUX, Duncan (Cont'd)

In these canvases the cube is rendered humourously by dissecting it and presenting a corner, or a top, or some other part of the cube in enormous proportions on a canvas 12' x 6'. In these statements de Kergommeaux searches for the relationship between colour and form which he finds exciting. The more he becomes involved in these forms the more he discovers new vistas. This discovery he feels is what creating is all about. The viewer is required to take more than the casual glance in order to grasp what the artist's statement is — and once he begins to study the work he becomes personally involved in making discoveries of his own relative to the subject at hand. While to the casual viewer de Kergommeaux's work might seem non-objective this is not true of his most recent geometric paintings. The cube is the object and it is presented in a diversified and creative series of statements. These huge dark areas of canvas give off the feeling of silence which radiates a conducive atmosphere for appreciation. His 'Cuberoute' series was presented in a one man show at the Galerie Denyse Delrue, Montreal, in February of 1969.[6] A large canvas from his 'Cuberoute' was recently purchased for the Memorial University Art Gallery, St. John's, Newfoundland. His textile banners are bright, well designed and range from medium to large sizes. He has taught the mechanics of painting, art appreciation, and the philosophical approach to painting, for the Extension Department of Carleton University and St. Patrick's College in Ottawa. He was also involved in design projects for the Canadian Pavilion at Expo '67 and was Director of the Canadian Pavilion Art Gallery. Other one man shows of his paintings were presented at the Art Gallery of Greater Victoria (1965); The Isaacs Gallery Toronto (1965); Fredericia and Copenhagen, Denmark (1965); McIntosh Memorial Gallery, University of Western Ontario (1966); Confederation Art Gallery and Museum, Charlottetown (1966). He is represented in the collections of the National Gallery of Canada;[7] Banff School of Fine Arts; Art Gallery of Greater Victoria; London Public Library and Art Gallery; Mendel Art Gallery, Saskatoon; and in private collections in Canada, United States, Mexico and Europe. A creative painter he continues to search for new forms in his 'painter's painter' paradise. He was the owner of the Lofthouse Gallery, Ottawa, which featured paintings, sculpture, jewellery, pottery and a wide variety of other interesting art objects. Now lives in London, Ontario.

References

[1] A visit with the artist in his studio

[2] as above

[3] as above

[4] *The Ottawa Citizen*, Monday, Feb. 20, 1961 "Artists In Action" by Carl Weiselberger

[5] *Canadian Art*, Vol. 20, No. 3 Art Reviews "Duncan de Kergommeaux at the Blue Barn Gallery, Ottawa" by Naomi Jackson Groves

[6] Exhibition notice "Duncan de Kergommeaux 'Cuberoute' " Feb. 3rd to Feb. 22nd, 1969 at Galerie Denyse Delrue

[7] *National Gallery of Canada Catalogue*, Vol. 3, P.157

see also

Catalogue — *de Niverville and de Kergommeaux presented by the National Gallery of Canada, 1967-68*

Catalogue — *Sixth Biennial Exhibition of Canadian Painting 1965 Organized and Circulated by the National Gallery of Canada*

KERNERMAN, Barry

A former Toronto area painter who is known mainly for his abstract art. He has exhibited in group shows and also at the Gallery of Contemporary Art (1959). In the *Globe & Mail* C.S. reviewing his 1959 solo exhibit noted "What is most striking are the evidences of reasoned order, and his deeply informed respect for color. His work radiates the glow of personal warmth of feeling. Not fitting neatly into any current category, his pictures are what he calls them: 'Memories' of things seen — sometimes paintings by El Greco and Goya, whom he greatly admires; sometimes sky, land or water scenes, figures in such settings, or merely representations in color of 'emotional glow' re-called from a visual experience." The late Pearl McCarthy noted his 1961 exhibit at the Here and Now Gallery as follows, "Mr. Kernerman's style is poetic, and I think that was bound to be the path where he would find himself . . . . This artist, formerly of Toronto, now has a gallery in Tel Aviv."

References
> *Globe & Mail*, April 11, 1959 "Kernerman Admiration Can Be Seen" by C.S.
> Ibid, Jan. 7, 1961 "Abstract Artist Emerges" by P. McCarthy

KERR, Estelle Muriel
b.1879

Born in Toronto, Ontario, she studied under M.E. Dignam, Laura Muntz in Toronto; at the Art Students' League of New York (2 years); and at the Académie de la Grande Chaumière, Paris, France (2 years).[1] During her summers she sketched and travelled in Italy, Switzerland, France, Belgium and Holland. It was in Holland that she acquired material for a child's book of rhymes and pictures, *Little Sam in Volendam*, published in New York.[2] By 1914 she was listed amongst Canadian women painters of note by E.F.B. Johnston[3] and in 1925 by Newton MacTavish.[4] During the First World War she served as a Red Cross driver in France. From this experience she later wrote the book *The Town Crier of Gevrey*. She contributed illustrated stories and verses to many Canadian and some United States publications. She illustrated some children's books and published a book of verse entitled *The Island*. She did many portraits of children as well as figure studies and landscapes. During 1948 she participated in a joint exhibition with Edgar Noffke at the Gavin Henderson galleries when *The Toronto Telegram*[5] noted, "Miss Kerr, who has always painted youth with success, brings a new and warm sensibility and round-ness to her paintings of Mexican youth . . . the canvas which of all Miss Kerr's present offerings impresses most is one marked by smoothly undulating rhythm, called by the artist 'Cuernavaca Boys'. The pattern created by their large hats has been most effectively integrated." Last reported Miss Kerr was living in Toronto.

References
[1] National Gallery of Canada Information rec'd May 30, 1944
[2] Biographical data from Photo Library of the Nat. Gal. Canada rec'd 1932
[3] *Canada And Its Provinces*, "Painting" by E.F.B. Johnston, 1914, P.627
[4] *The Fine Arts In Canada*, by Newton MacTavish, 1925, P.146
[5] *The Toronto Telegram*, Sept. 18, 1948 "Dazzling Mexican Sunshine Influences Art Ideologies"

KERR, Illingworth Holey

b.1905

Born in Lumsden, Saskatchewan, he made drawings of animals when very young and received some guidance from his mother an amateur water colourist.[1] In 1924 following high school and a summer spent as dump-wagon driver he went to Toronto with one hundred dollars in his pocket. He attended an art course at the Central Technical School and from there entered the Ontario College of Art (1924-27) where he studied under Arthur Lismer, J.E.H. MacDonald, F.H. Varley, and J.W. Beatty.[2] Of this period he wrote "Fortunately a childless uncle staked me when need arose in the following years at the Ontario College of Art. Lismer, MacDonald, Varley and Beatty were my chief instructors; but the Group of Seven approach to rendering landscape was not taught. I assimilated this in exhibitions at the Toronto Art Gallery, Hart House and in occasional visits to studios – which included those of A.Y. Jackson and Lawren Harris."[3] He returned to Saskatchewan in 1928 and established a studio above the local pool hall in Lumsden. He explains, "Canvases were usually based on field sketches. These had been done at every opportunity, while trapping and moose hunting in Northern Saskatchewan, while sign painting on the prairie, or while harvesting."[4] Dusan Bresky[5] explains, "He could not support himself by painting and earned his living as a farm hand, as a sign-writer, and as a hunter of pelts and stories. He had begun writing tales of adventure and humor . . . . " In this article[6] Illingworth Kerr's own account of trapping experiences was quoted as follows, "In the Qu'Apelle Valley I always covered my trapline by horseback. The North Country was tougher. Travelling on the main Saskatchewan River I camped with two partners in a small tent when there was three feet of snow. We were caught in a blizzard. Then we paddled down the Squaw Rapids dodging rocks rimmed with ice that could rip the bottom of a canoe in a second." These experiences in addition to drought and depression provided him with such a background that he was not afraid to take a chance for new experiences elsewhere. He went to Europe as a cattle hand on a cargo boat and arrived in England in 1936. He worked for John Grierson in documentary film productions and studied at the Westminister School of Art in London. From there he went to Scotland where he wrote his stories on Canada for Blackwood's Magazine. While there he also worked on four dioramas illustrating various phases of Canadian life and industry (scenes of – mining, western wheat fields, habitant life and ice hockey),[7] for the Canadian Government Display in the Empire Exhibition at Glasgow. In these ventures he received enough financial reward to be married and travel to France with his wife. They also went to Germany where they visited Munich and finally returned to Montreal. In Montreal Kerr worked during the winter months of 1939 on Canadian Government and Maritime Maps in preparation for the World Fair in New York and was supervisor of this work. Later that year he left Montreal with his wife for the west. He had purchased a car and with extra cash from his World's Fair work, travelled to the West Coast by stages, camping, writing, and painting. After reaching the west coast they settled in Vancouver, B.C. where in 1943-4 he worked in the illustration department of Boeing Aircraft Co. for the United States Navy. In 1945 he entered the Vancouver School of Art as a member of the faculty. His book *Gay Dogs and Dark Horses* which he also illustrated was published by the J.M. Dent & Sons, Canada (c)1946. In 1947 he was appointed Art Director at the Provincial Institute of Technology and Art, Calgary, Alberta, where he succeeded J.W.G. MacDonald who had joined the staff of the Ontario College of Art. Up until the summer of 1955 Kerr's painting had been mainly representational with a strong element of design. But following a summer course at the Hans

KERR, Illingworth Holey (Cont'd)

Hofmann School of Fine Art at Provincetown, Mass., his work became more abstract. He also became very interested in the work of Marc, Picasso, Braque, then totem forms of art in Canada, Africa, also totems of medieval times. But apart from his semi-abstract symbolism he is known as a landscape and animal painter. He was awarded a Canada Council senior fellowship in 1960 which enabled him to study and travel in United States, Spain, France, Italy, Germany and Great Britain. During his travel he was able to enlarge his experiences as a teacher and as a painter.[8] An exhibit of some of his paintings produced during his travel abroad took place at the Alberta College of Art in March of 1962. In 1963 an exhibition of his work was held at the Edmonton Art Gallery when Dorothy Barnhouse[9] of *The Edmonton Journal* noted, " . . . Mr. Kerr's work which is marked by a strong underlying design; and unerring balance of horizontals versus verticals and a discriminating use of color. This is as apparent in earlier works like 'Prairie Town, Early Morning' as it is in a mosaic-like abstract laid on with pallett knife in facets of hot glowing color. Several small oils — earlier works, reflect strongly The Group of Seven . . . . A sombreness of mood pervades much of this artist's work. He leans heavily on greys, frequently employing black or brown for underpainting; building on this with direct heavy brush strokes. Mr. Kerr is one of the few artists who knows how to use sand — not as a gimmick but as an integral part of the painting. The fluid grace of a recent line drawing of deer in brown on a speckled coppery background suggests Chinese brush drawings or the Cave drawings of Altamira." In 1969 his work was exhibited in eastern Canada which included a showing at the Arts and Culture Centre of Corner Brook, Newfoundland. Marian McNutt[10] of *The Western Star* noted "Making prairie landscape — the main subject of the collection — look interesting is surely no easy task. Kerr's solution is often to use the gently rolling yellow and buff farmland to draw the eye to the background interest of the foot-hills, where he 'let loose' with blue, mauve and pink shades. When the view is less panoramic, the prairies may be scarcely more than a defining line across the bottom of the paintings. In 'Prairie Sky', orange-red grain elevators point towards a magnificent sky replete with the rounded contours of billowing clouds outlined in mauve and blue. The sky is again the focus where the yellow orb of sun is reflected across a blue and mauve sky." Illingworth Kerr is a past member of the British Columbia Society of Artists, and the Alberta Society of Artists. He lives in Calgary, Alberta, where he continues to head the Alberta College of Art. He is represented in the permanent collections of the Norman Mackenzie Art Gallery, Regina; the Allied Art Centre, Calgary; The Glenbow Foundation, Calgary; the National Gallery of Canada and elsewhere.

References

[1] Document from artist

[2] Ibid, also National Gallery of Canada Information Form rec'd Jan., 1963

[3] *Illingworth Kerr* (booklet) chapter on "My Earlier Paintings"

[4] Ibid

[5] *The Calgary Herald*, Alta., Feb. 21, 1953 "Trapper Turned Artist, Now Heads School Here" by Dusan Bresky

[6] Ibid

[7] *The Gazette*, Mtl., P.Q., May 7, 1938 "Saskatchewan Artist One of Four Who Decorated Canadian Pavilion"

[8] *The Calgary Herald*, March 31, 1962 "College Displays 'Grant-Aided' Art" by Pat Bowker (Herald Staff Writer)

KERR, Illingworth Holey (Cont'd)

[9] *The Edmonton Journal*, Edmonton, Alta., Oct. 11, 1963 "Illingworth Kerr Paintings Amongst Current Display" by D.P. Barnhouse (Journal Art Critic)

[10] *The Western Star*, Corner Brook, Nfld., Jan. 14, 1969 "Kerr paints Canadian west" by Marian McNutt

see also

National Gallery of Canada Catalogue, Vol. 3, by R.H. Hubbard, NGC, 1960, 1967, P.157

Canadian Art, Vol. 20, No. 2, "Clement Greenberg's View of Art on the Prairies" by Clement Greenberg, P.96

Painting In Canada/A History by J. Russell Harper, U. of T. Press, P.329, 330, 331

KERTÉSZ-RÁCZ, Maria

b.1922

Born in Környe, Hungary, she left Budapest in 1946 and lived in Austria before coming to Canada in 1948.[1] She studied drawing and painting at the Ontario College of Art and graduated in 1965 (A.O.C.A.).[2] She had studied sculpture under Emanuel Hahn before his death in 1957. She participated in exhibits at the Terry National Art Institute, Miami, Florida (c.1954); Royal Ontario Museum, Tor. (1956), London Art Gallery, Ont. (1956), and the Cooling Gallery where she held a one man show in the summer of 1966. Viewing this exhibition Kay Kritzwiser[3] of the *Globe & Mail* noted, "Miss Kertész-Racz' work is strong, precise and scrupulously in tradition. She disdains the shortcuts that are almost automatic with young painters. 'I make my own gesso,' she said. 'I prepare my canvas. I make my own frames if I feel they will be a continuation of the painting.' She works with egg tempera until it becomes her subject; usually soft and lustrous for a bouquet of nasturtiums, loose and textured for the rough wood of an old barn. On her last visit to Europe, she searched through Italian shops to find her oil paints. 'I took a lousy job in Banff once to get those sketches.' she said, indicating the charming pastels of Indian babies." She is an instructor at the Toronto Central Technical School Adult Programme and has taught crippled children. She lives in Toronto, Ontario.

References

[1] National Gallery of Canada Information Form rec'd July 28, 1966 biography sheet – Cooling Galleries (Ont.) Ltd.

[2] Ibid

[3] *Globe & Mail*, June (?), 1966 "At The Galleries" by Kay Kritzwiser

see also

The Telegram, Tor., Ont., Sat., June 18, 1966 "Art & Artists"

KETTLE, Horace Garnard

b.1906

Born in London, England, he received his M.A. at Oxford University specializing in Natural Science. He came to Canada in 1932 and the same year was appointed Director of Arts and Crafts at Upper Canada College (1932-41). He became a member of the Canadian Society of Painters in Water Colour (1938) and the Canadian Society of Graphic Art (1939) and served as President of the latter society in

KETTLE, Horace Garnard (Cont'd)

1947. In recent years business has occupied most of his time and he has done little or no painting. He is a member of the firm of Massey-Ferguson Limited. He lives in Toronto, Ontario.

References
   National Gallery of Canada Information Form rec'd 1954
   Letter from Massey-Ferguson Limited dated Oct. 28, 1960

KETURAH, Elizabeth Steeves (Mrs. Fred John Cheesman)
b.1916

Born at Meadow Lake, Saskatchewan (near North Battleford), as a child she lived in many provinces in Canada (Alberta, Saskatchewan, Manitoba, Quebec) but her parents were originally from Albert County, N.B. She took up residence in Saint John, N.B. where she has been active in art circles. She is a member of the Maritime Art Association and was its Director of Exhibitions from 1953 to 1954. She studied under Garnet Hazard in Regina; and subsequently at the Art Gallery of Toronto (The Grange) as part of course of study at the University of Toronto, and a year apprenticeship at Ridpath's Interior Decorators, also under Julia Crawford in Saint John. She is represented in the New Brunswick Museum by a small oil "October Noon" purchased about 1950. She lives in Saint John, N.B.

Reference
   National Gallery of Canada Information Form rec'd May 21, 1957

KHAN, Ishrat Ali

An artist living in Vancouver, B.C., who was born in India and raised in Pakistan. Most of his work is of a semi abstract nature. He is represented in the Jacqueline Bouvier Kennedy Onassis and the late Dwight Eisenhower collections. His work can be seen at the Gallery of The Golden Key, Vancouver, B.C.

Source
   Denese J. Gordon, Assistant Director of the Gallery of The Golden Key, 8th Feb., 1967

KHANBEGIAN, Mrs. Jean MacNeil

Born at Glace Bay, N.S., she studied art in New York City at the Parsons School of Design, the School and Visual Art and at the Art Students' League.[1] She also studied commercial art and did some work for advertising agencies and fashion catalogues.[2] In her painting she works in a variety of media including water colour, oil, acrylic, ink, pastel and charcoal and has even done sculpture. She has exhibited her work at the Glace Bay Library, the Beaverbrook Art Gallery, Fredericton (in the Atlantic

KHANBEGIAN, Mrs. Jean MacNeil (Cont'd)

Province Exhibition) and in the Lynn Cottler Gallery, New York, also the John J. Myers Gallery, New York. During 1967 thirty-one of her paintings were exhibited in the Miners' Museum, Sydney, N.S. Viewing this exhibit Francis H. Stevens[3] of the *Cape Breton Post*, noted, "There isn't sufficient space on this page to say all that one would be pleased to say about Mrs. Khanbegian's work. To say it as concisely and briefly as possible, her victory is in conveying to the viewer the truth of atmosphere, the compelling touch of wind on water, voyaging clouds, the quality of rocks, the power of surf, and the feeling of the breeze on shore meadows. They range from the spectacular in size and content to the small and intimate. One of the latter, 'Quarry Point Road' has been purchased, for the Miners' Museum." She worked on the editorial staff of *The Artist* and is still a contributing author.[4] She is now living in Massachusetts where she exhibited at the Mount Saint Vincent University Art Gallery during April of 1968.[5]

References
[1] *Cape Breton Post*, Sydney, N.S., Nov. 17, 1967 "Art Show At Miners' Museum"
[2] Ibid
[3] Ibid, Nov. 23, 1967 "A Graphic Demonstration" by Francis H. Stevens
[4] *Halifax Mail Star*, April 13, 1968 "Khanbegian Exhibition At The Mount"
[5] Ibid

KHANNA, Bindoo

Born in India, she studied painting (oils, water colours), interior design, sculpture and batiks at the Santinkentan College of Fine Arts in Calcutta. Following graduation from the College she was employed by a department store in New Delhi where she worked on interior decoration. She married and came to Canada in 1968 with her husband and they have settled in Toronto. She has specialized in batiks and has had a showing at the Four Seasons hotel, Toronto, as part of the decor for an Indian Festival.

Reference
York Mills/Bayview Mirror, Toronto, Ontario, June 26, 1968 "Art holds life's greatest joys – Bindoo" by Phyllis Switzer

KIDDER, Jack

Born at Little Sioux, Iowa, he studied art in Los Angeles, California, and worked as a technical illustrator, draftsman designer and craftsman.[1] Ted Linberg[2] of the *Victoria Daily Times*, B.C., explains "As a painter he was formally schooled, plunged into the murky milieu of abstract expressionism of the fifties in southern California, and after a brief success, came to a temporary deadend. Gradually, he has worked into the constructivist persuasion, no doubt bolstered by his increased penchant for control and exactitude, a necessary prerequisite of the other vocations he has relied upon." Describing Kidder's current work Linberg[3] noted, "His sculpture is ultra-contemporary; a clean, incredibly immaculate use of such

KIDDER, Jack (Cont'd)

materials as Plexiglas, cast resins, stainless steel, lacquers, mirrors, wood and silver leaf, brought together in three-dimensional compositions of optical illusion; reality and visual aberration so skilfully woven that many of the pieces are really difficult to interpret in any single way." Don Gain[4] of *The Daily Colonist*, Victoria, explained, "The artist prefers to leave his works untitled or to give them names which bring to mind no particular meaning. 'I want people to bring to them something of themselves. Everybody sees something different." He held a one man show at the Print Gallery, Oak Bay, Victoria, B.C., during April of 1969. He lives in Victoria.

References
[1] *Victoria Daily Times*, Sat. Apr. 12, 1969 "Sculpture Frames A New Dimension" by Ted Lindberg
[2] Ibid
[3] Ibid
[4] *The Daily Colonist*, Victoria, B.C., Apr. 19, 1969 "Beauty Everywhere" by Don Gain

KIDICK, Tess

Formerly a public school art teacher she later studied at the Ontario College of Art and became a potter. Describing some of her work Joan Phillips of *The St. Catharines Standard* noted, "There's a talented artist in Jordan using earth to create rocks in stone . . . . The earth she uses is clay, some of it her own blend of clays for special purposes and the stone is the stoneware produced by the firing of the clay — the final product of her art. The rocks Miss Kidick was recreating through the medium of pottery are the jagged, massive rock walls rising from the water in the Lakehead region. The dark ridges and high-lighted outcroppings of these rock formations which she first saw about eight years ago have been the inspiration from some unusual and striking pieces of her work." Miss Kidick has done wall panels on which she creates landscapes in relief of the rock formations of the Lakehead region as well as vases and various other containers also based on these formations. She is able to produce the formations in 'Many variations on one theme.' She adds colour to the panels or other pieces before firing them. She is striving to capture such things as the movement of grass and other vegetation. She has been teaching pottery at the Mohawk College of Applied Arts and Technology, Hamilton, Ontario. She has exhibited her work at the Rodman Hall Art Centre and the Grantham Plaza Library in St. Catharines, Ontario.

Reference
St. Catharines Standard, Ont., May 9, 1969, World Of Art by Joan Phillips "From Clay Into Things Of Beauty"

KIERSTEAD, Dr. Karl

Born in South Africa of New Brunswick parents, he came to Canada where he completed his education. He entered the teaching profession and taught at Mount Allison University, New Brunswick where he became interested in art.[1] Then he

KIERSTEAD, Dr. Karl (Cont'd)

went to the United States where he graduated with his M.A. from Columbia University. He returned to Canada and settled in Quebec City in 1943 where he became a science teacher at Quebec High School.[2] He entered Laval University about 1949 and received his doctorate in bio-chemistry. In painting he studied under Albert Rousseau and Fielding Downes at Quebec City. The Quebec *Chronicle-Telegraph*[3] explains his work as an artist, "Dr. Kierstead's desire is to use art to interpret science and scientific ideas. Not as a dull lesson but in attractive pictures to delight the eye. If the viewer does not understand the lesson, he will still see a beautiful picture." Dr. Kierstead is a Fellow of the Canadian Institute of Chemists and is technical director of Lignosol Chemicals Limited. His paintings have been exhibited at Chalmers-Wesley church hall, Quebec (1960), Bishop's University, Lennoxville, Quebec (1968). He completes about one hundred paintings a year and favours acrylic on masonite or epoxy combined with dry colours.

References
[1] *Chronicle-Telegraph*, Quebec, P.Q. "Science Expressed in Art At Kierstead Exhibition"
[2] Ibid
[3] Ibid
   see also
   Sherbrooke Record, Que., Feb. 16, 1968 "Paintings relate art, science" by Hubert Bauch

KIJEK, Fred E.

b.1938

Stricken with polio in 1960, and almost completely paralysed, he has achieved remarkable success as a painter and is a member of the Association of Mouth and Foot Painting Artists (a world wide group with only eight Canadian members in 1967). He lives in Edmonton, Alberta at the University Hospital of Edmonton.

References
   clipping (probably from *Tribune*, Bonnyville, Alberta) Dec. 9, 1967 "Edmonton Mouth-painting Artist Gains International Recognition"
   Brochure – Rehandart Canada Ltd., Suite 507, 160 Bay St., Toronto 1, Ontario.

KILBOURN, Rosemary

b.1930

Born in Toronto, Ontario, she studied at the Ontario College of Art and then travelled to London, England, where she attended the Chelsea School of Art and the Slade School. In 1957 she completed a mural for University of Western Ontario described by *The London Free Press*[1] as follows, "A thousand young critics have been watching Toronto artist Rosemary Kilbourn at work this week on a huge mural in the new University of Western Ontario dining hall. Students surround her continually as she paints the story of Canadian universities on the corridor wall. Set on a stylized map of Canada, figures such as the one Miss Kilbourn works on here, illustrate the arts, sciences and other branches of university training." In 1960 she completed fourteen beautiful wood engravings for William Kilbourn's[2] *The*

KILBOURN, Rosemary (Cont'd)

Elements Combined. Her engravings have also appeared in the Canadian Society of Graphic Art shows and the National Gallery of Canada's "Canadian Water Colours, Drawings and Prints, 1966".[3] She received the C.W. Jefferys Award at the CSGA exhibit in 1962. She lives in Toronto.

References
[1] *The London Free Press*, London, Ont., Jan. 17, 1957 "Mural On University Wall" (photo and caption)
[2] *The Elements Combined* (a history of The Steel Company of Canada) by William Kilbourn, Clarke, Irwin & Co. Ltd., Tor, Ont. 1960, Wood Engravings by Rosemary Kilbourn (see beginning of each chapter and Appendices)
[3] *Canadian Water Colours, Drawings and Prints 1966* by Kathleen Fenwick and Pamela Osler

KILGOUR, Andrew Wilkie

1868-1930

Born at Kirkcaldy, Fifeshire, Scotland, he studied at the Glasgow School of Art under Francis Newbery, and the Heatherley School, London.[1] He came to Canada in 1910 and settled in Montreal. There he was active in art circles and became a charter member of the Arts Club of Montreal.[2] In that city he studied under William Brymner and Maurice Cullen.[3] In 1932 A.H. Robson[4] in his book *Canadian Landscape Painters* wrote "Wilkie Kilgour's work was just beginning to receive wide and popular recognition before his death, in 1930. He was another painter who used pastel with consummate skill." Kilgour was a regular exhibitor at the shows of the Royal Canadian Academy and of the Art Association of Montreal.[5] Many of his paintings were of the Laurentian country bordering Montreal.[6] He had a summer home at Strathmore, Quebec. The National Gallery of Canada acquired his canvas "Flecked By The Morning Sun" in 1914.[7] Wilkie Kilgour, because of the pressing commitments of his commercial art work, found little time for his painting in later years. He died at Strathmore, Quebec. He is represented in many private collections including those of: T.H. Edwards of Montreal and F.E. Winter, Ottawa.

References
[1] National Gallery of Canada Information Form (undated but c.1920's)
[2] Ibid
[3] Ibid
[4] *Canadian Landscape Painters* by A.H. Robson, Ryerson, Tor., 1932, P. 170
[5] *The Gazette*, Mtl., P.Q., May 30, 1930 "Montreal Artist Died Suddenly"
[6] *The Montreal Star*, May 30, 1930 "A.W. Kilgour Dies At Summer Home"
[7] [7] *National Gallery of Canada Catalogue, Volume 3,* by R.H. Hubbard, P. 157
see also
  The Herald, Mtl., P.Q., May 30, 1930 "Well Known Local Artist Died At 61"

KILLINS, Ada Gladys

c.1901-1963

Born in Caistor Township, County of Lincoln, Ontario, she attended Teachers' College and began teaching art at the Memorial School, Niagara Falls in 1924.[1]

KILLINS, Ada Gladys (Cont'd)

During the 1930's she studied painting under Franz Johnston and a little later (1935-38) summers at Geneva Park, Lake Couchiching under Carl Schaefer.[2] By 1938 her work was included in the Eleventh Annual Exhibition of the Canadian Society of Painters in Water Colour which took place at the Art Gallery of Toronto.[3] Around 1939 she made regular painting trips to Orangeville and Parry Sound districts. She also did many scenes of the Niagara district including "Town Hall" a study of the Stamford Township Hall which hangs in the new Niagara Falls City Hall.[4] Her painting "Factory Closed" which depicted a closed chemical factory at Longford, Ontario (a comment on the grim days of the depression), was exhibited at the Canadian National Exhibition, Toronto, where it received favourable attention from the critics.[5] In 1939 she was elected member of the Canadian Society of Painters in Water Colour.[6] Her paintings appeared almost regularly in the Society's exhibitions in the years that followed. In 1942 fifteen of her paintings were part of the exhibition "Four Canadian Painters" which included work by F.H. Brigden, W.J. Phillips and Thoreau MacDonald. In 1955 Ada Killins moved to Glen Cross, Ontario. She had given up teaching in 1947 to devote full time to painting. She frequently visited the Hockley Valley area where she produced many fine paintings.[7] In 1948 an exhibition of her work took place at the Niagara Falls Public Library when the Niagara Falls Evening Review[8] wrote a detailed article on the show and concluded by noting, "Her work is indeed individual and personal creating moods of which when once experienced by the spectator are not forgotten." In 1954 another exhibit of her work was held at the Gallery of Fine Arts in Owen Sound.[9] She then settled in Glen Cross, Ontario, where she continued to paint scenes of this beautiful region. She spent her final period at Dunchurch, about thirty miles northeast of Parry Sound. She died in 1963 and was buried in the Smithville cemetery near the homes of her parents. A memorial exhibition of her work was held at Oak Hall, Niagara Falls, under the auspices of the Niagara District Art Association. A catalogue was prepared for the show by Edward Phelps who also wrote a very informative text. Collectors of her paintings include: from Niagara Falls — Mrs. N. Douglas Clement, Mrs. Frances Corfield, Miss Barbara Escott, Miss R. Violet Gardner, Mr. Wesley Killins, Mrs. W.W. Laundy, Miss Helen M. Lothian, Miss Gertrude McKeown, Miss Joanne Murray, Mrs. Stanley Nanson, Mr. John Nott, Mr. Harold D. Rosberg, Mr. Joseph L. Rosberg; from other districts as shown — Miss Cora Bartlett, Smithville, Ontario; Mrs. Kenneth Lampman, Stoney Creek, Ont.; Mrs. Charles S. Phelps, Sarnia, Ont.; Miss Evangeline Wheatley, Grimsby, Ontario; in public collections at Niagara Falls Public Library; Memorial School, Niagara Falls; Canada Packers, Toronto. Miss Enid Alexander of Concord, Massachusetts, U.S.A. has been making a photographic record of Miss Killins' work with the purpose of compiling a full catalogue of known works by her. It is estimated that she may have produced about 100 finished paintings during her artistic career.[10]

References
[1] [1]National Gallery of Canada Information Form rec'd June 14, 1954

[2]*A Brief Sketch of The Life And Work Of The Late Ada Gladys Killins* by Edward Phelps, St. Catharines, Ontario, 1967, P. 2

[3]Ibid, P. 2

[4]Ibid, P. 3

[5]Ibid, P. 3

[6]see [1]

KILLINS, Ada Gladys (Cont'd)

[7] see [2] P. 3

[8] *The Evening Review,* Niagara Falls   Ont., July 19, 1948 "Water Colors Are Shown At Public Library"

[9] *The Orangeville Banner*, Ont. Thurs., Feb. 18, 1954 "Gallery Showing Watercolors By Glen Cross Artist"

[10] see [2] P. 4

KILLMAN, Murray

A professional artist who has been acclaimed for his painting in oils and water colours. He lives with his wife and children near Caledonia, Ontario, at a site centered in the heart of an ancient Neutral Indian Camp site. A few years ago he became interested in Canadian history. His ancestors were United Empire Loyalists and one of them, Robert Killman, fought in the battle of Lundy's Lane. After much research Murray Killman created forty paintings depicting the War of 1812 with emphasis on the Battle of Lundy's Lane. The original paintings were created for the production *Sound And Light* a historical attraction presented at Clifton Gate Building on the River Road near Niagara Falls under the auspices of the Niagara Parks Commission. He also produced twenty six paintings for a Centennial Calendar which has been very well received. Killman is also known for his animal paintings.

References

    Grand River Sachem, Caledonia, Ont., May 24, 1967 "Local Artist Originator of Novel Production"

    Review, Niagara Falls, Ont., May 20, 1967 (six photographs of Killman's historical paintings for *Sound And Light)*

KILPIN, Legh Mulhall
1855-1919

Born on the Isle of Wight, Ryde, England, he studied at the South Kensington School of Art, London, England, where he later became Art Master.[1] He came to Canada in 1906 with his wife and children and settled in Montreal. He did portraits, landscapes, miniatures, and etching. He was a member of The Art Association of Montreal (1906) and the Arts Club (1913). He exhibited at the Royal Academy, London, and the Royal Canadian Academy. Two of his paintings are in the collection of the National Gallery of Canada, one a water colour and the other an oil.[2] Legh Kilpin died suddenly in Montreal and was survived by his widow, two sons (Noel L.S. Kilpin, Mtl., and Eric T. Kilpin of Vernon, B.C.) and one daughter, Mrs. Chas. F. Mitchell of Westmount, Quebec.[3]

References

[1] National Gallery of Canada Information Form (undated) also another Form completed by his wife received Aug. of 1920.

[2] *National Gallery of Canada Catalogue, Vol. 3*, Can. School, by R.H. Hubbard, P. 424, 425

[3] *The Gazette*, Montreal, P.Q., Nov. 4, 1919 "Prominent Artist Died Suddenly"

KIMPTON, Allan

b.1921

Born in Toronto, Ontario, in his early youth he began to do portraits of famous personalities. One of the first subjects was "Red" Horner of the Toronto Maple Leafs. Kimpton received much encouragement from his father who was himself a water colourist. At fourteen he won a scholarship at the Ontario College of Art but due to his family move to Ottawa he did not complete his course of studies at the College. Specializing in realistic portrait studies he has done work in oils, water colours, and more often in pencil and charcoal. He admires very much the work of Norman Rockwell, one of the world's top artists. His work has been shown at the Central Canada Exhibition and in shops along Ottawa's Sparks Street. He has had his work accepted by the following: H.M. King George VI and Queen Elizabeth; Her Majesty Queen Elizabeth II; Field Marshal Alexander of Tunis; Field Marshal Montgomery of Alamein; Sir Winston Churchill; Sir Anthony Eden; H.R.H. the Duke of Kent; General Dwight Eisenhower; Madame Chiang Kai-shek; President Franklin Roosevelt; President Harry S. Truman; General Andrew McNaughton; Air Marshal W.A. "Billy" Bishop; Governor-General Roland Michener; Rt. Hon. William Lyon MacKenzie King; Rt. Hon Lester B. Pearson; and Rt. Hon. John Diefenbaker. Allan Kimpton in addition to his portrait work does Old English and Script printing and Scroll work and has produced scroll work for the Royal Canadian Legion and the Army, Navy and Air Force Veterans in Canada. He is employed in the design of forms for the Government of Canada in Ottawa where he lives.

References
> *The Ottawa Citizen*, Nov. 14, 1941 "Mr. King Takes Time Out To Receive Young Artist"
> Ibid, July 14, 1943 "Young Ottawa Artist Thanked By Mme Chiang for Portrait"
> Ibid, June 12, 1947 "Ottawa Artist Sketches United States President" by Harold A. Morrison
> Ibid, Nov. 1, 1949 "Lord Alexander Honors Artist Allan Kimpton"
> Document from artist

KING, Jimmy   (Chief Ka-Kwa-Ga-La of Kingcome Inlet)

A British Columbia Indian who is a creator of totem poles. He did two such poles for the portal of the Capilano Trailer Park in North Vancouver. Also a number of years ago he carved a pole for the entrance to Discovery Inn, Campbell River. No doubt he has done many other works. He was last reported living in North Vancouver.

Reference
> *Courier,* Campbell River, B.C. Aug. 13, 1969 "Jimmy King Has New Name"

KING, Laurence F.

A former president of the Sarnia Art Association who won first prize in a recent art exhibit by chemists in Chicago. Laurence King is a research chemist in Imperial

KING, Laurence F. (Cont'd)

Oil Enterprises Limited at Sarnia, Ontario. He has exhibited his painting with the following: Canadian Society of Painters in Water Colour; Chatham Kent Art Association show; Essex County Artists Exhibition at Willistead Art Gallery, Windsor, Ont., his work has also been shown at the Beaverbrook Gallery, Frederiction, N.B.; Canadian National Exhibition, Toronto; Western Art League Show, London, Ont.; Art Gallery of Hamilton; Western Ontario Fair; Sarnia Art Gallery; and he is represented in the permanent collections of the Sarnia Public Library and Art Gallery, and the Chatham Public Library art collection. He won the Purchase Award at the Western Art League Show in London, 1963. He has given talks on art in Sarnia and lives at Mooretown, Ontario.

References
   The London Free Press, May 4, 1963 "Russia's Violent Opposition to Abstract Art Poses Paradoxical Situation for Westerners"
   Observer, Sarnia, Ont. "Laurence King Local Artist Will Speak About Modern Japanese Art"
   Ibid, Oct. 21, 1967 "I.O.L. Chemist Paints Winners" by Marcella Brown

KINGAN, Edward Nathan
b.1927

Born at Lytham-St.-Annes, Lancs., England, he started serious study in art at the age of sixteen when he attended evening classes at the Avenham Institute, Preston, Lancashire. During the Second World War he served with the armed forces and afterwards continued art training under an Ex-Serviceman's Grant at the Blackpool School of Art (1948-52). He received an award of National Diploma In Design for painting at "Special Level". He was then qualified as teacher by the Ministry of Education (1952). He took further study at the Regional College of Art, Manchester, and upon graduation received his A.T.D. (Manc.). For a time he was a teacher in Mansfield Woodhouse, Notts. England, in secondary education. He came to Canada in 1959 and settled in North Vancouver where he has become a full time art specialist for junior high school. In his painting he has been influenced by the work of surrealists and more recently by a combination of surrealism and abstraction. He has been working mainly in oil but has also used gouache. He has exhibited at the Vancouver Art Gallery during jury showns and is a member of the British Columbia Society of Artists.

Source
   Document from artist

KINGSCOTE, Dr. Anthony
b.(c)1902

A former lecturer at OVC, he has been working as a parasitologist with the Food and Agricultural Organization of the United Nations where he has been employed to improve food supplies and to seek better ways to grow basic food. He has spent most of his time in the Philippines for the U.N. but has also been in Hong Kong, Fiji and mainland China. He has had a secret ambition to be an artist most of his life. He has mastered the extremely difficult art of Chinese brush-painting. He

KINGSCOTE, Dr. Anthony (Cont'd)

brought back to Canada well over 100 works which he did as a member of the Artist Guild of Manila. Most of his works are of flowers, birds, Buddhist temples and landscapes. When not serving the U.N he lives at Rockwood, Ontario.

Guelph Daily Mercury, Guelph, Ont., Aug. 14, 1969 "Serenity, Compassion Used To Solve Asian Food Problems" by George Ort

KINGSFORD, Winifred
1880-1947

Born in Toronto, Ontario, she studied at the Toronto Art School under William Cruikshank and G.A. Reid; also the Toronto Central Technical School under Mr. Banks. She went to France where she studied in Paris under Antoine Bourdelle. She returned to Toronto where she taught art at Havergal College. She died in Toronto at the age of 67.

References
National Gallery of Canada Information Form rec'd July 12, 1915 *The Ottawa Journal,* Feb. 5, 1947 "Prominent Sculptress Dies in Toronto"

KINNEAR, John H.

He studied under Charles Bell at the Northampton Technical School, England (1937) also with Frank Law, R.A., England. A painter, his work has been exhibited at the 25th Western Ontario Show (1965); three man show at the University of Guelph; three man show at the Raven Gallery, Detroit (1964); at the Royal Canadian Academy 87th Annual Exhibition (1966). He is represented in the permanent collection of the University of Windsor, the University of Guelph, the Art Gallery of Edmonton. His work can be seen at the Pollock Gallery, Toronto; Gallery Martin, Montreal; the Gallery of the Golden Key, Vancouver; and the Much-Taas Gallery, Toronto. He lives in London, Ontario.

References
Information supplied by the Gallery of The Golden Key, Vancouver, B.C.
Royal Canadian Academy 87th Annual Exhibition catalogue, entry 34 Canvas entitled "Red Land" 40 x 48.

KINNIS, William Gilbert
b.1921

Born at Trail, B.C., he studied at the Vancouver School of Art under Charles Scott, B.C. Binning, J.S. Shadbolt and in Montreal, where he settled, at the Montreal Art Association under Goodridge Roberts, the late Dr. Arthur Lismer and Jacques de Tonnancour.[1] He worked with the National Film Board in their graphics and display sections during the period 1944-46.[2] A member of the Federation of Cana-

KINNIS, William Gilbert (Cont'd)

dian Artists he was Chairman of this Society from 1949 to 1950.[3] He has exhibited with the B.C. Society of Artists, the Spring Show, Montreal, the Contemporary Canadian Arts Exhibition, Toronto, 1950, and has held one man shows at the Y.W.C.A., Montreal (1950) and at the Arts Club, Montreal (1961) when Dorothy Pfeiffer[4] of *The Gazette* noted, "Mr. Kinnis paints with refreshing zeal, using quick, nervous strokes of color and brush. His palette runs to various shades and intensities of green — mostly those of ripening olives, combined with nuances of beige, grey and rust . . . . William Kinnis has succeeded in enfolding sensations of fresh air and space into his spontaneous expressions. His work is knowledgeable, unostentatious and worthwhile."

References

[1] National Gallery of Canada Information form rec'd June 3, 1950
[2] Ibid
[3] Ibid
[4] *The Gazette*, Montreal, P.Q. "At The Arts Club" by Dorothy Pfeiffer

---

KINSMAN, Katharine Bell

b.1909

Born in Los Angeles, California, she studied at the Parsons School of Applied Art and in Paris under Ozenfant. She came to Canada in 1909 and continued to study art under Anne Savage.[1] She has painted scenes of old Montreal for over twenty-five years. Describing her interest in the city Laureen Hicks[2] of *The Montreal Star* explained, "Kay Kinsman waits for a sunny day without much wind. Then she bundles together her watercolors and sets off by bus from her Cote des Neiges apartment to the foot of McGill street where she explores along St. Paul to St. Gabriel, or Bonsecours, in search of something worth preserving. Something like a house with an ornate gable, a colorful front, a courtyard that stirs her imagination, or a house she heard was about to be torn down. There, in the heart of old Ville Marie just a stone's throw from the river, she persuades someone to lend her a crate to sit on while she reproduces hundreds of years of history onto her watercolor paper . . . . Sometimes she returns to find a place she painted a couple of weeks before, torn down . . . . Her interest in old Montreal was intensified when her husband took his MA from McGill in old Montreal history. 'We used to browse through the old newspapers and follow different people's lives. Then it was natural to wonder where and how they lived.' "

References

[1] National Gallery of Canada Information Form rec'd June 2, 1950
[2] *The Montreal Star*, Sept. 30, 1963 "Artist Tries to Preserve Old Montreal in Paintings" by Laureen Hicks

KINTON, Jerrine Wells

b.1892

Born in Waterloo, Ontario, she studied at the Ontario College of Art under J.W. Beatty, Robert Holmes and C.M. Manly. She exhibited her paintings at the Robert Simpson Company, Toronto, in 1938. She was known mainly for her landscapes and seascapes. She painted in many countries although living in Toronto.

References

National Gallery of Canada Information Form (undated)

The Saturday Night, Tor., Ont., May 7, 1938 (a short review of her work at the Robert Simpson Company)

KIPLING, Ann (Barbara Ann Kipling Epp)

b.1934

Born in Victoria, B.C., she studied painting under Jan Zack and Herbert Siebner and entered the Vancouver School of Art in 1955 where she studied for four years and graduated in 1960 with three scholarships — The Emily Carr Scholarship, Vancouver School of Art Travel Scholarship, and the Koerner Foundation Grant.[1] She studied graphics under Rudy Kovak while at the Vancouver School of Art.[2] She has done much work in pen-and-ink including coloured inks and has held several solo exhibits at the Bau-Xi Gallery in Vancouver including one in 1968 when Ann Rosenberg[3] of *The Vancouver Sun* described her portraits as follows, "Explosions of minutely fine lines multiply from the dense centres of heads and torsos to define in the most transient manner the character of faces and bodies. Inherent in each characterization is the possibility of change, not only in facial gesture but also mood. As one watches each portrait, a wealth of expression and feeling parades before the eye. Perhaps the richness within a series preoccupied with the exploration of a particular manner of drawing a very select subject range is best seen in the portraits of the artist herself. Minute alterations in density of the collections of lines and minute changes in the orchestration of internal growth of form suggest subtle variations the artist has found within herself at certain moments." Miss Rosenberg noted Miss Kipling's etchings which were also exhibited at that showing. Her landscapes have that same intimate calligraphic treatment as one sees in her portraits. She is represented in the permanent collection of the National Gallery of Canada by two woodcuts. She married Leonard Epp in 1961 and they live at Sunshine Falls, Burrard Inlet, B.C.[4]

References

[1] National Gallery of Canada Information Form rec'd October, 1965

[2] *Western Homes and Living*, Van., B.C., May, 1964

[3] *The Vancouver Sun*, Van., B.C., April 13, 1968 "Ann Kipling's Fine Lines Convey Wealth of Feeling" by Ann Rosenberg

[4] see [1]

KIRBY, Luther Henry

b.1882

Born in Oshawa, Ontario, he has been painting since 1914 and has sketched in many countries.[1] He has exhibited his paintings with the Ontario Society of Artists, the Royal Canadian Academy shows and has held solo exhibits of his work at his own

KIRBY, Luther Henry (Cont'd)

home in Toronto, Ontario.[2] He was for many years the head of the chemistry department at Oakwood Collegiate and after retirement from teaching turned to full time painting.[3] No recent information is available on him.

References

[1] *Globe & Mail*, Tor., Ont., Oct. 8, 1947 "His Hobby Is Painting, Sure Cure for Boredom"
[2] *Canadian Art, Its Origin and Development* by William Colgate, Ryerson Paperbacks, 1967, P.249, 250
[3] see [1]

KIRKLAND, Donald

Very little information can be provided here on this artist but he exhibited with the Manitoba Society of Artists in 1948 and a reproduction of his work exhibited, a landscape, appeared in the Winnipeg *Free Press*.

Reference

Free Press, Winnipeg, Man., April 17, 1948 (photo of painting approx. 4¼ x 6" with caption "Donald Kirkland's Manitoba Farm")

KIRWIN, Brian

Originally from Melville, Saskatchewan, he settled in Fort Nelson, B.C. He served with the Forestry Service, during which service he made many sketches of the countryside. He has done many scenes of British Columbia and in addition to landscapes is a painter of animals and portraits. An exhibition of his work took place in the Art Gallery of the Fort Nelson Hotel building in 1965 when the *Fort Nelson News* noted, "Mr. Kirwin, a teacher at the Carlson school, now has a permanent studio at the Art Gallery and this is the first of his shows to be seen at Fort Nelson. The paintings, . . . are all of scenes of B.C. painted since Easter from sketches made over the years. Capturing unusual lighting effects in many of the scenes, he excells in painting water falls and rushing swirling water. Using vivid shades he portrays the brightness of the blue skies and lush greenness of B.C. in scenes from the Cariboo, Golden, Stanley park and the Vancouver areas amongst others; . . . ."

References

Fort Nelson News, Fort Nelson, B.C., Wed., May 12, 1965 "Kirwin art show here this week"
Ibid, May 26, 1965 "Art show extended" (photo of artist with his work which accompanied an article on him)

KISS, Steven Joseph
b.1933

Born in Calgary, Alberta, he studied at the Provincial Institute of Technology and Art (Alberta College of Art), Calgary, 1950-54, and has been influenced by many artists including Maxwell Bates and Ronald Spickett. He makes his living as a

KISS, Steven Joseph (Cont'd)

commercial artist but as a painter favours abstracts and semi-abstracts and draws his main inspiration from landscapes. He works in the media of oils, water colours and tempera. He attended The Art Center School in Los Angeles, California, in 1962. A member of the Alberta Society of Artists, his home is in Calgary but no recent information is available on him.

References

National Gallery of Canada Information Form rec'd in February, 1962
Document from artist

KITSCO, Margaret Rose
b.1938

Born in Edmonton, Alberta, she studied art at the University of Alberta under H.G. Glyde, E.N. Yates, J.B. Taylor, W. Townsend (from the Slade School, London, Eng.). During her study she won the Alumni Association Prize in Fine Art (1961); Fuller Brush Scholarship in Art (1962); Provincial Government Cultural Development Branch Scholarship (1962 & 1963). She exhibited with the "All Alberta Exhibition" in May, 1963 at Edmonton. She lives in Edmonton.

KIYOOKA, Harry Mitsuo
b.1928

Born in Calgary, Alberta, a painter and graphic artist, his recent paintings include elements of geometrical and optical art, also other adventures in pure painting including mobile paintings, serigraphs using printing ink and a variety of other experiments. He has had several one man shows including a showing at the New Design Gallery in Vancouver and in a travelling exhibition of the Western Canada Art Circuit. Harry Kiyooka studied painting under H.G. Glyde at the University of Alberta, Edward Bawden at the Banff School of Fine Arts, W.A. McCloy and R. Bowman at the Winnipeg School of Art, R. Hendrickson, E. Brauner and J. DeMartelly (in lithography) at Michigan State University, and D. Weygandt at the University of Colorado.[2] During his studies he received the following degrees: B. Ed. (Art Education), Alta., 1953; B.F.A. (Fine Arts) Man., 1954; M.A. (Fine Arts) Michigan State, 1956; M.F.A. (Fine Arts) Colorado, 1957.[3] He has won a number of awards which include Prov. of Alberta Bursary, 1947; Sullivan Lake S.D. No. 9 Bursary, Alta. (Summer School), 1949; Birks Scholarship, Alta., 1950; Fuller Brush Art Scholarship, Alta., 1953; Graduate Assistantship, Michigan State, 1955; Graduate Assistantship, Colorado, 1956; Canada Council Scholarships 1958-59, 1959-60.[4] He studied and painted in Italy, 1958-61 and in Europe again in 1966. Also in 1966 he won First Prize in the Winnipeg Biennial, and had his work selected for exhibit in the Sixth and Seventh Biennials of Canadian Painting. He is represented in the following collections: The Victoria Art Gallery, The Museum of Contemporary Art, Montreal, The Mendel Collection, Saskatoon, The National Gallery of Canada, The Art Gallery of Ontario, the Winnipeg Art Gallery and in the Brock Hall Collection, Vancouver. He is a member of the Alberta Society of

KIYOOKA, Harry Mitsuo (Cont'd)

Artists (Pres. 1967-8). He is professor at the University of Alberta, and has taught art for many years. His home is in Calgary, Alberta.

References
   [1] *Vancouver Sun*, Jan. 26, 1966 "Art Preview Reception Set"
   [2] National Gallery of Canada Information Form Rec'd Nov. 2, 1961 also January, 1963
   [3] Ibid
   [4] Ibid
   see also
   The Calgary Herald, Apr. 26, 1966 "2 Calgary Artists Win Awards"
   Times-Herald, Moose Jaw, Sask. "Kiyooka Serigraph Show Displayed At Art Museum"
   Sixth Biennial Exhibition (catalogue) of Canadian Painting, 1965
   Seventh Biennial Exhibition (catalogue) of Canadian Painting, 1968

KIYOOKA, Roy Kenzie
b.1926

Born in Moose Jaw, Saskatchewan, he studied painting at the Provincial Institute of Technology and Art, Calgary, 1946-49 under J.W.G. MacDonald and I.H. Kerr; at the Instituto Allende, Mexico (on scholarship), 1955, where he studied with James Pinto; at the University of Saskatchewan Emma Lake Workshops with Barnett Newman and others.[1] During his study he received a Diploma in Fine Arts at the Institute of Technology and Art, Calgary, 1949.[2] His early work was representational and in 1950 he was winner of the O'Keefe scholarship.[3] In 1952 he exhibited his work with three other artists Gregory Arnold, George Mihalcheon, and Ronald Spickett. Viewing this four man show Lenore Crawford[4] of *The London Free Press* noted, "Roy Kiyooka has used palette knife and varnish effectively in several canvases. 'House by Night' has interesting greens and reds contrasted to give excellent comparison of the dreary cold of outside and the warmth and brightness of within. 'They Also Lived Here,' says something old satisfactorily and 'Fishermen' is a powerful study, replete with symbolism . . . . " By 1954 a change in his work was noted by Dr. R. W. Hedley[5] in *The Edmonton Journal* " . . . a visit to the Arts building of the University of Alberta to see the 19 pictures by Roy K. Kiyooka. The pictures range from the realistic style to the abstract, with a wide choice of subjects, and in a wide range in styles of expression. Some are very good and some are not so good. One fact stands out prominently, when he wishes to do so he can paint and paint well. He is a young man and is evidently exploring many styles and techniques . . . . and knows how to handle paint well . . . . Probably in time he will settle on one style which he finds is particularly appropriate to express himself. He should go far as an artist." He was now instructing at the Provincial Institute of Technology, Calgary, evenings while days he worked as a display artist with a local firm. Later he became an advertising manager for a supermarket firm in Nelson, B.C. It was then that he won a scholarship at the Institute San Miguel d'Allende in Mexico City. In 1955 his "The City" (an oil on masonite) was accepted in the First Biennial Exhibition of Canadian Painting and was reproduced in the exhibition catalogue.[6] It was acquired by the National Gallery and reproduced in the Gallery's catalogue of Canadian paintings.[7] In 1956 he became full-time instructor at the Regina College of Art; at night he taught there as well. Also that year his exhibition with Maxwell Bates, Janet Mitchell, Roy Stevenson took place at the Norman Mackenzie art gallery.[8] His work was selected for the Walker Biennial exhibition in Minneapolis in 1958. He also held a one man show of 21 water colours at the Norman Mackenzie art gallery and achieved success at the Winnipeg Show where he won a prize. These are only a few of his activities. Many one man shows followed; he held ten one man shows before 1957. In 1964 he exhibited with his brother artist Harry at the Alberta College of Art, Calgary, when *The Albertan*[9] noted, "Though the Kiyooka brothers have shown widely on an individual basis throughout North America this exhibition represents the first time their works have been shown together." It was in 1964 that Roy Kiyooka received a senior art fellowship from the Canada Council and took a year's leave of absence from the Vancouver School of Art where he had been teaching since 1960. He began his 'oval series' of paintings described by the *Western Homes & Living*[10] as follows, "When we caught him at his studio, an otherwise abandoned apartment over a furnace shop on Fourth Avenue, Roy Kiyooka was working on his 'Oval Series'. These are pure forms belonging to the world of art alone, but their inspiration can be traced to such prosaic sources as a neon sign seen through the slats of a bamboo blind, the moving pattern of shadows on his studio floor, or an oval panel of bevelled plate glass in an old West End door. All these things, and other aspects of modern urban life, hold a continuous fascination for Roy Kiyooka as he moves about the city or sits in his studio. 'Art is uniquely human experience; everything is possible and nothing is forbidden – in art', he explains. His uniquely personal expression of visual experience is producing some of the most stimulating art in Canada." At the close of 1964 he held a one man show of his paintings at The New Design Gallery. The year 1965 was an important year of achievement with his honourable mention award at the Eighth Biennial Exhibition at Sao Paulo, Brazil. He had also joined the staff of Sir George Williams University and held a one man show at Galerie du Siècle which *The Gazette*[11] noted as follows, "In his most characteristic, oft recurring image, composed into single or twin elliptic fields Kiyooka uses horizontal bars, joined by vertical, stem-like connections as in Roman numbers. His colors are strong, assertive blues and yellows, used with orange and sometimes green. Black and more often white enter into these combinations . . . . In public life, in industry, in the press and in commerce we desperately need more effective and more visually meaningful design. Granted time, an inspired teacher of Mr. Kiyooka's graphic ability could change the picture. We wish him good speed." In 1966 he was awarded a thousand dollars for his painting "Green Connecting" at the Winnipeg Show, also in 1966 an exhibition of his paintings took place at the Laing Galleries in Toronto. His visit to Vancouver in 1967 brought forth an extensive article by Joan Lowndes[12] in *The Province* which revealed Vancouver artists Michael Morris, Brian Fisher, Bodo Pfeifer, Claude Breeze, Jane Adams and Brent Gifford has studied under him at one time or another. In conclusion a passage of Kiyooka's credo was reproduced from a catalogue as follows, "I believe that 'dogma' whether political, religious, or personal is the despair of the painter. Insistently, his feelings overflow the rigidity of a prior concept. I see the aim of Art the vivification of Life. The rest is esthetics. To make Art for the pleasure and anguish of it. To give it away for the same reasons . . . The courage to do this . . . an Aspiration! Not to make monuments but to lay beside a mountain the fragility of a painting; the fragrance of a life, lived." A second article appeared in *The Province* in 1969 written by Richard Simmins[13] on the occasion of Kiyooka's visit to Vancouver to install three major sculptures at the Douglas Gallery where they were on view. These sculptures were part of a series of ten fibreglass three-dimensional creations which the artist had been working on since 1967. Kiyooka was quoted by Simmins[14] as follows, "I am really a painters' sculptor. My

KIYOOKA, Roy Kenzie (Cont'd)

works have a rectangular basis. They are floor sculptures, slab-like, containing configurations which are bounded by the edges, like a painting. Color is an integral part of all these new works and the finish is smooth, highly reflective and the surface as pristine as a painting. My sculpture as well as my painting is not abstract. It has always had reference to the physical reality which I have experienced . . . . " Simmins[15] felt however, "There seems no doubt, even in his first show, that the artist has it made as a sculptor. He has a profound understanding of weight, empty volumes which balance with precise form, color as a dimension which creates physical nuance and a profound understanding of line as related to mass. These are not just painterly works in a new medium, but a radical breakthrough in terms of working with contemporary materials and new forms." A mosaic muralist as well, he designed and executed commissions for the First Presbyterian Church, Regina, and the Biology Building of the University of Saskatchewan. He has also written two books of poems, *Kyoto Airs* and *Neverthless These Eyes*[16]. He is represented in the following public collections: University of Victoria; University of British Columbia; National Gallery of Canada; the Saskatchewan Arts Board; the Calgary Allied Art Centre, the Norman Mackenzie Art Gallery, Regina; Vancouver Art Gallery, Art Gallery of Ontario, Victoria Art Gallery, University of Alabama and in the private collections of Samuel Zacks, Joseph Hirshhorn and many others. He has also exhibited his work at the David Mirvish Gallery, Toronto, and R.C.A. shows.

References

[1] National Gallery of Canada Information Form rec'd 1968 and papers in his file in NGC Library.
[2] Ibid
[3] National Gallery of Canada Information Form rec'd Jan. 28, 1952
[4] *The London Free Press* Jan. 15, 1952 "Calgary Artists Exhibit in City"
[5] *The Edmonton Journal*, Feb. 8, 1954 "Youthful Alberta Artist Displays 18 Paintings" by Dr. R.W. Hedley
[6] *First Biennial Exhibition of Canadian Painting, 1955* (catalogue) NGC, P.29
[7] *The National Gallery of Canada Catalogue, Vol. 3, Can. School* by R.H. Hubbard, P.158
[8] *The Leader-Post*, Regina, Sask., Sept. 29, 1956
[9] *The Albertan*, Calgary, Alta., Jan. 18, 1964 "Kiyooka Brothers Exhibited at ACA"
[10] *Western Homes and Living*, Van., B.C., June, 1964 "B.C. Artists – Roy Kiyooka"
[11] *The Gazette*, Mtl., P.Q., Dec 4, 1965 "Kiyooka And . . . "
[12] *The Province*, Van., B.C., Nov. 17, 1967 "Return of visionary – Kiyooka – a factor in the sudden brilliance of the visual arts in this city" by Joan Lowndes
[13] Ibid, Feb. 14, 1969 "Art – The Kiyooka phenomenon" by Richard Simmins
[14] Ibid
[15] Ibid
[16] *Kyoto Airs* by Roy Kiyooka, Periwinkle Press, Van., B.C., 1964
Nevertheless These Eyes by Coach House Press, Tor., Ont., 1967
see also
The Victoria Daily Times, 7 April, 1954 "Art in Review" by Colin Graham
The Calgary Herald, April 1, 1955 "Calgary Artist Wins Award"
The New Canadian, May 25, 1955 "National Art Gallery Purchases Works Of Kazuo Nakamura, Kenzie Kiyooka"
Leader-Post, Regina, Sask., Sept. 27, 1958 "Roy Kiyooka watercolor display at art gallery" by R.L. Bloore
Ibid, Nov. 15, 1960 "Art teacher takes part in exhibit"
The Province, Van., B.C., Jan. 30, 1961 "Realm of art – He 'digs' exhibit but reservedly" by The Critic
Leader, Oak Bay, B.C., Sept. 25, 1963 "Kiyooka Collages Gallery Display" by Hyslop Ingram

KIYOOKA, Roy Kenzie (Cont'd)

The Vancouver Sun, Feb. 24, 1964 "City Artist Awarded Fellowship"
Ibid Sept. 23, 1964 "Kiyooka Paintings Bring Gay Note" by David Watmough
The Province, Van., B.C., Sept 26, 1964 "Art – Kiyooka's new paintings are calm and elegant" by Belinda McLeod
Leader-Post, Regina, Sask., Sept. 11, 1965 "Canadian artist honored"
Tribune, Winnipeg, Man., Nov. 4, 1966 "Calgary artist wins $1,000"
La Presse, Mtl., P.Q. "Kiyooka: evocations de l'accident dans l'infini"
Studio International, Vol. 176, No. 906, 1968 "The Canadian Scene, No. 3" by David Thomson
The Vancouver Sun, Van., B.C., Feb. 13, 1969 "Painter, Poet Turned Sculptor – Kiyooka's 'Illusions' Form Austere, Beautiful Set" by Charlotte Townsend
Canadian Art, Issue No. 78 Mar./Apr., 1962 "A Survey Of The Work of 21 More Canadian Artists – Roy K. Kiyooka" by Abraham Rogatnick
Painting In Canada/A History by J. Russell Harper, U. of T. Press, 1966, P.399, 400
Painting In Canada (catalogue) by Barry Lord, Queen's Printer, Ottawa, 1967,
Three Hundred Years of Canadian Art (catalogue), by R.H. Hubbard and J.R. Ostiguy, Queen's Printer, 1967
Fifth Biennial Exhibition of Canadian Painting, 1963 (Catalogue) P.21

KLAASSEN, Mrs. Jean (Mrs. William Klaassen)

She began painting early in her youth and later studied under Peter Goetz at Kitchener. She has won many prizes including: Major Newman Award for representational painting at the Central Ontario Art Association annual exhibition (1960); Grumbacher Award for Best Oil at the Guelph Outdoor exhibition (1962); Grumbacher Award for the Best Advanced Painting Prize at Guelph's "Painting on the Green" (1964); Honourable Mention at the Glenhurst Show (1964); First Prize in the Central Ontario Exhibition Fine Arts Contest at Kitchener (1968). She travelled and painted in Europe in 1965 and conducts classes in oils at the Galt YWCA. She lives at Preston, Ontario, where she has a framing business with her husband.

References
Evening Reporter, Galt, Ont., Jan. 15, 1964 story by Irene Baumgartner
The Guelph Guardian, Guelph, Ont., Fri., Aug. 13, 1965 "Painter's Profile"
The Guelph Mercury, Sat., Aug. 21, 1965 "Preston Painter Teaches As Well"
Evening Reporter, Galt, Ont., Sept. 3, 1968 "Area Artists Come First And Sell Winning Entries"

KLACHAN, Paul Peter

An artist from Bothwell, Ontario, of Czechoslovakian parents, who has been producing some remarkable paintings. He is a versatile painter of scenery and character studies. He studied under Mrs. Glen Atkinson of Merlin, Ont. (a former elementary school teacher). He is represented in a number of Canadian and European collections.

Reference
News, Chatham, Ontario, Nov. 6, 1967 "Kent County Painter Wins Attention of 400"

KLASSEN, Jacob Frank

b.1904

Born in the Village of Donskoi, Russia, he first studied art through a village school teacher J. Janzen (who later went to South America). Klassen came to Canada in 1924 and settled in Winnipeg, Manitoba. There he studied under Walter J. Phillips one of Canada's greatest water colourists. A painter of landscapes in realistic presentation, he has done water colours mainly and occasionally some tempera paintings. A member of the Manitoba Society of Artists he has exhibited with this society throughout the years, also the Winnipeg Sketch Club (former Pres.). He is no longer active with the Winnipeg Sketch Club but continues to exhibit with the Manitoba Society of Artists.

Source
> Document from artist

KLASSEN, John

A Brantford, Ontario artist who has done commercial art work and carving in soapstone and maple rock. His carving heritage is derived from his mother's side of the family as she is a Mic Mac Indian. Perhaps in the near future John will branch into making very large works of stone or other materials when he fulfills an ambition to become a sculptor. His carvings have been exhibited at the Brantford Public Library (1969) and he is represented in the collection of the Owen Sound Museum by a soapstone carving of an Eskimo skinning a seal. Reports are that he is full of creativity and has a very promising future.

Reference
> *Brantford Expositor*, Ont., June 28, 1969 "World of Sculptor Is Wonderful Place, Full of Images" by Dick Cross

---

KLEMMING, Maria Elisabeth (Maj-Lis)

b.1901

Born in Uleaborg, Finland, of Swedish parents, she came to Canada in 1925 and settled in Winnipeg. She studied at the Winnipeg School of Art under Miss E. Tedeschy and Miss E. Carter for Design and Still Life (1949-50), under Prof. W. A. McCloy for Life Painting (1950-51) under Prof. W.A. McCloy and Prof. R.I. Bowman for Oil Painting (1951-52).

References
> National Gallery of Canada Information Form rec'd April 8, 1952

KLIMOFF, Eugene
b.1901

Born in Mitau, Russia, he studied at the Academy of Fine Arts in Riga, Latvia, where he specialized in the History of Russian Art and graduated with his Master of Arts degree in 1929.[1] He took further study in Paris, Moscow, Italy, and Austria. In 1933 he became Secretary of the Arts Society "Akropolis", in Riga, Latvia, an office he held until 1940.[2] In 1941 he was appointed Chief of the Russian Section, Arts Museum, Riga, Latvia, and later its Vice-Director. All during this period he also developed as a painter and graphic artist. He was restorer of Russian ikons at the Kondokov Institute, Prague, 1944-1945.[3] He published a number of albums of lithographs including Ten Views of Cities (1928); City Views (1936); The region of Petsery, Estonia (1937); Views of Baltic States (1941); Italia (1941); Pskov, Russia (1943); Kitzingen, Germany (1944).[4] He came to Canada in 1949 and settled in Quebec City. In 1953 his first Canadian lithographs were produced with subject matter of Quebec. Others followed including scenes of Toronto (1955), Ports of Gaspé (1954), Touring Gaspesia (1955).[5] Solo exhibits of his paintings took place at the Three Rivers Library (Nov. 1949); Fisheries Training School, Grand-River, Gaspé-Sud (1954); Palais Montcalm, Quebec (1952, 1955, 1963); la salle Jefferson, Carling Avenue, Ottawa (1963); Centre audio-visuel de Quebec, Quebec City (1965) when Christiane Brunelle[6] noted that his work revealed him to be a naturalist and portraitist before all. She also noted that his paintings of the Holy Land and mosaics of holy figures had particular qualities of mysticism and all his works possessed luminous qualities. Much earlier in 1953 Pearl McCarthy[7] had referred to him as a skillful academic artist. In 1967 Mr. Klimoff presented a lecture on Russian Religious Painting in The Nineteenth Century, at Carleton University. The lecture was sponsored jointly by the Departments of Fine Arts, History and Modern Languages at Carleton University and the Humanities Association of Ottawa. He has held teaching positions in the field of Russian literature, history and art at a number of North American institutions, including: Laval University, Middlebury College, and Indiana University. He is represented in the Museum collections at Riga, Moscow, Leningrad and Quebec.

References

[1] National Gallery of Canada Information Form rec'd Aug. 23, 1965

[2] Ibid

[3] Ibid

[4] Ibid

[5] Ibid

[6] L'Evenement, Que., P.Q., Nov. 23, 1965 "Les toiles du peintre Eugene Klimoff lumière et clarté" par C. Brunelle

[7] The Globe & Mail, Tor, Ont., Oct. 31, 1953 "Russian Paintings and Ikons Show Traditions on the Move" by Pearl McCarthy

see also

L'Evenement, Que., P.Q., 10 Nov. 1952 "Eugène Klimoff expose au Palais Montcalm"

L'Action Catholique, Que. P.Q., 11 Nov., 1952 "Eugène Klimoff" par J.P.

Le Bien Public, Trois-Rivières, 21, Oct., 1955 "Une exposition Klimoff à Québec"

Le Droit, Ottawa, Ont., Mar. 29, 1963 "Eugène Klimoff expose"

Chronicle-Telegraph, Que, P.Q., Nov. 1, 1963 "Abstract Painting Said Sickness Of Our Period"

L'Evenement, Que. P.Q., Nov. 1, 1963 "Exposition rétrospective du peintre Klimoff"

L'Action, Que. P.Q., Nov. 2, 1963 "Rétrospective de 40 années de travail"

KLOEZEMAN, Gijsbertus (Bert)

b.1921

Born in Ipoh, Malaya, he studied at the Royal Academy of Fine Arts, The Hague — Holland, under Paul Citroen, Han Van Dam, Rÿndert Draayer, Henk Meyer, Willem Schrofer, Willem Rosendaal and privately under Stien Eelsigh. He came to Canada in 1952 and settled at Woodstock, Ontario, before moving to London, Ontario, in 1960.[1] A commercial artist he also specialized in portrait painting.[2] By 1957 he was exhibiting his work in a one man show at the Ingersoll Public Library and his work was noted by *The Ingersoll Tribune*[3] as follows, "Black and white predominate in this show and it is the first time the library has had such a large exhibit in graphic art, pencil, pen and ink, charcoal and etching. There are lively caricatures, a delicate etching, well modelled portrait studies, and many fine drawings in pencil and pen and ink, of landscape both European and Canadian. Of local interest are the many interpretations of Oxford county scene and it would be interesting to have these developed to a greater degree . . . . The paintings in the show while not numerous show a distinct break from the black and white style and are interesting in their qualities of colour and design." In 1960 he exhibited his work in London, Ontario, at the Fred Landon Branch library where Lenore Crawford[4] of *The London Free Press* noted, "Everything is fundamentally rhythmic, he claims, and color gives character, depth and expression to the rhythm. His paintings, which vary from large canvases to one about a foot square, attest to his convictions. They demonstrate his belief in rhythm as contrapuntally vertical and horizontal; occasional curves exist, but they are there more to emphasize the vertical and horizontal than for their own sake. Their use is skilful, often imaginative . . . . He uses recognizable forms as a means of expressing his thought, emotion and interpretation, . . . " But in his two murals for the London Airport (each mural 50 ft. long by four ft. high) he uses abstract presentations to convey the electronic systems of the communications media today in one, and in the other, a day's cycle in the world of flight.[5] The most recent news of this artist was his participation in a four man exhibition at the London Public Art Museum, Ontario, during March of 1969. Lenore Crawford[6] on viewing this show noted of his prints, " . . . Mr. Kloezeman's technical breadth has expanded also, he uses a variety of media now with ingenuity." He joined the art department of the H.B. Beal Secondary School in the fall of 1964 . Mr. Kloezeman is a member of the Society of Canadian Painter-Etchers and Engravers (1953); The Royal Academy of Fine Arts/The Hague — Holland (1939); The Hague Society of Fine Arts (1950).

References

[1] National Gallery of Canada Information Form received during the mid 1950's

[2] *The London Free Press*, Oct. 29, 1964 "Dutch-Born Artist Wins Job of Painting Airport Murals"

[3] *The Ingersoll Tribune*, Ingersoll, Ont., July 11, 1957 "One-Man Exhibition of Art At Ingersoll Public Library"

[4] *The London Free Press*, Jan. 30, 1960 "Woodstock Artist Exhibits Paintings" by Lenore Crawford

[5] see[2]

[6] *The London Free Press*, Mar. 3, 1969 "Display of 4 Artists' work offers technique contrasts" by Lenore Crawford

KNAPP, Stanley
b.1912

Born in Devonshire, England, he came to Canada in 1930 and joined the Hudson's Bay Company in charge of the Company's post 500 miles north of Frobisher Bay, Southern Baffin Land, N.W.T., at Clyde.[1] In 1934 Knapp made a gift of an oil painting he had done of his post, to H.S. Southam, Chairman of the Board of Trustees of The National Gallery of Canada. The gift was brought back from the north by Major D.L. McKeand, Commander of the Canadian government Arctic patrol.[2] The remarkable thing about the oil painting was that Knapp had no art supplies with him. He made brushes from hair on his own head, used cardboard for a canvas and common house paint.[3] This painting was later given to the Public Archives of Canada by the trustees of the Gallery because of its historical value. Knapp had forwarded a letter asking for art supplies and the next year the Gallery trustees forwarded a set of artist's paints and brushes by way of the *S.S. Nascopie*, Hudson's Bay Company ship.[4] Describing Knapp's life in the north Robert Reade[5] wrote the following, "He can wield a skinning knife as well as a palette-knife. He can tell at a glance whether a white fox was trapped in Baffin Land or Ungava or the Mackenzie River delta. He has experience of the trail as well as the trading post. He can drive a dog team with a 20 foot whip and has been up and down Baffin Land from Lake Harbor to Clyde Inlet to Pangnirtung and Pond Inlet. And he can build a snow house." In 1937 Knapp entered the Ontario College of Art where he studied painting and drawing until 1939.[6] His first one man show took place at the Picture Loan Society, Toronto, in April of 1939 when Graham McInnes[7] in the *Saturday Night* noted, "At the end of seven years, Stanley Knapp had saved enough money to go to the Ontario College of Art; for he was convinced that, self-taught, he could go only a certain distance. A year there has knocked off some of the charm and substituted Canadian Group-ish skies for the bitter and unearthly blue of his earlier period. But there have also emerged qualities which were hitherto dormant — richness, rhythmic line and a feeling for texture. Stanley Knapp's paintings are to be seen at the Picture Loan Society, 3 Charles Street West. You won't regret going. This is an unusual and fascinating show." Knapp returned north in 1939 and was quoted by *The Montreal Standard*[8] as saying, "I believe I can interpret the life of the Eskimos because during my ten years in the Hudson Straits and Bay, I have lived with them, worked, played, slept, ate and even starved with them." The article continued, "Mr. Knapp will leave the McLean at one of the first isolated points the ship reaches and head for the interior with the Eskimos. He will travel by Kayak, dog team and on foot, living exactly as the Eskimos do. He anticipated lengthy treks over the barren wastes carrying a 100 pound sketch box. He will rejoin the ship at some other post as she begins her return voyage." When he returned to Toronto Knapp held a one man show of his paintings at Eaton's Fine Art Galleries. This exhibit was well received.[9] No recent information is available on this artist.

References

[1] National Gallery of Canada artist's file in Library

[2] *The Ottawa Citizen*, Ottawa, Ont., April 27, 1935 "Young Northern Artist Given Recognition For His Efforts"

[3] *The Mail & Empire*, Tor., Ont., April 27, 1935 "National Gallery Rewards Resourceful Young Artist"

[4] *The Montreal Star*, Mtl, P.Q., April 29, 1935 "Young Artist in Northland Gets Official Encouragement"

[5] *The Toronto Star Weekly*, Dec. 18, 1937 article by Robert Reade

[6] Ibid

KNAPP, Stanley (Cont'd)

[7] *The Saturday Night*, Tor., Ont., April 22, 1939 "Reporter of the Northland" by Graham McInnes

[8] *The Montreal Standard*, July 29th, 1939 "Artist Proceeds North To Capture Eskimo Life With Brush and Canvas"

[9] *The Toronto Star*, May 25th, 1940 "Knapp's Arctic Show Almost Surrealistic"

KNIGHT, Cecil

A landscape artist who has exhibited at the Essex County Artists Exhibitions held annually in Southern Ontario. David Mawr of *The Windsor Daily Star* noted his work as follows, " 'Haunted House' by Cecil Knight shows a keen appreciation of pattern and composition and his color is well-chosen to carry out his particular subject." Knight's paintings are usually water colours. No recent information is available on this artist.

References
The Windsor Daily Star, Windsor, Ont., Sat., May 13, 1944 "Striking Art as Painted Along the Windsor Riverfront" (photo of Knight's painting)

Ibid, Feb. 12, 1949 "92 Exhibits In Essex County Show" by David Mawr (photo of Knight's "Haunted House")

KNIGHT, Charles

A political cartoonist for *The Windsor Daily Star* who exhibited his work at the Willistead Gallery, Windsor, in 1947, with nine other leading North American cartoonists. This exhibition was sponsored by the Public Library Board of Windsor in co-operation with the United Nations Society of that city.

Reference
The Windsor Daily Star, Windsor, Ont., Sept. 23, 1947 "Windsor Star Staff Cartoonist's Work on Display"

KNOPF, Miss Ernestine

Born in Toronto, Ontario, she studied under W.H. Taylor in Montreal, 1922; under John Y. Johnstone at the Council of Arts and Mfgs. classes from 1922 to 1925; under Edmond Dyonnet, 1929-30 at the Art Association of Montreal Classes and the R.C.A. Classes (from life); under Mr. Mahias, 1924, at the Ecole des Beaux Arts (water colours); received criticisms from G. Horne Russell; short course in pen and ink with the Langdon Correspondence School at Cleveland, Ohio; two years' modelling under Mr. Elzear Soucy at the Council of Arts and Mfgs. She won a number of honours during this period of study. From 1927 (8) when she submitted her paintings at the Montreal Art Association and the Royal Canadian Academy shows, they were always accepted. She went to New York City where she found a market for her portrait studies (genre), still life, and she did a few landscapes. She made thousands of quick sketches from life in red conte crayonne. In 1935 she

KNOPF, Miss Ernestine (Cont'd)

visited Canada and exhibited two portraits at the Montreal Art Association Spring Exhibition. She returned to Canada in 1940 and stayed in the Laurentians for over two years. No recent information is available on this artist. She was last reported living near Knowlton, Quebec, in 1949.

References

National Gallery of Canada Information Form (undated)

Letter to H.O. McCurry, Director NGC, dated Dec. 12, 1949 (see artist's file in NGC Library for copy of letter)

KNOWLES, Dorothy Elsie (Mrs. W. Perehudoff)
b.1927

Born in Unity, Saskatchewan, she received her B.A. at the University of Saskatchewan and afterwards worked as a laboratory technician. She first studied painting at the University of Saskatchewan, evenings, under Eli Bornstein and N. Bjelejac.[1] She then attended summer courses at Emma Lake where she studied under Will Barnett, Clement Greenberg, Jules Olitski, Joe Plaskett, Kenneth Noland and Lawrence Alloway. In 1951 she studied briefly at the Goldsmith School of Art in London, England. She married artist William Perehudoff and they travelled to France (Paris) and Italy in 1952. Returning to Canada with her husband she held her first one man show in 1954 at the Saskatoon Art Centre, others followed in the James Art Studio, Saskatoon (1962); Saskatoon Art Centre (1963); Regina Public Library (1963); The Mendel Art Gallery, Saskatoon (1964); The David Mirvish Gallery, Toronto (1965); Bonli Gallery, Toronto (1967); at the Moose Jaw art museum, Saskatchewan (1968) when the Moose Jaw *Times-Herald*[2] noted, "Her show consists of 12 paintings which are mainly of northern Saskatchewan and the Saskatoon area, 'I chose the paintings from my most recent work,' she said. Speaking at the opening were Mrs. Joan Rankin chairman of the art museum board and Mayor L.H. Lewry. Mrs. Rankin said Miss Knowles is 'one of the finest landscape artists in Canada. She proves to us that landscape painting is still a real and important art form." In 1967 Marie Nagel[3] of the *Star-Phoenix*, Saskatoon, explained, "She says she has beat the problem of mosquitoes flying into her paintings, and dust blowing onto them, by buying a large van from which she often paints. 'I tried to develop my own technique directly from nature,' said Mrs. Perehudoff, explaining that she tries to integrate her charcoal sketches on the canvas with the paint, using it very thinly so the charcoal shows through and becomes a part of it . . . . Mrs. Perehudoff says it takes her from a week to a month to complete a painting and there's more of it than just sketching and painting. Canvas sheets must be stretched over wooden stretcher frames, and must also be sized before they are ready to be painted on, she said. Besides painting, the Perehudoffs are collectors of paintings and pottery. They have a large art library, and find enjoyment through music and books . . . . " A fine reproduction of Dorothy Knowles' work appeared in *Canadian Art* for an article by Andrew Hudson.[4] He had referred to "the respectively limpid and staccato brushwork of Dorothy Knowles and Nonie Mulcaster (two women landscape painters from Saskatchewan whose work deserves to be more widely known in Canada), ... " She is represented in the following public collections: The Willistead Museum at Windsor, Ontario; the Hamilton Art Gallery; the Art Gallery of Ontario; the University of Saskatchewan; the Saskatchewan Arts Board collection and elsewhere. She and her husband live in Saskatoon, Sask.

KNOWLES, Dorothy Elsie (Cont'd)

References

[1] National Gallery of Canada Information Form rec'd during 1968 and Jan. 1963

[2] *Times-Herald*, Moose Jaw, Sask., June 21, 1968 "Saskatchewan Artist's Show Officially Open"

[3] *Star-Phoenix*, Saskatoon, Sask., Jan. 23, 1967 "Local artist's work exhibited in Toronto" by Marie Nagel

[4] *Canadian Art*, Vol. 22, No. 2, Mar./Apr., 1965 "The Paintings as Object" by Andrew Hudson, P.34

see also

Star-Phoenix, Sask., Sept. 27, 1957 "One-Man Show"

Ibid, Sept. 19, 1957 "Art Centre Reopens" (photo of artist)

Leader-Post, Regina, Sask., "Two Sask. women have art showing"

Star-Phoenix, Sask., July 29, 1964 "In Beautiful Qu'Appelle Valley"

Catalogue sheet for The David Mirvish Gallery, Toronto, Recent Landscapes (of Dorothy Knowles) text by Andrew Hudson 17 June, 1965 (Showing in July)

Canadian Art, Vol. 20, No. 2 "Clement Greenberg's View Of Art On The Prairies" by C.G., P.104

Ibid, Vol. 20, No. 3 Art Reviews "Dorothy Knowles Perehudoff at the James Art Studio Gallery, Sask." by Andrew Hudson, P.147

The Art Journal of Saskatoon Society of Education through Art 1966 (coloured reproduction)

KNOWLES, Elizabeth A. McGillivray

1866-1928

Born in Ottawa, Ontario, her maiden name was Elizabeth Beach and her family came from Oakley Hall in the South of England. She was a relative of Sir Michael Hicks-Beach. While attending school in Toronto she studied art under F. McGillivray Knowles who was then an A.R.C.A. and in 1890 they married.[1] They went to Europe where they both studied and travelled. By 1908 she was elected an Associate of the Royal Canadian Academy (her husband was then a full member). The same year her canvas "Nocturne" was exhibited at the R.C.A.'s annual show and purchased by the National Gallery of Canada a few months later. This paintings is of a country scene, a lane, trees and a moon in the background.[2] By 1912 she had achieved considerable recognition as a painter and her work was noted by the *Home Journal* and *The Canadian Magazine*.[3] In 1914 E.F.B. Johnston[4] included her among women painters in Canada that deserved recognition. In 1919 she was elected member of the National Association of Women Painters and Sculptors, New York.[5] By 1920 she and her husband were living in New York City. When they left Toronto a banquet was held for them by their many friends at the King Edward Hotel. They continued however to exhibit their works jointly in Canada at the Wilson's Art Gallery, Ottawa, and in Montreal at the Johnson Art Galleries. Their paintings continued to be shown at the Royal Canadian Academy shows. In a joint showing of their paintings at Johnston's in Montreal in 1921 *The Montreal Star*[6] noted, "Apart from its great artistic interest, the exhibition possesses an unusual fascination in that it affords a study in the interpretative methods of a husband and wife, both artists of high standard. Mrs. Knowles has become known as a landscape painter of the romantic school, and as a portrayer of rural scenes, while her husband's vigorous landscape painting and fine figure work is known throughout Canada . . . . Mrs. Knowles has sought and found her inspiration in the common life round the farm, and the beauty of everyday homely things. Her

KNOWLES, Elizabeth A. McGillivray (Cont'd)

favorite subjects are chickens, and she has studied them with the enthusiasm and sincerity of a naturalist, as well as the imagination of an artist. She shows the feathered beauties in all moods, against a background of weather-beaten old barns and quaint old farmhouses, and the result is at once intimate, characteristic and restful. Her work with one or two exceptions is carried out in oils, a medium well adapted to show the flamboyant beauty and coloring of her feathered subjects." Another joint showing by the Knowles in Ottawa was noted by *The Ottawa Journal*[7] as follows, "Elizabeth A. Knowles stands alone in her field of miniature and larger paintings of poultry. In these she gives a touch of the human that amuses and charms, while the rich color, fidelity to facts and spontaneous ease in technique make her work a delight both to artists and art lovers." Newton MacTavish[8] in his book *The Fine Arts In Canada*, mentions her after she had gone to the United States with her husband as follows, "Mrs. Elizabeth McGillivray Knowles, A.R.C.A., who, with her husband, was for many years prominent in the artistic life of Toronto, has displayed a real gift for landscapes in miniature and for clever little pictures of domestic animals, especially fowl. She has a deft way of handling these subjects and with them she has gained a wide reputation. Together with her husband she has painted in many parts of Canada; and these two, wherever they have gone, have entered whole-heartedly into artistic and social life." In 1928 at the age of sixty-two she died at her summer home in Riverton, New Hampshire, U.S.A.[9] She and her husband had just opened a new studio there. She also was a member of the following societies: Pennsylvania Society of Miniature Painters; Brooklyn Society of Miniature Painters, Washington Water Color Club; American Water color Society; League of American Pen Women (pen, brush and pencil). She is represented in a number of other public collections including the Agnes Etherington Art Centre, Queen's University, Kingston, as well as many private collections.

References
[1] *Canadian Men And Women Of The Time*, Ed. by H.J. Morgan, Briggs, Tor., 1912, P.621
[2] *National Gallery of Canada Catalogue, Vol. 3, Can. School* by R.H. Hubbard, 1960, P.158
[3] as in[1]
[4] *Canada and Its Provinces*, Vol. 12, "Painting" by E.F.B. Johnston, P.627
[5] National Gallery of Canada Information Form rec'd May 20, 1920
[6] *The Montreal Star*, Dec. 10, 1921 "Fine Exhibition By Toronto Painters"
[7] *The Ottawa Journal*, Apr. 19, 1922 "In The Realm Of Art"
[8] *The Fine Arts In Canada* by Newton MacTavish, MacMillan, Tor., 1925, P.143
[9] *The Globe*, Tor., Ont., Oct. 5, 1928 "Brush Is Laid Down By Talented Artist"
  see also
  The MacMillan Dictionary of Canadian Biography, Ed. by W. Stewart Wallace, MacMillan. Tor., 1963, P.373
  Agnes Etherington Art Centre (catalogue) *Permanent Collection*, by Frances K. Smith, Queen's University, 1968.

KNOWLES, Farquhar McGillivray Strachan Stewart
1859-1932

Born in Syracuse, N.Y., of Scottish ancestry, his family returned to Canada around 1863 (4) and he received his early education at Guelph, Ontario. He was raised under the influence of his military grandfather and entered West Point to take an artillery course about 1877.[1] A serious accident during his fourth year brought an end to the possibility of his following a military career. McGillivray Knowles however was more drawn to the arts and after his accident at the academy he got a job retouching photographs for a New York firm and followed art studies also in that city.[2] He returned to Canada and became employed by Messrs. Notman & Fraser, Toronto, and studied miniature painting and water colours under John A. Fraser, R.C.A. co-owner of the firm. Fraser was one of the most accomplished water colourists in Canada at that time, and Knowles soon benefited from his instruction. In 1889 Knowles was elected an Associate of the Royal Canadian Academy, an appointment according to E.J. Hathaway,[3] which was won on his reputation as a water colourist. His first wife Ada Cullen had died in 1887 and in 1890 he married Elizabeth Beach who had studied painting under him. In 1891 they went to Europe. In England he studied under Sir Hubert von Herkomer, R.A., two years, and then went on to Paris where he spent the next four years under the instruction of Benjamin Constant, Jean Paul Laurens, Henri Gervais and Veir Schmidt (in drafting).[4] Returning to Canada the Knowles opened a school of painting, design, ceramics, life classes, where many students received excellent training. Of this period Hathaway[5] wrote, "He was also keenly interested in literature, music, and in his moments of leisure indulged in a passion for carpentry, yachting, motoring, shooting and travel. Some years ago his beautiful studio in Toronto was filled with pictures, rugs, and quaint curios picked up in many parts of the world, and there he and his accomplished wife, herself also a musician and artist . . . kept open house, for they had a wide circle of friends and occupied a prominent place in the social life of the city." In 1916 the Knowles went to New York and lived on his yacht for a year and painted in the harbour of Manhattan. He was then fifty-seven years old. He returned to Toronto but in 1920 he moved with his wife to New York where they took up residence. They returned to Canada often and continued to participate in all the important exhibitions of the time, including the Royal Canadian Academy annuals. He was especially known for his marines, noted, as follows, by E.W.H. of *The Ottawa Citizen*[6] during a showing in that city, "In the United States he has a strong following of those who admire his pictures of the sea. There are a number of these on view at the present exhibition and a few of them represent his highest achievement in this direction. They are all notable for their freedom of movement and authentic atmosphere. One of these is 'Windswept,' a very successful rendering of air, sky and water as the tide begins to ebb on a bright boisterous day. Another is 'Shades of Evening,' which depicts a seaway set against a range of steep and sombre hills. The whitecaps dance and the wind carries the waves before it. It is close of day, and the last rays of the sun strike the summit of the hills in the background while a ghostly schooner runs for home in the shaded lee of the cliffs." By 1928 the Knowles had established a new studio at their summer home in Riverton, New Hampshire, where Elizabeth A. Knowles died the same year. McGillivray Knowles returned to Toronto and in 1931 married Lila Taylor, an artist in her own right, and former student of his. Several years later she became Art Director at Alma College, St. Thomas, Ontario. In 1932 however McGillivray Knowles died. Reviewing briefly his career, the *Mail & Empire*[7] noted, "His 'Titan Bathers' was for many years one of the most notable pictures in the Chicago Art Institute. Land and sea pictures from his brush are to be found in nearly all Toronto's seats of higher education and of his best known portraits might be mentioned those of Sir Robert Falconer, Hon. Chester Massey, Mrs. Timothy Eaton

KNOWLES, Farquhar McGillivray Strachan Stewart (Cont'd)

and Miss Addison. His series 'The History of Music' is in the deaconess home in this city, and the 'Finding of Leander by Hero' has been for years in the Ontario Art Museum." Knowles was survived by his wife Lila Taylor McGillivray Knowles, two brothers William Janes Knowles (Toronto) and Arthur Strachan Knowles (Sydney, Australia); four sisters: Mrs. Ray B. Howilster, Miss Emma and Miss Jessie Knowles (Pasadena, California, U.S.A.) and Mrs. Frank Franklin (Hollywood, Cal.). A Memorial Exhibition of F. McGillivray Knowles took place at The Art Gallery of Toronto in October of 1932.[8] It included paintings, prints, drawings and lithographs. The paintings were assembled from the collections of: Mr & Mrs. Henry Burgoyne (St. Catharines, Ont.); Burwash Hall (Toronto); Mr. & Mrs. Gordon Conn (Toronto); Mr. & Mrs. Walter Clemes (Toronto); Mr. & Mrs. R.J. Dilworth (Toronto); Mrs. Galbreaith (Hamilton, Ont.); Mrs. John Garvin (Toronto); Mrs. R.W. Leonard (St. Catherines, Ont.); Mr. & Mrs. R.S. McLaughlin (Oshawa, Ont.); Col. and Mrs. W.E. Phillips (Oshawa, Ont.); Miss Lorna Reid (Toronto); Mr. & Mrs. A. Ernest Richardson (Toronto); Mrs. H.D. Warren (Toronto); Mr. & Mrs. Van Every (St. Catharines); and many others. Subsequently, exhibitions of his work took place in the years that followed including: Mellors Galleries (Toronto) 1941; The Robert Simpson Co., Ltd. (Simpson's Canadian House of Art, Toronto) 1944, also in this exhibition were paintings by Elizabeth Knowles and Lila C. Knowles; Jerrold Morris International Gallery (Toronto), 1966 (Jerrold Morris' Gallery is now located on Prince Arthur Street, Toronto). He is represented in the National Gallery of Canada[9] by three or more paintings, also the Agnes Etherington Art Centre, Queen's University At Kingston by four canvases.[10]

References

[1] *Saturday Night*, April 16, 1932 "The Late McGillivray Knowles" by Ernest J. Hathaway (submitted after Mr. Hathaway's death and brought up to date by his widow Mrs. Maud S. Hathaway of Toronto)

[2] Ibid

[3] Ibid

[4] Ibid

[5] Ibid

[6] *The Ottawa Citizen*, April 17, 1922 "Exhibition of Paintings" by E.W.H.

[7] *Mail & Empire*, Tor., Ont., "Eminent Artist Taken By Death"

[8] *Catalogue of Memorial Exhibition of F. McGillivray Knowles, R.C.A.* . . . . October, 1932, The Art Gallery of Toronto, Grange Park.

[9] *National Gallery of Catalogue, Vol. 3* by R.H. Hubbard, P.158-9

[10] *Catalogue, The Permanent Collection of Paintings Sculpture & Drawings Agnes Etherington Art Centre Queen's University At Kingston* by Frances K. Smith, 1968

see also

Canadian Men and Women of the Time, Ed. by Henry James Morgan, Tor., 1912, P.621, 622

Canada And Its Provinces, Vol. 12 Toronto, 1914, Painting by E.F.B. Johnston, P.623

The Fine Arts In Canada by Newton MacTavish, 1925, P.134

Canadian Art by Graham McInnes, 1950, P.45

The Macmillan Dictionary of Canadian Biography, Ed. by W. Stewart Wallace, P.373

Canadian Who Was Who, Ed. Charles G.D. Roberts & Arthur L. Tunnell, 1934

KNOWLES, John

b.1932

A Kingston, Ontario, artist who studied under Fred Schonberger and William Muysson in Kingston. His work was described by the *Whig-Standard* as follows, "A

KNOWLES, John (Cont'd)

landscape artist whose soft grey-white canvasses are a striking contrast to today's trend to psycheledic colors . . . . Not only does the 36 – year – old Queen's University faculty member paint 'with pieces of cardboard,' but he also uses a trowel, putty knife and paint scraper. Occasionally, he uses a brush. But it's not the thin, pencil-line type one normally associates with an artist. Knowles uses the household variety in two to four – inch widths." The above note was written during his one man show at the Art-Graphic gallery in Kingston. Dr. John Knowles is a member of the psychology department at Queen's.

Reference

   Whig-Standard, Kingston, Ont., Feb. 3, 1958 "For artist Knowles – Anything's a brush"

KNOWLES, Mrs. Lila McGillivray (nee Lila Caroline Taylor)
b. (c) 1886

She studied under F. McGillivray Knowles at his Bloor Street Studio and at the Central Technical School, Toronto. She became a teacher at Alma College and in 1931 married F. McGillivray Knowles. She continued to teach at Alma College for thirty years and to remain in the community of St. Thomas. Her husband died in 1932. During the summers she made sketching trips to Colpoy's Bay near the Owen Sound area of Ontario and exhibited her work there in 1937.[1] She also exhibited her paintings at The Robert Simpson Company Ltd., Toronto (1944) with the work of F. McGillivray Knowles and Elizabeth Knowles,[2] at Alma College (1946) when the St. Thomas *Times-Journal*[3] noted, "The Canadian scene has a gifted exponent in Mrs. Knowles – not the stark and the bleak and forbidding aspects of the country's landscape (and it has those), but its beauty, its glorious color, its strength, its exquisite and its comfortable, homely aspects. This exhibition of over fifty pictures portrays them in all seasons of the year – comfortable farm homes, winding country roads, orchards in blossom time, the woods in maple sugar time, in deep winter, in summer and in fall, the fields in the ploughing season and at harvest. Many of the pictures have been painted on the shores of Northern Ontario's lovely blue lakes, where silver birches make a fairyland of the scene, and many portray this immediate district. There are several marines also, one large one showing the sea with the fog creeping in towards shore. And there are a number of interesting flower studies, which have their own appeal." She also painted at Cape Breton Island where she did marine studies which were exhibited in 1951 at The Little Gallery, Toronto.[4] Since then she has held a number of exhibitions at her own home in St. Thomas[5] also at the offices of the Ontario Loan and Debenture Company, St. Thomas (1967) when twenty-five of her paintings were exhibited to mark the first anniversary of that company's establishment in the St. Thomas area.[6]

[1] *Sun-Times*, Owen Sound, Ont., Aug. 3, 1937 "Mrs. McGillivray Knowles Sketches at Colpoy's Bay"

[2] Catalogue sheet From Frances Turner, The Robert Simpson Co., Ltd., an art exhibition which opened Nov. 16, 1944, in Simpson's Canadian House.

[3] *Times-Journal*, St. Thomas, Ont., Nov. 19, 1946 "Noteworthy Exhibition by Lila McGillivray Knowles"

[4] *The Evening Telegram*, Toronto, Ont., Mar. 31, 1951 "Her Brush Gives Life To Tumbling Waters" by Rose MacDonald

KNOWLES, Mrs. Lila McGillivray (Cont'd)

[5] *Times-Journal*, St. Thomas, Ont., Nov. 21, 1961 "Local Artist's Exhibit Has Appeal and Beauty"

Ibid, Nov. 7, 1963

[6] Ibid, Dec. 5, 1967 "Local Artist's Paintings Shown Here" (photo of Artist and her work)

KNOWLES, Maida Doris Parlow (Maida Parlow French)
b.1891

Born in Toronto, Ontario, she studied under F. McGillivray Knowles and became his assistant for two years. In 1918 she married Arthur Raymond Knowles of Buffalo, N.Y. After her husband died she settled on a pioneer farm (that had been in her family for generations) with her three sons. There she made her living from the sale of apples grown on the large orchard of the farm. She also wrote: *Boughs Bend Over*, (1944) a best seller in the United States and Canada, of the experiences of her loyalist ancestors in Canada; *All This to Keep* (1947) historical romances set in the early days of settlement in eastern Ontario. She specialized in childrens' portraits which she did mainly in pastels. She was a member of the Heliconian Club (1914) and the Toronto Art Gallery (1924). She was last reported living in Toronto.

References

National Gallery of Canada Information Form

The Gazette, Picton, Ontario, July 12, 1944 "Author of Famous Book Former Art Student Here"

The Oxford Companion to Canadian History and Literature by Norah Story Oxford University Press, Tor., 1967, P.266 (see Maida Parlow French)

KOCH, Jerry

A Mission City, B.C., artist who studied at the Ecole des Beaux Arts, Montreal; the Vancouver School of Art; the San Carlos School of Art, Mexico; and the Institute Allende, Mexico (1960).

Reference

Fraser Valley Record, Mission City, B.C., Aug. 17, 1960 "Local Artist Studying In Mexico"

KOCHANSKI, Vera

b.1928

Born in Oshawa, Ontario, she studied at the Central Technical School, Toronto, under Peter Haworth, Robert Ross, Charles Goldhammer, Doris McCarthy, Dawson Kennedy, Joselyn Taylor and Virginia Luz; also at the summer school of Queen's University, Kingston, Ont. under Carl Schaefer. She won the Jessie Dow prize at the Spring Exhibition, Montreal Museum of Fine Arts in 1951 (for water colours) and worked for the National Film Board, Ottawa, in the Film Strip Unit. No recent information is available on this artist. She was living in Ottawa in 1951.

Reference

National Gallery of Canada Information Form rec'd June 22, 1951

KOCI, Franz

A painter, commercial artist, art teacher, and sign painter who lives at Blairmore, Alberta, on the border of Alberta and British Columbia. He has done a 12 x 24 foot mural on the east side of his house and birds on the south side described by *The Lethbridge Herald Daily* as follows, "The mural done in bright blues, greens, browns and other natural colors is a rendition of abstract art which represents Alberta's wildlife from the mountains to the prairies. The crow seen in the large art work symbolizes the Crowsnest Pass. Lifelike paintings of Canadian birds have been done on a section of the south side of the artist's studio adding greatly to the appearance of the building."

Reference

The Lethbridge Herald Daily, Lethbridge Alta., May 10, 1969 (photo of artist at work on mural)

KODDO, Galina (Mrs.)

b.1916

Born in St. Petersbourg, Russia, she received her early training and encouragement from her father who was an artist. She made sketches of her teachers at school and was soon helping other students with their work during art lessons. Later she enrolled in the Tallinn Art School in Estonia and graduated in 1940. She studied then at Tartu, Estonia, in 1941, when she became acquainted with a Russian artist who influenced her work considerably. She was also influenced by the work of C. Klein, German artist. She came to Canada in 1947 and is a painter of portraits, landscapes, still life studies mainly in realistic style. Her media include oils, water colours, tempera, pastel, chalks and she taught ceramics for the Alberta Government at Jasper, Edson and Calgary. She is a member of the Alberta Society of Artists and lives in Calgary, Alberta.

Source

Document from artist

KOEHLER, Marie

b.1939

Born in Manchester, N.H., U.S.A., she studied at the Tufts University near Boston for three years and then at the Boston Museum School for a year. She came to Canada in 1962 and began serious brush-and-ink genre scenes. By October, 1963, she held her first one man show. At this time she did illustrations for a book of poetry. She also participated in a number of group shows. She illustrated another book of poetry and has had her paintings published in the following journals: *Trace* (U.S.A. & England); *El Corno Emplumado* (Mexico); *Edge* (Canada) and *Alphabet* (Canada). Her work has also been used on the C.B.C. T.V. Last reported she was preparing a portfolio of her drawings for publication in book form. Her work can be seen also at the Sobot Gallery where she has held solo exhibits.

Reference

Information supplied by Sobot Gallery, Toronto.

KOENIG, Kurt

Born in Austria, he studied in Vienna and in Paris and came to Canada in 1954. He studied in Montreal and Toronto and has held solo exhibits in Vancouver, Calgary, Montreal and Toronto. His recent work has been of Canadian Landscapes which includes Ontario scenes.

References

The Daily Sentinel-Review, Woodstock, Ont., March 12, 1968 "Artist Demonstrates For Sketch Club" (photo of artist with other artists at the Ingersoll Public Library)

Banner, Aurora, Ont., April 24, 1968 "Kleinburg showing Koenig paintings"

KOFLER, Ernest H.

Born in Austria, he attended the Academy of Fine Arts in Vienna, and held his first one man show in that city in 1947. He inspired a group of artists to free themselves from dictated art forms which prevailed in his country during the war years. This group became known as the Neuer Hargentbund group. In 1950 he received the Franco-Austrian Cultural Exchange Festival award. He came to Canada and settled in Montreal where he is now Art Director of an advertising agency. His painting (mixed oil and tempera) "Resurgence of Hope" executed in the magic realism form won him a Price Fine Arts Award for 1970. The Price awards were originated in 1965 to encourage Canadian commercial artists with an interest in fine art. "Resurgence of Hope" shows a desolated cityscape in background with a large ravine-like crack in the earth presumably made from a nuclear bomb blast, diagonally cutting its way through the centre of the composition with a survivor standing in the foreground in tattered trousers with his hand resting gently on a surviving plant. Behind him in the ravine are three huddled naked figures (two adults and a child) with only their backs showing, a short distance away from them in the ravine is another limp naked figure. Kofler seems to have used himself as a model for the lone standing figure, as he might appear after such a disaster. The Price Group of Companies have made a vital contribution to Canadian art in encouraging artists of the caliber of Ernest Kofler.

Reference

Price fine art awards 1970 (catalogue) and viewing of the sixteen works on exhibit at the Montreal Museum of Fine Arts

KOHLUND, Hans

Born in Freiburg, S.W. Germany, he studied music and acting in Berlin. He came to Canada in 1952 and joined the CBC TV station where he produced many short films and documentaries. He has been teaching Animation and Television Graphic Production at the Ontario College of Art since 1962 and in recent years has turned to full time teaching. He has also appeared in numerous recitals and CBC broadcasts as lutenist and harpsichordist. He lives at Don Mills, Ontario.

Reference

Glenhurst Arts Council, 1969 Summer Program

Ontario College of Art folder on Careers & programs calendar year 1967-68

KOHUSKA, Helen

b.1929

Born at Sioux Lookout, Ontario, she studied at the Winnipeg School of Art under Joseph Plaskett, William McCloy and others also at the Banff School of Fine Arts under Frederic Taubes. She won a Banff School Scholarship and other prizes. She is a member of the Winnipeg Sketch Club, Winnipeg Art League (Pres. 1951) and the Contemporary Arts Society. Last reported (1951) she was working in her own studio in the Music and Arts Building in Winnipeg.

Reference
> National Gallery of Canada Information Form rec'd Aug. 20, 1951

KOLAUT, Pacome

(c) 1926-1968

An Eskimo carver, he was a top notch hunter and was officially recognized in his community as a hunt leader. He married and had several children. In 1963 when the Co-Operative of Igloolik was founded he was elected its first president. He became a fine carver and is represented by his "Bear Hunt" in the collection of the National Museums of Canada. He died in 1968 when transporting with two other drivers, two D-8 Caterpillar tractors and an earth-moving scraper over 150 miles of land and ice from Bray Island to Igloolik. When only twelve miles from Igloolik the ice opened and his tractor slid backwards into 35'of water and he was drowned.

Reference
> *North*, September-October, 1968, pub. by Dept. Northern Affairs and National Resources, Ottawa, "Pacome Kolaut And The Igloolik Co-Operative" by Frans Van der Velde, P.33 (Fr. Van der Velde is an Oblate Missionary in the Canadian Arctic)

KOLISNYK, Peter Henry

b.1934

Born in Toronto, Ontario, he studied at the Western Technical School under Julius Griffith, G. Griffin, M. Aiken, F. Fraser and at the Ontario College of Art, evenings, under Carl Schaefer in the study of water colours.[1] He has travelled in Europe and Mexico and has taught art at Belleville, Elliot Lake and at Cobourg where he now has his studio on the outskirts. He has exhibited his plexiglas sculpture at the Pollock Gallery, Toronto. Describing his work in this regard Kay Kritzwiser of the *Globe & Mail*[2] explained, "His line is concerned with the refraction of space. On the cold shine of a freshly painted white floor and against white walls, the sheets of bronzy plexiglas stand, cut, polished by heat and glued with comb-like precision. But any movement back and forth beside them is fractured into vigorous movement, while the piece itself sets up exquisite pattern." Kolisnyk won a $3,000 award for one of his two sculptures entered in the Canadian Artists 1968 competition held at the Art Gallery of Ontario.[3] Twenty of his constructions were exhibited in a one man show at the Pollock Gallery in March of 1968, May (1969). He is represented in the collection of the Art Gallery of Ontario, the Sifton Construction Company of London, Ontario, and elsewhere. He is a member of the Canadian Society of Painters in Water Colour, and was the winner of their award in 1962.

KOLISNYK, Peter Henry (Cont'd)

References

[1] National Gallery of Canada Information Form rec'd August, 1956
  The Intelligencer, Belleville, Ontario, "Toronto Man To Teach Art In Belleville'
[2] *The Globe & Mail*, Tor., Ont., April 26, 1969 "The games Kolisnyk's light plays" by Kay Kritzwiser
[3] *The Cobourg Sentinel Star*, Cobourg, Ont. "Local Sculpture Brings $3,000.00"
  see also
  The Fourth Biennial Exhibition of Canadian Art 1961 (Catalogue) NGC No. 37
  The Pollock Gallery (Catalogue) The P.G., 599 Markham St., Tor. 4, Ont. (photo of Kolisnyk and his Plexiglas work)
  Standard, Elliot Lake, Ont., May 11, 1966 "Top Canadian Artists Signed to Teach Here"
  The Cobourg Sentinel Star, Cobourg, Ont., Nov. 20, 1968 "Canada Wide Competition Includes Local Art Pieces"
  The Evening Guide, Port Hope, Ont., Mar. 28, 1968 "Art Gallery Buys Three Local Works"
  Chronicle, Colborne, Ont., May 1, 1969 "Refractors In Toronto Gallery Foresee The Art Of Tomorrow"
  The Cobourg Sentinel Star, Cobourg, Ont. May 28, 1969 "Kolisnyk Refuses Job As Art Gallery Curator"
  Arts/Canada, October/November, 1968, No. 122/123 Exhibition Reviews − Toronto − by Gary Michael Dault

---

KONTSKI, Stefan

b. (c) 1898

Born in Poland he studied in Cracow, also in Florence and Paris. In 1939 he fled to England where he joined to Polish Free Army.[1] Before the war he had been assistant curator of art in Florence where he had worked on the restoration of the world's most famous frescoes. In 1933 he was one of the scientists who rediscovered the exact Moorish process for Cordovan leathercraft.[2] He came to Canada in 1948 and lived in Ottawa where he taught painting to children. It was there that he held a one man show of his paintings at the Little Gallery on Sparks Street. Viewing the work Carl Weiselberger of *The Ottawa Citizen*[3] noted, "In most of Mr. Kontski's canvasses the paint is applied in thick brush strokes, which give to many objects, particularly treetops, an aspect of solidity and firm texture in spite of their fanciful, unrealistic, distinctly French treatment. Some of these landscapes have the effect of colorful designs and sketches rather than naturalistic portrayals, for instance 'Trapped Logs, Ottawa River,' and the skies over such stylized scenes, handled in luminous blue, violet, arched strokes are obviously influenced by the hot, sensuous skies of Van Gogh.' It is interesting to note here that Kontski had no prices listed for his paintings in the exhibition catalogues.[4] He went to Montreal in 1950 on the invitation of Father F.R. Bernard of St. Mary's Polish Church in the east end of Montreal. John Ayer[5] writing about Kontski at St. Mary's explained, "He doesn't want a car, an eight-hour-day or a refrigerator. He never goes to the movies and he's quite content to wear an old suit of clothes. In fact, Konski spends most of his time in a church − St. Mary's Church, in Montreal's east end. There, for less than a skilled house-painter's wage, he paints the traditional masterpieces which brought him fame and fortune in his native Poland. Unmarried and living in a small room, the 54-year-old immigrant has spent two years on his task to date. Working far into the night, he thinks only of his art. Meals, which he eats with the parish priest, are hurried, 15 minute affairs. At dawn he sits on his bed making rough sketches for the coming day's work." Stanley Twardy in *Mayfair*[6] described the work as follows,

KONTSKI, Stefan (Cont'd)

" . . . Kontski has fervently and happily converted the bare walls of St. Mary's (together with the ceiling, pillars and all other surfaces) into a wondrous gallery of Biblical and Polish Roman Catholic religious history. Along with his luminous frescoes, Kontski is decorating the church with an art form that is unique — cordovan leatherwork. The technique of sculpture in calfskin, lost when the Moors were driven out of Spain, had been rediscovered by Kontski and a team of colleagues. Unfortunately for Kontski's wish to live and work like a hermit, the unique nature of his work brings more and more visitors and tourists to the church every year." In his fresco work Kontski used paint of an ancient formula which he believes will remain bright for a thousand years. While in Quebec Kontski inspected and cared for the Polish art treasures brought to Canada for safekeeping when Hitler invaded Poland. After completing the work in St. Mary's Church, he left for Long Island, New York where he was to decorate St. Adalbert Church.[8] No recent information is available on this artist.

References
[1] *The Gazette*, Mtl., P.Q., Mar. 1, 1952 "Beautifying Church Brings Painter Rare Contentment" by John Ayer (photo of artist at work on mural)
[2] *The Montreal Star*, Jan. 24, 1953 "Two-year Church Fresco Task Completed by Polish Artist" (photo of finished altar)
[3] *The Ottawa Citizen*, April 26, 1949 "Color Freshness Features Kontski's Paintings" by Carl Weiselberger
[4] Catalogue — *Exhibition: Oil Paintings by Stefan Kontski* at the Little Gallery — Photographic Stores, Limited, 65 Sparks St., Ottawa. April 25 – 30, 1949
[5] see[1]
[6] *Mayfair*, March, 1955 "Polish Painter-in-exile   creates medieval art in Montreal" by Stanley Twardy
[7] *Globe & Mail*, Tor., Ont., Jan. 26, 1953, "Polish Artist Ends Two-Year Task In Montreal Church"
[8] Ibid, see[2] also

KOOCHIN, William

b.1927

Born in Brilliant, B.C., he studied at the Vancouver School of Art between 1949 and 1951.[1] He joined the design department of the CBC television studio in Vancouver where he worked until his departure for France in 1955.[2] In Paris he studied drawing at the Grande Chaumière and worked in the centuries-old government-operated Manufacture de Sèvres, producer of fine porcelain, china, enamel ware and ceramics. In this factory he studied ceramic sculpture. He also travelled through Europe, returned to Paris and then arrived back in Canada in 1957. By 1958 he was creating metal sculpture with a welding torch. He produced three huge sculptures for the Canadian Pavilion at the Brussels International Exposition (a huge 18 foot high welded steel figure "Industrial Worker" for the manufacturing section, and two 9 foot high welded metal figures "Ballet Dancers" for the ballet and music section). A one man show of his work took place the same year at Galerie Agnes Lefort when Dorothy Pfeiffer[4] noted, " . . . from Mr. Koochin's welded birds one derives a feeling of optimism and strength as well as a sensation of almost overpowering and opulent majesty . . . in the figure of a young women standing with upraised arms and with delicate claw-like fingers gathers her wiry black hair into a chignon. The figure's arms, hands, fingers and legs are of rather roughcast steel cleverly contrasted to the body which is seductively modelled by a garment of

KOOCHIN, William (Cont'd)

finely-welded links outlining its form like a tightly-fitted gown or crocheted silk lamé. The two deceptively simple terra cotta heads might have been dug from the ruins of ancient Pompeii yet also are completely present day in feeling." Koochin was living in Ottawa during this period and worked on his welded steel creations in a garage. In the years that followed he returned to Vancouver and held one man shows in Toronto, Vancouver and Victoria. He also worked in the mediums of enamels, mosaics, terra-cotta, wood, and exhibited his drawings and woodcuts in the above cities. His subjects have been derived from bird forms, the human figure and animals in a style which he describes as 'realist-expressionist.' He taught sculpture at the University of British Columbia in 1962 and is now an instructor of design at the Vancouver School of Art. His sculpture has been exhibited at The New Design Gallery, Vancouver, The Vancouver Art Gallery, and in the Centennial Sculpture 67 show held at the Queen Elizabeth Theatre, Vancouver (arranged by the Federation of Canadian Artists and financed by Rothmans of Pall Mall Canada Ltd.). William Koochin is represented in the collections of the Vancouver Art Gallery, the University of Oregon Museum of Art, and elsewhere. He is a member of the British Columbia Society of Artists, and lives in West Vancouver, B.C., with his wife and children.

References

[1] Document from artist

[2] *Trail Daily Times*, Trail, B.C., Jan. 25, 1957 "Doukhobor Sculptor Returns From Paris"

[3] *Canadian Art*, Vol. 15, No. 3, Aug. 1958 "Designing the Exhibits: A Three-year Project" by T.C. Wood, P.181

[4] *The Gazette*, May 17, 1958 "Braised Brass And Welded Steel" by Dorothy Pfeiffer

see also

The Montreal Star, May (?), 1958 Art Notes "The Inevitability of Koochin" by Robert Ayre

Western Homes & Living, Van., B.C., Feb., 1964 B.C. Artists "Bill Koochin, Sculptor"

KOPMANIS, Augusts Arnolds

b.1910

Born at Riga, Latvia, he did small wood carvings, drawings and oil paintings as a boy of sixteen. His interest in art grew and he visited many galleries and attended exhibitions and in 1930 began wood carving classes which he attended for the next two years.[1] In 1933 he worked as an assistant to the Latvian sculptor, K. Zemdega. He then studied at the Academy of Fine Arts at Riga, 1938-44, when he became particularly interested in the work of French sculptors Maillol and Bourdelle and he tried to express himself in the unity of concepts from both of these famous artists.[2] Later he was most impressed with the work of Carl Milles a Swedish sculptor.[3] He began with idealized realistic figures and moved towards stylization and finally semi abstract presentations. Kopmanis came to Canada from England in 1951 and settled in Toronto. He was elected member of the Colour and Form Artists' Society in 1952 (Vice-Pres. 1959, 1960). By 1957 he was a Canadian citizen.[4] In this year he had received Honourable Mention in the Winnipeg Show for his sculptured 'Torso'. He was elected a member of the Sculptors' Society of Canada in 1958 and the next year he held his first one man show at the Upstairs Gallery, Toronto, of seventeen pieces of sculpture, noted by Colin Sabiston[5] of the *Globe & Mail* as follows, "He works in stone of all types, wood, modelled casts, hammered copper — any medium

KOPMANIS, Augusts Arnolds (Cont'd)

appropriate to his purpose. In all media his pieces are superbly conceived and finished, and each intelligibly conveys its message, whether derived from Norse or other mythologies, presents a single figure or group executed in a single piece, has a humorous purpose, or is designed primarily for decorative qualities . . . . Pieces derived from Norse mythology are from both the Sagas of the Gods and those of the Kings. They are strikingly effective. A simplified, modern type Torso, carved in wood, is very different, but equally expressive. His small 'In A Hurry' is an abstract figure suggesting headlong flight, clean, lean, dynamic. 'Surprised Bathers' shows children trying to hide in the folds of their mother's skirts. 'Fisherman' (purchased anonymously for the International Institute), is a small portrait like figure requiring no title . . . . There are other items of varied appeal, but the only real disappointment in the exhibition is the limited number of pieces." In 1961 he held another solo exhibit at the Upstairs Gallery;[6] at Huntsville in 1964 at the Copper Lantern;[7] in Montreal, Winnipeg, St. Catherines and Hamilton, and elsewhere. Among his other honours he received, Life Fellow, International Institute of Arts & Letters (Swiss Inc.) (1960); Government of Canada honourable mention for his new design of the 1964 Commemorative Dollar (1963). He has done many monuments, tombstones and decorative sculpture for buildings also portraits, statues and medals. His work has been exhibited with the Royal Canadian Academy, Sculptors' Society of Canada, and the Ontario Society of Artists and in many other exhibitions throughout Canada. He lives in Toronto with his wife and family in his combined studio and residence.

References

[1] Document from artist
[2] Ibid
[3] Ibid
[4] National Gallery of Canada Information Form rec'd Aug. 17, 1965
[5] *Globe & Mail*, Tor., Ont., April 11, 1959 "Kopmanis Sculptures Superbly Conceived" by Colin Sabiston
[6] Ibid, April 1, 1961 "Welded Works – Metal Artists Show Lyric, Epic in Styles"
[7] *Huntsville Forester*, Huntsville, Ont., Aug. 13, 1964 "To Exhibit Sculpture Here"
see also
Who's Who in American Art (Canadian Section)
The Canadian Who's Who
International Art Directory, IKA, Dessauer Strasse 6-7, Berlin 61, Germany
Royal Canadian Academy Of Arts 87th Annual Exhibition Catalogue, 1966 No. 80

KORNER, John Michael Anthony
b.1913

Born in Nový Jicín, Czechoslovakia, he had an early interest in art. Later he studied under Fritz Kausek in Prague (1931-34) and under Othon Friesz, Victor Tischler and Paul Colin in Paris (1938-39) and also studied the history and philosophy of art at the Sorbonne.[1] He came to Canada in 1939 and settled in Vancouver, B.C., and became a Canadian citizen in 1944.[2] He exhibited his oil paintings and water colours not long after he settled in Canada. In his painting he did representational work for many years and through a process of exploration became interested in abstract concepts. At first he was influenced by the work of Paul Klee, then Bonnard and Goya. In 1954 Colin Graham[4] noted of his work, " . . . When Mr.

KORNER, John Michael Anthony (Cont'd)

Korner paints a picture . . . he deliberately 'discovers' his picture on the canvas as he goes along. One shape leads to another, one intuition to the next. To allow a particular form or shape to be freighted with meaning on a number of levels, reaching down perhaps toward the last accessible strata of the mind, he depicts it through metaphor, allusion, or analogy, ... " During those early years in Vancouver he exhibited his paintings at the Kelly Galleries and the Victoria Art Centre and was also busy creating murals for homes in West Vancouver. By 1956 The Vancouver Art Gallery was holding a one man show of his paintings and drawings which were described by Palette[5] of *The Province* as follows, "His work is distinctive, thoughtful and poetic. Mr. Korner makes liberal use of his imagination in his 24 paintings and does not confine himself entirely to any specific place or time. However, British Columbia has apparently inspired him and especially Vancouver and its lofty buildings, with reflections along the waterfront." Impressed with this same show Mildred Thornton[6] of *The Vancouver Sun* noted, "Shimmering light and color is seen in glistening sails, richly colored logs, boats and buildings in a fine panoramic canvas called 'Island Passage.' Monumental compositions built on block-like patterns are the basis for several city scenes. Some are in warm tones of yellow, red and brown. Others equally effective, are in cool, mysterious blues and greens. All are full of curious inner vitality." In 1959 he held his first one man show at Laing's[7] and six months later he participated in a three man show at this same Gallery with Jack Shadbolt, and Gordon Smith. Pearl McCarthy[8] noted, "New paintings by John Korner form an important group in the showing of three Vancouver artists . . . now at the Laing Gallery. There are only four of these new Korners, all nocturnes, but every one of them is a distinguished autographic piece, as different from his former canvases as they are from the world's myriad often repetitive landscape abstractions." Many one man shows followed for Korner. He was one of twenty-one artists reviewed by *Canadian Art* in the Spring of 1962 when Abraham Rogatnick[9] noted his transition as follows, "John Korner was creating panoramas of remembered impressions of the cities of his European youth: Prague, Geneva, Paris. These soon merged with the mountains, trees and water of his West Coast adulthood; and, with the facing of the past, the overwhelming pressure of the British Columbia landscape brought a flood of canvases revealing a hypnotic obsession with the theme of a land mass floating in water, and backed by misty, hovering mountains expressed in small, orderly planes of colour. Korner was now irrevocably a British Columbia painter. He had completely absorbed the new world around him, and it had absorbed him. From a montage type of composition, representing glimpses of the specific surrounding landscape, he moved gradually through abstract impressions of remembered landscapes, such as 'Coast Glitter (30)', until now he has become intrigued, not with the memory of land, water and mountain, but with the direct expression of a kind of landscape of mood, a landscape of the soul which he calls 'Inscapes,' . . . . Like the neatness of his back-of-the-house studio in its suburban setting, a great deal of control and structuring has always dominated his technique, from the Cézannesque planar discipline of his earlier compositions, to the small-stroked, embroidered quality of his 'Coast Glitter' series. Even in 'Freescape', which is related to the Inscape series, the 'freeness' of the idea is restrained by the parallel planes of colour, whose regularized rectangles emphasize the surprising sauciness of the one or two planes which dance away from the dominant axis." His solo exhibit in Montreal at Galerie Agnes Lefort in 1964 was noted by Dorothy Pfeiffer[10] as follows, "Beneath the relaxed manner of

KORNER, John Michael Anthony (Cont'd)

Korner's technique lies carefully thought-out form and structure. Korner's paintings do not fall apart, as do so many other contemporary semi-abstractions. The longer one looks at Korner's works the more solidly built do they appear. . . . A contrast is provided by 'Burrard Inlet in 1872', a wintry reflection on those days when life was reduced to elementals. In this painting Korner has left portions of his primed canvas unpainted, a device which adds considerably to the lonely coldness of the dock-side painting." David Watmough[11] noted surrealistic tendencies in his work in 1966 as follows, "Ostensibly we have a combination of oil and restricted collage – but the esthetic and metaphysical truth of these canvases is remote from a mere technical agility. By integrating small-scale realistic images of such things as flowers from seed packets, cauliflowers, fruit, etc., into an overall painterly commentary or interpretation of garden life, the surrealistic tenor is made known. The results are not only impressive but emerge as some of Korner's most successful work to date . . . . But with such minor exceptions this new Korner show triumphantly espouses the incorporation of a variety of novel trends – from hard edge to surrealism. All of it though inhabits the context of that pervasive European sensibility which hangs about Korner's oeuvre in the manner of a subtle mist which even the harshest winds of contemporaneity cannot blow away." His metal mural "Star of Hope" constructed from anodized aluminum and measuring 28 feet by 16 feet, completed for the Cowichan District Hospital at Duncan, B.C., was described by Joan Lowndes[12] as follows, "In the daytime the trees around filter the light, creating a constant play on the sparkling surface of the Star against its soft blue tile wall." She went on to explain, " . . . a gentle yellow light shines through quarter of an inch perforations which prick out shapes like snowflakes in the central disc, rimmed with two neon tubes . . . . The actual production of the mural took only six weeks. It was manufactured by Ted Scroggs, of Scroggs and Associates, Designers, illustrating the new alliance between studio and factory. The Star, beautifully proportioned, is simple yet effective, and achieves the purpose . . . of mitigating institutionalism." A retrospective of his work was held at the Douglas Gallery in 1968 which followed a solo exhibit he had held there the year before.[13] Korner continues to explore new concepts in his work. He is represented in the following collections: National Gallery of Canada; Art Gallery of Ontario; The Montreal Museum of Fine Arts; Musée d'Art Contemporain, Montreal; London Public Library and Art Museum, London, Ontario; Art Gallery of Victoria, B.C.; Vancouver Art Gallery; Winnipeg Art Gallery; Edmonton Art Gallery; Seattle Art Museum, Seattle, Wash., U.S.A., Hart House, U. of T., Tor.; Agnes Etherington Art Centre, Kingston, Ont.; Willistead Art Gallery of Windsor, Ont.; Lord Beaverbrook Museum, Fredericton, N.B.; Government House, Victoria, B.C.; Municipality of Burnaby, B.C.; Department of External Affairs; University of British Columbia (four collections) and in many other collections including The C.I.L., Montreal; The Royal Bank of Canada, Tor.; The Readers' Digest, Tor., Ont. He has done murals in the homes or offices of the following in Vancouver; R.J. Young; D.H. Simpson; Radio Station C.H.Q.M.; H.B. MacDonald and others. He won prizes at The Winnipeg Show (1955, 1957, 1961), Burnaby Show (1958); British Columbia Centennial Award (1958); Vancouver Art Gallery (1959). He is a member of the following societies: Canadian Group of Painters (Vice-Pres. 1959-60); B.C. Society of Artists (Pres. 1956-58); Associate of the Royal Canadian Academy (1960); Vancouver Art Gallery (Council Member 1955-60). His work may be seen at the galleries of the following art dealers: Jerrold Morris Gallery, Toronto; Seligman Gallery, Seattle; New Design Gallery, Vancouver.

KORNER, John Michael Anthony (Cont'd)

References
[1] Document from artist
[2] Information sheet from Galerie Agnes Lefort (Galerie Godard Lefort)
[3] Document as in[1]
[4] *Times*, Victoria, B.C., June 26, 1954 "Art in Review" by Colin Graham
[5] *The Province*, Van., B.C., Nov. 9, 1956 "Korner's paintings excellent" by Palette
[6] *The Vancouver Sun*, Van., B.C., Nov. 10, 1956 "Shimmering Light, Color In Show" by Mildred Valley Thornton
[7] *Globe & Mail*, Feb. 21, 1959 "Abstracts by Korner Delightful" by Pearl McCarthy
[8] Ibid, Aug. 15, 1959 "Four New Paintings By Korner on View" Pearl McCarthy
[9] *Canadian Art*, Vol. 19, No. 2 "A Survey Of The Work Of 21 More Canadian Artists" John Korner by Abraham Rogatnick, P.134-5
[10] *The Gazette*, Montreal, P.Q., Mar. 7, 1964 "Korner At Galerie Lefort" by Dorothy Pfeiffer
[11] *The Vancouver Sun*, Feb. 4, 1966 "Surrealist Re-Emergence Stressed at Art Show" by David Watmough
[12] *The Province*, Van., B.C., Oct. 23, 1967 "Star of Hope – a dramatic light mural from John Korner" by Joan Lowndes
[13] Ibid, Dec. 15, 1967 "Korner – shows quiet brushwork" by Joan Lowndes
The Vancouver Sun, Sept. 27, 1968 "Exhibition Offers No Challenge" by Ann Rosenberg
see also
National Gallery of Canada Catalogue, Vol. 3, Can. School by R.H. Hubbard P.159-160
Painting In Canada/A History by J. Russell Harper, U. of T. Press, P.398
Agnes Etherington Art Centre, Queen's University At Kingston (catalogue) by Mrs. Frances K. Smith, No. 74

KORTT, Mikola

Born in Poland he left there with his wife after the Second World War and settled for a time in Australia. He came to Canada about 1956 and lived first in Toronto and then at Paisley, Ontario, in 1961. A wood carver he lives with his wife in the old Presbyterian manse on the edge of the town. Describing his studio Michael Keating of the Owen Sound *Sun-Times* explained, "One of his first touches in the former home for ministers was a mural, a gift to his wife celebrating her 'name day' and the flight of the Telestar communication satellite. By the tradition of the Polish Orthodox church Olga was named after a saint and she celebrates the day of her patron saint rather than the actual anniversary of her birth . . . . The studio is a forest of animals. Tall herons' beaks project above carved fish dorsals and the heads of deer and squirrels . . . . He starts each carving by examining the grain of the piece of cedar or walnut to decide what kind of animal it will become and what pose its wooden body will finally take. Saw, sanding disc, file and sandpaper join the traditional knives on the workbench to speed the tedious task of roughing out the figures. When a figure attains its shape under his hands, Mr. Kortt usually deliberately burns it. The burning is a careful process under the guided flame of a butane torch that first blackens the hard grain for a contrast of light and dark then eats away the soft grain if the flame plays across it long enough. With the smooth lines of the shape the flames turn the grain into fluted channels and whorls."

Reference
Sun-Times, Owen Sound, Ont., Feb. 19, 1966 "Paisley Artist Mikola Kortt Finds Good Market For His Stylized Animal Carvings" by Michael Keating

KOSEBA, Eddy

A Sault Ste. Marie, Ontario, artist who studied drawing and painting, two years at the Ontario College of Art (1956-58). He completed a large mural at St. Mary's College for a backdrop for the regular gatherings of the Centennial Hoedown Club. He has been working in poly-vinyl-acetates and as a result his paintings have great brilliance. In his early painting Koseba was influenced by the work of the Group of Seven, then the Impressionists — especially the work of Van Gogh. To-day he is concerned with portraying people in their daily activities although he has done paintings on religious themes, floral studies, all of which have the luminosity of stained glass. He held a joint exhibition with Ken MacDougall and Stan Miller in Sault Ste. Marie in 1960. No recent information has been received on this artist.

References
  Star, Sault Ste. Marie, Ont., April 24, 1959 "Using New Mediums" by Gwen Keatley
  Ibid, Jan. 20, 1960 "Koseba Has Completed Hoedown Mural" by Gwen Keatley
  Ibid, Aug. 4, 1960 "Art Exhibit Downtown" (photo of Koseba's "Apple Blossoms")

KOST, Robert Theodore
b.1936

Born in Lac Du Bonnet, Manitoba, he began painting in 1956 and has produced well over three hundred works. Maggie Hood[1] of the Winnipeg *Tribune* viewing his 1966 solo exhibit at The Bay in Winnipeg described his paintings as follows, "The works are a panorama of the Bird River and White-shell areas, gurgling falls, towering pines, contoured rocks, feathery sumac fronds, beaver dams, log cabins and log piles, snowdrifts, quiet lakes in seasonal moods and phases. Every one will have familiar overtones for any cottager, fisher, hunter, or camper who has spent time in the beautiful districts." He has exhibited his paintings at The Bay, and the Centennial Concert Hall, in Winnipeg. Kost has also had his paintings exhibited with the Manitoba Society of Artists. His paintings are on view all year round at his home at Lac Du Bonnet, Manitoba.

References
  [1] *The Tribune*, Winnipeg, Man., "His world is the wilderness" by Maggie Hood
  Springfield Leader, Lac Du Bonnet, Man., "Lac du Bonnet Artist Displays Paintings"
  Free Press, Winnipeg, Man., May 1, 1969 (large photo of artist with his work)
  Ibid, May 3, 1969 "Took Up Painting As A Hobby, Now It Provides His Livelihood"
  The Bay Presents Robert T. Kost (biography and list of paintings)
  National Gallery of Canada Information Form rec'd 21 June, 1966

KOSTYNIUK, Ronald Peter
b.1941

Born in Saskatchewan, he studied at the University of Saskatchewan under Eli Bornstein and at the University of Alberta. A structurist artist he has been creating structurist relief studies which he has exhibited at the Museum of Contemporary Arts in Chicago; the Herron Museum in Indianapolis; the Cranbrook Academy in Bloomfield Hills; the High Museum, Atlanta; Allied Art Centre. Brandon, Man.,

KOSTYNIUK, Ronald Peter (Cont'd)

1966; University of Manitoba, 1967; Lindfield College, McMinnville, Oregon, 1967; Kazimir Gallery, Chicago, 1967; Alberta Society of Artists Group show, 1967-68 (Calgary and Edmonton); Seventh Biennial of Canadian Painting at the National Gallery of Canada, 1968. He is represented in the permanent collection of the University of Manitoba and his work has appeared in the following publications: *The Structurist*, *Art Scene*, *Chicago Omnibus*. He lives in Edmonton, Alberta and is a member of the Alberta Society of Artists. He received a Canada Council Grant in 1969 to study at the Museum of Contemporary Arts, Chicago.

References

The Brandon Sun, Brandon, Man., Sept. 6, 1967 "Young Sculptor Attends Exhibit"
Ibid, Sept. 11, 1967 "Saskatoon Sculptor Finds Eager Audience In Brandon" by Kaye Rowe
Ibid, May 1, 1968 "People-Watching" by Kaye Rowe
Recorder, Wakaw, Sask., May 1, 1969 "$4000 Bursary To Ronald Kostyniuk"
The Structurist, No. 7, 1967, P.42, 43, 50
Seventh Biennial of Canadian Painting (Catalogue), 1968, P.62

KOUSAL, Matthew F.

Born in Czechoslovakia, he studied art there and came to Canada about 1927. He settled with his wife at Chatham where they farmed. Later they moved to Bridgeport and Mr. Kousal became known for his paintings and opened a school of art where he now teaches about 75 students. During one of his exhibitions at Bridgeport in 1958 the St. Thomas *Times-Journal* noted, "Mr. Kousal's seascapes are particularly good. The detail in the pictures is so accurate that many of the settings are quickly recognized by those who have actually been there. One picture made from a sketch of a spot near Peggy's Cove on the Atlantic coast is easily recognized. Many of Mr. Kousal's paintings are of Northern Ontario, and in them he has captured the rugged beauty of that country."

References

[1] *Times-Journal*, St. Thomas, Ont., Oct. 10, 1958 "Work of Bridgeport Artist Shown Here"
see also
News, Chatham, Ont., June 23, 1966 (Photo of artist's work)
Ibid, Mar. 17, 1967 "Famed Kousal Landscapes Being Displayed Tuesday"

KOVACH, Rudy
b.1929

Born in Yugoslavia, he came to Canada in 1938 and settled at Port Alberni, B.C.. He studied at the Vancouver School of Art, 1949-53 under Jack Shadbolt, Orville Fisher and others. He is a member of the Canadian Society of Graphic Art (1958); The Society of Canadian Painter-Etchers and Engravers (1953) and an Associate of the B.C. Society of Artists (1953).

Reference

National Gallery of Canada Information Form rec'd April 12, 1954

KOWAL, Ivan

Born in the Ukraine, he studied at the Institute of Art in L'vov (1942). From 1945 to 1948 he studied painting and sculpture in Munich, Germany. He came to Canada in 1948. He is recognized for his stained glass work, ceramics, sculpture, and paintings. He held his first one man show of his paintings and sculpture sponsored by Alpha Omega University of Manitoba graduates of Ukranian descent at the Ukrainian National Federation auditorium in Winnipeg, December of 1967. This show was also seen at the Public Library at East Kildonan, Manitoba.

References
Free Press, Winnipeg, Man., Nov. 29, 1967 "Roman Kowal Art Showing Opens Sunday"
Tribune, Winnipeg, Man., Dec. 1, 1967 "Ivan Kowal one man show"

KRAVJANSKY, Mikulas

Born in Czechoslovakia, he came to Canada in 1968. He created scenery for television and theatre productions in Bratislava. He was also chairman of the Slovak Art Union in that city. He was well known throughout Europe for his stagings of opera and dramatic presentations which included ancient and contemporary classics. He now lives in Toronto where he has exhibited his work several times.

References
Toronto Daily Star, Tor., Ont. "Czech artists show us talents" by Lotta Dempsey
News, Scarborough, Ont., June 5, 1969 "Public Art Preview" (a one man show of Kravjansky's work at the Scarborough Public Library)

KREYES, Marielouise (Mrs.) (nee Bodewein)
b.1925

Born in Lobberich, West Germany, she came to Canada in 1951 and by 1957 was a Canadian citizen. She studied at the University of Manitoba, School of Fine Arts, 1959-63, under Professors Swinton, Bjeljac, Eyre, Bruce, Williams and she was awarded her diploma in art in 1963. She held one man shows at the Albert White Galleries, Toronto (1965) and the Yellow Door Gallery, Winnipeg (1965). She exhibited in the Second Annual McLaren Acquisition Show (Winnipeg, 1966) and the Travelling Show of the Manitoba Society of Artists (1967). She won the Gold Medal and Grand Prix Du Salon International de Vichy (France) 1961 and an Award in Sculpture from the University of Manitoba in 1960. She lives in Selkirk, Manitoba.

Reference
National Gallery of Canada Information Form rec'd April, 1969

KRIEGHOFF, Cornelius David
1815-1872

Born in Amsterdam, Holland, the son of Johann Ernst Krieghoff (b.Uphoven, Germany) and Isabella Ludivica Wauters (b.Ghent, Belgium). His father, Johann, met Isabella in the city of Amsterdam, Holland, and they married May 12, 1811.[1] They had four children: Frederika Louisa (b.1811); Charlotta Sophia (b.1813); Cornelius David (b.1815) and Johann Ernst (b.1820).[2] The Krieghoffs moved to Dusseldorf sometime between 1815 and 1820 where Cornelius' father operated a carpet factory.[3] In 1822 they moved again, this time to Mainburg near Schweinfurt where Johann again established a carpet factory.[4] Later he was able to send his son Cornelius to university in Dusseldorf and Rotterdam where Cornelius studied botany, music and painting.[5] His son then earned his way through Europe as an itinerant musician and craftsman.[6] In 1837 Cornelius arrived in New York and joined the United States Army on July 5th of that year. He was assigned to Battery 1, 1st United States Artillery, with which unit he served until May 5, 1840.[7] We learn from his grand-nephew, William Krieghoff, an artist and illustrator with the *New York Herald* staff, in a letter to G.M. Fairchild,[8] that his grand-uncle served in Florida as follows, "The Seminole war breaking out he joined the U.S. army in order to observe and record the events of that sanguinary conflict in the Everglades of Florida. He made several hundreds of drawings and the U.S. Government commissioned him to make replicas of them for the War Department Archives, which he did in his studio at Rochester, New York, where he resided for several years." After being discharged from his unit May 5, 1840 at Burlington, Vermont, following three years' service, he re-enlisted, then deserted all on the same day.[9] Marius Barbeau[10] offered this explanation for Krieghoff's action, "We may surmise that Louise (Gauthier) had something to do with his need for freedom. For a little daughter, Emily, was born to them some time before March, 1841." He had met Louise Gauthier dit Saint-Germain, at a hotel in which he was staying in New York shortly after his arrival in United States. They must have kept in touch with one another or have even been married while he was in the army. His marriage might not have been recorded in the army records. His decision to enlist again with the possibility of being sent to another campaign was probably too much for Louise. The replicas of his drawings which he was supposed to have done in Rochester, New York, have never been located and most authorities are skeptical of the replicas' existence. His initial sketches of the Florida campaign were mentioned by G.M. Fairchild[11] when giving an account of Krieghoff's army service as follows, "The campaign (of Florida) to him was one of severe labour, for in addition to his sergeant duties he determined to make an exhaustive series of sketches illustrating every phase of the war and its participants. From these drawings Krieghoff made a large number of paintings for the U.S. Government. Whether these paintings are yet in the archives of the U.S. Government I do not know. The sketches which became the property of John S. Budden, Esq., were all destroyed in the great Quebec fire of June, 1881 . . . . " Krieghoff made his way with his bride out of Vermont to Rochester, New York, where he had a studio, and from there to Toronto, Canada, to visit his brother Ernst who had deserted from the American Navy earlier. From there Cornelius and Louise probably went to Longueuil where Louise's parents accepted them into their home. Just recently, a painting has been discovered which he must have done three or four years after his arrival in Canada (c.1844). It was found by Paul Duval and authenticated by Dr. Marius Barbeau.[12] At Longueil

KRIEGHOFF, Cornelius David (Cont'd)

Krieghoff began to depict life of the 'habitant' and of the Caughnawaga Indians. Dr. Barbeau[13] described this period as follows, "His French-Canadian interiors of the Longueuil period often show a beautiful young woman with her daughter, whom he was fond of using as models. They were Louise and Emily, his wife and young daughter. One of those pictures goes back to 1842 or 1843; the child was then about two years old. A reproduction of this was made in the form of a colour lithograph entitled 'Canadian Habitants Playing at Cards'. Of the year 1846 we have the 'Picture Pedlar' with the inscription 'Montreal, 1846', at the back of the canvas, and 'Habitant Sleigh'. In the first, a gentleman pedlar is showing chromos to some French-Canadians whom we recognize as 'le Vieux Lapocane', Louise's father, and his family. Emily, then a child in arms, is there with the others. The second picture is a large and delightful winter landscape where a group of people are seated in, or stand around, a red 'berline' on the ice in front of Longueuil; among them we see Louise, a pretty young woman in a fur bonnet and bright homespun cape, with Emily, a few years old, and 'Vieux Lapocane'. Cornelius himself is there, still young, long-haired, clean-shaven, and handsome, in a winter sporting costume." During this period Krieghoff went to the Caughnawaga Indian reserve to depict the daily life of the Indians — on their way to the hunt, or women going to market, sometimes on snowshoes, the men often with red toques and white Hudson's Bay blanket coats. Toboggans were often pulled by the subjects. He did summer scenes as well showing the subjects around their campfires, birch bark canoes by the shore, kettles over the fires, wigwams, dogs, all set in a forest background. Details of his Indian paintings are gathered under the "Catalogue Raisonée of Krieghoff's Paintings" pages 131 to 148 of Barbeau's[14] book *Cornelius Krieghoff, Pioneer Painter Of North America* published in 1934. Krieghoff had been reasonably successful at Longueuil where he had received the patronage of Lord Elgin in the printing of four lithographs based on his paintings entitled "Place D'Armes" (13-5/8 x 19-1/8), "Indian Wigwam in Lower Canada" (13½ x 19½), "Sledge Race Near Montreal" (13-3/8 x 19-1/8), "French-Canadian Habitants Playing At Cards" (14½ x 20½) all lithographed in colour by A. Borum, Munich, Germany, and printed by Thomas Kammerer.[14] He had also received the patronage of a chief engineer engaged in the building of the Victoria Bridge who bought forty or fifty of his paintings. He had friends like Henry Fletcher Joseph Jackson (grandfather of A.Y. Jackson) general freight agent for the Canada Atlantic Railway.[15] When Jackson left Longueuil he took along three of Krieghoff's paintings one of which is now in the permanent collection of the National Gallery of Canada.[16] The exodus of his patrons following the completion of various construction projects in the area as well as the anticipated move of Louise's parents to Ogdensburg, U.S.A., brought about his decision to move to Montreal.[17] There, he contemplated the patronage of wealthy merchants. After his move there he discovered to his disappointment that the wealthy of that growing centre were more interested in European art. To eat he was forced to turn to sign painting and to accepting commissions to paint portraits of steeds of the wealthy. He even decorated pieces of furniture including table tops (one, forty-two inches in diameter), also Victorian tilt-top tables with miniature landscapes. He sold his smaller canvases from door to door. He made copies of European paintings[18] for several of his patrons. During the period 1849 to 1853 he moved from place to place in Montreal: at Pied-du-Courant (1849); Beaver Hall (1850); Barclay Place (1852) and Aylmer House (1853). One of his sketch books of this period lost for many years was discovered in England and was purchased by Dr. Sigmund Samuel for the

KRIEGHOFF, Cornelius David (Cont'd)

Canadian collection of the Royal Ontario Museum of Archaeology, and shed much light on the life in Montreal during that period. It contains twenty-nine water colours and seven pencil sketches on sheets of Whatman paper (9½ x 12) water-marked 1831. There had been eleven additional pages in the book according to stubs of removed pages. At the bottom of the sketches in Krieghoff's handwriting are explanation's of his subjects which included "Canadian Selling Rolls of Baccy", "Selling Canadian Homespun Cloth, Montreal", "Canadian Woman with Maple Syrup", "Frozen Sheep, Market, Montreal", Montreal Swells", "Lady Swells, Officer and Muffin", "Canadian Wedding", "Celebrated Blind Fiddler" and others. Three of these sketches appeared in *Canadian Art* in 1952 when J. Russell Harper[19] wrote an article on the sketch book. They were also discussed in the Spring Issue of *New Frontiers*[20] the same year. In 1851 he had met John Budden for the first time, and in 1853 was persuaded by Budden to move to Quebec City with his wife and daughter. Budden, a Quebec City auctioneer, had sold some of Krieghoff's paintings which he bought from the artist on his 1851 visit to Montreal. He was a partner in the firm of Maxham and Company, auctioneers, and was well known in Quebec City. When the Krieghoffs arrived in Quebec they found a place to live at Budden's cottage located at Mount Pleasant on upper St. John Street.[23] During that winter Budden took Krieghoff to Montmorency Falls, a winter playground, where they met important people from the City. At the Falls even the Governor General climbed the Sugar Loaf and coasted on a toboggan at full speed down the ice cone coming to rest at the outlet of the river half a mile away.[21] Krieghoff was intro-duced to British Army Officers stationed at the Citadel, sportsmen, businessmen, and a host of other new friends. G.M. Fairchild, Jr.[22] explained this period as follows, "Stimulated and encouraged by the enthusiasm of Mr. Budden and the liberal purchases of his pictures by such men as James Gibb, J.R. Young, C.R. O'Connor, D.D. Young, J.J. Foote, and also by many of the British officers stationed in Quebec (who sent or took Krieghoff's paintings back to Britain), Krieghoff entered upon a most successful career. It is true his pictures at that date brought small prices, but again he was a rapid and prolific worker, and his output was very considerable. He had, however, the bad habit of making three or four replicas of any picture that pleased him. Portrait painting interested him not at all, although I have run across three or four bearing his signature." But nevertheless he did portraits of John Budden in 1853 (now in the collection of Mr. Esmond Peck, Montreal) and a fair number of others. He also did a series of paintings of the Mont-morency area including five canvases in the winter of 1853 one of which became the subject of a lithograph "The Ice Cone At The Falls Of Montmorency Near Quebec, Lower Canada, in 1853" produced by Day & Son, Lithographers to the Queen. W. Simpson of London, England actually did the work of engraving. The lithograph was then run off by Ackermann & Co. also of that city. During his career he did about 19 subjects which became lithographs. They are listed on page 126 of *Cornelius Krieghoff, Pioneer Painter Of North America* by Dr. Barbeau. Gerald Stevens[26] in his book *In A Canadian Attic* also lists these prints and cautions the prospective collector of Krieghoff works not to confuse the prints "Indian Hunter Calling Moose" and "Indian Hunter In Blizzard", which were mounted on canvas and given a heavy coat of varnish, with original paintings. Later a limited edition of mezzotints of an Indian encampment were produced by F. Petitjean "after Krieghoff" showing a male Indian sitting in front of his wigwam with a flintlock gun and an axe beside him. He is facing two squaws. Also in the picture are two children, a dog, and a man carrying a canoe. This type of print ("after Krieghoff") was in 1963 valued at fifty dollars or more and if in good condition worth double or triple that value.[27] When Krieghoff reached Europe with his wife he made copies of paintings in the Louvre by famous artists including "Lot's Daughters" after Rubens; "Romulus and Remus" after Champmartin; "The Harvesters of the Roman Marches" after Robert; "Approaching Storm" after Ruysdael. At the Luxembourg museum he made copies of "Strolling Actors" after Baird; "German Forester talking to Children in a Sleigh" after Wickembourg; "Marine View, Moonlight" after Grolig and perhaps others.[28] He probably had made other copies while travelling through Europe as a young man. He painted portraits of his wife and daughter who accompanied him on his trip to Europe and did original work apart from his copies.[29] After their return to Canada he did a self portrait (dated 1855) which is now in the collection of the National Gallery of Canada[30], also a portrait of Colonel J.F. Turnbull (coll. William P. Wolfe, Montreal); The Horse Fraser, Ridden By Mr. Miller (coll. Dominion Gallery, Montreal) as well as other portraits but he returned to the theme of the habitant which was to win for him a lasting place in the history of Canadian art. About 1850 he began his series of paintings about habitants cheating the toll with "Bilking The Toll" (12 x 17½) followed by "The Toll Bar" (11¼ x 20-3/4); "Cheating The Toll" (16½ x 24) dated 1857; "Cheating The Toll Gate" (15½ x 24½) 1857; "Running The Toll Gate"; "Toll Gate (17 x 25); "Running The Toll" (18 x 25½) 1860; "Running The Toll Gate" (12½ x 17) 1861; "Running The Toll Gate (11½ x 17½) 1862; one in this series was painted for his daughter Emily for her second marriage to Count de Wendt, who was born in Russia and settled in Chicago. (Emily's first husband, Hamilton Burnett, Esq., Lt. of the 17th Regiment, Quebec, died shortly after marriage). The de Wendt's gift was created in a Russian setting, including costumes, sleigh, horses and harness and general surroundings. When discovered by Norman Seagram (Toronto stockbroker) the setting seemed strange because of the Russian theme and had to be authenticated by William Watson, art collector and dealer from Montreal.[31] Another "The Toll Gate" valued at $10,000 was donated by Hugh P. Buchanan (Publisher, Lethbridge Herald) and the late Donald W. Buchanan (former Assoc. Director, NGC) with other paintings, to the City of Lethbridge on the condition that ample provision be made for their display; the City accepted the gift.[32] One "Bilking the Toll" was discovered in the basement of a home by Maxwell S. Novis, Toronto antique dealer, in 1961. This painting (14 x 22") dated 1862 brought one offer of $10,000.[33] Two other "Bilking the Tolls" were found in Australia bringing the known number of this series to fourteen.[34] Between 1847 and 1862 Krieghoff did many scenes of habitants driving sleighs in winter, usually three or four depending on the size of the sleigh and at other times with two sleighs engaged in a race. For the historians Krieghoff's paintings provide much detail on clothing and customs of the people of Quebec of his time. Many of his paintings deal with Indians at Caughnawaga and at Lorette. The Caughnawaga Reserve is outside Montreal and the Lorette Reserve outside Quebec City. The Caughnawaga area Indians are descendants of the Iroquois, and the Lorette area Indians of the Hurons. By the mid 1800's these tribes dressed much the same since they both bartered with the Hudson's Bay Company. The Hudson's Bay blanket coats were popular not only with the Indians but with the sportsmen and habitants as well. An oval painting of an Indian guide and hunter (10-5/8in. x 8-7/8in.) done about 1850, was sold for $2,000 by Fraser Brothers Limited, Montreal auctioneers, in 1963.[35] Another, of Caughnawaga Indians, was offered for sale at $12,000 by Jacoby's House of Antiques, Montreal, in 1969.[36] Many others have been sold through auctions at Sotheby's of London, England, who established a Canadian branch at Simpsons, Toronto, only recently. It was at Sotheby's Toronto branch that Dr. Morton Shulman sold seven Krieghoff oil paintings for $67,550. He had purchased these seven in 1955 for $20,000; Christie's also of London, England, have sold many Krieghoffs as well. About 1856 Krieghoff began to produce his merrymaking scenes and it is in this group of which there are five, that his masterpiece "Merrymakers" (34½ x 48") was created in 1860. It is not surprising that he gave his best in these creations for he himself was a merrymaker. He loved a gathering of good friends, music and dancing, and as a musician himself he probably contributed his fair share to the party atmosphere. Such parties took place at Mère Gendron's inn at Beauport just a few miles away from the winter playground of the Montmorency Falls. It was following one of these parties which often did not break up until the early hours of the morning, that Krieghoff was inspired to paint a large canvas in which many of the faces of his friends would appear. Many other friends however pleaded to be left out of the composition because of the fear that their reputations of school teachers, church wardens, inn keepers, and a dozen other occupations would be jeopardized.[37] A fictitious name for the inn "J. Bte. Jolifou" was invented and many familiar faces did not appear. The model for this inn, Gendron's at Beauport, just a few miles north east of Quebec City, was still in existence in 1934 although it had been much transformed.[38] "Merrymakers" was purchased from the artist by James Gibb, a friend and patron of Krieghoff. When Gibb died the painting became the property of his wife who later married David Ross. It was then inherited by J.T. Ross, Esq., of Quebec City, who sold it to Lord Beaverbrook in 1957 for $25,000.[39] Lord Beaverbrook made a gift of it to the Beaverbrook Art Gallery in Fredericton, N.B. This gallery founded by Beaverbrook and given to the Province of New Brunswick exhibited the largest collection of Krieghoff's ever assembled. The exhibition took place in 1961 through the co-operation of many public galleries and private collectors. A catalogue was prepared for the occasion with the text written by Edwy Cooke[40] who was then Curator of the gallery. Krieghoff did a series on a settler's log house in winter (eleven known) between 1856 and 1863; also on habitant homes in winter (twenty-two in this series), painted between 1845 and 1863. "Settler's Log House" from the former series (24½ x 36½) was painted in 1856 and is now in the collection of the Art Gallery of Ontario. It has been reproduced on several Canadian Christmas cards.[41] From the latter series the Hamilton Art Gallery acquired "The Habitant's Home" which was presented to the Gallery by Reginald W. Watkins of Erindale, Ontario in 1962.[42] "The Habitant Farm" (24 x 36") done in 1854 is owned by the National Gallery of Canada and was given to the Gallery by the Estate of the Hon. W.C. Edwards, Ottawa, in 1928.[43] Krieghoff produced a series of paintings on "Winter Road, Snowstorm, Blizzard" series. One of them "The Blacksmith's Shop" (22-1/4 x 36-1/4) owned by the Art Gallery of Ontario, was reproduced in *Great Canadian Painting* by Elizabeth Kilbourn, published in 1966.[44] Krieghoff did many other series which included summer and autumn scenes at Lake Beauport, Lake St. Charles, Jacques Cartier River, Lake Memphramagog and elsewhere. One such painting appeared in Dr. Barbeau's book *Cornelius Krieghoff* published by McClelland & Stewart in 1962, entitled "Owl's Head, Lake Memphramagog".[45] During Krieghoff's career it is estimated that he painted over seven hundred

KRIEGHOFF, Cornelius David (Cont'd)

canvases. His Quebec period (1853-1867) was his most prolific. His wife Louise, after their return from Europe disappeared from his life. It is known however that she lived in Denver, Colorado, until the early 1900's.[46] Krieghoff himself left Quebec around 1867 and went to live with his daughter and her husband in Chicago but he returned to Quebec later in 1871 and revisited Montreal and Quebec City.[47] It was in that year that he painted his last merrymaking scene "J.B. Jolifou, Aubergiste" (22 x 36") now owned by Mrs. W. Pitfield of Montreal; also the canvases "New Year's Day Parade" (25 x 42") "The Blacksmith's Shop" (mentioned above), "On The Quebec Heights" (17 x 25") and probably others. He then returned to Chicago where he died a few months later while writing a letter to his good friend John Budden. Today there are still living distant relatives of Cornelius Krieghoff. Mrs. Edwin Krieghoff of Gross Pointe, Michigan, U.S.A., whose late husband was the great-great-grand nephew of the artist, attended the 1963 exhibition of Krieghoff works held at the Willistead Art Gallery in Windsor, Ontario.

References

[1] *The Atlantic Advocate*, December, 1962 "Cornelius Krieghoff" by Louis Rombout

[2] Ibid

[3] Ibid (from the 1822 'Acts of the City Archives of Dusseldorf')

[4] Ibid

[5] Ibid

[6] Ibid

[7] Letter dated Dec. 1, 1928, from John S. Scholfield, War Office Department, Washington, D.C., to Miss Ethel Pinkerton, Art Association, Montreal (published in Dr. Barbeau's book below, P.88)

[8] *Cornelius Krieghoff, Pioneer Painter Of North America* by Marius Barbeau, MacMillan Co. of Canada Ltd., Toronto, 1934, "From Printed Records", P.86

[9] Ibid, P.88

[10] Ibid, P.3

[11] Ibid, P.86 (as extracted from Fairchild's My Quebec Scrapbook)

[12] *Weekend Magazine*, No. 21, 1966 "Portrait Of The Painter's Daughter"

[13] *Cornelius Krieghoff* as in[8], P.4

[14] Ibid, P.126

[15] *A Painter's Country* by A.Y. Jackson, Clarke, Irwin, Tor., 1958, P.1

[16] *National Gallery of Canada Cat. of Paintings & Sculpture, Vol. 3*, P.163

[17] *Cornelius Krieghoff* by Marius Barbeau, McClelland & Stewart, 1962, P.6

[18] *Painting In Canada/A History* by J. Russell Harper, U. of T. Press, 1966, P.124

[19] *Canadian Art*, Vol. 9, No. 4, Summer, 1952 "A Sketch-Book of Cornelius Krieghoff" by J. Russell Harper, P.163-4

[20] *New Frontiers*, Spring, 1952 "Krieghoff's Sketch-Book – A Discovery" P.25

[21] *Gleanings From Quebec* by G.M. Fairchild, Jr., Quebec, 1907 (see[8], P.87)

[22] see[8], P.87

[23] deleted

[24] deleted

[25] deleted

[26] *In A Canadian Attic* by Gerald Stevens, Tor., Ryerson, 1963, P.234, 235

[27] Ibid, P.235

[28] see[8], P.27

[29] see[8], P.28

[30] NGC Catalogue, P.161

[31] *MacLean's Magazine*, Dec. 24, 1955 "In The Editor's Confidence" (Illustration)

[32] *The Lethbridge Herald Daily*, Aug. 19, 1958 "Art Work For Lethbridge" (photo of painting)

[33] *The Gazette*, Mtl., P.Q., Mar. 15, 1961 "99-Year-Old Krieghoff Found By Antique Dealer In Cellar" (CP Tor).

KRIEGHOFF, Cornelius David (Cont'd)

[34] Ibid

[35] Ibid, Mtl., Dec. 21, 1963 "Krieghoff Work Sold"

[36] *La Presse*, Oct. 10, 1969 "Une Collection de $400,000 à l'encan"

[37] see[8], P.41

[38] see[8], P.109

[39] *The Gazette*, Oct. 28, 1957 "Beaverbrook Pays $25,000 For Krieghoff's Painting"

The Toronto Telegram, Tor., Ont., Oct. 26, 1957 "Beaverbrook Buys Finest Krieghoff Work"

[40] *Cornelius Krieghoff, 1815-1872*, Beaverbrook Art Gallery, 1961 (18 pages)

[41] *Catalogue – Art Gallery of Toronto, 1959*, P.33

[42] *The Hamilton Spectator*, Nov. 9, 1962, "Painting By Cornelius Krieghoff Donated To Hamilton Art Gallery"

[43] NGC Catalogue, Vol. 3, P.162

[44] *Great Canadian Painting* selected by Elizabeth Kilbourn, Frank Newfield/Text by Ken Lefolii, Wm. Kilbourn, Marjorie Harris, Sandra Scott, The Can. Centennial Lib., Weekend Magazine & McClelland & Stewart, 1966, P.6, 7

[45] see[17]

[46] *Painting In Canada/A History* as in[21]

[47] see[8], P.78

see also

The Fine Arts In Canada by Newton MacTavish, MacMillan, 1925, P.15, 16, 17

Canadian Landscape Painters by A.H. Rosbon, Ryerson, 1932, P.19, 21, 25, 28, 30, 32, 34, 35, 211

Canadian Painters by Donald W. Buchanan, Phaidon Press, 1945, P.5, 6

Cornelius Krieghoff by Marius Barbeau, Ryerson, Tor., 1948

Canadian Art by Graham McInnes, MacMillan, 1950, P.7, 21, 22, 26, 31, 33-34

The Growth Of Canadian Painting by Donald W. Buchanan, Collins, Tor., 1950, P.18, 22

The Development of Canadian Art by R.H. Hubbard, Queen's Printer, 1963, P.21, 47, 58-60, 63, 70

The MacMillan Dictionary of Canadian Biography Ed. by W. Stewart Wallace, MacMillan, 1963, P.374

A Century of Colonial Painting (catalogue) by J. Russell Harper, NGC, 1964.

Canadian Art, Its Origin And Development by William Colgate, Ryerson (1943) Ryerson Paperback, 1967, P.1 (see also index)

The Hart House Collection of Canadian Paintings by Jeremy Adamson, U. of T. Press, 1969, P.19, 95.

Some exhibitions of Krieghoff paintings

1934 January Art Gallery of Toronto (Catalogue Issued)

1934 February National Gallery of Canada (Catalogue Issued)

1934 March Art Association of Montreal (Catalogue Issued)

1961 September Beaverbrook Art Gallery, Fred. N.B. (Catalogue Issued)

1963 January Willistead Art Gallery, Windsor, Ont.

1966 February Laing Galleries, Toronto, Ontario (Catalogue Issued)

1968 October The Art Gallery of Brantford, Brantford, Ontario (Catalogue Issued)

KRISTMANSON, Hannah

Originally from Vancouver, B.C., she moved to Calgary, Alberta, where she studied at the Alberta College of Art and became known for her creative batiks. The Vernon *News* described her 1968 works as follows, "Hanna Kristmanson's collection of batiks seemed to have a predominate theme of circles, suns and animals. Such titles as 'Big Sun', 'Yellow Sun', 'Sun and Water', 'Fish', 'Golden Birds', reflected that theme. One particularly attractive batik was entitled 'Mother and Child', done in mauves and white." Mrs. Kristmanson's work has been exhibited at the Alberta College of Art, the Vancouver Art Gallery, and elsewhere on the Western Canadian Art Circuit, and also in eastern Canada.

KRISTMANSON, Hannah (Cont'd)

References
New Westminister Public Library Notice Oct. 25, 1967
News, Vernon, B.C., Jan. 22, 1968 "Exhibit combines old with the new"
The Amherst Daily News, Amherst, N.S., Oct. 21, 1968 "Batik Art Exhibition"
Halifax Mail Star, Halifax, N.S., Jan. 11, 1969 "Kristmanson Batiks At The Mount"

KRISTMANSON, Lawrence

On the staff of the Alberta College of Art he exhibited his paintings with George Mihalcheon at the Griffiths Gallery, Vancouver, in 1969 when Charlotte Townsend, art critic for *The Vancouver Sun* noted, "He also uses collage, and dabbled paint, to build up a dense texture for his landscape-derived abstractions. He has got a real feeling of depth, the regression of landscape forms perhaps, and an evasive atmosphere. The colors are softened with a lot of white, the translucent results the artist intends to transfer to plexiglass . . . . Kristmanson's etchings are expert. 'Float City' betrays an interest in commercial graphics; but 'Back Eddy' and 'Night Reflection' have a movement and space which invite a longer look."

Reference
The Vancouver Sun, Van., B.C., June 2, 1959 "Tolerance Versus Art" by Charlotte Townsend

KRIZAN, Sam

Born in Windsor, Ontario he completed his secondary school education in that city and then studied two years at the Ontario College of Art, Toronto; also two years at the Arts and Crafts School, Detroit, Mich. He won the Ann and Richard Drulard Memorial Award in 1962 for his "Figure No. 4" (a standing nude painted in thin washes of 'hot colour'. Kenneth Saltmarche in 1964 noted his work as follows, "The drawings of today continue to explore the possibilities of the figure but they do so less literally, with considerably more feeling and a more highly developed sense of style." Saltmarche was commenting on Krizan's exhibition of black ink line drawings, coloured pencil drawings, and chalk drawings. Krizan has exhibited with the "Young Contemporaries" exhibitions organized by the London Art Museum.

Reference
The Star, Windsor, Ontario, Feb. 1, 1964 article by Kenneth Saltmarche (with a photo of Sam Krizan in his studio)

KRPAN, Jason

A potter who worked with Jack Sures at the Studio Pottery firm in Winnipeg where he achieved a high degree of development in traditional pottery.[1] He studied at the School of Art, University of Manitoba, and has participated in joint exhibitions with Muriel Guest, first in 1968 when the *Free Press*[2] noted his work as follows, " . . . rolled slabs, precisely cut or with their edges left untrimmed, expressing their creation just as clearly as the indentations of the fingers on the spinning clay.

KRPAN, Jason (Cont'd)

These rawer forms evoke the qualities of bits of rock or lava with much the same appeal, asking to be picked up, to be pressed and squeezed and manipulated, by comparison to the more serene pots thrown on the wheel which ask to be caressed and turned." From his later joint show of December, 1968, the reviewer of the *Free Press*[3] expressed a hope that this potter would evolve from his almost total experimental period to a new level of development enriched by his experimentation.

References
[1] *Free Press*, Winnipeg, Man., June 15, 1968 "Potters Reveal Opposing Styles At Recent Winnipeg Two-Man Show" by Peter Crossley
[2] Ibid, June 12, 1968
[3] Ibid, Dec. 17, 1968

KUBOTA, Nobuo

b.1932

Born in Vancouver, B.C., he graduated from the School of Architecture, University of Toronto, in 1959. By 1969 he had moved from architecture to sculpture and held his first one man show at the Isaacs Gallery in the spring of that year. Kay Kritzwiser[1] of the *Globe & Mail* found the show full of 'polish, excitement, and originality' and Florence Diggins[2] of *The Ryersonian* in her article on the same show explained, "Kubota's approach seems to be taking geometrical forms that are symmetrical and working into them an asymmetrical twist. Most of the materials are wood which has been painted black. As an example of the artist's approach, Dissection III was the basic shape of a rectangular block broken up into several slices with a circular tube running through one corner of the rectangle to the centre of the other side. All the sculptings would serve as attractive pieces of furniture-art in a spacious room. Kubota left his architectural position to design and sculpt. He feels, 'Architects are usually too hung-up on their budget to give much thought to what many consider periphery frills.' " Harvey Cowan[3] in *Arts/Canada* felt that the overall impact of Kubota's show was 'one of professionalism and welcome attention to detail.' Kubota has participated in the following major group exhibitions: Sarah Lawrence College, N.Y. (USA) 1964; The Isaacs Gallery, Toronto, 1966; Sculpture '67, City Hall, Toronto (selected, but not completed in time); Canadian Sculpture Exhibition at Stratford, Ontario, 1968; Canadian Artists '68 at The Art Gallery of Ontario. He has joined The Artists' Jazz Band of Toronto, a quartet made up of Gordon Rayner, Graham Coughtry, Robert Markle and himself. Kubota plays alto sax, bag pipe, and other instruments. His large work which is untitled (a sculpture measuring 12' high, 18' long and 10' wide) created for Sculpture '67, held at the Toronto City Hall, was purchased by the City of Toronto as a playground piece for Bellevue Square in the Kensington Market in memory of Charlyn Howze, a dedicated social worker. A plaque was inscribed "For Charlyn Howze, from her friends, sculpture by Nobuo Kubota". Barrie Hale[4] viewing the work after its placement in the Bellevue Square noted, " . . . late last week, on a balmy June evening, Charlyn Howze's memorial was covered with kids. They were climbing all over it, exploring it, exploring its spaces, then jumping off to study it so they could attack it in a new way. Their elders would cross the park to watch them, and it, and on their faces was that curious innocence of people confronted with something new, something that has been outside their experience but is now so emphatically there that it must be

KUBOTA, Nobuo (Cont'd)

considered. And they considered it. At length. It was (and is) that rare thing – a public sculpture that is a work of art, a public sculpture used by the public." Kubota is represented in the private collections of Mr. Kenneth Lochhead, Mr. & Mrs. J. David Eaton, Mr. Robert Markle, Mr. Morley Markson and others.

References

[1] *Globe & Mail*, Tor., Ont., Mar.1, 1969 "Excitement, polish and Nobuo Kubota"

[2] *The Ryersonian*, Tor., Ont., Mar. 11, 1969/four "Architect goes Artist" by Florence Diggins

[3] *Arts-Canada*, Tor., Ont., June 1969, Issue No. 132/133 Exhibition Reviews "Nobuo Kubota – The Isaacs Gallery February-March, 1969" by Harvey Cowan

[4] *Toronto Daily Star*, Tor., Ontario, July 5, 1969 "A truly public work of art" by Barrie Hale
see also
Time, June 28, 1968 "The Arts"

KUCH, Peter

An artist and cartoonist for the Winnipeg *Free Press* who has exhibited his work at the Ukrainian Free Academy of Sciences art gallery in Winnipeg. The show was opened by Canadian sculptor Leo Mol, and featured Kuch's drawings, paintings and cartoons.

Source

Notice of exhibition (undated)

KUCHARSKI, Zig

b. (c) 1932

Born in Hamilton, Ontario, he studied art at the Hamilton Technical Institute (Central High School) and graduated at the age of sixteen. He jointed the firm of Standard Engravers, Hamilton, where he served a six-year apprenticeship while at home he worked steadily to perfect his colour techniques. He then moved to Toronto where he did colour illustrations for a number of studios and made periodical visits to New York City. In 1959 he was hired by a New York studio who were impressed with his automotive illustrations. It was with this firm that he worked on assignments for major American corporations engaged in the manufacture of components for space projects. He illustrated rockets, manned space-flight capsules and planets. In New York he learned to think fast and work quickly. At nights he followed a home-study course in art. In 1962 he returned to Toronto as a free-lance commercial artist, while he produced, on his own time, a series of paintings on space phenomena and when his work was discovered by officials of the McLaughlin Planetarium who were desperately seeking a qualified astronomical artist he was offered the assignment. Between his commercial assignments, he turned out all of the art work connected with the planetarium and is still engaged in the production of illustrations for its everchanging space exhibits. He designed the official map for Expo '67 and has done many other projects. He lives at Clarkson, Ontario, where he designed his own home located in the Rogers Woods Estate. There his studio is located in the basement of his split level house which has no

KUCHARSKI, Zig (Cont'd)

windows facing the street but all of the windows of his studio facing a picturesque ravine. He married Olga Wasylyshen of Hamilton, Ontario.

References

The South Peel Weekly, Port Credit, Ont., Oct. 16, 1968 "Re-creating Space Through A Telescope" by Ron Dennis

The Hamilton Spectator, Hamilton, Ont., Nov. 16, 1968 "So Zig finds a fortune among the stars" by Max Wicken

KUCHARSKY, Norman

b. (c) 1915

He studied nights at the Monument National and l'Ecole des Beaux Arts, at Montreal; in the American Art School, New York under Raphael Soyer, John Brackman, and Bill Cropper; summers at Columbia University in Chinese painting under Dong Kingman. During the Second World War he served overseas with the Canadian infantry in Holland, France and Belgium. He was wounded in the leg and during his recovery he made sketches of life in hospital. In the spring of 1944 his water colour painting "Sally Ann, Petawawa" appeared in *Canadian Art* as a result of its entry in the Canadian Army Art Exhibition. He also won Second Prize in the Canadian Auxiliary Services Contest which marked the beginning of his career. In recent years he has been employed with the Canadian Broadcasting Corporation as a graphic artist in the production of identification placards as well as illustrations for children's programs and other assignments. His paintings have been exhibited at the Dominion Square Art Exhibition in Montreal. He lives at St. Laurent, P.Q. in the City of Montreal area.

References

St. Laurent News, P.Q., July 28, 1960 "Art displays more a tourist lure than sign of progress in Canada"

Canadian Art, Vol. 1, No. 4, April-May, 1944 "Canadian Army Art Exhibition" P.137

KUCHMIJ, Nicholas

Born in Montreal he studied painting and pottery there, and in 1961-2 painted in London, Brussels and Rome. He has worked with ballet and theatrical groups in Canada and for television advertising. He has exhibited in Canada, the United States and Europe and held his first one man show in 1965 at the Galerie de la Place in old Montreal.

Reference

Town of Mont Royal Weekly Post, Montreal, P.Q., Thurs. Nov. 4, 1965

KUCZER, Michael J.

b.1910

Born in Winnipeg, Manitoba, he studied under L.L. Fitzgerald at the Winnipeg School of Art where he won three scholarships. From 1929 to 1949 he lived in London, England, and returned to Canada settling in Toronto in 1949. He has

KUCZER, Michael J. (Cont'd)

exhibited his paintings at the Picture Loan Gallery, Toronto. He does large canvases which are non-objective, reminiscent of the work of the late Jock MacDonald, a friend of the artist from 1955 until MacDonald's death.

Reference

Picture Loan Gallery circular announcing Kuczer's exhibition from Oct. 31, 1969 to Nov. 16, 1969

KUJUNDZIC, Zeljko Desider
b.1920

Born in Subotica, Yugoslavia, his father was of Turkish origin and his mother of Hungarian.[1] His father was a struggling sculptor who became a prosperous hotel keeper and had dreams of living among North American Indians but soon put aside his dreams when his business demanded his full attention. Zeljko Kujundzic however did what his father had only dreamed of doing.[2] But not before war intervened and he was forced to serve in labour camps of the Nazis. He escaped but then became a prisoner of the Russians and again escaped by going underwater and then trekking back a thousand miles through the Ukraine and Roumania to post-war Yugoslavia under Tito. He studied at the Royal College of Art, Budapest, Hungary, where he received his diploma in painting and sculpture and at the University of Budapest, Faculty of Fine Arts, for post graduate studies. He received a travelling scholarship awarded by the Hungarian Ministry of Education for study of folk art in Transylvania. He made his final move across the Hungarian border to the West in 1946 and made his way to Scotland where he lived and painted for ten years. There he lectured for the Arts Council and for the Extra-Mural Department of Edinburgh University. He became a critic for the *Weekly Scotsman*, took a Scottish bride and completed a post-graduate course in English literature at Edinburgh University. He wrote a manifesto *Art in the Modern World* which was published in 1956, and his autobiography *Torn Canvas* in 1957. He came to Canada with his wife and family in 1958 and on a stopover at Calgary was quoted by *The Calgary Herald*[3] as saying, " . . . I am almost overwhelmed with it all. It would take a blind person to miss the beauty around him in Canada. There is no lack of themes here for an artist." Following the establishment of his home at Cranbrook he painted amongst the Kootenay Indians. In the Spring of 1959 he held his first retrospective exhibition of paintings at the Waddington Galleries in Montreal.[4] Kujundzic is a very versatile artist who does sculpture, painting, carving, graphic work, tapestry, stained glass and ceramics. He was commissioned by the City of Cranbrook to build a memorial fountain for Central Park, Cranbrook's newest public park at the east end of Baker Street. He became art supervisor at Mount Baker High School in that city.[5] He then moved to Nelson, B.C., where he became Director and Exhibition Organizer of the Kootenay School of Fine Arts. In his own work he became greatly influenced by West Coast Indian art and some of his work of this period was exhibited at the Brabowski Gallery in London, S.W.3, England. This work was also exhibited in various Canadian galleries, and was comprised of oils, collages, acrylics with oils, and tempera with oils. His subjects included portraits, a crucifixion, and still life. His graphic work included monotypes, lithographs, linocuts and woodcuts.[6] By 1963 he had exhibited two tapestries which were well received at the Kelowna Regional Library along with a

KUJUNDZIC,Zeljko Desider (Cont'd)

number of oil paintings and other mixed media paintings.[7] He was chosen to do the commission of designing murals for the B.C. Institute of Technology, earlier he had designed a mural for the Peebles Motor Inn at Nelson, B.C., which was thought to be the largest mural in Canada. It was on the strength of the Peebles mural that he had been awarded the commission for the murals of the B.C. Institute of Technology.[8] He completed a number of other commissions (see below). In 1967 he was awarded a ten thousand dollar commission for the production of twelve thunderbird sculptures (each six feet high and weighing 2-1/2 tons) for the Thunderbird Stadium at the University of British Columbia.[9] He spent six weeks as a resident artist at the Institute of Fine Arts at San Miguel. In 1968 he was appointed visiting professor in art at the Pennsylvania State University,[10] and was later appointed head of the art department of this university.[11] Over the years he had held one man shows at the Edinburgh International Festival, 1958; K.B. Galleries, Oslo, Norway, 1958; Canadian Gallery, Calgary, Alberta, 1958; Waddington Galleries, Montreal, 1959; Chiltern Art Gallery, London, England; Washington State University Art Centre, 1960; New Design Gallery, Vancouver, 1961; Grabowski Gallery, London, England; 57 Gallery, Edinburgh, Scotland; Canvas Shack, Vancouver; and elsewhere. He has also participated in exhibitions at the following galleries: Crane Kalman, Manchester; Galleri Benezit, Paris; O'Hana Gallery, London; St. Georges, London; Leicester Galleries, London. Some of his other commissions include Stained Glass Window for the Wallyford Parish Church, Edinburgh; Bronze Statue and marble relief panel, Church of the Sacred Heart, Edinburgh; Altarpiece in tempera for the Greek Orthodox Chapel, Edinburgh; elm carving of St. Margaret and mural, for the Kilmahen Chapel, Kirkton, Scotland; fountain in reinforced concrete with copper relief panels for Cranbrook City Council; Fountain in welded and beaten copper for the Middlegate Shopping Centre, Vancouver; Mayor's Chain of Office in beaten silver with gold inlay for the Nelson City Council; mural in engraved walnut with welded copper for the Columbia Apts, Kelowna. His last address was Fayette Campus, Pennsylvania State University, Philadelphia, P.A., although he has returned to Kelowna, B.C., summers. His honours include: Judge for Pacific North West Art Exhibition, 1963, Scholarship for Institute Allende, Mexico, 1963 (didn't utilize this scholarship) and others.

References

[1] *The Montreal Star*, Apr. 2, 1959 "Artist Finds Canada Source of Inspiration" by Dusty Vineberg

[2] Ibid

[3] *The Calgary Herald*, Calgary, Alta., Aug. 19, 1958 "Opportunity Impresses Artist"

[4] *The Gazette*, Mtl., P.Q., Apr. 4, 1959 "Kujundzic Displays Works Here" by D.Y. Pfeiffer

[5] *The Nelson Daily News*, Nelson, B.C., June 25, 1959 (large photo of artist and his design for the fountain)

[6] *Vernon News*, Vernon, B.C., May 3, 1962 "Zeljko Kujundzic's Art On Show This Week"

[7] *Daily Courier*, Kelowna, B.C., Jan. 5, 1963 "Nelson Art School Director Exhibits Tapestries, Tempera"

[8] *Nelson Daily News*, Nelson, B.C., July 17, 1963 "City Mural Leads to Coast Art Projects"

[9] *Daily Courier*, Kelowna, B.C. "Artist Wins Commission"

[10] *The Province*, Van., B.C., "B.C. Artist to take new post at U.S. university"

[11] *Daily Courier*, Kelowna, B.C., June 24, 1969 "Artist Kujundzic Chosen For Tour"

see also
Young Artists of Promise, Studio Publications, London, England, 1957
Dictionary of International Biography 1964/5
Press Release, (The Art Centre, 1334 Richter St., Kelowna, B.C.) by Audrey Johnson

KULBACK, René
b. (c) 1901

Born in Russia, he hunted with his father in the forests of Estonia.[1] When his father died during the Bolshevik uprising, René then eleven years old, fled with his family to Germany using a circular route through countries along the Mediterranean. In Germany he had further enjoyment in the forests with his brothers. He acquired a knowledge of wild life which was to serve him later as an artist. He loved to paint from nature and also visit the zoos where he was able to perfect his sketches of animals. He attended school in Stuttgart for three years but in 1923 he returned to Estonia when that country became an independent republic.[2] He came to Canada from Estonia in 1928. For two years after arriving in this country he and his brother worked on prairie farms as hired hands. Then in 1930 he moved to Montreal where he became a commercial artist. He worked as well on the creation of batiks and hand paintings on silk fabrics. In 1936 he was in Toronto working for a display department of a large Toronto store. He also carried out free lance commercial art projects. He decorated the Crystal Ball Room of the Royal York Hotel with a 2,000 (sq.?) foot mural. He also decorated the walls of numerous large residences in Toronto as well as walls for department stores and industrial plants. During the Second World War he enlisted in the R.C.A.F. but his artistic skills were discovered and he was put to work decorating the officers' mess at Camp Borden, the library hall and Winter Gardens at the Trenton station and other projects. He returned to civilian life after the war and resumed his career as a commercial artist and muralist. His large mural for the main waiting room wall at Sunnybrook Hospital, Toronto, was begun by the artist powdering through perforations in a paper covering, onto the plaster. This step eliminated the necessity of making small squares in order to produce the cartoon. The mural (16-1/2 by 8 feet) was completed in three weeks.[3] William Sargent[4] described the mural as follows, "Across the huge painting the artist has spotted the crests of the provinces, and in the vicinity of each crest has skilfully placed life-like examples of birds, animals and fish familiar to each territory . . . . Perhaps one of the most striking things about this exquisite piece of work is the careful detail the artist has shown in striving for anatomic perfection in each figure."

References
[1] *Torch*, Toronto, June, 1948 "The Murals At Sunnybrook" by William Sargent
[2] *The Recorder & Times*, Brockville, Ont., July 27, 1948 "Canada's Foremost Mural Artist is Veteran of the R.C.A.F. Police Force"
[3] Ibid
[4] see[1]

KULMALA, George Arthur
1896-1940

Born in Pori, Finland, he came to Canada with his parents when he was eight years of age and they settled in Toronto.[1] He attended Cottingham Street School, Toronto, where he showed a talent for drawing and painting and soon caught the attention of his teachers.[2] He later attended the Ontario College of Art summer school at Port Hope under J.W. Beatty.[3] It was his hope to spend all his time as a professional painter but in order to make a living he conducted a fur business.[4] He spent many of his summers painting at his summer home in Muskoka, and a few years before his death bought forty acres of land near Lake Rosseau where he had

KULMALA, George Arthur (Cont'd)

planned to make a retreat for city artists. One of his paintings was exhibited at Wembley, another at the World's Fair in New York. He was president of theToronto Finnish Artists' Group and a member of the Ontario Society of Artists. Kulmala died at the young age of 44 and was survived by his wife Hulda Harkin Kulmala and one daughter Aileen.[5] His work was noted by the *Globe & Mail*[6] as follows, "Mr. Kulmala was a frequent exhibitor not only in Ontario, but also in England and in New York. A painter of colorful landscapes he chose for many of his subjects studies in Northern Ontario and numerous snow scenes."

References

[1] *Globe & Mail*, Tor., Ont., Feb. 23, 1940 "Geo. A. Kulmala Artist, Passes" also Nat. Gal. of Can. Info. Form rec'd Aug., 1925

[2] Ibid

[3] Ibid

[4] *The Toronto Star*, Tor., Ont., Feb. 23, 1940 "Artist Of Northland G.A. Kulmala Dead"

[5] see[1]

[6] see[1]

KUNDZINS, Pauls

b.1888

Born at Smiltene, Latvia, he took private lessons in water colours, charcoal, and oils, when he was fifteen and continued in this study for three years. In 1913, when he was twenty-five, he graduated from university in architecture. From 1919 to 1944 he was a professor of Architecture at the Latvian University in Riga. He received his doctorate in architecture in 1933. He practiced architecture in Latvia where he designed churches, community halls, schools, monuments and a number of interiors. In 1944 he fled communist occupied Estonia and settled for a time in West Germany. By 1949 he was doing architectural research and painting, in Sweden. He came to Canada in 1952 and settled in Halifax where he has been working in the office of an architect. He has also taken part in art exhibitions while he continues to work on his painting. He is a member of the Nova Scotia Society of Artists, Academy of Gustav Adolf, Uppsala, Sweden and the Association of Latvian Architects (of the West). A realistic artist Kundzins has been influenced by the landscapes of Latvian artist V. Purvits and generally in his water colours by German artist C. Klein. He is the author of treatises and essays on architecture and applied arts.

Source

Document from artist

KURELEK, Wasyl (William)

b.1927

Born at Whitford, Alberta, the son of Dmytro (b.Borivtsi, Ukrain) and Maria Huculiak (b.Willingdon-Vegreville district of Alberta) who had settled on a farm at Whitford, 75 miles northeast of Edmonton.[1] A victim of the depression his father lost his 160 acre homestead in 1932 when a mortgage company foreclosed on his

KURELEK, Wasyl (William) (Cont'd)

property.[2] The Kureleks then moved to Stonewall, 15 miles north of Winnipeg, where Dmytro invested his last savings on the purchase of another farm.[3] There William and his brother John were sent to school, and both did well. William however was keenly interested in drawing which allowed a release for his vivid imagination.[4] He spent more time dreaming and sketching and less time in the normal activities of a youth about the farm. His father, under the reality of the depression, was deeply concerned with William's moods and prodded him to be more active and less a dreamer. He even told his son to put aside his drawing.[5] But William didn't and when the Kurelek boys attended high school and lived in two attic rooms which his father has rented, William cluttered his walls with his drawings. Some of them even scared their landlady. By grade eleven William experienced severe eye pains whenever he painted or drew; this difficulty remained with him for many years. During the 1940's William attended the University of Manitoba where he graduated with his Bachelor of Arts in 1949. It was during this period he read James Joyce's *Portrait of the Artist as a Young Man* and as a result felt a new surge of independence to follow only the dictates of his own heart. His family had wanted him to study medicine but William wanted to study art. He worked in lumber camps to raise money for his art studies and did other odd jobs. He then studied six months at the Ontario College of Art but found he needed more freedom to develop at his own pace and interest.[7] He turned his attentions to Mexico and spent five months at the Instituto Allende and then decided to follow his own self study plan. He sailed for England in 1952 where he found a happier environment, a more tolerant acceptance for what he wanted to paint. He also apprenticed himself to a picture framer, Frederick Pollock, from whom he learned this exacting craft.[8] Stephen Franklin[9] in *Weekend Magazine* described his years in England as follows, "In seven years Kurelek found both happiness and sadness in London. His painstaking fool-the-eye paintings of pound notes and other objects found their way into three Royal Academy summer shows, but he was increasingly bothered by eye trouble for which there was no physical cause. He plumbed the depth of emotional despair, contemplated suicide and wound up in hospital for more than a year. It was here that he began his conversion — from boyhood membership in the Orthodox Church and subsequent atheism — to Catholicism which has deeply affected his life since." Kurelek began to illustrate the suffering of Christ from the Last Supper until his resurrection, as related in The Gospel According To St. Matthew (The Passion of St. Matthew). He journeyed to the Holy Land in 1959 where he spent five weeks doing research on the landscape, climate, architecture, and obtained from the Israeli press agency numerous photographs of the Israeli scene and the Jewish facial types.[10] He walked from Jerusalem to Bethlehem, visited the Sea of Galilee and other locations which he sketched and photographed.[12] He returned to Toronto, Canada in 1959, and visited Avrom Isaacs, looking for a job as picture framer. He had with him one of his own paintings framed. Although his framing was unquestionably professional it was his paintings which caught the eye of Isaacs (who became his art dealer). In 1960 Kurelek held his first one man show at the Isaacs Gallery. Pearl McCarthy[11] reviewing his work noted, "It is easy but perhaps misleading to note at once the affinity to the 15th Century Hieronymous Bosch. Mr. Kurelek is not imitating anybody. It just happens that the young Canadian of Ukrainian stock sees something similar in the problem of good and evil. He too, then, has some rather surrealist diableries in his pictures." In 1961 the women's committee of the Toronto Art

KURELEK, Wasyl (William) (Cont'd)

Gallery held its annual exhibition. The paintings were offered for sale. Alfred H. Barr, Director of the Museum of Modern Art, New York, was invited to the opening. He was offered, a painting of his choosing, by the committee, for his gallery. He chose one entitled "Hailstorm in Alberta" by William Kurelek which had been entered by Avrom Isaacs. Kurelek didn't know himself that the painting had been entered. He was summoned that evening by taxi from his Toronto rooming house and made his presence at the scene. It was an appearance not only for the evening, but on the Canadian art scene generally. Few art followers had heard of Kurelek until that evening, and were soon offering substantial amounts to possess better works by him. Today some of his paintings sell for two thousand dollars apiece. But his Passion of St. Matthew paintings are not for sale. They were created so that lantern slides could be made from them and used by missionaries. Peter Sypnowich[13] explained, " . . . the artist's aim is to portray such powerful spirituality in the face of Jesus that those who see it will be moved to faith." The artist has however painted many other scenes that are eagerly sought after by collectors. Jan Kamienski[14] art critic for the Winnipeg *Tribune* noted, "Personally, I like best Kurelek's paintings based on themes of Western Canada. One can quite easily let the eye wander about from detail to detail of a picture such as 'Manitoba Party' without losing sight of the Renaissance-like symmetry of design. It is almost like reading a map, going from point to point and wondering what there is beyond the horizon." Kurelek has done several series of paintings entitled "Farm Memories" exhibited at the Isaacs Gallery (1961) in water colours and thin oils; "Children's Games" (a dozen or so small pictures within one frame – exhibited in Montreal – Gallery XII, 1963); "Experiments In Didactic Art" shown at the Isaacs Gallery (1963); "An Immigrant Farms In Canada" shown at the Isaacs Gallery (1964) based on the life of a Ukrainian immigrant in Canada as exemplified by Kurelek's own father; "The Gospel Story According to the Passion of St. Matthew" (not for sale but exhibited at the McIntosh Memorial Art Gallery, University of Western Ontario, London, Ont., 1965); "Manitoba Bog Paintings". Agnes Lefort Gallery, Montreal (1967): "The Ukrainian Pioneer Woman In Canada", shown at the Isaacs Gallery, 1968. His actual one man shows were held at the Isaacs Gallery in 1962, 1963, 1964, 1966, 1968; the Edmonton Art Gallery, 1965; Agnes Lefort Gallery, Montreal, 1965, 1967; Trinity College (U. of Toronto), 1965; McIntosh Gallery (U. of Western Ontario) 1965; Winnipeg Art Gallery, 1965; The Yellow Door Gallery, Winnipeg, 1966; and Yellowstone Art Centre, Montana, 1967. He has participated in many group shows including the Biennial Exhibition of Canadian Art. The National Film Board released an eleven minute colour film entitled "Kurelek" which is based on the paintings of the artist. Collectors of his paintings include (collector & title of painting): The Rt. Hon. & Mrs. L.B. Pearson (Dairy Farming in Manitoba, 1963); Prof. & Mrs. B. Bixley (If on the Wings of Sorrows); Prof. & Mrs. P.W. Fox (Who Is She That Cometh Forth as the Morning Riseth); Prof & Mrs. J. Eayrs (Sunday Dinner Call in the Bush – also, Stooking); Mr. & Mrs. Rosenfeld (Hauling Grain In Winter); Mr. & Mrs. D. Draper (Green Sunday); Mr. & Mrs. L. Brouse (Remorse, 1953); Mr. Paul Arthur (Behold Man Without God, 1955); Mr. & Mrs. N. Olynyk (Still Life with Tomatoes and Eggs, 1955); Mrs. A. Isaacs (Haystack, 1961) (In Search of the True God, No. 5, 1964); Mr. M. Lesser (Russian Thistles Migrating, 1962); Mr. & Mrs. R.A. Hutchison (Gathering in the Garden before the Freeze-up, 1962); Mr. & Mrs. H. Gabriel (Dogs or People, 1962); The Hon. & Mrs. Walter Gordon (Stooking No. 2, 1963); Mr. & Mrs. S.J. Drache (The Auction Sale,

KURELEK, Wasyl (William) (Cont'd)

1963); Mr. & Mrs. M. Sprachman (Prairie Corn Roast, 1964); Mrs. W.G. McConnell (Abandoned Ukrainian Pioneer House, Komarno, Manitoba, 1964); Mr. D. Ritchie (The Unfinished Stack, 1965) and other collectors like Mr. & Mrs. Samuel J. Zacks and Dr. Evan Turner, Director Philadelphia Art Gallery. He is represented in the following public collections: The Museum of Modern Art, New York, U.S.A.; The Montreal Museum of Fine Arts; Philadelphia Museum of Art; National Gallery of Canada, Ottawa; The Art Gallery of Ontario, Toronto; Agnes Etherington Art Centre, Queen's University, Kingston, Ontario; Art Gallery of Hamilton, Hamilton, Ontario; McMaster University, Hamilton, Ontario; The Winnipeg Art Gallery, Winnipeg, Man.; Edmonton International Airport; Canadian Industries Limited, Montreal. William Kurelek lives in Toronto with his wife and children.

References

[1] *America* (English/Ukrainian), Philadelphia, Nov. 29, 1968, P.3
[2] *The Star Weekly*, April 13, 1963 "The Easter Story" by Peter Sypnowich, P.8
[3] Ibid, P.8
[4] Ibid, P.8
[5] Ibid, P.8
[6] A Ukrainian Publication from Winnipeg, article by Oksana Rozumna, March, 1966
[7] National Gallery of Canada Information Form rec'd during early 1960's
[8] *Weekend Magazine*, No. 4, 1968 "Painting The Simple Life" by Stephen Franklin, P.4
[9] Ibid, P.4
[10] See[2], P.13
[11] see[2], P.13
[12] *Globe & Mail*, Apr. 2, 1960 "Kurelek Show Significant One" by Pearl McCarthy
[13] *The Star Weekly*, April 13, 1963 as in[2]
[14] *Tribune*, Winnipeg, Man., Apr. 7, 1966 "His far horizons beckon" by Jan Kamienski
see also
Agnes Etherington Art Centre (Catalogue), *Queen's University*, by Frances K. Smith, 1968, No. 75
Painting In Canada/A History by J. Russell Harper, U. of T. Press, 1966, P.404
Great Canadian Painting/A Century of Art paintings selected by Elizabeth Kilbourn, Frank Newfeld, 1966 P.62, 63
Canadian Art, Mar./April, 1962, Vol. 19, No.2, "A Survey Of The Work Of 21 More Canadian Artists" William Kurelek by Elizabeth Kilbourn
Canadian Art, Sept./Oct., 1963, Vol. 20, No. 5 "Art Reviews" William Kurelek at the Isaacs Gallery, Toronto by J.R. Colombo P.270
The Ryersonian, Toronto, Ont., Nov. 6, 1969 "Painter, priest — poverty, protest" by Michelle Morey
William Kurelek, The Winnipeg Art Gallery, 1966 (catalogue) with Introduction by Ferdinand Echhardt, Director, The Winnipeg Art Gallery, a list of paintings with their owners.
The Globe Magazine, Jan. 20, 1968, "Kurelek" by Wendy Michener
The Toronto Daily Star, Tor., Ont., March 13, 1969 "At least one viewer is offended by artist Kurelek's paintings" by Gail Dexter
La Tribune, Que., P.Q., Nov. 4, 1968 "De la misère humaine au mysticisme"
Ibid, Nov. 2, 1968 "Exposition des oeuvres de Kurelek illustrant la vie des paysans de l'Ukraine et de l'Ouest canadien"

KUTHAN, George

b.1916

Born in Klatovy, Czechoslovakia, he entered medical school at the University of Prague and, in 1939 when he was in his third year the Nazis occupied his country

KUTHAN, George (Cont'd)

and the University closed. It was then that he started his artistic career. He enrolled in the School of Decorative Arts in Prague where he studied for six years. He studied mural and mosaics under Prof. J. Novak and graphic arts under Prof. F. Tichy. He was awarded an exchange scholarship by the French Government for one year of further study in the graphic arts in Paris. He then studied at the Ecole Supérieure des Beaux Arts, Paris, for three years in the graphic studio of Prof. Robert Cami where he learned Itaglio techniques, etching, drypoint, copper-engraving and other special studies. He received his certificate and letters from the Cami studio and next studied at the academy of André Lhote, Paris, for a year of painting. His last two years in Paris were spent at the Grande Chaumière, although this was not a continuous period of attendance at the school. In 1948 he produced a series of eight line etchings which were best sellers in the Print Department of the Louvre Museum in Paris. One of these etchings was purchased by the French Ministry of Education and later, in 1952, one was purchased by the National Gallery of Canada. Kuthan came to Canada in 1950 and stayed for a short time in Saskatchewan before settling in Vancouver, B.C., in 1951. In his work generally he is influenced by Czech folklore, medieval woodcuts and oriental miniatures. In the early spring of 1959 he held a one man show of his graphic art at the Vancouver Art Gallery when Mildred Valley Thornton[1] of *The Vancouver Sun* noted, "This is a large collection covering many phases of activity. Compositions are carefully organized, linework is decisive and well directed, techniques employed are skilful and inventive. A number of large decorative panels depicting British Columbia wild flowers are executed with masterly ease. There is a captivating set of illustrations for children's books. Another group features the Christmas theme . . . . Etchings, woodcuts and wood engravings are shown, and the tools used to make them. This fine exhibition will be on display till April 19." He exhibited in the summer of that year at the Victoria Art Gallery. Ethel Post[2] of the Vancouver *Province* found his 1960 show at the Vancouver Art Gallery one to recommend to her viewers as follows, "You don't have to 'understand' modern art to enjoy looking at his prints and drawings of such familiar subjects as flowers, birds, animals and people. I especially liked his sketches of downtown Vancouver, some with and some without last year's Centennial decorations. It's fun to study a street scene where you recognize the buildings. Makes you feel so cosmopolitan! " Other exhibitions of his work followed. Kuthan's work may be described as realistic to a degree, poetic, and decorative. He works in a wide range of graphic media including pen and ink drawings, linocutting, wood engraving, copper engraving, woodcutting and etching. His seventy-seven colour pen and brush drawings of wildflowers, mushrooms and insects were brought into existence by an award from the Leon & Thea Koerner Foundation, making possible his three week field trip in the province. This collection of drawings was purchased by the Glenbow Foundation, Calgary, and circulated in the Western Canada Art Circuit. From 1956 to 1961 he worked on the drawings for *Vancouver, Sights and Insights* with text by Donald Stainsby. This book was published by MacMillan of Canada, Toronto, in 1962, and is a fine example of a highly creative publication as a result of good writing and illustrating. Kuthan has also provided illustrations for the following books: *An Academic Symposium* (limited edition of 1000 copies) for which he did decorative initials, colour lino-cuts, for a record of the ceremonies and speeches held at the University of B.C. during the province's centennial, 1958; *Canadian Literature Quarterly* in which one will find his decorative linocuts in black, 1959; *Kuthan's Menagerie* (a children's book of Stanley Park Zoo animals) text, and colour

KUTHAN, George (Cont'd)

linocuts printed directly from lino blocks, were done by Kuthan. Only a limited edition of 130 copies, which were leather bound, were produced by the Nevermore Press, Vancouver, owned and operated by Robert R. Reid. This publication involved a Danish printer, a Dutch compositor, a German bookbinder and a Canadian typographer-publisher. George Kuthan is represented in the collections of the National Gallery of Canada, Vancouver Art Gallery, French Ministry of Education, Paris, public libraries and private collectors. He is a member of the British Columbia Society of Artists and the Vancouver Natural History Society.

References

[1] *The Vancouver Sun*, April 7, 1959 "Graphic Art Show Work of Craftsman" by Mildred Valley Thornton

[2] *The Province*, Van., B.C., April 15, 1960 "Graphic show not too 'arty' " by Ethel Post

see also

The Graphic Art Of George Kuthan, printed by Robert R. Reid (sample of artist's work and biography)

KUYVENHOVEN, Henry

An Owen Sound artist who is known for his landscapes, (which have been described as having exceptional beauty) as well as other subjects. He has worked in water colour, tempera, impasto, oil, brush drawing, felt-pen, charcoal and chalk. His subjects include areas near Owen Sound such as French Bay, Kelso Beach, Balmy Beach, Mary Miller Park, Harrison Park, and city scenes within Owen Sound. He has held several one man shows at the Tom Thomson Memorial Art Gallery and the Foto-Art Studio in Owen Sound. Mr. Kuyvenhoven also mounts and frames his own work.

References

Sun-Times, Owen Sound, Ont., Tues., Dec. 15, 1964 "Henry Kuyvenhoven Has Fine Exhibition in Gallery" (photo of artist and work)

Ibid, Mar. 10, 1966 "Local Scenes Views Inspire Artist's Brush"

Ibid, Mar. 21, 1966

Ibid, Apr. 14, 1967 "Local Artist Shows Many Moods in Work" (photo of artist and work)

KWARTLER, Alexander

b.1924

Born in Hungary, he studied at the Beaux Arts in Paris, and settled in Montreal in 1955.[1] His subjects include scenes of Montreal as well as landscapes and still life studies. He has held a number of one man shows in Montreal and is a member of the Independent Artists' Association. Dorothy Pfeiffer[2] on viewing his work in 1964 noted, "He is at his best in his rendition of windy skies and billowing foliage. His scenes of woodlands and parks encompass both space and atmosphere. Rhythm also plays its part in his strongly nervous brush and palette-knife strokes." His most recent exhibition was held at the Galerie Art Den, Montreal, in 1966. He is represented in the collection of The Rt. Hon. and Mrs. Lester B. Pearson, the Museum of Modern Art, Montreal, and important collections in the United States, Europe and Israel.[3]

698

KWARTLER, Alexander (Cont'd)

References
[1] *The Gazette*, Mtl., P.Q., Nov. 28, 1959 "Canadian Debut"
[2] Ibid, May 16, 1964 "Alexander Kwartler At Art Centre" by Dorothy Pfeiffer
[3] *Alexander Kwartler, Recent Paintings* (catalogue), Katz Art Gallery, 97 Dizengoff St., Tel-Aviv, Israel, 1965.
   see also
   Le Petit Journal, Mtl., P.Q., 29, May, 1966 (photo of artist and work)

KYLE, J. Fergus

(c) 1876-1941

Born in Hamilton, Ontario, the son of William Kyle of Stratford, he joined the staff of *The News* as a reporter.[1] He became a cartoonist and illustrator for *The Globe*, the *Toronto Daily Star*, and *Saturday Night*.[2] He toured England in 1911 with a party of newspaper writers. In 1916 during the First World War he joined the Canadian Army. He served overseas as a lieutenant (ammunication column) in the First Division. After the war he returned to Canada and his profession. The *Toronto Daily Star*[3] noted, "In many respects a born cartoonist he put the personal vitality of his ideas into anything he did, no matter how commercial it might be. He was always more interested in people and problems than in landscape. His figure work always had splendid vim and gusto. To mere decoration he was cold; to conventional landscapes critical; to the ultra-modern gadgeteer chucklingly contemptuous . . . . He did very little color work, though his few oil landscapes showed high vitality. He was much interested in spectacular scenarios. One big sweeping panoramic that he made of a pageant at the Coliseum is still remembered for its daring originality. In his later life he was considerably interested in stage matters." He was a member of the Little Billee Sketch Club[4] and of the Mahlstick Club.[5] At the time of his death he was survived by his widow, Charlotte Cotter (who was a member of the Shakespeare society); one son John; one sister, Mrs. S.H. Howard and two brothers, Major W.A. Kyle and A.T. Kyle, all of Toronto.[6]

References
[1] *Globe & Mail*, Tor., Ont., Sept. 29, 1941 "J. Fergus Kyle, Artist, Dies"
[2] Ibid
[3] *Toronto Daily Star*, Tor., Ont., Oct. 4, 1941 "Late Fergus Kyle Had Zest For Life"
[4] *Canadian Art, Its Origin and Development* by William Colgate, Ryerson Paperbacks 1967, P.68
[5] see[1]
[6] see[1]

LABA, Victor

b.1936

Born in Grimsby, Ontario, he studied at the Ontario College of Art, Toronto, and graduated in 1959. He worked as a commercial artist for the publication division of the Ontario Agricultural College, Guelph, from 1959 to 1961. He travelled in Europe in 1961 returning to Canada the next year. A one man show of his work was held at the Gallery House Sol, Charles Street, Toronto, in 1963, where his hard

LABA, Victor (Cont'd)

edge paintings of his "Journey" series were exhibited. Previously he had also exhibited his paintings at the Here and Now Gallery, Toronto.

Reference
    Herald, Georgetown, Ont., April 18, 1963 "Victor Laba Paintings Booked For House Sol"

LABBÉ, Françoise

Born at Baie St. Paul, she studied painting and ceramics at the Ecole des Beaux Arts, Quebec, where she received her diploma in 1956. Subsequently she studied in France on Quebec Government scholarships in 1962 and 1964. Her work has been shown in important international exhibitions and she is known especially for her enamel-on-copper panels and plates. Dorothy Pfeiffer[1] viewing her exhibition at Galerie Agnes Lefort in 1961 noted, "Her beautifully transparent background glazes, combined with non-figurative patterns of solidly glowing hues, show distinct affinity with paintings by Suzanne Bergeron, Jean-Guy Mongeau and Monique Charbonneau (Mrs. Pfeiffer clearly noted that these influences in no way dominated the artist's own individuality, and continued) . . . . Her technically knowledgeable creations have a life of their own. In fact, they easily fall into the unusual category of 'Enamel paintings.'" Françoise Labbé lives at Cte Charlevoix, Baie Saint-Paul, P.Q.

References
[1] *The Gazette,* Mtl., P.Q., Nov. 25, 1961 "Unusual Enamels" by D.Y.P.
    see also
    Le Droit, Ottawa, Ont., April 4, 1956 "Françoise Labbé" (photo of artist and her work)
    Le Nouveau, Mtl., P.Q., Nov. 14, 1961 "Françoise Labbé: des émaux sur cuivre au rang d'oeuvres d'art"
    Le Devoir, Mtl., P.Q., Nov. 16, 1961 "Emaux et art sacré" Par Laurent Lamy
    La Patrie, Mtl., P.Q., Feb. 25, 1962 "Françoise Labbé jeune artiste de Baie St-Paul, rajeunit l'art ancestral des émaux"
    Le Soleil, Mtl., P.Q., Jan. 15, 1966 "Françoise Labbé veut une carrière internationale" par Angéline Bouchard"
    La Malbaie, Que., P.Q., Feb. 2, 1966 (photo of artist and work)

LABBE, John

A muralist from Quebec City who has completed wall-length murals for The Royal Canadian Air Force Association's club rooms on St. Jean Street, Quebec City, and for the Sergeant's Mess, 57th Battery, Grande Allée armories. He is himself a member of the R.C.A.F.'s Quebec City Wing.

Reference
    Chronicle-Telegraph, Que., P.Q., Feb. 21, 1959 "New Interior Decoration For RCAF"

LABBÉ, Michel

From Quebec City his recent paintings have been described by Grazia Merler in *Le Soleil* as marvellous fantasies which are full of joy, life, spontaneity as well as moderation, reflection and hard work. His collages have aided him to discover colour, design and form. His last exhibition was held at Galerie Louis Jolliet, Quebec City, December of 1967. He took First Prize in a Quebec Provincial Competition. Usually Michel Labbé does not title his works in order to allow the viewers to form their own impressions.

Reference
> *Le Soleil,* Dec. 2, "Michel Labbé, beau conte de fées" par Grazia Merler.

LABELLE, Faye

She studied nights at the Ontario College of Art and has been working in abstract and symbolic concepts. She has exhibited her paintings at the Theatre of the Arts, University Gallery, University of Waterloo, and the Massey Library, Guelph, Ontario.

References
> *Kitchener-Waterloo Record,* Kitchener, Ont., Sat., Nov. 20, 1965 "University Gallery Featuring An Exhibit of Acrylic Medium" by John and Pamela Walter
> *The Guardian,* Guelph, Ont., Jan. 11, 1966 "Medium-Acrylic" by Ted Miller

LABELLE, Fernand

A painter from Cornwall, Ontario, whose work was shown at the Union of Canada Building, Dalhousie Street, Ottawa, in the late fall of 1969. Mr. Labelle is employed by the Quebec Ministry of Education. He is a painter of seascapes, village and city scenes, and a variety of other subjects.

References
> *Le Droit,* Ottawa, Ont., Nov. 26, 1969 (large photo of artist and his work)
> *Standard Freeholder,* Cornwall, Ont., "Cornwall Native" (photo of artist at work on a painting)
> *Le Droit,* Ottawa, Ont., Dec. 1, 1969 "Au fil des jours — une forme de patriotisme"

LABELLE, George A.

Born in Alberta, he served overseas in the RCAF for five years and returned home where he became a mink rancher. Later he moved to the Maritimes and attended the Agricultural College in Truro, N.S.[1] Following his graduation he attended MacDonald College, Quebec, and later accepted a position with St. Francis Xavier University in Antigonish, N.S., where he taught farmers and fishermen, in the extension department for adult education. He married

LABELLE, George A. (Cont'd)

and later purchased fourteen acres of land in Cocagne in 1949. In 1964 he attended the Provincial Handicraft Centre at Fredericton, N.B., where he studied pottery for just over a year. Vera Ayling[2] in the Saint John *Telegraph-Journal* described his work as follows, "For his earthenware, George LaBelle uses the reddish Cocagne clay, and mixes it with a coarser gray clay from Shubenacadie, N.S. He also takes clay from the Shediac and Scoudouc Rivers, and gets more from Musquodoboit, N.S., for use in his stoneware. Some of his finer stoneware bowls are very nearly on a par with those produced by the later Kjeld Deichman of Sussex. The clays are soaked for several hours before being screened and placed in old tubs Mr. LaBelle made from discarded electric washing machines to decant the water. And he equipped his potter's wheel with an electric motor to assist his foot power. When removed from the kilns, the green-ware has become bisque and then is ready for some of the hundreds of different glazes George LaBelle makes up. He keeps a record of each glaze test in his filing cabinets, and can check or vary each one at will. Nearby he strings small pottery circles like necklaces each one numbered for its different glaze test, ready to be copied when needed." See Miss Ayling's article for more details on this interesting and resourceful potter.[3] One of his vases was shown in the Atlantic Pavillion at Expo '67; he was one of three New Brunswick craftsmen whose work was chosen for this exhibition .

Reference

Telegraph-Journal, Saint John, N.B., Aug. 11, 1969 "Artist Becomes Mastercraftsman — Potter At Cocagne" by Vera Ayling

LABELLE, Leo

A young New Westminster artist whose canvases have been described as "highly expressive figurative paintings". He participated in a two man show at the Little Gallery, New Westminster, B.C. in 1966, with Bob Vaugeois. Labelle is director of the new Olympus art gallery in New Westminster where he features his work, and the work of other artists.

References

The Columbian, New Westminster, B.C., Nov. 30, 1966 "The pleasures of mad art" by Neil Godin (Columbian Staff Reporter)
Ibid, Feb. 27, 1969 (large photo of artist in his gallery)

LABELLE-OUELLET, Lise

A young artist who graduated from l'Ecole des Beaux Arts, Montreal, where she studied the plastic arts. She exhibited her paintings, drawings and engravings at the Saint-Jérôme Municipal Library in 1968. She also does sculpture, pottery and enamel on copper. She married Jean Ouellet and they live in Montreal.

Reference

L'Echo du Nord, St. Jérôme, P.Q., 11 Dec., 1968 "Exposition de livres, peintures, gravures et dessins jusqu'au 13" Page 15

LABERGE, Marie

She studied at the Ecole des Beaux Arts, Quebec, five years, and is a poet-artist who has held many showings of her paintings. She has painted many subjects in a variety of styles in her search for freedom as the Quebec *Chronicle-Telegraph*[1] noted "Marie Laberge describes her paintings as a search for spontaneity rather than a formal research. 'I paint the universe where I live. My paintings are not intellectual, not complicated. They are spontaneous.' " Marie Laberge is the author of the following books of poetry: *Les Passerelles du Matin,* Les Editions de l'Arc (1961); *Halte,* Les Editions de l'Arc (1965 when it won the Du Maurier prize);[2] *D'un cri à l'autre* (1966) *L'Hiver à Brûler,* Editions Garneau, Quebec (1968).[3] Her paintings are not intended to illustrate her poetry but in both forms of expression she seeks liberation for her spirit. Her paintings have been exhibited at La Huchette, Quebec (1960); Galerie Zanettin, Quebec (1962) (1963) (1965) (1966); Centre d'Art de Shawinigan (1964); Centre d'Art de Mégantic (1964); U. of Ottawa (1965); Galerie la Brique (1967); Galerie Kaléidoscope, Montreal (1967-8); Galerie Margo Fisher, Grand'Mère (1968); Galerie Champagne, Quebec (1968); Centre d'Art de Montmagny (1968) and in many group shows. She lives in Quebec City with her husband and children.

References

[1] *Chronicle-Telegraph,* Que., P.Q., Sept. 24, 1966 "Local Artist Stages Her Fifth Annual Exhibition"

[2] *L'Action,* Que., P.Q. 12 Nov. 1965 "Marie Laberge – Prix de Poésie 1965 – à la rencontre des poètes du Quebec" par Jean Royer

[3] *Le Devoir,* Mtl., P.Q., 21 Dec., 1968 "Tendresse de Marie Laberge Sobriété d'Andrée Chédid" par Jean-Guy Pilon

see also

La Presse, Mtl., P.Q., Sept., 1960 "A la Huchette – Exposition qui gagne à être vue mais dont la formule serait peut – être à modifier"

Le Soleil, Que., P.Q., May, 1960 " 'Etre ou ne pas être' artiste prend sa signification avec Marie Laberge" par Paule France Dufaux

Le Carabin, 26 Oct., 1961 "Marie Laberge" par J.-Claude Cossette

Le Droit, Ottawa, Ont., Dec. 19, 1962 "La Vie Artistique – Le rideau se lève. . ." par Edgar Demers

Chronicle-Telegraph, Sept. 21, 1963 "Disciplined Touch Lends Charm to 'Non-Landscapes' " by R.T.

L'Evénement, Que., P.Q. Sept. 23, 1963 "M. Laberge – Harmonies limineuses" par Paule France Dufaux

Le Nouvelliste, Trois Rivières, P.Q., Nov. 6, 1963 "Marie Laberge et Louis Perrier exposeront à l'hôtel de ville"

Le Soleil, Que., P.Q., May 5, 1965 "Marie Laberge expose à la Galerie Zanettin" par G. L'H.

Actualité, November, 1964 "Notre Femme du Mois: Marie Laberge" par Pauline Beaudry

L'Action, Nov., 1965 "Avec Marie Laberge; la difficulté d'être femme et celle d'être poète"

Chronicle-Telegraph, Que., P.Q., May 3, 1965 "Quebec Artist Changes Style" by F.J.P.

Le Soleil, Que. P.Q., 15 June, 1968 "Le Centre d'art de Saint-Laurent, Ile d'Orléans, ouvrira ses portes ce soir"

Echo-Vedette, 12 Oct., 1968 "Marie Laberge, peintre et poète" par Gergette Lacroix

Le Soleil, 18 Oct., 1968 (photo of artist with group on the occasion of the publishing of *L'Hiver à Brûler*)

Le Progrès, 10 Nov., 1968 "Marie Laberge à l'Art Canadien Chicoutimi" (and photo of her work "Les Pacifistes")

Le Soleil, 28 Sept., 1968 "Les images symboliques de Marie Laberge"

Ibid, 29 Mar., 1968 "Deux peintres de Quebec exposent à Montreal" par Guy Robert, P. 22

Le Nouvelliste, Dec. 5, 1969 "Marie Laberge parle de l'Art" par Doris Hamel

LABROSSE, dit Paul Jourdain
1697-1769

Born (most likely) in Montreal where his family were known as highly skilled joiners and carvers.[1] The Labrosse family and its tradition originated with Guillaume Jourdain (called Labrosse) a skilled craftsman brought from France by Bishop Laval when Laval established the Ecole des Arts et Métiers at Cap Tourmente (30 miles down the St. Lawrence from Quebec City) where a group of highly skilled craftsmen worked on decorations of churches and edifices and trained apprentices to follow in their footsteps.[2] Paul Labrosse carved among other things a number of madonnas, one of which is in the collection of Hôtel-Dieu, Montreal, entitled "The Virgin and Child" (wood 42" high), on the back of this work he signed his name with the date 'Paul Labrosse, 1755'.[3] He was active by 1704 in the Montreal area (Sault-au-Recollect 1739; Longueuil 1741). He carved an altar-piece with a set of apostle statuettes for a church at Longueuil (these statuettes were reproduced in Dr. R.H. Hubbard's book *The Development of Canadian Art,* Plate 52).[4] Another work, "The Virgin and Child" attributed to Labrosse is done in elm wood and was a gift to the Art Gallery of Toronto by Walter C. Laidlaw in 1935.[5] Very little work remains today, that can be attributed to Paul Labrosse or to other members of his family.[6]

References
[1] *Three Hundred Years of Canadian Art* (catalogue) by R.H. Hubbard and J.R. Ostiguy, Queen's Printer/NGC, 1967, P. 239
[2] *Canadian Art* by Graham McInnes, MacMillan, 1950, P. 11
[3] see [1]
[4] *The Development of Canadian Art* by R.H. Hubbard, Queen's Printer, Ottawa, 1963, P. 40
[5] *The Art Gallery Of Toronto* (catalogue), 1959, P. 46 (see *The Devel. of Can. Art* above P. 41)
[6] *The Arts In Canada,* Dept. Citizenship & Immigration, Ottawa, Queen's Printer, 1958, P. 27

LACELIN, Philippe
b.1938

Born in Montreal, P.Q., he received his Master of Arts from the University of Montreal in 1966 and his teacher's certificate in 1967. He taught for six years (1963-69) and did research in painting and engraving and exhibited his own paintings at the College de Joliette and Collège de Sainte-Thérèse in 1966. He travelled in France during 1967-8 where he enrolled in l'Ecole des Beaux-Arts, in the Province of Aix (1967) and he also studied engraving with Suzy David. He participated in a group show at Aix in 1968. On his return to Canada he continued in his studies and received a Quebec Cultural Affairs Bursary, 1969-70. He held a one man show at Galerie Artlenders de Montreal in April of 1969 and Galerie d'Europe, Quebec City, 1969. He lives in Montreal.

Reference
Biographical notes by Galerie Champagne enr., 16 rue Petit Champlain, Quebec 2, P.Q., for La Galerie d'Europe, Oct. 1969.
Le Soleil, Que., P.Q., Oct. 29, 1969 (photo of painting by Lacelin)

LACELLE, Beatrice

A folk painter from Spanish, Ontario, discovered in 1969 by Fred Owen, an artist co-ordinator for the Elliot Lake Centre for Continuing Education. Two other members of her family also paint. Her paintings were exhibited with those of her brother and sister (see below) at the Centre gallery in Spanish in July of 1969.

Reference

The Standard, Elliot Lake, Ont., July 24, 1969 "Works of Spanish Artists Become Exhibition Feature"

LACELLE, Florence

A folk painter from Spanish, Ontario, discovered in 1969 by Fred Owen, an artist co-ordinator for the Elliot Lake Centre for Continuing Education. Two other members of her family also paint. Her paintings were exhibited with those of her brother and sister at the Centre gallery in Spanish in July of 1969.

Reference

The Standard, Elliot Lake, Ont., July 24, 1969 "Works of Spanish Artists Become Exhibition Feature"

LACELLE, William

A farmer from Spanish, Ontario, who very early in his school years began sketching animals. His teachers on seeing his work advised him to become a commercial artist. This advice he never managed to follow. In 1946 while looking for work in Toronto, he was able to visit a number of galleries and began to paint. When he returned home to Spanish he continued to paint in his leisure hours and later offered his paintings for sale through a sign "Oil Paintings for Sale." It was through this sign that he was discovered by Fred Owen, an artist co-ordinator for Elliot Lake Centre. An exhibition of his work, and the work of his sisters, Florence and Beatrice, took place at the Centre gallery in Spanish in July of 1969.

Reference

The Standard, Elliot Lake, Ont., July 24, 1969 "Works of Spanish Artists Become Exhibition Feature"

LACROIX, Jacques

Born in Chicoutimi, P.Q., he attended the school of sculpture under the direction of Jean-Julien Bourgault for two years. In 1969 he held a one man show at Galerie Libre, Montreal, entitled "L'Exposition '2000' " and his cast iron pieces impressed Robert Ayre[1] as a potentially powerful abstract sculptural medium. The paper *Le Lingot* described Lacroix's semi mobile aluminium sculptures for the shop Lessard sur la côte as follows, "If you have been shopping in Chicoutimi recently...

LACROIX, Jacques (Cont'd)

you might have been intrigued by the four moving aluminum sculptures which catch the eye on entering the shop. Suspended on large wooden beams across the ceiling, each of these sculptures have both fixed and moving parts. They are eight feet in diameter and made from 1/8 inch thick aluminum sheet. In addition each has a gold coloured rim of about 10 inches in width and 25 feet in circumference. The fixed part is bright natural aluminum, reflecting light and illuminating the entire set. Each sculpture is suspended from the ceiling beams by three metal shafts held together by a chain link, allowing them to sway with the smallest air current." Raymond Lessard, owner of the shop commissioned Lacroix and Industries Couture of Chicoutimi to make the decorations.

References

[1] *The Montreal Star,* May 30, 1969

[2] *Le Lingot,* Arvida, P.Q., Nov. 7, 1969 "Fashions in Aluminum" (photo of sculpture)
see also
Le Courrier de Laviolette, Grand'Mère, P.Q., Oct. 22, 1969
Le Nouvelliste, Trois Rivières, April 4, 1968

LACROIX, Joseph Samuel Richard (Richard Lacroix)
b.1939

Born in Montreal, P.Q., he studied three years (1957-60) at l'Institut des Arts Graphiques, Montreal, under Albert Dumouchel, where he received his diploma in 1960[1]. Also in 1960 he received his certificate in teaching and in methodology at l'Ecole des Beaux-Arts, Montreal, and a certificate in aesthetics and history of art from l'Institut des Arts Appliqués, Montreal; he also became a professor in engraving at the Ecole des Beaux-Arts, Montreal.[2] He received a Canada Council grant for the period 1961-62 to study in different European engraving workshops, including Atelier 17, Paris, of printmaker Stanley William Hayter.[3] On his return to Canada in 1964 he founded L'Atelier Libre de Recherches Graphiques, with the assistance of the Ministry of Cultural Affairs of Quebec, and he also became co-founder of *Fusion Des Arts, Inc.* the same year. Robert Ayre[3] reviewing his prints at Galerie Agnes Lefort in 1963 noted, "Richard Lacroix's two years with Stanley Hayter at Atelier 17 in Paris have greatly enriched this young Montreal artist . . . . Lacroix has been seen at the Museum's Spring Show every year since 1960 and he received the Purchase Award last year; he was the only Canadian printmaker in the second Paris Biennial and has been in group exhibitions in Paris, New York and the Scandinavian countries. I remember a showing of his 'Bestiaire' and a few other prints at L'Art Français, but he has not had a full-scale one-man exhibition until now. He has scarcely had time. Its smallness — 17 or 18 prints out of two years' work — testifies to his seriousness and his discrimination. In the course of his experiments with plates, rollers and inks, he must have discarded many proofs and destroyed masses of paper . . . . Formerly, the print required as many plates and printings as there were colors, Lacroix uses one plate . . . . After spreading the first color, the artist takes advantage of intaglio and relief by using hard rollers to apply the ink to the highest surfaces and soft rollers to get another color into the hollows. There is more

706

LACROIX, Joseph Samuel Richard (Richard Lacroix) (Cont'd)

to it than that of course and one of the most fascinating, and rewarding, problems is preventing the inks from mixing with each other by using those with antagonistic oil consistencies. In this process, the print is conceived and brought into being as a whole, like a painting on canvas." The following year Marjorie Harris[4] in her article on printmaking in Quebec for *Canadian Art* explained, "Richard Lacroix returned to Canada from Paris in 1963 with two antique printing presses he had found in France, a set of gelatin rollers and little else. He spent the next two years concentrating on printing his own plates. Lacroix has gained a reputation as one of the finest print-makers in the country for the purity and clarity of his editions." in 1966 Lacroix founded The Graphic Guild with the assistance of the Ministry of Cultural Affairs of Quebec. In 1967 he turned his attentions to sculpture to create in co-operation with skilled technicians, "Synthesis of the Arts" under the joint credit of Fusion Des Arts, Inc. (Director, Richard Lacroix; participators: H. Saze, F. Souch, F. Rousseau, G. Gagnon and Y. Robillard) which was situated on the Forecourt of of the Art Gallery and Theatre of the Canadian Pavilion of Expo '67. This sculpture was made up of large discs of translucent acrylic on a concrete base with programmed lighting and music. For the Theatre Of The Youth Pavilion, Expo '67, he created "Les Méchaniques" (ten sculptural/kinetic/musical instruments for the active participation of spectators), and a mobile sculpture for the Montreal International Airport also one for Radio Québec. Over the years Lacroix has held one man shows at the following galleries: Galerie l'Art Français, Montreal (1961); Maison du Canada, Paris, France (1962); Dorothy Cameron Gallery, Toronto (1963); Galerie Agnès Lefort, Montreal (1963); Galerie XII, Montreal Museum of Fine Arts (1964); Camp des Jeunesses Musicales, Mont-Orford, Quebec (1966); Fleet Galleries, Winnipeg (1966); Triangle Gallery, San Francisco (1968); Dunkelman Gallery Toronto (1968). His work has been exhibited in many important shows including: Paris Biennial (1961); The International Biennial of Engraving, Yugoslavia (1963, 1965); Primera Biennial Americana de Grabado, Santiago Du Chile (1964); Triennial International of Engraving, Grenchen, Switzerland (1964, 1967); International Biennial of Engraving, Lugano, Switzerland (1964); International Biennial of Engraving, Cracow, Poland (1966); Three Hundred Years of Canadian Art at the National Gallery of Canada (1967); Retrospective of Quebec Painting at the Museum of Contemporary Art, Montreal (1967); Plastics at The Art Gallery of Ontario (1967); Graphics, Calgary (1967); Artistic Competition of Quebec (1965, 66, 67, 68, 69), Seventh Biennial of Canadian Painting (1968). He is represented in the following public collections: The National Gallery of Canada, Ottawa; The Montreal Museum of Fine Arts; The Arts Room, National Library, Paris; The Ministry of Cultural Affairs, Quebec; External Affairs, Ottawa; The Art Gallery of Ontario; The Museum of Contemporary Art, Montreal; Victoria and Albert Museum, London, England; Museum of Modern Art, New York, U.S.A.; Sherbrooke University; Sir George Williams University, Montreal; Queen's University, Kingston, Ont.; Hart House, U. of T.; University of Victoria, B.C. He has won many prizes for his paintings including: First Prize, "Festival of Flowers" contest, Montreal Museum of Fine Arts (1962) (Honourable Mention, 1964); Prize, Second National Print Show, Burnaby (1963); Prize, Canadian Graphic Art Show (1964); Prize at International Biennial of Engraving, Lugano (1964); Honourable Mention, International Triennial of Engraving, Grenchen (1964); First Prize, Painting section, Hadassah Exhibition, Montreal (1965) (Second Prize, 1966). He was made an Honourary Member, Engraving section, Accademia Fiorentina delle Arti del Disegno, Florence, Italy (1965). He lives in Montreal.

LACROIX, Joseph Samuel Richard (Richard Lacroix) (Cont'd)

References

[1] National Gallery of Canada Information Form rec'd May 29, 1962
[2] Information sheet from the artist in response to a questionnaire
[3] *The Montreal Star,* Dec. 14, 1963 "A High Opinion of Our Canadian Printmakers" by Robert Ayre
[4] *Canadian Art,* Sept/Oct 1965 "Print-making in Quebec" by Marjorie Harris, P. 20, 21
[5] *Canadian Sculpture, Expo '67* Introduction by William Withrow, Photography by Bruno Massenet, Graph, Montreal, 1967, Plate 45

see Also

Seventh Biennial of Canadian Painting, 1968, NGC/Queen's Printer, Exhibit No. 103 "Pointe à diamant VII" acrylic on canvas (60 x 60")
The Hart House Collection of Canadian Paintings by Jeremy Adamson, U. of T. Press, 1969, P. 95 Exhibit No. 63 "Variante (1965)" acrylic and oil on canvas (32 x 32")
Three Hundred Years Of Canadian Art by R.H. Hubbard and J.R. Ostiguy, NGC/Queen's Printer, 1967, P. 218, 219, No. 375 "Variante IV-N" Serigraph (18" x 18")
Vie Des Arts, Number 44, Autumn, 1966 "Montreal aujourd'hui par Yves Robillard, P. 50
Arts/Canada
Architecture/Canada
numerous other publications.

Deluxe Editions
Sept Eaux-Fortes (1959)
Pierres Du Soleil (1960)
Bestiaire (1961)

LACROIX, Paul

b.1929

Born at Sainte-Marie de Beauce, P.Q., he studied at the Ecole des Beaux-Arts, Quebec and at the Ecole des Beaux-Arts, Montreal under Alfred Pellan.[1] He then studied sculpture in Paris with Zadkine and also attended the Académie Brera de Milan where he studied with Marino Marini. Lacroix works in a wide range of media and has completed some important commissions. In 1949 he was awarded second prize by the Province of Quebec for his sculpture. He has exhibited his paintings and drawings at the Galerie Zanettin, Quebec City, for many years and in 1965 when F.J.P.[2] of the *Chronicle-Telegraph* noted, "The drawings – drawings from life and abstract compositions – make use of a new technique discovered, quite by accident, four months ago. Dry pigment of the sort that is combined with oil to make oil paint or egg to make gouache is applied with the hand and its pure form. The result is an incredible transparency and clarity of color and a softness similar to that found in pastel drawings. Lacroix's figure drawings combine a rhythmic interplay of a few simple lines with an ever so subtle use of distorties and of gentle coloring . . . . The abstract compositions in the collection are a free play with color itself. Colors are bright but never annoying to the eye. They glow with luminosity made possible by pigment in its pure state." In September of 1965 Lacroix was busy completing a large mural for the Royal Bank of Canada, d'Youville Square, Upper Town, Quebec City (110 ft. long by 11 1/2 ft. deep) composed of copper sheeting figures in relief on a multi-coloured Byzantine mosaic background depicting the economic development of the Province of Quebec from the first ships to enter the St. Lawrence to the completion of the Manicouagan Dam. In 1966 an exhibition of his paintings and drawings was held at the Musée de Québec when Jean Royer of *L'Action*[3] was very favourably impressed. Recently he made designs for tapestries, three of which

LACROIX, Paul (Cont'd)

were made in the workshops of Suzanne Goubely at Aubusson, France, and two in the workshops of Sister Monique Mercier of Quebec City. One of these tapestries entitled "Les Ombelles" made by Sister Mercier's workshop is in the collection of Laval University.[4] These five tapestries were exhibited at Galerie Zanettin in the fall of 1969.[5] Paul Lacroix is a professor of fine arts at the Ecole des Beaux-Arts, Quebec, and professor of architectural design and draughting at Laval University. Three of his sculptures decorate the Laval Campus buildings. He has also done set designing for Théâtre Lyrique de Nouvelle-France. His mobile creations have been included in a National Gallery of Canada travelling exhibition.

References

[1] National Gallery of Canada Information Form rec'd January, 1963
[2] *Chronicle-Telegraph*, Que., P.Q., Jan. 30, 1965 "Dry Pigment Helps Make Fine Pastel – like Works" by F.J.P.
[3] *L'Action Sociale Ltée.*, Que., P.Q., "Chronique des arts" par Jean Royer
[4] *Le Soleil*, Que., P.Q. "Tapisseries de Paul Lacroix" par Colette Auger
[5] *Chronicle-Telegraph*, Sept. 29, 1969 "Lacroix Works On Display" (photo of 'Le Follette')
see also
Le Soleil, P.Q., 30 Jan., 1965 "La douceur de la vie se dégage des oeuvres de Paul Lacroix" par Gaston L'Heureux
Le Guide, 15 April, 1965 "Paul Lacroix Exécute Les Décors De L'Opéra 'Mireille' Et Travaille Simultanément A Bon Nombre De Projets"
Chronicle-Telegraph, Que., P.Q., Sept. 27, 1965 "Fashioning Immense Mural Takes Dexterity, Strength"
Le Nouvelliste, Trois-Rivières, 20 Oct., 1965 "Gamanch – triomphe des apparences Lacroix – une certaine plénitude"
Chronicle-Telegraph, 22 Oct., 1966 "Lacroix Exhibitions Free Exercise in Imagination" by R.T.
Le Soleil, Que., P.Q., 22 Oct., 1966 "Peintures Et Dessins De Paul Lacroix Au Musée Et A La Galerie Zanettin"
Le Petit Journal, Mtl., P.Q., 28 Aug., 1966 "Paul Lacroix, un peintre de couleur et de l'amour . . ." par Yolande Rivard
Le Soleil, Que., P.Q., 15 Jan., 1966 "La Murale de Paul Lacroix"
La Presse, Mtl., P.Q. 8 Jan., 1966 "Paul Lacroix: Sculptures Sur Commande" par Jean O'Neil
Le Grand Livre de la Tapisserie edited by Bibliotheque des Arts, Paris (a history of tapestry)

LAFFIN, Heinz Gerhard
b.1926

Born in Germany, he came to Canada in 1953 and settled for a time in Quebec. He studied pottery at the Vancouver School of Art under R. Waghsteen; University of British Columbia under John Reeve and under Paul Saldner in Northwest Seattle, U.S.A. His pottery has been exhibited in the following shows, B.C. Craftsman (1962) (1964), Vancouver; Canadian Handicrafts Guild, Montreal (1963) (1967); Canadian Fine Crafts, National Gallery of Canada, Ottawa, 1967; Canadian Travel Exhibition abroad (1964). He visited Hornby Island, B.C., in November of 1968 when he presented jointly with Wayne Ngan a wheel pottery throw. He lives in Vancouver, B.C., where he taught ceramics at the Vancouver School of Art (1965-67).

LAFFIN, Heinz Gerhard (Cont'd)

National Gallery of Canada Information form rec'd July 5, 1967

The Upper Islander, Campbell River, B.C., Nov. 20, 1968 (large photo of artist's work on display)

The National Gallery of Canada, Canadian Fine Crafts catalogue, 1966-67 "Pottery" Cat. No. 63, jar with lid (stoneware) Cat. No. 64, Small pitcher, stoneware

LAFLAMME, Hélène

She studied engraving under Albert Dumouchel in Montreal and received a bursary from the Province of Quebec Arts Council to continue her studies in France and has exhibited her interesting works at the following galleries: Hélène de Champlain, Group Show (1960); galerie l'Etable, Group Show (1962); privately, organized by Claude Haeffely (1965); Galerie Jason-Teff, Montreal (1966); McGill University (1967); Galerie Kaléidoscope (1967); Galerie Soleil, Old Montreal (1967) privately by M. J.-M. Ritcher; Galerie Restaurant d'Europe de Quebec, (1968). She was last reported studying in Vaud, Switzerland.

References

*Photo-Journal,*Montreal, P.Q., Oct. 19, 1966 "Le talent devrait passer avant l'âge" par Michelle Tisseyre

Le Soleil, Que., P.Q., "Les animaux stylisés de Hélène Laflamme" par Grazia Merler

Notice of exhibit by Michel Champagne for Galerie Restaurant d'Europe, 1968

LAFLAMME, Roger

b.1925

Born in Montreal, P.Q., he studied under Ozias Leduc and Adrien Hébert.[1] He has exhibited his paintings at the following places: l'Auberge des Deux Lanternes, Cap St. Martin (near Montreal) (1947); Cercle Universitaire, Montreal (1948); Amis de l'Art (1948).[2] He is known for his landscapes and is represented in important collections in Montreal and Toronto. He is a member of the Art Association of Montreal. No recent information is available on this artist.

References

[1] National Gallery of Canada Information Form rec'd July 5, 1949

[2] Ibid

see also

Photo-Journal, April 29, 1948 "L'Exposition de Roger Laflamme témoigne des progrès de l'artiste" par L.L.M.

LAFLEUR, Claude

Born in Montreal, he studied at Mount St. Louis College, and painting at the Montreal School of Fine Arts. He became interested in plastic sculpture and Guatemalan art when studying architecture. He became Director of the University of

LAFLEUR, Claude (Cont'd)

Sherbrooke Art Gallery in 1964 and subsequently taught design and composition at the Montreal School of Fine Arts (1965-67). In 1969 he collaborated with Michel Denis, a ceramist, in the creation of a large mural (C. 20 x 10 ft.) depicting the Virgin Mary in a Canadian landscape, for the International Basilica of Nazareth, a Catholic church in Israel. The contract for the work was handled by Reverend Father Alfonso Calbrese of the Centro Propaganda Stampa di Terra Santa. The work was chosen so that a Canadian creation would be included in the decoration of the church. The mural was done on fifty 12 x 12 inch pieces of ceramic tile.

References
Record, Sherbrooke, P.Q., March 7, 1969 "North Hatley artists make mural for Basilica" see also
La Voix de l'Est, Granby, P.Q., March 6, 1969 "Deux artistes de North Hatley créeront une murale à Nazareth"
La Presse, Mtl., P.Q., Sept. 20, 1969 "Le Canada A Nazareth" par Huguette O'Neil

LAFLEUR, Pierre

His surrealistic paintings and drawings were exhibited at La galerie Kaléidoscope in Montreal. His work is of good quality although little or no information is available on this artist.

Reference
Exhibition notice from La galerie Kaléidoscope (reproduction of artist's work)

LAFONTAINE, Yvan

He has set up a workshop in the basement of his home at Ste-Foy, Quebec, where he is doing graphic research with other engravers. His own engravings were shown at Laval University.

References
Le Soleil, Que., P.Q., April 29, 1967 "Avenir de la gravure" par Claude Daigneault

LAFORGE, Jean

b.1911

Born in Belgium, he was a prisoner of the Germans in the Second World War. He later came to Canada and settled in Chicoutimi and held a one man show of his work at Galerie L'Art Français in the winter of 1965.

References
The Gazette, Mtl., P.Q., Feb. 27, 1965, Art, "A Fanciful Imagination" by R.M.
The Montreal Star, Mtl., P.Q., Feb. 20, 1965 "An Individualist From Chicoutimi" by Michael Ballantyne
Le Phare, Chicoutimi, P.Q., 24 Feb., 1965 "Un artiste de Chicoutimi-Nord tient avec succès une première exposition à Montréal"

LAING, Shayna (Mrs. Frederick Michaels)

Born and educated in Montreal she later studied at the Ecole des Beaux Arts, Montreal (c.1949), and the Instituto de San Miguel de Allende, Mexico, and has exhibited her paintings at the following galleries: YM-YWHA, Westbury Avenue, Montreal (1964); The Cowansville Art Centre, Cowansville, P.Q. (1964); L'Art Français Montreal (1966); Wiener Gallery, New York, U.S.A. (1967); Galerie Martal, Montreal (1968) when Michael Ballantyne[1] of *The Montreal Star* noted, "Miss Laing has always been an accomplished draughtsman and something of an experimenter as well. She works in something she calls a 'mixed aqueous' formula which gives the paintings a lush, reverberant quality and a texture not unlike the surface depth of a print." Mr. Ballantyne also noted that his preference was with her drawings. Her work can also be seen at the Carmen Lamanna Gallery in Toronto. She signs her paintings "Shayna". She lives in Montreal with her husband and children.

References

[1] *The Montreal Star*, Mtl., P.Q., April 6, 1968 "Sherry Grauer, Laing exhibitions" by Michael Ballantyne

see also

The Montreal Star, Mtl., P.Q., Jan. 2, 1964 article on artist by Laureen Hicks

The Monitor, Mtl., P.Q., Jan. 9, 1964 "Oil display"

Eastern Townships Advertiser, July 8, 1964 "Shayna Laing Exhibition"

The Suburban, Mtl., P.Q., Feb. 17, 1966 "Artists Shayna Laing Exhibits"

News, St. Laurent, P.Q., Feb. 17, 1966 "St. Laurent exhibitor has showing"

The Montreal Star, Sept. 13, 1967 "Montreal artist has one man show in New York Gallery" by Sheila Arnopoulos

Montrealer, Mtl., P.Q., June, 1968 "Art Profile; Shayna Laing" by Alex Mogelon

LAJAMBE, Denise

b.1928

Born in Montreal, P.Q., she studied at the Ecole des Beaux Arts, there, from 1943 to 1945 under Charles Mallard and others. Later, after her marriage to a Canadian soldier she lived in Germany where she studied at the Dusseldorf Academy with Professor Otta Pankok. She held a one man show of her paintings at the Arts and Crafts Shop, near Cataraqui, Ontario, just outside Kingston (1958) and at the Serge Moresco Art Gallery, Quebec City (1959). She was last reported living in Quebec City, her husband, an army officer being stationed at Camp Valcartier.

References

Whig-Standard, Kingston, Ont., Aug. 27, 1958 "Artist and Art Have Charmed Me!" by Jean Edwards

Chronicle-Telegraph, Que., P.Q., Sept. 22, 1959 "Canadian Artist Arrives At A Satisfying Maturity"

L'Evénement Journal, Que., P.Q. Sept. 22, 1959 "Denise Lajambe, peintre de l'âme humaine, donne sa note" par Pierre Godin

L'Action Catholique, Que., P.Q. Sept. 23, 1959 "La Galerie Moresco inaugure sa saison d'hiver avec Denise Lajambe" par Nicole Blouin

LAJEUNIE, Jean-Claude
b.1943

Born in Eaubonne, France, he came to Canada in 1951 and later studied sculpture at the Ecole des Beaux Arts, Montreal, under Louis Archambault and Armand Filion (1961-65), receiving his diploma in sculpture in 1965; he continued with free studies in sculpture there for an additional year. He has participated in a number of exhibitions including the Quebec Provincial Competition held at the Museum of Contemporary Art, Montreal, where he won the purchase award in 1966; Perspective '67, Toronto, where he also won a prize; Youth Pavilion at Expo '67 by three sculptures; Critics' Choice, The Art Centre, Mount Royal (chosen by Claude Jasmin in 1966 and Yves Robillard in 1967). He has received other honours. He is represented in the Museum of Contemporary Art, Montreal by his steel and plastic sculpture entitled "L'Emissaire" and in other collections. He lives in Montreal and has been Sculptor (Assistant Decorator) at L'Oratoire St. Joseph Du Mont Royal since October, 1967.

Reference

   National Gallery of Canada Information Form rec'd 15 March, 1968

LALIBERTÉ, Alfred
1878-1953

Born at Ste. Élizabeth, Arthabaska, the son of Joseph Laliberté and Marie Richard. His father had been a woodcutter, farmer, and finally a miller.[1] Alfred was the eldest in the family and about the age of fifteen began carving with his pocket knife during his free moments from chores at home.[2] He later attended the Conseil des Arts et Métiers, in Montreal.[3] When he was twenty-four, a public subscription helped finance his study in Europe and one of his greatest supporters was Sir Wilfred Laurier.[4] Through this support, Alfred Laliberté studied at the Ecole des Beaux Arts in Paris in 1902 under Gabriel Jules Thomas and Antoine Injalbert.[5] In 1904 he exhibited his sculpture at the Salon de Paris and received 'special mention' for his "Jeunes Indiens Chassant" (Young Indians Hunting) now in the National Gallery of Canada.[6] He also exhibited in Paris in 1905 and 1906. He returned home but made visits to France in 1910, 1917 and 1923. He was elected an Associate of the Royal Canadian Academy in 1912 and became a full member in 1919. One of his most remarkable undertakings was a series of bronze figures depicting the history of French Canadians. The series was divided into three categories: crafts, customs, and legends. They were modelled in clay and then cast in bronze. This series, which included 215 subjects, was purchased by the Province of Quebec and placed in the Quebec Provincial Museum. The whole project from its earliest conception, through planning and realization took Laliberté nearly fifteen years. But the series was only a part of his life's work of 700 works. He did about 200 paintings, 100 or so silver rings and other items such as pendants, bracelets, shoe and belt buckles. He wrote his memoirs in four parts: *Mémoires* (Vol. 1), *Artistes de mon temps* (Vol. 2), *Les hommes et les choses* (Vol. 3), and *Réflexions* (Vol. 4).[7] Laliberté established a workshop at 3531 rue Sainte Famille which he built in 1920. In an article on this studio building Robert Ayre[8] in 1962 noted, "What will become of this great storehouse of Canada's past? As the old buildings of Montreal go down to make way for skyscrapers and wider streets and parking lots, our sense of history is quickened and our consciences have been disturbed . . . . Let us be

LALIBERTÉ, Alfred (Cont'd)

aware of the studio Laliberté built in 1920 and the accumulation of the work he left in it. And let's not forget how much of the history of art in Canada was made elsewhere in this old house at 3531. Joseph Franchère, Maurice Cullen, Robert Pilot, Sherriff Scott, Jean Palardy, Jori Smith and Mario Merola all worked under its roof." At this point Laliberté's studio had been untouched for eight years following Laliberté's death. It was Laliberté's great wish that his house and workshop should become a museum. He purchased about 100 paintings of other Canadian artists and was regarded as being generous and noble.[9] He encouraged many artists and was a professor at the Ecole des Beaux Arts in Montreal. Some fine examples of his larger works include: the statue of "Dollard des Ormeaux" (leader of the heroes of the Long Sault), Lafontaine Park, Montreal (also one at Carillon, Quebec); "Louis Hébert", Quebec City; Sir Wilfrid Laurier's tomb in Notre Dame Cemetry, Ottawa; Christ The King (Christ Roi) at Roberval, Quebec; "Les Patriotes de 1837", Quebec City; a public fountain at the Parliament Buildings, Quebec City, dedicated to Maisonneuve; Sir Wilfrid Laurier's monument at Arthabaska and other large works. His bronze figures where exhibited in the French pavilion at Man and His World in 1968.[10] At the time of Alfred Laliberté's death the following comments appeared in *The Montreal Star*,[11] "Mr. Laliberté worked for the most part on the monumental scale and will be remembered best for his work in this field, but, scattered about the world, recognized as fine work, are many of his portrait busts, medallions and medals. He will be remembered here, too, for having created on Ste. Famille Street something that became an art center in the city. It was he who built the studio building there which housed artists of such renown as Cullen and Pilot and still served another generation of painters and sculptors. Quebec is rich in artists who pursue the historical tradition. Alfred Laliberté was not the least of these." Alfred Laliberté was survived by his wife who until her death lived at the Ste. Famille studio building which has tragically fallen victim to the wrecker's hammer. Laliberté received an Honorary Doctorate from the University of Montreal (1940); Member l'Académie des Beaux-Arts de l'Institut de France, Sculpture Section (1948). In 1934 a book entitled *Légendes-Coutumes, Métiers De La Nouvelle-France, Bronzes D'Alfred Laliberté*[12] was published by Librairie Beauchemin Limitée, Montreal, in a limited edition of 3,000 copies. Today it is very difficult to find copies of this edition. Where they have all disappeared remains a mystery.

References

[1] *La Revue Moderne*, Paris, France, Feb., 1938 "Laliberté, Sculpteur Du Terroir Canadien" par Albert Laberge

[2] *The Montrealer*, Mtl., P.Q., January, 1962 "Laliberté's Studio" by Robert Ayre (photographs by Sam Tata)

[3] see[1]

[4] see[1]

[5] Nat. Gal. of Can. Info. Form rec'd 1930, also info. sheet rec'd Aug, 1946

[6] *Nat. Gal. of Can. Catalogue, Vol. 3* by R.H. Hubbard, P.351

[7] see[5]

[8] see[2]

[9] see[1]

[10] *La Presse*, Mtl., P.Q., Sept. 7, 1968 "Nos Ancêtres À L'Age Du Bronze" par Noella Desjardins

[11] *The Montreal Star*, Mtl., P.Q., Jan. 14 "Alfred Laliberté, R.C.A."

LALIBERTÉ, Alfred (Cont'd)

[12] *Légendes-Coutumes, Métiers De La Nouvelle-France Bronzes D'Alfred Laliberté*, Preface by Charles Maillard, Directeur général des Beaux Arts de la province de Québec, Librairie Beauchemin Limitée, Mtl., P.Q., 1934.
see also
Le Droit, Ottawa, Ont., June 24, 1920 "Un Monument Érigé À Dollard Au Parc Lafontaine, Montréal"
The Canadian Magazine, August, 1920
The Globe, Tor., Ont., Aug. 24, 1921 "Art and Artists"
Mon Magazine, March, 1931 "Les Artistes de chez nous – Monsieur Alfred Laliberté"
La Presse Mtl., P.Q., Nov. 20, 1922 "Sa Meilleure Oeuvre"
The Ottawa Journal, Jan. 29, 1942 "Senator Dandurand Honored By Colleagues at Presentation" (a bronze bust of Dandurand by A. Laliberté)
The Montreal Gazette, Jan. 29, 1942 "Bronze Bust Given to Dandurand In Ceremony in Upper Chamber"
Ibid, Jan. 14, 1953 "Noted Sculptor Dies at Home Here"
La Patrie, Mtl., P.Q., Jan. 14, 1953 "Décès du sculpteur Alfred Laliberté"
The Ottawa Citizen, Jan. 14, 1953 "A. Laliberté, Sculptor, Dies"
The Star, Sudbury, Ont., Jan. 19, 1953 "Province With Culture"
La Patrie, Mtl., P.Q., 27 May, 1962 "Où Iront Les Oeuvres Du Grand Sculpteur A. Laliberté? "
Le Petit Journal, Mtl., P.Q. Dec. 22, 1963
Ibid, Dec. 22, 1963 "Attend-on que le feu rase le Musée Alfred Laliberté? "
The Fine Arts In Canada by Newton MacTavish, MacMillan, Tor., 1925, P.82-3
Yearbook Of The Arts In Canada, 1928-1929, Edited by Bertram Brooker, MacMillan, Tor., 1929, P.97
Who's Who In Canada, 1940-41, P.748
Canadian Art by Graham McInnes, MacMillan, Tor., 1950, P.93
The Arts In Canada, Ed. by Malcolm Ross, "Sculpture" by William S.A. Dale, P.36
Canadian Art, Its Origin And Development by William Colgate, Ryerson Paperbacks, Tor., 1967, P.127, 198, 200, 208

LALIBERTÉ, Joseph Laurent Guy (Guy Laliberté)
b.1930

Born in Hull, Quebec, he studied drawing under Professor M. Bernard Lefort at the Ecole Technique de Hull in 1952.[1] He won first prize for drawing and second prize for painting in "Les Compagnons de l'Art" competition, Hull, P.Q. in 1956.[2] He did a portrait of Princess Grace of Monaco based on other studies and the work was accepted by her.[3] He completed three murals[4] in 1958 for the Knights of Columbus, Hull, entitled "The Prospector", "The Rockies", "The Trappers" also another for the Villeneuve Room (Fortier & Sherbrooke, Hull) in 1959.[5] More recently he has been creating surrealistic paintings[6] and small sculpture. His work has been praised by Alfred Pellan, noted Canadian painter.

References
[1] Nat. Gal. of Can. Info. Form rec'd Nov. 16, 1962
[2] Ibid
[3] *The Ottawa Citizen*, Jan. 23, 1958 "Princess Grace Accepts Hull Artist's Painting"
[4] *Le Droit*, Ottawa, Ont., Apr. 10, 1958 "Murales de Guy Laliberté au local de Hull des C. de C.
[5] Ibid, Apr. 15, 1959
[6] *The Ottawa Journal*, Feb. 5, 1968 "Surrealism Striking In Hull Art Exhibit"

LALIBERTÉ, Joseph Laurent Guy (Guy Laliberté) (Cont'd)

see also
Le Droit, May 3, 1969 "Les arts visuels – Coincidences" par Pierre Pelletier
Ibid, Dec. 13, 1969 "Laliberté Les Pieds À Terre"

LALIBERTÉ, Madeleine

Born at Victoriaville, Que., she studied at the Ecole des Beaux-Arts in Quebec. She then went to Paris where she worked at the Grande Chaumière and with Marcel Gromaire in painting. Returning to Canada she went on to the United States and Mexico where she spent six weeks at the School of Fine Arts in Mexico City. She returned to Canada and exhibited jointly with Jean Soucy in Quebec City in 1940. In 1942 she was the winner of three first prizes at the Quebec provincial art competition. She studied in New York under Amedée Ozenfant in the winters between 1942 and 1944. Jean-Paul Lemieux writing in *Canadian Art* in 1944 noted, "Madeleine Laliberté is a versatile painter. She is at home in any subject: portraits, landscapes, still-life, nudes. Her colour and design are excellent. Her art is very much alive. Influenced by Gromaire's architectural arrangements her paintings were at first very brilliant in colour, but a little flat in treatment. She soon lost that flatness however by her intensive study of line and volume, which is the credo of Ozenfant's art. Now she is working by herself and creating something of her own, something deep and profound and at the same time extremely characteristic of her charming personality." In 1950 she exhibited 80 of her works at the Compagnie Paquet Limitée in Quebec City. No recent information is available on her.

References
   Canadian Art, December-January, 1943-1944 Coast To Coast In Art "Quebec – The Museum of the Province of Quebec" by Jean-Paul Lemieux
   Le Soleil, June 1, 1950 "Exposition De Peintures: Mlle Madeleine Laliberté" (Photo of artist and work)
   L'Union Des Cantons, Arthabaska, P.Q., July 27, 1950 "Une artiste-peintre de chez-nous! "

LALIBERTÉ, Norman
b.1925
Born in Worcester, Mass., U.S.A., of French-Canadian parents, he was raised in Montreal.[1] He studied in the Worcester Museum in Massachusetts and the Institute of Design in Chicago (1947-48). He won a painting scholarship to the Cranbrook Academy, Bloomfield, Mich. (1948-50),[2] and received his MS degree in Art Education at the Institute of Design at the Illinois Institute of Technology (mid 50's).[3] He taught at the Kansas City Art Institute; St. Mary's College in Notre Dame, Indiana and at the Rhode Island School of Design.[4] He began making banners while a resident artist at St. Mary's College in 1959 after having seen decorative banners at the Siena Festivals in Italy. From 1963-65 he was Design Consultant for the Vatican Pavilion, New York World's Fair during which time he created and executed 88 large banners.[5] In the spring of 1965 he held his first one man show in Canada at the Waddington Galleries, Montreal, of his drawings and banners, subsequently he exhibited at the Galerie Dresdnere, Toronto (1966);

LALIBERTÉ, Norman (Cont'd)

Robertson Galleries, Ottawa (1967); Gallery Moos, Mtl. (1969) and elsewhere in the United States.[6] He is the author of nine books.[7] He was last listed as living in Ossining, New York.

References

[1] Information sheet, Waddington Galleries, 1966
[2] *Canadian Art*, Nov./Dec., 1965 "Banners with that Festive Look" by Alex Mogelon
[3] Ibid
[4] Ibid
[5] see [1]
[6] Information sheet, Waddington Galleries, 1968
[7] *The History of The Cross* by Norman Laliberté, Macmillan, 1960
Banners and Hangings by Norman Laliberté and Sterling McIlheny, Reinhold Pub., 1966
Wooden Images by Norman Laliberté and Maureen Jones, Reinhold, 1966
The Crayon Book by Norman Laliberté, Reinhold, 1967
Silhouettes and Shadow by Norman Laliberté, Reinhold, 1968
Art: Of Wonder and a World, design consultant, Art Education, Inc., 1967
The Brayer Technique by Norman Laliberté, Reinhold, 1968
Pencil by Norman Laliberté, Reinhold, 1968
Ink by Norman Laliberté, Reinhold, 1969
see also
The Gazette, Mtl., P.Q., May 15, 1965 "The Spell Is Inescapable" by Réa Montbizon
The Montreal Star, May 15, 1965 "Norman Laliberté A Religious Art" by Robert Ayre
Montreal-Matin, Nov. 4, 1969 "Un Aquarelliste Expose" (photo of artist and M. Walter Moos – also caption)
The Gazette, Mtl., P.Q., Nov. 8, 1969 "Laliberté's contagious quality of joy" by Ann Capper

---

LAMARCHE, Gail

A Montreal artist who studied at the Ecole des Beaux-Arts (Mtl.) and the Montreal Museum of Fine Arts school.[1] She has done painting, ceramics, but in 1961 on a visit to Zurich, she discovered the possibilities of batik creations and has been working in this medium ever since.[2] Lisa Balfour[3] reviewing her work in 1964 noted, "She admits to being influenced by all sorts of creations whether traditional or primitive, oriental or western, but prefers to control the liberty of her choice of influence. 'My primary reactions are set down in my first sketches,' she said, adding that it might take three weeks before she had succeeded in composing a design which seemed a totality of her expression . . . . Symbols, such as the sun, appear often in her batik murals. One, in reds and golds, is dedicated to Paul Varley, whose verse 'A l'Aurore' is described across the surface of a huge crimson sun. Other examples bear abstract titles such as 'Improvisation II' or 'Introspection.' 'High Mass,' recalls the form and richness of an embroidered church vestment, its basic color being royal purple." Two examples of her batiks were chosen by the Federal Government for the display in the Artisans' Exhibition in Florence, Italy, also in Germany. Her work has been shown at the Artlenders gallery, Westmount, Quebec; the Montreal Museum of Fine Arts; Stratford, Ontario; Toronto, Ont.; New York City, U.S.A., and elsewhere. She has been teaching design to children in primary schools in Montreal.

LAMARCHE, Gail (Cont'd)

References
[1] *The Montreal Star*, June 30, 1964 "Artist's Batiks Going to Europe" by Lisa Balfour
[2] Ibid
[3] Ibid
see also
La Terre de Chez Nous, Mtl., P.Q., May 5, 1965 "Galerie de talents féminins" par Jacqueline April
Le Devoir, Mtl., P.Q., April 8, 1967 "Gail Lamarche"

LAMARCHE, Ulric
1867-1921

Born in Oakland, California, U.S.A., he arrived in Canada in 1874. He later studied in Paris at the Ecole des Beaux-Arts under Jean Leon Gérôme. He returned to Canada and lived in Montreal where he worked and died. His widow willed six of his small sketches to the Art Association of Montreal. These sketches were handed over to the Association in 1939 by his niece.

References
National Gallery of Canada Infor. Form (undated)

L'AMARRE, Pierre
b.1915

Born in Germany, he studied art and architecture at the Academies of Fine Arts in Dresden, Leipsig, Paris and Berlin. He worked as a stage designer, illustrator and satirical cartoonist in several European countries.[1] He has held one man exhibitions of his paintings in Germany, Hungary, Switzerland and Italy.[2] He came to Canada in 1951 and joined the staff of the National Film Board where he became art director.[3] He was commissioned to illustrate a Bible owned by Cardinal Leger.[4] At various times his caricatures have appeared in many Canadian newspapers and magazines. His paintings have been exhibited at Galerie Agnes Lefort (1958); Galerias Excelsior, Mexico City (1962); Gemst Gallery (1966) and elsewhere. In 1958 Dorothy Pfeiffer noted his work as follows, "Pierre l'Amarre's eighteen paintings . . . are emotionally alive and vibrant with color. Although non-representational in intent they are exactly the reverse in feeling. For strangely enough, each individual painting tells its own story clearly. Many of the works have a definitely religious quality. Others are drenched in nostalgic memories. Several of them give one the impression of theatre. While some have been painted only for the joy of form and color relationship."

References
[1] *The Gazette*, Mtl., P.Q., April 12, 1958 "Pierre L'Amarre Exhibition" by Dorothy Pfeiffer
[2] Ibid
[3] *The Monitor* Mtl., Feb. 17, 1966 "Art exhibit features Mexico"
[4] see[1]
[5] see[1]

LAMARSH, Rhoda E. (Mrs. W.C. LaMarsh)
c.1892-1960
A Niagara Falls artist who exhibited with the Niagara District Art Association. She was the widow of W. Clayton Lamarsh, a lawyer, and mother of Judy V. LaMarsh former Secretary of State of Canada.

Reference
>Globe & Mail, March 7, 1960 "Artist Noted In Niagara Area"

LAMARTINE, Gert Louis
1898-1965
He studied painting at the University of Heidelberg and the Academy of Fine Arts, Karlsruhe, Germany. After he arrived in Canada he established an interior decorating studio in Montreal from which studio he worked for more than forty years. Under his direction his firm decorated numerous houses in the Montreal district as well as the famous hotels Chateau Frontenac, Quebec City; Chateau Laurier, Ottawa; Chateau Lake Louise, Banff, Alberta; Queen Elizabeth Hotel, Montreal. His paintings are impressionistic and abstract. He did portraits, figures studies, landscapes and still life studies, and chose his subjects from many countries where he has travelled (Japan, China, Caribbean, Portugal, Spain and elsewhere). His work was exhibited at various places including the Montreal Museum of Fine Arts (Gallery XII), 1959, and Toit de Chaume gallery, Piedmont outside Montreal (1964). He did mosaics and sculpture as well.

References
>The Gazette, Mtl., P.Q., Dec (?), 1959 "Gallery XII" by D.Y.P.
>L'Echo du Nord, St. Jerome, P.Q., June 3, 1964 "Un peintre international expose"

LAMB, Harold Mortimer
b.1872
Born at Leatherhead, Surrey, England, he came to Canada and settled first in Montreal where he became a friend of A.Y. Jackson.[1] Later he moved to Vancouver, B.C., and contributed articles to the Bureau of Information, B.C., Government. He became Sec.-Treas. of the Provincial Mining Association of B.C.; Secretary of the Canadian Mining Inst. and served on the staff of the Department of Mines in Ottawa. He was founder and publisher of the Boundary Creek Times (1895); Managing Editor B.C. Mining Record (1897-1904); Editor Canadian Mining Review (1905); author of the B.C. Government Bulletins (1902-3), etc. As an art critic he wrote in defence of the Group of Seven when most other critics attacked their work.[2] After his retirement he took up painting about 1942 although he had been interested in the arts many years before. His paintings and photography were displayed at the Vancouver Art Gallery in 1952 when "Palette"[3] of The Province noted, "Mr. Lamb's current small but highly interesting one-man exhibition of oil paintings, and also some pictorial photographs, will come as a surprise to many art lovers unaware of a genuine talent seriously developed only during the past ten years. In a colorful manner, mingling poetic imagination with lively realism in the joy of expressing himself in paint, the artist provides rich entertainment with his group of

LAMB, Harold Mortimer (Cont'd)

pictures influenced by neo-impressionism but with the personality of their creator emerging very clearly." His daughter is the well known Canadian painter Molly Lamb Bobak (see Vol. 1 of this publication).

References
[1] *Canadian Men And Women of The Time*, Morgan, 1912, P.630
A Painter's Country by A.Y. Jackson, Clarke, Irwin, Tor., P.47
[2] *September Gale* by John A.B. McLeish, J.M. Dent, London, P.54
[3] *The Province*, Van., B.C., June 14, 1952 "80-Year-Old's Show Highly Interesting" by Palette
The Sun, Van., B.C., June 9, 1952 "Businessman's Collection – Thousandth Show For Art Gallery"
Ibid, Sept. 22, 1960 (photo of portrait of Lamb, done by another artist, which is now in the collection of the Vancouver Art Gallery)
The Province, Van., B.C., July 29, 1967 (review of artist's work)

LAMBERT, Jacques

He first started painting in 1957 and studied under Hugh John Barrett at the Ecole des Beaux-Arts, Arvida from 1960 on and held his first one man show in 1963 at Galerie de l'Oeil, Chicoutimi. A prolific artist of drawings, gouaches, water colours, oils, inks and compositions from diverse materials, some of his work is reminiscent of Paul Klee. He is also a musician and plays the flute and clarinet. Is a member of the philharmonic society of Chicoutimi. He studied music for two years at the Chicoutimi conservatory. He was an announcer for Station CBJ of the CBC and is now director of several regular radio shows. His taste in music reflects itself in his abstract painting. He speaks Spanish fluently. He has exhibited his paintings at La Maison La Sauvegarde, Montreal (1966); the Cultural Centre of Jonquière (1969) and elsewhere. He has won a number of prizes for his work. He lives in Chicoutimi, P.Q.

References
Le Lingot, Arvida, Sept. 5, 1963 "Jacques Lambert à l'honneur au cours national d'art"
L'Industrie, (Jonquière-Kenogami-Arvida) Dec. 15, 1965 "Jacques Lambert, de Chicoutimi, un homme à multiples facettes"
Le Petit Journal, Mtl., P.Q. Jan. 16, 1966 " 'La Maison' reçoit un artiste de Chicoutimi" par Paul Gladu
Le Soleil, Que., P.Q., Jan. 18, 1969 "Jacques Lambert sait faire vivre ses toiles"
Progrès-Dimanche, Chicoutimi, P.Q. Jan. 19, 1969 (photo and caption)

LAMBERT, Jane

b.1950

The daughter of Rev. and Mrs. Richard Lambert, she obtained her Jr. Matriculation in Montreal and Sr. Matriculation at Central Secondary School in London, Ontario. She graduated in Fine Art at Sir George Williams University in Montreal and went on to the Beal Technical School, London, Ontario, where she took a special art course for two years. She exhibited her work at the London Public Art Gallery Art Mart and Western Ontario Exhibition. She has opened a studio at Watford, Ontario, where she will also conduct art classes.

LAMBERT, Jane (Cont'd)

Reference
>   *Guide-Advocate*, Watford, Ont., Aug. 14, 1969 "Will Open Studio Here"

LAMBERT, Richard Tullie

b.1923

Born in London, England, he came to Canada in 1939 and settled in Toronto. He served with the RCAF during the Second World War and resided in England from 1948 to 1952. He studied at the School of Art and Design in Montreal under Dr. Arthur Lismer. He has exhibited in London and Paris and was last reported as working as scenic artist for the CBC-TV in Toronto. He is a member of the Society of Mural Painters, England (1949/Treas. 1951-52).

Reference
>   National Gallery of Canada Information Form rec'd Jan. 19, 1954

LAMBERT, Ronald

An Oshawa, Ontario, artist who studied under Miss Van Luven at the O.C.V.L. Art Department; Banff School of Fine Arts; and under Hans Hofmann at Provincetown, Massachusetts. He is a realistic and abstract painter. For his landscapes he has drawn much of his subject matter from the Ontario countryside. In his abstract work he has found expression through concentration on volume in space, planes, line, texture and colour.

Reference
>   *Times-Gazette*, Oshawa, Ont., Oct. 16, 1950 "Work of Local Artist On Display At C.R.A."

LAMBTON, Gwenda

Born in Wilhelmshaven, Germany, of Scottish father and English mother. Her travel in Spain, Italy, and in London, England where she studied at the Westminister School of Art, provided her with an ideal background in the arts. She married, just before the Second World War, in London and came to Canada where she taught art and languages. She took post graduate studies at the School for Social Work in Toronto and worked for three years as assistant advisor in art for the Adult Education Branch of the Ontario Department of Education. Later she developed her skills in the graphic arts and did illustrations and writing for the Canadian Broadcasting Corporation and the Toronto *Globe and Mail*. She travelled in Europe from 1961 to 1966 (Spain, Scotland, France and Germany) and returned to Canada before visiting Brazil where she made drawings in some of the oldest towns. These drawings were subjects for her 1967 engravings. She lectured part-time at the National Gallery of Canada. Since 1969 she has been teaching print-making at the High School of Commerce, Ottawa, evenings. An exhibition of her engravings and etchings took place at the Germany Institute and Library in Ottawa in November of 1969.

LAMBTON, Gwenda (Cont'd)

References

The Ottawa Journal, Nov. 6, 1969 "Lambton Etchings On View" by WQK
Le Droit, Nov. 15, 1969 "A l'Institut allemand"
Catalogue sheet for her November show, 1969.

LAMER, Gilles
b.1928

A painter from Baie-du-Febvre, Que., he studied at l'Ecole des Beaux Arts, Montreal, and at the School of Fine Arts and Crafts, London, England. He spent two years in Spain where he studied under Andres Fabregat and exhibited in Madrid with great success. He travelled in Italy and Austria, where he studied at the Kunstakademi of Vienna under Prof. Drobroski. Returning to Canada he has been teaching at the Art Centre at Three Rivers since 1958.

References

L'Evénement Journal, Que., P.Q., 3 Nov. 1953 "De Baie-du-Febvre à Florence"
Le Nouvelliste, Trois Rivières, P.Q., May 26, 1962 (photo of artist and announcement of his return to Quebec after study abroad)

LAMONT, Gwen Kortright (nee Hutton)
b.1909

Born at Fort Macleod, Alberta, she studied at the Ontario College of Art, Toronto, under Arthur Lismer, Frederick Haines, Emanuel Hahn, Robert Holmes, J.E.H. MacDonald, H.H. Stansfield, Yvonne McKague Housser, G.A. Reid, J.W. Beatty, F.S. Challener, Allan Barr and received a scholarship each year during the four year course.[1] She graduated with her A.O.C.A. in 1929. Subsequently she attended the Banff School of Fine Arts where she studied theatre design under Mrs. Haines, and Mr. Cohen; and in Victoria, B.C. under Mrs. John Kincaid in puppet theatre.[2] In 1933 her portrait of a young Edmonton girl was hung in the National Gallery of Canada. She held her first solo show at the Vancouver Art Gallery in 1938 when the Vancouver *News-Herald*[3] noted, "Her sketches of her twin children are among the most charming shown. She has ventured also into the realm of oils, a difficult medium. Perhaps what will make the greatest appeal however, are examples of design for theatrical work, and her marionette designs and models are examples of unusual merit." An exhibition of her portraits at the Kelowna Library Room in 1960 included an oil of Leon Gillard (nephew of famous Gillard who named Kelowna, B.C.); pen drawing of Dr. Marius Barbeau (anthropologist); Bill Meloor (dressed in Indian Medicine Man clothes) and many others. Describing one study Salulika[4] of the *Daily Courier* noted, "There is a small portrait of a rather frail looking lad in a large dark hat, against a background of green. Among all the other portraits, this little work holds its own and shows a quality of feeling – something more than a mere likeness – which only a gifted artist can portray." In 1961 she completed a large ceramic mural (16' x 2') depicting the life work of Dr. W.J. Knox for the Dr. Knox Junior-Senior High School, Kelowna. The mural was the idea of architect John Woodworth. Mrs. Lamont received the assistance of Mr. and Mrs.

LAMONT, Gwen Kortright (nee Hutton) (Cont'd)

Frank Sidebotham in the ceramic work. The mural was unveiled by Premier W.A.C. Bennett on March 30th, 1961. She is very interested in teaching children and has illustrated books for children including a children's book of plays published by J.M. Dent & Sons, Toronto. She has also worked as a commercial artist and she costumed a full scale production of *Midsummer Night's Dream* for the St. James Players Guild of Vancouver. She lives at Okanagan Mission, Kelowna, B.C.

References
[1] National Gallery of Canada Info. Form rec'd April 20, 1961
[2] Ibid
[3] *News-Herald*, Van., B.C. Feb. 24, 1938 "Clever Artist Presents Show"
[4] *Daily Courier*, Kelowna, B.C., Oct. 24, 1960 "Exhibition of Portraits By Well-known Valley Artist" by Salulika
[5] Ibid, Apr. 7, 1961 " 'Deception' In Friendship Justifiable Says Artist" by Eric Green (The artist, a life long friend of the Doctor, did not let him know the information she wanted was for a mural. The Doctor thought all the time it was for the local historical society — even when she made several sketches of him.)

LAMPE, Walter

A Winnipeg artist who at the age of eight attended Saturday Morning Classes at the Winnipeg Art Gallery. Years later he studied under George Eliason at the Winnipeg School of Art.[1] He received his degree in social work at the University of Manitoba then went on to post graduate studies in Toronto.[2] He returned to Winnipeg where he is a Professor at the School of Social Work in the University of Manitoba. In the summer of 1967 he travelled to British Columbia where he spent much of his time in a Chinese community with two Oriental artists.[4] Pat Hannon[5] of the Winnipeg *Tribune* noted of him, "Prof. Lampe seems to continue to paint anything and everything that carries special meaning for him but he will continue to paint in such a way that will force viewers to trust their own judgement when they 'look at my work, I want them to see what they want to see and not what they think I'd like them to observe.' " He has been working with oil and lacquer in combination with a palette knife spreading his colours in a variety of ways achieving, when he wants to, an almost water colour effect. His paintings have been exhibited in galleries in Montreal, Winnipeg and Vancouver.

References
[1] *Free Press*, Winnipeg, Man., March 31, 1967 "Walter Lampe" by Peter Crossley
[2] Ibid
[3] Ibid
[4] Ibid, June 22, 1968 "Latent desire makes painter" by Pat Hanna
[5] Ibid

LAMPMAN, Helen Winifred (Mrs. Archibald Otto Lampman)
(nee MacKenzie)
b.1898

Born at Lakefield, Ontario, she studied under Miss Mary Wrinch, J.W. Beatty, F.H. Varley, R. York Wilson also at Bishop Strachan School, Port Hope Art School, and

LAMPMAN, Helen Winifred (Mrs. Archibald Otto Lampman)

the Doon School of Fine Arts. She has been active with the Peterborough Group of Painters. No recent information on this artist.

Reference

Nat. Gal. of Can. Info. Form rec'd June 25, 1958

LAMPRECHT, Gisela Helene Louise (née Von Eicken)
b.1899

Born in Munich, Germany, she took teacher training and in 1917 married and became a Polish citizen.[1] In 1936 she began to model in clay and learned to draw under the advice of Prof. Stanislaw Gilcuski of Crakow, Poland; Roland Von Bohr taught her the Munich-Method (it makes possible the firing of original sculpture without further manipulation of casting in plaster); studied anatomy under Prof. W. Tank and others; five years in portrait-sculpture under Kurt Eckard.[2] She left Poland with her husband and children and arrived in Canada in 1945.[3] She was matron at King's Hall Boarding School for young girls and later taught sculpture classes at the YWCA (Sherbrooke Street) Montreal.[4] She finally established her own studio where she works and teaches. She also kept in touch with artistic activity at Audrey Tailor's Workshop and the Art Centre in Montreal. She exhibited her work jointly with painter Moe Reinblatt at Gallery XII of the Montreal Museum of Fine Arts when *The Montreal Star*[5] noted, "Gisela Lamprecht's contribution consists of about two dozen portrait heads. Without knowing the sitters, one would assume that they are good likenesses, for likeness is the thing, not experiment with form or the creation of symbols. The sculptor appears to be particularly sensitive to the contours and expression of youth."

References

[1] The National Gallery of Canada Info. Form rec'd Apr. 13, 1954
[2] Ibid
[3] Ibid
[4] Ibid
[5] *The Montreal Star*, Mtl., P.Q., Mar. 31, 1956 "Lamprecht, Reinblatt Exhibits in Gallery XII" (photo of Lamprecht's portrait-sculpture of painter Gentile Tondino"

LANC, Paul (Paul Lancz)

b. (c) 1919

He began carving at the age of twelve and later studied at the Budapest School of Fine Arts. For three years he worked with Professor Kisfaludy Szigmond, noted Hungarian sculptor. Lanc came to Canada with his wife in 1956. One of his first important commissions was a bust of Abraham Bronfman, Montreal philanthropist, for Mount Sinai Hospital, Ste. Agathe, Quebec. In the following years he has done busts of actresses Zsa Zsa Gabor and Jayne Mansfield; former mayor of Toronto, Nathan Phillips; the late John F. Kennedy, 35th President of United States of America (bust was placed in the Kennedy Library at Harvard University on approval of the President's widow); former Prime Minister of Israel, David Ben-Gurion (bust was presented to the Israeli pavilion at Expo '67 by the artist), and many other commissions including a statue of a young boy sitting cross-legged with his head

LANC, Paul (Cont'd)

bowed, for the Garden of Wonders, Lafontaine Park, Montreal; works for numerous churches and millionaire businessmen. Paul Lanc is a sculptor of unusual ability.

References
> *The Ottawa Citizen*, June 17, 1967 "Patience, perseverance are sculptor's key tools" by Karin Moser
> *see also*
> *The Montreal Star*, Nov. 20, 1964 "Onlookers Struck By Kennedy Bust" by Dusty Vineberg (photo of Kennedy bust)
> *The Toronto Telegram*, Aug. 22, 1960 "The Mayor Had A Secret — In Clay" (photo of Lanc at work on bust of Nathan Phillips)

LANCEMAN, Audrey

Born in London, England, she studied at Nottingham College of Art; exhibited in group shows in London; two man shows, Sweden (1957); one man show, London (1959); came to Canada in 1960; solo show in Ottawa (1964); solo show, Toronto, at the Upstairs Gallery (1964) of realistic city scenes in oils.

Reference
> Exhibition Oils — June 1st to June 14th, 1964 "Audrey Lanceman" at the Upstairs Gallery, Toronto (folder with illustration)

LANDORI, Eva (Mrs. Eva Landori Hoffmann)
b.1912

Born in Budapest, Hungary, she studied at the School of Fine Arts, Budapest, under Almos Jaschik for three years. She became an illustrator, theatre decorator, designer and later ceramist. She worked for several Hungarian daily newspapers and periodicals and for the Muvesz Szinpad theatre.[1] During the Second World War her home was bombed and she lost almost everything she owned.[2] In 1946 she went to Paris where she lived for five years and studied at the Académie de la Grande Chaumière and attended seminars of André Lhote.[3] She started oil painting in 1948 and in 1951 held a solo exhibit of work at Galerie Ariel, Paris.[4] Later that year she came to Canada and in 1952 exhibited six paintings in the collection of Modern French Art at the Antoine Art Gallery in Montreal.[5] In the autumn of 1953 she presented a solo exhibit at the Robertson Galleries, Ottawa; at Agnes Lefort Gallery, Montreal (1955) (1958); joint show with Marjorie Winslow (sculptor) at Montreal Museum of Fine Arts, Gallery XII (1959) also a solo show there (1965). Much of her painting in recent years has been of an abstract nature. Réa Montbizon[6] noted of her graphics, " . . . its rich kinesthetic feeling appears to have matured into an assured personal style . . . . " In addressing the Herman Abramowitz Chapter of Hadassah in 1960 Eva Landori noted that freedom in modern art is often seen as disorder and explained, "But it is exactly that freedom that determines its spirituality. Freedom to say anything, freedom to invent, to create a personal style, freedom to prefer dissonance to consonance, freedom to choose or to reject the rule. It is in fact that freedom that has revealed those rich, original personalities who have made modern art the wonderful new expression of the beautiful."[7] She lives in Montreal with her husband and children.

LANDORI, Eva (Mrs. Eva Landori Hoffmann) (Cont'd)

References
[1] Nat. Gal. of Canada Info. Form rec'd April 9, 1953
[2] Ibid
[3] Ibid
[4] Exhibition sheet, Galerie Aeriel 1 Avenue De Messine, Paris Oct. 19 to Nov. 3, 1951
[5] see[1]
[6] *The Gazette*, Mtl., P.Q., "Eva Landori, Betty Goodwin" by R.M.
[7] Ibid, Nov. 16, 1960 "Modern Art Topic Of Discussion"
see also
N.D.G. Monitor, Mtl., P.Q., Feb. 13, 1958 "Imagination"
The Gazette, Mtl., P.Q., Nov. 1, 1960 "Among Current Exhibitions" by Dorothy Stewart
Ibid, Jan. 31, 1959 "Paint Away Your Troubles Is Artistic Prescription" by Julian Armstrong
N.D.G. Monitor, Nov. 7, 1959 "Landori – Winslow"
Ibid, Nov. 16, 1960 "Modern Art Topic Of Discussion"

LANDRY, Paul

b.1933

Born in Halifax, N.S., the son of Dr. and Mrs. J.T. Landry, he attended St. Patrick's High School and the Nova Scotia College of Art and was considerably influenced by William DeGarth.[1] Landry apprenticed himself to a photo engraver while studying art in Halifax.[2] After leaving Halifax he studied in New York City with the Art Students' League.[3] He is employed by the Chemical Color Plate Corporation at Bridgeport, Conn., U.S.A. but each summer has returned to visit relatives in Halifax and sketch Nova Scotian scenes.[4] He exhibits his work in Canada and has won numerous prizes in Canada and the United States. He has been honoured by the Salmagundi Club (oldest art assoc. in U.S.). Lives at Westport, Conn.[5]

References
[1] *Mail-Star*, Halifax, N.S., July 25, 1967 "Returns To Sketch N.S. Scenes"
[2] Ibid
[3] Ibid
[4] Ibid
[5] Ibid
see also
Mail-Star, Oct. 23, 1963 "Halifax Artist Wins Award"

LANDRY, Pierre

b.1939

Born in Three Rivers, P.Q., he studied at l'Ecole des Beaux-Arts, Montreal (1959-64) where he received his diploma in sculpture and in pedagogy in plastic arts. He travelled and studied in Mexico (1960) and in Europe (1962). He was greatly impressed with the religious work of the ancient civilizations of the Indians of Mexico. He has been influenced by Michelangelo, Augustus Rodin, Henry Moore and Constantin Brancusi. His sculpture has been exhibited at Quebec provincial competitions; Art Centre of Three Rivers; Cultural Centre, Shawinigan; Carrousel des Arts, Three Rivers; Grenier des Artistes, St. Jacques-des-Piles; Galerie Fantasmagorique, Three Rivers and elsewhere. His commissions in Three Rivers

LANDRY, Pierre (Cont'd)

include: three works for the interior of the City Hall and three murals for the facade of the same building (90' x 4' x 18"); a non-figurative work for la Place Royale on the site of the old Rousseau House; a work for the exterior wall of the Cultural Centre auditorium; a tabernacle, chandeliers, cross for the sanctuary, canopy for the altar for the chapel of the Dominicans "Ville Joie St. Dominique". In Louiseville, P.Q., he did a sculpture for Bortos du Canada (50' x 20' x 5') and he has done several works outside Quebec. His smaller works have been shown at la Galerie du Vieux, Three Rivers, and La Maison des Arts La Sauvegarde, Montreal. He lives at Saint-Joseph de Sorel, Richelieu, P.Q.

References

Le Nouvelliste, Trois-Rivières, P.Q., 27 Oct., 1964 "Depuis son entrance, Pierre Landry rêvait du sculpture" par Claire Roy

Ibid, Nov. 24, 1965 "Sculpture non-figurative montée à la Place Royale? "

Ibid, July 29, 1967 "La Sculpture qui ornera la façade du nouvel hôtel de ville réalisée par Pierre Landry" par Georges Lamon

Ibid, Feb. 8, 1969 "Exposition conjointe de Pierre Landry et Richard Normandin"

La Presse, Mtl., P.Q., June 28, 1969 "Quand un artiste hésite . . . "

The Gazette, June 28, 1969 "Sprung steel and alumachromes" by I.H.

The Montreal Star, July 4, 1969 "Group shows, young artists" by Michael White

---

LANDRY, Yvan

b.1932

Born in Quebec City, he studied five years at the Ecole des Beaux-Arts, Quebec (1949-54) and obtained his diploma in ceramics with distinction. He studied as well, design, drawing, decoration and modelling. He travelled to Mexico, with his wife, where he studied mosaic under Chaves Morado (creator of mosaics for Univ. Mexico). The Canadian Embassy to Mexico offered him a scholarship; also an offer from the School of Fine Arts, Mexico, to direct the ceramics section of the school was declined by him. He returned to Quebec where he conducted courses for adults in an old garage at Limoilou. In 1956 he taught at the school of pedagogy and in 1960 became professor of artistic education at the Centre de Culture Populaire de l'Université Laval. He has shown his works at Quebec, Montreal, Toronto, Washington, Mexico, Paris, and is represented in museums and collections around the world. In 1958 he became member of l'Association professionnelle des artisans du Quebec (Pres. 1950), and Directeur Associé des Ecoles d'Arts Decoratifs, Quebec (C.1960). His ceramics have been shown at La Lanterne, Côte de la Montagne, and at the Palais Montcalm, Quebec.

References

l'Evénement Journal, Que., P.Q., July 30, 1955 "Yvan Landry expose des céramiques"

La Presse, Mtl., P.Q., Dec. 21, 1959 "Exposition Yvan Landry: art et décoration en céramique"

Le Reveil, Jonquière, P.Q., Aug. 24, 1960 "Yvan Landry, professeur et artiste"

Le Lingot, Arvida, P.Q., Sept. 1, 1960 "Nouveau professeur de céramique à l'Institut des beaux-arts de Jonquière"

Le Canada Français, St. Jean, P.Q., Nov. 16, 1961 "Yvan Landry – Céramiste"

Le Soleil, Que., P.Q., Nov. 18, 1961 "Une exposition du céramiste Landryvan" par Paule France Dufaux

LANDSLEY, Patrick Alfred
b.1926

Born in Winnipeg, Manitoba, he studied at the Winnipeg School of Art under L.L. Fitzgerald and Joseph Plaskett (1948-50) and at the School of Art and Design, Montreal Museum of Fine Arts under Arthur Lismer, Jacques de Tonnancour and Gordon Webber (1950-51). In 1951 he went to Paris on a Canada Foundation Scholarship and studied at the Académie Montmartre under Fernand Léger; also at the Académie Ranson under Gustav Singier. After two and a half years in Europe he returned to Canada and settled in Montreal. He taught for three years at Lower Canada College (1955-58) and since 1954 at the Montreal Museum of Fine Arts. He taught one term at MacDonald College (1957) and since 1960 he has been teaching at McGill University, Department of Fine Arts. His influences were first derived from the work of Gustave Singier and later by the School of Paris. Landsley was associated with the Non-Figurative Artists' Association of Montreal. He exhibited in various group exhibitions across Canada including the Fourth Biennial Exhibition of Canadian Art (1961), Canadian Water Colours Drawings and Prints (1966) and annual spring exhibitions at the Montreal Museum of Fine Arts, Annual Winnipeg Shows, Ont. Soc. of Artists, Canadian Group of Painters (member). Has held one man shows at Delrue Gallery, Penthouse Gallery, McGill University, Montreal. He twice exhibited in two-man shows at the Montreal Museum of Fine Arts, and with Owen Chicoine in a travelling exhibition in 1965 organized and circulated by The National Gallery of Canada. He is represented in the Museum of the Province of Quebec, Sir George Williams University, Montreal, and in many private collections.

References

National Gallery of Can. Info. Form rec'd July 7, 1958
Globe & Mail, Tor., Ont., July 21, 1951 "Scholarships Enable Three Study Abroad"
The Gazette, Mtl. P.Q. July 20, 1951 "CAHA Helps Three Artists With Funds For Studies"
La Presse, Mtl., P.Q., May 17, 1955 "Au Musée, un tableau qui ouvre des horizons"
The Montreal Star, Mtl., P.Q., Sept 18, 1957 "Praises 'New Deal' For Young Artists"
The Vancouver Sun, Van., B.C., Oct. 2, 1957 "Cold, Flies, People Test Outdoor Artist (from *The Gazette*, Mtl.)
The Gazette, Mtl., P.Q., Nov. 28, 1959 "Patrick Landsley Show"
La Presse, Mtl., P.Q., Nov. 28, 1959 "Patrick Landsley"
The Brandon Sun, Brandon, Man. July 15, 1965 "Two-Man Show To Open Today" By Kaye Rowe (Sun Staff Writer)
Catalogues
Sir George Williams University Collection of Art
The Fourth Biennial Exhibition of Canadian Art, 1961 (NGC)
Canadian Water Colours Drawings and Prints, 1966 (NGC)
Chicoine/Landsley – exhibition *Organized and Circulated By the NGC*

LANG, Byllee Fay
1908-1966

Born at Didsbury, Alberta[1], she was brought up on her father's ranch in Alberta. Ben Lepkin[2] of the Winnipeg *Free Press* explained, "She showed none of the annoying premature semi-development of the child prodigy. Her childhood was the healthy normal life of an Alberta Rancher's daughter. She could handle a .22 rifle long before she ever saw a sculptor's tool, and she was expert with a saddle before she even knew of the existence of an armature." She studied painting at the School of Art, Winnipeg (then in the old Board of Trade building). But not finding the satisfaction in painting that she had hoped for she switched to sculpture. With no sculpture courses in Winnipeg she moved to Toronto where she studied at the Ontario College of Art under Emanuel Hahn. She then travelled to Europe where she took further study at the State Academy, Munich, Germany (Akademie der Bilden Kumste) and later under Professor Baldfritsch in Berlin. She also travelled in Vienna, Budapest, Florence, Bologna, Rome, Venice and Paris. War clouds in Europe finally brought about her return to Canada. She arrived back in Winnipeg where she had first begun her art studies. She established a private school of sculpture in 1936.[3] But in 1939 she joined the staff of the Winnipeg School of Art. By 1945 she was living in Montreal. In Europe and Canada she had done many portraits of prominent sitters including I. Ramzy Bey (Minister of Education in Cairo), Senor J.J. Trallere (world famous worker with rare gems), George Bornoff (violinist and teacher of Winnipeg); Senator the Hon. T.D. Bouchard of Quebec and others. About 1946 she went to Bermuda where she worked at many things in the commercial field, design and execution of floral floats for various pageants, and in her sculpture she did figures of Christ and his Apostles for the Bermuda Cathedral, perhaps one of her more important undertakings. Describing her style Jack Williamson[4] in the *Canada-West Indies Magazine* wrote, "Soon Byllee Lang became one of the leaders of a rugged, honest school of Canadian sculpture of which Elizabeth Wyn Wood was to say: 'There are qualities of awkwardness in Canadian sculpture because it is the art of those who have forsaken the megalopolitan way of life with its smartness and its bric-a-brac. Here is a simple art – not the folk art of the peasant, – but the straightforward art of those who have deliberately rejected the suave." Her work was twice selected to represent the Commonwealth abroad. Graham McInnes[5] noted in 1950, " . . . in the firmly realized character studies of Byllee Lang, there is both a simple and massive nobility." She is represented in the collection of the Winnipeg Art Gallery by a bronze head "Old Woman". She was a member of the Manitoba Society of Artists (1938); Sculptors' Society of Canada (1942); Federation of Canadian Artists (1942). She died in Bermuda at the age of fifty-eight. *The Bermuda Sun*[6] warmly wrote, "With the death of Byllee Lang . . . the Colony lost more than a devoted patron of the arts, and more than a gifted sculptress. It lost a remarkable human being whose love of people warmed all around her like a living flame. To know Byllee was to love her, and through her the world of the arts which she held so dear . . . . To the young she gave advice and instruction, to the not so young she set an example of dedication and unselfishness . . . . Their lives have been deprived, with tragic suddenness, of something very fine and very noble."

References

[1] Nat. Gal. of Can. Info. Form rec'd Jan. 25, 1943

[2] *The Free Press*, Winnipeg, Man., Feb. 4, 1938 "Local Sculptor Builds Enviable Reputation"

[3] Ibid

[4] *Canada – West Indies*, Aug., 1959 "Mid-Atlantic-Bermuda/Byllee Lang . . . Canadian Sculptor in Bermuda" by Jack Williamson

[5] *Canadian Art* by Graham McInnes, MacMillan, Tor., 1950, P.95

[6] *The Bermuda Sun*, Dec. 10, 1966 "In Memoriam" large photo of Byllee Lang in her studio
see also
News Pictorial (Pub. by Mid-Ocean News) 3 Nov., 1962 "Byllee Lang's Reply To Critics – Reredos For Cathedral Go On Show" by Harry Rose

LANGDALE, Stella

She studied in Glasgow, Scotland, under Maurice Greiffenhagen and Frank Newberry. She came to Canada during the late thirties. She is known as a painter, etcher, illustrator of books, and also a sculptor. At the time of her arrival in Victoria she was in poor health and it is not known if she produced art work after her recovery. She illustrated the following British books: *Dream of Gerontius* by John Henry Newman, *Christ in Hades* by Stephen Phillips, *Hound of Heaven* by Francis Thompson (1922 edition by Dodd, Mead & Co.). She exhibited in the Paris Salon and the Brook Street Art Gallery, London, England. She was a member of the Print Society (an international society), also was associated in the capacity of illustrator, with John Lane Publishing Company, London.

References
> *The Daily Colonist*, Victoria, B.C., Jan. 28, 1940 "An Artist Comes to Stay" by J.E.M. Bruce

LANGE, Detta

Potter, painter, and print-maker who exhibited at the Jacox Galleries in Edmonton, Alberta, some of her work in print-making, ink and wash, collage, oil, mosaic and clay. Dorothy Barnhouse noted of her work, "The imaginative quality that enlivens Mrs. Lange's prints is only slightly less evident in her pottery and sculpture. I never could work up much excitement over the transportation of gears, pot handles and so on, to a foreign environment, be it clay, canvas or whatever, but this artist does it better than most. She integrates them firmly with fired tile in several large mosaic sculptures."

Reference
> *The Edmonton Daily Journal*, Jan. 17, 1964 "Detta Lange's Work Has Individualism" by Dorothy Barnhouse (Journal Art Critic)

LANGEVILLE, Adrien

A Quebec artist who created a fine sculpture of two birds (doves?) for a new elementary school at Saint-Cyrille de Lessard, County of L'Islet, Quebec. A photo of the sculpture appeared in *Le Soleil*.

Reference
> *Le Soleil*, Quebec, P.Q., "Pour Une Ecole Nouvelle" (photo of Langeville's sculpture exhibited on the portico of the Museum of the Province of Quebec during Easter Week, 1966).

LANGEVIN, Claude
b.1942
Born in Montreal, P.Q., he began painting at an early age, attended the University of Montreal for a brief period for medical studies, turned to painting and is known

LANGEVIN, Claude (Cont'd)

for his landscapes, still lifes and floral studies. He achieves a three-dimensional effect by first applying a white paste to his canvas. He is the son of Dr. Langevin of Montreal. Does about 300 paintings a year which sell in New York as well as in Canada.

References
> *The Canadian Magazine,* May 23, 1970 "The fastest brush in the East" by Barry Conn Hughes
> biographical sheet (undated)

LANGEVIN, Roger

A Mont Laurier, Quebec, sculptor, who took classical studies in Quebec City for six years and then enrolled at the Ecole des Beaux Arts, Montreal, where he studied painting, sculpture, mural decoration, theatre set design, for five years. His wife also a painter, studied at the Ecole des Beaux-Arts. He has completed several commissions in Mont Laurier including a mural for the corridor of the Annex of the St. Joseph Seminary; a sculpture for another building by architects Ryan and Simon; a Christ on the cross for the Chaplain of Bénédictines Dom Mercure and others. He admires the work of sculptor Zadkine and painter Cézanne.

References
> *L'Echo de la Lièvre,* Mont Laurier, Que., Feb. 17, 1966 "Roger Langevin – un gars bien de chez nous" par Lionel Nazaire

LANGLAIS, Thérèse

She studied at l'Ecole des Beaux-Arts, Quebec, and exhibited her oils, pastels, and drawings at the Palais Montcalm, Quebec. Among her subjects are scenes of old streets of Quebec City.

Reference
> *L'Evénement-Journal,* Quebec, P.Q., Feb. 1, 1960 "Crayons et pastels de Mlle Langlais" par Paule France Dufaux

LANGLOIS, Claude
b.1918

Born in Montreal, P.Q., he studied painting in Montreal with Fernand Faniel (1932-35) and with Paul-Emile Borduas (1935-38) while at the same time he followed studies in philosophy at the University of Montreal. He spent three years in Paris where he studied painting and the history of art at l'Ecole des Beaux Arts with André Lhote. He obtained a bursary to study the plastic arts from the Ministry of Cultural Affairs of France. From 1955 to 1963 he taught the history of contemporary art in Montreal. In 1964 he was appointed director of the plastic arts department at the Collège Jean de Brébeuf.

Reference
> *Le Droit,* Ottawa, Ont., Nov. 10, 1967 "Le peintre Claude Langlois"

LANGLOIS, Denyse (Mme. Denyse Langlois-Chenevert)

A copper enamellist, she studied oil painting with the Sisters of Immaculate Conception at Cénacle and ceramics and copper enamelling under Yvan Landry. In September of 1957 she exhibited 300 of her works at the Quebec Provincial Exhibition and sold them all. She has created religious pieces, jewellery, plates and other items which are in the collections of famous people like Dr. Wilder Penfield and Nicole Germain. She has taught students in copper enamelling. Has exhibited her work also at the Palais du Commerce, Montreal. She lives at Beauport, Quebec.

References
   Progrès-Dimanche, Chicoutimi, P.Q., April 6, 1960 "Deux artistes (Denyse Langlois et Yvan Landry) exposent à Chicoutimi" par Jean-Claude Boudreault
   Le Soleil, Quebec, P.Q., Mar. 27, 1958 "Denyse Langlois, émailliste québécoise, se donne toute à un métier exigeant" par Michèle Stanton

LANGLOIS, Jean
b.1916
Born in Montreal, P.Q., he studied at the school of the Montreal Museum of Fine Arts under Adam Sheriff Scott. He exhibited his work at the New York World's Fair (1939) also with the Royal Canadian Academy, Canadian Group of Painters, Montreal Spring Shows, and held a solo exhibit at the Art Gallery of Toronto and the Montreal Museum of Fine Arts. He lived in Montreal also St. Eustache sur-le-Lac, P.Q.

Reference
   Nat. Gal. of Can. Info. Form rec'd Aug. 9, 1945

LANGLOIS, Sheila (Mrs.)

She studied at the Ontario College of Art and teaches art to evening classes at Kirkland Lake Collegiate and Vocational Institute. Her paintings have been exhibited at the "Operation Ontario Art '67" a travelling show (July 1 to Dec. 31, 1967) and Northern Ontario Art Association in Kirkland Lake. She lives in Kirkland Lake, Ontario.

Reference
   Northern Daily News, Kirkland Lake, Ont., May 9, 1967 "Painting By Tech Woman Chosen For Ontario Tour"

LANKAU, Hans Gottfried Edita
b.1897
Born in Berlin, Germany, he studied at the Staatlichen Kunstgewerbe Museum under sculptors Leonard Jamaer, Willie Roetger, Friedrich Zuchantke and he received the Friedrich-Scholarship for Industrial and Fine Art (1919). In Germany he specialized in restoration of old and precious oil paintings and sculpture. He came to Canada and settled in Vancouver, B.C. in 1951. He does a wide range of sculpture including architectural, memorial, portrait, in the media of stone, bronze,

LANKAU, Hans Gottfried Edita (Cont'd)

aluminum and wood. His commissions include: 11 ft. plaque in bronze over the main entrance of the Canadian Imperial Bank of Commerce, Van. (1954); 10 ft. high enameled bronze coat of arms over the main entrance of the new Court-House, Calgary (1961); coat of arms for the new Bank of Canada, Van. (1965); 4 ft. bronze and aluminum circular crest for R.C.M.P. Building, Regina; works for city hospitals at Edmonton, Lethbridge and Calgary, Alberta; memorial plaque with portrait of Sen. Pat Burns, Calgary; portrait of Mr. Winch, MP of Vancouver; memorial plaque with portrait of bush pilot Russell Baker; several portraits of Charles Woodward (of Woodward Dept. Stores); 12 ft. high and 11 ft. wide coat of arms of Canada (3,000 lbs. wt.) ceremoniously inagurated at Confederation Garden Court, Victoria, B.C. (this work required the fashioning of numerous individual parts in such a fashion that all parts fitted together neatly), considered to be one of his finest works. Hans Lankau lives in West Vancouver, B.C.

References

Nat. Gal. of Can. Info. Form rec'd (c) 1967

Der Courier, Winnipeg, Man., 13 July, 1967 (German language newspaper) title in English "German-Canadian Created Centennial Work of Art"

LANSDOWNE, James Fenwick
b.1937

Born in Hong Kong of English parents, his father was an engineer employed by Jardine, Matheson, a British trading company.[1] When the artist was only eleven months old he was stricken with polio.[2] War in China reached their area finally and they were evacuated to Victoria, B.C. in 1940.[3] His father returned to his job in Hong Kong but was taken prisoner (for four years) by the Japanese.[4] In Victoria his mother worked very hard to provide proper care for her convalescing son. When he was seven his mother, an accomplished artist in her own right, sat by his bed and painted pictures for him. He soon began to experiment on his own.[5] He watched birds from his bedroom window and by the time he was 14 he had become so interested in birds he began sketching them. He attended Victoria High School and for three summers worked as a lab assistant at the British Columbia Museum where he studied the anatomy of birds.[6] Colour slides of his illustrations were seen one day by the director of the Canadian Audubon Society, John Livingston, who was so impressed with the young man's work that he arranged a showing of his paintings in Toronto, at the Royal Ontario Museum in connection with International Museums Week, 1956. At that time T.M. Shortt (one of Canada's top wildlife illustrators) as well as John Livingston, rated Lansdowne's work as brilliant.[9] Up to this time only one other showing of his paintings had been seen by the public — at the B.C. Provincial Library in 1950. Lansdowne had been selling his work to friends for as little as two dollars or less. But an article in *Time* magazine noted that his work could command higher than the $30 to $50 a painting he was getting at the time of his Toronto showing.[10] *Maclean's* a little earlier, had published a portfolio of his work with an article on the artist.[11] His first non-Canadian exhibition took place in New York City at the headquarters of the National Audubon Society where he was introduced by the president of the society John H. Baker.[12] Art critic Pearl McCarthy[13] in 1959 noted, "His work is now a Canadian contribution to that culture which links a science and art, to the advantage of each, and he is to be congratulated." His paintings were shown at the Canadian National Exhibition by The Star Weekly Birds of Canada and reproductions of them were made available to the public at a low cost, by this publishing company.[14] His 1960 appearance at the Royal Ontario Museum on the occasion of an exhibit of his work and a reception for him was attended by about 750 persons including government heads, civic dignitaries, and celebrities who warmly applauded him. Paul Duval[15] in describing the paintings for *The Telegram* noted, "Like all of his paintings, they are in the exact, transparent watercolor technique. He uses this traditional method in a crips, realistic style. Most impressive of the works in this exhibit are the dramatic action portraits of the Groshawk, Common Crow and Skylark. His unerring instinct for design is apparent in the silhouettes of the Greater Scaup and the Marsh Hawk. Though he has achieved such triumphs while still a very young man, I am confident that Lansdowne's greatest achievements remain ahead. He will almost certainly become the world's foremost bird painter of his time." Shortly afterwards Lansdowne went to England where he sketched birds, in their natural habitats in preparation for more detailed work of them. His English studies dealt with the small birds rather than the game birds depicted by the majority of English bird artists. It was then that arrangements were made for a showing of his Birds of Britain and Canada at The Tyron Gallery, London. In the fall of 1960 he exhibited at the Art Gallery of Greater Victoria, and in the spring of 1961, his Tyron exhibition took place and was met with the greatest enthusiasm. Critics ranked him among the world's leading painters of birds.[16] By 1961 his paintings were valued from $250 to $750.[17] His one man exhibitions at the Kennedy Galleries in New York City, Brooke Bond Canada Ltd. tea centres in Montreal and Toronto of 123 paintings sold out within a week for a total of $25,000 averaging about $200 a picture.[18] This showing and most of his others were a result of a contract which had been drawn up between Bud Feheley of TDF Advertising Artists (Toronto), and Lansdowne shortly after his first Toronto showing. Feheley prebought the entire output of Lansdowne by agreeing to pay the artist a basic salary of $4,000 in return for 40 paintings a year.[19] Lansdowne is free to devote himself to his art. *The London Free Press*[20] in recording the events of May 9th, 1964 noted, "Mr. Lansdowne — his friends call him Fen — was in London (Ont.) yesterday for a brief reception at the home of Tom Hayman, London naturalist and long-time admirer of Lansdowne bird paintings. Then, with a party that included Mr. and Mrs. Hayman and Mr. Feheley, he headed for Point Pelee and a weekend that combined — for Fen — business and pleasure, bird-watching." Through Feheley arrangements were made for the publishing of Lansdowne's paintings in a series of six books by McClelland & Stewart. *Birds of the Northern Forest* with 56 plates and text by J. Livingston appeared in 1966 and *Birds of the Eastern Forest: 1* with 52 plates in 1968.[21] Both books have been very well received and together already have sold 62,000 copies grossing the publisher more than a million dollars.[22] By 1969 his paintings were selling for $2,500 each in centres like New York, London and Toronto. Olion Sewall Pettingill, Jr., Director of the Cornell Laboratory of Ornithology was quoted as having said that Lansdowne's paintings are far superior to those of John James Audubon, father of avian art. Pettingill, however, in all fairness to Audubon, made clear that he was not comparing the overall knowledge of both men. David MacDonald[23] of Victoria, B.C., has written the most complete article on Lansdowne to date which appeared in *The Reader's Digest* in 1969 accompanied

LANSDOWNE, James Fenwick (Cont'd)

by twelve illustrations on birds. Lansdowne is represented in the following public collections: The Royal Ontario Museum; Beaverbrook Art Gallery; Audubon House, New York; Montreal Museum of Fine Arts; Art Gallery of Greater Victoria; Ulster Museum, Belfast and many others; also in the collections of Mr. & Mrs. Samuel Bronfman; Princess Royal; Duke of Edinburgh; Carling Breweries Limited; private collectors in Britain, United States, Canada and elsewhere. Still cripped from polio he travels the countryside in a specially adapted car, and walks with crutches.

References

[1] *Time*, N.Y.C (Canadian Edition), Oct. 29, 1956

[2] *Canadian Art*, Vol. 21, Jan./Feb., 1964 "J. Fenwick Lansdowne" by Peggy Ellis Livingston P.36-39

[3] *Reader's Digest*, August, 1959 "The Stunning Birds of Fen Lansdowne" by David MacDonald P.29-34

[4] Ibid

[5] *The Ottawa Journal*, Dec. 18, 1961 "Youthful Bird Illustrator Wins Wide Acclaim Abroad" by Tom Wat (Victoria, B.C.)

[6] *Times*, Fort Frances, Ont., Aug. 6, 1969 "Young Canadian Painter Rated As One of Best Wildlife Artists; Termed Superior to Audubon"

[7] Ibid

[8] *MacLean's Magazine*, Tor., Ont., Jan. 26, 1963 "In an art market" by Joan Allen

[9] see [4]

[10] see [1]

[11] *Victoria Daily Times*, Aug. 12, 1957 "Famed Painter Of Bird Life To Make Trip"

[12] *The Ottawa Citizen*, Nov. 8, 1958 "Paints Birds On Recovery From Polio"

[13] *Globe & Mail*, Tor., Ont., Jan. 24, 1959 "Bird Paintings By Lansdowne"

[14] *The Toronto Daily Star*, Sept. 11, 1959 "Star's Bird Pictures Popular at CNE" (The public obtained these reproductions by sending one dollar to The Star Weekly, 80 King St. W., Toronto)

[15] *The Telegram*, Tor., Ont., May 28, 1960 "Accent On Art – He's An Amazing 'natural' " by Paul Duval

[16] *The Ottawa Journal*, Dec. 18, 1961 "Youthful Bird Illustrator Wins Wide Acclaim Abroad"

[17] *Wine, Beer and Spirits In Canada*, Dec., 1961 "Lansdowne painting for Carling Collection" also *Campbellton Tribune*, Feb. 28, 1962 "Bird Painter Wins Acclaim In London"

[18] *MacLean's Magazine*, Tor., Ont., Jan. 26, 1963 "In An Art Market"

[19] Ibid

[20] *The London Free Press*, London, Ont., May 9, 1964 "Artist, Businessman Join Forces To 'Sell' Canadian's Bird Paintings" by Del Bell (Free Press Staff Reporter) also *Post & News*, Leamington, Ont., May 14, 1964

[21] *Birds Of The Northern Forest* by J.F. Lansdowne with John A. Livingston, McClelland & Stewart Ltd., Tor./Mtl., 1966
Birds of the Eastern Forest/1, Paintings by J. Fenwick Lansdowne, text by John A. Livingston, McClelland & Stewart Ltd., Tor./Mtl., 1968

[22] see [6]

[23] see [3]

see also
Weekend Magazine, Vol. 12, No. 46, Nov. 17, 1962 "Canada's Superb Painter Of Birds"
Portfolios of his bird paintings have been published from time to time.

LAPALME, Pierre Gaboriau (b.1932 see Vol. 2, GABORIAU, Pierre)

LA PALME, Robert
b.1908

Born in Montreal, Quebec, his father moved to the Peace River district in Alberta where he operated a butcher shop. There Robert attended school, helped his father in the shop, and spent much of his spare time making caricatures.[1] When the La Palmes returned to Montreal Robert became a cartoonist. He was hired by *La Patrie* in 1928 as sports cartoonist and later turned to free lance work. He married and in 1935 went with his wife Nanette to New York where they lived for two years. Returning to Quebec he founded the Municipal Gallery in 1937.[2] He joined the faculty of science of Laval University, Quebec where he taught art. It was during this period that the officer commanding the training centre at Valcartier, Lt. Col. Adolf Dansereau, commissioned him to decorate a drop curtain for the stage in the drill hall of the Royal 22nd Regiment. Dansereau was so pleased with La Palme's work that he asked him to decorate the walls of the entire hall.[3] Before the actual work had begun Dansereau was transferred to England and the commission was dropped by the succeeding O.C. La Palme kept working on the sketches and when he had completed them he exhibited the entire series at the Bonestell Gallery on 57th Street in New York City.[4] Robert Ayre[5] in Canadian Art explained how they were received, "This show of projected murals, which he called 'There is No Secret Weapon! ' caused a stir. The *Times* said: 'In gay colours and with semi-abstract approach he depicts ancient more or less military legends with wit and point. Judith, Genghis Khan and the Revolt of the Angels are treated with due irreverence.' " Ayre quoted a number of other papers' reactions and noted, "For a little fellow (he is less than five feet tall and says he's rationed) and a shy little fellow at that, Robert La Palme has a terrific punch, as those who see his daily caricatures in *Le Canada* know . . . . With his wit and a few strokes of that wiggly line of his, he tears them apart, the petty politicians and the big-shots. Hitler and Mussolini have been easy victims of his ridicule, and the famous cartoon 'L'Approche de la tempête, ' in the travelling exhibition of British Commonwealth war cartoons circulated by the National Gallery was only one of many. The other day in *Le Canada* he showed a stout and amiable Russian bear back from hunting and holding up the pelt of a ludicrous looking Fuehrer." In the article, four of La Palme's cartoons were reproduced. Pearl McCarthy[6] of the *Globe & Mail* was equally impressed with his work and in her column wrote, "Canada has a cartoonist, or painter-satirist, of international importance, but there has been little opportunity to see his work in Toronto. He is the French-Canadian, Robert La Palme. He has a well-stocked brain and taste, plus a sense of what is art, so that his fantasies are always more than literary illustrations . . . when intellectual taste is both good and French, it is excellent. This applies to Mr. La Palme's very humorous pictures in gouache which will be shown in the fine art galleries of Eaton's College St. this coming week. You must see them. The general title is 'Nothing New Under the Sun'." This series was shown as well in Montreal, Rome, Italy, Brazil, and France. Michael Forster[7] in 1950 wrote, "By no means a wealthy man, he is of the select company that can go into Montreal's best restaurants and command a meal on the strength of his signature. Talkative and friendly behind a long cigar, Bob relishes the delights of good food, fine wine and well-favored women, and if you know of any other source of interest and enjoyment he is keen to learn about it." Forster had mentioned in the article that La Palme had established himself a considerable reputation as a commercial designer, cartoonist and painter and was looking forward to new ventures in a career that had barely begun at the age of 40. In the summer of 1950 La Palme completed an unusual assignment for the Ste. Adèle Chamber of

LA PALME, Robert (Cont'd)

Commerce on the occasion of the Laurentian Night Festival. Sketching the outlines of an allegorical painting along 900 feet of road he was followed by 20 volunteer painters using 500 pounds of paint. The work was completed in 24 hours and was reported in detail by many newspapers.[8] The road painting was expected to last several months. In November of 1950 he exhibited his "The History of War" and "The History of Medicine" at the Agnes Lefort gallery in Montreal, the latter series being shown for the first time at that exhibition. Robert Ayre[9] reviewing the work noted, "He may not have much respect for history, but he has been at some pains to reveal the essential character of each age through its proper costumes, tools, utensils and other details. It is the same in his War series. Just for devilment he adds details of his own — a kitten playing with a roll of mummy tape in Egypt; an athlete reading the 'Policus Gazettus' at the Roman bath; whisky and soda and a box of bonbons in the tent where Judith (the first commando) beheads Holofernes . . . banners, shields, spears, swords and all the gear and tackle of human enterprise, with animals and flowers, stars and symbols, animate the whole surface of La Palme's paintings in a gorgeous efflorescence, delighting the eye as the ideas delight the mind." His book *The First Twenty Years of The Canadian Caricaturist* was published in 1951 when *The Standard*[10] noted, "It contains . . . drawings of the world-famous as well as the leaders of Quebec's creative and political life. Bob's drawings have never been deliberately malicious although his revelation of character should make some of his subjects squirm. Scattered throughout, like a recurrent chuckle, are two of his favorite subjects; the Dionnes, père, mère and the famous five, and Camillien Houde in all the aspects of his beauty." In the book are his first series of twelve stylized caricatures constructed of cubes and other geometrical shapes published in the *Almanach de la langue française* of Montreal in 1933 which attracted wide attention of critics. From 1959 to 1961 he was on the staff of *La Presse* and then with *Le Nouveau Journal* from 1961-2. La Palme has travelled to Europe several times and to New York City every four years where he is stimulated by the activity of this large progressive centre. His entry into the field of mural design probably started with his commission to decorate The Botanical Garden restaurant in Montreal depicting the coming of the Europeans to North America. The actual work was executed in ceramic tile by Mr. and Mrs. Claude Vermette of Ste. Adèle. Other commissions followed including a fresco (40 x 6 ft.) for the Cercle des Journalistes, Montreal, showing the history of the eight daily newspapers in that city. This work required six months of research in old newspapers going back 100 years; one for the Montreal policemen depicts Maigret (Belgian detective of fiction), Sherlock Holmes, Dick Tracy, Fearless Fosdick, Keystone Cops, a Montreal policeman and a Paris policeman all looking for a thief who has snatched a woman's purse — all except the Montreal policeman who is handing out a parking ticket to some poor driver.[11] Next was his mural of Orpheus (god of music) visiting Dionysus (god of wine) for a drink, executed on a tapestry made in France from his design (8 x 19 ft.). This work hangs on the wall above the bar in the concert hall's main lounge. His design for the large mural "Quebec at Work" for the Place Crémazie, Montreal, was executed in ceramic tile by Jean Claude Gagnon. In 1967 he completed three murals for the reception centre at Expo '67 and the same year he became the director of the program to turn Montreal's new subway stations into an art showplace of 75 murals executed by over thirty Montreal artists. The murals were installed on blank walls of 23 stations along the 16 mile Metro system under Montreal streets. La Palme himself did a mural in bas relief telling the general

LA PALME, Robert (Cont'd)

history of Montreal from its earliest days to Confederation (1967). Each mural was sponsored by a firm who paid the artist's fee for the work. Credit to the contributing firm is given on an attached plaque.[12] La Palme's Expo Poster received first prize of a gold plaque by the Japanese Master Printers' Association and was presented by Expo '67 advertising director Paul Break. La Palme continues to excel in every new challenge.

References

[1] National Gallery of Canada Info. Form rec'd Oct. 12, 1943 also *Maclean's Magazine*, June 1, 1946 "Robert La Palme" by Gerald Anglin

[2] *The First Twenty Years Of The Canadian Caricaturist La Palme*, text by Jean-Louis Gagnon, Le Cercle Du Livre De France (Montreal, Paris, New York), 1950.

[3] *Canadian Art*, Vol. 2, No. 4, April-May, 1945 "Bravo! La Palme" by Robert Ayre

[4] Ibid

[5] Ibid

[6] *Globe & Mail*, Tor., Ont., Feb. 28, 1946 "Art and Artists — Brilliant Work" by Pearl McCarthy

[7] *The Standard*, Mtl., P.Q., July 15, 1950 "Art Notes — Able Painter La Palme Also Great Showman"

[8] *The Herald*, Mtl., P.Q., Aug. 9, 1950 "Mountainside Painting Has 900-foot Scope"

Globe & Mail, Tor., Ont., Aug. 17, 1950 (large photo of road painting)

Star, Windsor, Ont., Aug. 19, 1950 "An Orgy of Art"

The Standard, Mtl., P.Q., Sept. 2, 1950 "Mountainside Painting"

[9] *The Montreal Star*, Mtl., P.Q., Nov. 4, 1950 "La Palme Exhibit Marvellously Entertaining in Design and Color" by Robert Ayre

[10] *The Standard*, Mtl., P.Q., Jan. 13, 1951 "La Palme Book" also see[2]

[11] *The Ottawa Journal*, April 9, 1963 "For Place Des Arts — Top Canadian Caricaturist Tackles Mural Challenge" by Alexander Farrell (CP) repeated in many other papers.

[12] *Evening Times-Globe*, St. John, N.B., Feb. 27, 1967 "Montreal Plans To Beautify City's New Subway Stations" by William Stewart (CP)

see also

Saturday Night, Tor., Ont., Mar. 9, 1946 "Robert La Palme's Paintings Are Witty Comment on Warfare" by Paul Duval

Le Canada, Mtl., P.Q., Jan. 9, 1950 "Les Arts — Robert La Palme expose à Paris" par R.B.

Le Soleil, Que., P.Q., Jan. 10, 1950 "Une Exposition de Robert La Palme suscite un vif intérêt à Paris"

L'Evénement-Journal, Que., P.Q., Jan. 12, 1950 "L'exposition de Robert La Palme bien accueillie par les Parisiens" par Jean Gachon (AFP)

Le Droit, Ottawa, Ont., Sept. 1, 1953 "Peintres canadiens à Sao Paulo"

La Presse, Mtl., P.Q., Jan. 21, 1952 "Drôle et piquante histoire de huit papiers à nouvelles"

Ibid, Sept. 1, 1959 "Bourses à La Palme, Anna Malenfant et Félix Leclerc"

Le Devoir, Mtl., P.Q., Quand un caricaturiste, Lapalme, peint une murale pour la future Place des Arts" par Alexander Farrell

Weekend Magazine, Vol. 13, No. 49 Dec. 7, 1963 "Montreal's Proud Place Des Arts"

Canadian Art, Vol. 7, No. 3, Spring 1950 "The Difficult Art of Caricature" by Robert La Palme

---

LA PIERRE, Thomas

b.1930

Born in Toronto, Ontario, he studied at the Ontario College of Art under John Alfsen, Frederick Hagan, Eric Freifeld and Carl Schaefer and won a travelling scholarship at graduation. With this money he travelled to Paris, where he attended the Ecole des Beaux-Arts and later went on to Mexico.[2] Returning home he taught

LA PIERRE, Thomas (Cont'd)

oil painting classes for the Etobicoke Recreation Committee and held an exhibition of paintings and prints at the Hayter Gallery, Toronto, in the fall of 1957.[3] His subjects included still-life, and nudes in representational style. He joined the staff of the Ontario College of Art in 1959 where he instructs in drawing and painting. In 1960 he exhibited jointly with Rita Briansky at the Upstairs Gallery when the *Globe & Mail*[4] noted, "The La Pierre watercolors range from misty impressions of Mexico, through pictures from whose patterns of color realistic scenes appear to be emerging, to a few frankly representational urban and mountain scenes in forceful color for carefully delineated components . . . . In a particular sense the water-colors are literary — they tell the viewer a good deal about the artist's emotional response to the Mexican scenery. His lithos, pen, pencil, wash drawings and wood-cuts are skilled in workmanship, with fluent lines of great economy in figure drawings having free but expressive shading lines." In 1961 he became a member of the Canadian Society of Painters in Water Colour and in 1965 won an honour award from this society at its 39th annual exhibition at the Art Gallery of Ontario.[5] His work was chosen for the 'Canada at Sao Paulo' exhibition in 1963[6] and selected for showing at the Royal Canadian Academy 90th Exhibition, 1970.[7] He won a Price Fine Arts Award for his oil painting "Loved One Departed" also in 1970[8], as well as holding two simultaneous exhibitions in Toronto at Hart House and the Roberts Gallery which William McElcheran in a review for *artscanada* noted, "The paintings, drawings and graphics of 39 year old Toronto artist Tom La Pierre, recently shown . . . convey, with powerful imagery, a view of life which few people are willing to share. In a multitude of symbols and poetic references, he cuts beneath the surface to reveal some underlying realities from which we insulate ourselves. Without compromise, he reaches deeply within and touches the raw nerve, the visceral, primitive, biological self inside each of us, revealing, to those who do not turn away, the demons of death, lust, and violence with which the history of man has been in constant dialogue. Like Hieronymus Bosch and Breughel, he is a realist, not a surrealist. Even his most extravagant images spring from a very conscious objective mind. He uses beautifully drawn visual symbols as Dylan Thomas uses poetic images to make statements about what he sees, feels and understands . . . The intensity of the drawings carries over into the paintings where colour becomes another symbolic element. With his powerful imagery and pene-trating ideas, Tom Lapierre adds an important, darker note to Canadian art . . . . With magnificent draughtsmanship, he has gained freedom to move in the common domain of uncommon talents."

References

[1] National Gallery of Canada Info. Form rec'd Jan., 1963

[2] Ibid

[3] *The Etobicoke Press*, Etobicoke, Ont., Sept. 26, 1957 "Fine Art Exhibit By Tom Lapierre"

[4] *Globe & Mail*, Tor., Ont. Mar. 5, 1960 "Something To Admire"

[5] Ibid, Jan. 9, 1965 "La Pierre Deep Sea A Winner"

[6] *Canada at Sao Paulo*, 1963 (Exhibition Catalogue)

[7] *90th Annual Exhibition 1970 Royal Canadian Academy of Artists* (catalogue (Cat. No. 40)

[8] *Price Fine Art Awards 1970* (catalogue) reproduction and biography

[9] *arts/canada*, June 1970 "Tom LaPierre; a dialogue with demons, Roberts Gallery, Hart House, University of Toronto, March-April 1970" by William McElcheran

see also

Brampton Times & Conservator, Brampton, Ont., Feb. 3, 1965 "Art Group '59 Instructor"

LAPINE, Andreas Christian Gottfried (André Lapine)
1868-1952

Born in Shujen, Province of Riga, Russia, he studied there under Professor Rosé of the Imperial Academy of Petrograd.[1] He then was reported to have travelled with Rosé to London and Paris.[2] In France he spent two years then went on to Belgium and Holland.[3] He studied under Prof. Allebé at the Royal Academy of Fine Arts in Amsterdam, Holland, and was married in that country.[4] He came to Canada with his wife in 1907 and farmed for a time in the west and about a year later settled in Toronto. Among the many subjects he painted were horses and he did them exceptionally well. His work was reproduced in magazines like the *Canadian Magazine* and *Saturday Night*, and others. By 1919 he was an associate of the Royal Canadian Academy, and, shortly after its founding in 1925 he became a member of the Canadian Society of Painters in Water Colour.[5] In 1934 he was struck by an automobile and the *Mail & Empire*[6] carried the following account of the accident, "The rather small painter, who excels in the delineation of horses, was crossing the highway near his home two weeks ago. He saw an auto coming from one direction, stepped backward and was knocked down by another car travelling in the opposite direction." The article also mentioned that his friends were appealing for money to aid the artist in meeting his medical expenses. *The Star Weekly*[7] almost a month later announced that a committee had been formed headed by Sir Wyly Grier who was then President of the Royal Canadian Academy, to organize a sale of paintings contributed by artists in Ontario to help pay for Lapine's medical bills. Actually, L.A.C. Panton, President of the Ontario Society of Artists, was a co-organizer of the benefit exhibition. The showing took place at the T. Eaton Fine Art Galleries and the Robert Simpson Co. under the patronage of His Honour, the Lieutenant-Governor and Mrs. Bruce and forty-one other distinguished families including Lady Baillie, Lady Eaton, Hon. Vincent and Mrs. Massey, Mrs. Lawren Harris, Col. and Mrs. J.B. MacLean, Mr. & Mrs. A.H. Robson, Dr. and Mrs. Sigmund Samuel. Lapine who was in serious condition recovered and returned to his easel. In 1939 a second serious accident almost took his life. *The Toronto Star*[8] related his own story of what happened at his South Lake farm near Minden, Haliburton country, as follows, "I was digging a hole to bury a boulder that was too large for the horses to drag out of the field . . . . It was six feet high, five wide and three feet thick, and I thought we could easily tumble it into a hole dug alongside of it. I had the hole about two feet deep when I struck a large slab of rock about three feet long and three inches thick. I had lifted this up and was talking to Mrs. W. Hamilton, at whose farm I live, when I felt something moving against my back. Immediately I realized the big stone was moving on top of me and there was no chance of getting out of the hole before it would crush me. Somehow I managed to shove the slab I held in my hands against the big stone as it fell, and by a chance it propped the big stone up while I crawled out from under the arch they formed." The story appeared in other papers. It was in 1944 that he held his next one man show after a period of eight years. The showing took place at the Malloney Gallery and was reviewed by *The Toronto Star*[9] as follows, "Andre's current show is a revel in the luminous pageantry of nature: red foxes at play in a Haliburton forest; colonnades of gray larches etched against splashes of cloud-colors; a sandy high-road among rich blazes of maple foliage; a Whistleresque gray-poplar gleam of ice-cutters; a misty symphony of grays; cattle-herds as naturalistic as his horses used to be . . . for touches of portraiture, a luminous figure of his mother and a vivid cheerio of Pearce, naturalist in a glorious ensemble of clothes-colors even to the glistening rubber of his overshoes." He held subsequent solo shows at Malloney's. At the age

LAPINE, Andreas Christian Gottfried (Cont'd)

of 84 he died at his home in Minden, Ontario, and his passing was noted by *The Telegram*[10] as follows, "Few of his paintings ever changed hands after they were bought. Adversities which befell him from time to time had no effect on his mood of painting. It remained gallant. Prior to his 80th birthday, he did a series of pictures of an old Ontario village following the scene through spring and summer." Lapine is represented in the National Gallery of Canada[11], The Agnes Etherington Art Centre (Queen's University, Kingston)[12] and elsewhere, also in many important private collections.

References

[1] National Gallery of Canada Info. Form

[2] *The Fine Arts In Canada* by Newton MacTavish, MacMillan, Tor., 1925, P.172

[3] Ibid

[4] Ibid, see also[1]

[5] *Canadian Water Colour Painting* by Paul Duval, Burns & MacEachern, Tor., 1954, 16th page of text.

[6] *Mail & Empire*, Tor., Ont., July 17, 1934 "Artist Hurt In Crash Is Fighting For Life"

[7] *Star Weekly*, Tor., Ont. Aug. 11, 1934 "Artists To Give Sale Aiding André Lapine"

[8] *The Toronto Star*, Nov. 20, 1939 " 'Miracle Man of Hospital' Nearly Digs Own Grave"

[9] Ibid, Nov. 14, 1944 "Latvian Artist Has First Show Since '36"

[10] *The Telegram*, Tor., Ont., Feb. 27, 1952 "André Lapine Gentle Cavalier Artist Dead"

[11] *National Gallery of Can.* Cat., Vol. 3, by R.H. Hubbard, P.165

[12] *Agnes Etherington Art Centre Catalogue Permanent Collection*, 1968 by Francis K. Smith

see also

The Toronto Star, Sept. 17, 1934 "Benefit Art Exhibit To Aid André Lapine"

The Globe, Toronto, Sept. 17, 1934 "Sale of Pictures Arranged For Benefit of André Lapine"

Saturday Night, Toronto, Ont., Sept. 22, 1934 "The André Lapine Fund"

Watchman-Warder, Lindsay, Ont., Nov. 23, 1939 "Aged Russian Artist Nearly Dug Own Grave Near Minden"

The Telegram, Tor., Ont., Nov. 10, 1945 "At The Galleries – Splendor Of Nature Lives In Paintings Of Ontario"

Globe & Mail, Tor., Ont., Nov. 10, 1945 "Lapine's Painting Young in Spirit" by Pearl McCarthy

The Toronto Star, Nov. 10, 1945 "André Lapine Paints Miracles Of Magic" by Augustus Bridle

The Telegram, Tor., Ont., Nov. 2, 1946 "Brilliant Work Is Shown By Octogenarian Artist"

Globe & Mail, Tor., Ont., Nov. 8, 1947 "Art and Artists – André Lapine, at 80, Paints Ontario Scene With Youthful Warmth" by Pearl McCarthy

The Telegram, Tor., Ont., Nov. 8, 1947 "At The Galleries – Luminous Paintings Depict Joyous Ontario Landscapes"

Globe & Mail, Tor., Ont., Feb. 27, 1952 "Gentle Cavalier – Toronto Art Circles Lose Unique Link With Past" by Pearl McCarthy

---

LAPOINTE, André

A painter who held an exhibition at the Maison des Arts in Chicoutimi, Quebec. His work which is surrealistic also contains audio visual effects. He is Professor of Plastic Arts at Lafontaine School, Chicoutimi.

LAPOINTE, André (Cont'd)

Reference

Progrès-Dimanche, Chicoutimi, P.Q. Feb. 2, 1969 "Une Exposition CHOC" (photo of artist with work)

Ibid, Feb. 9, 1969 "Exposition André Lapointe" par Andrée Rainville

LAPORTE, Denis

A painter from the Grand'Mère or St. Georges-de Champlain settlement who creates rural scenes (farmes, sugar bushes, etc.) and who has won several prizes for his work at exhibitions across the Province of Quebec including First Prize at the Quebec Provincial Competition of 1964. He has exhibited his paintings at 'Galerie du vieux Trois-Rivières' (1967) where he is permanently represented; at the Cultural Centre of Shawinigan (1968), Cultural Centre of Jonquière (1968), and elsewhere.

References

Le Réveil, Jonquière-Kenogami, P.Q., Oct. 16, 1968 "Le peintre naturel Denis Laporte expose ses toiles"

Le Soleil, Quebec, P.Q., Oct. 19, 1968 "Le peintre Denis Laporte a été très bien accueilli"

Le Nouvelliste, Trois-Rivières, P.Q., Oct. 23, 1968 "Les oeuvres du peintre Laporte bien accueillies à Jonquière"

LAPORTE, Paul Carmel

b.1885

Born in Verchères, Quebec, his boyhood ambitions were to serve mankind and to be active in the arts.[1] He studied under private instructors of sculpture, painting and fine arts in general during his early school years and graduated from high school at the age of fourteen — too early to enter medical school.[2] He apprenticed himself to a Montreal woodcarver and cabinetmaker for three years. He also attended night classes under the auspices of the Société St. Jean Baptiste at the Monument National, Montreal with fellow students Elzear Soucy and Norman Laliberté, where he studied modelling, drawing, music and elocution. He then entered medicine at Laval University and graduated "cum laude", 1909.[3] He practised at Grand Falls where his territory extended for seventy-five miles; Connors Claire where he opened a private hospital under the auspices of the Red Cross, and in Edmundston with his brother Dr. R.H. Laporte who became Minister of Health for New Brunswick.[4] Dr. Paul Laporte set up a workshop in the basement of his home where he spent much of his leisure time (the little he had) carving illustrations often in colour and sometimes based on experiences within the field of medicine. His work which is influenced partly by Phillipe Hébert and Suzor-Coté is done realistically in bas relief in many types of wood, plaster of Paris, and metal embossing. He was the recipient of the American Physician's Art Association Award and other awards. He has given direction to many young people including Albert Nadeau, Claude Rouselle and Claude Picard.[6] On his retirement from medical practice he directed his energies to woodcarving. He founded a private school where he taught up to 36 pupils a week, giving free tuition to all, young and old. He conducted a survey of wood-carvers in Canada and with the assistance of Frank E. Whale and Commander H.W.S. Soulsby of Victoria, B.C., formed the Federation of Canadian Woodcarvers

LAPORTE, Paul Carmel (Cont'd)

and was elected its first president. He prepared a booklet on the art of woodcarving in easy to follow stages. He is a strong supporter for the theory that a hobby rests one area of the brain while exercising another. This reduces susceptibility to psychoneuroses, so common in our society to-day. Dr. Laporte was elected President of the New Brunswick Medical Council (two terms); lectured for the Red Cross and the St. John's Ambulance; promoted Victory Loan drives during the Second World War and held office as chairman of the military medical board during two world wars for which services he was awarded the M.B.E.[7] He lives in Edmundston, N.B.

References
[1] Document from artist
[2] Columbia (B.C.?), September, 1954 "The Doctor Thought He Had Retired" by Eugene Shevlin
[3] Ibid
[4] Ibid
[5] Ibid
[6] Ibid
[7] Ibid, P.23

LARCHEVÊQUE, André

He has been doing paintings of streets and buildings of Quebec City for the Tourist Branch of the Province of Quebec. These paintings are beautifully conceived both in colour and composition and combine the best of impressionistic and realistic styles. His street scenes are full of life — children tugging at parents' arms, shoppers, tourists, automobiles and horse drawn carriages all in colourful historical settings.

Reference
Canadian Weekly (Province of Quebec tourist ads)

LARIVIÈRE, Roger

Born in Ottawa, he studied at the Garneau School and the University of Ottawa where he obtained his bachelor of arts. Subsequently he studied painting under Henri Masson. In 1950 Carl Weiselberger[1] noticed his work as follows, "Only a few weeks ago, visiting an exhibition of paintings by pupils of Henri Masson, we were particularly impressed with the work of Roger Larivière and expressed hope to see more paintings by this young Ottawa artist . . . his latest show reveals that he already has developed a personal style of painting and of thinking in color. Whether he does portraits, still lifes, figure studies or landscape, Roger Larivière impresses the visitor of his show with the freshness and vigor of his moderately modern idiom. His draughtsmanship is sound, the color harmonies particularly in his still lifes — are effective and the objects have been arranged with taste and imagination . . . . In all, a show of splendid painting, which holds great promise for the future! ". He won the Purchase Award at the St. Catharines and District Arts Council in 1953 for his "Fleurs Fanées" and the following year exhibited jointly with R. York Wilson at

LARIVIÈRE, Roger (Cont'd)

the Williams Memorial Art Museum, London, where his work was again well received by the London *Free Press* as follows, "Roger Larivière, of Ottawa, is younger than Wilson in years and experience. The importance of his show is that although some of the canvases attest he is a student of Henri Masson, others reveal a definite and interesting individuality. The rhythm is flowing and although sometimes it asserts itself too forcefully, there is no doubt about its interest . . . . The paintings are remarkable for predominating blues used with a nice feeling for their capacity for etherealism, starkness, softness and blatancy. We particularly liked 'The Iron Chair,' because of the many blues combined with poetic sensitiveness of feeling. The soft glow of pinks, on the contrary, lends character to 'Still Life with Negro Statuette.' " He exhibited at the Robertson Gallery, Ottawa, in 1955, and again in 1959 when L'Association des femmes universitaires, Ottawa-Hull, sponsored an exhibition of his work which was warmly received by the press. In 1961 an article on the artist appeared in *Le Droit*.[3]

References
[1] *The Ottawa Citizen*, June 15, 1950 "Roger Larivière Paintings Show Distinctive Stylings" by Carl Weiselberger
[2] *The Free Press*, London, Ont., Mar. 20, 1954 "Canadian in Mexico, Canadian In Canada"
[3] *Le Droit*, Ottawa, Ont., Aug. 5, 1961 "Portraits — Une rencontre avec le peintre Roger Larivière" par Madeleine Leblanc
see also
Le Droit, Oct. 7, 1950 "Larivière"
Ibid, 24 Mar., 1955 "Remarquable exposition de peintures et céramiques à la galerie Robertson"
Standard-Freeholder Cornwall, Ont., Mar. 22, 1957 "Well-known Artist Paints Portrait At Art Meeting"
Le Droit, April 25, 1959 "Peintures de R. Larivière à la galerie Robertson" Par Darquise Parent
Ibid, May 12, 1959 "Exposition Roger Larivière"
The Ottawa Citizen, May 12, 1959 "Ottawa Artist At Best In His Figure-Painting" by Carl Weiselberger

LAROCQUE, Sylvio
b. (c) 1935

A Sudbury, Ontario, artist who studied at the Sacred Heart College and later completed Grade 13 at Sudbury High School. He then entered the Ontario College of Art in Toronto and in his third year won a cash bursary for his high standing in romantic abstract painting. With seven other students he helped establish a gallery called "The Garret" where students exhibited their paintings. In 1958 Larocque's ambition was to revive romantic abstract art.

Reference
Star, Sudbury, Ont., April 9, 1958 " 'Romantic Dream Painter' From Sudbury Featured in Novel 'Garret' Art Gallery"

LAROSE, Leo

A Montreal artist who painted two canvases of churches in Montreal for the St. Patrick's Society of that city. Prime Minister Diefenbaker presented these canvases

LAROSE, Leo (Cont'd)

to the Prime Ministers of Northern and Southern Ireland during his visit to these countries. The two canvases were of the historical Montreal churches — Christ Church Cathedral (presented to Prime Minister of Northern Ireland) and St. Patrick's Church (presented to the Prime Minister of Eire).

References

The Gazette, Mtl., P.Q., Feb. 25, 1961 "Two Gifts For The Irish"

La Presse, Mtl., P.Q., Feb. 21, 1961 "Present De La Société St. Patrice A L'Irlande" (large photo of artist working on one of the paintings)

LAROSE, Ludger

1868-1915

Born in Montreal, P.Q., he studied drawing at the Ecole des Beaux Arts, Paris, from 1887 to 1894, under Jean Paul Laurens and Gustave Moreau and won a prize in the evening school.[1] He returned to Montreal and taught drawing at the Ecole du Plateau (1894-1910) and Westmount public schools (1912-1915).[2] He did landscapes of the Laurentian area as well as other subjects.[3] He decorated the Sacred Heart Chapel of Notre Dame Church, Montreal.[4] Some of his work has passed through the hands of the Dominion Gallery, Montreal. Larose died in Montreal at the young age of 47.[5]

References

[1] National Gallery of Canada Information Form (undated)

[2] Ibid

[3] *The Gazette*, Mtl., P.Q., June 18, 1949 (photo of his canvas "St. Faustin" painted in 1899 and then owned by the Dominion Gallery)

[4] *Photo-Journal*, Mtl., P.Q., April 5, 1967 (large photo of one of Larose's paintings, a scene of Venice, which we assume to be the property of Salons funeraires Boudrias et Cormier, Saint-Laurent, P.Q.)

[5] see [1]

LARSON, Orland M.F.

b.1931

Born in Shaunovon, Saskatchewan, he entered the teaching profession and specialized in art. He studied painting with Jan Zack at the Banff School of Fine Arts while he continued to teach in the Saskatoon area. He travelled to England in 1954 where he taught elementary school in London for five months and travelled extensively on the Continent from northern Norway to North Africa visiting museums, galleries and sketching. He then studied pottery in London at the Central School of Arts and Crafts before returning to Canada in 1955. He received his Master's degree in art from the University of Wisconsin, U.S.A., where he studied oil painting, graphics and the making of jewellery. During 1960-61 he taught Eskimo children on Baffin Island and was granted a special certificate to teach art by the Saskatchewan Department of Education. He became a Curriculum Specialist in Art Education and Art Supervisor for the Northwest Territories for the Department of Northern Affairs (1961-63). He developed six readers oriented for Eskimo children and these were published by the Queen's Printer. He received a Canada Council Grant for the

LARSON, Orland M.F. (Cont'd)

period 1963-64. He then studied with the Danish jeweller Adda Hueted-Anderssen at Columbia University (1963-4); silversmithing with Hans Christensen at the School for American Craftsmen in Rochester, N.Y. (summer 1965). Was principal of an Eskimo school on Baffin Island (1964-66) where he and his wife also conducted a doctoral research programme. He worked with the goldsmith Stanley Letchzin, at Temple University, Philadelphia, Pa., (1966-67). During the period 1967-68 he carried out independent study and research as a jeweller working in Nova Scotia and exhibited his jewellery in a one-man show in Montreal. He was awarded a prize for his sterling comb exhibited at the "Craft Dimensions Canada" exhibition held at the Royal Ontario Museum, Toronto, in 1969. He lives with his wife at Petite-Rivière Bridge, Nova Scotia.

References

Information sheet from NGC Library file on artist
Chronicle-Herald, Halifax, N.S., Sept. 23, 1969 "Wins Award"

LASNIER, Raymond
1924-1968

Born in Quebec City, he was a victim of polio before he was four years old and was paralyzed in both his legs.[1] He was encouraged by his mother in creative activity which allowed his artistic talent to develop early.[2] He drew aeroplanes and later when he was attending school he was given the job of making geography maps and special projects such as posters. He mixed well with his school friends and never became isolated.[3] He took a correspondence course in drawing and on his first assignment his teachers were surprised at the good quality of his work. Later he studied under Mrs. Geraldine Bourbeau of Montreal, Jordi Bonet and Léon Bellefleur and received his diploma from the Ecole des Beaux-Arts, Quebec. He settled in Three Rivers, Quebec, where he received many honours and was held in high esteem. He won honourable mention in the 1957 Quebec Provincial Competition.[5] Gerald Godin[6] in 1959 noted how he had been influenced by Augustus Renoir and Claude Monet during one period of his career. But Lasnier moved from the Impressionist style to compositions of a more solid nature.[7] In 1960 he took first prize in the Quebec Provincial Competition for his painting "Lac Saint-Pierre".[8] A self sufficient man he lived in his own apartment where he enjoyed gourmet cooking, literature, philosophy and music.[9] He was an avid reader with an interest in international politics, books on travel, poetry and novels. It was his own belief that an artist does not need to be an eccentric or be isolated.[10] From 1960 to 1962 he painted night scenes of the river where he lived and was particularly fascinated with the reflections on the water. Many of his other scenes were of the spring break up on the St. Maurice River; of the old quarter of Three Rivers; early morning in little fishing ports or farms.[11] He was keenly interested in the outdoors, loved sailing and was skilful at the wheel. Many of his canvases were about boating and boats.[12] For a brief period before his death (1966-68) he did non-figurative canvases using acrylics. Acrylics were not new to him since he had used them for his still life studies. One reviewer of his abstract work felt the presence of water, the mournful, mysterious beauty of a harbour, of ships at anchor and of the docks.[13] Lasnier was recognized as one of Quebec's better artists and his paintings were

LASNIER, Raymond (Cont'd)

reproduced on Christmas cards, tourist folders and he had great success with his serigraphs.[14] Hydro-Quebec reproduced his painting Des Ursulines Street showing the Ursuline convent for their 1966 Christmas Card.[15] Some of his larger paintings are on permanent display such as his "Madonna" (8 ft. x 6 ft.) purchased for Chenaux Park at Le Cap-de-la-Madeleine. One of his paintings of the Ursuline Convent was presented to the late Daniel Johnson during a political rally at Three Rivers in 1962. His paintings are in private collections in Montreal, Quebec, Halifax, Toronto, Three Rivers and he is represented in the Museum of the Province of Quebec and other public collections. He was a member of the Cultural Centre Commission of Three Rivers and was also in charge of the course in art history at the Centre for University Studies in Three Rivers. He participated in the following exhibitions: Concours Artistiques, Musée du Québec (1950); Ecole Technique de Trois-Rivières (1952); Château de Blois, de Trois-Rivières (1960); Centre d'Art de Trois-Rivières (1960); Exposition Provinciale de Québec (1960); Salon du Printemps de Montréal (1961); Hôtel de Ville de Trois-Rivières (1958); Séminaire de Trois-Rivières (1962); Galerie Zanettin de Québec (1962); Galerie Margo Fisher-Richer de Grand'Mère (1964); Centre d'Art de Shawinigan (1965); Musée du Québec (1966); Centre d'Art de Shawinigan (1966); Centre d'Art St-Laurent, Ile d'Orléans (1967); Galerie du Vieux-Trois-Rivières (1968); l'Exposition Itinérante Raymond Lasnier sous la distinguée présidence de l'Honorable Jean-Noel Tremblay, du Centre Culturel de Trois-Rivières (1969). News of his death at the age of 44 came as a great shock to his many friends and acquaintances. He was survived by his parents Mr. & Mrs. D. Lasnier, and a brother and sister Pierre and Denise.

References

[1] *Le Nouvelliste*, Trois Rivières, P.Q., 19 Jan., 1961 "Raymond Lasnier, l'homme et l'artiste" par Claire Roy

[2] Ibid

[3] Ibid

[4] Nat. Gal. Can. Info. Form rec'd 10 Oct., 1965

[5] Ibid

[6] see[1]

[7] *Le Nouvelliste*, 16 Sept., 1959 "Un Peintre trifluvien – Raymond Lasnier" par Gerald Godin

[8] *Le Bien Public*, Trois Rivières, 9 Sept., 1960 "Raymond Lasnier, Grand Prix De L'Exposition De Quebec"

[9] see[1]

[10] see[1]

[11] Commentaires Sur l'Oeuvre De Raymond Lasnier par Louise Panneton

[12] *The St. Maurice Valley Chronicle*, Trois Rivières, P.Q., Feb, 1968 "Landscapes, A Lasnier Forte"

[13] *Chronicle Telegraph*, Que., P.Q. (Nov., 1962) "Five Young PQ Artists In Joint Showing Here" by F.J.P.

[14] see[11]

[15] *Le Nouvelliste*, 9 Dec., 1966 "Une toile de Lasnier servira à porter aux quatre coins de l'univers les voeux de Noël de l'Hydro"

see also

Le Nouvelliste, 6 Juin, 1960 "Les élèves de R. Lasnier exposent leurs travaux" par G.G.

La Presse, Mtl, P.Q., Sept. 3, 1960 "Le Premier Prix Du Concours National De l'Exposition Provinciale"

Le Nouvelliste, 25 Avril, 1961 "Raymond Lasnier expose et vend une toile au 78e Salon annuel du Printemps" par Louis Caron

Ibid, 23 Jan., 1961 "Des tableaux de Lasnier au Musée de la province"

LASNIER, Raymond (Cont'd)

Le Soleil, Que., P.Q. Nov. 1962 "Les peintres de Trois-Rivières exposent dans la Vieille Capitale" par Paule France Dufaux
Le Bien Public, 8 Feb., 1963 "Raymond Lasnier, peintre trifluvien" par Louise de Cotret-Panneton
Le Nouvelliste, 30 Jan., 1967 "Lasnier repense la nature" par Pierre Baril
Ibid, 15 Feb., 1968 "Hommage" par Mamie
Ibid, 12 Feb., 1968 "Peintre de grand talent Lasnier n'est plus" par Pierre Baril
Ibid, 10 Avril, 1968 "Au Centre culturel – Une salle portera le nom du peintre Raymond Lasnier"
Ibid, 21 Jan., 1969 "Raymond Lasnier, tel qu'en Lui-même" par Claire Roy
Ibid, jeudi le 1er mai, 1969 "Le ministre Tremblay au vernissage de l'exposition Lasnier – Ses toiles racontent le courage et la force d'un homme" par Jean-Marc Beaudoin

LASSZNER, Gabor

Born in Hungary he studied art in Budapest, Prague and Rome, and came to Canada in 1961. He settled in Toronto and later travelled across Canada in a mobile studio stopping at many communities where he painted portraits of interesting and enterprising Canadians. He financed his travel by portrait commissions of people from all walks of life. He completed about 2,000 portraits from which he selected about 100 for a tour across Canada. Before coming to Canada he spent eleven years in Brazil. He has won major awards for his work in Europe and South America.

References

The Free Press, London, Ont., Aug. 26, 1961 (photo of artist with work)
Tillsonburg News, Tillsonburg, Ont., March 11, 1964 "Canada's Faces On Canvas" (a portrait of Harold D'Arcy by Lasszner)
News, Chatham, Ont., Sept. 2, 1965 "Hungarian Artist Offers Travelling Art Exhibits"
Etobicoke Adv. Guardian, Islington, Ont., March 20, 1969 "Portraits on view"

LATTER, (Mrs.) Helen

An artist from Morden, Manitoba, who painted 16 mural panels (4 x 8 ft.) depicting the History of Morden and the Pembina Valley. They were undertaken by Mrs. Latter as a Manitoba Centennial project and 12 of the panels were exhibited at The National Arts Centre, Ottawa, on the occasion of Manitoba Day.

References

Times, Morden, Manitoba, Jan. 7, 1970 "Morden Artist's Murals To Be Displayed – National Arts Centre"
Ibid, Feb. 4, 1970 "Morden Murals Cause Comment in Capitol"

LAUBENTHAL, (Mrs.) Sybil

Born in Halle, Germany, where she studied pottery on a four year apprenticeship then worked as a potter for four years before coming to Canada. She is a teacher at Victoria Composite High School, Edmonton, Alberta, and for special classes at the

LAUBENTHAL, (Mrs.) Sybil (Cont'd)

University of Alberta. She was the first Canadian potter ever to receive a prize at the Ceramic National at the 19th Annual Ceramic National, Syracuse Museum of Fine Arts, Syracuse, N.Y., in 1956. For a number of years she has also won prizes at the Canadian Ceramics exhibition held in Toronto. Her work was shown at the First Fine Crafts Exhibition at the National Gallery of Canada and at the 1958 Brussels World's Fair. She is the wife of architect Charles Laubenthal. They have two children, Cornelius and Sabine. Lives in Edmonton.

References

The Edmonton Journal, Edmonton, Alta., Dec. 6, 1956 "Prize Winning Skill" (photo of artist at work)
Ibid, June 27, 1957 "Work Of Edmonton Potter To Be Shown At Brussels"

L'AUBINIÈRE, C.A. (Mme. C.A. de L'Aubinière / nee Steeple)

Daughter of John Steeple, an English water-colourist. She studied under Corot and Gérôme in France; travelled in England, France, United States and Canada with her husband, holding exhibitions, lectures, and painting in the places she visited. She settled in Montreal for many years and painted at Montmorency in 1888. The Dominion Gallery had, and may still have some of her canvases.

References

The Gazette, Mtl., P.Q., July 8, 1950 (photo of her painting "Springtime, Montmorency" dated 1888)
NGC Library file on artist

LAUDA, Georges J.

b.1925

Born in Prague, Czechoslovakia, he studied four years in Art Education at University; two and a half years at l'Ecole des Beaux Arts, Paris, under Prof. R. Jaudon. He came to Canada in 1951 and settled in Montreal where he received his diploma of Professor of Drawing from L'Ecole des Beaux Arts, Montreal in 1952.

Reference
NGC Information Form rec'd April 14, 1953

LAUDER, James (Jim)

Born in Toronto, Ont., he studied at the Ontario College of Art and later settled near Wakefield, Quebec, not far from Ottawa. He was a landscape painter for about two years and taught classes in painting to supplement his income. He attended Carleton University where he received his Bachelor of Arts. He became interested in sculpture with found objects, especially from old machinery parts left behind on deserted farms, which he fashions into highly creative and successful pieces. Judy Barrie[1] of The Ottawa Citizen on her visit to the artist's workshop noted, "Stuffed into a decrepit lean-to below the house are Jim Lauder's art materials — pitch forks,

LAUDER, James (Jim) (Cont'd)

wiring, chains, weather pumps, wheels, an old golf course lawn mower, even an ancient cream separator. Stacks upon stacks of musty junk. Ideally, he creates what the objects suggest to him, thus making 'ultimate use' of them. Sometimes he conceives the idea first, but never cuts a piece unless absolutely necessary. He will spend many hours searching for an item with just the right twist, just the right angle . . . . 'There is nothing originally nice about the stuff I use,' he said, 'but it gains character and beauty with age.' " W.Q. Ketchum[2] of *The Ottawa Journal* noted his 1967 exhibition at the Elmdale Theatre as follows, "The sculptures are ingeniously contrived from found objects including parts of agricultural implements. For his paintings, the artist derives his inspiration from Wakefield, Ramsay's Crossing, Cascades and Kirks Ferry. We particularly liked a large canvas 'Brooding Girl.' In the landscapes 'Sapling, Wind and Water' is splendid. His brushes have conveyed to canvas the beautiful Gatineau country in all its moods. A number of small polymer prints are especially attractive." His work is on exhibit at Galerie Martin, Montreal.

References

[1] *The Ottawa Citizen*, Ottawa, Ont., Dec. 7, 1968 "The path to paradise – Paved with rusty junk" by Judy Barrie
[2] *The Ottawa Journal*, Aug. 23, 1967 "Lauder Shows Work At Theatre" by W.Q. Ketchum
see also
The Ottawa Journal, June 10, 1969 "Mall Attention Grabber" (large photo of Lauder's "African mother and child" on the Sparks Street Mall, Ottawa)

LAUR, Edgar Lee
1867-19--

Born near Aylmer, Elgin County, Ontario, he attended the Central Ontario School of Art under William Cruikshank.[1] He also studied under Frederick S. Challener. He was a school teacher, then telegrapher for the Michigan Central Railroad.[2] Whether he studied art before or after the above employment is not indicated on any of the references given below but he entered the field of black and white illustration full time. He never did any professional colour work since he had defective colour vision but he became well known for his etchings and mezzotints. He lived in Woodbridge, Ontario, in a cottage which served as his home and studio.[3] He was a member of the Little Billee Sketch Club.[4] Represented in the National Gallery of Canada, Ottawa, Department of Prints and Drawings.

References

[1] NGC Info. Form rec'd May 19, 1920
[2] Biographical sketch on reverse side of his press portrait in artist's file, NGC Library.
[3] *The Toronto Star*, Tor., Ont., July 26, 1930 "Canadian Artist Prospers Finds Opportunity At Home"
[4] *Canadian Art, Its Origin And Development* by William Colgate, Ryerson, Paperbacks 1967, P.68 (mentioned as Edward Laur)

LAUTERMAN, Dinah
1900-19--

Born in Montreal, P.Q., she studied drawing at the Montreal Art Association School under Randolph Hewton and drawing and sculpture at the Ecole des Beaux Arts,

LAUTERMAN, Dinah (Cont'd)

Montreal, under Maurice Felix, H. Albert Laliberté, Edwin Holgate, H. Charpentier, and Charles Maillard. After four years at the Beaux Arts where she won several medals for her work she entered the field of sculpture with total dedication. After her death an exhibition of her sculpture was held at the Redpath Library of McGill University, Montreal, to commemorate the establishment of an endowed special collection to be known as The Dinah Lauterman Library of Art. The exhibit included twenty-two designs in plaster including one of Dr. Howard T. Barnes who was a distinguished member of the Physics Department of the University.

Reference
National Gallery of Canada Info. Form
The Montreal Star, April 29, 1947 "A Fitting Memorial — Work of Late Montreal Artist Exhibited at Redpath Library "

LAUZON, Larry

He studied at the Ontario College of Art for three years and then travelled to Mexico in 1968. Paul Russell described his work on show at the Pollack Phase II Gallery as follows, "His drawing is hard and precise on white ground — a counterpoint to the jumping color of surrounding areas. The compositions are strikingly simple, asymmetrical in most cases, and always exhibit a certain finesse. His imagery is contemporary, and ranges through pop music, politics, and art, from Paul McCartney and a bowl of apples to Salvador Dali and a pair of scissors . . . . A painting of Lyndon Johnson's head and hand draped in a flat blue area sliding off the right side of the canvas, is the most enigmatic, most interesting work, and the one most free from Daliesque clutter."

Reference
The Globe & Mail, Tor., Ont., July 5, 1969 "At The Galleries — Two young artists clamor for color" by Paul Russell

LAUZON, Normand
b.1925

Born in Montreal, P.Q., he studied at the Ecole des Beaux Arts under Jean Simard, Stanley Cosgrove and Sylvia Daoust. He exhibited his work at the Annual Spring Show at the Montreal Museum of Fine Arts in 1954. Last reported working as a commercial artist with the firm of Bomac in Montreal.

Reference
Nat. Gal. of Can. Info. Form rec'd April, 1954

LAVOYE, Juliette de (Miss Marie Ann Juliette Lavoie)
b.1903

Born in Montreal, P.Q., she studied philosophy (1925-26); then learned fine colouring and drawing at the Koehne Studio, Chicago, where she took a six weeks' course (1926); returning to Montreal she worked as a free lance display artist for the C.P.R., the C.N.R., and the Bell Telephone (1928-39). She took a further eight months study at the Grand Central Art School, New York (1931).[1] Then she continued free lance work while in her spare time she drew and copied photographs on porcelain.[2] In 1933 she had obtained such a marked degree of proficiency in miniature work that she was commissioned by Lord Bessborough to paint a miniature of his young son. In 1935 she was then authorized to use "By appointment of their Excellencies the Governor-General and the Countess of Bessborough."[3] F. Cleveland Morgan of Henry Morgan and Co., commissioned her to paint miniatures of Princess Elizabeth and Margaret Rose. In 1939, a year later, the King and Queen visited Canada and these miniatures were placed in the Royal Suite of the Windsor Hotel. The Royal couple were so taken with her fine work that the President of the Windsor Hotel (J. Alderic Raymond) presented the miniatures to them before their return to England. Shortly afterwards Miss de Lavoye received a letter from the Queen thanking her for her beautiful miniatures. A large portrait of the Queen (or Queen Mother as she is known today) was subsequently completed by Miss de Lavoye and accepted by the Queen. During the Second World War Miss de Lavoye studied drafting evenings at Sir George Williams College (1941-46) and she worked days in the war effort as a draftsman for the Angus Shops (CPR) and Noordyn Aircraft Company. In 1946 she returned to the field of miniature portraiture. Writing in *The Ottawa Journal* in 1957 Garry Carroll[5] noted, "Her work was received with much excitement in Britain. Instead of using the traditional gilt frames for her work she designs all her own frames from fine Canadian blended wood . . . . Miss de Lavoye uses fine feathers to paint and all of her work is done on imported ivory. She also designs and paints miniature jewelry." In 1953 she became the first Canadian to be admitted to the Royal Society of Miniature Painters, Sculptors and Gravers, London. One of her most important undertakings was to paint miniature portraits of the Fathers of Confederation which she began in 1960 by visiting the National Archives in Ottawa to study likenesses of the fathers.[6] The paper on which the work in the Archives was done had reached such a marked degree of deterioration that it was important that her work was undertaken then. Ivory on which the miniatures are done is considered the most successful material to conserve likenesses over a long period. She went to Paris where after an exhausting search she found the right ivory which is a special hard type, and a vibrant burgundy velvet for mounting the work which allows the portraits to maintain a rugged character and liveliness. The shadow-box type frames were chosen in order to protect the work as much as possible from direct light. Her water colours were obtained from England, and for fine detail work a feather of a bird was obtained from Poland. Commissioned by Samuel Bronfman, LL.D., founder of The House of Seagram, the portraits after their national tour were deposited in the Parliament Buildings, Ottawa. An exhibition catalogue was published for the tour by Seagrams Limited with foreword by Samuel Bronfman, text by Joseph Schull and reproductions of Miss Lavoye's thirty-four miniatures.[7] Miss Lavoye is a member of the Royal Institute, London, England; Montreal Museum of Fine Arts; Women's Art Society, Montreal; Detroit Museum of Fine Arts Founders Society. She has done portraits of many important Canadians including the late Vincent Massey.[8] Her proper family name is Lavoie but to avoid confusion with several other Juliette

LAVOYE, Juliette de (Miss Marie Ann Juliette Lavoie) (Cont'd)

Lavoies she has been using the ancestoral spelling of her family name – Lavoye. She lives in Montreal.

References

[1] Information sheet in NGC Library, see artists file also NGC Info. Sheet and *The Montreal Standard* below

[2] *The Montreal Standard*, Mtl., P.Q., Aug. 17, 1946 "Painter of Miniatures At Top of Profession" by Kenneth Lunny

[3] Ibid, also as in [1]

[4] Ibid

[5] *The Ottawa Journal*, Ottawa, Ont., Feb. 23, 1957 "Juliette De Lavoye – Miniature Painters' School Her Dream" by Garry Carroll

[6] *The Globe & Mail*, Tor., Ont., June 3, 1967 "Seven years' work involved in painting of miniatures"

[7] Catalogue – *Henceforth We Shall Rank Among The Nations*, text by Joseph Schull, foreword by Samuel Bronfman, reproductions of miniatures of Fathers of Confederation by Juliette de Lavoye, Distillers Corp. – Seagrams Ltd., 1967

[8] Portrait of Vincent Massey is in the collection of the Montreal Museum of Fine Arts

see also
The Gazette, Mtl., P.Q., April 10, 1943 "Miniature Painter Follows New Line"
Le Canada, Mtl., P.Q., June 5, 1952 "Mlle Juliette Delavoye, miniaturiste Canadienne parle de son art délicat" par Odette Oligny
Saturday Night, Tor., Ont., Aug. 14, 1954 "Montreal Miniaturist"
Le Soleil, 12 Août, 1967 "Un art oublié, la miniature" par C.D.

LAW, Charles Anthony Francis

b.1916

Born in London, England, the son of Major and Mrs. A.S. Law, both Canadians.[1] His father had been with the Canadian Expeditionary Forces during the First World War. He arrived in Canada with his parents in 1917, and they settled in Quebec City. A year later he was taken to the summer home in Muskoka of his paternal grandfather, Captain F.C. Law, R.N. retired.[2] His grandfather in his daily routine ran his island summer home like a battleship and in the years that followed imparted a sense of seamanship to the boy.[3] On the other side of his family his maternal grandfather, the Hon. Justice L.A. Audotte, a Judge of the Exchequer Court, had his summer home at Rivière du Loup where at the age of fourteen the boy built his first sailing boat.[4] An Upper Canada College student (1928-31) he was part owner of an old 21 foot yacht at the age of sixteen. Sharing in the ownership were his fifteen year old brother Stuart, and a friend Peter Cossette who was fourteen.[5] They sailed in the St. Lawrence unaware that they were gaining valuable experience for the demanding years that lay ahead. But not all his development was in this direction. His grandfather Captain Law was also an accomplished painter and the boy's own talent was discovered and encouraged by Dr. Marius Barbeau. At the age of eighteen he studied under Franklin Brownell, F.H. Varley at the Ottawa Art Association (1934-37) while he studied at the University of Ottawa (1931-36). It was in Ottawa that he became a friend of Frank Hennessey with whom he painted in the Gatineau and Gaspé areas (1935-39). At home in Quebec City, he received instruction from Percival Tudor-Hart who like Brownell had studied at the Julian academy in Paris.[6] In 1937 he held his first one man show in Quebec City.[7] His goal in painting was to create a true conception of Canadian landscape in bold, and vigorous realism. In 1939 he was awarded the Jessie Dow Prize for landscape in oils for his canvas "Cold Winter Day, P.Q." *The Gazette* reproduced the canvas with the caption which included the following remarks, "The forms are broadly handled, the design effective and the color crisp and clean . . . . Law, whose marked natural talent was developed by personal determination and industry, has in the last few years benefited by some spasmodic professional training . . . ." In 1937 he had joined the Royal Canadian Ordnance Corps as Lieutenant and in the last week of August, 1939, was sailing in his new yacht along the Saguenay River and painting some of the beautiful countryside as he went. When he returned to Tadoussac the last week in August he learned war was not far off and immediately set sail for Quebec City. Travelling night and day he arrived at Quebec on September 1, and reported for duty the next morning. In March of the next year he transferred to the Royal Canadian Naval Volunteer Reserve and within a week sailed for England where he served on big ships for a brief period before joining the Motor Torpedo Boat Command of the Royal Navy at Dover. He was handed command of M.T.B. No. 48 which he took into action against Nazi warships escaping from Brest in 1941. The squadron of Torpedo Boats advanced through the fire of the Nazi escort vessels and fighters overhead. His boat managed to fire two torpedoes and the Prinz Eugen (heavy cruiser) was hit. Getting back safely under the deadly fire of the Sharnhorst and Gneisnau was something short of a miracle. For his part in the attack he was mentioned in despatches.[10] He was able to reconstruct the action on canvas the next day. In the months that followed he continued to record his experiences on canvas. Later in 1942 he was appointed Commander of M.T.B. 629 and was again mentioned in despatches for a probable sinking of a Flak Trawler off the Dutch coast. In 1944 he became Senior Officer of the 29th Canadian M.T.B. Flotilla which took part in the invasion of Normandy. He was awarded the Distinguished Service Cross for his part in various engagements during the invasion. A year later he was appointed Official War Artist and completed twenty-nine large oil paintings and seventy-five oil sketches. Most of these works are in the National Gallery of Canada Second World War Collection.[11] As early as 1942 his war paintings went on tour in Canada in connection with the Navy exhibition.[12] In 1946 he was transferred to the permanent Navy with the rank of Lieutenant. He was commanding officer of the frigate *Antigonish* and was promoted to Lieutenant Commander. Later he joined the staff of the Defence Secretary at National Defence Headquarters in Ottawa. He held two one man shows in 1950 at the Little Gallery, Ottawa; another at the Odeon Theatre Gallery in 1951 before taking up his duties of first Lieutenant-Commander aboard the aircraft carrier *Magnificent*.[13] Even aboard the carrier when duty permitted he formed an art club among the officers and men. In 1955 he became second-in-command of the Arctic patrol ship *Labrador*. Travelling north he made many sketches and in 1957 many of these paintings were exhibited at The Citadel Branch of the Provincial Museum in Halifax. The *Mail-Star*[14] noted the exhibition as follows, "Bold in execution and with effective use of vivid colors the scenes of the northern fringe of this continent are eye-catching and give a real appreciation of the ruggedness of coastline and vast wastes of ice and snow encountered on such a patrol tour." His Arctic paintings were on view at the Robertson Gallery, Ottawa, in 1961. That year he took command of the destroyer H.M.C.S. *Sioux* and also became Commander of the Third Escort Squadron and Senior Officer. Next he commanded the mobile repair ship H.M.C.S. *Cape Scott*

LAW, Charles Anthony Francis (Cont'd)

which went on the medical expedition to Easter Island from November 16, 1964 to March 17, 1965. This was his last command before his retirement from the Navy in 1966. He became Chairman of the Centennial Visual Arts Sub-Committee for Nova Scotia. Since his retirement he has devoted his full time to painting. In 1967 he became resident artist of St. Mary's University, Halifax, N.S., where he is Curator of Art, consultant, and supervisor of many other activities which make available to students as much art as possible. A retrospective exhibition of his paintings was held at the Nova Scotia Museum of Fine Arts Centennial Art Gallery during November, 1968.[15] He held a one man show at Zwicker's Granville Street Gallery in early December of 1969.[16] He married Jane Shaw of Berlin, N.H., U.S.A., in 1942, an artist in her own right. He is represented in the Quebec Provincial Museum, Nova Scotia Provincial Museum and the National Gallery of Canada as mentioned. He is a member of the Nova Scotia Society of Artists.

References

[1] Nat. Gal. of Can. Info. Form rec'd October, 1965

[2] Ibid

[3] *The Gazette*, Mtl., P.Q., Jan. 29, 1943 "Attack on German Battleships Painted by Officer Who Took Part"

[4] Ibid

[5] Ibid

[6] Questionnaire form, NGC Library, see artist's file, form dated Aug. 10/46

[7] *The Gazette*, April 1, 1939 "Awarded Jessie Down Prize For Landscape In Oils" (photo of Law's canvas "Cold Winter Day, P.Q.")

[8] see [3]

[9] see [3]

[10] *The Gazette*, June 13, 1942 (CP) London, Eng. "Quebec Artist, Lt. C. Anthony Law, Paints Nazi Warships' Brest Dash"

[11] *Check List of The War Collections* by R.F. Wodehouse, NGC, 1968, P.125-6-7 Tor., Ont.

[12] *Globe & Mail*, Tor., Ont., Dec. 15, 1942 "Unique Naval Mixed Exhibit Goes On Tour"
The Toronto Star, Tor., Ont., Dec. 30, 1942 "15 Tons Of Navy Display In Show"

[13] *The Ottawa Journal*, Oct. 23, 1952 " 'Maggie's' Sea-Going Artists Display Talent in Halifax Show"

[14] *Mail-Star*, Halifax, N.S., May 15, 1957 "Paintings Of Arctic Are On Exhibition At Citadel"

[15] *Catalogue-Retrospective Exhibition of Paintings* by Anthony Law, November, 1968 with introduction by John D. Reppetaux, Curator, Nova Scotia Museum Of Fine Art Centennial Art Gallery.

[16] *Mail-Star*, Halifax, N.S., Dec. 9, 1969 "Art Shows Law's Love of Nature" by Gretchen Pierce
see also
Canadian Art by Graham McInnes, MacMillan, 1950, P.83
National Gallery of Canada Catalogue of Paintings and Sculpture, Vol. 3, P.433

LAWLEY, Douglas

b.1906

Born at Glace Bay, N.S., he graduated from Glace Bay High School; Mount Allison University; McGill University.[1] He taught for many years and specialized in Latin. Later he became Principal of Westmount High School, Montreal.[2] After his retirement he continued to teach Latin at Lower Canada College, Montreal. Painting first interested him in 1937 and he gave serious consideration to becoming an artist but teaching won out as a first occupation. He studied painting under Agnes Lefort in Montreal and Albro Hibbard of the American National Academy.[3] For many years

LAWLEY, Douglas (Cont'd)

he painted scenes in and around Montreal and became known for his Mount Royal studies livened with cab horses. Horses were of special interest to him and one of his ambitions was to visit Sable Island to paint the legendary wild ponies. Finally he received permission from the Department of Fisheries to visit the Island. He had done extensive research into the origin of the ponies and found their history very probably went back to the year 1518 when Baron de Lery of France left some domestic animals on the island after attempting to establish a settlement there.[4] The Island subsequently became the scene of some 250 shipwrecks which caused the loss of ten thousand lives.[5] Lawley flew over the Island several times before landing to study the ponies close up. He did a series of paintings of the ponies wandering among the sand dunes which sometimes rise to a height of seventy or eighty feet. The Island is now occupied by nine men and one woman from the meteorological division of the Government of Canada. His Sable Island paintings were exhibited at his first one man show, held at the Dominion Gallery, Montreal, in April of 1962. The next year at Cowansville, Quebec, Fred Pattemore[6] noted his work as follows, "A trifle conservative, the canvases do, nevertheless trap the movement of the horse, making a sensible sacrifice of detail to make this effect even more pronounced. He occasionally strays from Sable Island to Montreal and Quebec City, quite aptly capturing the blue haze over the metropolis and the quaint charm of our provincial capital. Even here the horse creeps in, whether hitched to a calèche or a sleigh, in spring or in winter. In these paintings the colorful dress of the calèche drivers of Quebec, the raccoon coats and so on provide a good deal of life and interest to his works." He is represented in the collection of the Royal Trust Company, Montreal; Glace Bay Miners' Museum Foundation and elsewhere as well as in many private collections. His work can be seen at the Dominion Galleries, Sherbrooke Street, Montreal. Lives in Montreal.

References

[1] *Cape Breton Post*, Sydney, N.S., July 17, 1965 "Donates Painting" (large photo of Lawley and painting also Nina Cohen, Chairman, Museum Committee of Glace Bay Miners' Museum Foundation) and article.

[2] Ibid

[3] Ibid

[4] *The Gazette*, Mtl., P.Q., Mar. 24, 1962 "Boyhood Dream To Visit Sable Island, See Horses Achieved; Paintings Result" by Bill Bantey

[5] Ibid

[6] *The Record*, Sherbrooke, P.Q., Oct. 7, 1963 "Enjoyable and worth a visit" by Fred Pattemore

LAWRENCE, Mary C. (Mrs.)

b.1899

Born at the Island of Mull, Scotland, she came to Canada in 1908 but didn't start serious painting until her fifty-first year. She received her training through the Department of Extension of the University of Alberta. She won scholarships to study at the Banff School of Fine Arts in the years 1951, 1954, 1955, where she studied under H.G. Glyde. She was first influenced by Braque and Cézanne but later found the work of her teacher H.G. Glyde of particular interest and inspiration. A painter of landscapes, still lifes, and abstracts she works mainly in the medium of oils although she also uses some water colours. She is represented in the Calgary

LAWRENCE, Mary C. (Mrs.) (Cont'd)

Allied Arts Centre; the Edmonton Museum; Banff School of Fine Arts and the Canadian Pacific Railway. She is a member of the Alberta Society of Artists and the Red Deer Art Club. Lives in Red Deer, Alberta.

References
   Document from artist
   see also
   The Red Deer Advocate, April 30, 1965 "Mrs. Mary Lawrence To Exhibit Paintings In One-Day Show"

LAWRENCE, Mollie Cruickshank

Born in Regina, she studied with W.J. Phillips, André Biéler, Lawrence Alloway, Frank Stella and others.[1] Her off-prints from oil paintings caught the attention of Clement Greenberg during his tour of the Prairie provinces for Canadian Art in 1963. Greenberg described her prints as "Chinese-tinged, largely abstract landscape fantasies" which he felt deserved a much wider public.[2] Andrew Hudson[3] also received her work well, noting " . . . Thanks to an inspired relaxation and a giving in to the quirks and whims of her medium (the oil paint can print puddles or herring-bone furrows where it pleases) the final work has a freshness, vitality and intuitive life of its own . . . . The leaving of so much untouched, blank paper and the casual way in which the printed area meets, or runs over the edge of the page, make for a feeling of openness and spaciousness that I find exhilarating." She has exhibited her work at the following shows: Serigraphs with the Society of Canadian Painter-Etchers and Engravers; Prairie Painters exhibit, Norman Mackenzie Art Gallery (1963); Saskatchewan Art Show, Ohio (1965); Sask. Jubilee Art Exhibit (1965); U. of Sask. Regina Show (1966); International Print Show, Knox-Albright Gallery, Buffalo, New York (1964); Western Printmakers (1967); Canadian Crafts Exhibit Expo '67 where her West Over Jacket, Slippers, Hat and Gloves where shown;[4] Bonli Gallery, Toronto (1966-67) and many other showings. Her first one man show of Prints was held at the Isaacs Gallery, Toronto (1964). She has been Art Supervisor for Elementary Schools, Regina Board of Education. She is represented in the Saskatchewan Arts Board collection; Art Gallery of the Regina Public Library and in private collections in New York, Washington, Vancouver, Toronto and London. She lives in Regina.

References
   [1] M. Cruickshank Lawrence (catalogue for exhibition in the Art Gallery of Regina Public Library)
   [2] *Canadian Art*, No. 84, Mar./Apr. 1963 "Clement Greenberg's View of Art on the Prairies" by Clement Greenberg P.105
   [3] *The Leader Post*, Regina, Sask., Feb. 1, 1964 "Local artist's work 'product of Regina' " by Andrew Hudson
   [4] *Canadian Fine Crafts* (at Expo 67) an exhibition collected by Moncrieff Williamson, Queen's Printer, 1967, P.32 (no illustration)

LAWS, Eve (née Eva Maria Huldschinsky) (Mrs. S. Gossage)

b. (c) 1917

Born in Berlin, Germany, she later studied at the Art Academy of Berlin. She lived in Alexandria, Egypt, for a number of years where she painted portraits and did display design and interior decorating. She came to Canada about 1939 and established a display studio in Montreal. It was in Montreal that she met and married Stevenson Gossage in 1956. In 1962 they moved to Winnipeg where her husband was Vice-President of the CPR prairie region. Later they moved to Victoria, B.C., before returning to Montreal. In 1966 she held a one man show at the Gemst gallery, Montreal. Her subjects include old Montreal streets, railway shops, the western prairie, ballet and portraits.

References

Tribune, Winnipeg, Man., Dec. 5, 1962 "Eve's Views – From portraits to studies to comment on art aspects"

The Montreal Star, Mtl., P.Q., Mar. 29, 1966 "Eve Laws Exhibition At Gemst" by Robert Ayre

---

LAWSON, Ernest

1873-1939

Born in Halifax, N.S., the son of Annie (nee Mitchell) and Dr. Archibald Lawson.[1] His parents moved to Kansas City where his father set up a practice of medicine. Ernest was left behind at Kingston, Ontario, with his maternal aunt Jessie Grant, wife of Dr. George Munro Grant, principal of Queen's College.[2] As a boy Ernest had begun to paint pictures of animals and to make studies of things that interested him.[3] In 1888 he left Kingston and arrived in Kansas City where he enrolled in the Art Institute of Chicago.[4] There he met Ella Holman a teacher at the school. After he left the Institute and lived with his father and mother in Mexico City he kept up correspondence with Miss Holman. His father was the Medical Officer to Pearson & Co., American civil engineers who were engaged in large construction projects in Mexico. Ernest was hired as an assistant draftsman by the Pearson firm.[5] Despite his father's disapproval of art as a career Ernest attended the Santa Clara Art Academy in his spare time. He lived with his parents saving money until his eighteenth birthday when he struck out on his own to study art in New York. It is believed that he studied at the Art Students' League shortly after 1891 although it is not known for sure because many records at the Institute were destroyed by fire. He then studied under John N. Twachtman and Alden Weir at their summer school at Cos Cob, Connecticut, before leaving for France in 1893.[6] He studied in Paris at the Académie Julian for a short period before following his own study course. The styles of the Impressionists came under his scrutiny. He also found the work of James Whistler of particular interest.[7] He continued to paint in his own particular strain of impressionism. In 1894 two of his paintings were accepted in the 'Salon des Artistes Français'. He also met with Sisley and held this artist in high esteem for it was noted that he painted a landscape entitled "Church at Moret-sur-Loing" taken from the area where Sisley lived and signed his name "Lawson" omitting his initial in the fashion of Sisley.[8] He experimented as well in the Seurat idiom. He returned to America in 1894.[9] During his stay in Paris he had become acquainted with Somerset Maugham as well as many great painters. Shortly after his arrival in United States he married his former teacher Ella Holman at Philadelphia and they returned to Paris on their honeymoon.[10] After a two year stay in France he arrived

LAWSON, Ernest (Cont'd)

in Toronto with his wife and baby daughter. His impressionistic styled paintings were not accepted in Canada and he soon decided to leave. Later he accepted a teaching post at Columbus, Georgia, after a second daughter was born to them.[11] In 1898 he moved with his family to New York City first at Washington Heights and later in MacDougal Alley, Greenwich Village.[12] He painted several portraits but one or two experiences with certain patrons gave him no encouragement to move into this field. Instead his landscape work and his new surroundings gave him a fulfilment described by Barbara O'Neill of the National Gallery of Canada as follows: " . . . Washington Heights and its surroundings now provided Lawson with landscape themes which suited him, and the great city offered him for the first time the congenial society of other artists. Through his friend William Glackens he met John Sloan, Everett Shinn, and George Luks. They formed part of a group of artists and newspaper reporters who were protégés of the artist and teacher Robert Henri and who became known as the Realists." He held a one man show at Pennsylvania Academy, Philadelphia in 1907. Although Lawson's style was quite different from theirs he shared a common interest in the contemporary American scene. The National Academy of Design rejected works by Luks, Glackens, and Shinn, and turned down Lawson's nomination for associate membership. The stage was set for the banding together of these men and others. By 1908 the exhibition of *The Eight* had taken place at the Macbeth Gallery, an event which was to command wide attention. This group was made up of the following artists: Arthur B. Davies, William Glackens, Robert Henri, Ernest Lawson, George Luks, Maurice Prendergast, Everett Shinn and John Sloan. *The Eight* were eventually accepted by the National Academy and Lawson received his status of Associate Member the same year. His association with *The Eight* brought his eyes closer to the city in search of some of his subjects. In 1910 he participated in the exhibition of Independent Artists and served on one of the committees which made arrangements for the great Armory Show of 1913, where three of his paintings were shown, "Clouds and Shadows", "Weeds and Willow Trees" and "Harlem River-Winter". He found much of his subject matter along the Harlem River. One of his winter Harlem scenes was later purchased for the Walter P. Chrysler collection. By 1911 he was exhibiting with the Canadian Art Club in Toronto and had his first painting purchased by the National Gallery of Canada. He exhibited jointly with Bryson Burroughs at Galerie Levasque, Paris in 1914; won a Gold Medal for excellence of his entire showing at the Panama-Pacific International Exposition at the Palace of Fine Arts, San Francisco, 1915, and later that year was awarded the National Academy 'Altman' prize; from a one man showing of 18 paintings his "Harlem River-Winter" was purchased by the Metropolitan Museum of Art, New York.[14] He had been mentioned by E.F.B. Johnston[15] as a native of Halifax and member of the Canadian Art Club in *Canada And Its Provinces*, published in 1914. His winning of a Silver Medal and cash prize at the Sixth Biennial Exhibition of Contemporary American Paintings for his "Boathouse-Winter, Harlem River" made possible his trip to Spain, his choice over other European Countries most of which were engaged in the First World War. It was here that he declared himself born in San Francisco, and an American citizen (Americans were still considered neutrals). Arriving in Spain with his wife and children he painted with Max Kuehne in Segovia. His new environment caused a change in his style and a more rhythmic quality in his brushwork which he continued to develop after his return to the United States.[16] In 1917 he was elected full member of the National Academy of Design, New York, an academy much like

759

the Royal Canadian Academy. Because most of his activity and exhibitions took place in United States no real opportunity arose for him becoming a member of the Royal Canadian Academy. He did however, visit Canada several times including the year 1924 at Halifax, Nova Scotia, when he painted the surrounding coves and villages in at least three different styles as noted by Barbara O'Neal:[17] a flat manner, a strongly rhythmical style developed in Spain, a heavy impasto employing simple structure reminiscent of the work of Albert P. Ryder who had done many seascapes.[18] Lawson's exhibit at the Ferargil Galleries (NYC) in April, 1925, received warm praise from the *New York Times*[18(a)] whose reviewer concluded, "Every composition has a linear bone for its firm flesh of colours." During this period Lawson's activities did not escape the attention of Newton MacTavish[19] who in his *The Fine Arts In Canada* noted, "His work is of an unusually high order, being notable for its exquisite colour values, its tone and vibrating quality. By metropolitan critics he is accounted one of the greatest of living American painters." Lawson taught at the Kansas City Art Institute (1926), Broadmoor Academy, Colorado Springs (1927) where he found the mountains a subject to paint but not always successfully; however he received a prize at the National Academy of Design exhibition in 1930 for his "Gold Mining, Cripple Creek" a point located about twenty miles from Colorado Springs. Lawson kept moving to new environments in the succeeding years but rheumatoid arthritis finally drove him to the warmer climate of Florida and in 1936 he settled more or less there at Coral Gables with his friends Mr. and Mrs. Royce Powell. (His wife was not living with him any longer although he was still in love with her. She took the children to France in 1926 but later returned to the U.S.). The depression had come down equally hard on those in the art world and Lawson despite his many prizes suffered pressures from lack of funds; in addition one of his daughters had died while on a visit to Egypt with her mother, and he was alone. He turned to liquor to numb his anguish. The Powells with whom he stayed often over the years made possible during the closing years of his life a certain comfort in which he continued to produce paintings which would most surely not have come into existence had he been left alone. Other friends like Edith Glackens encouraged him on, and arranged the sale of his paintings while keeping in touch also with the Powells[20], also Samuel Shaw.[21] Newlin Price, President of the Ferargil Galleries was his faithful New York art dealer who did his best to sell his work and encourage the artist over difficult periods.[22] Lawson did one large mural for the Post Office at Short Hills, New Jersey, measuring four feet high, by twelve feet wide, of gently rolling countryside surrounding a way-side station and an approaching train, all bathed in sunshine.[23] He did this work in Florida in 1939 and completed it before he died suddenly on December 18th, 1939, while walking on the beach at Miami.[24] The mural was shipped to Short Hills by the Powells and installed in the building. Ironically the mural, the largest work as well as the last work he completed was demolished by accident when an addition was made to the Short Hills Post Office building in 1963.[25] Lawson did many small canvases when money was scarce by cutting his larger canvases into sections. As well he painted over many old canvases given him by Ira Glackens which had been done by his father in his student days.[26] Lawson is survived today by his daughter Mrs. Margaret Bensco of Ojai, California. A number of Lawson exhibitions have taken place in recent years including one by the National Gallery of Canada in 1967 when sixty-nine of his canvases were shown and were then sent on a travelling exhibition to various other Canadian Galleries. Lenders to this exhibition included

LAWSON, Ernest (Cont'd)

the following public galleries and private collectors: The Art Gallery of Ontario, Tor.; The Art Institute of Chicago; The Art Museum, Princeton University; Babcock Galleries, New York City; Berry-Hill Galleries Inc., New York City; City Art Museum of St. Louis; The Corcoran Gallery of Art, Washington, D.C.; The Engineers' Club, New York City; Columbus Gallery of Fine Arts, Col., Ohio; The Joseph H. Hirshhorn Foundation, New York; Hopkins Center Art Galleries, Dartmouth College, Hanover, New Hampshire; Milwaukee Art Center; The Minneapolis Institute of Arts; The Montclair Art Museum, Montclair, New Jersey; Munson-Williams-Proctor Institute, Utica, N.Y.; Museum of Art, Carnegie Institute, Pittsburgh; National Academy of Design, New York; National Collection of Fine Arts, Smithsonian Inst., Washington, D.C.; Nelson Gallery-Atkins Museum, Kansas City, Missouri; The Newark Museum, Newark, New Jersey; Norton Gallery and School of Art, West Palm Beach, Florida; Nova Scotia College of Art, Halifax; Pennsylvania Academy of the Fine Arts, Philadelphia; The Phillips Collection, Washington, D.C.; Santa Barbara Museum of Art; Telfair Academy of Arts and Sciences Inc., Savannah, Georgia; The Toledo Museum of Art, Toledo, Ohio; University of Nebraska Art Galleries, Lincoln, Nebraska; Wadsworth Atheneum, Hartford, Connecticut; Whitney Museum of American Art, New York: private collectors, Miss Nina Berman, Allentown, Penn., U.S.A.; Mr. & Mrs. Philip I. Berman, Allentown, Penn.; Lucien Brownstone, Esq., New York; Mr. & Mrs. Charles F. Burroughs, Jr., Norfolk, Virginia; Jean Nison Cuyler, New York City; Ira and Nancy Glackens, Center Conway, New Hampshire; Mr. & Mrs. Robert C. Graham, Stamford, Conn.; Dr. & Mrs. Jos. M. Klein, Wilkes-Barre, Penn; Dr. & Mrs. Theodore Leshner, Brooklyn, N.Y.; Major-General & Mrs. A. Bruce Matthews, Willowdale, Ont.; Charles C. Mitchell, Esq., Halifax, N.S.; Edwin C. Nelson, Esq., San Francisco; Mr. & Mrs. Dan Oppenheimer, San Antonio, Texas; Mr. & Mrs. J. Stuart Roy, Bedford, N.S.; Dr. & Mrs. Irwin Schoen, Los Angeles, Calif.; Dr. & Mrs. Joseph L. Shaw, Arlington, Mass.; Victor D. Spark, Esq., New York City; Anita & Joseph Steckler, Brooklyn, N.Y.; Mrs. E.W. Stinson, Southport, Conn.; L.J. Zwicker, Esq., Halifax, N.S., and he is represented in the collections of many others.

References

[1] *Halifax Weekly Citizen*, 29 March, 1873, Column 1, Page 8 "Births" for Mar. 22nd also NGC Info. Form rec'd May 17, 1920

[2] *Ernest Lawson, American Impressionist* by Henry & Sidney Berry-Hill, F. Lewis, Publishers, Ltd., Leigh-on-Sea, England, 1968, P.19 SBN 853170819

[3] Ibid, P.20

[4] Ibid, P.20

[5] Ibid, P.20

[6] Ibid, P.20

[7] Ibid, P.20

[8] Ibid, P.20

[9] Ibid, P.21

[10] Ibid, P.23

[11] Ibid, P.25

[12] *Ernest Lawson, 1873-1939*, Catalogue of an exhibition organized by the NGC, 1967 text by Barbara O'Neal, P.9

[13] Ibid

[14] see[2], P.34

LAWSON, Ernest (Cont'd)

[15] *Canada & Its Provinces*, 1914, Vol. 12, Painting by E.F.B. Johnston, P.619

[16] see [12], P.9

[17] see [12], P.9

[18] see [12], P.9, see also *Albert P. Ryder* by Lloyd Goodrich, Geo. Braziller, Inc., New York, 1959 (Great American Artists Series)

[18] (a) *Echo*, Halifax, N.S., Apr. 14, 1925 "Color and Form"

[19] *The Fine Arts In Canada* by Newton MacTavish, MacMillan, Tor., 1925, P.125

[20] see [2], P.52

[21] see [2], P.57

[22] see [2], P.53

[23] see [2], P.57

[24] *New York Times*, 19 Dec., 1939 "Ernest Lawson Drowns At Miami"

[25] see [2], P.63

[26] see [2], P.54

see also

Ernest Lawson Canadian-American by F. Newlin Price, Ferargil Inc., NYC, 1930

The Development of Canadian Art by R.H. Hubbard, Queen's Printer, Ott., 1963, P.84, Pl.135

Canadian Art, Its Origin and Development by William Colgate, Ryerson Paperbacks, Tor., 1967, P.168-9

The National Gallery of Canada Catalogue, Vol. 3, Can. School by R.H. Hubbard, U. of T. Press, 1960, P.165-6-7

The Controversial Century; 1850-1950 (Paintings from the Collection of Walter P. Chrysler, Jr.) Chrysler Art Museum of Provincetown, Mass., U.S.A./The National Gallery of Canada, Ottawa, 1962

Three Hundred Years of Canadian Art by R.H. Hubbard and J.R. Ostiguy, NGC/Queen's Printer, Ott., 1967, P.114, 115

Ernest Lawson 1873-1939 (cat.) Retrospective Exhibition, ACA Heritage Gallery Inc., 63 East 47 St., New York, N.Y. 10022

A Bibliography On Ernest Lawson, 1873-1939 by Margaret G. Andrew (Term Essay presented to the Library School, University of Ottawa, as partial fulfillment of the requirements for Course BLS 243), Ottawa, Ont., 1967 (copy in NGC Library)

Newspaper and magazine articles

Arts And Decoration, September, 1916 "Ernest Lawson, Optimist" by Guy Pene Du Bois, P.505-507

International Studio, July, 1916 "Ernest Lawson" by A.E. Gallatin

The American Magazine of Art, Vol. 7, May, 1917, No. 7 "Ernest Lawson" by Duncan Phillips, P.257-263

Shadowland, March, 1922 "Ernest Lawson and His America" by Edgar Holger Cahill, P.23, Cont'd on P.72

International Studio, Vol. 72, February, 1921 "Landscape Painting in America" by Ameen Rihani, P.114-117

The Art Digest, 15th April, 1932 "Ernest Lawson Wins High Praise of Critics"

Ibid, Jan. 1st, 1940 "As Ever, Ernest" – "Lawson Is Gone", P.10

Ibid, May, 1940 "Vibrant Lawson Landscape for Minneapolis"

Ibid, March, 1945 "Ernest Lawson Through Fifty Years" by J.K.R.

The Montreal Star, Feb. 11, 1967 "Ernest Lawson – An Early Expatriate; Contemporary Exchanges" by Robert Ayre

Halifax Mail-Star, March 31, 1967 "Exhibition of Ernest Lawson Paintings is Opened" by Marion Moore

Star-Phoenix, Sask., May 5, 1967 "Wide range of displays prominent at art gallery"

Ibid, May 23, 1967 "Artist's daughter, grandaughter travel here to see his paintings"

Whig-Standard, Kingston, Ont., Sept. 15, 1967 "Short-term Kingston Resident Has Showing at Etherington Centre"

LAWSON, Wendell (Arthur Wendell Phillips Lawson)
1898-1952

Born in Toronto, Ontario, he graduated from the University of Toronto with his Bachelor of Architecture in 1924 and Master of Architecture in 1925.[1] He studied drawing and water colours under C.W. Jefferys.[2] During his study he received a scholarship from the Ontario Government to study at the Ecole des Beaux-Arts, Paris (1924).[3] He also travelled in England and the Continent sketching in water colours, pen and ink, and other media (1924-25).[4] Returning to Canada he settled at Leaside, Ontario, and also became Assistant Professor of Architectural Design at Pennsylvania State College (1929-32).[5] He became a member of the Society of Canadian Painter-Etchers and Engravers (Sec. Treas. 1935-36); conducted a summer school in art at Leaside, Ontario, in 1934;[6] did fifty pen and ink drawings of the history of Nova Scotia for a manuscript of G.G. Campbell.[7] The drawings for the original work were never published. Sixteen of the sketches were given to the Provincial Archives, Halifax, about 1937[8] and another ten were donated to the same place much later.[9] These historical scenes of Nova Scotia included the old Ordnance Building, Halifax; Sally port of Fort Anne at Annapolis Royal; Mantello Tower, Point Pleasant Park, Halifax; Windsor blockhouse, Windsor, N.S.; house of Captain Silvanus Cobb, Liverpool, N.S.; Louisburg lighthouse; and other sites.

References

[1] Nat. Gal. of Can. Information Form rec'd June 1936 also Feb. 18, 1927
[2] Ibid
[3] Ibid
[4] Ibid
[5] Ibid
[6] Ibid
[7] *Saturday Night*, Tor., Ont., May 15, 1937 (Caption and reproductions of his "Fog At Peggy's Cove")
[8] *Times-Herald*, Moose Jaw, Sask., June 28, 1937 "Famous Spots Preserved In Pen Sketches"
[9] *Mail-Star*, Halifax, N.S., Dec. 11, 1965 "Archives Exhibit Wendell Lawson Sketches"
see also
books by Ryerson Press; Royal Architectural Institute of Canada Journal, 1928; books by A.L. Guptill, N.Y.; *Pencil Points*, N.Y.
Note
Lawson exhibited his work at the Art Gallery of Toronto between 1926-44; with exhibitions of the Canadian Society of Graphic Arts;
The Ontario Society of Artists; Royal Canadian Academy and Society of Canadian Painter-Etchers and Engravers.

LAWTON, Pierre
b. (c) 1933

Originally from Chicoutimi, Quebec, he studied at Sir George Williams University School of Art and the Montreal Museum of Fine Arts. He has done many seascapes and scenes of the old quarter of Montreal in oils, water colours, and drawings. He has also produced a series of lithographs. Taught art at youth camps in the Gaspé and St. Lawrence River regions. Exhibited in the Annual Spring Show of the Montreal Museum of Fine Arts and held solo exhibits of his work at his own studio in Montreal. Has worked as a proofreader.

LAWTON, Pierre (Cont'd)

References
> *The Gazette*, Mtl., P.Q., Nov. 4, 1967 "Ink Studies Of Old Quarter On Display Next Friday"
> *Westmount Examiner*, Westmount, P.Q., Sept. 26, 1968 "An odd experiment – Art and Appliances"

LAXTON, Harold McLean

b.1922

Born in Hamilton, Ontario, his interest in art began in early childhood and he later studied at the Hamilton Technical School under Hortense Gordon. He served with the Canadian Army five years during the Second World War and while overseas was able to spend three months at the Farnham School of Fine Arts, England, before his return to Canada. He studied at the Ontario College of Art with a D.V.A. grant (veteran's grant) under John Alfsen, Will Ogilvie, Manly MacDonald and George Pepper and graduated with honours in 1949. He became interested specifically in experiments with oils and mural work. In 1949 he became a member of the Contemporary Artists of Hamilton and exhibited as well in the Annual Western Ontario Exhibition at London, Ontario, also the Hamilton Art Gallery Annual Exhibitions (1949-50). He moved to Vancouver, B.C. around 1950.

Reference
> National Gallery of Canada Information Form rec'd Aug. 2, 1951

LAZAR, Patricia

She graduated from West Hill High School in 1962 and attended the Montreal Museum's School of Art and Design, drawing class under L. Schalk. She worked with the Artists' Colony in Safad, Israel, also exhibited her work in group shows. She received a Bat Yam Academy Scholarship and subsequently studied stone-cut printing under Stanley Lewis and sculpture under Yvette Bisson. Her paintings, drawings, sculptures, copper repoussés, stone-cut prints were exhibited at the Stable Gallery, Montreal (Galerie De L'Étable) 1968 and she has also shown her work at Gallery Moos, Montreal; Gallery Kaleidoscope, Montreal and elsewhere.

Reference
> Information circular from the Stable Gallery, Mtl., P.Q., 1968

LAZEAR, Ann (nee Tarantour)

b.1927

Born in Montreal, P.Q., she received her Bachelor of Arts degree in 1949 from Carleton University. She married Art Lazear, an Ottawa displayman and artist in 1948 and after her graduation she worked with her husband on newspaper illustration, decorative art and papier mâché work (1951-53). They held a joint exhibition of their paintings at the Odeon Theatre in 1956; she held her first solo

LAZEAR, Ann (nee Tarantour) (Cont'd)

exhibit at the Little Gallery, Ottawa, in 1959, of winter scenes and still life studies. She participated in a group show with Kathleen Anderson, Ralph Burton, Mrs. Marjorie Craik, Maurice Haycock, E.B. Reynolds and Roger Saint-Denis. She taught Social Studies for Grades Seven and Eight (1961-68) attended the Ontario College of Art summers (1961, 62, 63, 66) and received her Supervisor-Specialist Certificate in Art. She also painted under the instruction of John Hall in Toronto; Henri Masson, Larry Halpin, Miss Eli Kish in Ottawa. Her portrait of Dr. MacOdrum was presented by the Alumni Assoc. of Carleton to that University in 1957. She lives in Ottawa, with her husband and three children.

References

National Gallery of Canada Info. Form rec'd May 11, 1960 and Nov., 1967
Le Droit, Ottawa, Ont., Oct. 7, 1959 "Le rideau se lève . . . " par Edgar Demers
The Ottawa Citizen, Ottawa, Ont., Mar. 6, 1956

LEA, Allan
b. (c) 1941

Studied at the Daniel MacIntyre Collegiate Institute, Winnipeg, under Miss J.D. Hunt. He won the Founder's prize at the 63rd Annual Exhibition of the Royal Drawing Society at the Guildhall Art Gallery, London, England. The painting, a water colour, was discovered by his art teacher Miss Hunt after Allan had left it lying on a cupboard in the school art room. He was the first Canadian winner of the Founder's prize in sixty-seven years.

References

The Columbian, New Westminister, B.C., April 28, 1958 "Young Canadian Artist Wins Founder's Prize"
Examiner, Peterborough, Ont., May 6, 1958 "Biblical Student Wins U.K. Prize For Painting" (from Winnipeg – CP –)
The Ottawa Citizen, Ottawa, Ont., May 10, 1958 "Canadian Youth Wins Art Prize In London"
Tribune, Winnipeg, Man., May 12, 1958 "Prize-Winning Landscape" (large photo 'The Cart' described by Miss Hunt as "a picture of rolling country with row upon row of hills, a gleam of light falling on a farmer's cart")

LEACH, John

Born in Toronto, Ontario, he graduated from the Northern Technical School and the Ontario College of Art, Toronto. He has travelled throughout Canada, Europe, and the Middle East also in the United States where he visited Hollywood and did portraits of Bob Hope, Dan Rowan, Dinah Shore and others. Was director of a leading Canadian advertising agency. Also was Arts and Crafts Instructor at Pickering College (1966-68). Settled in Newmarket, Ontario, where he entered the field of portrait painting usually at $1,000 a portrait. His patrons include Eartha Kitt (American singer), Mr. & Mrs. Trent Frayne (did portrait of their daughter Jennifer); Robert Stevens (portraits of Miss Judith Stevens) and many others. A private showing of his portraits at his home at Newmarket was attended by the Fraynes (both writers); Dr. Peter Swan (Royal Ontario Museum); Mackenzie Porter

LEACH, John (Cont'd)

(Toronto *Telegram*); Mr. & Mrs. Derek Phillips (Mrs. is Nancy, writer); Rudolphe (Toronto dress designer); Mr. & Mrs. Roman Bartkiw (Mr. is the Markdale potter); Dr. & Mrs. Norman Mortimer; Mr. & Mrs. A.B. Gillard; Mr. & Mrs. Eric Veale, and others. John Leach designed and executed two murals for Sherwood School, Hamilton, has exhibited his work at the Collector's Cabinet, Toronto and is known for his fine nude studies.

References

The Era, Newmarket, Ont., Sept. 18, 1968 (article and large photo taken during the private showing mentioned above)

Tribune, Winnipeg, Man., Sept 27, 1968 "Art director quits for life as painter"

The Globe & Mail, Tor., Ont., Dec. 24, 1968 "Artist shows Eartha without nightclub glamor" by Kay Kritzwiser

The Era, Nov. 19, 1969 (photo of artist in his gallery with Dr. & Mrs. Peter Levers)

LEACOCK, Ethel

An Ottawa ceramist who studied at the University of Syracuse, the University of California and New York State College of Ceramics. Her work was described by Sheila Moodie of *The Ottawa Citizen* in 1955 as follows, "Outstanding in the show of all original work is a sculpture, the small figure of a man molded from clay coils. Made on strong, sure lines, it embodies powerful feelings and is realistic in appearance. Also eye-catching in display are a set of long-legged giraffes, bowls, jars and plates . . . . She particularly likes to make coil figures of people and animals, which she does very quickly, almost spontaneously. In her work, which is mostly earthenware and stoneware, Miss Leacock uses primarily two types of clay — white and red. The clay comes from Canada (Kingston, Ont.), England and the United States. She makes nearly all her own glazes, and a fine example of what she has done is a jewel-glazed bowl, with a brilliant turquoise center. This bowl gives a shiny, cracked effect, pretty to look at, because the glaze was mixed dry before the bowl was fired." Miss Leacock has exhibited her work at the Central Canada Exhibition, Toronto (women's handicraft section), also in Ottawa and Montreal.

Reference

The Ottawa Citizen, Aug. 20, 1955 "Ottawa Ceramist Shows Original Art At 'Ex' " by Sheila Moodie

LEADBEATER, Roy

b.1928

Born in Ashbourne, Derbyshire, England, his father was an artist (painter). When Roy was eight he lost both his parents and was brought up in an orphanage. He then worked in a pottery until he was fifteen when he became an apprentice engineer.[1] In 1943 he entered the British Merchant Marine where he ultimately served as a Marine Engineer (1945-46).[2] He then spent fifteen months in the Middle East (1946-48) on the Palestine Police Force and was attached to Government House where he transmitted secret documents. He returned to sea for two years

LEADBEATER, Roy (Cont'd)

(1950-2)[3] and for a while lived in Australia and New Zealand. Subsequently he studied mechanical engineering in England and attended night classes in drawing at the Birmingham School of Art.[4] He came to Canada in 1953 with his wife and settled in Edmonton, Alberta, and worked for a short period with the Provincial Government before going into the Oil and Gas Industry as a Power Engineer. He attended the University of Alberta, part-time, where he studied drawing under Professor Glyde. He moved to Calgary where he was hired in the Engineering Department of The Royal Globe Insurance Group while he spent every available moment at the Calgary Allied Arts Centre working on sculpture.[5] At first he worked in wood but when a fellow sculpture student noticed his work he offered Leadbeater the opportunity of working in steel. The student turned out to be William Garrick, General Manager of Dominion Bridge, who was looking for ways to demonstrate the uses of steel.[6] After meeting and seeing Leadbeater's sculpture he made an arrangement for Leadbeater to work in his plant with an adequate stock of materials, welding equipment, supplied by Dominion Bridge.[7] Leadbeater set to work in his new surroundings producing among other works, a ten foot diameter moon for the Calgary Planetarium (steel shows the cold lifelessness of the moon); Celestial Flower for the Genevieve Yates Memorial Centre (Lethbridge); polished steel sculpture for the Civic Centennial Library (Edmonton); a huge mobile machine sculpture for the Four Western Provinces Pavilion at Expo '67; sculpture for the Bradie Building (Calgary); Crown Trust Building (Calgary); Science Building (Lethbridge); Clinical Sciences Building (University of Alberta, Edmonton) and he has exhibited his work in the following Canadian centres: Ottawa, Quebec City, Winnipeg, Charlottetown, Willowdale (Ont.) and elsewhere. Won Sixth Place for a Pen and Ink Drawing at the Quebec Provincial Exposition of 1960; had his drawings exhibited at the Alberta Crafts Exhibition at the Jubilee Auditorium, Edmonton, Alberta in 1960, and has been receiving many important commissions for his exceptionally fine work. Lives in Calgary, Alberta where he has exhibited his work at The Canadian Art Galleries.

References

[1] *The Albertan*, Calgary, Alta., June 15, 1963 "Engineer Dreams Of Being Sculptor" by Linda Curtis also *The Edmonton Journal*, Aug. 30, 1966

[2] Ibid

[3] Ibid

[4] National Gallery of Canada Info. Forms rec'd 1964, 1965 also *The Edmonton Journal*, Aug. 30, 1966

[5] Letter of biographical details dated 4th May, 1962, in NGC Library see artist's file.

[6] *The Edmonton Journal*, 30 Aug., 1966 "Romance With Steel"

[7] Ibid

see also

The Calgary Herald, Calgary, Alta., June 26, 1965 "Art Show Staged At Furniture Store" by David Thompson

Ibid, Oct. 18, 1965 "City Art Gallery Opens Show With New Owner, Decorations" by David Thomson

The Albertan, Calgary, Alta., June 25, 1965 "Space and Sculptured Steel — Leadbeater On Exhibit" by Inger Voitk

Ibid, Nov. 5, 1966 (large photo of Leadbeater's "Celestial Flower")

The Calgary Herald, Alta., May 27, 1966 "City Sculptor Gets New Job"

The Albertan, Calgary, Alta., June 11, 1966 "Calgary sculptor creates Western symbol for 'Expo'" by George Lyttik

The Calgary Herald, Alta., Oct. 24, 1968 "Two Calgary Sculptors Depict Striking Range Of Subjects"

LEADBEATER, Roy (Cont'd)

Lethbridge Herald, Alta., Oct. 25, 1969 "Sculpture To Aid Fund"
The Medicine Hat News, Alta., Jan. 7, 1970 "Noted sculptor showing here" by Ethel Gilbert

---

LEAGH, Raine

A Lander, B.C., ceramist who has exhibited his work with the Canadian Handicrafts Guild and who is represented in the Guild's Canadian permanent arts and crafts collection by a bowl. The bowl has a matt glaze in off-white with an under glaze of a crackle design with an overall transparent glaze. He has exhibited in the Canadian Ceramics show, 1963 and has received special mention with six other Canadian potters in the eighth International Exhibition of Ceramic Art at the Smithsonian Institute, Washington, D.C. He teaches art at the Delta Secondary School in Lander, B.C.

Reference
Optimist, Lander, B.C., April 17, 1963 "Guild purchased Leagh pottery"

LEANING, John Dalton
b.1926

Born in London, England, he studied architecture at Liverpool University and graduated with his Bachelor of Architecture.[1] In 1951 he worked under the well known French architect Le Corbusier in Paris, designing a hospital for French Equatorial Africa, the Universal Exhibition in Casablanca and the Unité d'Habitation in Marseille. He married a Swedish girl the same year and moved to Stockholm where he learned the language and designed a large enclosed stadium at Malmo as well as the first designs for a town centre outside Stockholm. Following a three year stay in Sweden (1953-55) he decided to come to Canada and arrived with his wife in Montreal in 1955.[2] There he enrolled in McGill University where among other things he did special studies in community planning and graduated with his Master of Architecture.[3] He worked in Calgary for a time then joined the National Capital Commission in Ottawa in 1959.[4] He won an award from the Ontario Association of Architects for his design of the National Capital Commission information offices at 531 Sussex Drive, Ottawa, and was the originator of many new colour schemes on federal projects in the Capital.[5] He also helped prepare the preliminary master plan for Algonquin College on Woodroffe Avenue, Ottawa, and his other achievements in the field of architecture are many.[6] His drawings and paintings have come out of his activities as an architect. Part of this work has taken the form of murals in the lobby of the Executive Apartments on Metcalfe St., Ottawa, and on the exterior of a house on the adjoining lot beside his own Ottawa home. Many of his paintings are abstract forms and patterns used in architecture. A selection of his oils and pen and ink drawings were shown at the Robertson Galleries in 1958 under the title "55 Inventions" noted by Carl Weiselberger[7] as follows, "The artist's drawings, which form the bulk of the exhibition, are quite remarkable and enjoyable for their rich imagination and and cartoon-like humor. The fine sensitive line is often reminiscent of Paul Klee's calligraphic inventions, but

LEANING, John Dalton (Cont'd)

the satire has the artist's own stamp and derives its themes from Canadian subjects." Another exhibition of his work was held at Robertson's in 1960 when his drawings were again found by Weiselberger[8] to be "poetic, playful, humorous, sometimes satirical . . . . " His mobiles and stabiles were also shown at that show. Leaning was elected Chairman of the Ottawa Chapter, Ontario Association of Architects (1965). As Chief Architect for the National Capital Commission he was responsible for the outdoor auditorium for "Son et Lumière" (1967) and the development of Confederation Square (1967).[9] He is now a private consultant in Ottawa. Presently with the Canadian International Development Agency in Tanzania, Africa.

References

[1] National Gallery of Canada Information Form rec'd October, 1965
[2] Ibid
[3] Ibid
[4] *The Ottawa Citizen*, Dec. 13, 1967 "Swinging city architect's idea" by Burt Heward
[5] Ibid
[6] Ibid
[7] Ibid, July 7, 1958 "An Artist Reveals His 'Inventions' " by C.W.
[8] Ibid, June 15, 1960 "Exhibition By Leaning Attractive" by Carl Weiselberger
[9] see [4]

see also
The Ottawa Journal, July 3, 1958 "John Leaning Paintings Whimsy, Individualistic" by W.Q.K.
The Ottawa Citizen, Sat., Mar. 16, 1968 "Ottawa facelift" by Bill Neddow (Board and batten disguise)

LEATHERS, Winston

b.1932

Born in Miami, Manitoba, he attended children's art classes when he was about twelve and was further encouraged in junior high school. He won a Winnipeg Sketch Club Scholarship in 1953 and received University of Manitoba Student Teaching Scholarships (1954-55). He studied Fine Arts graduating from the University's Manitoba School of Art in 1956. He then went to Mexico (1957-58) where he worked for the Mexican Government Archaeological Society under Dr. Carmen Cook De Leonard. In 1958 he graduated from the Manitoba Teachers' College where he majored in Art Education. He continued in Art Education at the University of Manitoba from 1959-60. In 1960 he was elected full member of the Manitoba Society of Artists. In 1961 he won a Festival of the Arts Scholarship to the University of British Columbia to work with Prof. Ulfert Wilke from the University of Louisville. His one man exhibitions took place at Mexico City (1957), Alty Gallery, Winnipeg (1960); University of British Columbia (1961); Alty Gallery, Toronto (1962); Point Gallery, Victoria (1963); Grant Gallery, Winnipeg (1964); Western Canadian Art Circuit (1966-67); Yellow Door Gallery, Winnipeg (1967); Winnipeg Art Gallery (1968); Brandon University, School of Music foyer (1969) when Kaye Rowe[1] of *The Brandon Sun* quoted Leathers as working to evoke, "Some sense of the wonder in what I see around me — not as a pictorial souvenir nor as an equivalent of what I see, but as a personal statement of wonder and beauty." Ms. Rowe continued, "He is particularly moved, he relates, by those aspects of nature that are wild, that seemingly haphazard look that is yet inevitable

LEATHERS, Winston (Cont'd)

and complete. Landscape is his initial impetus. Selection and rejection in any given work determines its final form, a matter of months rather than days in finishing a canvas or plate. He finds that working in different media — in collo, plastics, in metal collages, in the embossed surfaces and the serigraph — as a relief and a diversion rather than a obstacle. It is impossible to describe in words the precise nature and complexity of Mr. Leathers' unique experiments in print-making." Earlier Peter Crossley[2] in *The Free Press* had noted, "Winston Leathers shows a great deal of sympathy towards Oriental philosophy. His interest in Haiku poetry and its simplicity of symbolism is carried over very emphatically in all his works. His awareness of the circle as a powerful symbol is always evident." His two man shows are as follows: Esler & Leathers (Grant Gallery, Winnipeg, 1964) (Point Gallery, Victoria, 1964) (Alberta College of Art, Calgary, 1964); Mikuska & Leathers (Grant Gallery, Winnipeg, 1964); Esler & Leathers (Ontario Art Circuit, 1965); Esler & Leathers (University of Manitoba, 1966). He has exhibited in many group shows including the following: Winnipeg Shows; Canadian Young Contemporaries; Montreal Spring Show; Manitoba Society of Artists (hon. mention, 1966); Western Ontario Exhibitions; Royal Canadian Academy Annuals (86th, 87th, 88th) and Travelling Exhibitions; Burnaby National Prints Shows and Travelling Exhibition (1st, 2nd, 3rd); Ontario Society of Artists; Canadian Society of Painter-Etchers and Engravers; Northwest Printmakers International Graphics Exhibition, Seattle, Washington, U.S.A.; Winnipeg Art Gallery Centennial Exhibition (One Hundred Years of Canadian Art); 32nd Exhibition of the British Federation of Printmakers, London, England and his prizes include 2nd Prize in oils — Winnipeg Show, 1960; 1st Prize in oils — Canadian Young Contemporaries Exhibition, 1961; Purchase Prize — Calgary Graphics, 1964; Purchase Prize, 25th Western Ontario Exhibition, 1965; 1st Prize in oils, Red River Exhibition, 1965 and he received a Senior Canada Council Grant (1967-68). He is represented in the following permanent collections: Art Gallery of Victoria; Art Gallery of Alberta College of Art; Winnipeg Art Gallery; Sir George Williams University, Montreal; Art Gallery of London, Ontario; Canada Council Collection; Imperial Oil Collection; University of Calgary Collection; Regina Public Library Collection; Simon Fraser University Collection, and in numerous private collections throughout Canada, United States, England and Mexico. He has been teaching environmental studies, on the faculty of architecture, University of Manitoba.

References

[1] *The Brandon Sun*, Brandon, Manitoba, Feb. 13, 1969 "Distinctive originality in print-making exhibit" by Kaye Rowe

[2] *The Free Press*, Winnipeg, Man., May 19, 1967 article by Peter Crossley

see also

The Free Press, London, Ont., Nov. 4, 1961 "Jury Picks 21 Works To Represent Canada's Rising Young Painters" by Lenore Crawford

The Mail-Star, Halifax, N.S., Nov. 25, 1965 "N.S. College of Art Displays Fifth Annual Calgary Graphic Exhibition" by Martin Kemp

The Province, Van., B.C., April 28, 1967 "Little gallery with big ideas that pay off"

The Free Press, Winnipeg, Man., Mar. 18, 1967 "Artist, Writer Here Share Council Awards"

Leader-Post, Regina, Sask., June 8, 1967

The Free Press, Winnipeg, Man., June 9, 1967 "Local Artist's First" by Peter Crossley

Ibid, Sept. 7, 1968 "Local Artists Awarded"

The Brandon Sun, Manitoba, Feb. 8, 1969 "Artist opens show in city of his work"

LEATHERS, Winston (Cont'd)

Canadian Art, Issue No. 84 (Mar/Apr 1963) "Clement Greenberg's View Of Art On The Prairies" by C. Greenberg, P.97

The Canada Council Collection (catalogue) A travelling exhibition of the National Gallery of Canada, Ottawa, 1969, Fourth last page of check-list

Sir George Williams University Collection of Art (catalogue) 1967, P.122

LEBEL, Maurice

1898-1963

Born in Montreal, Quebec, he studied painting under Suzor-Côté and Dyonnet in Montreal, probably under Dyonnet at the Monument National where Lebel won first prize for drawing in 1915. He also won first prize for drawing at the Conseil des Arts the same year. He took part in the first exhibition of wood-cuts held at the Art Association of Montreal in 1924. Also exhibiting were Edwin Holgate and Ivan Jobin. Lebel taught at the Ecole Supérieure Le Plateau (1929-42) and at the Ecole Normale Jacques-Cartier in Montreal and in 1942 was nominated director of drawing education at the Commission des Ecoles Catholiques de Montréal. He exhibited for many years at the spring exhibitions of the Montreal Museum of Fine Arts and at the Royal Canadian Academy shows. An exhibition of his work was held at La Galerie l'Art Vivant, Montreal in September of 1965. Lebel was an artist of great ability. He is represented in the Quebec Provincial Museum and the National Gallery of Canada.

References

Le Progrès du Golfe, Rimouski, P.Q., Nov. 2, 1951 "Oeuvres d'artistes du Québec – Sous les auspices des Compagnons de l'Art – Elle se terminera dimanche soir."

Le Devoir, Mtl., P.Q., 27 Juin, 1963 "Décès, à Montréal, de M. Maurice Lebel"

La Patrie, Mtl., P.Q., Oct. 10, 1965 "L'Art Pour Tous – Galerie 'L'Art Vivant': Maurice Lebel"

Le Petit Journal, Mtl., P.Q., Sunday, Sept. 12, 1965 "Maurice Le Bel a été un artiste sincère et dévoué" par Paul Gladu

Maurice Lebel (folder or catalogue) La Galerie 'L'Art Vivant', Montreal 22 Sept., 1965

LEBEUF, Jean Guy

b.1932

Born in Quebec, P.Q., he studied at the Ecole des Beaux-Arts, Quebec, under Jean Paul Lemieux and Marius Plamondon. He travelled in Spain and France (1954-55) and in France several times afterwards. He was influenced greatly by the work of Balthus and Carzou. He returned to Canada, and in 1957 took Second Prize for engraving at the Quebec Provincial exhibition, and the following year won First Prize in the Windmill Point Inc., art competition where over two hundred entries were submitted. An exhibit of his work took place at Atelier Renée Lesieur in Quebec City in 1960 when Raymond Doubille, under-secretary of the Province of Quebec officially opened the show. Another solo show of his work took place at Denise Boucher, i.d., gallery in Ottawa in March of 1961. Basically his work is realistic.

LEBEUF, Jean Guy (Cont'd)

References

National Gallery of Canada Information Form rec'd July 23 19—
Le Devoir, Mtl., P.Q., June 28, 1958 "Jean Le Beuf, gagnant d'un concours de peinture"
Globe & Mail, Tor., Ont., July 5, 1958 "Quebec Artist $600 Winner"
L'Evénement-Journal, Que., P.Q., July 19, 1958 "La toile d'un jeune peintre de chez-nous remporte le 1er prix" par André Fortin
Ibid, March 30, 1960 "Exposition des toiles de Jean Le Beuf: du neuf, du personnel, de l'art vivant . . . "
Chronicle-Telegraph, Que., P.Q., Mar. 30, 1960 "1-Man Show At Atelier"
Le Soleil, P.Q., July 23, 1960 "Visages d'artistes de chez nous" par Paule France Dufaux
Le Devoir, Mtl., P.Q., Oct. 19, 1961 "Jean Le Beuf à l'Estanco"

LEBOW, Julius Leonard

b.1920

Born in Toronto, Ontario, his interest in art began while he was a patient at the Christie Street Veterans' Hospital in Toronto in 1945. Later he enrolled at the Ontario College of Art and graduated from there in 1951. Subsequently he exhibited in annual exhibitions of the Hamilton Art Gallery, the Ontario Society of Artists and the Canadian Society of Graphic Arts. Has taught art and lives in Hamilton where he is the owner of the Westdale Gallery. Is represented in the collection of the Hamilton Public Library and elsewhere.

Reference

National Gallery of Canada Information Form rec'd June 11, 1951
Visit to the Westdale Gallery in Hamilton.

LEBRUN, Roland

An artist from Victoriaville, P.Q., who is known for his landscapes, bird and animal studies. His work was described by R.T.[1] of the Quebec *Chronicle-Telegraph* as follows, "Essentially a painter of the gentler side of nature, Lebrun employs a leisurely brush, a style which is meticulous without being pedantic and a subdued color scale. Even the titles of his paintings are disarming — 'Vision d'Hiver,' 'Printemps', 'Trois Pichets'. But this is not to say that Lebrun's work is either wooden or photographic. Behind the formality, which is more apparent than real, is a genuineness of feeling and a kinship with his subject which do not fail to register on the spectator." His work has been shown at the Palais Montcalm, Quebec City; Chateau Louis, Louiseville, and elsewhere.

References

[1] *Chronicle-Telegraph*, Que., P.Q. Nov. 26, 1960 "Artist Revels In Nature In Her Gentler Moments" by R.T.
see also
La Patrie, Mtl., P.Q. "Roland Lebrun et ses toiles"
Le Progrès du Richelieu, Sorel, P.Q., May 12 "Hommage à Lebrun" par F.D.R.
L'Evénement Journal, Que., P.Q., Nov. 25, 1960 "Le peintre Roland Lebrun expose ses huiles au Palais Montcalm"

LEBRUN, Roland (Cont'd)

L'Action Catholique, Que., P.Q., Nov. 26, 1960 "Roland Lebrun expose au Palais Montcalm"
L'Evénement-Journal, Que., P.Q., Nov. 24, 1961 "Une exposition honnête du peintre R. Lebrun" par Paule France Dufaux
Le Soleil, Que., P.Q., Nov. 24, 1961 "Exposition du peintre Roland Lebrun" par Paule France Dufaux
L'Action Catholique, Que., P.Q., Nov. 25, 1961 "Oeuvres de R. Lebrun exposées au Palais Montcalm"
Le Nouvelliste, Trois Rivières, P.Q. Dec. 7, 1962 (large photo of artist during his Louise-ville exhibition with guests)

LECLAIRE, Pierrette

She studied in New York under a Danish enamellist and received the Prix de l'Artisane in 1965. She lives at Saint Bruno, P.Q. One of her works was offered to the Shah of Iran at the time of his trip to Montreal.

Reference
Photo-Journal, Mtl., P.Q., June 2, 1965 "L'Artisane de l'année dans l'intimité . . .

LECOCQ, Doris

Born in London, England, the daughter of western Canadian journalist, W.A.R. LeCocq of Lethbridge, Alta. She spent her early life in Lethbridge but went to England to study painting, pottery, and sculpture at the Central School of Art in London where she graduated. She then went on to study at the Royal College of Art at South Kensington under Prof. Garbe, R.A., F.R.B.S., A.R.C.A. and later became his assistant. Subsequently she taught sculpture in London County Council Schools and exhibited with the Royal Academy of Art, London; The Royal Institute of Art, Glasgow; and the Monza Exhibition at Milan, Italy. After travelling widely in Europe studying ancient and modern pottery she returned to Canada and became an instructor at the Provincial School of Technology, Calgary, Alta. In 1939 she moved to Vancouver where she taught summer school while continuing to work at pottery. She discovered a seam of clay at the bottom of Burrard Inlet on the Pacific Coast after a long and careful search. Extracting the clay from the bottom of the Inlet by a long pole with a rake-like scoop she returned to her studio where she created pottery of unusual translucency which was admired by connoisseurs. She also developed many fine glazes including one known as "Water-of-the-Sea" described as "a green shot with blue which gives the effect of the combers breaking against the Pacific Coast". She found other clays in various parts of the country each yielding a unique type of pottery. For a time she taught at the Vancouver School of Art. Among her pottery items were animals like the Arctic fox, mule deer, pack horses, fish and other wild life. No recent information is available on this artist.

References
The Calgary Herald, Calgary, Alta., Nov. 26, 1932 "H.M. Queen Mary Praises Work Of Alberta Artist"

LECOCQ, Doris (Cont'd)

Saturday Night, Tor., Ont., Aug. 31, 1935 "Canadian Sculptress" by C. Frank Steele
The Montreal Herald, Mtl., P.Q., Aug. 14, 1937 "A Canadian Sculptress"
Financial Times, Mtl., P.Q., Dec. 7, 1949 Home and Fireside "Beautiful Pottery From the Sea" by Marion Angus

LECOMTE, Pierre

b.1935

Born at Magog, P.Q., he completed his classical studies at Saint Charles Borromée in Sherbrooke and at l'Ecole des Beaux Arts in Montreal. A professor of plastic arts, he exhibited his paintings at the University of Sherbrooke in 1966 and 1968.

Reference
Record, Sherbrooke, P.Q., Oct. 9, 1968 "U of S art centre is giving ET talent a helpful boost"

LECORRE, Paul (Tex)

His father was from Brittany, France, and came to Canada as a Jesuit missionary, became a painter, served in the Canadian Army overseas and was wounded during the First World War. Paul Lecorre studied at the Ecole des Beaux Arts, Montreal, and during the summers operated tourist boats at Gaspé. He earned his captain's papers and spent some time in the merchant marine serving first at the age of eighteen on the Great Lakes ships. Lecorre is a poet, painter and singer and has written about 118 songs. He lives alone with his dog and has many friends. He has his studio in the Galerie-Cafe in the Bonsecours Market, Montreal, where he paints portraits and other subjects.

References
Le Journal des Vedettes, Montreal, P.Q., Sat., Jan. 23, 1965 "Tex, Le Poète, Le Peintre, L'Original, . . . "
Photo-Journal, the week of 21 to 28 June, 1967 "Tex c'est aussi le peintre Lecor et le capitaine-caboteur Lecorre! " par Rudel-Tessier

LECOUTEY, André

He studied under Maurice Denis and was an artist by profession before becoming a priest. He has continued as an artist with religious paintings which show a lightness and freshness of colour as well as an ethereal atmosphere. His still lifes and scenes were described by Jean Dénéchaud as having a dazzling sensation of colour. Lecoutey's works have been exhibited at Cercle Universitaire, Montreal. He is assistant director of the magazine *Arts et Pensée*.

Reference
La Presse, Mtl., P.Q., Feb. 24, 1951 "L'exposition d'un ensemble de toiles d'André Lecoutey" par Jean Dénéchaud

LEDAIN, Bruce

b.1928

Born in Montreal, P.Q., his work was selected in 1936 for the International Children's Art Exhibition, U.S.A. By 1946 he had enrolled at Sir George Williams University to study fine art. His work was accepted by the Montreal Museum of Fine Arts Spring Shows in 1949, 1952, 1953. From 1953 to 1957 he lived in London, England, where he attended St. Martin's School of Art. He also studied and travelled in Europe and returned to Canada and settled in Montreal where he is a director of the art department of a public relations firm. He exhibited with the Royal Canadian Academy in 1966 and won First Prize for his paintings shown in the Price Fine Arts Award for the years 1967 and 1969. One of his paintings was presented to the former Prime Minister of Canada, Lester B. Pearson, by the City of Montreal at Expo '67; another of his paintings was presented to a dignitary by the City of Montreal during the same year.

References

Information supplied by the Continental Galleries, Montreal

Le Soleil, Que., P.Q., May 12, 1969 "Bruce Le Dain, lauréat du concours des Beaux-Arts Price"

Le Droit, Ottawa, Ont., May 13, 1969 "Prix de $1,000 à Bruce Le Dain"

Royal Canadian Academy of Arts 87th Annual Exhibition (catalogue), 1966

LEDSON, Sidney Albert James

b.1925

Born in London, England, he arrived in Toronto, Canada, with his parents Mr. and Mrs. David Ledson in 1927.[1] He was interested in art at an early age.[2] He served with the R.C.A.F. during the Second World War as a wireless mechanic (1943-45) and afterwards studied at the Ontario College of Art on a veteran's educational grant.[3] At the College he took instruction from John Alfsen, Fred Finley, Archibald Barnes, Rowley Murphy, Gerald Roling, Manly MacDonald, George Pepper, Eric Freifeld and Will Ogilvie, and graduated with his A.O.C.A. in 1950. He also continued with his own research and study in many fields of art with a particular interest in portrait painting. In this field he was influenced to a certain degree by the work of Sir Henry Raeburn and John Singer Sargent. He developed a particular skill in the use of charcoal and pastels although he employed many other mediums in his work. As early as 1955 Carl Weiselberger[5] art critic for *The Ottawa Citizen* referred to Ledson's work as " . . . revealing the artist's solid craftsmanship and, in many instances, his deft ability to transmit the typical character and expression of the sitter." Ledson served with the R.C.A.F. again from 1953 to 1956 in Europe as a graphic artist and photographer when he also managed to paint fifty portraits. For a time he was associated with Pierre Guibert Limited and the Fairbairn Studio in Ottawa. He returned to Europe, and to Hollywood, California, in 1961 on assignment for *The Ottawa Citizen* to meet and sketch famous film personalities. Some of the sketches appeared in the *Citizen* of November 29th, 1961.[6] Earlier that year he was guest artist at the Central Canada Exhibition in Ottawa where he did hundreds of quick portraits. He did a series of water colours of Ottawa churches and more recently has concentrated on some wonderful seascapes. Sidney Ledson has worked in a variety of occupations and has even played professionally in a band as he is an accomplished musician of clarinet, piano

LEDSON, Sidney Albert James (Cont'd)

and other instruments. He has painted portraits of the following notables: Yousuf Karsh (internationally famous photographer); Nicholas Monsarrat (novelist); I. Norman Smith (Editor of The Ottawa Journal); John Marlyn (Canadian writer); Lorne Greene (actor); Rt. Hon. Lester B. Pearson (former Prime Minister of Canada); Brooke Claxton (former Minister of Defence, Canada); Air Vice-Marshal Hugh Campbell (R.C.A.F.); Dean Kelly (jet acrobat and wartime ace); Bernard Braden (radio and TV star); Pat O'Brien (actor); the late Jayne Mansfield (actress); Clifton Webb (actor) Vincent Price (actor and art connoisseur); Pamela Curran (actress); Richard Beymer (actor); George Montgomery (actor), and many others. Ledson has exhibited with the Canadian Society of Painters in Water Colour, The Canadian National Exhibition, the Royal Canadian Academy, the Royal Society of Portrait Painters, London, England, The Paris Salon and elsewhere. He has recently invented a game to learn languages in the form of a book in which he has done all the art work. This publication should appear on the market soon.[7]

References

[1] National Gallery of Canada Information Form rec'd Feb. 4, 1952 and *Le Droit*, Ottawa, Feb. 15, 1956

[2] Document from artist dated 1961

[3] *The Ottawa Citizen*, Ottawa, Ont., Oct. 17, 1955 "Skilful Craftsmanship Shown by R.C.A.F. Artist" by Carl Weiselberger

[4] see[1]

[5] see[3]

[6] *The Ottawa Citizen*, Wed., Nov. 20, 1961 "Footloose In Hollywood . . . Local Artist Calls On Stars And Finds That Faces Change" by Norman Avery, P.17

[7] *The Ottawa Journal*, Sat., July 11, 1970 – Business & Finance – P.9

see also

The Ottawa Citizen, Mar. 26, 1958 "Art Exhibit In Restaurant Is Success"

Whig-Standard, Kingston, Ont., Aug. 15, 1969 "Sidney Ledson Has Added European Flavor To Picton Event" by Jack Brett (large photo of artist at work)

LEDUC, Fernand

b.1916

Born in Montreal, P.Q., he studied there at the Ecole des Beaux-Arts. He met Paul Emile Borduas in 1940 and in 1943 they participated in the exhibition of the "Sagittaires" which Père Couturier had organized at the Dominion Gallery.[1] It was in 1942 that he was profoundly influenced by the exhibition of fifty or so paintings in gouache by Borduas which ranged from the representational to the non-objective or automatic work.[2] When Borduas completed his *Refus Global* (later published in August, 1948) Leduc was one of fourteen artists who signed in support of the ideals of freedom to explore new horizons beyond the rigidity of the old education system of Quebec. Leduc had been exhibiting with the automatist group as early as 1943 and even after his departure to Paris, France in 1947. He had taught for the Catholic School Commission in Montreal from 1944 to 1947 at the College of St. Denis and College Notre Dame.[3] In France he studied under Jean Bazaine and others, and in 1947 helped organize and exhibited in the Automatisme exhibition with Borduas, Riopelle, Mousseau and Barbeau.[4] In 1948 he participated in the Salon des

LEDUC, Fernand (Cont'd)

Surindépendants; Galerie Creuze, 1950, 1951; Salon de Mai, 1952 and he returned to Montreal in 1953 and held an exhibition at his own home of about thirty works including a dozen water colours done during his last two years in Paris.[5] These water colours displayed remarkable luminous qualities. Also in 1953 he helped establish with Robert Roussil the Place des Artistes at Montreal's old Gaiety Theatre on St. Catherine Street where he held a joint exhibition with Roussil.[6] In 1954 he was invited to exhibit in Belgium and he also organized "La Matière Chante" at the Musée des Beaux-Arts, Montreal. He became a founding member and President of the Non-Figurative Artists' Association of Montreal, a group whose activity was based mainly around Galerie l'Actuelle owned by Guido Molinari.[7] This group received the attention of *Weekend Magazine* in 1956 which featured an article on them with photos of key members, their wives and works. Leduc and his wife Therese Renaud (CBC-TV singer) were in one of these photos with the background of Leduc's "Garden In Brazil" a large brilliantly coloured canvas of angular or geometric shapes.[8] Also during this period Leduc did many types of art work including tapestry designs which were executed by Mme. Marlette Rousseau-Vermette, Gaby Pinsonneault and other craftswomen.[9] He designed and executed as well a series of collages described by *The Gazette*[10] as "highly-colored felts which framed and covered with glass, would look well almost anywhere as decoration." He exhibited in the show "Canadian Abstract Paintings" at the National Gallery of Canada which toured the U.S.A. and "Canadian Artists Abroad" at London, Ontario, which toured other centres. The National Gallery of Canada purchased his canvas "Noeud Papillion".[11] He participated in many other exhibitions in the following years and won the Quebec Provincial Prize in 1957 for Decorative Arts. In 1959 he returned to Paris on a Canada Council Grant. It was this year that his work first appeared in the Canadian Biennials with his large painting "Haute fidélité".[12] His work again appeared in the Fifth (1963) and Sixth (1965) Biennials of Canadian Painting.[13] Robert Ayre[14] in viewing his work at Galerie Soixante in 1963 noted, "The color is still clean, smooth and luminous; resonant black, living orange and red, a green that is as vivid as grass, and a blue like the shining sky. There is a new approach to color and surface, too, in a number of small compositions in oil and pastel, granulated and vibrating. Altogether, a show that comes at you simply and directly, giving you a lift without making demands." The year 1965 was a busy one which included the showing of his work in the following exhibitions: "20ième Salon des Réalités Nouvelles" (Paris); Galerie Soixante (Mtl.); Sixth Biennial (Ottawa); and Ecole de Montreal at the Museum of Contemporary Art (Mtl.). The following year a retrospective show of his work took place at the Montreal Museum of Contemporary Art of about forty of his large size canvases representing the years 1960-65. This show traced his development from the hard edge geometrical compositions of the early '60s through the more supple period of 1963 of curves and freer forms, warmer contrasts of colours to the more subtly harmonious elements of his work in the mid sixties. For a long time he painted with only two colours and has returned to this bi-chromatism described in 1968 by Joan Lowndes[15] of the Vancouver *Province* as follows, "His latest formats are mostly horizontal. Winding across them are more organic forms, suggestive of the female figure or of an estuary. Leduc does not use masking tape, which he finds too mechanical, but his edges are faultless. Thus, in a style noted for its severity, he has arrived at something quite personal: a lyrical hard-edge." While Leduc lives in Paris he makes visits to Montreal where his work is on view at the various galleries,

LEDUC, Fernand (Cont'd)

including the permanent collection of Montreal Museum of Contemporary Art, the
Ecoles des Beaux Arts of Montreal and Quebec.

References

[1] *Le Droit*, May 29, 1961 "Leduc tente de faire connaitre la peinture canadienne à Paris"

[2] Ibid

[3] National Gallery of Canada Information Form rec'd April 7, 1953

[4] see [1]

[5] *La Presse*, Mtl., P.Q., May 23, 1953 "Un peintre de l'existence" par R. de Repentigny

[6] see [1]

[7] *Weekend Magazine*, Vol. 6, No. 36, 1956 also *The Non-figurative Artists' Association of Montreal* (Cat. NGC) 1960

[8] *Weekend Magazine* (as above)

[9] *The Gazette*, Mtl., P.Q., May 31, 1958 " 'Tapestries' By Fernand Leduc"

[10] Ibid

[11] *National Gallery of Canada Catalogue of Paintings and Sculpture Vol.3* by R.H. Hubbard, P.168

[12] *The Third Biennial Exhibition of Canadian Art* (cat.) 1959, No.32

[13] *The Fifth Biennial of Canadian Painting* (cat.) 1963, No. 35
The Sixth Biennial of Canadian Painting (cat.) 1965, No. 53 and 54

[14] *The Montreal Star*, Dec. 2, 1963 "The Art Scene – Abstract Exhibition" by Robert Ayre

[15] *The Province*, Van., B.C., March 12, 1968 "Art – Why the artist is drawn to Paris – by Leduc" by Joan Lowndes

see also

The Arts In Canada, Edited by Malcolm Ross, MacMillan, 1958, "Painting" by Robert Ayre, P. 15, 29

École de Montréal by Guy Robert, Editions Du Centre de Psychologie et De Pédagogie, 1964, P.16, 22, 23, 56

Vie Des Arts, Automne, 1966 "le dynamisme des plasticiens de Montréal" par Fernande Saint-Martin, P.46

Painting In Canada/A History by J. Russell Harper, U. of T.; U of Laval, 1966, P.375

Three Hundred Years of Canadian Art by R.H. Hubbard and J.R. Ostiguy, NGC Ottawa, 1967, P.184, 185

La Presse, Nov. 11, 1950 "Importantes expositions des oeuvres de F. Leduc, Schjerfbeck et Corinth"

Ibid, April 16, 1955 "Quelques oeuvres magistrales de Leduc" par R. de Repentigny

Ibid, Sept. 3, 1955 "Chez Fernand Leduc et André Jasmin" par R. de Repentigny

L'Autnité, Beauceville, Que., May 23, 1953 "Fernand Leduc et Babinsky"

La Presse, 16 Oct., 1956 "Exposition Fernand Leduc à L'Actuelle"

Ibid, 20 Oct., 1956 "L'exposition de Fernand Leduc" par R. de Repentigny

Ibid, 31 May, 1958 "Un peintre sort de son cadre" par R. de Repentigny

Le Devoir, 9 July, 1958 "Formes et Couleurs" par René Chicoine

Ibid, 9 March, 1959 "Fernand Leduc à la galerie Artek"

Ibid, 17 March, 1959 "Formes et Couleurs" par René Chicoine

La Presse, 10 June, 1961 "Fernand Leduc: 60 toiles par an" par Paquerette Villeneuve

Ibid, 10 May, 1962 "Fernand Leduc expose à Paris"

Le Devoir, 26 Nov., 1963 "Fernand Leduc à la Galerie Soixante"

Le Soleil, 9 April, 1966 "A la rencontre de Fernand Leduc" par Claude Daigneault

Le Devoir, Mtl., P.Q., 23 April, 1966 "Une rétrospective Fernand Leduc" par Laurent Lamy

---

LEDUC, Ozias

1864-1955

Born at St. Hilaire, Quebec, he began to paint with Luigi Cappello in the decoration
of Saint-Paul l'Ermite church.[1] Cappello was an Italian painter who had done

church decoration for many churches in Quebec. Later Leduc became associated with Adolphe Rho in the decoration of the church of Yamachiche, including the painting of a copy of Raphael's "Transfiguration" and, a picture entitled "Baptême du Christ" destined for the church of Saint-Jean-in-Montana, Jerusalem.[2] Although this last painting was done by Leduc it was a commission given to Rho and done in his shops and therefore signed by Rho.[3] An engraving after this painting was made but was not a faithful reproduction of the original work.[4] Most of Leduc's art training was acquired through the process of observation and self teaching. By the age of twenty-three Leduc was producing beautiful still life studies bathed in warm candle light or from the light of a distant window. A painting from this period entitled "Les Trois Pommes" was given to Paul-Emile Borduas by the artist as Borduas was his assistant for many years in the decoration of churches and a life long friend. Now the property of Mme. Borduas the painting was reproduced in J. Russell Harper's *Painting In Canada/A History*.[5] In 1892 Leduc entered a painting in the Art Association of Montreal annual show and won a prize for the best work done by an artist under thirty. It was during this year and the next that he did decorations for the Joliette Cathedral. In 1897 he sailed for France in the company of Suzor-Côté. There Leduc became considerably impressed with three lessor known Impressionists, René Ménard, Alfons Mucha and Le Sidaner also Maurice Denis in religious art especially. He returned to Canada after eight months and set to work on decorations for the church at St. Hilaire.[6] Noting the effect of the Impressionists on Leduc's work Jean René Ostiguy[7] explained, "But the techniques of French impressionism, when transplanted to Saint-Hilaire, bore a very different fruit. For Leduc they were the means for weaving reveries and for expressing the tenderness which he felt before all life and all created things. His drawing, the care he devoted to his surfaces, show his early influences. But the real difference came in the handling of light. For him light was the symbol of another, an ideal world. He saw nature in the light of his dreams, and there is good reason for associating him with the surrealist tendency which is sometimes to be found in Renaissance painting. Because his development took this unusual course, Leduc's paintings are not modern in the ordinary sense. Yet in a deeper sense they are completely contemporary in spirit. His insistence on the poetic basis of art and his strongly personal manner of expression are qualities which contemporary painters revere and seek as essential elements in their work." Also commenting on the artist Gilles Corbeil[8] noted, "The extraordinary care which Ozias Leduc lavished on his paintings is almost unbelievable. He seems at every moment to have been conscious of some moral responsibility for the way he treated his canvases and handled his brush and his colours. Nothing was left undone; no care was too great. Everything which went into the making of a picture, from the preparation of the stretcher for the canvas, was the work of his own hands. One begins to wonder what brush could have been soft enough, what palette smooth enough, to have been employed in the creation of such exquisite paintings. But the really touching thing about Leduc is the tenderness, even sanctity, which seems to govern all his work. For him painting was never merely a manual craft but a flowering of character, an act of grace. For him the paint itself seemed sensitive, and perhaps it was for fear of violating it that he treated it with such gentleness." Corbeil went on to explain that throughout his life Leduc painted only some twenty still life studies of simple everyday things such as a candlestick, a loaf of bread, apples, a book, violin, a knife or spoon beside a bowl but he never painted flowers in these studies. Corbeil equated Leduc's treatment of objects with that of Jean Baptiste Simeon Chardin (1699-1779) the French master who also endowed his still lifes with a certain dignity although Chardin was a more wordly and sophisticated painter. Corbeil thought too, that the enchanted austerity of Leduc's paintings might be better compared to the Dutch still life painter Willem Claesz Heda (1594-1682). Heda however, unlike Leduc included flowers in his compositions but he achieved that aura of silence that Leduc always created in his still lifes. During the earlier part of his life Leduc did a number of portraits as well as landscapes. He made his living mainly from church decorations of which he did more than one hundred and fifty paintings for about twenty-eight cathedrals, churches, or chapels.[10] A few of his portraits include: Madame Lebrun (dated 1916); self portrait (1899); Marie-Madeleine Repentante (1901); his mother; Guy Delahaye (1912); Madame Labonté (1944); Robert Rocquebrune (undated charcoal) and many others. The portraits and other works were done with oil on paper, oil on cardboard, oil on canvas. He did a surprising number of oil on cardboard paintings. He kept track of his pencil drawings which were at times done on the back of envelopes and sometimes numbered.[9] In 1916 he was elected Associate of the Royal Canadian Academy and in 1938 received the degree of Doctor Honoris Causa from the University of Montreal. He illustrated the following books: *Claude Paysan* by Ernest Choquette (novel published 1898, Montreal); *Mignonne, allons voir si la rose* by Guy Delahaye (Guillaume Lahaise) (a poet's answer to his critics, and parodied romantic verse published 1912); *La Campagne canadienne: croquis et leçons* by Adelard Dugre (published 1927); *Contes vrais* by Pamphile Lemay (folklore and accounts of peasant life, published 1899); and *Le Père Buteux* by Abbé Tessier. Leduc's church decorations in Quebec included: mural of Saint Charles Borromée (15 ft x 11 ft) dated 1891, after the engraving by C. Lebrun for the church at Lachenaile; large painting of Christ descended from the cross (8 ft x 4 ft 6 in.) dated 1891, after an original work by Ary Schaeffer for Notre-Dame-de-la-Paix, Verdun; painting of the Martyrdom of Saint Julie (12 ft x 5 ft 6 in.) c.1903 for the church Sainte-Julie at Chambly; portrait of Father Rodrique Desnoyers, dated 1906, taken from a photograph in the Seminary of Saint-Hyacinthe; several paintings in the church of Saint-Enfant-Jesus, Montreal; a painting of the Exaltation of the Cross in the chapel of the convent at Saint-Hilaire; a painting of Christ Calming the Tempest in Joliette Cathedral; The Angels Carrying the Tablets of the Law, for the Cathedral at Antigonish; a painting of the Crowning of the Virgin and the Stigmata of Saint Francis of Assisi, a decoration, for the church at Farnham; and other works at the following churches and cathedrals: Saints-Anges, Lachine; church at Saint-Genevieve; church at l'Ile Bizard; Notre-Dame, Montreal; Bishop's Palace, Sherbrooke; church at Pierrefonds; church of Saint-Hilaire, Rouville and elsewhere. Nineteen of these were destroyed in the fire at the church of Rougemont in 1930.[11] There have been three important showings of Leduc's work as follows: at the St. Suplice Library, Montreal in 1916; a retrospective exhibition at the Lycée Pierre Corneille, Montreal in 1954 and a retrospective exhibition organized by Jean René Ostiguy for the National Gallery of Canada which included forty-one oil, charcoal, and coloured crayon drawings and paintings. Leduc was still active at the age of ninty, overseeing the work for the decoration of the church at Almaville-en-Bas near Shawinigan Falls.[12] He died at St. Hyacinthe aged ninety-one. Collectors of his works include: Père Wilfrid Corbeil, C.S.V. (Joliette, P.Q.); M. Jacques Auger (Montreal); M. Paul Gouin (Montreal); Mlle. Gabrielle Messier (St. Hilaire, P.Q.); M. Luc Choquette (Montreal);

LEDUC, Ozias (Cont'd)

M. Gerard Lortie (Montreal); M. Edouard Clerk (St. Hilaire); M. Jean Désy (Paris); M. Gilles Corbeil (Montreal); Dr. Guy Lahaise (Montreal); M. L.-J. Barcelo (Montreal); Mgr. Olivier Maurault, P.D. (Montreal); Mgr. Albert Tessier, P.D. (Montreal); Dr. Jules Brahy (Montreal); Abbé Filion (Montreal); M. Pierre de Ligny Boudreau (Paris); M. René Bergeron (Chicoutimi); and other private collectors of his works. He is represented in the following public collections: Museum of the Province of Quebec; The Montreal Museum of Fine Arts; and the National Gallery of Canada by landscapes "Neige Dorée" (54" x 30"); a still life "Le Repas Du Colon" (14" x 18") which was beautifully reproduced on the back cover of *Vie Des Arts*, Winter 1967; a close up study of part of an apple tree "Pommes Vertes" (24½" x 36½"); a head and shoulders study of "Endymion Et Séléné" (9¼ x 10-3/4") two characters of Greek mythology, Séléné (Moon Goddess) and Endymion (a beautiful youth).[13]

References

[1] Notes by Jules Bazin and Gérard Morisset at the time of their visit with Ozias Leduc, 10 August, 1937, also *Painting In Canada* by J. Russell Harper, 1966; *Bulletin Du Musée Du Quebec, No. 5, 1967*

[2] Ibid

[3] Ibid

[4] Ibid

[5] *Painting In Canada/A History* by J. Russell Harper, P.236

[6] *Ozias Leduc*, 1864-1955, Catalogue for the exhibition organized by the National Gallery of Canada, 1956

[7] Ibid

[8] Ibid

[9] see[1]

[10] *Le Voix de l'Est*, Granby, P.Q., Nov. 17, 1954 "Bien qu' âgé de 90 ans, M. Ozias Leduc, artiste peintre renommé continue de brosser ses tableaux"

[11] Ibid

[12] Ibid

[13] *National Gallery of Canada Catalogue, Vol. 3* by R.H. Hubbard, P.168-9

see also

Canadian Landscape Painters by A.H. Robson, 1932, P.166

Canadian Art, Its Origin and Development by William Colgate, Orig, Pub. 1943, Paperback 1967, P.221

Canadian Art by Graham McInnes, 1950, P.78

Canadian Painting 1850-1950, NGC Travelling Exhibition, 1967-8

The Growth of Canadian Painting by Donald W. Buchanan, 1950, P.100

The Arts in Canada, Dept. Citizenship & Immigration, Ottawa 1958, P.61-2

The Arts in Canada, Ed. by Malcolm Ross, Painting by Robert Ayre, 1958, P.30

The Development of Canadian Art, by R.H. Hubbard, 1963, P.76-7

Ecole de montréal by Guy Robert, 1964, P.10

Vie Des Arts, No. 29, Winter 1962-63 "Ozias Leduc, Peintre Independant" par Jean-Rene Ostiguy, P.16

Bulletin Du Musée Du Quebec, Numero 5, 1967 (Ministère Des Affaires Culturelles)

Le Nouvelliste, Three Rivers, April 10, 1952 (photos of work by Leduc at Almaville church)

The Herald, Mtl. P.Q. June 18, 1954 "Gallery Notes" by C.G. MacDonald

La Presse, July 1, 1954 "Le plus canadien et le plus universel de nos peintres" par Rodolphe de Repentigny

Le Droit, Nov. 17, 1954 "Arts et pensée" par Frederic Phaneuf

L'Evénement, Que., P.Q., May 21, 1955 "Les Arts" par Claude Picher

The Montreal Star, June 17, 1955 "Noted Quebec Painter Dies"

LEDUC, Ozias (Cont'd)

Le Droit, Ottawa, June 18, 1955 "Peintre décédé"
Le Nouvelliste, June 18, 1955 "Secrets De Polichinelle"
La Presse, June 21, 1955 "Ozias Leduc repose a l'ombre du mont St-Hilaire, où il vécut"
La Tribune, Sherbrooke, June 27, 1955 "Ozias Leduc aura laissé de belles peintures chez nous! "
Tribune, Winnipeg, Man., Jan. 12, 1956 "Humble Quebec Artist's Work On Tour"
The Ottawa Citizen, Jan. 14, 1956 "Artist From Obscurity Into National Gallery" by Don Peacock
Le Devoir, 14. Jan., 1956 "Un hommage au peintre Ozias Leduc, 1864-1955" par Noël Lajoie

The Montreal Star, Jan. 14, 1956 "Ozias Leduc's Serene Life Beside the St. Lawrence" by Robert Ayre
The Gazette, Mtl., P.Q., Feb. 4, 1956 "Ozias Leduc Works At L'Art Français"
The Hamilton Spectator, Hamilton, Ont., April 4, 1956 "Quebec Artist's Work Displayed For Month" by Mary Mason
The Calgary Herald, Calgary, Alta., Sept. 27, 1956 "Quebec Artist Is Revived"
Le Progrès, Chicoutimi, P.Q., March 25, 1958 "Un film de l'ONF sur Osias Leduc"
The Montreal Star, Mtl., P.Q., Sept. 23, 1967 "Ozias Leduc at the Sauvegarde" by Michael Ballantyne
La Voix de L'Est, Granby, P.Q. Aug. 11, 1969 "Ozias Leduc a décoré de son vivant au moins 28 églises"

LEDUC-BARRETT, Camille (Camille Barrett)

She studied at the Ontario College of Art, Toronto, and the Ecole des Beaux-Arts, Montreal, and held her first one man show at l'Institut des Arts, ecole Treffle-Gauthier at Jonquière, P.Q. She has given courses in design and decoration at the Ecole des Beaux-Arts at Arvida and teaches art to pre-school children and students at the Atelier-Ecole du Cercle des Arts de Chicoutimi. She is a painter of landscapes.

References

Le Lingot, Arvida, Mar. 5, 1964 "Deux expositions importantes pour Camille Barrett"
Le Reveil, Jonquière, P.Q., Mar. 11, 1964 "Exposition-solo de Camille Leduc"

LEE, Abel Alexander
b.1918

Born in Estonia, he studied at the Estonian State Art School at Tallinn and specialized in graphic art under G. Reindorff but also studied figure drawing under Wabbe and painting under Jansen. He came to Canada in 1951 and settled in Maple, Ontario. He is the founder of the "Colour and Form" society. Exhibited his latest work of wood constructions, made of patterns and textures of woods, at the Ruthe Calverley Gallery, Yonge Street, Toronto.

References

National Gallery of Canada Information Form rec'd Dec. 12, 1951
Liberal, Richmond Hill, Ont., April 27, 1967 "Unique Art Form On Display"
Free Estonian, Jan. 4, 1968 "Abel Lee at Yonge Gallery" by E. Koks
Ibid, Oct. 12, 1968 "Abel Lee at Fifty" by Hannes Oja

LEE, Byng

He graduated from the Winnipeg School of Art and the Ontario College of Art and is known for his paintings which have an Oriental theme. He exhibited in France, United States, and in Hong Kong where he spent several years. He was last reported living in Lethbridge, Alberta, where he exhibited his paintings in the Lethbridge Public Library.

Reference

   The Lethbridge Herald Daily, Lethbridge, Alta., April 22, 1960 "Water Colors On Display"

LEE, Eu Jeanne Park (Mrs. John Lee)
b.1940

Born in Seoul, Korea, she studied at the College of Fine Art, Seoul National University, where she received her Bachelor of Arts degree in 1962. She was awarded the top prize and medal for her Oriental art works at the annual national art exhibition in Korea in 1962, 1963, and 1964. She held a solo showing of her work in Seoul in 1963 and 1964, and in Tokyo, Japan in 1965. She settled in Saint John, New Brunswick in 1967 with her husband Dr. John Lee who is an anesthetist at the Saint John General Hospital. In addition to her traditional Oriental paintings she has done portraits and scenes of Saint John which were described by the *Evening Times Globe* as follows, "Mrs. Lee's impressions of Saint John are fascinating. They project the feeling that Mrs. Lee has found in Saint John something that is often missed by its inhabitants. She has a delicate sense of color and design that has not been stifled by the discipline of her Oriental art." She received a Canada Council Grant in 1969 to continue her painting.

References

   Evening Times Globe Saint John, N.B., May 14, 1969 "Art Show Scheduled"
   Ibid, May 17, 1969 "Art Show Opened"
   Ibid, May 21, 1969 "Exhibition Of Paintings At YMCA – A Delicate Touch Of Oriental Art"

LEE, Frederick W.

He was believed to be a Fellow of The Royal Academy. He painted extensively in England before coming to Canada around 1900. He settled in the Chilliwack district where he painted for approximately forty years. He also taught others. Many of his paintings were sold through a shop in Chilliwack. Some of his water colours dating in the early twenties were acquired by the Chilliwack and District museum.

   Progress, Chilliwack, B.C., Aug. 22, 1961 "Paintings On View"

LEE-GRAYSON, Joseph Henry
1875-19 - -

Born in Harrogate, Yorkshire, England, he studied at the South Kensington art school, London, and in Paris at the Académie Julian also in the Ecole des Beaux-Arts, Brussels. Belgium. He came to Canada in 1906 and spent two years in Montreal. Travelling West he did farming until 1914 when he joined the Canadian Expeditionary Force and served overseas where he lost his right eye. He returned home to Regina and subsequently worked in the Saskatchewan provincial service. He continued to paint the Saskatchewan landscape and exhibited his work with the Art Association of Montreal. He was active in art circles around Regina and was President of the Regina Junior Art League (1930-31-32).

References
    National Gallery of Canada Information Form rec'd May 31, 1932
    The Regina Star, Regina, Sask., April 26, 1932 "Ottawa Recognizes Lee-Grayson's Art"

LEE-NOVA, Gary (Gary Nairn)
b.1943

Born in Toronto, Ontario, he studied at the Vancouver School of Art (1960-61 and 1962-63) and at the Coventry College of Art, England (1961-62) during which time he discovered the work of Peter Phillips.[1] Since 1963 he has exhibited his work in group shows and one man shows in Vancouver, Toronto and London. He started working with electronic media and films in addition to his print-making and painting. He held a joint exhibition (probably others) with Claude Breeze, an artist who had helped him in his development.[2] Attention to his work perhaps did not register in a significant way until 1967 when *arts/canada* carried Richard Simmins'[3] preview of his Toronto exhibition of which the following is an excerpt, "Gary Lee-Nova steps effortlessly into the mainstream of Canadian art with his first Toronto exhibition at the Carmen Lamanna Gallery. 15 paintings and 10 drawings by this 23-year-old artist reflect a poise, assurance and consistently high level of execution which is rare for a man of his age. . . . His idiom is international, a fusing of New York and London influences. In an artist of lesser statue this eclecticism could be diminishing, but Lee-Nova adds something unique and personal. Disarmingly simple on the surface, his paintings possess a geometric, optical order and balance which is highly complex. Cubes and rectangles hang from invisible sky-hooks, in themselves isolated but related to background which is either geometric or flat landscape. Colour is solid, dynamic, contrasting – with after-image effects which are forceful without being garish. . . . Gary Lee-Nova is one of the most promising painters to appear from the west coast in recent years. While some works in the show are stronger and more powerful than others, there is no stumbling, faltering or hedged padding." His "Outskirts of the City" (Aquatex on canvas) was chosen for exhibit in the "Seventh Biennial of Canadian Painting." This work, painted in 1966, was purchased by The Agnes Etherington Art Centre, Queen's University, Kingston. In 1968 in co-operation with Michael Morris, Gary Lee-Nova presented "Prisma: an environment" discribed by Marguerite Pinney[5] as ". . . a confinement which expands the chimerical possibilities. Within, programmed light, music, and colour cause deliberate time and mood sequences. So encompassed is the illusion of infinite space, it calls into being a mind-world, an enclosure of boundlessness. Heptagonal, it is somewhat the size of a large *summer-house* – a strange and curious one. One enters through a black facade to be greeted by

LEE-NOVA, Gary (Gary Nairn) (Cont'd)

glittering phantasmagoria. When the door slides closed behind one, he is totally immersed, surrounded by mirrored walls, ceiling and floor – alternately plunged into darkness – eerily illuminated." In April of 1969 *arts/canada* published excerpts from an interview by Alvin Balkind[6] with Gary Lee-Nova covering a wide range of topics about himself including: recurring images in his work (images of boxes, circles, arcs, tangents of circles, pyramids, triangles skies, sunsets, rays of light, lightbands – with which he is fascinated); his sculpture (fibreglas and metal flake lacquer from which he makes geometrically related forms); media in painting (the use of oil paint – oil mixed with lacquer, using the oil paint to tint the lacquer base); films (he started making films in 1965 and produced *Steel Mushrooms* (in collaboration with Dallis Selman in 1967), *Magic Circle* and later *Flipbook* (collaboration with Al Neill), he has become interested in loops, loop animation, cell animation, collage animation; other subjects. With the interview were accompanying photos of Lee-Nova at work, and reproductions of his paintings. Immediately following this article was another on the artist by Gerry Gilbert,[7] a Vancouver poet, filmmaker, and editor of *radiofreerainforest*. In Issue No. 142/143 of *arts/canada* Gene Youngblood[8], Los Angeles film critic and faculty member of the California Institute of the Arts, discussed his findings on independent cinema of young artists-filmmakers in London and Vancouver, and what he found in viewing forty-five minutes of unedited footage by Gary Lee-Nova. To say the least he was impressed with the advancement of the artist and felt that he was "on the verge of a fairly important interface between film and the other plastic arts." Lee-Nova was also mentioned in an article on "World Game: the artist as ecologist" by Youngblood[9] for arts/canada's August, 1970 issue. Gary Lee-Nova lives in Vancouver, B.C. He is represented in the following collections: The National Gallery of Canada, Ottawa; The Agnes Etherington Art Centre (as above); London Public Library and Art Museum; the Vancouver Art Gallery, and elsewhere.

References

[1] *Canadian Art Today* by William Townsend, Studio International, London, England, 1970, P. 110

[2] *arts/canada*, January, 1967, No. 104, (record on plastic disc of interview of Claude Breeze by Barry Lord

[3] Ibid, April, 1967, No. 107 (*artscan*, P. 4 "Toronto – Gary Lee-Nova – Carmen Lamanna Gallery" previewed by Richard Simmins in Vancouver

[4] *Seventh Biennial of Canadian Painting*, 1968 (catalogue) P. 53

[5] *arts/canada*, August, 1968, No. 120/121 "arts/scan – Exhibition reviews – Prisma: an environment by Michael Morris and Gary Lee-Nova, Vancouver Art Gallery" by Marguerite Pinney

[6] Ibid, April, 1969, No. 130/131 "Gary Lee-Nova – Frustrums, Fragments and Spaces" by Alvin Balkind

[7] Ibid, "1000 words on Lee-Nova" by Gerry Gilbert

[8] Ibid, April, 1970, No. 142/143 "the new Canadian cinema: images from the age of paradox" by Gene Youngblood, P. 9, 10, 11

[9] Ibid, August, 1970, No. 146/147 "World Game: the artist as ecologist" by Gene Youngblood, P. 46 (first column

see also

arts/canada, February, 1969, No. 128/129 "Conservation of the Contemporary", by Nathan Stolow, P. 14-18.

Ibid, October, 1969, No. 136/137 "The language of the eyes – Windows and Mirrors" by Ross Mendes, P. 20-25

Ibid, December, 1969, No. 138/139 "The New Art of Vancouver, Newport Harbor Art Museum, Newport California, October-November, 1969

Ibid, October/November, 1970, No. 148/149 "drawing reconsidered" by John Noel Chandler, P. 31 (middle column)

LEEQUAFIK, Charlie (Charlie Seeguapik)

A sculptor from Povungnituk who was the first Eskimo to be admitted to the Sculptors' Society of Canada.

References
La Presse, Mtl, P.Q., May 6, 1958 "Un artiste esquimau est élu membre de la Société des sculpteurs"
Leader-Post, Regina, Sask., May 8, 1958 "Native Craftsman Honored" (photo of artist)
Independent, Windthorst, Sask., June 4, 1958 "Eskimos Honored"
The Globe, Tor., Ont., Mar. 28, 1959 "Leequafik Standards Set High"

le FEBURE, Jean

b.1930

Born in Montreal, P.Q., he studied at the Ecole des Beaux-Arts (1949) under Paul Emile Borduas (1949-52).[1] From 1950-52 he exhibited in group shows with Borduas, Ferron, Mousseau, Barbeau and others.[2] He then studied in Paris (1952) at the Académie Ranson with Henri Goetz. He spent six months visiting exhibitions of art and then travelled to Spain where he lived in a small fishing village near a beach. There he came in contact with gypsies who invited him to accompany them on many trips and gatherings. He completed a number of paintings which he exhibited in Madrid through the assistance of Camilo Jose Cela, a member of the Royal Society of Spain. He returned to Paris where he was taken by his teacher Henri Goetz to the Cote d'Azure to meet Picasso and Pignon. Back in Paris he married a French girl from Perigord and they owned and operated a bookstore. He continued to paint during his slack moments. After their first child they sold the store and moved into a large house in the heart of the Latin Quarter of Paris. In 1958 he was awarded a large contract to design the colour scheme for a large factory and this led to other jobs. He also participated in the following exhibitions: Salon des Réalités Nouvelles, Paris, 1954; group show at Iris Clert gallery, Paris, 1955; solo show at Cannes, 1961; Galerie Arditti, Paris, 1962; Galerie Levi, Milan, 1962; Galerie Semia Huber, Zurick, Germany, 1962; Festival at Spoleto, Italy, 1962; La Galerie Soixante, Montreal, 1963, 1965. There is much in Jean Le Febure's work which reminds one of canvases of Paul-Emile Borduas.

References
[1] National Gallery of Canada Information Form rec'd January, 1963
[2] Ibid
La Presse, March 28, 1953 "Peintre montréalais remarqué en Espagne"
The Ottawa Citizen, May 25, 1960 "Montreal Artist Turns To Industrial Painting" by Paquerette Villeneuve (Canadian Press Staff Writer)
The Gazette, Mtl., P.Q., Oct. 26, 1963 "Art Notes"
Le Journal de Montreal, Montreal, Que., Wednesday, Nov. 17, 1965 "La Vogue Des Galeries De Peinture Augmente Dans La Métropole"

LEFEBVRE, Henri

1974-1965

His grandfather was a church builder and decorator in Laprairie, Quebec. He watched his grandfather at work and through his watching learned much about

LEFEBVRE, Henri (Cont'd)

decoration. In 1899 he received his degree in engineering and began work immediately as a cartographer for the building of the Victoria Museum in Ottawa. Later as painter and designer he did animal paintings and sculptures with exceptional effects. Subsequently he taught drawing and sculpture for the Hull Technical School, Quebec, for almost twelve years. He also made furniture and was influenced by the supple lines of Louis XV style. As well he made clocks, mirrors, paintings and their frames and for fifty years worked at wood sculpture. He made the high altar in oak for Collège Saint-Alexandre, Ottawa; a baptismal font in cottonwood for Sacred Heart Church, Hull and completed many other commissions. He was as well, the author of a collection of poems entitled "En courant les bois" which he illustrated with his own water colours. One of his students was his son Marcel Lefebvre, the well known sculptor, church decorator and maker of violins and lutes.

References
Le Droit (article dated around 1951) "Professeur a l'École technique de Hull" par Pierre Charpentier

LEFEBVRE, Marcel Victor
b.1914

Born in Ottawa, Ontario the son of Henri Lefebvre, noted sculptor and teacher, he began woodcarving about the age of eight.[1] He learned from his father all the techniques involved in woodcarving including the curing of wood, colouring and finishing. He studied clay modelling, casting, and form, under Lionel Fosbery and Robert Darby at the Ottawa Technical School (1935-36).[2] He again studied colour and form at the Chicago Art Institute in 1937 and took advanced courses in anatomy. Back at Chicago he took ceramics and glazing the following year.[3] In 1952 he studied painting including composition and analysis, then copper enamel work, semi-precious stone cutting, siversmithing, mosaics, and stained glass. He has never begun the actual work on his subjects until he has completed his idea on the drawing board. The creative process therefore has been laid out on paper and not when he begins to carve or to do any other type of work. He has been influenced by the art of Ancient Greece also of El Greco and Rouault while also adapting modern styles to his work when appropriate. Ken Parks[4] of The Ottawa Journal noted his sculpture as follows, "Most of his pieces based on human figures are stylized to some extent though to date he has stayed away from abstract forms that are produced by many modern artists. Almost everything he has carved has been purchased before long by admirers of his work and it took considerable 'rounding up' to get together the collection shown . . . . " The article included a photo of Lefebvre and many pieces of his sculpture. Recently he has been working with bronze and copper in sculpture. Lefebvre turned to the study of violin-making and after three and a half years of research — talking to people, consulting various books on the subject, and taking a violin apart and rebuilding it, he began making his own.[5] After seven months he finished his first violin and has since made four others. Arthritis finally made the finishing touches of the ornamental border, called purfling, too difficult for him. He turned to making lutes and has completed ten of them: one of teak in Morocco covering; two laminated in suede covering and seven finished in laminated semi precious wood. He has also made a bass fiddle in the

LEFEBVRE, Marcel Victor (Cont'd)

shape of a lute. For twenty-three years he has worked with Central Mortgage and Housing Corporation, Ottawa, where he is Chief Translator. With this Corporation he compiled and edited a bilingual dictionary of building terms published in 1965 under the joint sponsorship of the Central Mortgage and Housing Corporation and the Division of Building Research of the National Research Council.[6] During the Second World War Lefebvre served in the Navy and afterwards worked as a translator with the Wartime Prices and Trade Board before joining the Central Mortgage and Housing Corporation. He has given public and private lectures, has taught for many years, has been interviewed on film and television in Montreal, Toronto, and Ottawa. He has given some thirty-five fifteen minute talks for radio, completed commissions for churches including the altar, tabernacle, and other decorations for Saint-Médard Church at Deschênes, P.Q., which he has recently redecorated with a new altar and a life size statue of the Risen Christ of solid teakwood weighing almost half-a-ton, three candelabras of teakwood mounted on wrought iron brackets, a tabernacle entirely built from black wrought iron; a mosaic (10' x 12') and stations of the cross also of mosaic and ceramic figures for the church at Luskville, P.Q., and works for other institutions. He has demonstrated soapstone carving and woodcarving on T.V., and has participated in many other activities. His sculpture can be found in collections in Australia, Spain, France, Mexico, U.S.A., England, Switzerland, Japan and India. He lives in Lucerne, Quebec, near Hull.

References
[1] Document from artist
[2] Ibid
[3] Ibid
[4] *The Ottawa Journal*, Feb. 4, 1956 "With Wood and Chisel, Deschenes Sculptor Winning Reputation as Master Carver" by Ken Parks
[5] *Le Droit*, Ottawa, Ont., Sat., Dec. 12, 1964 "Un artiste de chez nous: Marcel Lefebvre" par Darquise Timmerman
[6] *dictionnaire du Bâtiment/Building terms dictionary* by Marcel Lefebvre, Central Mortgage and Housing Corporation/Building Research Div., National Research Council of Canada, 1965 (Les Éditions Leméac)
see also
Le Droit, Ottawa, Ont., 6 Mar., 1957 (Large photo of artist with work)
Ibid, June 10, 1954 "De la traduction à la sculpture" par Pierre Rainville
The Ottawa Journal, June 5, 1954 "Translator Turns His Talents To Wood Carver's Fine Art" by Shirley Gillespie

---

LEFKOVITZ, Sylvia

b.1924

Born in Montreal, Quebec, she received encouragement from Anne Savage to study art when very young.[1] She attended classes at the Ecole des Beaux-Arts, Montreal and the Montreal Museum of Fine Arts (1942-46) under Eldon Grier, then attended Columbia University, New York, where she studied under Malloy and Malderelli.[2] She went to France where she studied at the Académie Julian, Paris, and then to Spain, Italy, and Mexico in 1956 where she painted, and studied the major historical murals done in lacquer.[3] Returning to Canada she applied the newly acquired knowledge on a series of Canadian historical murals about the Riel rebellion commissioned by the Redpath Museum of McGill University. This work "Riel Rebellion" was purchased later by the Department of Northern Affairs (Parks Branch) for The

National Historic Park at Fort Battleford, Saskatchewan.[4] She did another work of fifteen panels of masonite, each four feet by six feet, in lacquer, on the theme of the Acadians in five chapters (three panels to each chapter). They were described by *The Montreal Star*[5] as follows, "First, the beginnings of their country, with the Vikings accepted as visitors if not inhabitants, and Cartier and Champlain shown among the Indians. The Acadians are seen arriving and then after a sort of pastoral (scene) illustrating their peaceful and industrious life, comes to the drama of the expulsion, the sober black and white of the composition broken by a few glints of scarlet coats. The story closes with the return, on a note of thanksgiving." She exhibited as well studies of mother and child or children, train travellers, and generally studies of people. It was in 1958 that she was awarded a fellowship by The Canada Council making possible a year's study in Mexico with Prof. Jose Guierrez of the Polytechnic Institute. In Mexico she was able to devote her full time to art for the first time in her life. She also painted many scenes of life in Mexico in the market place, day-by-day Mexican living as well as scenes of bull-fights, children, apprentice glass blowers, flower vendors, and others.[6] In 1960 she went to Italy after giving up the security of her job as a bookkeeper. There she painted and worked in a bronze foundry learning the craft of casting in bronze; the art of terra cotta in ceramic factories; and stone sculpturing in the Vallechi Studio in Florence; where she also learned to speak Italian fluently. She won the Porcellino Award in 1962 for best artist of the year. After two years she returned to Montreal with nine cases of her work in marble, terra cotta and bronze also paintings. In the autumn of 1962 she held a solo exhibit of fifty-one oil paintings and five sculptures at the Waddington Galleries in Montreal reviewed by Dorothy Pfeiffer[7] as follows, "Since Miss Lefkovitz is essentially a disciple of the classical tradition in art, it appears only natural that her paintings – almost without exception – project overtly sculptural qualities and dimensions. Her palette is equipped with the dryly rich blues, browns, golds and green nuances, of the Italian Renaissance. Her work demonstrates an innate feeling for centuries-old Italian hillside fields and vineyards; for the fiercely-proud bearing of the Italian populace and for a mutual adoration of antiquity . . . in 1961 . . . she turned serious attention to sculpture. First, in wax – when she is said to have astounded art circles in Florence by her rapid mastery of the 'lost wax' technique . . . whereby the original work is modeled in wax, then enclosed in a mound of refactory earth and fired. Then, following a cooling process, hot metal is poured into the mould which melts the wax and preserves its light and subtle quality and by which even details of the sculptor's fingerprints are seen. Such a method of casting limits each work to one example only." Miss Pfeiffer went on to comment favourably on the artist's sculpture. It was on November 13, 1962, that the National Film Board released their photostory of Sylvia Lefkovitz showing her sculpture, paintings, and activities in Italy and Montreal.[8] She set to work carving in Canadian wood but in the spring of 1963 left again for Italy where she produced through the "lost wax process" Dante's "Divine Comedy" based on the famous epic poem dealing with the *Inferno*, *Purgatory* and *Paradise*. Her study consisted of thirty-three groups of bronze figures, comprising in all 80 individual figures. The work was modelled in wax then cast in bronze, every piece being unique in that no copies of the original were to be made. This work was then exhibited in the Dante Room of the Royal Palace in Milan on the occasion of the seventh hundredth anniversary of Dante's birth in 1265. The exhibition was sponsored by the International Art Book Fair (Mostra Internazionale del Libro

LEFKOVITZ, Sylvia (Cont'd)

d'Arte e della Bibliofilia).[9] Her "Divine Comedy" was purchased by the Canadian government and put on travelling exhibit. As her career has progressed she has spent more and more time on sculpture and has been working in Milan. It was from there that she was successful in her entry for the competition set up to obtain a "centrepiece of confederation" used in the Confederation Chamber of the various Confederation caravans which toured Canada in 1967. This work was described by the press[10] as follows, "In the centre of the sculpture is a stationary platform on which stand frock-coated figures symbolizing the 36 Fathers of Confederation. Around the circular platform, another platform rotates slowly at a lower level. On it are figures of the people of Canada, united when the British North America Act came into force July 1, 1867; farmers, businessmen, women, children, kilted Scots from the Maritimes, hunters and trappers from the northern woods of Quebec and Ontario. The impact of the sculpture is emphasized by a lone spot-light on it in the Confederation Chamber." She completed a bronze work of four women figures standing side by side for the plaza of the new Westmount Square entitled "The Chorus" unveiled by Ambassador F. Bacusci Rizzo, commissioner general of the Italian pavilion at Expo 67 in October of 1967. Describing this work for *The Montreal Star* Dusty Vineberg[11] noted, "Although it is only six feet tall, the bronze, with its black patina, holds its own against the black towers which are spaced so that mountain, sky and plaza also come into play . . . . 'The Chorus' weighs a ton; Miss Lefkovitz worked on it where it was cast, in the Milan foundry of Valcamonica & Visigalli, one of the best Italian foundries. The wooden base is temporary; eventually it will rest on black granite." Mary Green[12] writing of an interview with the artist for *The Montreal Star* in 1969 quoted Miss Lefkovitz as follows "Sylvia Lefkovitz stays in Italy 'because by temperament I like the Italian people.' But she says that her roots are in Quebec, 'I'm a Québécoise,' she hastened to say '. . . I feel I belong to Montreal — my home town. And when I meet a French Canadian here, we speak of home'. "

References

[1] National Gallery of Canada information sheet and Information Form dated Oct. 1965; Letter from Mrs. A. Samuels of Montreal dated April 22nd, 1963; *The Gazette*, Mtl., Mar. 20, 1959 "Facts and Fancies" by Harriet Hill

[2] Ibid

[3] Ibid

[4] *The Montreal Star*, Sept. 13, 1969 "Now Here This" by Mary Green

[5] Ibid, Jan. 26, 1957

[6] *The Gazette*, Mtl., P.Q., Mar. 20, 1959 "Facts and Fancies" by Harriet Hill

[7] Ibid, 27 Oct., 1962 "One-Woman Show" by Dorothy Pfeiffer

[8] *National Film Board Photostory No. 324* "Italian Critics Acclaim Montreal Sculptor — Canadian Artist Wins Fame In Florence" (Nov. 13, 1964)

[9] *The Gazette*, Mtl., P.Q., Oct. 9, 1964 "Local Artist In Milan"
The Montreal Star, Oct. 17, 1964 "Dantesque Sculpture"

[10] *Progress*, Atikokan, Ont., Apr. 20, 1967 "Sculptured Figures a Highlight" (photo of work being viewed by public)
The Ottawa Journal, May 5, 1967 "Sculpture Is Symbol Of Canadian Pioneers" by Gloria Barrett

[11] *The Montreal Star*, Oct. 5, 1967 "The Chorus stars in the latest show" by Dusty Vineberg
see also
The Gazette, Mtl. P.Q., Oct. 25, 1958 "Wins Fellowship"
Le Petit Journal, Mtl, P.Q., July 12, 1959 "Sa seule patrie: la peinture" par Madeleine Vaillancourt

LEFKOVITZ, Sylvia (Cont'd)

The Montreal Star, 30 July, 1962 "Artist's Luggage Weighs Two Tons" by Joyce Goodman
La Presse, Mtl., P.Q., 3 Nov., 1962 "Sylvia Lefkovitz"
Photo-Journal, Mtl., P.Q., Nov. 10, 1962 "Un matériau résistant: quel défi! " par Michelle Tisseyre
Springfield Leader, Lac du Bonnet, Manitoba, Tues. Dec. 4, 1962 "Critics Acclaim Montreal Sculptor – Canadian Artist Wins Fame In Florence"
Globe & Mail, Nov. 27, 1962 "Montreal Sculptor Wins Italian Award"
Elizabethan, Mtl., P.Q., February, 1963 "Bravo, Sylvia! " portrait by Gaby
L'Evangeline, Moncton, N.B., Feb. 9, 1963 "Sylvia Lefkovitz, sculpteur canadien de grand talent"
Le Droit, Ottawa, Ont., 14 July, 1967 "La sculpture des Pères de la Confédération de Sylvia Lefkovitz admirée par les Canadiens"

LEFORT, Elizabeth
b.1914

Born at Point Cross, Nova Scotia, she learned how to hook wool yarn as a small girl under the direction of her mother.[1] Later she developed dyeing, colour and proportion senses on her own.[2] About 1940 she received a Christmas card which she liked and decided to try and reproduce the card by weaving its design into a rug. This was her first attempt at tapestry work which she now creates by making a rough line sketch on fine grade burlap to approximately the size of the desired finished work.[3] She then dyes two-ply fine yarn to all the shades she expects to use in the scene or portrait (she applies moth-proofing in the dye-bath at this stage).[4] She begins hand hooking with a tiny hand-made hook from a common nail. It is at this stage that she makes corrections or alterations of her original sketch. When completed her work can almost be taken for an oil painting at a distance of five feet. Elizabeth Lefort was discovered in 1954 by Kenneth Hansford, owner of a Cape Breton tourist gift shop who handles the sale of her tapestries and portraits or other commissions through his "Paul Prix Shop" at Margaree Harbour, Nova Scotia.[5] Since 1954 she has completed over 126 works of which the following are a few: portrait of Pope Pius XII (presented to the Apostolic Delegate to Canada in 1959 – now hangs in the Vatican Fine Arts Gallery); portrait of President Eisenhower (presented by the artist herself upon invitation, to the President at the White House, in 1957); portrait of Queen Elizabeth (personally presented to Her Majesty on her visit to Sydney, N.S., in July, 1959); portrait of President John F. Kennedy (personally presented to him at Phoenix, Arizona, in 1961) also a portrait of his wife; portrait of President Lyndon Johnson (presented to the President in the Rose Garden of the White House); portrait of former Prime Minister John Diefenbaker (1965), and Prime Minister Pierre Elliott Trudeau (1969). Other works by the artist include "The Last Supper" (8' long by 4½' high) after the painting by Leonardo da Vinci, which required the dyeing and blending of 154 colours; "My Country, 'Tis of Thee" which took her six months to complete is a 6'3" x 10'3" summary of United States of America's presidential history (this work toured the Eastern States Exposition of September 12 to 21st, 1969); a series of tapestries from the life of Christ which include: "The Nativity", "The Boy Jesus", "The Youth Jesus", "Life Size Figure of Christ", "The Last Supper" (as mentioned above), "Crucifixion" and she was last reported working on the "Resurrection" which by now may be completed. During the past ten years her work has been shown in Toronto, Montreal, St. John, Moncton, Sydney, San Diego, Phoenix, and

LEFORT, Elizabeth (Cont'd)

elsewhere. The National Film Board spent a week at her studio making a fifteen minute film on the artist. Six colour movie travelogues were circulated on her work. The artist's studio is located at Point Cross (or at the "Paul Prix Shop", Margaree Harbour), where she spends her summers and at Phoenix, Arizona, during the winter months, where the bright light enables her to continue her work which is now internationally known.

References
[1] National Gallery of Canada Information Form rec'd Aug. 18, 1965
[2] Ibid
[3] Ibid
[4] Ibid
[5] *Elizabeth Lefort, Canada's Artist In Wool* (Booklet)
see also
Cape Breton Post, Sydney, N.S., June 11, 1960 "Elizabeth Lefort Canada's Artist In Wool"
Ibid, July 4, 1960
Ibid, June 5, 1964 "Canada's Artist In Wool' Returns"
Chatham Commercial-World, Chatham, N.B., Oct. 21, 1964 "N.S. Has Only All-Tapestry Art Gallery"
Cape Breton Post, Sydney, N.S., Aug. 26, 1969 "World Tapestry Artist" (large photo of Elizabeth Lefort's "My Country 'Tis of Thee")
Canso Breeze, Truro, N.S., Aug. 27, 1969 "Portrait In Wool" (large photo of artist's presentation of Prime Minister Trudeau's portrait to the Prime Minister)

LEFORT, Marie Agnès

b.1891

Born at Saint-Remi, Napierville County, P.Q., she attended the Ursuline Convent school at Three Rivers and later studied drawing at the Council of Arts (Monument National) in Montreal under Joseph St. Charles, Charles Gill and Edmond Dyonnet; also took further study in portrait painting under St. Charles at his studio in Montreal, and studio and outdoor classes in landscape painting under J.Y. Johnstone.[1] She was awarded the yearly medal of The Council of Arts for drawing in 1917.[2] Subsequently she made study trips to France, Italy and England.[3] She began to exhibit her work with the Art Association of Montreal and the Royal Canadian Academy annual exhibitions in 1923 and more regularly after 1932.[4] In 1935 she held a large solo show of her paintings (81 paintings) of portraits, nudes, landscapes, genre scenes and still lifes, at the Eaton's Art Galleries in Montreal. Many of her landscapes were of scenes of the canal at Lachine, points in and around Shawinigan, street scenes of Montreal, and other points in Quebec.[5] Three of her four portraits were done in pastel. The majority of her paintings of this show were probably done in oils. The following year her work was chosen for the Royal Canadian Academy Touring Exhibition also R.C.A. tours in 1937 and 1938. Her paintings were accepted for showing in the exhibition "Canadian Art In Brazil" at Rio de Janeiro and Sao Paulo which took place during December 1944 to January 1945. Sergio Milliet[6] of the newspaper *O Estado de Sao Paulo* noted "The Canadian exhibition also presented us some impressionists, one of which, Lefort, has force and imagination. Her painting, 'Masques' has nothing disagreeable and would please even more without the symbolic intention." José Augusto De Macedo Soares[7] was also delighted with her work when he noted in the *Correio da Manha* "Agnes Lefort shows us 'Port de Peche, Cap Breton', painted in a free and vibrant

LEFORT, Marie Agnès (Cont'd)

manner, in harmony with the artist's spirit." In the years that followed she did advertisement copy writing, radio talks on the History of Art and conducted classes in her own studio. In 1949 she exhibited her work at L'Art Français gallery in Montreal, where *The Montreal Star* reviewer H.P.B.[8] noted, "The Montreal painter, Agnès Lefort, whose representational pictures have been seen in many exhibitions, has now taken to another and newer style of painting, as she shows in the collection of her recent work at L'Art Français on Laurier Avenue. A few of these are highly stylized landscapes, which have interesting suggestions and some decorative color . . . . " The reviewer however seemed to indicate that he was not too appreciative of abstract work in general and elaborated very little on the whole show. Charles Doyon[9] on the other hand devoted two columns to this same show in which he noted that Miss Lefort was influenced by Lhote, and to a lessor extent by Braque and Ozenfant (all whose works had tighty organized compositions with less concern in the achievement of depth and more on the play of design and colour). Doyon clearly noted that she knew her craft and had executed her studies in solidly constructed canvases rich in substance. He also mentioned that he preferred her earlier more traditional works. Agnès Lefort also taught painting at the Miss Edgar and Miss Cramp School Inc. in Montreal. In November of 1950 the heading "New Art Gallery Will Show Local Painters" in *The Standard*[10] heralded her entry into a new enterprise of art dealer and owner of the Agnès Lefort Gallery. She opened her gallery with a showing of gouaches on the History of Medicine and the History of War by Robert La Palme.[11] It was not long before her gallery was widely respected and known for its high quality work. She had of course, no more time for painting but only the thought of returning to her easel after her retirement. Her gallery has since been taken over by Myra Goddard who named her gallery Galerie Godard Lefort, specializing in contemporary Canadian artists and twentieth century masters. Agnès Lefort is represented in the following galleries: Museum of the Province of Quebec, Canadian Embassy in Brazil, Museum of Seminary of Joliette, Museum of College Grasset and elsewhere.

References

[1] National Gallery of Canada Information Forms Aug. 12, 1943 and one date not legible. An information sheet also on file dated Aug. 7, 1946

[2] Ibid

[3] Ibid

[4] Ibid

[5] *Exposition de Peintures (catalogue), Agnès Lefort*, Eaton Art Galleries, 16 to 29 September, 1935

[6] *O Estado de Sao Paulo*, 14 Jan., 1945 "Peinture Canadienne" par Sergio Milliet (*Canadian Art In Brazil*)

[7] *Correio da Manha*, 7 Dec., 1944 "Peinture Canadienne" par José Augusto De Macedo Soares (*Canadian Art In Brazil*)

[8] *The Montreal Star*, Nov. 22, 1949 "A New Departure By Agnes Lefort" by H.P.B.

[9] *Le Clairon*, St. Hyacinthe, P.Q., Dec. 9, 1949 "Agnès Lefort A L'Art Français"

[10] *The Montreal Standard*, Nov. 4, 1950 "Speaking of Art – New Art Gallery Will Show Local Painters" by Michael Forster

[11] Ibid

see also

École de Montréal by Guy Robert, Editions Du Centre De Psychologie Et De Pédagogie, Montreal, P.Q., 1964, P.4

La Presse, Mtl., P.Q., Nov. 26, 1949 "Agnès Lefort et ses études"

The Herald, Mtl., P.Q., June 27, 1950 "Speaking of Women" by Helen Murphy

LEFORT, Marie Agnès (Cont'd)

The Gazette, Mtl., P.Q., Mar. 7, 1951 "Art Gallery Owner Receive Summons In Statue Dispute" (unclad figures of a man and a woman topped with doves symbolizing peace)
L'Autorité, Beauceville, P.Q., Aug. 15, 1953 "L'unique Rubens de Montréal"
Le Foyer, Mtl., P.Q., Sept. 24, 1955 "Agnès Lefort, Peintresse – Animatrice d'avant-garde"
The Gazette, July 27, 1960 "Curator Looks For Winners" by Julian Armstrong

---

LÉGARÉ, Joseph

1795-1855

Born in Quebec City,[1] he is considered Canada's first landscape painter.[2] He was interested in painting as a youth and began in his early twenties to copy paintings in churches and religious institutions around Quebec City.[3] Most of his first works were copies and he did as well, considerable restoration of paintings sent to Canada by Abbé Desjardins around the time of the French revolution when many great works were wantonly destroyed.[4] The Desjardins collection at Quebec was auctioned in 1817 when much of it was purchased by Légaré.[5] Légaré also produced a number of pictures on Indian life including several tragic scenes of scalpings. It was in 1828 that one of his Indian studies "Le Désespoir d'Une Indienne" was awarded a medal by the Montreal Society for the Encouragement of Science and Art.[6] Légaré did a variety of subjects even processional banners, and in 1832 decorations for the Theatre Royal in Quebec City. Working with him from 1819 to 1825 was an apprentice by the name of Antoine Plamondon who became one of Quebec's great painters.[7] Légaré recorded historical events which won him the reputation of being Canada's first historical painter as in his painting of the great landslide at Cape Diamond in 1848 which crushed many dwellings at the foot of the cliff ("Éboulis du Cap-aux-Diamants" collection, Quebec Seminary); or the cholera plague at Quebec, a result of an epidemic from India around 1826 which spread to Europe and through European immigrants hit Quebec City after 1832 ("The Cholera Plague at Quebec", Nat. Gal. Can. collection) and other events. Some of his paintings like "The Falls at Saint-Ferréol"[8] or "The Artist's House At Gentilly, P.Q."[9] have a decided primitive look to them although others like "Les Ruines après l'incendie du Faubourg Saint-Roch"[10] or "Éboulis du Cap-aux-Diamants"[11] show the artist's fine handling of perspective and dramatic presentation. As a young man Légaré was quite involved in politics, was a strong supporter of Louis Joseph Papineau, was arrested during the rebellion of 1937 but fortunately released five days later on the guarantee of good behaviour by his father. Much later in life he was esteemed to the degree that he was appointed to the Quebec Legislature as Councillor in 1855 a few months before his death. The painting of his home at Gentilly was loaned by his great grand-daughter Madame Pierre Duhamel of Deschambault, P.Q., when it was exhibited for the first time at the Albany Institute of History and Art in 1946. Légaré's large collection of paintings was exhibited publicly in 1838 and 1852 and was finally acquired by Laval University after his death.[12] He is also represented in the collections of the Museum of the Province of Quebec, and many churches. He did hundreds of religious paintings for religious institutions based on French originals.

References

[1] *Canadian Art, Its Origin and Development* by William Colgate (1943, paperbacks 1967), P.108
[2] *Painting In Canada/A History* by J. Russell Harper (1966), P.81

LÉGARÉ, Joseph (Cont'd)

[3] see[1]
[4] see[2], P.82
[5] see[2], P.82 also *The Fine Arts In Canada* by Newton MacTavish (1925) P.8
[6] see[2] P.82
[7] see[2], P.83
[8] *Three Hundred Years of Canadian Art* by R.H. Hubbard and J.R. Ostiguy (1967), P.56, 57
[9] *Painting In Canada/A Selective Historical Survey* by John Davis Hatch Jr., Albany Institute of History and Art, Albany, N.Y. (1946), P.27
[10] see[2], P.85
[11] see[2], P.83
[12] see[1], P.109

see also
Artistes-peintres canadiens-français by G. Bellerive (1925)
Canadian Landscape Painters by A.H. Robson (1932) P.18, 20
Encyclopedia of Canada, Vol. 4, Gen Ed., W. Stewart Wallace (1948), P.59
The Development of Canadian Art by R.H. Hubbard (1963) P.55, 56
The MacMillan Dictionary of Canadian Biography, Ed. W. Stewart Wallace (1963), P.404
Encyclopedia Canadiana, Grolier (1962), P.114

LÉGARÉ, Juliette

b.1937

A Montrealer and daughter of a Canadian architect, she studied at the Ecole des Beaux-Arts, Montreal, and at McGill University. Her first exhibitions were mainly of houses or buildings in simplified or abstract patterns. By 1962 she was working on stained glass windows commissioned by a Belgian firm for a Montreal building. These particular windows were constructed so that the glass was embedded in a concrete frame. During the same year she exhibited paintings she did in Mexico and Scotland which were very well received by critics. She then began creating pictures in stainless steel for business establishments. These murals were done by cutting a design in steel sheets using an electric drill. One of these works was for the head office of a steel firm in Welland, Ontario. She was reported under contract with the El Greco gallery in Montreal, where other works by her could be seen. The remarkable thing about Juliette Légaré is her versatility. She is also a high-fashion model, part time actress, and sports car racer (took part in Shell 4000 race from Vancouver to Montreal). She is a member of Montreal's MG Club. Her murals and paintings have been exhibited in the United States, Spain, Italy and England. She is represented in the Halifax Museum and elsewhere.

References

La Presse, Dec. 8, 1961 "Juliette Légaré à 'Ars Classica' " par Claude Jasmin
Examiner, Westmount, Que., Jan. 5, 1962 "Local artist imparts warmth to paintings"
The Gazette, Mtl., P.Q. Sat., June 22, 1963, Canadian Weekly section "Glamor girl on the go" (photos by Sam Tata)
Photo-Journal, Mtl, P.Q., June 15, 1966 "Un vitrail amusant de Juliette Légaré" par Michelle Tisseyre

LEGAULT, Joseph-Onésime

1882-1944

He studied under William Brymner, Joseph Franchère, and Edmond Dyonnet and did many paintings of rural Quebec, old homes, country roads with wayside crosses, still lifes, and portraits, in the media of oil, pencil, charcoal, and pen and ink. His work was so realistic that he was criticized for this quality. About 1941 he exhibited first with a group of painters known as "peintres de la montée Saint-Michel". Their first showing took place in a store on Ste. Catherine Street, Montreal, during 1941 and presumably there were other showings of his work. His paintings were chosen to illustrate calendars of the Saint Joseph Chapel which were sold throughout Canada and the United States. He did other calendar illustrations as well. He died suddenly in Montreal at the age of sixty-two. It is not certain if he was survived by members of his family other than his daughter Jeannine.

Reference

Le Petit Journal, Mtl, P.Q., Oct. 13, 1963 "Quelques artistes de chez nous – J.-O. Legault, peintre oublié? " par Emile Falardeau, de la Société historique de Montreal

LEGAULT, Pierre

A potter in the Ottawa-Hull area who exhibited thirty works at the Hull Municipal Library under the auspices of the Henry-Desjardins Cultural Centre. The show included twenty-one vases, a bowl, a wine service, and a jar.

Reference

Le Droit, Ottawa, Ont., Feb. 24, 1970 "Le Centre Culturel Henry-Desjardins" (large photo of artist)

Ibid, March 2, 1970 "Une Exposition De Poteries" (photo of artist and his work)

LEGENDRE, Irène

b.1904

Born at Fall River, Mass., U.S.A., of Canadian parents, she studied at the Ecole des Beaux-Arts of Quebec (1929-32) under Yvan Neilson and Lucien Martial and in New York (1939-43) with Alexandre Archipenko (sculpture) and Amédée Ozenfant (painting). In 1941 she participated in a group show in New York and the same year and the year following, was awarded a Quebec Provincial Government grant.[2] In 1945 she won first prize for painting in the Quebec Provincial competition, and the same year participated in a show of Quebec painters. In 1946 she gave a series of five talks on modern painting over Radio-Canada and exhibited in the Montreal Spring Show at the Montreal Museum of Fine Arts. She held a solo show of paintings and pastels under the patronage of the Canadian Council of Arts at Cercle Universitaire, Montreal, in November of 1950.

References

National Gallery of Canada Information Form rec'd June 28, 1946

The Standard, Mtl., Nov. 25, 1950 "Speaking of Art – Irene Legendre Show; Paintings From Paris" by Michael Forster

La Presse, Mtl., Nov. 25, 1950 "Présentation d'une rétrospective des tableau d'Irène Legendre" par Jean Dénéchaud

LEHTO, Joyce (Mrs. Robert J. Kaiser)
b.1928

Born in Sudbury, Ontario, she studied in Detroit and at the Ontario College of Art, Toronto, and is known for her wall hangings or tapestries. Her work has been exhibited at the Dorothy Cameron Gallery in Toronto (1965), the Canadian Fine Crafts Show (1966-67) at the National Gallery, and at Expo '67 in Montreal. She is represented in the collections of Mr. & Mrs. J. Markson, Dr. & Mrs. F. Mustard; Mr. & Mrs. J.D. Eaton; Mr. & Mrs. Jeremy Brown; Mr. S. Ross; Marjorie Harris; Anna Cameron; Mr. M. Teitelbaum; Dr. & Mrs. Myers; Mr. Winston Gray; Dept. of External Affairs (Canada); Shell Oil; Cadillac Construction and many others. She lives in Toronto with her husband and three sons.

References

National Gallery of Canada Information Form rec'd August, 1967
Exhibition notice dated March 8, 1965 Tapestries by Lehto, Dorothy Cameron Gallery Ltd. (This gallery closed several years back)
Canadian Fine Crafts, 1966-67 (catalogue by the NGC), P.13, Cat. No. 133

LEIBL, Lee (Mrs. Philip Heilig)

Born and educated in Plzen, Czechoslovakia, she attended the School of Graphic Arts there for three years. Arriving in Canada in 1950 she continued her art studies in Victoria, B.C. and later in Montreal under Leslie L. Schalk and held her first solo exhibition in 1963 at the School of Architecture of McGill University. Other solo shows followed at the Penthouse Gallery (1964), Gallery 1640 (1964) when Lisa Balfour of *The Montreal Star* noted, "As a starting off point, Mrs. Leibl admits her work is inspired by natural forms in nature, – shifting sands, branches, hanging forms and the human figure. Recently, however, she observed that a surrealistic and more subjective, expressionistic vision had emerged in her drawings. 'I admire Alfred Pellan's work because he combines intellect and passion in such harmonious balance,'. she said, partly in explanation. One drawing, The Innocents, depicting three female nudes in an architectural setting, washed over with water-color, recalls a mediaeval stained-glass window, as Mrs. Leibl pointed out." In addition to painting and drawing she has done tapestry work from scraps of materials and continues to search for new forms of expression and new materials.

References

The Montreal Star, Feb. 15, 1964
Ibid, March 2, 1964 "Pen and Ink Drawings – Memories of Past Affect Her Work" by Lisa Balfour
The Gazette, Mtl, P.Q., Feb. 20, 1968 "Woman Today – Limbs And Faces Painter's Latest Canvas"

LEIBOVITCH, Norman
b.1913

Born in Montreal, Quebec, he studied in New York City at the American People's Schools under Carl Nelson and the Art Students' League under William Zorach and

LEIBOVITCH, Norman (Cont'd)

was awarded a scholarship in sculpture at the league.[1] Returning to Montreal in 1937 he did some set designing and other work. By 1943 he was exhibiting decorative panels of animals and modelled pottery of animal figures, also landscapes and portraits. He held a one man show in 1945 at L'Art Français, Montreal, of oils and drawings when *The Gazette*[2] noted his work as follows, "This young artist paints with directness and force and seems equally at home in grey or in sunny weather. His composition is generally effective and his handling of architectural forms is marked by summary freedom. He can employ bright color very effectively as is evidenced in the work called 'Fletcher's Field' in which trees in summer leaf, near which figures stand, are flushed with bright sunlight . . . . His travels have taken him to Mont Tremblant, Labelle and other points. He is open-minded in the selection of subjects as is clear by such titles as 'The Church', 'Warehouse', 'Harvest Time', 'Street Scene', 'Fences', 'Haystack' and 'Stubble', while figures have not been overlooked." He visited Mexico in 1946 and brought back many paintings which he exhibited at Brebeuf College, Montreal in 1947. All of the major Montreal papers received this show favourably. In 1948 he exhibited twenty-two paintings at the Norlyst Gallery in New York City; 1950 at Brebeuf College; 1951 at the West End Gallery, Montreal (scenes of Israel); 1962, Penthouse Gallery, Westmount (abstracts, non-figuratives, figurative paintings).

References

[1] The National Gallery of Canada Information Form rec'd June 21, 1940
[2] *The Gazette*, Mtl., P.Q., Feb. 17, 1945 "N. Leibovitch Shows Works at L'Art Français"
see also
The Montreal Star, Feb. 24, 1943 "New Exhibition At Arts Club"
Canadian Jewish Review, February, 1943
The Gazette, Mtl, P.Q., Feb. 27, 1943 "Leibovitch Exhibits At The Arts Club"

Ibid, Apr. 26, 1947 "Leibovitch Showing Paintings of Mexico"
The Montreal Star, Apr. 30, 1947 "Mexican Scenes In Exhibition"
The Herald, Mtl., P.Q., May 5, 1947 "Leibovitch Art on Display At College Jean de Brebeuf"
Ibid, Nov. 1, 1947 "Art Exhibit Date Set Here"
The Gazette, Mtl., P.Q., Dec. 11, 1947 "Norman Leibovitch To Show in New York"
The Standard, Mtl, P.Q., Jan. 10, 1948 "Young Montreal Artist Holding N.Y. Exhibition"
La Presse, Mtl., P.Q., Mar. 11, 1950 "Exposition de paysages du peintre Norman Leibovitch"
The Gazette, Dec. 1, 1951 "Leibovitch Displays Paintings of Israel"
Ibid, Sept. 8, 1962 "At The Penthouse" by Dorothy Pfeiffer

LEIGH, David Leroy

b.1927

Born in Toronto, Ontario, he studied at the Central Technical School and the Ontario College of Art (both Toronto) under Carl Schaefer, Doris McCarthy, John Martin and Sidney Watson. He travelled to England for further study in stained glass techniques (1954-55); Graphic Art and Film Animation (1955-60); Design Directing and Stage Designing (1960-65). Was reported in 1963 to be working as art director for a television station in Ottawa. His paintings range from religious to intriguing nude studies in casein. He lives in Ottawa.

LEIGH, David Leroy (Cont'd)

References

National Gallery of Canada Information Forms rec'd April 16, 1952 and November, 1965
N.D.G. Monitor, Montreal, Feb. 14, 1963 "Wandering with Wanda – Art Exhibit here 'striking' " by Wanda Boytscha

---

LEIGHTON, A.C.

1901-1965

Born in Hastings, Sussex, England, he received his formal education at Hastings, and in London at the Hornsey School.[1] He had no formal painting lessons but received advice and criticism from a friend, E. Leslie Badham, R.B.A.[2] Leighton did paintings for a commercial organization. It was while he was filling a commission for this firm at Mansion House and Temple Bar in London that Badham who had dropped in for a cup of tea, discovered his work and advised him to try for the exhibition of the Royal Society of British Artists.[3] Leighton entered two pictures in the exhibition and his work was well received. As a result he was elected an Associate of the Academy. He was in London from 1920 to 1927. During that period he taught classes, filled commissions and visited Canada in 1925. On his second visit in 1928 he was commissioned by the Canadian Pacific Railway to paint a series of scenes of the prairies and Rockies. He travelled by pack train in the mountains making all his paintings out-of-doors. He spent most of the summer on the trail and then after a solo showing in Calgary where he sold twelve or so paintings, he arrived in Vancouver to continue the C.P.R. commission to paint scenes of the C.P.R. docks, and of that city, also of Victoria. He exhibited his work at the James Leyland galleries in Vancouver in the autumn of 1928 and by 1930 had settled in Calgary where among other things he was an instructor at the Institute of Technology and Art. In 1929 he became full member of the Royal Society of British Artists. He held an exhibition of forty-four water colours in the Elizabethan room of the Hudson's Bay store, Calgary, in 1930.[4] This show included many of the paintings he had done that summer also a canvas "Lake of the Hanging Glaciers" which he had completed in 1928 and exhibited in the Paris salon in 1929. In the show as well, were a number of paintings completed in Victoria, B.C., which were used as illustrations for a publication presented by the C.P.R. and purchased later by J. Murray Gibbon. In the years that followed Leighton exhibited many times in Calgary, Edmonton, and in other cities in Canada. He became a member of the Canadian Society of Painters in Water Colour in 1930 and himself founded the Alberta Society of Artists in 1931. By 1934 he had attracted the attention of the Toronto *Saturday Night* who carried the news that he was holding summer art classes for selected art students, from the Province of Alberta, at the Brewster Dude Ranch near Banff.[5] This same year he had the unusual distinction of having three of his water colours accepted for showing at the Royal Academy Exhibition in London, England.[6] In 1935 he was elected Associate of the Royal Canadian Academy. In 1936 an exhibition of one hundred of his water colours was on view at the Fine Art Galleries of the T. Eaton Company, Montreal, including scenes which he had also done in Britain. *The Gazette*[7] in review of the exhibition noted, "The charm of the picturesque has much to do with the appeal of his windmills, his old buildings and boats, his bridges and castles . . . . He has brought his appreciation of the colorful to Canada, too, and he

LEIGHTON, A.C. (Cont'd)

shows in a romantic light the drydocks at Vancouver, the ferry there, an old paddlewheeler at New Westminister, and even the grain elevators of the prairies . . . he is able to do justice to the Rockies, and his views of Cathedral Mountain, Mount Assiniboine, the Crow's Nest Pass, Floe Lake and Tumbling Glacier, are notable for a bulk and solidity that are not always found in water colors. Whatever his subject, whether castle or windmill, Sussex village or ridge in the Rockies, Mr. Leighton builds it up into a substantial well-integrated design and he does it with an uncompromising line and a sureness of color." Leighton did a number of oil paintings as well of landscapes and flower studies;he also worked in pastels. His paintings were reproduced in *The Studio, The Sphere* of London, England, and in *La Revue Moderne* of Paris. He had completed paintings for English Railways, Vickers Limited (London, Eng.), as well as the C.P.R.; illustrated two books *Far Horizons* and *Victoria, B.C.*; had organized the Calgary Sketch Club and the Medicine Hat Sketch Club, given lectures on art appreciation for the University of Alberta also on art and industry. He remained Head of the art department of the Provincial Institute of Technology and Art until 1938 when he retired. He spent several years in Britain then settled on a ranch near Midnapore south of Calgary. The Gainsborough Galleries in Calgary exhibited forty of his paintings in 1964 the year before his death. A.C. Leighton is represented in the following collections: National Gallery of Canada, Ottawa; The Vancouver Art Gallery; Winnipeg Art Gallery; Edmonton Art Gallery; the New York Central Reference Library; International Business Machines; The Seagram Collection of Paintings and in Britain at Eastbourne, Hastings, Brighton, Hull and Glasgow. He is represented in many private collections as well, particularly in the Calgary area. He was a cousin of the noted British painter Frederic Leighton (Lord Leighton of Stretton/1830-1896).

References

[1] National Gallery of Canada Information Form rec'd June, 1934

[2] *The Evening Sun*, Van., B.C., Oct. 29, 1928 "Youthful Artist Suffers Hardships To Get Pictures"

[3] Ibid

[4] *The Calgary Herald*, Calgary, Alta., Nov. 19, 1930 "Leighton Water Colors Displayed"

[5] *Saturday Night*, Tor., Ont., Mar. 3, 1934 "Will Hold Summer School" (photo of Leighton at work on a painting)

[6] *The Calgary Herald*, May 17, 1934 "A.C. Leighton's Work Recognized By Royal Academy"

[7] *The Gazette*, Mtl, P.Q., Mar. 24, 1936 "Leighton Pictures Are On Exhibition"

see also

Canadian Landscape Painters by A.H. Robson, Ryerson, 1932, P.186

Painting In Canada/A History by J. Russell Harper, U. of T. Press, 1966, P.342, 346

The National Gallery of Canada Catalogue, Vol. 3, 1960, P.170

Bulletin, Edmonton, Alta., Wed., July 29, 1931 "Water Color Exhibition by A.C. Leighton of Interest"

The Edmonton Journal, July 29, 1931 "Leighton's Show New Galleries Museum of Art"

The Calgary Herald, May 6, 1933 "A.C. Leighton Arranges Outdoor Sketching Trip"

Tribune, Winnipeg, Man., May 22, 1936 "This Man Leighton" by Walter J. Phillips, R.C.A.

The Calgary Herald, Feb. 23, 1942 "Artists Pay Tribute To A.C. Leighton"

The Albertan, Calgary, Alta., Oct. 15, 1947 "Character Seen In Rockies Art"

The Medicine Hat News, Medicine Hat, Alta., Nov. 22, 1956 "Leighton Art Exhibit Showing at the Library"

The Edmonton Journal, Feb. 2, 1957 "Leighton Works On Display Here"

The Albertan, Calgary, Alta., May 9, 1964 "In the limelight" by Linda Curtis

LEIGHTON, Thomas Charles

b.1909

Born in Toronto, Ontario, he studied there at the Ontario College of Art under F.S. Haines, Robert Holmes and Franz Johnston, also in the studios of John Russell and was assistant to John Russell during the period 1934-35. He studied as well, in London, England, and Chicago, U.S.A. He was known for his portrait and still life paintings. He was represented in collections in New York, Chicago, Los Angeles, Toronto, Hamilton, Welland, St. Catharines, Calgary, and Niagara Falls where he settled. He was Director, Dept. Fine Arts, Ridley College (1935–); was President of the Niagara Falls Art Club (1936-37); and Director of the Dept. of Fine Arts, Niagara Falls High School, Ont. (1938–). He was as well director of his own schools in Niagara Falls, Ont., and at St. Catharines, Ont. He exhibited with the Royal Canadian Academy for the first time in 1938 when his flower study "White Peonies and Yellow Lillies", a pastel (36" x 32") and a portrait of Dr. W.E. Olmsted, were accepted by the Academy. He is represented in the collection of the Wakefield Art Gallery, England (1930); Welland County Hall, Welland, Ontario and elsewhere. Related to Lord Leighton (British painter) and A.C. Leighton.

References

National Gallery of Canada Information Form rec'd Jan. 9, 1939
The Standard, St. Catharines, Ont., Nov. 18, 1938
Niagara Falls Review, Ont., Nov. 15, 1938

LEITCH, Peggy (Mrs. John D. Leitch)

Born in Toronto, Ontario, she first attended Saturday Morning Classes at the Art Gallery of Ontario in 1928. She began painting seriously in the late 1950's and studied with Mashel Teitelbaum at the New School of Art, Toronto. By 1969 she held an important solo show at the Albert White Gallery when Gillian Robertson[1] of *The Toronto Telegram* noted, "Although she is a world traveller, most of her landscapes are of areas around Georgian Bay where they have a cottage, and the family country home at Thornhill." Mrs. Leitch was described as an "assiduous and meritorious painter."[2] She is active in many fields of the arts and was past president of the Canadian Opera Women's Committee and for three years headed York University's drive for a theatre in north Toronto resulting in the building of the Burton Auditorium. Attending her show at the Albert White Gallery were: Col. & Mrs. K.C.B. Corbett; Lady Henrietta Banting; Miss Cec Long; Mrs. Ed. Mirvish; Mr. & Mrs. David Kinnear; Mr. & Mrs. Graham McLachlan; Dr. Murray Ross (Pres., York Univ.); Mrs. Bud Bunnett; Mrs. George Gardiner; Mrs. Charles Tidy; Dr. John T. Saywell (Dean, Faculty of Arts & Science, York Univ.); Dr. James M. Gillies (Dean, Faculty of Administrative Studies, York Univ.); Mrs. John Godfrey; Mrs. Keiller MacKay and her son Alistair MacKay and many others. Wife of John D. Leitch (shipping industrialist), and daughter of Hon. John Cartwright (Chief Justice of Canada).

References

[1] *The Toronto Telegram*, Ont., Jan. 9, 1969 "A preview of Peggy Leitch's new works" by Gillian Robertson
[2] Ibid, Jan. 6, 1969 "Bargain"
see also
Globe & Mail, Tor., Ont., Sept. 16, 1965

LEITCH, Peggy (Mrs. John D. Leitch((Cont'd)

The Star, Sault Ste. Marie, Ont., May 7, 1969 "Show Leitch Paintings"
The Standard, Elliott Lake, Ont., May 15, 1969 "Artist Of Note" (photo of Peggy Leitch and work)
The Star, Sault Ste. Marie, Oct. 18, 1969 "Allied Arts news – Library will show Leitch art"

LEMAY, Marcien

b.1927

He studied sculpture at the Forum Art Institute, Winnipeg, under Nicholas Bjelajac, and was successful in a competition for a statue of Louis Riel to be placed in the city of Winnipeg. The over all plans, developed by architect Etienne Gaboury and Lemay, consisted of an outer shell thirty feet high, actually the shape of a cylinder split in two from top to bottom. Inside the shell is Lemay's fifteen foot high statue of Riel. On each half of the outer surfaces of the cylinder are inscriptions in English and French. The cost of the design was estimated at $35,000 including the foundation. Lemay is employed by the city of St. Boniface as a fireman. His eight foot version of Riel caused a minor sensation at the 44th Annual Manitoba Society of Artists' Exhibition at the Winnipeg Art Gallery.

References
    The Winnipeg Tribune, Man., April 19, 1969 "Lemay's Louis – result of reading" by Ritchie Gage
    Lake Centre News (Manitouwapa Times), Arborg, Man., May 29, 1970 "Riel Statue Design Chosen"

LEMIEUX, Emile

b.1889

Born in Montreal, Quebec, he studied at the Monument National and in Toronto. He then travelled to the United States where he took further art training in New York and Chicago; later to France at the Colorossi and La Grande Chaumière in Paris. Lemieux painted mainly landscapes in the Laurentians and on the Island of Montreal. He joined the T. Eaton Company in Montreal in 1911 and as Art Director served this firm many years until his retirement.

References
    National Gallery of Canada Information Forms rec'd June 15, 1936 and Jan. 26, 1946
    The Montreal Star, March 8, 1934 (review of his show at Eaton's Gallery, Montreal)

LEMIEUX, Jean Paul

b.1904

Born in Quebec City, his parents were originally from that region.[1] His father was with the Greenshields Company for many years and later became agent for the Regent Knitting Mills. They lived in Quebec City until Jean Paul was eleven. During those years they spent their summers near Montmorency Falls and Kent House which had been built in 1784 by the Governor General of Lower Canada, General

LEMIEUX, Jean Paul (Cont'd)

Halimand.[2] Later Kent House became a hotel where in 1914 Jean Paul met an American painter named Parnell. Parnell had a studio in the hotel where he painted large murals for its decoration. After many hours watching Parnell, Jean Paul began to sketch on his own. In 1916 the Lemieux family moved to Berkeley, California. His sister had been suffering from rheumatism and the dry warm climate helped her through a difficult period. There he studied with the Brothers of the Christian Schools. During his summer holidays he travelled through California with his family. In 1917 the Lemieuxs returned to Canada and settled in Montreal where the boy attended College Mont-Saint-Louis (two years) and later Loyola College. Having firmly decided to become an artist he enrolled in l'Ecole des Beaux-Arts, Montreal, in 1926, and spent the next three years studying under Charles Maillard, Edwin Holgate, Maurice Felix and others.[3] In 1929 he travelled to Europe with his mother and in Paris he studied advertising art under a Mr. Seltz of the Dorland Publicity Firm.[4] He also followed courses at la Grande Chaumière and the Colarossi. It was in Paris that he met Clarence Gagnon who was then working on his illustrations for *Maria Chapdelaine*.[5] Lemieux lived in the Montparnasse district of Paris and frequented the terrasse du Dome where he met his artistic colleagues.[6] He returned to Montreal in 1930 where he set up a commercial art studio with Jean Palardy and other associates but after six months, with the country in depression, they were not able to see their way clear and the studio closed. He went to California where he sketched and painted then returned to Montreal and the Ecole des Beaux Arts, where he received his diploma in 1934. He was awarded Second Prize in the Brymner Competition at the Art Association of Montreal.[7] He stayed on at the Beaux Arts in Montreal as teacher. In 1935 he moved to the Ecole du Meuble where he continued to teach drawing and painting. He became a frequent visitor to the studio of Edwin Holgate a former teacher. Through his admiration for Holgate's work his own landscapes like "Paysage en Charlevoix" (Coll. M. Jean-Marie Gauvreau, Mtl.) bear an affinity to Holgate's paintings. Both men were interested in portrait and figure work and during this period Lemieux did some fine studies of Madeleine Desrosiers like "Tête", a pencil drawing (Coll. artist) and a portrait of her in oils (Coll. artist), both of which have been reproduced in catalogues and books.[8] In 1937 he moved to Quebec where he resumed his teaching career at l'Ecole des Beaux-Arts de Quebec. It was in this year that he married Madeleine Desrosiers. They had met at the Ecole des Beaux-Arts in Montreal and he exhibited with her at the Chez Morency in Quebec City in 1938.[9] His teaching post at l'Ecole du Meuble was then filled by Paul Emile Borduas. It was Lemieux who introduced Borduas to Alfred Pellan in 1940. In general, Lemieux's paintings up until 1940 were derived from a realistic and decorative style. As with many artists the influence of Cézanne also played an important role in his early work but he was to leave this behind by the beginning of the 1940's. A complete change in his work was evident for instance in the large canvas "Lazare" which he painted in 1941. This widely reproduced work owned by the Art Gallery of Ontario is an allegorical work which seems to depict isolationism of old Quebec during the period of the Second World War (the War depicted in the upper left hand corner of the canvas). The painting is roughly divided diagonally from the upper right hand corner to the lower left by the border of Quebec. The Province is depicted by a cutaway view of a church in which a priest imparts a sermon on Lazarus to his congregation. In the upper right hand corner of the painting Lazarus is seen to be brought back to life by a gentle Christ in modern clothes while an astonished grave digger witnesses the miracle. A winding country road leading to the graveyard bears a funeral procession of an early period horse drawn hurse. A raven sits on a lower right hand corner wall of the church perhaps to forewarn of the impending change of old Quebec under the 'Quiet Revolution'. Lemieux seems to infer by the drifting war clouds of the 20th Century that his beloved province will be caught up in the impending events of the present. Could the funeral procession be that of old Quebec? A remarkable reproduction of this painting can be found in the book *Great Canadian Painting*,[10] works selected by Elizabeth Kilbourn and Frank Newfeld. Discussion of the same painting can be found in Guy Robert's book *Jean Paul Lemieux*.[11] Other of his allegories are more direct with a lessor degree of symbolism like "Etude pour Emmaus", "Etude pour la Fête-Dieu", "Les Disciples d'Emmaus" and others. Describing his work of this period Dr. Marius Barbeau[12] explained, "No other method and technique than that of primitive or folk imagery could be more appropriate and fruitful. The spirit and naiveté of those images furnish a clue to much of Lemieux's later work as a painter. Under a peculiar light Lemieux looks at the people, in town, convent or country, and exposes their activities and strivings. When down the river he spends a summer vacation, he responds to the good humour of the pioneers in the midst of stumps and poverty; he catches them on the fling, as it were, posing for him in the manner of bourgeois, whose daguerrotypes fill a family album." By 1951 a new and simplified style of almost cubistic structure was to herald a dramatic change in his work. Also in 1951 he won first prize in the Quebec Painting Contest for his "Les Ursulines" (Coll. Quebec Prov. Museum) which shows a group of nuns sitting in a courtyard surrounded by houses. In this painting there is a great play of design of each of the elements that go to make up the whole. The rectangular shapes of the sides of the houses, the forms of the nuns themselves, the courtyard, even the wall along one side of the courtyard present almost an abstract composition. But Lemieux never goes beyond the highly simplified point. This work as well as others are reminiscent of the American painter Niles Spencer.[13] In 1954 Lemieux went to France on a Canada Council Scholarship but found little original inspiration. Everything he painted was reminiscent of Monet or Matisse. But when he returned to Canada a complete change in his work took place. By the 1960's Lemieux's paintings were mainly of quaint lonely figures in austere landscapes. These landscapes were made up of little more than a horizon line to suggest a division between earth and sky although each of a different colour. Until recently he seldom painted blue skies. Often they would be amber as in a late summer day, or steel grey of an approaching storm.[14] During an exhibition in Toronto in 1960 at the Roberts Gallery his work was described by the *Globe & Mail*[15] as follows, "There is a haunting loneness and sense of space in his paintings of figures against far, flat land; of roads ending in a point of vision; of landscape bounded by a far city's skyline. His White Angel done last year has quality. It is not gay art but it is vastly communicative." Lemieux[16] once stated, "I have no theories, and like everyone else who paints, I am never satisfied with my work. I am especially interested in conveying the solitude of man and the ever flowing passing of time. I try to express in my landscapes and my figures this solitude, this silence in which we all move . . . in every new painting my inner world of recollections. The physical world around me interests me only because it allows me to picture my inner self." To Patrick Nagle[17] he said "I'm not a landscape painter. Don't call me that. I like painting figures too much. When I get tired of landscapes I paint figures. I never use models; I couldn't. I try to convey a remembrance, the feeling of

LEMIEUX, Jean Paul (Cont'd)

generations. I sometimes see myself as the central figure, but as a child in the continuity of generations. I like the feeling of summer in the old days, the feeling of old newsreels or photographs. You get the feeling of fading away." In 1965 when his one-man show opened at the Agnes Lefort Gallery Robert Ayre[18] remarked, "It says something about the state of Canadian art that people should queue up during a painter's lifetime to buy his work. This is what happened to Jean Paul Lemieux of Quebec at the opening of his one-man show at Galerie Agnes Lefort. More than an hour and a half before the doors were unlocked, the crowds had begun to gather outside, some of the collectors supplied with books to while away the time, for all the world like fans waiting for hockey tickets or rush seats to the opera. When they gained admittance, they made a scramble for the paintings, quickly filling up the galleries so that you could hardly see pictures for people and in 15 minutes they were all reserved . . . . The subject of all the excitement is a quiet man, both as person and painter, who is so little interested in the limelight that he didn't come to Montreal to see his show hung, and avoided the crush of the opening. He has always gone his own way, untouched by the changing fashions of painting, from the automatist to the optical, and one of the reasons for the driving demand for his work is the short supply, he is not prolific. Most of the works in his last show here, . . . were lent from private collections." Lemieux retired from his teaching post at the Ecole des Beaux Arts in 1965 after twenty-eight years association with the school and now spends most of the year at Ile-aux-Coudres, Quebec. He was honoured by Montreal Museum of Fine Arts by a retrospective exhibition in the fall of 1967. This show of 108 works was then exhibited at the Musée du Quebec and the National Gallery of Canada[19] In 1968 he was honoured with the Companion of the Order of Canada. He is a member of the Royal Canadian Academy (A.R.C.A., 1951) (R.C.A., 1956). His paintings are in the following public and private collections: National Gallery of Canada, Ottawa; Art Gallery of Ontario, Tor., Ont.; Art Gallery of Hamilton, Ont.; London Public Library and Art Museum, Ont.; Montreal Museum of Fine Arts, P.Q.; Musée du Quebec, Que., P.Q.; Royal Bank of Canada, Tor., Ont.; Hart House, Univ. of Tor., Tor., Ont.; private collections of: H.M. Queen Elizabeth; Son Excellence M. Jules Leger, Paris, France; Mr. & Mrs. Robert Ayre, Mtl. P.Q.; Mr. R.S. Bennett, Mtl., P.Q.; M. Henri-Pierre Bourque, Lucerne, P.Q.; Dr. & Mrs. Marcel Carbotte, Que., P.Q.; Dr. Yvon Chartrand, Mtl., P.Q.; Mr. & Mrs. Willie Chevalier, Mtl., P.Q.; Andrée & Maurice Corbeil Coll., Mtl., P.Q.; Mr. & Mrs. Dagenais-Perusse, Mtl., P.Q.; Mrs. Frank Endean, Tor., Ont.; Mrs. Françoise Faucher, Mtl., P.Q.; Mr. & Mrs. Fraser M. Bell, Don Mills, Ont.; Mr. Germain Gauthier, Sillery, Que.; Mr. Jean-Marie Gauvreau, Mtl., P.Q.; Mr. & Mrs. Amedée Geoffrion, Mt., P.Q.; Miss Diane Giguère, Mtl., P.Q.; Mrs. Mira Godard, Mtl., P.Q.; Mr. Camille-R. Hebert, Mtl., P.Q., Mr. R.M. Hogarth, Willowdale, Ont.; Mr. Stephen Jarislowsky, Mtl., P.Q.; Mr. & Mrs. Geo. P. Kidd, Wash., D.C.; Mr. & Mrs. W. S. Kirkpatrick, Mtl., Mr. Luc Lacourcière, Beaumont, P.Q.; Mr. Jean-C. Lallemand, Mtl., P.Q.; Miss Jeanne Lapointe, Que., P.Q.; Mr. & Mrs. Jack Lazare, Beaconsfield, P.Q.; Mrs. Jean Leahy, Que., P.Q.; Mr. & Mrs. J. Gordon Littlejohn, Tor., Ont.; Mr. & Mrs. Jules Loeb, Hull, P.Q.; Mr. & Mrs. C.W. McConnell, Mtl, P.Q.; Mr. James Maxwell, Mtl., P.Q.; Mr. Edmund Meredith, Tor., Ont.; Mr. & Mrs. J.H. Moore, London, Ont.; Mrs. H.B. Norris, Mtl., P.Q.; Mr. & Mrs. Gordon E. Pfeiffer, Rosemere, P.Q.; Mr. Yves Pratte, Sillery, P.Q.; Mr. Louis Rasminsky, Ottawa, Ont.; Dr. A. Ritchie, Tor., Ont.; Mr. Hubert Rogeau, Sherbrooke, P.Q.; Mr. & Mrs. J.M. I. Scott, Mtl., P.Q.; Mr. & Mrs. Wm. Sofin, Mtl.,

LEMIEUX, Jean Paul (Cont'd)

P.Q.; Mr. & Mrs. Alan Steiner, Tor., Ont.; Mr. Yvon-R. Tasse, Sillery, P.Q.; Mr. & Mrs. Johnny Wayne, Tor., Ont.; Mr. & Mrs. L.S. Wildridge, Tor., Ont.; Mr. Gerard Zanettin, Que., P.Q.

References

[1] *Jean Paul Lemieux* (catalogue) An exhibition organized by the Montreal Museum of Fine Arts, 1967

[2] Ibid

[3] Nat. Gal. Canada Information Form rec'd Sept. 15, 1942 also 1963

[4] Ibid

[5] see [1]

[6] see [1]

[7] see [3]

[8] *Jean Paul Lemieux* by Guy Robert, Editions Garneau, Quebec City, 1968, P.18, 19 also see [1], P.7, 10

[9] *Le Soleil*, Quebec City, P.Q., Nov. 12, 1938 "Exposition des tableaux de deux peintres canadiens bien connus"

Ibid, Nov. 14, 1938 "Une Exposition" par Gerard Morisset

[10] *Great Canadian Painting* by Elizabeth Kilbourn, Frank Newfeld, Text by Ken Lefolii-Research by William Kilbourn, Marjorie Harris, Sandra Scott; The Canadian Centennial Publishing Company Ltd. (Weekend Magazine – McClelland & Stewart Ltd.) P.60

[11] *Jean Paul Lemieux* by Guy Robert, P.31

[12] *Painters of Quebec* by Marius Barbeau, Ryerson, Tor., 1945, P.36, 37

[13] *Dictionary of Modern Painting* "Niles Spencer" by John Asbery, Tudor Pub., NYC, 1955, P.456

[14] *Weekend Magazine*, No. 10, 1963 "Timeless Painter From Quebec" by Patrick Nagle, P.18-20

[15] *Globe & Mail*, Tor., Ont., Mar. 12, 1960 "Important Show – Lemieux of Quebec Vastly Communicative"

[16] *Jean-Paul Lemieux* as in [1]

[17] see [14], P.19

[18] *The Montreal Star*, Mtl., P.Q., Jan. 12, 1965 "Lemieux Exhibit at the Galerie Lefort" by Robert Ayre

[19] see [1]

see also

Coup d'Oeil sur les Arts en Nouvelle-France par Gerard Morisset, Que., 1941

Who's Who in American Art, 1956, P.531

Royal Architectural Institute of Canada, August, 1957

The Arts In Canada, Dept. of Citizenship & Immigration, Ottawa, 1958, P.101

The Arts In Canada by Malcolm Ross, MacMillan Co. of Can. Ltd., 1958, P.30 Ill. P.26

The Art Gallery of Toronto (Catalogue) of Painting & Sculpture, 1959, P.80

Nat. Gal. of Can. Cat. of Painting & Sculpture, Vol. 3, by R.H. Hubbard, 1963, P.171-2

Ecole de Montréal by Guy Robert, Editions Du Centre De Psychologie Et De Pédagogie, 1964, P.96-7

An Anthology of Canadian Art by R.H. Hubbard, Toronto, 1959

The Development of Canadian Art by R.H. Hubbard, Queen's Printer, 1963, P.115

Painting In Canada/A History by J. Russell Harper, U. of T., Press, Tor., 1966, P.333

Three Hundred Years of Canadian Art by R.H. Hubbard and J.R. Ostiguy, NGC, 1967, P.180-1

The Hart House Collection of Canadian Painting by Jeremy Adamson, 1969, P.95

Canadian Art, Mar. 1957, Aug., 1958; July, 1960; Nov., 1962; July, 1963; Sept., 1963; Nov., 1963; May, 1964; July, 1964; Mar., 1965; May, 1965

Vie des Arts, No. 1, Jan., Feb., 1956; été, 1958; hiver, 1963; No. 34 printemps, 1964;

LEMIEUX, Marguerite

b.1899

Born in Montreal, P.Q., she studied there under Joseph Saint-Charles, Joseph-Charles Franchère, Edmond Dyonnet, Albert Laliberté and in Paris at the Académie Julian with J-P. Laurens, M. Benner, Guillonnet, P. Ersback, and V. Charreton; at the Académie de Biloul l'Aquarelle under Carlier, Vignal, H. Charrousset; received her diploma from the National Society of Horticulture (a section of the Ecole des Beaux Arts in Paris). She made five trips to Europe to learn new techniques in decoration.[1] In 1927 she held a solo exhibit of 250 works (water colours, oils, enamel and leather works) at the Saint Sulpice Library in Montreal.[2] By 1930 she enjoyed an enviable reputation as a painter and artisan in leather, wood and ceramics. In her painting her subjects included flower studies, landscapes, portraits. Her works were also exhibited at the Montreal Spring Shows and other exhibitions.

References

[1] National Gallery of Canada Information Form rec'd June 18, 1930

[2] Catalogue – *Exposition – Aquarelles, Peintures, Travaux D'Art Décoratif de Marguerite Lemieux – 14 Nov. au 1 Dec., 1927*, Bibliotheque St. Sulpice, 1700 Rue St. Denis, Montreal, P.Q.

see also
La Presse, Mtl., P.Q., Fri., Oct. 5, 1928 "Une Belle Chose Humaine Passe, Mais Non Une Oeuvre Artistique, Qui Demeure Et Charme L'Esprit"

Le Petit Journal, Mtl., Nov. 24, 1964 "Quelques artistes de chez nous – Talent créateur de Marguerite Lemieux" par Emile Falardeau, de la Société Historique de Montréal

LEMIEUX, Maurice

b. (c) 1932

A sculptor from Valleyfield, Quebec, self taught, he created one of the biggest metal sculptures in Canada on the exterior wall of the auditorium of the Seminary of Saint-Jean-d'Iberville. He worked for three months on his two-and-a-half ton creation. Originally he intended using 1/4" steel sheets but this would have doubled its weight. He chose 1/8 inch steel sheets and then reinforced the work with a framework similar to that used in an aeroplane wing. The sculpture which stands 35 feet high by 20 feet wide symbolizes the motto of the Seminary "Let us love one another". Lemieux has exhibited his work at the University of Montreal and the Biennial of Madrid in 1957; Saint Helene Island, 1958; Artek Gallery, 1959; Galerie Libre permanently since 1959.

References

Architecture-Batiment-Construction, Mtl., P.Q., April, 1959 "A la Galerie Artek"

La Voix de L'Est, Granby, Que., Sept. 25, 1961 "Une gigantesque sculpture est accrochée au Seminaire"

Globe & Mail, Tor., Ont., Sept. 23, 1961

Perspectives, 2 Dec., 1961 "Sculpture Monumentale"

La Voix de l'Est, May 1, 1969 (photo and caption)

LEMOINE, Edmond

1877-1922

Born at Quebec City, the son of Edouard Le Moine, notary, and Dame Victoria Buies, he studied under Charles Huot for four years. In 1898 he went to Europe where he studied drawing and painting at the Royal Academy of Fine Arts in

LEMOINE, Edmond (Cont'd)

Anvers. In the same Academy he continued his studies at the Institut Superieur in the workshop of Julian de Vriendt, director of the Academy. Returning to Quebec he painted many portraits and genre scenes. He taught drawing and painting at the Ecole des Arts in Quebec and made a second trip to Europe in 1913. He married Hortense Charlebois in 1921. A retrospective exhibition of his work was held at the Quebec Seminary in November of 1922. He was commissioned in 1911 to paint a scene of Wolf's Cove in connection with a monument to Montcalm. This painting was exhibited at the Museum at Nimes, France. He left more than three hundred paintings and many sketches. He did several excellent portraits, a good number of landscapes, habitant interiors and still lifes. Some of these paintings are in Toronto, Montreal and Ottawa but most of them are in Quebec City.

References
  Le Terroir, Que., P.Q., February, 1920 "Le Coin Des Peintres" by Hormisdas Magnan P. 292-296
  Ibid, October, 1922
  Ibid, April, 1923
  Catalogue M. Edmond Lemoine dated 25 May, 1909

LEMONDE, Serge
b (c) 1945

Originally from St. Hyacinthe, he studied at the Ecole des Beaux-Arts, Montreal, and in painting has worked in many styles including dadaism, surrealism, neo-realism, pop-art, and others. During his exhibit at Galerie Libre in 1968 his paintings were described as having freshness, virtuosity and tenderness. This 1968 exhibition was entitled "The event of The Century. Pictures of an extra-terrestrial painter" and was made up of fifteen paintings representing diverse animals. A previous show dealt with the machine and sex (bare breasted models working in an industrial complex) of which The Montreal Star noted, "Mr. Lemonde . . . has a good deal of witty fun with his models. His sense of design lifts this kind of thing above the level of what might have been just an undergraduate jape . . . ." Lemonde is employed as a set decorator for various theatres.

References
  The Montreal Star, May 20, 1967 "Exhibitions around town" by Michael Ballantyne
  Le Clairon, May 18, 1967 "Une peintre maskoutain S. Lemonde expose à Montréal" par Jean-Claude Robert
  Ibid, Dec. 11, 1968 "Serge Lemonde expose"
  La Presse, Dec. 14, 1968 "d'une exposition à l'autre"
  La Patrie, Mtl., P.Q., Dec. 22, 1968 "Des peintures 'extra-terrestres' trouvées a St. Hyacinthe dans la soucoupe volante d'un savant du cosmos"

LENDVAY, Istvan Stephen
b.1929

Born in Csorna, Hungary, he studied at the Technical University of Budapest (architectural artist course) and graduated with his "Diploma of Architect-Engineer". He came to Canada in 1957 and subsequently became a member of the

LENDVAY, Istvan Stephen (Cont'd)

Ontario Association of Architects. Holds the diploma of M.R.A.I.C. In his painting and drawing he has explored Canadian landscapes and exhibited his work at the Upstairs Gallery in Toronto.

Reference

National Gallery of Canada Information Form rec'd Mar. 20, 1961

LENNARD, John Barry
b.1937

Born in Barrie, Ontario, he studied at the Ontario College of Art (1956-59) under Jock MacDonald and Alan Collier also at the Art Students' League of New York (1959-61) under Morris Kantor. Lennard is known for his drawings and paintings which he has exhibited at the Ontario Society of Artists Show (1961); Canadian Biennial of Art (1961); Montreal Museum of Fine Arts (c.1963); Art Gallery of Ontario; Hamilton Art Gallery, Ont. (1962); The Winnipeg Show at the Winnipeg Art Gallery (1961); The Pennsylvania Academy of Fine Arts Annual (1964). His first one man show of paintings was held at the Nordness Gallery, New York City, in the spring of 1964. He has been living in New York City temporarily having moved there from Toronto.

References

National Gallery of Canada Information Form rec'd 1962

The Fourth Biennial Exhibition of Canadian Art, 1961 (catalogue), NGC/Queen's Printer, No. 42

John Lennard, Recent Paintings (small catalogue of his first one man show held March 10 – March 28, 1964) Nordness Gallery, 831 Madison Ave., New York 10021, N.Y., U.S.A.

LENNIE, Beatrice (Edith Beatrice Catharine Lennie)
b.1905

Born in Nelson, B.C., she entered the Vancouver School of Art in 1925 where she studied drawing, composition, painting under F.H. Varley, design with J.W.G. Macdonald, costume design with Mrs. Sharland, modelling, anatomy and sculpture under Charles Marega; graduated with her diploma in 1929.[1] Subsequently she took post graduate study at the California School of Fine Arts, San Francisco, in modelling, stone carving, wood sculpture, under Ralph Stackpole, Spencer MacKay, Lee Randolph and Lucien Labouy.[2] She also took private lessons with Harry Tauber in stage design, scenario, puppetry, stage costume; lessons in animal study from Kate A. Smith; landscape and portrait drawing from F.H. Varley.[3] In the years that followed her paintings were exhibited with the Royal Canadian Academy and she gained a reputation for fine theatre design. Sculpture however has been her forte. She exhibited in a solo show at The Gables (Arts & Cultural Centre) on University Boulevard, Vancouver, in 1948.[4] She completed the following commissions: Architectural details, fireplaces for Hotel Vancouver, Van., B.C. (1932); Bronze Dedication Plaque for Pattullo Bridge, New Westminister, B.C. (1937); Bronze Details for Federal Building, Van., B.C. (1938); 12 ft. panel "Ascension" for the Main Lobby of Hotel Vancouver (1939); two sculptured stone panels, 8 x 5 ft.

LENNIE, Beatrice (Edith Beatrice Catharine Lennie) (Cont'd)

each, for the Shaughnessy Military Hospital,[5] Van., B.C., Main Entrance (1940); 17 stone panels of Indian designs for the exterior of the Lipsett Indian Museum, Hastings Park, Van., B.C. (1941); sculptured mural, 20 ft. long by 7 ft. high for The Labor Temple,[6] Van., B.C. (1949); Baptisimal Font for St. John's Anglican Memorial Church,[7] Shaughnessy Heights, also the bell tower, facade and other details for this church (1950); stone carving for the Main Entrance of the Ryerson Memorial Centre[8] on the theme "Suffer little children to come unto Me." which is the inscription on the base of the stone relief carving of Christ and five children of different ages, the figures are life size (1950); free stone relief statue of Hippocrates (father of medicine) in heroic-size, for the Academy of Medicine,[9] Van., B.C. (1951); her sculptural portrait commissions include those of: Col. H.T. Goodland (Victoria, B.C.); Mrs. Moody "Lorraine" (Winnipeg, Man.); G. Aley Wiers (Van., B.C.); Moira Drummond (Montreal, P.Q.) and many others. She also created the Phyllis Schuldt Trophy for the B.C. Musical Festival (Modern Composition Class); Mrs. Stearn Music Trophy (Seattle, Washington) and many other works privately owned. She has exhibited in many group shows and with the Royal Canadian Academy; National Gallery of Canada; Canadian National Exhibition, Tor., Ont.; Montreal Art Association; San Francisco Art Association; North West Artists Association, Seattle Wash.; B.C. Society of Artists at Vancouver, B.C. and has exhibited her Theatre Masks and Theatre Designs at the Picture Loan Society, Tor. (1937); Pacific Drama Festival, Victoria, B.C. (1938); University of B.C., Van. (1939); Canadian Pacific Exhibition, Van. (1939); Univ. of B.C. Van. (1941); and elsewhere. She has taught and lectured with the B.C. College of Art; Director of Children's Saturday Morning Classes at Vancouver Art Gallery (ten years); Special Art Class Crofton House School (seven years); several summers with the Extension Department of UBC in Sculpture, Masks and Theatre Arts, Puppetry; Art Director for films for National War Finance; her art has also been used for charities (esp. her puppets and masks). She was Tour Guide for Wright's Travel Service tour through Florence, Siena, and Rome to show the treasures of Italy to enrich the appreciation of those on tour for the arts and to study first hand the works of masters, old and new (1961,–). Last reported living in West Vancouver.

References

[1] National Gallery of Canada Information Form rec'd 1961, 1950, 1942
[2] Ibid
[3] Ibid
[4] *The Province*, Van., B.C., April 8, 1948 "In The Realm Of Art – Vancouver Sculptor's Work on Display Soon" by Palette
The Vancouver Sun, Van., B.C., May 1, 1948 "Sculptor's Art On Display" By Mildred Valley Thornton
[5] *The Province*, Dec. 21, 1940 "Symbolic Figures To Grace New Hospital"
[6] Ibid, May 14, 1949 "In The Realm Of Art – Labor Temple Mural Symbolizes Industry" by Palette
[7] *CBC Times*, Tor., Ont., July 2, 1950 "The Noted Sculptress"
[8] *The Province*, Nov. 18, 1950 "In The Realm Of Art – City Sculptor's Work Shows Human Aspect" by Palette
[9] Ibid, June 2, 1951 "In The Realm Of Art – Hippocrates Statue Has Simple Majesty" by Palette
see also
The Nelson Daily News, B.C., Feb. 25, 1961 "Miss Beatrice Lennie, Nelson-Born Sculptor, To Conduct Study Tour"
Lions Gate Times, Mar. 3, 1961 "For Camera or Brush – Italian Tour Starts April"

LENT, Dora Geneva

b.1904

Born in Elmvale, Ontario, the daughter of the late W.F.W. Lent, K.C. and Carrie Belyea Lent, she studied from the age of six with various water colour artists; later under Victor Reid; A.C. Leighton, R.B.A.; and Nickola de Grandmaison for work in pastel.[1] In 1933 she had two of her flower studies (water colours) hung at the Ontario Society of Artists Show. Also during the early thirties she made an extensive study of primitive art concentrating on British Columbian Indians. Six of her paintings of ancient tribal dance masks were acquired for the permanent collection of the National Museum of Canada, Ottawa.[2] Subsequently she made "needle-paintings" fashioned from wool of live sheep — to preserve resilience and natural oils of the wool. Pigments in the colouring of the wool were taken from natural sources such as lichens, dogwood, elder, oak galls, mignonette, hollyhock, all yielding their unique colours.[3] In this process she made a special study of natural dyes created by peoples of the world. Describing her work in 1946 the Victoria *Colonist*[4] noted, "Miss Lent's needle pictures are actually masculine and bold, though delicately colored. Her huge needle-painting of Moraine Lake won a special award from the city of Montreal for all Canada. A member of the national needle-work committee of the Canadian Handicraft Guild, she believes in preserving and stimulating all that is best in the national cultures of the myriad groups which make up the Canadian peoples." She made a series of documentary paintings on British Columbia and Alberta Indian life and artifacts which were exhibited in 1962 at the Hudson's Bay Company's Douglas Room in Victoria.[5] Another showing of her work took place at the Banff School of Fine Arts in 1966 when the Victoria *Times*[6] explained, "Miss Lent attempts to tell a story in her paintings, as well as to depict the traits and customs of the ethnic group she is portraying. She explains one painting, one of her works on Eskimo life, as showing, step by step, how igloos are made. Her paintings are done through research, 'study with depth, intensity — with purpose, with a trained and disciplined mind.' " During her career she has written two books: *Needle Point As A Hobby*, 1942; *West of the Mountains*, 1962 (made possible through a Ford Foundation Grant). Most of the research for her last book was done in the British Museum and the Hudson's Bay Company Archives. She was honoured by the nomination of member of the Hudson's Bay Records Society which gives her immediate access to the complete records.

References

[1] Nat. Gal. of Can. Info. Form rec'd May 19, 1933

[2] *The Albertan*, Calgary, Alta., 27 June, 1933 "National Museum Acquires Paintings of Local Artist"

[3] *The Daily Colonist*, Victoria, B.C., Aug. 24, 1946 "Artist, Author and Lecturer Calgary's Geneva Lent Is Here"

[4] Ibid

[5] *The Times*, Victoria, B.C., Aug. 11, 1962

[6] Ibid, July 15, 1966 "Tells World Of 'Canadiana' " by Penny Murphy

see also

The Calgary Herald, Calgary, Alta., Sept. 29, 1942 "Miss Geneva Lent Is Chairman New Arts Group"

LEONARD, John

A Toronto artist noted by the *Globe & Mail* as follows, "John Leonard's work appears simultaneously in three Toronto galleries, a fact which qualifies him for attention. He is a young painter who likes to paint objects, but his work happens to have that blend of paint and photo realism which is shaping up, currently, as a recognizable trend of the Seventies . . . . In Realisms 70 at the Art Gallery of Ontario, Leonard's huge Ruger Single Six in acrylic on canvas stands up better than some of the work there, in finding a relationship between abstraction and description. At Hart House Art Gallery, Leonard's big blowups of contemporary pop faces — the Beatles, Raquel Welch — are allied with objects — the gun again, or a blue Volkswagen. And again there is a coolheaded collaboration between color painting and recognizable objects."

Reference
> *Globe & Mail*, Tor., Ont., Sept 5, 1970 "Young Realist"
> (Leonard exhibited his work as well at the Albert White Gallery, Tor.)

LEONARD, Rose (Mrs. R.D. Davies)

Born on a farm near St. Paul, Alberta, she married in the early 1940's during the war and was later faced with supporting her small son and herself on her own. She worked at a number of jobs which included display advertising and began to sell paintings she did in her spare time. She remarried in the 1950's and was able to give up her advertising job and devote her full time to painting and has achieved remarkable results in landscapes, portraits, flower studies and other subjects. She is represented in the collections of Her Majesty Queen Elizabeth and Lady Churchill and in many homes in Edmonton, Vancouver, Toronto, New York, San Francisco, Los Angeles and Chicago. For a Centennial project she completed twelve paintings of Canadian Provincial Flowers of which ten were reproduced on Austin-Marshall Hasti-Notes, a Toronto firm which has been reproducing her work on Christmas Cards and Hasti-Notes for over fifteen years. She works in the media of pastels, oils and water colours. She lives in Edmonton, Alberta.

Reference
> *Rose Leonard* (brochure) C.1969 (reproductions of her work including a photo of her beside one of her paintings)

LEONARD, Ted (Reginald Haviland Ted Leonard)

Originally from Toronto, he graduated as a commercial artist in the early 1930's during the depression. He found it impossible to make a living from his art training during this difficult period and for many years he was a reporter and news photographer for *The Toronto Star* covering events in a large part of southern Ontario. About 1963 he left his reporting job to go into full time writing of fiction books but he turned to marine painting after he had settled in his new bungalow on the Old Homestead Road at Keswick, Ontario, on the southern shore of Lake Simcoe. In 1966 his painting of the yacht "Skirl" caught the attention of officials of the Shipbuilding Branch, Department of Transport, Ottawa, and subsequently he

LEONARD, Ted (Reginald Haviland Ted Leonard (Cont'd)

received his first commission from the Canadian government. Since that time he has painted scores of Department of Transport ships including oceanographic-weatherships, ice breakers, search and rescue vessels, a sounding vessel and other Canadian Coast Guard Ships. His finished paintings hang in Canadian government buildings in Ottawa. A few of his ship paintings include: CCGS "Vancouver"; CCGS "Quadra"; CCGS "Louis S. St. Laurent"; CCGS "John A. MacDonald"; CCGS "Robert Foulis"; CCGS "Norman McLeod Rogers"; CCGS "Tracy" and others including C.N.R. passenger vessels. Ted Leonard is known for his high degree of accuracy in recording details in his marine art. He is the first marine artist to be elected to the 8,000 member world-wide Society of Naval Architects and Marine Engineers. His membership was proposed to this Society by the Department of Transport shipbuilding officials as follows, "on the basis that his work accurately and dramatically depicts the final visual stage of naval architect's plans and designs which is the vessel itself".

References
The Era, Newmarket, Ont., June 28, 1967 "A Marine Artist From Keswick – Linked With Canada's Present"

Ibid, Feb. 28, 1968 "Artist honored"

Lake Simcoe Advocate, West, Sutton, Ont., Feb. 11, 1970 "Keswick Artist Paints Icebreaker"

LEONARD, Vera
b.1927

Born in Sydney, Nova Scotia, she studied under Ruth Wainwright at Halifax, N.S., and Gentile Tondino at the N.S. School of Community Arts at Tatamagouche. She is a member of the Nova Scotia Society of Artists and has exhibited her realistic and semi abstract oils with this Society. She lives in Halifax.

Source
Document from artist

LE PAGE, Denis

Born in Vancouver, B.C., he studied at the Vancouver School of Art under Gordon A. Smith, Bruno Bobak and Jack Shadbolt (1955-59) and received an Emily Carr and a Leon Koerner Foundation Award in 1959. He exhibited his works in the North West Show, Seattle, Washington, also in 1959, and the following year at the Spring Show of the Montreal Museum of Fine Arts and the Winnipeg Show. He travelled throughout the United States and much of Europe before settling in London, England, for four years (1961-65). Returning to Canada he has been living in Toronto and has exhibited his work at the Art Gallery of Ontario (1968); the Spring Show, Kingston, Ont. (1969); Color and Form Exhibition, Hart House, Toronto (1969). In 1969 a one man show of his work was held at the Wells Gallery, Ottawa, when Barry F. Walsh in his foreword to the exhibition catalogue stated, "He is drawn to subjects that embody movement, life, inherent power, 'dynamis'. But the romantic in him remains strong and sets his limits. Within these bounds his

LE PAGE, Denis (Cont'd)

choice is wide, allowing him to give his chosen subjects the special attention that comes from love and admiration. He sees the signs, on road and street, sings the spirit of open highway . . . . Le Page shows us our cult images and their trappings, points the harmonies of their forms and gives the icons of locomotion to radiate their own environment." W.Q. Ketchum viewing this show noted, "Introduced to gallery-goers as 'High-Speed Signals' the works all are interrelated. The exhibiting artist displays what he terms sculpture bas-relief cars. Three were on view. The work is beautifully integrated and reveals the artist's sense of color and his imaginative qualities." Le Page is represented in the permanent collections of the Sarnia Public Library and Art Gallery, and the Agnes Etherington Art Centre, Queen's University, Kingston, Ontario.

References

Catalogue – *High-Speed Signals, Denis Lepage*, September 12-27, 1969, The Wells Gallery, Ottawa "Denis Le Page" by Barry F. Walsh (biography and list of works included)

The Ottawa Journal, Sept. 12, 1969 "One-Man Show Of Interest To Racing Buffs" by W.Q. Ketchum

see also

Le Droit, Ottawa, Sept. 13, 1969 (photo of artist and his work, also caption).

LE PAGE, Marc
b. (c) 1947

A Montreal artist who graduated from the Ecole des Beaux-Arts of that city in design and graphic communications who has recently introduced murals of his creation in washable polymer paints. He also makes them in three dimension but feels they ought not to be called murals but rather environmental paintings. Cynthia Gunn of *The Montreal Star* described them as follows, "Although Marc's paintings are his own style, he believes they should go with a client's furniture and room arrangement. So, when he receives a commission, he offers several possible designs and then consults with the client. His style tends toward shape and color rather than intricate naturalistic presentations. It is modern in mood, but depending on the subject can also be old worldly or avant garde."

Reference

The Montreal Star, Aug. 25, 1970, "Inside/Outside – Walls are made for painting on . . . aren't they? " by Cynthia Gunn

---

LEQUESNE, Donald Corbel
b.1932

Born in Montreal, P.Q., he lived for a time in Gaspé and in northern Quebec near the Labrador border. He studied at Mount Allison University under Lawren P. Harris and Edward Pulford and graduated with his Bachelor of Fine Arts.[1] He travelled in Europe for a year then worked a year in display with the Montreal branch of Simpson's.[2] He moved to Toronto where he taught for five years in secondary schools as well as instructing three summers at the Ontario College of Art.[3] Subsequently he took his master's degree from the University of Georgia before joining the staff of the Brandon College, Manitoba. There he held a one man

LEQUESNE, Donald Corbel (Cont'd)

show at the Music and Fine Arts building in 1965 where his work was well received for its essential honesty. Kaye Rowe[4] of *The Brandon Sun* noted, "His landscapes and old building studies will win wide approval in the evocation of mood and a kind of emotional vibrancy. Fairly realistic, the study of a barn at the Douglas-Shilo turn-off standing lone amid the dun-colored hummocky ground of late fall. Mr. LeQuesne manages to speak the language of the prairie – of great space, the threat of winter, the isolation of building, of spirit. Nothing fancy or pretty or Tretchicoff – but honest! " This showing consisted of twenty pieces including painting (oils and Polymer acrylic paint), etchings and drawings. LeQuesne moved to the Toronto area where he is presently living. He was guest lecturer on design at the three-day weavers' workshop held at the Fred Landon Library, London, Ontario, under the sponsorship of the London District Weavers in co-operation with the community program branch of the Ontario Department of Education.[5]

References
   [1] National Gallery of Canada Information Form rec'd April 5, 1954
   [2] *The Brandon Sun*, Friday, April 23, 1965 "City Artist Plans One-Man Show" by Kaye Rowe
   [3] Ibid
   [4] Ibid
   [5] *The London Evening Free Press*, London, Ont., Feb. 27, 1968 "Artist-lecturer at weavers' workshop teaches students to use originality" by George Blumson

LERCH, Tosca

Born in Bohemia, Czechoslovakia, she came to Canada in 1939 and subsequently studied with Margaretta Stevens, Dorothy Stevens, Aba Bayefsky, Jas. Williamson, Hayward Veal (from Pitman College of Art, London, Eng.) and Mashel Teitelbaum of the New School, Toronto. *The Forest Hill Journal* described her work as follows, "The paintings of Tosca Lerch are abstract landscape studies. Mood of seasons and an impassioned use of personal colour are trade-marks of this gifted painter. Over a period of years, she has developed from the representational studies of flowers and nature to the joyous tone poems on the Canadian Seasons." She has exhibited her work at the East York Public Library, the Canadian National Exhibition, the Pollock Gallery, and Eaton's Fine Art Gallery.

Reference
   Forest Hill Journal, Tor., Ont. "East York Public Library Exhibits The Fine Paintings Of Tosca Lerch"

LEROUX-GUILLAUME, Janine
b.1927

Born at St. Hermas, County of Deux-Montagnes, P.Q., she studied engraving at the School of Graphic Arts in Montreal and at the Ecole des Beaux Arts under Madame Charlebois and Albert Dumouchel (graduated from the Beaux-Arts, 1954); travelled in Europe and studied at the Atelier Lacourière in Paris in 1959.[1] Exhibited at Ljubljana, Yugoslavia, in 1960 where she was one of five Canadian engravers to

LEROUX-GUILLAUME, Janine (Cont'd)

have her work chosen for the show. By 1966 she had gained an enviable reputation as evidenced by the following review in the Montreal *Gazette*[2], "It is always a sunny day in the life of an art critic when a visit to an exhibition amounts to an encounter that goes to the heart. One is all too rarely moved to speak in such terms, having almost forgotten that it is one of art's vital functions to stir the emotions on the most intimate non-verbal level. The art of Janine Leroux-Guillaume does just that . . . . Janine Leroux-Guillaume is a printmaker of admirable skills in the intricate traditions of her craft, and it is reassuring to know that she is applying her talents as an educator in addition to building up an imaginative oeuvre of her own . . . . The artist is especially fond of the soft, ungraded half-tones achieved by the aquatint, using the textured ground of varied grain in combination with the dry point or burin. But there are a few pure aquatints in the show also, in which she may have interrupted the etching process and proceeded by stopping out some areas before returning her plate to the acids for more action. In some of her aquatints she achieves effects as soft as Goya's." She has exhibited her work at the Montreal Museum of Fine Arts; the Canadian Society of Painters Etchers and Engravers, also at Winnipeg, Hamilton, and Toronto. She has illustrated books of poetry. In 1964 she received a scholarship from the Department of Education of Quebec. Her engravings are in the following collections: McMaster University (Hamilton, Ont.); Museum of Contemporary Art (Montreal) and the National Gallery of Canada (Ottawa). She has been teaching plastic arts for the Catholic School Commission for a number of years also engraving at the Ecole des Beaux-Arts, Montreal. Her aquatint "Le Canoe blessé" was exhibited at Canadian Water Colours, Drawings and Prints, 1966.[3]

References

[1] National Gallery of Canada Information Form rec'd Oct. 31, 1965

[2] *The Gazette*, Mtl., P.Q., Oct. 29, 1966 "Saluting A Fine Printmaker"

[3] *Canadian Water Colours, Drawings and Prints, 1966*, NGC/Queen's Printer, Cat. No. 87

see also
Watchman, Lachute, P.Q., June 20, 1957 "Young Lady Artist Proves Specialist In Engraving"

Ibid, April 18, 1957, "Former Lachute Artist Honored In 'One-Man' Exhibit"

Le Devoir, Mtl., P.Q., 18 April, 1964

La Presse, Mtl., P.Q., Oct. 21, 1966 "Exposition au Centre d'art"

L'Argenteuil, Lachute, P.Q., Mar. 19, 1969 "Expositions au Centre d'Art"

LEROY, Hugh Alexander

b.1939

Born in Montreal, P.Q., he studied under Arthur Lismer at the School of Art and Design of the Montreal Museum of Fine Arts, also under Arthur Pinsky at the Sir George Williams University art school.[1] His earlier sculpture was not objective in the sense that he created a figure, a head, a bust, an animal but rather natural shapes he would only slightly alter so that the viewer could imagine an object, or a person. Robert Ayre[2] explains this further while reviewing Leroy's 1963 exhibit at the Waddington Galleries, as follows, "His concepts are inspired by an appreciation of natural organic shapes and a delightful wit. He can take, the stone, as you might take driftwood, see something in it, and with just a touch here and there, make something of it, called, perhaps, 'Bone and Flesh,' or 'Torso — Inside, Outside' —

and it almost does seem to turn itself inside out, like some boneless sea creature. He can on the other hand, construct a 'Sun God' in geometrical terms. This, and the 'King', which ends in the prong of the crown, are chiselled out of the grey stone, unpolished, but most of his pieces are of the deep and lustrous green. And it might be said here that they owe nothing whatever to the Eskimos." By 1967 he was experimenting with shapes under stress as he himself explains during a taped interview with Dorothy Cameron,[3] "I am really a carpenter at heart, except that I don't enjoy making doors or windows; I just enjoy making things, useless things, which happen now to fit into a social scheme or way of life called 'contemporary art' by our fickle culture assessors. That is why I am against intellectualizing about art, especially about minimal art or sculpture, where such an elaborate framework of justification is demanded . . . I began a private search for fundamental truth. Just as (Arthur) Miller (referring to Miller's play *Death of a Salesman*) understood humanity, I wanted to investigate and understand the elements of sculpture . . . . My new consciousness led me to the theory of 'form-resulting-from-force', which introduced me to the idea of the *rational object*; . . . . " Using his work "Four Elements Column" as an example he continued,"'Four Elements Column' illustrates this theory of form-resulting-from-force. The first 'element' is the cylinder itself; the second is a perpendicular slit; the third is compression, and the fourth is a twist. Because I was disciplined throughout the making of this piece by the natural and inevitable results of force, I could push the twist no further without distortion . . . . " In 1969 he exhibited his recent work at the Galerie Godard Lefort, Montreal, when Patricia Railing[4] reviewed the showing — of which the following are review excerpts, "In reaching towards a new simplicity, LeRoy pursues his seeming fascination with the cylindrical form, and uses it in four ways: he also turns to natural wood and 'intuites' proportions. In every case, the shapes are arbitrary in size and could go on longer or higher. It is important, however, that each of the four is conceived as 'man-sized,' regardless of the fact that the shapes are basic to our world of engineering and construction and consequently, usually recognized as colossal. LeRoy's objects may be monumental, but they are not colossal . . . . This fourth one-man show of the objects of Hugh LeRoy reveals within the range of the total production (minus one) of a year, the changes and development towards a one-element concern, a 'concern with the closeness of (the artist's) vision with that of others.' This concern is especially relevant in regard to the last wood pieces. They all possess the quality of colour which penetrates and is not additive, but is highly nuanced due to wood's natural variety and harmony. Further, they possess the rigidity of one shape, one form that has no ending. This search for the infinite possibilities . . . in a simple object reflects LeRoy's profound desire to give value to the ordinary aspects visible to us all, to the ordinary elements which make up our ordinary lives." In 1967 LeRoy was appointed Dean of the School of Art and Design of the Montreal Museum of Fine Arts and lectures in fine arts at Sir George Williams University. He is represented in the permanent collection of Sir George Williams University; The Canada Council; The Museum of Contemporary Art of Montreal and the Ontario Arts Council. He was awarded grants from the Canada Council in 1966 and 1967, and received first prize in the Centennial Commission Exhibition "Perspective '67". Lives in Montreal.

References
[1] National Gallery of Canada Information Form rec'd April 20, 1967
[2] *The Montreal Star*, Mtl., P.Q., June 15, 1963 "Fun With Soapstone" by Robert Ayre

LEROY, Hugh Alexander (Cont'd)

[3]*Sculpture '67* (catalogue) An open-air exhibition of Canadian Sculpture presented by the National Gallery of Canada as part of its Centennial program at the City Hall of Toronto, Summer, 1967, Coordination and Catalogue by Dorothy Cameron, P.8, 9

[4]*Artscanada*, August, 1969 No. 134/135 "Exhibition Reviews Montreal, Hugh LeRoy, Galerie Godard Lefort, May-June, 1969" by Patricia Railing

see also
École de Montréal by Guy Robert, Éditions Du Centre De Psychologie Et De Pédagogie, Montreal, P.Q., 1964, P.107, 120, 121

Sir George Williams University Collection of Art (Catalogue) c.1969

The Canada Council Collection — A travelling exhibition of the National Gallery of Canada, Ottawa, 1969 (catalogue)

Canadian Art Today, Editor, William Townsend, 1970, Studio International, London, England, P.97

La Presse, Mtl., P.Q., June 15, 1963 "hugh leroy"

The Gazette, Mtl., P.Q., "Hugh LeRoy Sculptures" by Dorothy Pfeiffer

Ibid, Feb. 26, 1966 "Stark And Symmetrical Sculpture" by Susan Altschul

La Presse, Mtl., P.Q., May 31, 1969 "Sculptures non sculptées — A la Galerie Godard Lefort; sculptures de Hugh Leroy"

The Montreal Star, Mar. 21, 1970 "The impossible dream" by Arthur Bardo

La Presse, Mtl., P.Q., Sept. 3, 1970 "La 'Colonne à quatro éléments' est installée"

LESLIE, Bailey (Mrs.)

b.1904

Born in Lodz, Poland, she came to Canada with her parents in 1910 and they settled at Cobalt, Ontario. She studied pottery at the Central Technical School in Toronto under Mrs. Peter Haworth while she also attended the University of Toronto where she graduated with her B.A. in 1926. She took her M.A. in 1928, trained at St. George's Nursery School and in 1940 published the paper, *Clays for Young Children in a Progressive School*. She joined the staff of Windy Ridge Progressive School where for fifteen years she was in charge of clay classes for children. In 1945 she attended summer school at Alfred, N.Y., where she worked with stoneware and porcelain. She became a founding member of the Canadian Guild of Potters and served as its president, twice, and was on the executive and held other offices until 1967. She has exhibited her pottery with the Canadian Guild of Potters Biennials and received awards for stoneware and porcelain in 1957, 1959, 1961, 1963, and 1965. She also won Honorable Mention in the Ceramic National, Syracuse, N.Y. (1952); Silver Medal, International Ceramic, Prague (1962); Silver Medal for glaze effects, International Ceramic, Geneva (1965). She has also exhibited with the Canadian Handicraft Society in Toronto, Montreal; Stratford Festival; Smithsonian Inst., Wash., D.C.; Brussels World's Fair (1958); Expo '67, and at many other showings and occasions. She is represented in the permanent collection of the Canadian Handicraft Guild, Montreal; Arana Museum, Geneva, Switzerland; Museum of the Americas, Madrid, Spain. Lives in Toronto. Married Samuel William Leslie, D.D.S., M.D., F.I.C.D., 1926, two sons.

References

Nat. Gal. of Can. Info. Form rec'd July 13, 1967
The Five Potters (Two films shown on C.B.C.)

L'ESPÉRANCE, Alphonse

b.1914

Born in Montreal, he began his studies in that city at the Ecole des Beaux-Arts under Edmond Dyonnet and others. About 1934 he travelled to Italy where he studied at the Royal Academy of Rome under De Simoni, Mizzana and Ridolfi. After a stay of ten years he returned to Canada and has completed commissions for portraits of celebrated and historic personnages, several murals for churches and has restored several precious works of art. He is also known for his still lifes, landscapes, nudes. His portraits are mostly of children, adolescents and old men of which the eyes are particularly expressive. He does not attach himself to any school, although the form of his art is inspired by both impressionism and expressionism. He has exhibited his work in Quebec at Sherbrooke, St. Jérome, Le Reginal-Chicoutimi, Three Rivers and elsewhere. His paintings vary in size from 12" x 18" to 4 x 6 ft.

References

Le Soleil, Que., P.Q., 30 May, 1964 "Chez Les Hospitalières"
Ibid, 5 Sept., 1964 "Nouvelle peinture de la vénérable Catherine de Saint-Augustin'"
Courrier du Sud, Longueuil, P.Q., Apr. 6, 1966 "Succès d'un artiste de chez-nous Alphonse Lespérance" par Rachel Jodoin
Le Nouvelliste, Trois Rivières, P.Q., Apr. 23, 1966 "Le peintre Lespérance transmet au portrait l'image exacte de son sujet" par Renée Lecoursière
La Tribune, Sherbrooke, P.Q., April 19, 1968 "Exposition de peintures au domaine Howard"
L'Echo du Nord, St. Jerome, P.Q., May 8, 1968 "Un Jovitois expose"
La Tribune, Sherbrooke, P.Q., April 22, 1968 "Une oeuvre a la fois secrète et sereine! "

LESTER, Barbara (Mrs.)

An artist from Dartmouth, N.S., who favours landscapes, but also paints flower studies, portraits and still lifes. She works mainly in oils but also uses polymer tempera and egg tempera. Her paintings have been exhibited in the Chenil Galleries, Chelsea, London, Eng.; Doon School of Fine Arts annuals; Annual Canadian National Exposition, Quebec City; The Maritime Art Association annuals; Beaverbrook Gallery, Fred., N.B.; The Tatamagouche Festival Award Show and the Art Instruction Schools Annual International Competition for students and professionals in Minneapolis, Minn., U.S.A., where she won first prize in oil painting in 1963 and 1964. She also conducts classes at the Dartmouth Y.M.C.A. and in her own studio at Whyduholme Avenue in Dartmouth.

References

Free Press, Dartmouth, N.S., Thurs. March 18, 1965
Halifax Mail-Star, Halifax, N.S., Mar. 25, 1965 "Art Display Draws Large Attendance" by Greg Cook

---

LETARTE, Jean Paul

b.1933

Born in Montreal, P.Q., he studied under Paul-Emile Borduas at Beloeil; the Ecole des Beaux-Arts, Quebec, under Jean Dallaire, Benoit East, Rene Thibault, Jean-Paul

LETARTE, Jean Paul (Cont'd)

Lemieux; under J. Simard, Charpentier, Marcotte in Montreal. In 1953 he participated in the group show at the Quebec Provincial Museum, and in 1954 at the Spring Show of the Montreal Museum of Fine Arts, Montreal. A man of many interests he has been set designer for T.V.; painter; engraver; singer; guitarist; composer; film maker and even a radar technician with the Reserve R.C.A.F. He received a Canada Council Award and lived two-and-a-half years in Paris where he worked in different film studios, did several animated films including "Smaragdin" which won two mentions (one at Annecy, the other at Karlovy-Vary, Czechoslovakia); gave two concerts at the famous Pleyel Salon in Paris; designed draperies. His wife Lucille helps him in his studio. He studied film research and animation in Europe. He represented Canada at Annecy and Karlovy Vary Festival, Czechoslovakia in 1958. He has worked as director in T.V. for Radio Canada for over seven years and held his first one man show at Galerie du Gobelet, Montreal in 1968.

References

National Gallery of Canada Information Form rec'd April 8, 1954
Le Nouveau Journal, Mtl., P.Q., April 7, 1962 "Jean Letarte – Un cinéaste hors-carde et, peut-être, hors pair" par Michel Brule
Progrès de Villeray, Mtl., P.Q., Nov. 27, 1968 "Jean Letarte expose à la Galerie du Gobelet"

LETELLIER, André

b. (c) 1944

An Ottawa artist who studied under Roger Larivière and is known for his sculpture which has been described as audacious, clean and sober. He admires the work of Rodin although he himself works in the abstract showing only the realistic outline of his subject. For example his "Christ à la croix" for Saint-Pius X Church in Ottawa, is a figure of Christ composed of a series of wires which one can see through, although its outline is realistic and beautifully executed. He has done other commissions including decorations for churches. In 1965 his paintings of figures, portraits and scenes were shown at St. Pius X. Another showing of his work took place at Britannia Pavilion during the Eighth Ottawa Summer Festival. In 1966 he held his first one man show at the Galerie de la Côte-de-Sable, Nelson Street, Ottawa.

References

The Ottawa Citizen, Ottawa, Ont., Mar. 17, 1965 "Art exhibition"
Le Droit, Ottawa, Ont., Nov. 16, 1965 "La Vie Artistique – Le rideau se lève . . . " par Edgar Demers
Ibid, June 25, 1966 "André Letellier exposera ses sculptures"
Ibid, June 28, 1966 "Les oeuvres de Letellier reflètent la sincérité" par Jean-Jacques Fleury

LETENDRE, Rita

b.1929

Born in Drummondville, Quebec, of Iroquois descent, her interest in art began about the age of fifteen through her discovery of Watteau and Grunewald.[1] Partly self taught she entered the Ecole des Beaux-Arts, Montreal, where she studied for a year and a half.[2] But in art school she had difficulty finding herself as a painter and for this reason she left the school and began a search for her identity. During

LETENDRE, Rita (Cont'd)

her study at the Beaux-Arts, Borduas, Mousseau, and Ferron were in the midst of their revolution when they distributed pamphlets announcing where their paintings could be seen. It was at these stimulating exhibitions that Miss Letendre found the possibilities of her own painting. She explained in *The Montrealer*[3] "Then we discovered our contemporaries. People with whom we would develop our talents. For me there was Ulysse Comptois . . . Gilles Groux, the filmmaker, among others. I was convinced that I was going to revolutionize the universe, and all my friends thought the same about themselves. The problem was to find someplace to exhibit. We used to visit each other's studios and compare notes, but the galleries kept their doors closed to all but sure moneymakers." In 1952 and 1953 she exhibited with the automatistes and in 1955 again with this group under the title "Espace 1955" at the Montreal Museum of Fine Arts. In 1956 she shared a studio with Comptois, painter and sculptor, and they and others were the subject of an article in *Weekend Magazine*[4] on non-objective painters of Montreal. In 1957 her works were shown at the Parma Gallery, New York City, and in 1959 again in New York at Canada House with the exhibition "Aspects of Canadian Painting", then in Montreal at the Denyse Delrue Gallery.[5] In 1959 her work was included in The Third Biennial Exhibition of Canadian Art.[6] This was followed in 1960 by another important event the "Non-Figurative Artists of Montreal" a show organized by the National Gallery of Canada and put on the road to various centres across Canada. For the exhibition a catalogue was made by the Gallery with a short biography and photograph of each artist. It contributed much to the awareness of the public to this new movement and to the personal identity of its members.[7] Miss Letendre's paintings then appeared in three successive Spring Shows at the Montreal Museum of Fine Arts (1960, 1961, 1962). She won the Young Painters Prize at Montreal (1959) and the Rodolphe de Repentigny Prize in Montreal (1960) and the Province of Quebec Award, Quebec City (1962). Her solo show at the Here and Now Gallery in Toronto was not as enthusiastically accepted as had been her individual works because of the style which Robert Fulford[8] described, " . . . Characterized by rough, wide strokes, heavily encrusted paint and unsubtle color has in many places fallen on bad times . . . The approach, it would seem, is wearing out. But the fact that there is still enormous life in it is demonstrated decisively by Rita Letendre, the Montreal artist, in her first local one-woman show, at the Here and Now Gallery. Miss Letendre works in the roughest, widest of strokes, she builds up the paint in thick crusts and her color is often used violently. But in her work, these commonplaces of the 1950s and 1960s are assimilated into an intense personal vision. She rises beyond her earlier influences . . . . 'Victoire,' the largest picture in the exhibition, is also the *pièce de résistance* . . . . The brutal strokes, building up in thick horizontal waves of paint, and the blunt composition (layers, from top to bottom, of red, black, white, black again, then red again, all apparently threatening to consume each other) work together perfectly as an expression of an intransigent and genuinely original personality. (Like so many other good recent pictures, 'Victoire' has gone into the Waxer collection, which is becoming a definite record of Canadian artistic excellence in this period.)" Later in 1962 she showed her work jointly with Comtois at the Montreal Museum of Fine Arts and the show was reviewed by Guy Viau[9] in *Canadian Art*. She also participated in the exhibition "Twenty-Five years of painting in French Canada" shown at Spoleto, Italy, also British Commonwealth Travelling Show "Contemporary Canadian Art". A special issue of *Canadian Art* (No. 78) brought before the public a survey of the

LETENDRE, Rita (Cont'd)

work of 21 Canadian artists in which Miss Letendre's work was discussed by Guy Viau[10] and a large photo by Tess Boudreau of Miss Letendre standing before one of her sizable canvases as well as reproductions of two other works accompanied the article. Ulysse Comtois[11] was a subject also in this issue with four photos accompanying the article written by Guy Viau. In 1962 Rita Letendre received a travelling grant from the Canada Council and went to Paris, also Italy and Israel with side trips to Spain, Belgium and Germany. Returning home in 1963 she exhibited the fruits of her travels at Galerie Camille Hebert and the show was reviewed by Robert Ayre.[12] Her home-coming was also noted by the following publications and others: *Le Quartier Latin; The Montreal Star*; and *Canada Month*.[13] Her oil on canvas "Reflêt d'août" was exhibited at the 5th Biennial Exhibition of Canadian Painting, 1963,[14] and her "Terra Feconde" in the 84th Annual Exhibition of the Royal Canadian Academy in 1964.[15] In '64 Guy Robert's fine book *École de Montréal* was published in which he noted her work under "The Lyrical Abstract" as having the mixture of elements of the fiery, the graceful, the crude and the supple, the trenchant and the nuance (see P. 29 for this passage and P. 88, 89 for her work). She held a solo exhibit of her work in Paris at Galerie Arnaud in 1964 and the following year she painted a 21 by 24 ft. Epoxy mural on the wall of Long Beach State College as her contribution to the International Symposium of Sculpture which her sculptor husband, Kosso Eloul, was attending. This mural entitled "Sunforce" required a special request to the Flex-Coat Corporation, at Paramount, California, for two new products, a brilliant cadmium yellow and a matte varnish. Describing the mural Elise Emery[16] in a press release for the Symposium, noted, "In the painting, vivid yellow areas pierce and burst against a black background. Quoting Miss Letendre, she went on, 'The conception is mass and force in action, provoking new, continuous action — before, now and after action. The force of life is marvelous to me. We see the same force in the sea, the sun, all around us. It is the same strength that makes human beings dream — to want to go to the moon — to accomplish the impossible.' " While in California she was Guest Printer at the Tamarind Lithography Workshop in Los Angeles, and the following year Guest Printer at Gemini Ltd., in the same city. In 1966 she held a solo exhibit at Galerie Agnes Lefort and her show was reviewed by Michelle Tisseyre of the *Photo-Journal*, Anne Gilbert of *L'Information Médicale et Paramédicale*, J.B. of *Le Devoir*.[17] In 1967 she exhibited 21 of her prints at Gallery Pascal, actually serigraphs based on a theme "Un Carnet de Voyage". In 1969 she exhibited jointly with her husband Kosso Eloul at Galerie Sherbrooke when Irene Heywood[18] of *The Gazette* described her painting as follows, "In Letendre's painting sharp speeding darts of color angle across the canvas omitting rays which held the sensation of speed. Her involvement with natural forces is felt before we see titles such as 'Northern Light' and 'Sun Song.' In 'Sunburst' the angles push toward what seems to be a natural horizon. But only in 'Infinite' do the angles meet exactly. In some works these lines curve, as nature curves the straight, in many they seem to miss as if by accident." Gilles Henault[19] reviewed this show as well in *Arts/canada*. By 1970 she had collected the following additional honours: Canada Council Grant (1963); Province of Quebec Arts Council Grant (1967); Artists Choice (Prize for Painting), Toronto, 1968; Prize for Prints, Ladies Committee Show, Ottawa (1968); The Purchase Award of the President's Committee of the Robert McLaughlin Gallery at the 98th Annual Open Exhibition of the Ontario Society of Artists (1970) for her 'Sun Mist"; a painting chosen for

LETENDRE, Rita (Cont'd)

exhibit at Expo '70, Osaka, Japan. Her solo exhibit at Roberts Gallery, Toronto, during March, 1970, was well received by Kay Kritzwiser of *The Globe*, and Bernadette Andrews of *The Toronto Telegram*. One of her large paintings of this period "Lode Star 1970" (12 ft. by 9 ft.) was too large for the Roberts Gallery but was reproduced on the exhibition invitation card in beautiful colour with the artist standing in front of her work. The painting was kept in her apartment which has a high ceiling. Describing this work Kay Kritzwiser noted, "The moment the door swings open on the penthouse apartment . . . an outerworldly thing happens. A comet of light speeds your eye upward, out through the slanting glass roof and into the black infinity above. This is what Lode Star 1970 does — . . . which spells out the major theme of Miss Letendre's exhibition at Roberts Gallery . . . ." She is represented in the following collections: Montreal Museum of Fine Arts; Quebec Provincial Museum; Vancouver Art Gallery; Department of External Affairs (Ottawa); Speed Museum, Kentucky, U.S.A.; Museum of Contemporary Art, Montreal; Sir George Williams University, Montreal; Long Beach Museum of Fine Arts, Calif.; Art Gallery of Ontario; Brandeis University Museum of Art; Toronto Dominion Bank (Tor.); Canadian Industries Ltd., Montreal; Quebec House, Paris; Northern Gas Company, Toronto, and private collections of Hon. Robert Macauley (Tor.); Wilson G. McConnell (Tor.); Guy Robert (Mtl.); Mr. & Mrs. Percy Waxer (Tor.) and many others.

References

[1] Document from artist, also NGC Info. Form rec'd 1962

[2] Ibid

[3] *Montrealer*, Mtl, P.Q. January, 1962

[4] *Weekend Magazine*, Mtl., P.Q., Vol. 6, No. 36, 1956 "Their Objective Is Non-Objective" P. 15

[5] *Le Devoir*, Mtl., P.Q., Nov. 2, 1959 "Rita Letendre à la galerie Delrue"

[6] *The Third Biennial Exhibition of Canadian Art, 1959*, NGC

[7] *The Non-Figurative Artists' Association of Montreal* (catalogue) December, 1960, NGC/ Queen's Printer.

[8] *The Toronto Star*, Mar. 24, 1962 "World Of Art — Letendre" by Robert Fulford

[9] *Canadian Art*, Vol. 19, No. 1, No. 77 (1962) "Reviews" P. 11 "Rita Letendre et Ulysse Comtois à la galerie Norton, Musée des Beaux-Arts de Montréal" par Guy Viau

[10] Ibid, Vol. 19, No. 2 (No. 78) "Rita Letendre" par Guy Viau, P. 138, 139

[11] Ibid, Vol. 19, No. 2, P. 116, 117

[12] *The Toronto Star*, Nov. 16, 1963 "Home Thoughts From Abroad" by Robert Ayre

[13] *Le Quartier Latin*, Mtl., P.Q., 21 Nov., 1963 "Rita Letendre Expose"

The Montreal Star, Nov. 25, 1963 "Widening of Horizons Chief Gain for Painter In Europe" by Laureen Hicks

Canada Month, Guelph, Ont., February, 1964

[14] *5th Biennial Exhibition of Canadian Painting*, 1963 (catalogue)

[15] 84th Annual Exhibition, R.C.A. 1964 (catalogue)

[16] Release from California State College, Long Beach, for the Internat. Sculpture Symposium, Aug. 14, 1965 "Rita Letendre's Art Far From Static — Walk Into Her Painting" by Elise Emery

[17] *Le Devoir*, Mtl., P.Q., Oct. 11, 1966 "Rita Letendre: 'J'enseignerai la Vie' " par J.B.

Photo-Journal, Mtl., P.Q., Oct. 12, 1966 "le billet de michelle tisseyre — Une Rita Letendre toute transformée"

L'Information Médicale et Paramédicale, Mtl., P.Q., Oct. 18, 1966 "Entretiens Sur L'Art Moderne" par Anne Gilbert

[18] *The Gazette*, Mtl., P.Q., Oct. 18, 1969 "Letendre, Kosso are compared" by Irene Heywood

[19] *Arts/canada*, December, 1969 No. 138/139 "Rita Letendre and Kosso, Galerie Sherbrooke, Montreal, September-October, 1969" by Gilles Hénault P.64

LETENDRE, Rita (Cont'd)

see also
Ecole de Montréal by Guy Robert, Editions Du Centre De Psychologie Et De Pédagogie, Mtl., P.Q. 1964

Painting In Canada/A History by J. Russell Harper, Tor., 1966, P.385

Vie Des Arts, No. 44, Autumn, 1966 "Génération, 1950-1960" par Guy Robert P.43

Ibid, Winter 1969-1970 "Rita Letendre" par Claude-Lyse Gagnon, P.57

Great Canadian Painting by Elizabeth Kilbourn, Frank Newfeld; text by Ken Lefolii Research Wm. Kilbourn, Marjorie Harris, Sandra Scott, P.103

Sir George Williams University Collection of Art (catalogue) P. 124, 125, 126

Seventh Biennial of Canadian Painting (catalogue), 1968, NGC, Ottawa, P.49, 51

90th Annual Exhibition, 1970, Royal Canadian Academy of Arts, Cat. No. 44

Le Nouveau Journal, Mtl., P.Q., Oct. 28, 1961 "Peinture Fraiche" par Jean Sarrazin

Ibid, Nov. 6, 1961 "A la Galerie XII du Musée Rita Letendre: prête . . . " par Jean Sarrazin

Perspectives, No. 19, 12 May, 1962 "Inventer des formes et des couleurs! Chez Rita Letendre, c'est ainsi que s'écrit l'histoire" par Guy Fournier

Photo-Journal, Mtl., P.Q., Jan. 19, 1963 "Quatre femmes peintres (3) "J'aime les enfants, mais j'y . . . . " par Guy Robert

La Presse, Mtl., P.Q., Nov. 7, 1963 "Rita Letendre retour d'Europe . . . . " par Madeleine Doyon

The Toronto Star, Nov. 16, 1963 "Home Thoughts From Abroad" by Robert Ayre

La Presse, Mtl., P.Q. Oct. 11, 1969 "Arts Plastiques – Rita Letendre: la marche lumineuse" par Normand Thériault

Oshawa Journal, May 13, 1970 "Letendre painting wins purchase award" by Paul Bennett

The Globe & Mail, Tor., Ont., May 11, 1970 "Toronto painter wins $900 award" by Kay Kritzwiser

---

LEVASSEUR, François-Noël

1703-1794

Son of Noël Levasseur, he worked in his father's shop assisting with various commissions for churches and other institutions.

References

The Arts in Canada, Dept. Citizenship & Immigration, Ottawa, 1958, P.25

The Ottawa Journal, Dec. 23, 1969 "Editorial Page (photo of François-Noël Levasseur's carving "Kneeling Angel" 32-1/2")

LEVASSEUR, Jacqueline

An artist from the Shawinigan, P.Q., area, who studied painting five years under Alban Dufresne, Louis Parent, Jean-Marie Bastien, Marcel Bellervive. She has taken part in several group shows at the Margo Fisher Gallery in Grand'Mère, and at Bronte, Ontario. She held her first solo show at the Shawinigan City Hall under the auspices of the Shawinigan Art Centre. Her work is figurative and non-figurative.

References

La Voix de Shawinigan, Mar. 17, 1965 "Une artiste de Shawinigan expose à l'Hôtel de Ville"

Ibid, March 31, 1965 "A L'Exposition Des Peintures De Mme. Jacqueline Levasseur" (photo of exhibition in progress)

L'Echo du St. Maurice, Shawinigan, P.Q., March 17, 1965 "Exposition Jacqueline Levasseur"

LEVASSEUR, Jacqueline (Cont'd)

La Voix de Shawinigan, P.Q., March 24, 1965 "L'exposition Jacqueline Levasseur remporte un beau succès"
Le Nouvelliste, Trois Rivières, P.Q., March 22, 1965 "L'exposition Jacqueline Levasseur nous permet d'apprécier une artiste locale"

LEVASSEUR, Jean-Baptiste Antoine
1717-1775
Son of Noël Levasseur he worked in his father's shop carrying out commissions of carvings and other work for churches and institutions.

Reference
The Arts in Canada, Dept. Citizenship & Immigration, Ottawa, 1957, P.25

LEVASSEUR, Noël
1680-1740
Born in Quebec City, from a family of carvers and joiners, he worked in Montreal for a time where he was married in 1701 and came in contact with sculptor Charles Chaboillez who made carvings for several monastic houses in that area. Levasseur returned to Quebec City where he was active until his death. He carved the altar-piece in the chapel of the Hôpital Général (1721) and the altar-wall of the Ursuline Chapel (1732) in Quebec. Noël Lavasseur was assisted in his workshop by members of his family as well as his cousin Pierre-Noël Levasseur.

References
Canadian Art by Graham McInnes, MacMillan (Can.), Tor., 1950, P.12
The Arts in Canada by Dept. Citizenship & Immigration, Ottawa, 1958, P.25
The Development of Canadian Art by R.H. Hubbard, NGC/Queen's Printer, 1963, P.36, 37, 38.
Three Hundred Years of Canadian Art by R.H. Hubbard and J.R. Ostiguy, NGC/Queen's Printer, 1967, P.16, 241

LEVASSEUR, Pierre-Noël
1690-1770
He worked in the shop of carver Noël Levasseur and was his cousin. Pierre-Noël was known for his figure carving. He is represented in the collection of the Museum of the Province of Quebec.

References
The Arts in Canada, Dept. Citizenship & Immigration, Ottawa, 1958, P.25
The Development of Canadian Art by R.H. Hubbard, NGC/Queen's Printer, 1963, P.39
Three Hundred Years of Canadian Art by R.H. Hubbard and J.R. Ostiguy, NGC/Queen's Printer, 1967, P.241
Canadian Art, Autumn, 1959, Vol. 16, No. 4, "Early Sculpture of Quebec" by Jean-Paul Morisset, P.265
Le Droit, Ottawa, Ont., Jan. 19, 1952 (photo of his work "Saint Joseph" in the permanent collection of the Museum of the Province of Quebec)

LEVASSEUR, Pierre-Noël (Cont'd)

La Presse, Mtl., P.Q., Aug. 13, 1960 (photo of a madonna done by him around 1740)
Le Soleil, Que., P.Q., Sept. 9, 1961 (photo of one of his kneeling angels done around 1775 for the church at Lotbinière. This work shows a robust Canadian tradition plus delicate French tradition as well as an incontestably oriental spirit in the overlay. His brothers had been in China and India)
Le Quartier Latin, Mtl., P.Q., Jan. 11, 1962 "Pierre-Noël Levasseur" par Jean-Paul Morisset
Le Clarion, St. Hyacinthe, P.Q., Jan. 18, 1962 "Pierre Levasseur, sculpteur" par Jean-Paul Morisset

---

LEVER, Harry

b (c) 1920

An artist from Richmond Hill, Ontario, who studied under Professor Angelo Berini at the Prato Academy of Fine Arts, Italy. He came to Canada in 1963. A painter of landscapes, still life and portraits. He was born in England, travelled in Europe and has recently set out on a tour of North America with the intention of returning to Richmond Hill with his wife, where he will continue to paint full time.

Reference
The Liberal, Richmond Hill, Ont., Aug. 14, 1969 "Plan Life In A Trailer" (photo of artist with his wife and one of his paintings)

LÉVESQUE, Andrée

A young painter from Mont-Joli, P.Q., who held her first solo show at the Matane college. She studied at the Ecole des Beaux-Arts, Montreal, and has been interested in developing line, light and space in her work.

Reference
Nouvelles, Mont-Joli, P.Q., June 19, 1969 "Mlle. Andrée Lévesque et deux de ses oeuvres"

LÉVESQUE, Claire

An artist from Montreal, P.Q., who worked and studied in Europe including six months in Florence where she learned about ceramics. In Canada she studied under the late Raymond Lasnier. In painting she has worked in pastel and charcoal and other media. Her abstracts are free, dynamic and she is trying to achieve balance and movement in her work.

References
Le Petit Journal, Mtl., P.Q., Oct. 18, 1964 "Une jeune artiste expose dans une jeune galerie" par Paul Gladu (at Galerie Claude Haeffely, Mtl.)
Le Nouvelliste, Trois Rivières, P.Q., July 8, 1967 (review by P.B. of her show at Galerie Fantasmagorique)

LÉVESQUE, Solange
b.1946

Born in Quebec City, she studied at the College Notre-Dame de l'Assomption de Nicolet and the Ecole des Beaux-Arts de Québec (1966-69). Her show at Galerie Restaurant d'Europe in 1969 of sixteen paintings was described by Grazia Merler of *Le Soleil* as having lively fantasy, fresh vision, and good technical mastery. Merler also described her work as revealing a relation to the lyricism of Miró and the influence of Chagall and surrealists.

References

Solange Lévesque (exhibition notice), La Galerie du Restaurant d'Europe, 27 rue Ste-Angele, Quebec City

Le Soleil, Quebec, P.Q., May 31, 1969 "La féérie de l'imagination" par Grazia Merler

LEVINE, Les (Leslie Leopold Levine)
b.1936

Born in Dublin, Ireland, his interest in photography started at the age of eight and at twelve he was entering his work in competitions. At fifteen he enrolled at the Central School of Arts and Crafts where he studied fine arts for a year and industrial design for a year. He then worked as a fashion photographer in Ireland and came to Canada in 1957. He settled in Toronto where he attended the New School for two months under the guidance of Mashel Teitelbaum.[1] He travelled in the United States during 1961 and 1962 and returned to Toronto where he participated in a group show at the David Mirvish Gallery under the title of "Exhibition 8". He also exhibited jointly in London, Ontario, at the University of Western Ontario. He held a solo show at Hart House which received the attention of Kay Kritzwiser[2] who found he had changed the art gallery into something resembling "a pink abattoir". She went on to describe the show as follows, "Hanging by chains from wooden structures resembling gibbets, Mr. Levine's pieces are shaped from broken chairs, cloth-covered and painted. They resemble nothing so much as a row of shiny pink carcasses neatly encased in clear plastic bags . . . . Mr. Levine buys quantities of old chairs, breaks them into rungs and slats, saws their back in two, rips off their rockers. Then laboriously and with a kind of genius, he forms them again, using the chair shapes for his armatures. He covers them with cloth, weaves them together with thick nylon thread and then paints with many, many coats of plastic paint until he gets the high-gloss finish of the assembly line. He also gets curved surfaces and filigree effects that are undeniably beautiful. The pink loops and coils in plastic bags have real significance to Mr. Levine. They represent to him this antiseptic, germ-free world where emphasis on cleanliness has, he believes, taken over from Godliness . . . . A group of highly imaginative, highly decorative oils accompany Mr. Levine's structures." His show then went on to Ottawa and was shown at the Blue Barn Gallery.[3] His next important creation was called "Slipcover — An Environment" which caused a minor sensation. Elizabeth Kilbourn[4] described the show as follows, "The walls and ceiling are covered with heavy silvery plastic material able to reflect with almost mirror-like clarity — but in wild distortion. The floor is covered with the same material in a shade I can only describe as magenta. Lights programmed at 30-minute intervals flash on and off constantly in cool colors of green, orchid, yellow and blue. They shift and shimmer, and reflect endlessly in the silvery walls and ceiling. Just before you enter the room, any sound you make is picked up and distorted and then replayed over and over a few seconds later inside. There is also a closed circuit television which projects on a screen anyone who comes within the camera's range. The effect on entering is like going into a fun house but whose simple crudities in Levine's hands become fantistic, exotic, sophisticated and electronic but with the disorientation of perception a fun house provides . . . . He has created a little silvery universe with its own mysteriously flashing lights, its own breathing, heaving forms and strange language. I felt that I and other ordinary mortals were even more out of place in this environment than in nature with a capital N." By now Levine was living in New York City where he held his first one man show at the Fischback Gallery. Harry Malcolmson[5] noted in this show that Levine had exhibited three works plus some disposable art objects. Describing the three pieces, Malcolmson continued, "One of them was a 10-foot-high transparent plastic bubble called Star Chamber into which the spectator could put himself, then inspect and be inspected by his companions. The other two pieces were sculptures in Levine's familiar technique of the stretching plastic spray-painted cloth over a wood frame. The larger piece consisted of five identical units whose shapes brought refrigerators to mind. The smaller piece was a sequence of eight chairs . . . . I say the show is more direct than other Levine exhibitions because he downgrades subsidiary ideas such as the ghost-like threatening character of the locked-in skeleton shapes. Instead, he concentrates on his point that industrial products are objects of great beauty. Levine tells us what containerization means to this society. The plastic bubble Star Chamber refers to the plastic or glass front of the TV set and the images that are packed inside. The other sculptures insist that machine-made refrigerators and automobile hoods have the qualities we call 'hand-made' to a greater extent than hand-made products ever had." As part of this show Levine had made about 3,000 flimsy square plastic sheets with the impression of bottles, radios, kitchen utensils and other pop articles which were sold for three dollars each. His disposables were also featured at the Castelli Gallery in that city. In the spring of 1967 his "The Star Garden; A Place" came into being. This work exhibited at the Museum of Modern Art, New York, was made possible by the support of the American Cyanamid Company (Bldg. Prod. Div.) of Wakefield, Massachusetts, who supplied the material. Levine explained his work as follows, "because the piece has no importance without people – the viewer enters and becomes the 'star'. The piece is concerned with physical experience rather than visual contemplation, it has no validity until someone is inside it, not simply looking at it. The work is almost invisible – intentionally. The viewer is more aware of his own physiognomy and of the people and objects outside 'The Star Garden; A Place' not in a visual way but in a sensory way, than of the piece itself. It is intended literally as a place to be in, rather than an object. It packages people in endless space and makes them more beautiful, shiny and new."[6] The creation was also shown at Levine's one man show at the Walker Art Center, Minneapolis with his "Slipcover". A related work "All Star Cast; A Place" was part of "Sculpture '67" organized by Dorothy Cameron under the auspices of the National Gallery of Canada, at the site of the Toronto City Hall.[7] It was also in 1967 that *The Aspen Times*[8] featured an article on Levine under the heading "Les Levine; the image breaker" in which his ideas for disposable houses and many other of his theories were discussed. Robert Fulford[9] described Levine recently in the *Toronto Daily Star* at the time of Levine's solo show at the Isaacs Gallery. Good accounts were also carried in *The Globe & Mail* and *The Telegram*.[10] In 1968 Levine produced "Photon: Strangeness 4" in cooperation with a research

LEVINE, Les (Leslie Leopold Levine) (Cont'd)

director at the IBM Lab in Yorktown, New York, named George Fan. The work was made up of vibrating wires, moving fish eye mirrors, and image identification equipment producing the image of viewers in a variety of sizes, as a pair of vidicon cameras scanned the same space giving them the sensation of having the space move in all directions at once. This work was exhibited under the auspices of The Junior Council of The Museum of Modern Art of New York, The New York State Council on the Arts and The National Council on the Arts, at the Theatre Workshop for Students on West 65th Street. It was shown in a number of other exhibitions. Also in 1968 he produced "Electric Shock" which was described as "a mesh of overhead wires which crackled and emitted a shock to anyone who touched them." I.B.M. computers solved the problem of how much electricity could be conducted safely through the wires without causing physical harm to the viewers. This was achieved by the transfer of 1,000 bolts of static electricity generated by cattle prodders (or riot control sticks) which were hung above the wires, transferring the electric energy from the sticks to the grid of wires.[12] Many other projects by Levine followed: "Systems Burn-Off and Residual Software"; "Iris" (six television monitors stacked in a bronze plastic cabinet 7-1/2 ft. high and 5 ft. wide. Between the middle row of monitors are the lenses — telephoto, normal, and wide angle for three television cameras which project on the monitors whatever appears before the unit). From the cameras come: one close-up, one profile and one distance view of the person in front of the unit. This creates unusual mixes on the six T.V. cameras which swirl and dissolve to create a new image. "Iris" was commissioned by Mr. & Mrs. Robert Kardon of Philadelphia for their home at a cost of $15,000. Gulf and Western, New York, commissioned Levine to build a large version of "Iris" for the lobby of their new world headquarters. This work contains 18 screens, and nine cameras, and should be completed by 1972.[13] "The Process of Elimination" in early 1969 consisted of 300 plastic disposable curves measuring 48 x 30 inches strewn over a vacant lot. Ten of these pieces were removed each day by the artist for thirty days until all had disappeared; "Body Colour" followed, and was made up of fifteen pairs of acrylic plastic domes, each pair a different colour large enough to walk through giving a variety of colour sensations; at the Fischback Gallery, N.Y.C., "White Sight" (two high intensity monochromatic sodium vapour lights in a vacant room — about light itself — these lights drain away all colour in the room so that visitors show up as black and white subjects. Their profiles and clothing outlines seem sharper); "Window" (disposable windows 12" x 19¼" which can be placed anywhere; "Retrofocus" an attempt to create an area in which the viewer would be unable to focus clearly, through the use of acrylic optical fibres and acrylic patterned sheets arranged in such a way as to make the space no longer definable in terms of perpendicular angles and focusable edges, providing the viewer moves around the area to achieve this effect). In August of 1969 Levine published his first edition of *Culture Hero* a monthly magazine devoted to personalities in the arts including fine art, classical music, theatre and poetry, commercial design, rock, movies, journalism, television, fashion and food. The magazine places emphases on photographs and information. In late 1969 his exhibition "Paint" opened at the Molly Barnes Gallery, Los Angeles, California, and consisted of pouring a gallon of different colours of paint into a trough on the floor of the gallery until thirty gallons were poured, each gallon adding a new colour. An automatic camera then photographed the proceedings and the photographs were presented as the finished work of art. In the spring of 1970 he exhibited at the

LEVINE, Les (Leslie Leopold Levine (Cont'd)

Isaacs Gallery, Toronto, "Body Control Systems" (three works presenting the body as a universal technological and ecological system) and "John & Mini's Book Of Love" (a video play of two people engaged in sexual love and discussing their sex life as they watch their own images on the television screen – explained by Levine as an attempt at an open and honest presentation of the physical act of lovemaking within marriage). Other units were shown in this exhibition. While busy on his one man shows he was also contributing to countless group shows both national and international for which there is no space here to list them. Levine is represented in the following public collections: National Gallery of Canada; Hart House, University of Toronto; Museum of Modern Art, New York; Vancouver Art Gallery; Winnipeg Art Gallery; Edmonton Art Gallery; Art Gallery of Ontario; Montreal Museum of Fine Arts; Philadelphia Museum of Art; University of Waterloo, Ontario; Norman Mackenzie Art Gallery, Regina, Sask.; Confederation Art Gallery & Museum, Prince Edward Island; Agnes Etherington Art Centre at Queen's University, Kingston, Ont.; Willistead Art Gallery, Windsor, Ont.; McMaster University, Hamilton, Ont.; and in the private collections of Dr. S. Wax; Mrs. J. Florence; Mr. S. Silverman; Mr. Jared Sable; Mr. Irving Grossman; Mr. Walter Moos; Mr. David Mirvish and others. He lives with his Japanese-Canadian wife in the Bowery section of New York. He opened a restaurant in New York called "Levine's" located between Chelsea and Gramercy Park, billed as the only Canadian restaurant in New York, and offering 20 percent off to all patrons by the name of Levine. This restaurant is equally unique for its decoration.

References
[1] National Gallery of Canada Information Form rec'd 1964 also The Aspen Times, Aspen, Colo., U.S.A., Aug. 17, 1967, P.7-C
[2] *Globe & Mail*, Tor., Ont., Sept. 30, 1964 "Clean Godliness – Free, Pink, Over 21, Hangs Around; Broken Chairs Depict World" by Kay Kritzwiser
[3] *The Ottawa Citizen*, Thurs. Nov. 5, 1964 "Display of 'pink' sculptures" by Carl Weiselberger
[4] *Toronto Daily Star*, Tor., Ont., Oct. 8, 1966 "Little silver universe with forms of its own" by Elizabeth Kilbourn
[5] *The Telegram*, Tor., Ont., Nov. 19, 1966 "Harry Malcolmson – New York"
[6] Museum of Modern Art Press Release No. 36, April 21, 1967
[7] *Sculpture '67* by Dorothy Cameron, NGC/Queen's Printer, Ottawa, 1968, P.90, P.91
[8] see [1]
[9] *Toronto Daily Star*, Oct. 31, 1967 "The special joys of new plastics" by Robert Fulford
[10] *Globe & Mail*, Tor., Ont., Oct. 28, 1967 "At The Galleries – Two resplendent artists flash upon ... " by Kay Kritzwiser
The Telegram, Tor., Ont., Oct. 27, 1967 "Art – As many as one wants" by Barrie Hale
[11] *The Province*, Van., B.C., Mar. 2, 1968 "Art – Levine jolts art gallery with shocking display" by Maija Bismanis
[12] *The Vancouver Sun*, Mar. 11, 1968 "Wires, Energy – This Art Shocks" by Ann Rosenberg
[13] *This Week Magazine*, Long Island Press, N.Y., Dec. 29, 1968 "Ahead of His Time" by Leslie Lieber
see also
Canadian Art Today Edited by William Townsend, Studio International, 1970, P.39
Canadian Art, July, 1966, Issue No. 102 "Liking things for what they are" by Jill Johnston, P.15-17
Ibid, July/August, 1964, Issue No. 92 "The Scope of Sculpture in '64" by Hugo McPherson, P.234
Ibid, February, 1967, Issue No. 105 "Les Levine's Slipcover" by P. Russell

LEVINE, Les (Leslie Leopold Levine) (Cont'd)

Second Canadian Sculpture Exhibition, 1964 (Catalogue, No. 8 & 9)
Globe & Mail, Tor., Ont., Nov. 19, 1965 "Levine tries space-age art" by Kay Kritzwiser
Ibid, Sept. 22, 1966 "Levine returns with wall-to-wall Levine"
The Telegram, Sept. 24, 1966 "Slipcover: A Theatrical Place"
Saturday Night, November, 1966 "Art skin and bones" by Harry Malcolmson, P.70-73
The Telegram, Oct. 12, 1966 "Cool, yes. Refrigerators no! " by Susan Kastner
Le Droit, Ottawa, Ont., Dec. 3, 1966 "Des oeuvres d'art que l'on jette comme des mouchoirs de papier! " par Denise Cote
The Telegram, Dec. 31, 1966 "Art" by Barrie Hale
Canadian Interiors, Tor., Ont., Jan., 1967 "Les Levine" by Bernadette Andrews
The Telegram, Apr. 3, 1967 "Art – Levine receives N.Y. commission" by Barrie Hale
Time, May 5, 1967 "Tiptoe Through the Silver"
Toronto Daily Star, July 1, 1967 "The new artists: Audacious rebels in a rich market" by Robert Fulford
The Aspen Times, Aspen, N.Y., Aug. 17, 1967 "Les Levine: the image breaker" by D.G.
Gleaner, Fredericton, N.B., Dec. 4, 1967 "The Lively Arts" by Charlotte Townsend
Saturday Night, Tor., Ont., Jan., 1968 "Sculpture" by Harry Malcolmson
The Telegram, Oct. 4, 1968 "Sculptor Les Levine and a . . . " by Bernadette Andrews
The Canadian Magazine, Tor., Ont., June 7, 1969 "This man admits he's crazy" by Barrie Hale
The Village Voice, NYC, Thurs. Jan. 30, 1969 "Seeing a Man about an Octopus "
The Telegram, Tor., Ont., "Art" by Bernadette Andrews
Ibid, May 10, 1969 "Each and every Levine gets 20 percent off" by Merle Shain
News – The Architectural League of New York
New York, Vol. 2, No. 6 Feb. 10, 1969 "Plastic Man Meets Plastic Man" by David Bourdon
Slipcover/a place, Art Gallery of Ontario, "An Interview With Les Levine" by Brydon Smith, 1966, P.1-4
VIᵉ Biennale de Paris, Musée d'Art Moderne de la Ville de Paris, 2 Oct. – 2 Nov., 1969 (catalogue sheet)
Globe & Mail, Tor., Ont. April 9, 1970 "The body in the technology age" by Kay Kritzwiser
Toronto Daily Star, April 10, 1970 "A one-man art show aimed at forces that control us" by Barry Lord
Ibid, Oct. 24, 1970 "Artistic master of the put-on Les Levine opens a new show" by Paul Russell
The Telegram, Tor., Ont., July 18, 1970 "The installation was the message" by Bernadette Andrews

----

LEVINE, Marilyn Ann

b.1935

Born at Medicine Hat, Alberta, she graduated from the University of Alberta, in 1959, with a M.Sc. in Chemistry. Her husband is also a chemist and when they moved to Regina they could not both be employed by the same department of the University of Alberta. It was then that she turned to pottery and by 1964 was on the organizational committee of the Western Potters' Organization. By 1966 she was a member of the Canadian Craftsmen's Association and the Canadian Guild of Potters. Previously she had studied art at the University of Alberta under Henry Glyde (1955-56), and at the University of Saskatchewan under Kenneth Lochhead, Arthur McKay and a potter, Beth Hone (1961-62) also at the U. of Sask. under W.E. Godwin, R.V.S. Gomez and J. Sures (1964-66). She has shown her work at the International Ceramic Exhibition, Istanbul, Turkey; HemisFair '68, San Antonio, Texas, U.S.A.; Expo '67, Montreal, P.Q.; Canadian Ceramics '67; Canadian Fine

LEVINE, Marilyn Ann (Cont'd)

Crafts, 1966-67 at the National Gallery of Canada. She has won prizes for her stoneware. Lives in Regina, Alberta.

References
> National Gallery of Canada Information Form rec'd Feb. 25, 1968
> *Le Soleil*, Que., P.Q., May 22, 1968 "Un passe-temps devenu rentable"
> *Barrie Examiner*, Ont., June 5, 1968 "Chemist's Pottery On Display From Istanbul To San Antonio"

LEVINSOHN, Lisl

b.1924

Born in Vienna, Austria, she was brought up in the United States.[1] There she lived in New York and attended the George Washington High School in Brooklyn. Later she became a model; then a professional ice skater (with "Holiday on Ice"); advertising manager for a department store on Fifth Avenue, New York; engineering draftsman; architectural designer; interior designer; industrial designer of textiles; graphic designer; and mathematician.[2] She moved to Toronto about 1964 where she later joined the staff of the Royal Ontario Museum in the display department.[3] She started doing her pen and ink drawings about 1966 and held her first one man show at the Isaacs Gallery in the winter of 1968.[4] This first show was a complete sell out. Subsequently her drawings interested the Royal Ontario Museum and she designed the ROM poster "Many Worlds" (20 x 28 inches) which is available to the public for only three dollars. Then she was invited to design a Christmas card (1969) for The Museum of Modern Art, New York. Talking about her work to Pat Annesley,[5] Lisl Levinsohn commented, " . . . I literally wanted to put the whole universe into every single drawing. Each one is a book, really. So that the Japanese could look at it, and understand, as well as North Americans. And I always feel I do exactly right. I hardly ever spoil a drawing (some of which not only take four months, but consist of as many as 67,000 intricately plotted lines)." Concluding her article on the artist Pat Annesley[6] noted, "Now the girl with hang-ups about her high-school education can visit her friends, the New York intellectuals, who used to make her feel inferior, and meet them on equal ground. Her drawings, so early in her career, are selling for more than $500 . . . collectors like Raymond Moriyama are grabbing up her work."

References
[1] National Gallery of Canada Information Form rec'd Feb. 23, 1968
[2] *The Telegram*, Tor., Ont., May 16, 1970 "Portrait of the woman as an artist"
[3] Ibid
[4] see [1]
[5] see [2]
[6] see [2]

see also
The Telegram, Sat., March 7, 1970 "Art" by Bernadette Andrews, P.56

LEVITT, Marvin Richard
b.1915
Born in Macklin, Saskatchewan, he attended the Institute of Technology and Art, Calgary, Alberta, following his discharge from the services at the end of the Second World War. At the Institute he studied under H.G. Glyde, W.J. Phillips, and sculpture under L. Lindo, then sculpture again under Jan Zack at Victoria, B.C. He has specialized in architectural and garden sculpture which he creates from the media of stone, wood, cast stone and concrete. Most of his work is for private homes and gardens. He has exhibited in juried shows at Vancouver, Victoria, Portland (Oregon, USA) and Seattle (Washington, USA). He exhibited in the outdoor show in Quebec City in the summer of 1960, and on the campus of the University of British Columbia, the same year. He is a charter member of the Northwest Institute of Sculpture (1954) (Pres. 1958-59; Executive member, 1961-62). He is represented in the permanent collection of the Vancouver Art Gallery.

References
National Gallery of Canada Information Form rec'd 1963
The Ottawa Citizen, Ottawa, Ont., Aug. 13, 1960 "About Art" by Carl Weiselberger (photo of Levitt's "Seabird Form")

LEW, Fon
b. (c) 1940
Born in China, he came to Canada in 1952 to be reunited with his father at Richmond Hill, Ontario. At that time he could only speak Chinese. He joined the grade four class of Richmond Hill Public School (Lillian McConaghy School) in the class of Mrs. Alice Unger who recognized his aptitude for art and encouraged him to develop his abilities. During his years of development he helped his father at his Town Inn Restaurant while he attended the Ontario College of Art under J.E.H. MacDonald. When his father died Fon Lew became the manager of the Town Inn. It had been his intention to become a commercial artist specializing in advertising and illustration. But with his responsibilities of restaurant owner and father of two children he has turned to landscape painting when the opportunity permits. His landscapes have been praised by Thoreau MacDonald. In 1965 he exhibited fifteen paintings under the auspices of the Civitan Club of Richmond Hill and he has shown his paintings elsewhere. His favourite sketching places include Georgian Bay and the Muskoka areas. In his Richmond Hill restaurant he specializes in authentic Cantonese food which his patrons enjoy to a background of soft lighting from Chinese lanterns, bamboo and red burlap covered walls, and music.

Reference
Liberal, Richmond Hill, Ont., Oct. 5, 1967 "Rambling Around" by Elizabeth Kelson

---

LEWICKI, Walter (Wladimir Lewicki)
b.1921
Born in Tuapse, Russia, he first studied art in 1938 in his home town where he attended evening classes sponsored by the local art school.[1] In 1939 he was drafted into the Russian army and was on active service in 1941. He was taken prisoner of the German army in 1942 and was sent to Germany where he was released in 1945.[2]

LEWICKI, Walter (Wladimir Lewicki) (Cont'd)

He continued his art studies in the refugee camp in Germany where he was staying after the war and came to Canada in 1951.[3] Later he settled in Noranda, Quebec, where he worked as a daily labourer in the mines while he continued to paint in his off hours.[4] He entered his work in competitions and won the following prizes: Northwestern Quebec Exposition, Rouyn, Quebec, 1957 (Grand Prize and First Prize), 1959 (First Prize), 1960 (Grand Prize, two First Prizes, Second Prize), 1961 (Grand Prize, First Prize, Second Prize), 1962 (Grand Prize, two First Prizes). He held his first one man show in Noranda in 1958.[5] In 1960 he entered his work in the Northern Ontario Art Association Exhibition where he won Honorable Mention, and in 1961 won the "Noranda Mines Award". In 1964 one of his paintings was acquired by the Department of External Affairs, Ottawa. His first one man show in Montreal was held at the Waddington Galleries in 1965 when George Waddington[6] noted, "His are paintings that reflect a love of nature — fields, meadows, mountains, orchards in blossom — created with warmth and sensitivity . . . " and a second show there in 1967 when Robert Ayre[7] of *The Montreal Star* noted, "There are more than 50 works in this show, oils and oil pastels, some really little more than colored sketches but all displaying great vivaciousness and a singular way of looking at the world around us. There are also, to be sure, echoes from the past, reminders that Mr. Lewicki has seen Cézanne and Van Gogh, but they are fleeting and generally sublimated to his purposes . . . . So far as color goes, Mr. Lewicki has come alive (as the Pepsi people say) in this last year quite obviously relishing the rich juxtapositions which his views of cosy European town and countryside afford. His is the innocent eye at work unfettered by the dogmas of the 1960s." Lewicki lives in Montreal with his wife and children. He met his wife Marthe when they both worked for the International Relief Organization in Arolsen, Hessen, Germany, after the war. Lewicki came to Canada to work on the Quebec Hydro project at St. Jean. He was later joined by his wife. They had been married about 1950 just about six months before he left for Canada.[8]

References

[1] National Gallery of Canada Information Form rec'd Mar. 20, 1961

[2] Ibid

[3] Ibid

[4] *L'Echo D'Abitibi Ouest*, La Sarre, P.Q., June 14, 1962 "Lewicki: peintre du temps revécu" par Raoul Duguay

[5] see[1]

[6] Exhibition notice, First Montreal Exhibition of Walter Lewicki at the Waddington Galleries, March 29th to April 10th, 1965.

[7] *The Montreal Star*, Dec. 2, 1967 "At Waddington's" by Robert Ayre

[8] *Rouyn-Noranda Frontière*, Rouyn, P.Q., April 1, 1965 "Walter Lewicki expose aux Galeries Waddington, de Montréal, du 29 au 10"

see also

Le Progrès, Rouyn-Noranda, Que., May 21, 1959 "Un peintre néo-canadien et l'histoire de sa vie . . . " par Lucette Lafrenière

Rouyn Noranda Press, Rouyn, P.Q., Mar. 16, 1961 "W. Lewicki Wins Top Prize At Northern Ontario Art Showing Held In Sudbury"

Ibid, Dec. 7, 1961 "W. Lewiki's Paintings Exhibited In Rouyn" (photo of artist with paintings)

Rouyn-Noranda Frontière, Jan. 17, 1963 "L'âme de la peinture, c'est le silence" Une interview de Jocelyne Dugas

LEWIS, Glenn

b.1935

Born in Chemainus, B.C., he did modelling and drawing as a child. In high school he became seriously interested in art and received encouragement from his high school art teacher, Mrs. Gwen Lamont.[1] He entered the Vancouver School of Art in 1954 and graduated with honours in drawing and painting in 1958.[2] He put himself through school with odd jobs and scholarships and in 1959 took a teacher training course at the University of British Columbia. He taught high school for two years; also adult night school classes in oil painting; and summer classes for children.[3] He spent two years at the Leach Pottery at St. Ives, Cornwall, England, under Bernard Leach (1961-63) and then worked independently with John Reeve and Warren McKenzie (pottery) at Hennock, Devon, England (1963-64).[4] Returning home to Vancouver he held an exhibit of his ceramic work at the Bau-Xi Gallery when David Watmough[5] of *The Vancouver Sun* noted, "Glenn Lewis is the latest to show his wares and his extensive display affirms an emphatically superior craftsmanship in a context emphasizing a down-to-earth practicality and masculine idiom. Lewis's colors are generally muted and there is a gritty assurance to his pieces that is a refreshing defiance of so much in our glossy and slick world." By 1968 he was producing totally untraditional works such as his "Vault of Treasured Music and Milky Way Room Freshener" and ceramic pieces in his "Fairy Ring" series. Viewing his 1968 show at the Douglas Gallery in Vancouver Joan Lowndes[6] noted, "Through the cooperation of Canadian Pittsburgh Industries Ltd., which has lent thousands of dollars' worth of stock, the Douglas Gallery has been lined with plate-glass. Into this sparkling ambiance Glenn Lewis has introduced his small white porcelain sculptures. They are of the type which caused some raised eyebrows when he won a $1,000 prize in Perspective 67, the national competition-exhibition for artists under 35. They subvert in a half-playful, half-mocking way the practical use of cups, plates and saucers, crumpling and ripping them as though they were paper. To indicate that his Perspective 67 entry was to be considered not as pottery but as sculpture Glenn Lewis, at a time when sculptors generally are abolishing the pedestal, re-instated it. His cup and saucer were elevated on a plexiglass stem with a small plexiglass top. Now he has asserted his sculptural intention even more strongly by large oblong pedestals of plexiglass or plate-glass. Upon these handsome bases he has fitted Larry Bell boxes of tinted plexiglass inside which, upon cylinders of clear plexiglass, he has lightly placed his dishes of visual puns. The plate-glass has destroyed the walls of the gallery. As you look into them your eye rides the reflections of overlapping constructivist sequences of chartreuse, blue and pink cubes . . . . This architectonic broadening of Glenn Lewis' vision is a welcome corrective to a fantasy which can sometimes verge on the precious." Lewis also exhibited his miniature beauty boxes which were described by Joan Lowndes as follows, "He may build this inner-world around a painted shell, a small Japanese vase or an old hand-mirror, treated with nostalgic tenderness. He lights them imaginatively placing the shell, for example, in a blue box evocative of undersea dimness." In 1969 he exhibited his creations with graph paper and other works at Ace (Canada) in Vancouver.[7] His mural of 128 handmade salt shakers, eight by twenty-two feet, (phallic in shape), commissioned for Expo 70, proved too controversial to officials to let it be shown in the Canada Pavilion.[8] Also in 1970 he exhibited at the Vancouver Art Gallery jointly with Gathie Falk, a former student of his. Lewis' work consisted of eight untitled plywood closets, lined up in two rows, in each of which a semi-mirrored light box was mounted on a black plexiglass stand, containing some art relic created or collected by Lewis. Joan Lowndes[9]

LEWIS, Glenn (Cont'd)

described them as follows, "As one peers into the light boxes, one sees a pile of ashes from Lewis' immolated graphs at his last show at Ace (Canada); 1000-year-old shards dug up in Japan; crumbled bits of raw clay arranged like a Japanese rock garden . . . . And these microscopic objects are repeated in the semi-mirrored plexi in a triple avenue that reaches into infinity: moonscapes above which one suddenly catches sight of one's own hovering reflected half-face." He also exhibited photographs of a closet in various locations around Vancouver (the photos were taken by Michael de Courcy). The effect of these photos assembled, gives the impression that the backgrounds have been changed to create a new scene for the closets rather than the closets being moved from place to place.[10] Richard Simmins[11] in describing the artist in 1970 noted, "A key to understanding Lewis is to accept his expanding environment from pots to sculpture to film to taping city blocks to claiming a slag mountain to enclosing everything again in a plywood closet." Lewis is represented in the permanent collection of the Faculty Club of Queen's University, Kingston (by a painting) and other collections including a number of private collections. He is a member of the Federation of Canadian Artists; B.C. Society of Artists (1965); Canadian Council For the Environmental Arts (1965); B.C. Potters' Guild (1965); American Craftsmen's Council (1964).

References

[1] Document from artist and letter dated Jan. 10, 1962 and National Gallery of Canada Information Form rec'd April 20, 1965
[2] Ibid
[3] Ibid
[4] Ibid
[5] *The Vancouver Sun*, Van., B.C., Sept. 10, 1965 "Grit and Charm Paired at Gallery" by David Watmough
[6] *The Province*, Van., B.C., May 10, 1968 "Glenn Lewis" by Joan Lowndes, P.10
[7] Ibid, Dec. 1, 1969, "Art and Artists – Madness flavors breakfast opening of the Lewis show" by Joan Lowndes
[8] *Georgia Straight*, Van. B.C., May 27, 1970 "Englescoop"
[9] *The Vancouver Sun*, June 18, 1970 "Falk, Lewis sculptures keep gallery in touch" by Joan Lowndes also see below
[10] *Arts/Canada*, June, 1970, P.35
[11] Ibid

see also
Arts/Canada, December, 1969 Issue No. 138/139 "The New Art of Vancouver, Newport Harbor Art Museum, Newport, California, October-November, 1969 by Susan Ginsburg, P.58

Ibid, December/January, 1971, "Some thoughts-theoretical and practical-on gifts artists make" by Clyde McConnell, P. 40

Canadian Art Today, Edited by William Townsend, Studio International, 1970, "The Vancouver Scene" by Doris Shadbolt, P.63, 68

The Vancouver Sun, Dec. 27, 1968 " . . . . The Artists"

Ibid, Jan. 18, 1969 "Artists' Six New Works Show Air of Distinction" by Charlotte Townsend

Ibid, July 12, 1969

Ibid, July 3, 1970, P.10A

Ibid, (date unknown) "Glenn Lewis – Who Talks In Caps about Nonsense and his new mural" by Charlotte Townsend

LEWIS, Harriet

b.1940

Born in Montreal, P.Q., she studied drawing and painting at the Ecole des Beaux-Arts, Montreal (three years); and the Montreal Museum of Fine Arts School (one year); at the Bronfman Centre under Stanley Lewis (one year) for stone engraving. She has taken part in group shows sponsored by the City of Montreal.

Reference
    Exhibition notice from la maison des arts la sauvegarde, 160 est, notre-dame, Mtl., 23 Oct. to 24 Nov., 1969

LEWIS, Ivor Rhys

Born in Wales, he came to Canada as a boy; later he entered the employ of the T. Eaton Company and rose to be director of the company in 1942. During his years of service with Eaton's he was known for his academic painting and first-rate portraits, also sculpture. He did the large bronze statue of Timothy Eaton which stands in the main store, also the First World War Memorial to employees who were killed in the services. He was an actor and singer and performed on the amateur stage and radio. He received the Lady Tweedsmuir award as the best actor in the Dominion Drama Festival of 1936. Died in 1958.

Reference
    The Telegram, Tor., Ont., Nov. 27, 1958 "I.R. Lewis Ex-Director Of Eaton's"

LEWIS, Marion

b.1910

Born in Poland, she came to Canada and settled in Hamilton, Ontario, in 1920. She studied at the Central Technical School, Toronto, under Elizabeth Wyn Wood and Mrs. Peter Haworth. She is known for her sculptural forms. A member of a group called "Five Potters Studio" she collaborated with the group in the making of a mural for the Peel County Court House at Brampton, Ontario and pottery decoration for the stairway of the Medical Centre at Sault Ste. Marie, Ontario. Her work has been exhibited in the Emerson Museum of Art, Syracuse, N.Y.; Vicenza, Florence and Rome, Italy; Ostende, Belgium; Smithsonian Institute, Washington, D.C., USA; Stratford, Ont.; Prague, Czechoslovakia. She won a Gold Medal for Sculpture in Prague in 1962, also an Award for sculpture at Canadian Ceramics 1965 and 1967. She lives in Hamilton, and is married with two children.

Reference
    National Gallery of Canada Information Form rec'd July 20, 1967

LEWIS, Maude

1903-1970

Born in Ohio, Yarmouth County, N.S., she was the daughter of Jack and Agnes (L. German) Dowley.[1] Her father was a harness maker. She started painting as a child and did hundreds of hand painted Christmas cards with her mother every year which they sold on the streets of Yarmouth.[2] When her parents died she went to live with an aunt in Digby, N.S. In 1938 she married Everett Lewis and they made their home in a 10 by 12 foot, one-room cabin near No. 2 Highway four miles west of Digby, at a place called Marshalltown. Everett bought a Model T Ford and took his wife on trips from village to village. While he sold fish, she sometimes sold her cards. Her husband encouraged her to do larger works. He bought artists' supplies from a summer resident returning to winter quarters and collected plywood from a lumber dealer, also wall board, and cut them into panels of a size which would allow her to work within the limited space of her polio-afflicted arms and arthritic condition. Most summer mornings Maude Lewis could be seen sitting in the doorway of her tiny home busy on a painting.[3] She did usually one or even two paintings a day then placed them in the warm oven to dry. She used her oil colours straight out of the tube and seldom if ever mixed her colours. Soon people were coming to her door to buy her work. By 1965 her reputation had spread beyond her district, and the *Moncton Times*[4] carried the following story, "Maude Lewis is a natural primitive Canadian artist whose surely executed, simple Nova Scotia scenes in gay colors are flavored with a humor unbelievably sophisticated in one so shy, simple and untouched by 20th-century complexities. She lives a fairy-tale existence without electricity, plumbing, radio or other comforts we take for granted, and the outside world scarcely exists for her. Perhaps because of this, her work has an irresistable charm and happy quality that appeals to both tourists and artists of discrimination from many parts of the country Maude Lewis has never heard of. She paints entirely from her own everyday experience, depicting farm animals. cottages, folds of hills and gardens with a simple directness that most people find refreshingly cozy in a world of superficiality." The article went on to describe her husband and their home in these words, " . . . in the little cabin, which was built originally for a man five feet tall, . . . Everett Lewis can never stand up perfectly straight inside. He bakes the bread, hunts and traps for the stew-pot on the big black range, does the cooking, and encourages his little wife in her artistic work, playing a big, gaunt Darby, unlettered but shrewd and protective, to his gently determined, fragile Joan." Her paintings had become so well known and so loved that CBC-TV's Telescope visited her home in 1965 and produced the programme "The Once-Upon-a-Time World of Maude Lewis". This programme was directed by George Ronald, produced by Peter Kelly, with host Fletcher Markle. Appearing in the documentary were: Bill Ferguson and Claire Stenning, co-owners of the Ten Mile House gallery, who became interested in her work; John Cook, a Halifax artist who commented on her work and others who assisted behind the scenes. In 1967 her work was shown at the Centennial Exhibition of Primitive Art in New Brunswick at the Beaverbrook House, Saint John, under the auspices of the Saint John Art Club. In August of 1970 she passed away at the Digby General Hospital at the age of 67. She is survived by her husband Everett and her brother Charles Dowley of Halifax. Collectors of her paintings include R.L. Stanfield (former premier of Nova Scotia and leader of the Conservative Party of Canada); Richard Nixon (President of the United States) and many others. Her paintings are in the White House and the Legislative Buildings of the Province of Nova Scotia.[5] Some forgeries of her work were produced and signed MAUDLEWIS instead of MAUD LEWIS.[6] She sold her paintings directly to patrons for $4.50, then $5.00 and later $10.00. Dealers in Toronto were selling her works for $25.00 framed.[7] Bill Ferguson at Ten Mile House in suburban Halifax probably handled most of her other works for resale apart from what she sold

LEWIS, Maude (Cont'd)

herself. On Telescope Ferguson commented, "Her use of colour is daring and her composition almost faultless. Like every good artist, though, she breaks the rules and she gets away with it beautifully." Doris McCoy[8] in *The Atlantic Advocate* concluded an article on Maude in these words, "In her lifetime she has painted hundreds of pictures, all of them in demand, but she does not consider them to be works of art. Rather she regards them with the same feeling an average housewife would have about an attractive apron she'd completed for the fall fair. The frail woman with the bold brush has great talent and completely genuine humility."

References

[1] *Digby Courier*, Digby, N.S., Aug. 6, 1970 "Digby's Artist, Maude Lewis, Laid To Rest"

[2] *The Star Weekly*, Tor., Ont., Sat., July 10, 1965 "The Little Old Lady Who Paints Pretty Pictures" by Murray Barnard (photos by Bob Brooks)

[3] Ibid

[4] *Moncton Times*, Sat., Nov. 20, 1965 "Once-Upon-A-Time World of Maude Lewis"

[5] *Mississauga News*, Mississauga, Ont., Dec. 17, 1969 "It's Your Castle" by Margo Gamsby

[6] Ibid

[7] Ibid

[8] *The Atlantic Advocate*, Fred., N.B., January, 1967 "Frail Woman With A Bold Brush" by Doris McCoy, P.36, 37, 39

see also

Times, Port Alberni, B.C., Dec. 1, 1965 "The Sketch Pad" by Jean Vowel

Yarmouth Herald, Yarmouth, N.S., Nov. 24, 1965 "Telescope Visits Painter Maude Lewis Of Digby"

Digby Courier, N.S., Mar. 27, 1969 "Maude In Hospital"

Chronicle-Herald, Halifax, N.S., Aug. 1, 1970 "Digby's artist, Mrs. Maude Lewis dies"

Mail-Star, Halifax, N.S., Aug. 1, 1970 "Digby artist dies; her primitive style paintings in the White House"

Spectator, Annapolis Royal, N.S., Aug. 4, 1970 "Digby's Artist, Mrs. Maude Lewis Dies"

Digby Courier, Aug. 6, 1970, "About This and That — The Passing Of Maude"

Chronicle Herald, Halifax, N.S., Aug. 6, 1970 "The Maude Lewis touch"

LEWIS, Stanley

b.1930

Born in Montreal, P.Q., he collected rocks from all over the world during his high school days at Strathcona Academy.[1] Following high school he entered the Montreal Museum of Fine Arts School of Arts and Design where he studied under Marion Scott, Jacques de Tonnancour, Gordon Webber, Louis Archambault, Eldon Grier, John Byers and Arthur Lismer. He received a scholarship in painting (1949), graphics (1950), and graduated as top student with an Honours Diploma in graphics, design, and sculpture (1951).[2] His first one man show of etchings was held at the Y.W.C.A., Montreal in 1952. He then received a post graduate scholarship to study one year at the Instituto Allende, San Miguel, Mexico. Roy Shields[3] noted his Mexican scholarship as follows, "Stanley . . . sees in the Mexico award (he is one of four on the North American Continent to receive an invitation to study) a chance to build up a little much-needed experience with fellow sculptors. As a matter of fact, he is anxious to find out what they will think of his method of work. Being an artist with a straightforward viewpoint and with few of the traditional artistic inhibitions that might hinder others, he doesn't often sit about pecking at a hunk of granite with hammer and chisel any more. He figures the small pneumatic drill he used is a lot more effective, besides being three or four times as fast . . . . He also stated that he feels the real place for sculpture is out-of-doors. 'That's the natural place and granite stands up the best,' he added. For this reason he has experimented in different kinds of granite. To date the best he has come across is the Standstead variety since its crystals are smaller. This makes it easier to control with the drill, because, as he said, 'with granite you have to crush crystals rather than chip the stone." In Mexico he found fully developed ideas in the work of the Mexican primitive sculptures also strength and simplicity. In an interview with Peter Olwyler [4] Lewis explained, "Before, it had always been city life. I'd been away from the elements. I found them in Mexico. The sudden downpours of rain. The wind gusts. The full faces of women. All these elements throw themselves open for you to look at. You can't help it. There's simplicity everywhere — the way they build their abode huts of mud, the way they fit in with the earth they walk barefooted on — all these things have really opened my eyes to nature again. I've revitalized my senses. Mexico opens you up. It releases the best in you. You don't feel at home." At the Instituto Allende, Lewis created five sculptures which were assigned a permanent place on the grounds of the Instituto: "La Molendera" (Indian woman grinding corn, made of veined marble); "Standing Woman" (marble); "Sleeping Head" (carved from volcanic boulder); "Standing Figure (pink sandstone); one work of which the title is not known (pink sandstone).[5] His "La Molendera" (The Corn-grinder) was officially unveiled by the Canadian Ambassador to Mexico, Douglas S. Cole. In 1953 he had received a continuation of studies grant from the Canada Foundation and at the same time he was granted an additional scholarship of tuition, board, and room at the Instituto Allende. He returned to Montreal during Christmas of 1954 when he held a solo show of drawings and lithographs done in Mexico at the Agnes Lefort gallery. He had instructed students in lithography at the Instituto Allende while also working on his sculpture. He continued his studies in Mexico and in 1955 returned to Montreal when he held another show of his litho-graphs also sculptures at Lefort's under the patronage of the Consulate General of Mexico. The remarkable thing about his Mexican sculpture is that he used a handful of primitive tools in making them. In 1956 he received an Elizabeth T. Greenshields Memorial Foundation Grant for studies in Italy. There he worked and lived for three years and did extensive research on Michelangelo. He retraced the steps of the great master and recreated his sculpturing tools so that he was then able to copy his bas-relief "Madonna and Child". He discovered Michelangelo's techniques by examining inch by inch his work in museums and churches. He took photographs and studied enlargements of small sections of statues. He talked with stone-masons, artists, and museum directors and discovered that Michelangelo used a special system of strokes or parallel lines (cross-hatching) in his sculpture and painting.[6] Other intricate handling of tools were discovered as well. In Italy at the same time as Lewis, was author Irving Stone, doing research for his novel on Michelangelo. Lewis provided Stone with technical information which was woven into *The Agony and The Ecstacy*.[7] Stone had produced the story of another great artist Vincent Van Gogh entitled *Lust for Life* which was later made into a movie. Lewis' copy of Michelangelo's "Madonna and Child" was taken into the collection of the Montreal Museum of Fine Arts. Returning to Montreal Lewis continued to show his work at: Montreal Museum of Fine Arts (1959); Galerie Dresdnere (Mtl. — 1960); Here and Now Art Gallery (Tor. — 1960); Galerie Libre (Mtl. — 1961); Galerie Agnes Lefort (Mtl. — 1962); Penthouse Gallery (1962). Over this period not only did he develop

LEWIS, Stanley (Cont'd)

his sculpture but he had developed the art of making stone-cut prints. The only other Canadians working in this medium were the Eskimos. In 1959 he won second prize for sculpture in the Concours Artistiques de Quebec; 1960 a prize for sculpture in the National Art and Photography Exhibition; 1962 (in the latter competition) for stone-cut prints. In 1963 he received a grant from the Canadian Jewish Congress to do research in Israel on archaeological discoveries in Biblical art to enable him to create and publish a portfolio of black and white stonecut prints illustrating the Ten Commandments. He travelled throughout Israel for a month then lived in the artists' colony of Ein Hod, a short distance from Haifa. There he set to work carving in stone his impressions of the Holy Land. In ten days he completed eleven works of the Commandments and thirteen days after that had finished the printing of one hundred portfolios of this work. He then went to work developing multi-coloured stone-cuts in which he had to do separate stone-cuts for each colour, employing transparent inks to achieve subtle relationships with a minimum of colour. Lewis is the Canadian pioneer in colour stone-cut prints. Both his stone-cut prints "Mystery of Man and Space" (coloured prints) and "The Ten Commandments" (black and white) were exhibited in May of 1965 at The Exhibition Rooms of the Israel Art Auction Galleries in Tel-Aviv under the patronage of the Canadian Embassy in Israel. In 1968 he held a retrospective of his prints covering the period 1961-1968 at the Mount Royal Art Centre, Montreal, and later that year spent six weeks on the Island of Santorini, a volcanic island north of Crete. There he did a series of water colours on heavy English ragpaper. His subject was the rich produce of the land against the background of jagged volcanic shaped stones. He collected pumice from the Island to use in his work. He used pumice dust in two of his fifteen multi-coloured stone-cut prints on the theme of "Air Pollution" the balance of the prints were surfaced with emery dust. Both dusts were used symbolically to evoke as realistically as possible air pollution. His "Air Pollution" prints were exhibited in various galleries. Stanley Lewis continues to develop his sculpture and prints with the highest of professional standards. He is a member of the Sculptors' Society of Canada (1960). Lives in Montreal.

References

[1] *The Gazette*, Mtl, P.Q., Nov. 5, 1954 "Every Block of Stone Has a Carving Inside" by Peter Desarats

[2] National Gallery of Canada Information Form rec'd April 6, 1953

[3] *The Monitor*, Mtl., P.Q., Dec. 11, 1952 "Young Sculptor Stanley Lewis Wins Scholarship To Mexico" by Roy Shields

[4] *Canadian Art*, Vol. 13, No. 1 (Autumn, 1955) "A Canadian Sculptor in Mexico" by Peter Olwyler, P.198

[5] Ibid

[6] *The Ottawa Journal*, Oct. 31, 1959 "Uncovers Secrets Of Michelangelo" by Robert Rice (Canadian Press Staff Writer) also *The Gazette*, April 20, 1959 "Michelangelo's Skills Recaptured"

see also

Saturday Night, 1955, October Issue "Canada's Art Colony In Mexico" by Earle Birney

Vie des Arts, 1959 Summer Issue "L'Ame de la Matière" by Folch

The Montrealer, 1960, February Issue, Interview with Lawrence Sabbath

Le Petit Journal, semaine du 14 janvier, 1962 "Renaissance d'une technique" par Paul Gladu

see also

La Presse, Mtl, P.Q., Oct. 30, 1954 "Stanley Lewis"

The Montreal Star, Mtl., P.Q., Oct. 30, 1954 (photo of Lewis working on a lava boulder in Mexico)

LEWIS, Stanley (Cont'd)

La Presse, Nov. 4, 1954 "Stanley Lewis cherche à renouer avec les cultures américaines" par R. de Repentigny

The Montreal Star, Nov. 6, 1954 "Mexico Has Strong Attraction For Young Canadian Artists"

La Presse, May 3, 1955 "Un artiste canadien expose au Mexique"

The Herald, Mtl., P.Q., June 2, 1955 "Montreal Sculptor's Work Rises Over Mexican Plain"

Cape Breton Post, Sydney, Oct. 29, 1959 "Claims Uncovering Of Michelangelo's Secrets" by Robert Rice

The Montreal Star, Oct. 20, 1959 "Alumnae To Hear Sculptor"

Le Droit, Ottawa, Ont., Nov. 16, 1959 "Un jeune sculpteur découvre certains secrets de Michel-Ange" par Robert Rice

Toronto Daily Star, Dec. 3, 1960 "Innocent of Life"

Le Devoir, Mtl, P.Q., Feb. 25, 1960 "Moins de métier, et plus de spontanéité" par Françoise de Repentigny

The Gazette, Feb. 29, 1960 "Canadian Sculpture" by Dorothy Pfeiffer

Ibid, May 27, 1961 "Lewis Prints And Sculptures" by Dorothy Pfeiffer

Le Petit Journal, May 28, 1961 "Bien peigné, pas de barbe, mais beaucoup de talent" par Paul Gladu

The Gazette, Jan. 20, 1962 "New Sculpture By Lewis" by Dorothy Pfeiffer

La Presse, Mtl, P.Q., 27 Jan., 1962 "Stanley Lewis, Sculpteur"

The Montreal Star, June 2, 1962 (photo of Lewis' sculpture "The Fissure")

Ibid, Mar. 16, 1963 (photo of Lewis' sculpture "Moon With Lovers")

The Gazette, Aug. 28, 1963 "Stanley Lewis Receives Grant, Goes To Israel"

Ibid, Sept. 7, 1963 "Lewis Sculpture"

Ibid, Dec. 4, 1964 "Sculptor Does Research In Israel" by Bill Bantey

La Presse, Mtl., P.Q., "d'une exposition a l'autre"

The Gazette, Sept. 7, 1968 "Montreal artist Stanley Lewis plans to carve volcanic stone" by David Tafler

Winnipeg Free Press, Feb. 18, 1969 "Prints, Drawings Contrast In Style" by John W. Graham

La Presse, Mar. 9, 1968 "Plus beau que les expositions, le centre Bronfman lui-même"

LEWIS, Virginia

An artist from Victoria, B.C., who studied under Arthur Lismer at the old Grange in Toronto and with Jan Zack when he was in Victoria. One of her paintings is in the lounge of the old rectory of St. John's Anglican Church in Victoria. Her paintings have been exhibited in a one woman show in the Art Gallery of Greater Victoria.

Reference

The Daily Colonist, Victoria, B.C., Dec. 7, 1968 "Modern Paintings Depicts Impressions of Church" by Don Gain

---

LI, Chi Tam (Mrs.)

Born in Shanghai, China, she was educated there and studied art under Yet Chungyuen Jong, well known Chinese artist. She later started teaching at the Kwong Sue Academy of Shanghai and continued teaching private lessons in Hong Kong. She came to Canada in 1968 and settled in Montreal. A solo show of her work was presented at the Chinese Presbyterian Church of Montreal where Francis

LI, Chi Tam (Mrs.) (Cont'd)

Allen described the exhibition as follows, "Mrs. Li has known the hardships of occupation . . . the terrors of the civil war . . . . Yet, throughout these massive upheavals she has quietly and calmly painted the birds and plants and landscapes of the country she loved so well, and which she found so beautiful . . . . Her own style of painting, done mostly with a brush, is devoted to landscapes and foliage. According to the subject and extent of each work she may devote nearly a whole day or simply an hour or two to each painting. The subtleties of color are so acute, she notes, that a Chinese artist uses seven shades of black, for instance, and a connoisseur of this kind of art can recognize and distinguish each shade."

Reference

The Montreal Star, Mtl., P.Q., Oct. 18, 1969 "Chinese painter displays art in church hall" by Francis Allen

LICASTRO, Joseph

He studied in Toronto at the Ontario College of Art under Charles Goldhamer, Carl Schaefer, Peter Haworth and Arthur Lismer. He served in the armed forces during the Second World War and exhibited in the first army show and won first prize for a still life study. During 1951 he exhibited his work at the Odeon Theatre, Ottawa, jointly with Lawrence Hyde. His water colours, for which he had been known for years, were best received. His oil paintings were also shown at this show. Licastro's subjects included landscapes and city scenes particularly Ottawa-Hull area scenes and Gatineau autumn scenes. No recent information on this artist.

References

Film News, Vol. XI, No. 6 "New Canadian Filmstrips"
The Ottawa Journal, May 15, 1951 "Water Colors by Joe Licastro Appealing, Vigorous and Free" by R.B.C.
Le Droit, 20 April, 1956 (photo of J. W. Pickersgill and Joseph Licastro)

LICUSHINE, Dimitry Semenoff
b.1896

Born in Rostov, on the Don River, Russia, he graduated from high school and attended a commercial college for two years. Also graduated from Military Academy and served on the Russian frontiers as an officer of the Russian Imperial Army for four and a half years during the Great and Civil wars. He came to Canada in 1923 and settled in Montreal, Quebec. There he studied painting under Adam Sheriff Scott and at the Beaux Arts. He exhibited his work at the Royal Canadian Academy shows, spring shows of the Art Association of Montreal and held a solo show at the T. Eaton Company of Montreal. He painted a wide variety of subjects including still lifes, seascapes, landscapes, city scenes, figure studies and interiors.

References

National Gallery of Canada Information Form rec'd June 16, 1934
The Gazette, Mtl, P.Q., Jan. 29, 1938 "Dimitry Licushine Opens Show Monday"

LIÉBERT, Phillipe
1732-1804
Born at Nemours, France, a carver and painter, he came to Montreal, Canada, some time before 1761. He did a great amount of decorative carving work in the Montreal area for churches although little of it remains today. A few surviving pieces can be located at Sault au Récollet; St. Michel at Vaudreuil, and St. Martin on the Ile-Jesus (both attributed to Liébert); Hôpital Général, Mtl.; St. Andrew West Roman Catholic Church near Cornwall, Ontario (this work had historians mystified as to its whereabouts for years) and elsewhere.

References
>Phillipe Liébert by Gerard Morisset, Quebec, 1943
>The Arts In Canada, Canadian Citizenship Series Phamphlet No. 6, Queen's Printer, Ottawa, 1958, P. 27, 28
>The Development of Canadian Art by R.H. Hubbard, Queen's Printer, Ottawa, 1963, P.40
>The Ottawa Citizen, Sat., July 18, 1964 "Priceless art lay in attic for century" by Alex Mullin
>Three Hundred Years of Canadian Art by R.H. Hubbard and J.R. Ostiguy, NGC/Queen's Printer, 1967, P.32, 33, 241

LIEBICH, Kathleen Chipman Sweeny (Mrs.)
b.1892
Born in Toronto, Ontario, the daughter of Archibishop Sweeny of Toronto, she studied art for three years under Mary Wrinch at Bishop Strachan School; at the Grange, Toronto, for two years under G.A. Reid; in Montreal under Adam Sheriff Scott. After 1936 she exhibited her work at Eaton's Fine Art Galleries (Mtl.); Montreal Art Association's Spring Exhibitions and at the Watson's Art Galleries. She painted portraits, still lifes and other subjects. She was a member of the Women's Art Association of Montreal (1935) and participated in their annual exhibitions at the Art Association of Mtl. and the Dominion Gallery. She was also a member of the Independent Art Association Inc. (1938). Last reported living in Westmount, Quebec.

References
>National Gallery of Canada Information Form rec'd May 14, 1937 and Feb. 17, 1948

LIGHTBODY, Maria Antoinette (Maya Lightbody)
b.1933
Born in Lwow, Poland, her mother was a botanical artist, her father a military attache.[1] They lived in many countries and Maria received her early education from private tutors.[2] Later she studied fine arts at the University of London, England, for one year.[3] She came to Canada in 1951 and settled in Montreal. There she studied at the Montreal Museum of Fine Arts School of Arts and Design (Diploma Course – 3 yrs.) under Goodridge Roberts, Jacques de Tonnancour, Moe Reinblatt, Gordon Weber and Dr. Arthur Lismer.[4] She won an art scholarship each year at the school and graduated with honours in Graphic Art.[5] She held her first solo show at the Upstairs Gallery in Toronto in 1960 and a second show there the following year. Subsequently she held solo shows at the Galerie Libre in 1962, 1963,

LIGHTBODY, Maria Antoinette (Maya Lightbody) (Cont'd)

1966 and 1968 when Virginia Lambe[6] noted, "Space is the overall theme of Maya Lightbody's show. . . . Altogether, besides being colorful and attractive, it is a stimulating and satisfying exhibition. Besides paintings, Miss Lightbody is now constructing three-dimensional cubes and oblongs, and she also has a cut-out spaceman suspended from the ceiling. One reason for this — besides the artist's natural desire to explore — is that she feels too many people don't bother looking at the paintings on their walls. But these cubes will 'have to be picked up and dusted'. . . . Miss Lightbody's colors are bright and defined. There is obviously a good deal of pop in these cubes, but they are by no means exclusively so. In some, such as 'Totem to Six Suns,' three cubes stacked on top of one another, the designs include a face and hard-edge circular sun symbols on a bright shiny surface. Here, and in some of the other non-spacemen cubes the effect is more high class decorative than anything else. Despite the three-dimensional excitement the paintings are the strongest thing in the show. Miss Lightbody uses stark monolithic faces and torsos, essentially repeating the same one. This style has been a trap to many painters, especially evident when you see a whole group of such paintings together. But Maya Lightbody pretty well avoids the trap, making her figures part of a valid overall pictorial conception rather than letting them stand (and fall) on their own." She also exhibited her "People Boxes" at the Albert White Gallery, Toronto, the same year. In April of 1970 her oils, ceramics and itaglio and polyester mediums were shown at Gallery 93, Ottawa, where they were well received. One of her hobbies is flying gliders. Her husband is also a glider pilot and they met at the glider club. Maria Lightbody has exhibited in many group shows and is represented in the following collections: The Montreal Museum of Fine Arts (Bronfman Collection); Sir George Williams University, Mtl.; Museum of the Province of Quebec, Que., P.Q.; Canadian Industries Limited, Mtl.; MacMillan Publishing, Tor.; Department of External Affairs of Canada; W.G. McConnell, Mtl., and many private collections in Europe, U.S.A. and Canada. Her honours include First Prize in Graphic Art at the Province of Quebec Exhibition, 1960; First Prize, hors concours, at the same Exhibition in 1962. Lives in Knowlton, Quebec, in her combined home and studio with her husband who is a Bell Canada engineer.

References
[1] *The Ottawa Journal,* April 21, 1970 "Versitility Pays Off For Quebec Artist" by Alixe Carter
[2] Ibid
[3] National Gallery of Canada Information rec'd June 23, 1958
[4] Ibid
[5] Ibid
[6] *The Gazette,* Mtl., P.Q., Mar. 23, 1968 "Lightbody: Stimulating, Satisfying" by Virginia Lambe
see also
La Presse, Mtl., P.Q., May 26, 1962 "les beaux-arts — Maya Lightbody" by Claude Jasmin
Le Nouveau Journal, May 26, 1962 "Maya Lightbody: souvenirs rupestres"
The Montreal Star, Sept. 25, 1963 "Two Graphic Exhibits At Montreal Galleries" by Robert Ayre
La Presse, Mtl., P.Q., Sept. 28, 1963 "le retour de maya lightbody"
The Montreal Gazette, Sept. 28, 1963 "Maya" by Dorothy Pfeiffer
Ibid, 20 Nov., 1965 "Maya" by Réa Montbizon
Sherbrooke Record, Que., Feb. 3, 1968 "Knowlton artist discusses total involvement in art"

LIGHTBODY, Maria Antoinette (Maya Lightbody) (Cont'd)

The Montreal Star, Mar. 30, 1968 "Space age figures" by Michael Ballantyne
Le Droit, Ottawa, Ont., May 2, 1970 "Le tour des. . . . . ."
The Ottawa Journal, Ottawa, Ont., April 22, 1970 "Quebec Artist Opens Exhibit At Gallery 93" by W.Q. Ketchum

LIGNY-BOUDREAU, Pierre de (see BOUDREAU, Pierre Deligny)

LIM, John

A sculptor who held a solo show at the Shaw-Rimmington Gallery, Toronto. His work was noted by the *Globe & Mail* as follows, "John Lim has ventured into his first bronzes, then modestly limited them to an edition of one only. One assumes it's modesty because his bronzes are fine enough to tempt a number of owners. Lim is cautious, restricting himself to a safe vocabulary. All sculptors eventually have to do a Daedalus and a Mother and Child and a Reclining Figure. But with these exercises he's finding his way into the real ideas — the tension he asks of a suspended torso or the strong way, in Eros, that he roughly splits a column to get his two figures."

Reference
Globe & Mail, Nov. 29, 1969

LIMA, Tom

b.(c)1925

Born in Toronto, Ontario, he served as medical assistant in the R.C.A.F. during the Second World War. In training for his job he studied anatomy and during his duty made sketches which were used in medical conferences. When he was posted to St. John's, Newfoundland, he assisted the recreational section in providing fine arts and crafts instruction to R.C.A.F. personnel and in return was given a place to use as a studio for his own painting. In 1943 he exhibited twenty of his canvases in St. John's. After the war he studied ballet under Rita Warne at the Toronto Ballet and later with the New Dance Theatre Group appeared in performances at Massey Hall, Royal Alexandra, Eaton Auditorium, and Hart House. Through his stage performances he became interested in set designing, making props, costumes and posters and finally he turned to recording activities of the performers on canvas. He studied in his spare time at the Ontario College of Art. In 1955 a serious motor vehicle accident brought an end to his dancing career and consequently he turned more and more to painting. His first important solo show took place in the foyer of the Towne Cinema, Toronto, in March of 1957. His subjects included figures, genre scenes, and dancers in oils, pen-and-ink washes, mixed drawing media (ink, wax, and crayons), water colours. In May of that same year he exhibited forty works in the Union Hall, Sudbury. In 1958 he joined the Society of Co-operative Artists which includes about thirty members from the Toronto area and he continues to exhibit with them.

References
Globe & Mail, Tor., Ont., Feb. 21, 1957 "Person to Person — Paintings Reveal Love of Dancing" by Lotta Dempsey

LIMA, Tom (Cont'd)

The Telegram, Tor., Ont., Feb. 22, 1957 "Once Top Dancer Now He's Artist" by James Hanney

The Toronto Star, Mar. 1, 1957 "By George! — Knowledge of Dancing Is Helpful to Create Movement on Canvas" by George Bryant

Ryersonian, Tor., Ont., Mar. 12, 1957 "(large photo of artist and work)

Ibid, Mar. 15, 1957 "Artist's bold, direct style wins Toronto recognition" by Paul King

Sudbury Daily Star, May 27, 1957 (large photo of artist, his sister, and three paintings)

The Toronto Star, April (?), 1958 "Art Colony — Steelworkers To The Rescue" by Roy Greenaway

Ibid, Nov. 12, 1959

LIND, Carl Werner

1891-1961

Born in Sweden, he left home at the age of fifteen and went to sea. After visiting many ports he arrived in the United States in 1907. For a time he worked on a ranch in Texas then moved north to Canada first at Prince Albert, Saskatchewan, in 1910. The next year he took up a homestead at Spruce Bluff not far from Prince Albert. Later he joined the Northwest Mounted Police in Battleford, Saskatchewan, and went overseas. He returned to Canada as an employee of the Hudson's Bay Company and became a store agent and purchasing agent. He travelled throughout the Canadian north and became familiar with the wild life and the country. This experience gave him inspiration for his paintings of animal life and the wilderness. He settled in St. Walburg, Saskatchewan, where he died at the age of seventy. Some of his work can be found in the Battleford and St. Walburg areas.

Reference

Enterprise, St. Walburg, Sask., Sept. 8, 1961 "Famed Wild Life Painter Carl Werner Lind Dies"

LINDEMERE, Gladys (Mrs.)

b.(c)1887

A New Westminister artist who came to Canada in 1911 from Yorkshire, England. She lived at Eden and Battleford districts of Saskatchewan until 1932 when she settled in British Columbia. As a child in Yorkshire she took lessons in Leeds in water colours from Gilbert Foster. She started to paint seriously in 1953 when she attended painting classes at the University of British Columbia, and the Vancouver School of Art. She has travelled in the interior of British Columbia reaching such points as North Thompson River, Lillooet, Lytton, Squamish, Pemberton and over the Mission Mountain to the deserted Indian reserve. Her paintings have been shown in B.C. at the following places: Clubhouse of JC Ettes, New Westminister; Gallery of B.C. Arts, West Vancouver; Little Green Gallery, New Westminister; Studio Workshop, Williams Lake, B.C. Mrs. Lindemere has become known for her waterfront, coastal, and Indian village scenes. Her paintings have been hung in offices, public institutions and private homes in British Columbia. One of her patrons is her son Gordon who opened a new business in New Westminister and chose ten of her paintings to hang in his office. She is a member of the B.C. Society of Artists and the Federation of Canadian Artists. Her paintings have also been shown in the

LINDEMERE, Gladys (Mrs.) (Cont'd)

Vancouver Art Gallery and the Art Gallery of Ontario. She had three daughters and two sons. Her son 'Billy' was killed in action while serving in the Canadian Merchant Navy.

References

The Columbian, New Westminister, B.C., Nov. 18, 1957 "Artist Shows Watercolors"

Ibid, Dec. 7, 1962, "Art exhibit to highlight Council tea"

Vancouver West Ender, Van., B.C., Nov. 17, 1965 "Travels retained in Water Colours"

The Columbian, B.C., Apr. 22, 1968 "81 – year – old local artist exhibits favorite scenes" by Winnifred Thorpe

Williams Lake News, B.C., Oct. 1, 1968 "Artist, 81, Paintings On Display Sat., Sun."

Columbian's This Week, New Westminister, B.C., Apr. 25, 1968 "81 – year – old local artist exhibits favorite scenes" by Winnifred Thorpe

Williams Lake Tribune, B.C., Oct. 2, 1968 "Lindermere paintings on exhibit this week"

LINDEMERE, Richard
b.(c)1881

Born in London, England, he was brought up in Paris, France, where he studied painting (1896-1899) under James Walker. He returned to London and became a member of the London Stock Exchange for the next five years. He took a trip to Canada in 1904 as a holiday and stayed on. In 1905 he brought horses across country from Medicine Hat to Battleford. For fifteen summers afterwards he rode in the wake of cow herds and painted his experiences in the winters. Settling near Battleford, Saskatchewan, he homesteaded, operated a livery stable, hunted, rode, was a sheriff's officer, collected for a farm implement company and recorded on canvas the history of his province during available periods. He became a friend of the Indians and listened to stories about early settlers. He visited ruins of old forts and with the aid of aged Indians and former residents reconstructed historical paintings. He also did a number of portraits of Indians. An exhibit of his paintings took place in the summer of 1929 at the art section of the Calgary exhibition and the following year at The Legislative Buildings, Regina, when he displayed his scenes of early history in Saskatchewan under the Royal Canadian Mounted Police. Lindemere is represented in the Lloydminster Barr Colony Museum, Lloydminster, Sask., and other collections both public and private. His paintings were reproduced in Saskatchewan school history books.

References

The Herald, Calgary, Alta., July 9, 1929 "Battleford Artist Has Exhibit Here – Richard Lindemere Shows Twenty-four Pictures of Early Life in West"

The Star, Regina, Sask., Feb. 17, 1930 "Art Gallery For Province Is Proposed – R. Lindemere, Battleford Artist, Makes Interesting Suggestion"

The Columbian, New Westminster, B.C., July 15, 1950 "To Paint Dust, You've Got To Eat It – Richard Lindemere" by Jimmie McPhee

Lloydminster Times, Lloydmstr., Sask., Oct. 6, 1965 "Historical Painting Loaned"

LINDGREN, Charlotte
b. 1931

Born in Toronto, Ont., she attended the Universities of Toronto, Wisconsin, Michigan (B.Sc.), Delaware.[1] She became Design lecturer at the University of Manitoba intermittently from 1957-63. In 1964 she received a scholarship to study under Jack Lenor Larsen at Haystack School in Deere Isle, Maine, U.S.A., and the

LINDGREN, Charlotte (Cont'd)

following year a Canada Council Arts Scholarship to study in Finland, Sweden and England.[2] She began exhibiting her weaving and stitchery in the form of wall hangings at the Rourke Gallery, Moorhead, Minnesota, in 1964, when F.G. Schoff, critic of the *Fargo Forum* noted, "Her designs are abstract, and sometimes in an abstract-expressionist vein except for an element of classical restraint. They can be stitched on fabrics with relatively complex patterns that are indescribable but fascinating, or extremely simple ones suggesting an eye for Chinese effects. Or they can be part of the weaving process, formed from loops drawn out of warp or weft threads, or perhaps from omitting the latter in one area . . . ." These comments were carried in the *Craft Horizons*[3] which also noted her 1965 exhibition at the School of Architecture, Nova Scotia Technical College, Halifax, when Carol Fraser[4] observed, "Charlotte Lindgren nearly always starts with a suggestive image and relates color, texture, shape, and size to this image either representationally, as in 'Seaweed,' a large (14" x 14" x 76") brown-green three-dimensional hanging woven of twine and silk suspended from an iron hoop, or by free association, as in 'Winnipeg Wedding' (10" x 70"), which contrasts soft, bulky puffs of unspun wool weft with the sheer, brittle elegance of a white linen warp . . . . There is a nice cohesiveness to these works in spite of their variety. Perhaps it is the insistence on experimentation which permeates every piece. Perhaps it is the way in which the aesthetic leavening of the loom has been used to control as well as excite design. Most likely it is a happy combination of the two." In 1965 she also held one man shows in New York City; Confederation Centre, Charlottetown; School of Art, U. of Manitoba, Winnipeg, and she participated in a group show at the Dorothy Cameron Gallery in Toronto. In 1966 she exhibited at the Montreal Museum of Fine Arts where her work was 'Critics' Choice' at Visua 66; she also exhibited in Paris, France; Maine, U.S.A.; and at the Festival of the Arts, Nova Scotia. The year 1967 was one of her most successful when she represented Canada at Lausanne, Switzerland, in the Biennial International Tapestry Exhibition; received a $3,000 prize in the fine crafts section of Perspective '67 under the auspices of the Canadian Centennial Commission.[5] This prize was won for her wall hanging of a young girl with golden braids. She also won a prize in Canada Crafts '67 Competition. Her work was twice noticed by *arts/canada*[6]. Her "Tunnel of Love" was selected by an international jury for exhibition at the Fourth International Biennial of Ancient and Modern Tapestry held in 1969 at the Canton Museum of Fine Arts, Lausanne. She was commissioned to do one of her three-dimentional forms of metalized plastic for the Canadian Pavilion at Osaka 70. She lives in Halifax, N.S. with her husband, an architect, (teacher at the Nova Scotia Technical College School of Architecture) and two children. She is represented in the following collections: The Canada Council; Montreal Museum of Fine Arts; New Brunswick Museum; Canadian High Commissioner in London, England and private collections in Canada, U.S.A. and Brazil.

References
[1] National Gallery of Canada Information Form rec'd 19 April, 1966 also 12 Sept., 1967
[2] Ibid
[3] *Craft Horizons,* May, 1964
[4] Ibid, May/June, 1965 "Exhibitions – Charlotte Lindgren" by Carol Fraser
[5] *Chronicle-Herald,* Halifax, N.S., July 13, 1967 "Weaver Wins $3,000 Prize"
[6] *arts/canada,* January, 1967, No. 104 "1967 – The Moment of Truth for Canadian Crafts" by Dorothy Todd Henaut, P. 20
Ibid, June/July, 1967 No. 109/110 "Two Halifax Artists"

LINDGREN, Charlotte (Cont'd)

see also

The Evening Patriot, Charlottetown, P.E.I., April 17, 1965 "Lindgren exhibition has something for everyone" by Jane Lapsley

American Fabrics, Winter, 1966 "The Work of Charlotte Lindgren Is Playful Yet Disciplined"

Catalogue, Charlotte Lindgren, Woven Hangings, The Winnipeg Art Gallery with introduction by Illi-Maria Harff, Curator, Dec., 1966

Free Press, Winnipeg, Man., Dec. 8, 1966 "Warp Like Summer's Dawn Gets Woof Of Cellophane" by Edith Paterson

Mail-Star, Halifax, N.S., July 13, 1967 "$3,000 Prize To Artist In Wool"

Ibid, May 26, 1969 "Weaving Is Believing . . . Mind Bending And Always Expressive . . ." by Sheila Urquhart

---

LINDNER, Ernest
b. 1897

Born in Vienna, Austria, the youngest of thirteen children, his father was a professional wood turner and carver who later established a factory of luxury articles in Vienna.[1] Ernest studied drawing and painting at preparatory school in his native city. When he was eighteen he served with the Austrian army and airforce during the First World War and was wounded in an air crash in 1916.[2] At the end of the war he started to study architecture but abandoned this when his father died. He then worked as a bank clerk for a short period and then as a designer in the family business of a small factory producing ornate items. Among these items were parasol-handles and canes and in 1921 Linder won a gold medal in a fashion design section at the Industrial Fair at Stuttgart with his entry of a parasol.[3] He left the family business and became a partner in a candy factory.[4] When the Italian lira fell in 1926, his firm was wiped out.[5] He came to Canada in 1926 as a farm labourer and worked in Saskatchewan.[6] After two summers work at farm labour he settled permanently in Saskatoon. He took special study under Augustus Kenderdine in 1928.[7] In 1931 he became a Canadian citizen.[8] He did some house-painting, illustration work for the University of Saskatchewan, free-lance commercial art work while he attended night classes in art at the Technical Collegiate.[9] He continued his night studies until 1935. In 1936 he became art instructor and head of the Art Department at the Technical Collegiate in Saskatoon, a position he held until his retirement in 1962. In 1933 one of his paintings was accepted for showing in the 50th Spring Show of the Art Association of Montreal.[10] His water colour "The Silent Audience" was accepted by the Royal Canadian Academy of Arts 60th Annual Exhibition at Montreal. This work was described by Nonie Mulcaster[11] as follows, "This is a fanciful impression of the little 'snow people' who inhabit the island throughout the winter. Tiny spruce wearing rounded fluffs of snow take the form of winter elves, crouched in a circle to watch the dancing figure of a slender maiden spruce. The soft-lit gloom of winter woods forms a fitting background and adds to the feeling of hushed suspense. The subtle colors of sunlit snow, the exquisite design in every shape, and the impish spirit that prevades this highly imaginative piece of work combine to make this one of Mr. Lindner's most popular pictures." In 1940 he became a member of the Federation of Canadian Artists. By 1941 Lindner had attracted the attention of the Society of Canadian Painter-Etchers and Engravers for his linoleum cuts entered in their 25th annual exhibition and as a result was invited to become a member.[12] In 1944 he donated one of his paintings of the Twenty-fifth Street Bridge in Saskatoon for presentation to Saskatoon's adopted Russian City of Romny.[13] His exhibition in Calgary during 1945 was noted

LINDNER, Ernest (Cont'd)

by The Albertan[14] as follows, "One of the most interesting phases of this exhibition has been the accentuation of drawings and paintings by the artist of his wife 'Bodil.' He has found in her attractive profile and characterful face an inspiration for a number of his works. In this he is repeating the trend of many artists, such as Frans Hals, amongst the masters, and Gerald Brockhurst, A.R.A., representing the moderns. In perhaps the finest large water color in the exhibition Lindner (who brings to western Canada the meticulous technique of Middle European art training) gives a fine portrait of his wife . . . . Lindner's other love is for the interiors of spruce woods, where he finds strange living forms, and intriguing aspects of decay. This phase of his work is making him well known in exhibitions across Canada." He produced carvings from spruce although his painting and drawing received more of his attention. In 1959 he received a Canada Council Grant for a year's study in Europe. He took a five months course in etching and wood sculpture at the Academy for Applied Arts in Vienna. He travelled in England, France, The Netherlands, Germany, Italy, and Switzerland.[15] After he returned to Canada he continued to develop his art and exhibited his work at: Norman Mackenzie Art Gallery, Regina, Sask. (1962); Saskatoon Art Centre, Sask. (1963); The Alberta College of Art, Calgary (1963); Brandon Allied Arts Centre, Brandon, Man. (1964); Moose Jaw Public Library, Moose Jaw, Sask. (1964); Banfer Gallery, New York City (1965); Mendal Art Gallery (retrospective exhibition – 1970) when Florence Pratt[16] noted, "Hung in chronological order the sketches, water colors, oils and acrylics tell their own story of a steadily maturing talent. Portraying with ever deepening insight and interest the varied facets of nature and the human form, these works reveal also both the strength and vulnerable gentility of the man himself. He has looked on nature, raw and rugged as she often is, yet found beauty in all her aspects. The grain and form of microscopic bits of bark or the great, grey swirl of prairie storm clouds, at varying periods, have found equal attraction and interest. Lindner's concern lay more with nature than with people. Yet in the few portraits and nudes in the show, it is clear the perceptive eye of the artist saw well beyond the form." Lindner painted in oils, water colours, tempera, casein; did sculpture in clay, wood, metals; engraved with stone lithography, acquatint and etching. He did illustrations for John McNaughton's book *Jungle Wise and Otherwise*. Five of his water colours were chosen for showing at the Seventh Biennial of Canadian Painting and one "The Fledgling" was reproduced in the exhibition catalogue.[17] Today Lindner's remarkable paintings remind us that if nature is given half a chance, she will renew herself as does the sapling from the decayed tree trunk on the forest bed. He is represented in the following collections: Grand Central Galleries, New York City; International Business Machine Corp., New York City; London Public Library and Art Museum, London, Ont.; Royal Ontario Museum, Tor., Ont.; Hart House (U. of T.) Toronto; Norman Mackenzie Art Gallery, Regina, Sask.; Beaverbrook Gallery, Fredericton, N.B.; Sir George Williams University, Montreal, P.Q.; Vincent Massey Collection (NGC); University of Saskatchewan, Saskatoon; F.S. Mendel Collection, Saskatoon; F.S. Mendel Collection, Sidney, Australia; Academy of Applied Art, Vienna, Austria; Clement Greenberg Collection; Saskatoon Gallery & Conservatory Corp., Saskatoon; Art Gallery of Ontario, Tor., Ont. In Saskatoon he completed eleven hammered copper reliefs and murals for the T. Eaton Company also murals for the Senator Hotel. Although no longer active with art organizations he was a member of the Saskatoon Art Association (1935); Saskatchewan Society for Education Through Art (1960); C.P.E.

LINDNER, Ernest (Cont'd)

(1942); Canadian Society of Graphic Art (1944); Saskatchewan Arts Board; Saskatoon Art Centre; Canadian Arts Council and others.

References

[1] biographical notes in NGC Library file

[2] Ibid

[3] The Sheaf, Saskatoon, Sask., Feb. 17, 1950 "Ernest Lindner" by G.G.

[4] arts/canada, June, 1970 "An Ernest Lindner retrospective" by C.S. McConnell, p. 30

[5] Ibid

[6] Ibid

[7] NGC Info. Form rec'd May 18, 1933

[8] see [1]

[9] see [1]

[10] Star-Phoenix, Saskatoon, Sask., Mar. 18, 1933 "Lindner Picture Accepted For Montreal Spring Show"

[11] Ibid, Dec. 1, 1939 "Lindner's Winter Picture of Fairy Island Show At Montreal by Royal Canadian Academy of Arts" by Nonie Mulcaster

[12] Ibid, May 17, 1941 "Artist Honored by Society of Etchers"

[13] Ibid, Aug. 2, 1944 "Illuminated Greeting, and A Painting of Saskatoon, Will Be Sent to Romny"

[14] The Albertan, Calgary, Alta., May 3, 1945 "Artist's Wife Provides Theme for Exhibition" by D. Geneva Lent

[15] Star-Phoenix, Saskatoon, Sask., Aug. 29, 1960 "Ernie Lindner Back After Year of European Studies"

[16] Ibid, April 13, 1970 "Fine tribute to Lindner hanging on gallery walls" by Florence Pratt

[17] Seventh Biennial of Canadian Painting (catalogue), Queen's Printer, Ottawa, 1968

see also

Canadian Drawings And Prints by Paul Duval, Burns & MacEachern, Tor., 1952, Plate 35

Canadian Art, Vol. 20, No. 2, March/April, 1963, "Clement Greenberg's View Of Art On The Prairies" P. 104, 105

Canadian Art Today, Editor: William Townsend, Studio International, London, England, 1970, P. 50, 51

arts/canada, June, 1970, No. 144/145 "A note on Ernest Lindner" by Ronald L. Bloore

Star-Phoenix, Saskatoon, Sask., Mar. 18, 1933

Ibid, Dec. 1, 1939 "Lindner's Winter Picture of Fairy Island Show At Montreal by Royal Canadian Academy of Arts"

Ibid, No. 9, 1939 "Practical Uses of Art Training Outlined for Club by E. Lindner"

Ibid, Sept. 7, 1940 "Northern Clouds Featured Largely In New Painting by Ernest Lindner"

Ibid, Oct. 29, 1941 "Lindner President Of Art Association"

Ibid, June 3, 1944 "Lindner on Executive Of Canadian Artists"

The Vancouver Sun, Van., B.C., Mar. 9, 1946 "Sharp Contrasts In Art Exhibits" by Mildred Valley Thornton

Star-Phoenix, Saskatoon, Sask., April 27, 1949 (photo of Lindner's carved spruce work "Four Figures")

Leader-Post, Regina, Sask., "Best painting by E. Lindner"

Star-Phoenix, Saskatoon, Sask., June 13, 1959 "Dean of Saskatoon Artists Prepares for Trip Overseas"

Leader-Post, Dec. 1, 1962 "Works by famed artist on exhibit"

Ibid, Dec. 5, 1962 "Artist termed man of courage"

The Brandon Sun, Brandon, Man., Mar. 21, 1964 "Lindner Collection Will Be Popular"

Ibid, Mar. 25, 1964 "Lindner Pictures Hang At Gallery" by Kaye Rowe

Moose Jaw Times-Herald, Moose Jaw, Sask., May 1, 1964 "Paintings By Sask. Artist Highly Rated Display Here"

Star-Phoenix, Mar. 6, 1965 "Lindner to Have One-Man Art Show In New York City"

E. Lindner (catalogue) Banfer Gallery, 23 East 67 Street, New York, Mar. 10 – 27, 1965

Leader-Post, Nov. 8, 1968 "Strong static quality seen in Lindner art at library" by Katie Fitzrandolph

LINDOE, Luke Orton
b. 1913

Born in Bashaw, Alberta, he studied in schools in Canada and the United States.[1] He worked periodically in a coal mine to finance his studies at the Provincial Institute of Technology and Art where he took four years of painting and sculpture, and at the Ontario College of Art, for an additional year's study in sculpture.[2] At first he made his living as an instrument man for Imperial Oil Limited and lived with his wife and child for several years in a small summer tent from May until November.[3] Although trained as a sculptor Lindoe at this point had no facilities or storage space for his work. He did however do some painting in water colours. In 1939 he became an Associate Member of the Alberta Society of Artists. His nomadic life came to an end when he was appointed Instructor of Sculpture and Ceramics at the Provincial Institute of Technology and Art in 1940. He became a member of the Canadian Society of Painters in Water Colour in 1946. By 1951 he had been elected Second Vice-President of the C.S.P.W.C. and also Chairman of the Alberta Society of Artists (1949-50). He exhibited his sculpture and ceramics at the Coste House, Calgary, when *The Herald*[4] noted, "His intimate art is a result of an unconventional compromise between a potter's and sculptor's technique and his polished works done mostly of glazed clay can produce an atmosphere of unexpected beauty in any average Canadian home. Functional and decorative pottery included in the show reveal the artist's universal craftsmanship. Mr. Lindoe, who is at present interested in the Korean high temperature ceramics, commented on difficulties pertaining to its technique." In 1956 his design for decoration of St. Mary's Roman Catholic Cathedral in Calgary, depicting the Virgin Mary and Child Jesus was constructed in seven separate pieces. Assembled it makes an impressive work twenty-one feet high weighing seven tons. Another commission in 1959 was awarded to him in a competition which included seven other prairie sculptors for the decoration of the Calgary Allied Arts Council building. The work, a wall-like structure, is made up of a series of ceramic plaques depicting on one side, primitive people travelling and conveying ideas by pictographs, and on the other, the Province of Alberta in a symbolic presentation. Financed by the Canada Council the work was unveiled in early January of 1960.[5] His other commissions include: Dr. Dan McCharles Memorial in Medicine Hat; the Alberta Museum and Archives facade, Edmonton; Medicine Hat Community Art Club's centennial gift of sculpture to the Medicine Hat Public Library. In recent years he has become known particularly for his fine pottery and has been a member of the Canadian Guild of Potters for over a decade. His works have been included in numerous national exhibitions and have won him honors and awards at international shows in Prague, Geneva, Istanbul and Ostend, Belgium. He shared the Potters' Club of Montreal award in 1967 and was one of five potters invited to participate in the Canadian Guild of Potters' exhibition "Invitation I". His work is not usually for sale in art shops as he prefers to invite a few acquaintances to his studio when he has enough work for sale and in this way sells everything. He lives in Medicine Hat with his wife who is also a painter.

References
[1] National Gallery of Canada Information From received August, 1961
[2] Ibid, also *The Medicine Hat News*, April 30, 1970 "A potter's philosophy . . . 'Accept nothing but the best' " by Carolyne Rittinger
[3] *The Edmonton Journal*, Edmonton, Alta., Feb. 17, 1953 "Sculptor Seeks New Approach In Canadian Art"
[4] *The Calgary Herald*, Calgary, Alta., Feb. 21, 1953 "Intimate Art Features Show"

LINDOE, Luke Orton (Cont'd)

[5] Ibid, Jan. 6, 1960 "Sculpture Unveiling Marks New Arts Centre Opening"
see also
The Calgary Herald, Calgary, Alta., May 30, 1950 "Calgarian Holds Top Art Position"
Leader-Post, Regina, Sask., Nov. 15, 1952 "Clay sculpture, pottery from Calgary on exhibit"
The Calgary Herald, Feb. 3, 1953 "Murals May Replace Pictures in Houses" by Dushan Bresky
Le Droit, Ottawa, Ont., Feb. 20, 1953 (photo of Lindoe at work)
The Record, Kitchener, Ont., Feb. 20, 1953 "New Art Approach Said Needed"
The Evening Tribune, Welland, Ont., Feb. 21, 1953 "Prairie Painter Looks For New Approach To Canadian Art"
Medicine Hat News, Medicine Hat, Alta., June 24, 1959 "$2,000 Art Award To City Sculptor"
The Calgary Herald, Calgary, Alta, June 25, 1959 "Ceramist Awarded Prize"
Medicine Hat News, Oct. 17, 1959 "Art Display Set Sunday"
The Albertan, Calgary, Alta., Jan. 6, 1960 " 'Major Step Forward' Taken by Arts Centre"
The Edmonton Journal, Edmonton, Alta., July 9, 1965 "Two Sculptors Commissioned By Cabinet"
A Bulletin Published By The Adult Education Division, Department of Education, and The Saskatchewan Arts Board, Vol 3, No. 9, April 30, 1952 (Queen's Printer For Saskatchewan) "Saskatchewan Art, How Some Artists Work" by Luke Lindoe

---

LINDSAY, Bertrand

A Grimsby, Ontario, sculptor, who studied art history and design theory at the Hamilton Technical College and the Toronto Central Technical School. He has been strongly influenced by classical sculpture. His "Viking's Head" won second prize at the 102 Festival of Art at Niagara-on-the-Lake in 1969. His subjects include figures and head studies. He works almost exclusively in cherrywood which he obtains from a local orchard. For a number of years he painted in oils and pastels. A teacher for thirty-five years he taught in schools at Hespeler, St. Catharines, Ottawa and Grimsby and retired from Park School, Grimsby, where he was principal for twelve years.

Reference

Independent, Grimsby, Ont., June 25, 1969 "Independent People – Grimsby's conventional sculptor" by Ron Gabriel
Express, Beamsville, Ont., July 30, 1969 "Prize carvings from cherrywood"
Herald, Georgetown, Ont., Aug. 7, 1969 "Cherrywood Sculpture Retirement Project for Georgetown Native"
The St. Catharines Standard, St. Catharines, Ont., July 18, 1969 "World of Art – No Material Shortage For Grimsby Sculptor" by Joan Phillips

---

LINDSAY, Doreen

Born in London, Ontario, she received a scholarship to study at the Instituto de Allende, Mexico, in 1956. She continued her studies and in 1960 settled in Montreal where she has taught for several years at the Montreal Museum of Fine Arts School. She held a solo show in 1962 at Galerie Huot, Montreal, where her work was well received by *La Presse* critic Claude Jasmin. This exhibition included her figurative oils, charcoal sketches, monoprints (oils painted on a sheet of glass and transferred on to heavy absorbent rice paper), and one collage entitled "Composition" which received particular praise.

LINDSAY, Doreen (Cont'd)

Reference

La Presse, Mtl., P.Q., June 16, 1962 "les beaux-arts — Un peintre qui se cherche: Doré Lindsay" par Claude Jasmin

LINDSAY, Ellen Trider
b. 1900

Born in Saint John, N.B., she studied at the Nova Scotia College of Art, Halifax, under Elizabeth S. Nutt and at the Parson's School of Design, New York City. She became a member of the Nova Scotia Society of Artists in 1939 and served as Treasurer (1946-49), President (1945-46, 1951-52), Exhibition Secretary (1955). Her work has also been shown in jury shows of the Canadian Society of Painters in Water Colour, Nova Scotia Society of Artists, at the Art Gallery of Hamilton, Montreal Museum of Fine Arts, Maritime Art Association and Nova Scotia Department of Education Travelling Exhibitions.

Reference

National Gallery of Canada Information Forms rec'd July 21, 1955 and June 26, 1959

LINDSAY, Isobel

A Toronto, Ontario, artist who held a large exhibition of water colours at the Burlington Public Library in the spring of 1958. Her work was noted by *The Hamilton Spectator* as follows, "Impulsive and dynamic in her style, Miss Lindsay is capable of communicating with zest the fresh country air and rich vegetation of forest regions. Trees and underbrush are slashed in a bursting but accurate stroke. Although executed with an apparently rapid and spontaneous hand, her paintings retain an appealing sensitiveness and delicacy. Her most 'noteworthy' canvases are those of churches, old mills and houses brooding behind a delicate mist. The lofty steeples seem to reach out of the haze to grasp a deeper spiritual essence." Miss Lindsay is head of the fine arts department at the R.H. King Collegiate Institute in Scarboro, Ontario.

Reference

The Hamilton Spectator, Hamilton, Ont., April 14, 1958 "Impulsive And Dynamic Paintings Are Featured"

LINDSAY, Robert Henry
1868-1938

Born in Prescott, Ontario, the son of George Lindsay, he was brought to Brockville as a boy where his family settled. He was employed as a painter by the James Smart Manufacturing Company and studied under Percy F. Woodcock, R.C.A. He succeeded Woodcock as instructor at an Ontario Government school in Brockville. He also taught drawing in St. Alban's Boys School. He became a member of the Arts Club of Montreal in 1911. He sketched with Harold A. Pearl of Toronto sometimes in the Newboro-Westport District and also did many pencil sketches of Brockville which are now of historical value. Following his death in 1938 his widow Margaret Boucher Lindsay presented about forty of his pencil sketches to

LINDSAY, Robert Henry (Cont'd)

the Brockville Public Library. He exhibited his oils and water colours with the Royal Canadian Academy, Ontario Society of Artists, Montreal Art Association also in Chicago, Winnipeg and Belfast, Ireland.

References

National Gallery of Canada Information Form rec'd April 15, 1935

Recorder & Times, Brockville, Ont., Oct. 9, 1931 "Scenery In Leeds Delights Artists — Sketching Done In Newboro-Westport District by Messrs. Lindsay and Pearl"

Globe & Mail, March 31, 1938 "Noted Artist of Brockville Dies, Aged 71"

The Recorder & Times, June 20, 1967 "Artist Lindsay Looks At Brockville" (eight of his drawings of Brockville reproduced)

LINDSTROM, Matt

b. 1890

Born in Finland of Swedish parents, he loved to paint as a child. He earned his living as a police detective and later a private investigator. He was not entirely happy with this work and decided to emigrate to Canada. He arrived in 1929 during the depression and made his way to a community north of Edmonton. He worked at various jobs but found it almost impossible to make ends meet. Finally he went to Edmonton where he got a job painting signs in a small department store but it too was affected by the bad times and he again found himself unemployed. Next he worked in a hardware store. While walking along vacant storefronts in downtown Edmonton he discovered a shop which sold paintings and went to work there. He then began to paint scenes. He moved to Calgary in 1932 and stayed at a chicken farm where the owner gave him food and a bench in the hatchery to sleep on until he was able to make some money at painting signs for confectioners. Later he became an interior painter and made enough money to stay at a lodge. Each evening he turned to painting at his easel. After several people advised him that he should paint scenes full time he enrolled in art classes at the Institute of Technology and Art then housed in the Coste House. He received scholarships to study at the Banff School of Fine Arts and in 1945 at the age of fifty-five began his new career. For the past few years his studio has been a room in the Wales Hotel, Calgary. Most of his paintings are landscapes but he is able to do a wide range of subjects. He was a friend of the late Roland Gissing and they often went sketching together. Describing his work in 1970 Bill Musselwhite noted, ". . . most of his sketches and his paintings deal with scenes familiar to Calgarians — foothills and mountains west of the city . . . . He especially loves trees . . . ." Lindstrom was doing a series of paintings in 1945 to record the history of the West, a project on which he had spent many hours of research. A fire in the building where he had his studio destroyed all the work he had managed to complete. Now over eighty years old he still produces enough canvases to hold two one man shows a year. He is a life member of the Calgary Sketch Club.

References

The Lethbridge Herald, Lethbridge, Alta., May 9, 1969 "Calgary Artist Going Strong at 81" by Joan Bowman

The Calgary Herald, Calgary, Alta., April 17, 1970 "Personality of The Week" by Bill Musselwhite

LINES, Beryl Jones

Born in Port Arthur, Ontario, she attended high school in Edmonton, Alberta, where her family settled. She won several awards for her art during these years and following her graduation from high school she attended a private art school in Edmonton. In 1942 she received her teacher's certificate from the Vancouver School of Art. Later she studied under visiting artists, summers, at Jasper. She has given instruction to many pupils at craft rooms across Canada during her husband's service in the army. In the summer her paintings are available in a family gift shop at Maligne Canyon about nine miles from Jasper. She is represented in many collections throughout the world. She lives at Camp Chilliwack, B.C., with her husband Lieutenant Lines, and they plan to retire in Chilliwack and spend their summers at Maligne Canyon. She is a member of the Fraser Valley Brush and Palette Club (Pres. 1962).

References
Progress, Chilliwack, B.C., April 14, 1965 "Just The Right Recipe For a Happy Home"

LINHART, Luba & Mila

Originally from Czechoslovakia, Luba and Mila Linhart came to Canada in 1949 and operated a display business. Later they opened a pottery near Gelert, Ontario (they live on the Drag River, on the Irondale Road, south of Gelert) in Haliburton County. They have studied the history of art including that of the Aztecs, Incas, Mayans, whom they feel have influenced North American Indian art. All their pottery is hand moulded and hand painted. As well they are influenced by the forests of Canada but most of their creations are derived from Canada's native races.

References
Le Droit, Ottawa, Ont., May 13, 1965 (photo of Lou Linhart with work)
Progress, Minden, Ont., Nov. 7, 1968 "Haliburton Pottery — A Place Of Distinction"

LINLEY, Joan

A Weyburn, Saskatchewan, artist who designed and supervised the making of a large wheel consisting of ten panels. Each panel depicts ten different periods in Weyburn's history dating back to the period of the Cree Indians and the buffalo. The wheel has a diameter of thirteen feet and weighs more than two thousand pounds. Miss Linley used Italian glass tile, hand-cut to one centimeter, in ninety different colours. She was assisted in the mosaic by Mrs. Russ Pennock and Al Wiebe of Weyburn. The work was unveiled in the Weyburn City Hall in 1965. Subsequently she was awarded a prize at Ceramics 69 at the Vancouver Art Gallery for her slab construction stoneware bottle.

References
Leader-Post, Regina, Sask., Nov. 1, 1965 "Mosaic designed by a local artist" by Pete Wenger (large photo of work)

LINLEY, Joan (Cont'd)

Weyburn Review, Weyburn, Sask., Nov. 4, 1965 "Festival City dedicates mural by local artist during jubilee program"
Ibid, Nov. 11, 1965 "Festival was turning point in local artist's life"
Ibid, April 11, 1968 (large photo of one of her pottery pieces)
Ibid, April 3, 1969 "Joan Linley wins ceramics award in Vancouver"

LIPARI, Frank A. (François Amedeo Lipari)

Born in Montreal, Quebec, he was an apprentice typographer (1942-46) then studied Life Drawing (1946), Fine Art (1947) at Sir George Williams School of Art; Academic Portrait under Francesco Iacurto, privately (1948).[1] From 1948-55 he was junior designer, then designer, and creative designer in graphics.[2] In 1955 he attended a post graduate course in advertising design, graphic design, and other subjects at the Art Centre School of Los Angeles under Miss B. Polifka and Harry Thomson, and others.[3] In 1957 he did special studies in motion picture and T.V. film production. Lipari is active as an illustrator, painter, graphic designer, master typographer and art director. His graphic designs have won him scores of awards (see below). He held his first one man show of drawings and paintings at the Arts Club, Montreal in 1958. The following year he exhibited jointly with Michel Kouliche at the Helene de Champlain Gallery on St. Helen's Island, Montreal, when Dorothy Pfeiffer[4] noted, "Lipari is primarily a painter of observation, wit and always of human reaction and emotion, whether he disguises his intention by designing lyrical forms of fish or birds, or expresses it in intense blue skies or snowy landscapes. This young painter has singleness of purpose, an almost childlike delight in chaste simplicity and subtle color and a most thought-provoking manner of interpretation . . . . Lipari's art is entirely personal. Far from being merely decorative – which it also undoubtedly is, his paintings advance ideas and contain a deeply persuasive philosophy . . . . Lipari works at his embellished drawings in a white heat of creative inspiration. He cannot rest until the idea itself is expressed on canvas or paper. There is therefore a feeling of spontaneity in nearly everything he draws or paints." In 1960 he held a solo show of his drawings and paintings at the Montreal Museum of Fine Arts in Gallery XII. His awards include: Best Cover, New York Financial Post, N.Y. (1952); Magazine Design Certificate of Merit from International Council of Industrial Editors (1952); Direct Mail Design Award from DMAA (1953); Magazine Cover Award from CDMLC (1953); Story Board Design for Film Award from Hollywood, Calif. (1955); Cover Art Award from Toronto Art Directors' Club Exhib. (1955); Direct Mail Design Award from CDMLC (1956); Design of Stationery Award from Lithographers' National Assoc., U.S. (1958); 15 Certificates of Merit Awards for booklet design from "Typography '58" (1958); 4 Certificates of Merit from "Typography '59" (1959); Booklet Design Award from Lithographers' Nat. Assoc., U.S. (1959); Magazine Design Award from Lithographers' Nat. Assoc., U.S. (1959); Christmas Cards Award, Lithographers' Nat. Assoc., U.S. (1960); Certificate of Merit Award from "Typography '60" (1960); Business Stationery Award, Lithographers' Nat. Assoc., U.S. (1961); Magazine Cover Award, Lithographers' Nat. Assoc., U.S. (1962); Stationery Award Lithographers' Nat. Assoc., U.S. (1962); 6 Certificates of Merit from "Typography '62" (1962); Magazine Design Award, Lithographers' Nat. Assoc., U.S. (1963); Excellence in Literature, Building Products Award (1964); Design of Booklet, Peter Barratt Award (1965); and others. He is a member of the following societies: Art

LIPARI, Frank A. (François Amedeo Lipari) (Cont'd)

Directors' Club of Montreal (1953); National Society of Art Directors (1954); Typographical Designer Society of Canada. He is a consultant art director for the Gazette Printing Co. Ltd., Montreal. He has participated in group shows too numerous to mention here.

References

[1] National Gallery of Canada Information Form, 1965 and 1958

[2] Ibid

[3] Ibid

[4] *The Gazette,* Mtl, P.Q., May 30, 1959 "Lipari-Kouliche Exhibition" by Dorothy Pfeiffer
see also
The Gazette, Mtl, P.Q., April 26, 1958 "One-Man Show"
La Presse, Mtl. P.Q., May 14, 1958 "Frank Lipari"
Globe & Mail, Tor., Ont. "Startling Variety in New Displays"
Petit Journal, Mtl, P.Q., Nov. 9, 1958
The Gazette, May 16, 1959 "At St. Helen's Island"
Le Devoir, Mtl., P.Q., May 23, 1959 "La forme et le sentiment" par R. Chicoine
The Montreal Star, Mtl., P.Q., "Art as Well as Letters Is Displayed In New Fraser-Hickson Institute" by Robert Ayre
The Gazette, April 19, 1960 "Gazette Designer To Exhibit"
N.D.G. Monitor, Mtl., P.Q., April 18, 1963 "Montreal West man wins two art awards"
Ibid, Sept. 15, 1966 "Local artist receives commission"
Publimondial, France, 1953, P. 56
Vie des Arts, Mtl., P.Q., Summer, 1958, P. 46
Canadian Printer & Publisher, Sept. 1958, P. 67, 1963, P. 54
Art in America, No. 1, 1960, P. 112
Canadian Art, May, 1960, P. 147
Format, Canada, 1964
Catalogue – Fourth Biennial Exhibition of Canadian Art, 1961, No. 43

LIPPERT, Jane Elizabeth

b. 1924

Born in Kitchener, Ontario, she studied at the Ontario College of Art, Toronto; Der Akademie der Bilden Kunst, Vienna, Austria; La Grande Chaumière, Paris, France; was apprenticed with Prof. A. Winternitz in mosaic church work in Madrid, Spain. She received scholarships from the Women's Art Association of Canada; received honour diploma from the Academy in Vienna for mosaic and fresco work and murals. After her return from Europe she specialized in mural work principally in Toronto. Her etchings were also exhibited with the Society of Canadian Painter-Etchers and Engravers. Was living in Toronto in 1954.

Reference

National Gallery of Canada Information Form rec'd 1954

LISHMAN, Bill

b. 1940

Born in Pickering Township, he started making sculpture seriously about 1964 although he had always been interested in this type of art. He turned to the construction of huge metal animals using a variety of objects. *The Mississauga News*

LISHMAN, Bill (Cont'd)

described one of his works as follows, "At one time it may have been littered around a scrap metal yard — now it's a prized work of art. It is the life-sized Iron Horse which graces the swimming pool surroundings at the home of Bruce McLaughlin of Lochlin Trail, Mississauga. Made out of odd scraps of iron — including nuts, bolts, old engine parts and even a car tail pipe — it portrays magnificently a stallion in swift motion, tail and mane flowing." Lishman has also done a variety of other subjects. His sculpture entitled "Yellow Dandelions in a Green Field" consists of two columns rising 25 feet. They are straight with the exception of a graceful curve in each of the two stems. This work won the Webb Zerafa Menkes cash award for the best sculpture at the 8th annual Toronto Outdoor Art Exhibition at Nathan Phillips Square, City Hall, Toronto. It was later purchased by the Robert McLaughlin Gallery, Oshawa. Two of his animal sculptures were purchased by *The Western Fair Board,* one, a large race horse, decorates the facade of the grandstand, the other, a large bull, is on display in front of the livestock barns. In another work he collected fifteen tons of junk in order to make an eight-ton mural worth $15,000 for an exterior wall of a hardware store in Ottawa. A few of the items that went into the work include: a plow, collection of old wrenches, sewing machines, antique items, and thousands of other pieces. He worked in a Mexican metal-working shop in 1966 and found that experience invaluable for his sculpture. An exhibition of his work took place at the Adams and Yves Gallery, Markham Street, Toronto, in April of 1969. He lives at Brougham, Ontario, where he and his wife Paula have made a home out of an old school house.

References

The London Free Press, London, Ont., April 11, 1868 "$5,500 iron horse adds new touch to WFR gateway"

The Mississauga News, Mississauga, Ont., July 10, 1968 "Midweek — This horse has a tail pipe"

Tribune, Stouffville, Ont., Aug. 22, 1968 (photo of Lishman's work of a large bull)

New Advertiser, Ajax, Ont., Sept. 26, 1968 (photo of a section of his eight ton mural earmarked for an Ottawa hardware store)

Ibid, Jan. 30, 1969 "Sure, people think that I'm a hippie" by Karen Parker

Globe & Mail, Tor., Ont., April 3, 1969 "The nuts and bolts and rust of Bill Lishman" by Kay Kritzwiser

Times, Oshawa, Ont., July 4, 1969 "Yellow Dandelions In A Green Field"

Tribune, Stouffville, Ont., July 24, 1969 (photo of artist and his sculpture "Yellow Dandelions . . .")

Free Press, London, Ont., Aug. 28, 1969 (photo of Lishman's sculpture of a bull purchased by The Western Fair Board)

LISMER, Arthur

1885-1969

Born in Sheffield, Yorkshire, England, the son of a draper, and one of six children, he was the only one in the family who wanted to become an artist.[1] At the age of nine he was continually sketching and making cartoons.[2] His father took an interest in his work and carried his sketches under his coat to the shop to show his fellow employees.[3] When Arthur was old enough he attended the Sheffield Central High School, and at the age of thirteen won a scholarship to study nights at the Sheffield School of Art. During the day he served his apprenticeship (seven years) in the printing business. When he was fifteen he took the post as illustrator for the *Sheffield Independent* in addition to his schooling and apprenticeship.[4] At the

LISMER, Arthur (Cont'd)

Sheffield School of Art he found the instruction almost dull and wanted to experiment more freely, but nevertheless he was receiving a thorough grounding in basic fundamentals of drawing, design, and general knowledge of the visual arts.[5] His job as illustrator took him to meetings and events to sketch people like George Bernard Shaw, Winston Churchill, evangelists Reuben Torrey and Charles McCallon Alexander and many others.[6] When he was only sixteen Lismer became secretary to The Heeley Art Club. Its membership was made up mainly of cutler's engravers who spent the weekends roaming the moors in search of subjects to sketch. In the evenings they would adjourn to the local pub to philosophize.[7] Their association continued for another nine years. Lismer completed his apprenticeship with the Eadon Engraving Company and also his scholarship course at the Sheffield School of Art with distinction. Of particular interest to him was the work of John Constable (1776-1837), and he collected reproductions of Constable's paintings. In 1906 Lismer went to Antwerp on the invitation of a friend who was a professor in the Berlitz School of Languages. He stayed with him and his wife while attending the Académie des Beaux-Arts. He rented a small studio over a baker's shop where he worked on his painting. He remained in Antwerp for a year and a half (1906-7) while making trips to Paris and London. He visited the galleries and viewed the works of Cézanne, Van Gogh, Daubigny, Corot, and others. On his return to Sheffield following his studies he opened his own business of pictorial publicity and also took in an apprentice.[9] He found it very hard to make ends meet but carried on for three years.[10] Pictorial publicity did not come into its own for another ten years. Near the end of this three year period Lismer's attentions were gradually turned to Canada. He received encouraging reports from William Broadhead who had gone out to Canada and found a job with the Grip Engraving Company. His interest intensified when several other men from Canadian engraving firms arrived in Sheffield in search of trained engravers. He was approached by a man named Grew (from Rolph-Clarke-Stone), then Fred Brigden and his father (Toronto Engraving Co.; later Brigden's). After some hesitation he made his decision to go to Canada. He left his young fiancée Esther Mawson behind until he settled in a new job. Sailing on the *S.S. Corsican* he arrived at Halifax and finally reached Toronto in January of 1911. There he was hired by David Smith and Company.[11] The manager of this firm made conditions so intolerable for Lismer that one day he quit on the spot with great justification. The following day (20th Feb., 1911) he joined Grip. The manager of this firm, Albert Robson, was sympathetic to his employees but also demanding.[12] Lismer was introduced to his fellow employees including J.E.H. MacDonald, Tom Thomson, Frank Johnston, and others. He renewed his his acquaintance with William Broadhead and met his friend Tom MacLean. It was Tom MacLean who invited Lismer to join the Arts and Letters Club.[13] There the cultural spirit of Toronto flourished within its walls, while without, the city moved through its dreary routine unaware of the Club's existence. It was at the Club that Lismer met Lawren Harris and A.Y. Jackson. The stage was now set for the exciting events which were to follow.[14] In 1912 Lismer had saved enough money to return to Sheffield and marry Esther. They returned to Toronto and settled in a small house on Delaware Avenue. Lismer had been inspired by tales of Thomson and Broadhead after their canoe trip through many rivers and lakes ending along the Mississagi River and on to Bruce Mines where they boarded a ship for Midland. Lismer had listened keenly to their descriptions of sunsets, huge water falls, mountains, rapids, and soon longed to venture forth himself. He did his early sketching with Tom Thomson in and around Toronto. Each artist probably helped the other. Thomson's great feeling for the north country would help immensely Lismer's understanding of a land he wanted to know more about. Lismer's thorough training at the Sheffield School of Art and his further study and travel in Europe coupled with an exceptional analytical faculty, probably made him an invaluable critic of Thomson's early paintings. Of course Thomson was receiving advice from others in the Grip circle and in turn was imparting his deep feeling of the north country to them. In 1912 Robson changed firms and went to Rous and Mann taking Carmichael, Johnston, Lismer, Varley and Thomson with him. In May of 1913 Lismer's only child Marjorie was born,[16] and within four months he received an invitation to spend part of September at Dr. MacCallum's summer home at Go Home Bay in the Georgian Bay area. MacCallum had become a patron of Canadian artists interested in painting open country, bushlands and lakes. The Lismers departed and soon arrived at Penetanguishene where they were picked up by an open speed boat. After putting up for the night because of stormy water they arrived the following day at MacCallum's Island to spend the next two weeks.[17] It was here that he experienced for the first time a spiritual awakening towards the Canadian landscape.[18] He made a number of sketches.[19] In 1913 he had accepted an offer to teach summers in art for Ontario teachers under the directorship of G.A. Reid. The classes were held under the auspices of the Ontario College of Art. Money was scarce and it gave him a reliable income. Equally important, it introduced him to a role which was to take up more of his time as the years went by. In May of 1914 Lismer made his first visit to Algonquin Park in the company of Tom Thomson.[20] They set up their main camp on Molly's Island in Smoke Lake and for three weeks they visited Ragged Lake, Wolf Lake and Crown Lake, lived in a pup tent and travelled by canoe.[21] Lismer made several sketches. Two are reproduced in Dennis Reid's *The Group of Seven* and one in R.H. Hubbard's *National Gallery of Canada Catalogue, Volume Three.*[22] Lismer returned to Toronto to his job at Rous and Mann.[23] But in the autumn of that same year, he was back in the Park with his wife and daughter. They joined forces with A.Y. Jackson, Varley, and Thomson. On this memorable occasion a photograph was taken of Thomson, Jackson, Lismer, on one side of a picnic table; Varley, Mrs. Lismer and her baby daughter (foreground) on the other.[24] Mrs. Lismer and baby probably stayed at Mowat Lodge or might have returned to Toronto. Varley and Lismer camped at one site, Jackson and Thomson at another. Many sketches were made that fall from which important canvases were produced. Lismer painted "The Guide's Home" and Jackson "The Red Maple"; both paintings have been reproduced in many publications. "The Guide's Home" was done in the French impressionist technique reminiscent perhaps of Pissaro. It was sketched at the mouth of Potter and Joe Creeks and was in fact the home of George Rowe and Larry Dickson.[25] When Lismer returned to Toronto he did the large canvas which was then exhibited in the Royal Canadian Academy show and acquired by the National Gallery shortly afterwards.[26] A fine reproduction of it appears in Peter Mellen's book.[27] In March of 1915 Lismer visited Dr. MacCallum's Island and he also seems to have continued to paint canvases based on his Algonquin trip, or a visit to Huntsville nearby. "Sumach and Maple, Huntsville" dated 1915 is reproduced in very good colour in Harper's *Painting In Canada/A History.*[28] Lismer moved to St. John Street, Thornhill in September 1915 and lived next door to J.E.H. MacDonald.[29] During March of 1915 he visited Dr. MacCallum at Go Home Bay. In the fall the Doctor commissioned J.E.H. MacDonald, Thomson, and Lismer to paint decorative wall panels for the living room of the cottage.[30] The wall space was measured and the artists went to work in the Studio Building that winter.[31] In April of 1916 the panels (beaverboard) were installed as a birthday surprise for Mrs. MacCallum. Lismer's part included six panels "The Picnic", "The Campers", "The Ducks", "The Sea Gulls", "The Fishermen" and "The 'Skinny-dip' ". A.Y. Jackson completed the decorations in 1953 (all panels were given to the National Gallery of Canada in 1968 by the present owners of the cottage, Mr. & Mrs. H.R. Jackman). In the late summer of 1916 Lismer departed with his family to Halifax where he became principal of the Victoria School of Art and Design.[32] During his stay of four years the school grew to about one hundred and fifty students which included some soldiers and sailors who were either waiting for overseas transport, or were on extended disembarkation leave.[33] He also opened, for the first time, his Saturday morning art classes for high school and elementary school pupils. He gave art instruction as well to the handicapped. The Lismers settled in a house ten miles beyond the city limits of Halifax. Luckily he missed his train the morning of the Halifax explosion.[34] But the shock of the explosion blew in the windows of their home. Although many schools were demolished the Victoria School of Art was only moderately damaged but was still a scene of horror as bodies were brought in from the streets to be thawed out beside the large furnace in the school basement. Lismer found himself climbing over empty coffins to get into his office. One of his best students had been killed and others suffered serious injuries. When he was not on relief work he kept from being overcome by the tragic events by making sketches of the city for the *Canadian Courier* in Toronto.[35] After enquiring from The National Gallery, Lismer received a commission from the Canadian War Records in June of 1918, to paint the activities of the Canadian armed forces around Halifax. During this period he did several large canvases "The 'Olympic' with Returned Soldiers" (48" x 64"), "Mine Sweepers, Halifax" (48" x 64"), "Convoy in Bedford Basin" (36" x 102"), "Halifax Harbour – Time of War" (42" x 52"), several black chalk drawings, and about seventeen lithographs with scenes of ships and seaplanes.[36] His large war paintings (above) are bold in design through Lismer's play on the ships' camouflage. He also did many drawings and paintings apart from his War Records commission.[37] Perhaps of greater importance was his development of techniques in child art education. In July of 1919 he exhibited fifty-three canvases at the Victoria School of Art and Design. In August he moved back to Toronto with his family in preparation to take over his duties of vice-principal of the Ontario College of Art, the job having been offered to him in April by G.A. Reid, principal.[38] Before leaving Halifax he had recommended to the board of the Victoria School of Art and Design the name of Elizabeth Nutt of Sheffield to take over in his place. This she did with great ability and forcefulness. During this year Lismer was elected Associate of the Royal Canadian Academy. The war had left its mark in Toronto particularly at the Arts and Letters Club where some of the absentees had been killed, while others were still on duty and had not yet been released. Lismer purchased a house which his wife had chosen. He made the purchase despite the fact that there was little room for his studio. Buying the house at all was made possible by a cheque from the National Gallery of Canada for War Records work. Lismer found studio space with A.Y. Jackson at the Studio Building and they continued to paint War Records until October when Lismer took up his duties at the Ontario College of Art. In the spring of 1920 however he joined Jackson, Harris,

MacDonald and Dr. MacCallum on a trip to Algoma country. They travelled on the Algoma Central Railway in a special railway freight car fitted out with windows, lamps, bunks, stove, water-tank, sink and cupboards. Harris had made arrangements with the railroad on two previous trips for a special boxcar to the same region with Dr. MacCallum, MacDonald and Frank Johnston in mid-September of 1918 and again in the fall of 1919 with Jackson, MacDonald and Johnston. The boxcar A.C.R. 10557 was in effect a studio on wheels. Lismer returned to Algoma in the spring and autumn of 1921 and the spring of 1924 and 1925. He also returned to Georgian Bay in 1920 with Varley and Dr. MacCallum. It was then that he made his first sketch (acquired by Dr. J. Parnell, Van. B.C.) for his large canvas "A September Gale, Georgian Bay". A larger study was made from the sketch (acquired by NGC from Vincent Massey bequest, 1968) and finally the canvas itself which was acquired by the National Gallery of Canada in 1926.[39] At the same time Varley developed his "Stormy Weather, Georgian Bay" but completed it later than Lismer's work. Lismer exhibited sixteen of his works in his First Group of Seven show at the Art Gallery of Ontario in 1920. In 1922 he completed "Isles of Spruce" (47" x 64") purchased by the Hart House Committee of 1927-8.[40] The sketch for this work was made at Sand Lake, Algoma, in 1921, and the final work in 1922.[41] This painting is of a northern lake in complete calm with a cluster of spruce trees on a low rocky island casting a reflection on the water. The viewer feels not a living thing stirs under a blue sky with high floating clouds, giving a sense of isolation and silence which is perhaps broken by the sound of a distant crow or loon. The clear air is scented by the smell of spruce, pine, and the dry leaves of autumn. A reproduction of this work was made by Sampson-Matthews of Toronto, and in September, 1970, the Canadian Post Office Department issued a six cent stamp featuring this work to commemorate the 50th anniversary of the founding of the Group of Seven. The stamp was reproduced by Ashton-Potter Ltd. of Toronto in 36,000,000 copies. Lismer did hundreds of sketches and drawings on his trips to Georgian Bay, Algoma, the Maritimes, and around Toronto. Through his deft caricatures we are given informal glimpses of Thomson, Harris, Jackson, and others as well as their critics. During these years he continued to teach at the Ontario College of Art but unable to implement all his teaching methods and concepts of discipline, he resigned as vice-principal of the College in 1927 although he continued with his duties as principal of the College's summer school.[42] The same year he was offered and accepted the post of educational supervisor of the Art Gallery of Toronto. In this capacity he was able to implement ideas on child and adult art education which he had begun to develop in Halifax. He was influenced in this work by the great Viennese teacher and artist, Franz Cizek. Cizek felt that children should not be taught art in order to provide them with something useful in adult life or to be trained to become future artists. But children should be allowed to have a profound spiritual experience through their own creativeness, and freedom to express their thoughts and instinctive feelings. To Cizek great artists were men who preserved spiritual attributes from the world of the child. It was in 1927 that Lismer arranged for a large travelling exhibition of the Cizek children's drawings and paintings to be shown at the Art Gallery of Toronto. Also he organized his Saturday morning classes through the co-operation of schools who submitted names of interested children. With an excellent group of teachers the classes were launched. Later the Art Centre for Children was initiated. His responsibilities also required him to give informal gallery talks to thousands of visitors, study groups and members of the Gallery; classes for teachers from public and private schools and the setting up of reading and reference room facilities. A loan system was also initiated for slides and films. During the summers of 1927, 1928, 1929 and 1930 he sketched in the Gaspé Peninsula, Rocky Mountains, McGregor Bay (at Georgian Bay), New Brunswick and Nova Scotia. From his Rocky Mountain trip he did the canvas "Cathedral Mountain" (48-1/4" x 56-1/4") which was acquired by the Montreal Museum of Fine Arts. In March of 1932 under the auspices of the National Gallery of Canada, Lismer set out on a tour across Canada to deliver a number of lectures including "The Necessity of Art", "Art Appreciation", "Art in Canada", "Education Through Art", "Art and the Child" and "Canadian Painting To-day". His tour was a great success. He also talked with informal luncheon groups and casual audiences. His wife accompanied him throughout the tour. In 1932 he was invited to the New Educational Fellowship conferences in France and England and South Africa in 1934; United States in 1935 and 1936; Australia and New Zealand in 1937. Also in 1936-7, at the request of the government, he lectured to teachers and established children's art classes in South Africa. At all these places during his free hours he invariably sketched. It was in South Africa that he used water colours extensively for the first time because they were more easily carried.[43] In 1938-39 he was a visiting professor at Teachers' College, Columbia University, where he taught four courses and devoted the balance of his time to visiting New York City schools and colleges. It was at these schools and colleges that he studied the conceptions of art education. These trips took him further afield to Milwaukee and Iowa also to Massachusetts and New Jersey. He spent long hours with Dr. Frederick Keppel discussing his findings. It was Dr. Keppel who had made possible a grant from the Carnegie Foundation to support Lismer's Saturday classes and also for the Child Art Centre. His daughter Marjorie attended Columbia University at the same time, where she took a post graduate course in anthropology. While at Columbia University he accepted a post in Ottawa at the National Gallery. He arrived there to take up his new duties in October of 1939. The plan was to set up a national art programme which had been originated by Eric Brown but shortly after Lismer's arrival Eric Brown died. The plan was never fully realized. By then the outbreak of the Second World War drastically reduced the activities of the Gallery. But Lismer gave lectures on "Peter Brueghel", "Goya", "Daumier", "Cézanne", "Van Gogh" and lectures based on his 1932 tour but enriched by his travelling and teaching experiences. In 1940 he became Educational Supervisor for the Montreal Museum of Fine Arts. In 1946 was elected full member of the Royal Canadian Academy. He became Assistant Professor of the Department of Fine Arts at McGill University in 1948. He received from Dalhousie University, N.S., an Honorary Diploma of LL.D. (1941); McGill University, Honorary LL.D. (1963). Relating a story which happened at the time he received his first LL.D. he recalled, "An hour after I got it I stopped in a little store to make a phone call and tried out the sound of it. The storekeeper said 'O, doctor, I'm so glad you're here, my baby is sick.' I told her I was a horse doctor."[44] A man of keen humour he once explained when he did his serious paintings as follows, "I spend six weeks in the wilds of British Columbia, where there's no telephone and not a child within 90 miles. I make enough sketches to keep me painting the rest of the year. I usually work when there are dishes to be done, so I've got in the habit of painting a picture as fast as my wife can wash the dishes."[45] For well over a decade Lismer and his wife spent about a month at Long Beach, B.C., using as his base Wickanninish Lodge. R.E. Baker[46] of Long Beach

LISMER, Arthur (Cont'd)

recalled in *The Vancouver Sun,* "We rarely saw him painting. I think the treasure trove of his sketch book sustained his work during the grim winters of the Eastern city. But two summers ago we came across him painting on a height above the beach. My small boy crept up quietly behind him to take a peek at his work. Without turning his head or staying his brush, Arthur Lismer said, 'That'll cost you $5 a peek.' My boy jumped back but was soon disarmed when Lismer turned his head to reveal the merry twinkle in his eyes that penetrated the thick bush of his eyebrows." In later years he exhibited his paintings at the Dominion Gallery, Mtl.; Laing Galleries, Tor. (1959); Galerie Agnes Lefort (1963)[47]; Galerie Martal, Mtl. (1965)[48] and probably elsewhere. He was further honoured by a Canada Council Medal presented to him by the late George P. Vanier, Governor-General of Canada. Lismer died in 1969 at the age of eighty-three. He is survived by his wife Esther and daughter, Mrs. Philip Bridges of Ashton, Md., U.S.A. A retrospective exhibition of his work was held at the National Gallery of Canada in May of 1969 and was organized by Pierre Theberge, assistant curator of Canadian art. Lismer is represented in most Canadian Public Collections including: National Gallery of Canada (Ott.); Art Gallery of Ontario (Tor.); Hart House, U. of T. (Tor.); The McMichael Conservation Collection (Kleinburg, Ont.); Agnes Etherington Art Centre, Queen's Univ. (Kingston, Ont.); London Public Library and Art Museum (Lond., Ont.); Winnipeg Art Gallery (Winnipeg, Man.); University of Sask. (Saskatoon); Montreal Museum of Fine Arts; Sir George Williams Univ. (Mtl.); The New Brunswick Museum, Saint John, N.B.; Dalhousie Art Gallery, Dalhousie Univ., Halifax, N.S.; and in the private collections of: John Parnell (Van., B.C.); Mr. & Mrs. J.S. McLean (Tor., Ont.); Mr. & Mrs. A.R. Laing (Tor., Ont.); C.S. Band (Tor., Ont.); J.S. Vaughan (Tor., Ont.); Mrs. John D. Eaton (Tor., Ont.); Mr. & Mrs. Erichsen Brown (Tor., Ont.); Mr. & Mrs. Jules Loeb (Lucerne, P.Q.); Miss K.M. Fenwick (Ott., Ont.); Mr. Walter Klinkhoff (Mtl., P.Q.) and many other collections.

References

[1] *September Gale* by John A.B. McLeish, J.M. Dent & Sons Ltd., London, England, P. 2
[2] Ibid, P. 2
[3] Ibid, P. 2
[4] Ibid, P. 7
[5] Ibid, P. 6
[6] Ibid, P. 8
[7] Ibid, P. 11
[8] Ibid, P. 12, 13
[9] Ibid, P. 16
[10] Ibid, P. 16
[11] Ibid, P. 23
[12] Ibid, P. 24
[13] Ibid, P. 26
[14] *A Painter's Country* by A.Y. Jackson, Clarke, Irwin, Tor. (1958) 1963, P. 22
[15] *A Canadian Art Movement* by F.B. Housser, MacMillan, Tor., 1926, P. 31
[16] see[1], P. 30
[17] see[1], P. 31
[18] see[1], P. 31, 32
[19] *The Group of Seven* by Peter Mellen, McClelland & Stewart Ltd., 1970, Tor., P. 32, Plate 46
   The Group of Seven Dennis Reid, NGC, P. 65, Plate 37
   National Gallery of Canada Catalogue, Vol. 3, P. 179, Cat. No. 6403
[20] *Tom Thomson, The Algonquin Years* by Ottelyn Addison In Collaboration With Elizabeth Harwood, The Ryerson Press, Tor., 1969, P. 28

LISMER, Arthur (Cont'd)

The Group of Seven by Peter Mellen, McClelland & Stewart Ltd., Tor., 1970, P. 39

The Group of Seven by Dennis Reid, NGC, 1970, P. 68

[21] *Tom Thomson, The Algonquin Years* as above, P. 28

[22] *The Group of Seven* by Dennis Reid, NGC, P. 74 (Plates 42 & 43)
National Gallery of Canada Catalogue, Vol. 3 by R.H. Hubbard, P. 179
September Gale by McLeish, P. 205 (listing only)

[23] writer's assumption only

[24] see[19], P. 100

[25] *The Tom Thomson Mystery* by William T. Little, P. 31

[26] *The National Gallery of Canada Catalogue,* Vol. 3, by R.H. Hubbard, P. 173

[27] *The Group of Seven* by Peter Mellen, Page 43 (Plate 57)

[28] *Painting In Canada/A History* by J. Russell Harper, U. of T., 1966, P. 270 (Plate 244)

[29] see[1], P. 55, *Art Gallery of Ontario/The Canadian Collection,* P. 245 Cat. No. 50/51

[30] *The MacCallum/Jackman Donations* by Dennis Reid, NGC, 1969 (cat.) P. 59

[31] Ibid

[32] see[1], P. 55

[33] see[1], P. 58

[34] see[1], P. 60

[35] see[1], P. 61

[36] *Check List of The War Collections* by R.F. Wodehouse, NGC, 1968, P. 37, 38 Also *Group of Seven* by Peter Mellen, P. 77

[37] see[1], P. 63, also *Art Gallery of Ontario/The Canadian Collection* P. 246-248

[38] see[1], P. 64, 65

[39] *The Group of Seven* by Dennis Reid, P. 154, 155
The Group of Seven by Peter Mellen, P. 128-131

[40] *The Hart House Collection of Canadian Paintings,* U. of T. Press, 1969, P. 96 (Cat. No. 66)

[41] *A Canadian Art Movement* by F.B. Housser, 1926, P. 178, 189
Canadian Paintings In Hart House by J.R. Harper, 1955, P. 31
Group of Seven Drawings by Paul Duval, 1965, Plate 17
The Group of Seven by Peter Mellen, P. 135 (Plate 154)

[42] *September Gale* by J.A.B. McLeish, P. 100, 101, 102
The Group of Seven by Peter Mellen, P. 202

[43] *Arthur Lismer/Paintings 1913-1949* AGT/NGC, 1950, Introduction by Sydney Key, P. 6

[44] *Maclean's Magazine,* May 7, 1960 "A Canadian art master meets and teaches a new generation" pictorial by Don Newlands, story by Cathie Breslin

[45] Ibid

[46] *The Vancouver Sun,* Van., B.C., May 10, 1969 "Lismer Recalled" by R.E. Barker

[47] *The Montreal Star,* Sept. 18, 1963 "Two Sketch Collections By Arthur Lismer" by Robert Ayre

[48] Ibid, Dec. 11, 1965 "Arthur Lismer, Moe Reinblatt and International Lithos" by Michael Ballantyne

see also

The McMichael Conservation Collection by Paul Duval, Sampson Matthews, Tor., 1970, see text, section on artist and catalogue in back section of book.

Agnes Etherington Art Centre by Frances K. Smith, Queen's Univ., Kingston, 1968, No. 81

The McMichael Conservation Collection by Paul Duval, Clarke Irwin, 1967, *Canadian Painting/1850-1950* by Clare Bice, NGC Travelling Exhibition Catalogue, 1967, P. 19, 20, 24

Great Canadian Painting by Elizabeth Kilbourn and Frank Newfeld, Text, Ken Lefolii/ Research Wm. Kilbourn, Marjorie Harris, Sandra Scott, P. 39

Sir Geroge Williams University Collection of Art with Foreword by Edwy F. Cooke, P. 130

Breaking Barriers by F. Maud Brown, Soc. for Art Publications, 1964, Inside jacket, P. 39, 40, 41, 42, 43, 45, 46, 51, 67, 73

The Development of Canadian Art by R.H. Hubbard, Queen's Printer, 1963, P. 88, 91, 95 Plates 159, 160

The Montreal Museum of Fine Arts (catalogue), 1960, P. 146
One Hundred Years of Canadian Painting, Laing Galleries, 1959, P. 22
Canadian Paintings In Hart House by J. Russell Harper, 1955, P. 31
Canadian Water Colour Painting by Paul Duval, Burns & MacEachern, Tor., Plate 31

LISMER, Arthur (Cont'd)

Canadian Drawings and Prints by Paul Duval, Burns & MacEachern, Tor., Plates 22 & 23

The Growth of Canadian Painting by Donald W. Buchanan, Collins, Tor., P. 36

Canadian Art, Vol. 7, No. 3, Spring 1950 "Arthur Lismer – His Contribution to Canadian Art" by A.Y. Jackson, P. 89 "Lismer's Painting from 1913 to 1949 in Review" by Andrew Bell, P. 91

Canadian Art by Graham McInnes, MacMillan, 1950, P. 16, 53, 57, 58, 61, 69

The Group of Seven by Thoreau MacDonald, Ryerson, 1944, P. 2, 6, 12, 26

The Fine Arts In Canada by Newton MacTavish, MacMillan, P. 155, 158, 172

Canadian Art, Its Origin and Development by William Colgate, Ryerson Paperbacks, 1967 (see index)

SEE extensive bibliography in *The Group of Seven* by Peter Mellen, P. 225

Toronto Star Weekly, May 30, 1931 "His Work Is Fashioning Our Artists of To-Morrow"

Free Press, Winnipeg, Man., Mar. 17, 1932 "Need of Art Gallery In Winnipeg Stressed by Toronto Lecturer"

Mail & Empire, Tor., Ont., May 31, 1934 "Educational System Attacked By Lismer – Teaching of Art in Schools Antiquated, He Says"

The Ottawa Citizen, Oct. 6, 1934 "Inspiring Story of Artistic Development in South Africa"

Mail & Empire, May 4, 1935 "Lismer Exhibition Wins High Praise – Artist's First One-man Show at the Malloney Galleries"

The Gazette, Mtl., P.Q., Nov. 2, 1936 "Works of Lismer At Scott Gallery"

The Montreal Standard, Mtl., P.Q., Sept. 17, 1938 "Canadian Art and Artists – Leaving Canada to Accept Appointment As Professor of Fine Arts At Columbia"

Ibid, Oct. 14, 1939 "Art News And Reviews – 'They Start With Reality, Not Imitating, But Making a Picture'; Children's Work At Art Association" by Robert Ayre

Saturday Night, Tor., Ont., Oct. 13, 1945 "Art and Artists – Arthur Lismer, Canadian Artist, Led World in Art Education" by Paul Duval

Ibid, Feb. 16, 1946 "Fascinating Evolution Seen in Lismer Exhibit" (Eaton's Fine Art Galleries, Tor.)

Evening Telegram, Tor., Ont., Jan. 14, 1950 "At The Galleries – Art Gallery Exhibition Honors Work Of Lismer" by Rose MacDonald

Globe & Mail, Tor., Ont., Jan. 14, 1950 "Admirers Pay Homage to Artist And Educator" by Pearl McCarthy

The Montreal Standard, Mtl., P.Q., Feb. 11, 1950 "Artist's Dinner – Art World Pays Homage To Arthur Lismer" Story by Bill Brown, Photos by Page Toles (photos of Lismer, Nicholas Hornyansky, Bertram Brooker, Charles Comfort, Dorothy Stevens, A.Y. Jackson, Martin Baldwin)

The Ottawa Citizen, April 14, 1950 "Alexander Officially Opens Lismer Painting Exhibition"

Ibid, "Arthur Lismer Paintings Cultured, Impressionistic" by Carl Weiselberger

The Calgary Herald, Calgary, Alta., June 2, 1951 "Arthur Lismer Exhibit At Coste House Sunday"

The Ottawa Citizen, Ott., Ont., Feb. 14, 1952 "Lismer's Life And Work Now Recorded On Film" by C.W.

The Province, Van., B.C., Aug. 4, 1953 "Gets Dreamy About B.C. – Arthur Lismer, Scenic Artist, Starts Paintings Of Scenery In Gulf Isles" by Dan Illingworth

The Ottawa Citizen, Feb. 15, 1954 "At Robertson Galleries – Lismer 'Captures' Beaches, Forest Of Vancouver Island" by C.W.

Times, Victoria, B.C., Aug. 15, 1956 "Fight Uniformity Warns Art Expert" by Audrey St. D. Johnson

Globe & Mail, Tor., Ont., Mar. 16, 1959 "45 Years in Retrospect – Bold Art Cavalier, Arthur Lismer Unchanged" by Pearl McCarthy

The Toronto Star, Mar. 28, 1959 "World Of Art – Later Lismer Works Disappointing" by Robert Fulford

The Gazette, Mtl., P.Q., Feb. 13, 1960 "In The Norton Gallery" by Dorothy Pfeiffer

Ibid, Feb. 25, 1960 "Fire Personal Loss To Lismer As Art, Precious Records Go" by Bill Bantey

The Montreal Gazette, May 2, 1963 "McGill To Honor Five At Spring Convocation May 31" by Gordon Pape

The Montreal Star, Sept. 18, 1963 "The Art Scene – Two Sketch Collections by Arthur Lismer" by Robert Ayre

LISMER, Arthur (Cont'd)

Time (Canada), Jan. 27, 1967 "The Arts — One-Man Show"
Globe & Mail, Tor., Ont., Mar. 23, 1969 "Group of Seven founder famed as teacher" (obituary)
The Ottawa Journal, Ott., Ont., Mar. 25, 1969 "Group of Seven Art Pioneer Dies"
Le Devoir, Mtl., P.Q., Mar. 25, 1969 "Décès du peintre Lismer, du célèbre groupe des Sept"
Victoria Times, B.C., Mar. 26, 1969 "Canada on Canvas" (obituary)
Star, Windsor, Ont., Mar. 29, 1969 "A Lismer memoir" by Ken Saltmarche
Coin Stamp Antique News, Tor., Ont. Sept. 5, 1970 "Canada Post Office Marks Group of Seven Painting — Lismer Art Chosen"
Films on Art compiled by Beatrice H. Trainor (1960) revised by Shirley A. Webb, Nat. Film bd., Library & Info. Service, 1762 Carling Ave., Ottawa, Ont., P. 58 "Lismer" 16mm 20 mins. sd. colour (NGC Collection)
Art Films At the National Gallery of Canada (1961) catalogue of films available free of charge, except for transportation, to any responsible institution or group, obtainable from Canadian Film Inst.